AUSTRALIA

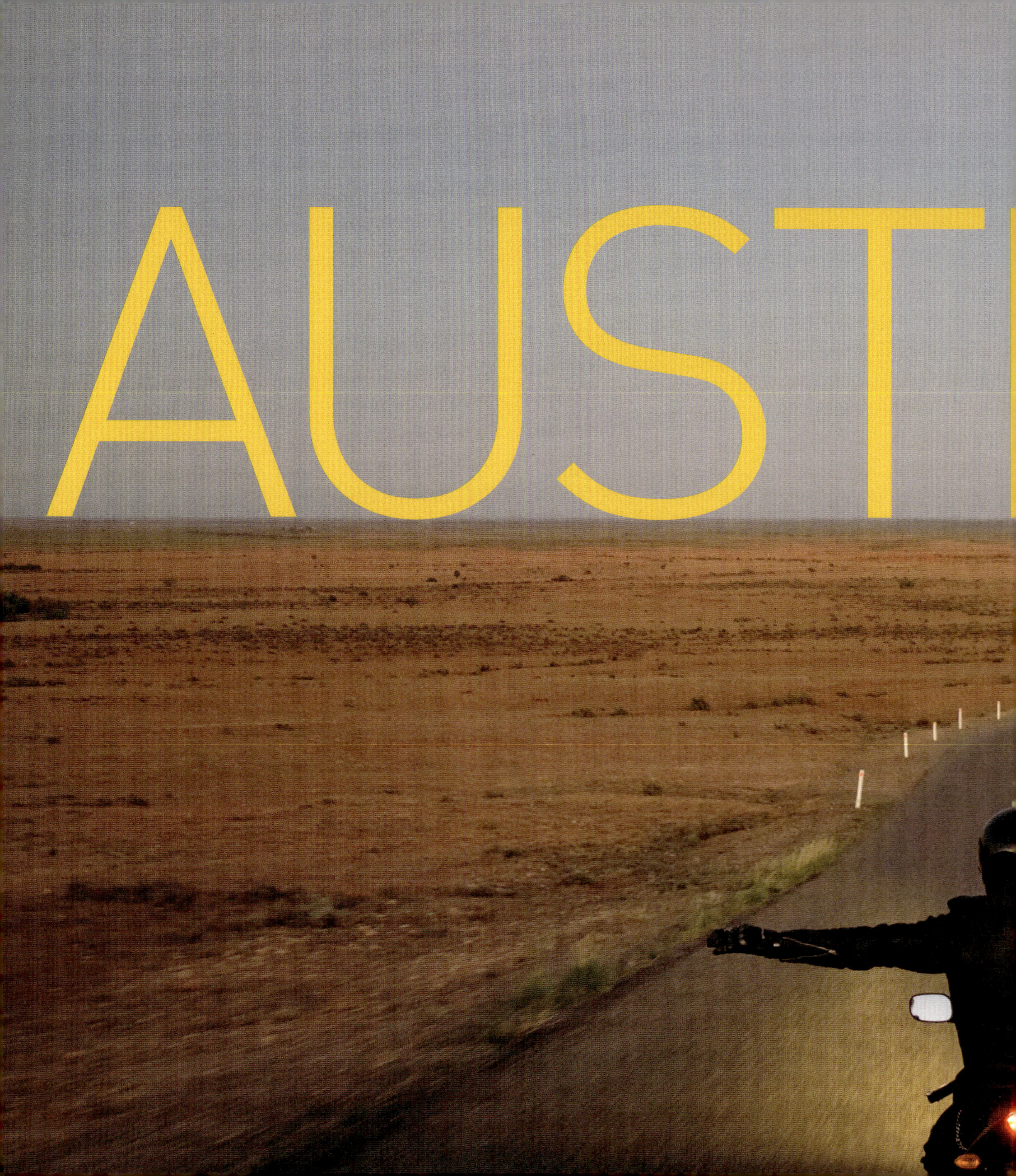
AUST

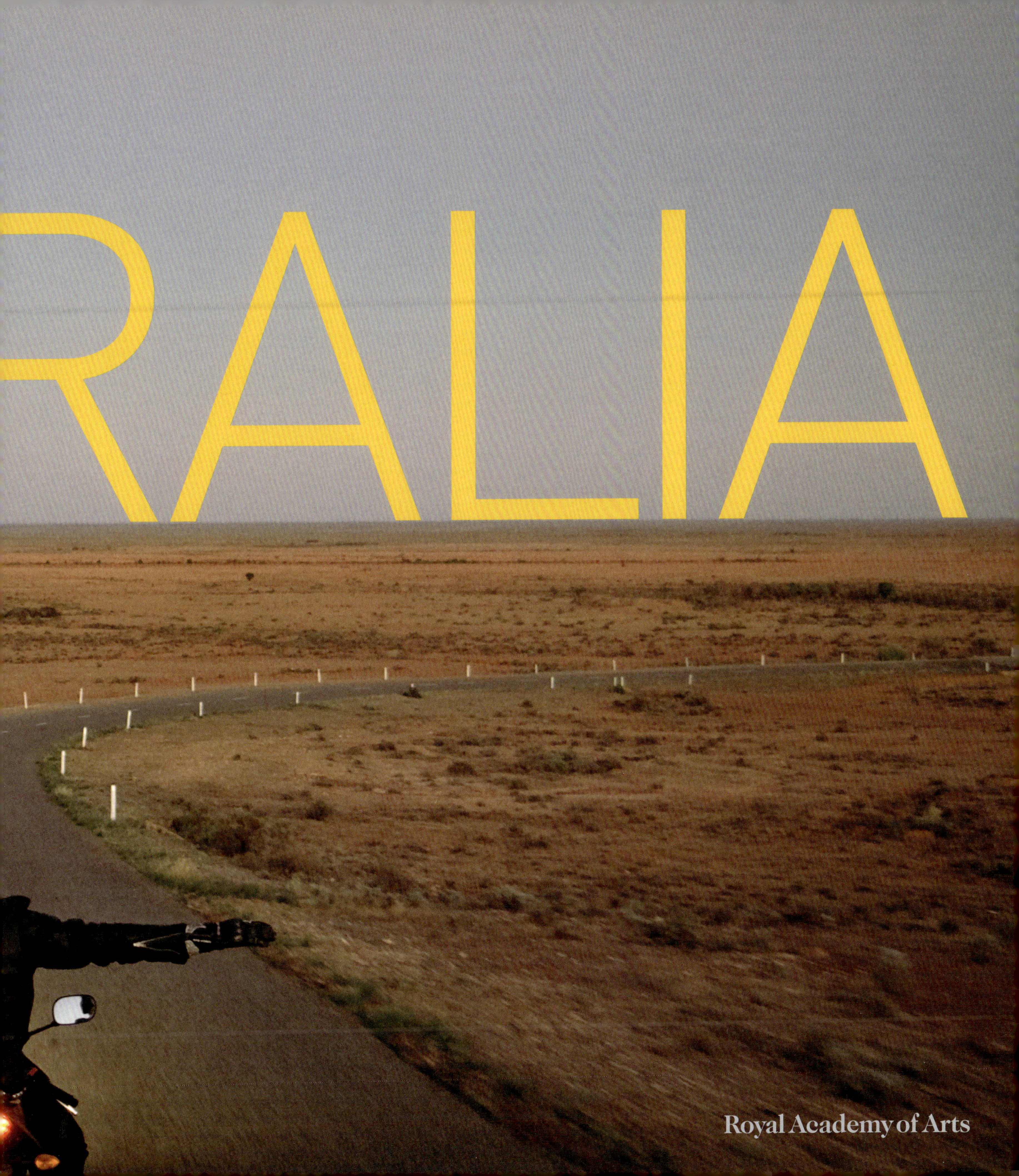

RALIA
Royal Academy of Arts

First published on the occasion of the exhibition 'Australia'

Royal Academy of Arts, London
21 September – 8 December 2013

Organised with the National Gallery of Australia

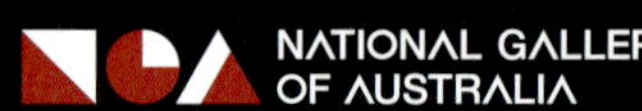

Supported by

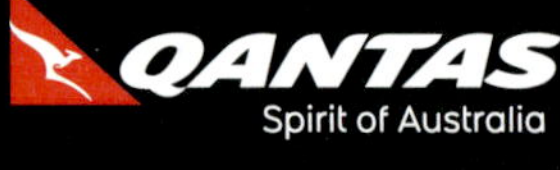

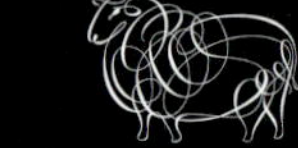

Supported by
The Campaign for Wool

THE CAMPAIGN FOR WOOL
Patron: HRH The Prince of Wales

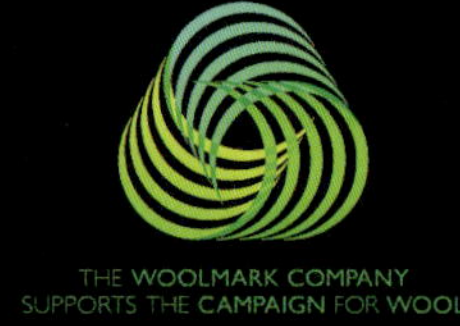

British Library Cataloguing-in-Publication Data

A catalogue record for this book is available from the British Library

ISBN 978-1-907533-44-0 (paperback)
ISBN 978-1-907533-45-7 (hardback)

Distributed outside the United States and Canada by Thames & Hudson Ltd, London

Distributed in the United States and Canada by Harry N. Abrams, Inc., New York

This exhibition has been made possible by the provision of insurance through the Government Indemnity Scheme. The Royal Academy of Arts would like to thank HM Government for providing Government Indemnity and the Department for Culture, Media and Sport and Arts Council England for arranging the indemnity.

The National Gallery of Australia is grateful to the Australian Government for support of the exhibition through the Department of Foreign Affairs and Trade.

EXHIBITION

CURATORS
Anne Gray
Ron Radford
Kathleen Soriano

ASSISTED BY
Roger Butler
Wally Caruana
Franchesca Cubillo
Deborah Hart
Gael Newton
Katia Pisvin

EXHIBITION MANAGEMENT
Idoya Beitia
assisted by Elana Woodgate

PHOTOGRAPHIC AND COPYRIGHT CO-ORDINATION
Kitty Corbet Milward

EXHIBITION CATALOGUE

ROYAL ACADEMY PUBLICATIONS
Beatrice Gullström
Alison Hissey
Elizabeth Horne
Carola Krueger
Peter Sawbridge
Nick Tite

COPY-EDITING AND PROOFREADING
Rosalind Neely

PICTURE RESEARCH
Sara Ayad

COLOUR ORIGINATION
DawkinsColour

BOOK DESIGN AND CARTOGRAPHY
Isambard Thomas, London

Printed in Italy by Graphicom

EDITORS' NOTE

In many Indigenous communities custom forbids mention of the names of the deceased and viewing of photographs that depict them. Members of Indigenous communities are respectfully advised that a number of individuals named in this book and shown in photographs have now passed away.

The Royal Academy of Arts and the National Gallery of Australia much regret that it has proved impossible to reach an agreement with the artist's copyright owner concerning the inclusion in this catalogue of plates of the two fine watercolours by Albert Namatjira selected for this exhibition from the collection of the National Gallery of Australia, Canberra: *Gum Tree and Sandhill* (*c.*1938) and *Love's Creek, MacDonnell Ranges* (*c.*1948).

Dimensions of all works of art are given in centimetres, height before width (before depth). For watercolours, lithographs and stencil prints, dimensions are sheet measurements, and for etchings, they are plate measurements.

ILLUSTRATIONS

Pages 2–3: detail of cat.197
Pages 6–7: detail of cat.29
Page 10: detail of cat.76
Page 13: detail of cat.161
Page 14: detail of cat.203
Page 17: detail of cat.168
Pages 18–19: detail of cat.158
Pages 28–29: detail of cat.21
Page 41: detail of cat.32
Page 91: detail of cat.55
Page 147: detail of cat.108
Page 185: detail of cat.128
Page 227: detail of cat.165

This catalogue is dedicated
to the memory of

ROBERT HUGHES AO

Honorary Fellow of the Royal Academy
1938–2012

ACKNOWLEDGEMENTS

All those concerned with the making of this exhibition and its catalogue would like to thank the following individuals for their invaluable assistance: Vivien Allimonos, Sue Backhouse, Murray Bail, Glenn Barkley, Natalie Beattie, Bill Bleathman, Alison Bracker, Michael Brand, Carl Bridge, Margie Bryant, Kate Buckingham, Christopher Butler, Alex Byrne, Edmund Capon, Stefano Carboni, Wally Caruana, the Clore Leadership Programme (notably Dame Vivien Duffield, Lord Smith of Finsbury, Robert Hewison and Sue Hoyle), Hugo Chapman, Stephen Coppel, Michael Dagostino, Rebecca Daniels, Kate Darian-Smith, Andrew Dempsey, Caroline Downer, Erica Drew, Clare Drysdale, Deborah Edwards, Geoffrey Edwards, Tony Ellwood, Tracey Emin RA, Simon Elliott, Helen Ennis, Stephen Farthing RA, Angela Goddard, Anthony Green RA, Sir Nicholas Grimshaw PPRA, Kate Groves, Charmane Head, Michael Hedger, Ian Henderson, Oscar Humphries, Sophie Hunter, Philip Jones, Magda Keaney, Thomas Keneally, Brian Kennedy, Caroline Kha, Michael Landy RA, Colin and Liz Laverty, Frances Lindsay, Tracey Lock-Weir, Julie Lomax, Michael Lynch, Elizabeth Ann Macgregor, Nicki Mackay-Sim, the British High Commissioner to Australia Paul Madden, Terence Maloon, Naomi Milgrom, Andrew and Hal Missingham, Nick Mitzevich, Gordon Morrison, Justine van Mourik, Rupert Myer, Peter and Renate Nahum, Shanthini Naidoo, Richard Neville, Nick Nicholson, Hetti Perkins, Simon Pierse, Timothy Potts, Alessandra Pretto, Ron Ramsey, the Australian High Commissioner to the UK the Hon. Mike Rann and Sasha Carruozzo, Thérèse Rein, Dennis Richardson, Liz Rideal, Sue Roberts, Jan Robison, Brett Rogers, Michael Rosenthal, Ann Ryan, Jude Savage, Andrew Sayers, Nancy Sever, Desmond Shawe-Taylor, Anne-Marie Schwirtlich, Kerry Styles, Kevin Sumption, Natalie Sweet, Elena Taylor, Daniel Thomas, Nicholas Thomas, the Australian Deputy High Commissioner to the UK Andrew Todd, Wayne Tunnicliffe, Mark Van Veen, Gerard Vaughan, Maryanne Voyazis, Jonathan Watkins, Liz Wilson, Tim Winton, Adam Worrall, Janet Worth, and Bill and Hilary Wright.

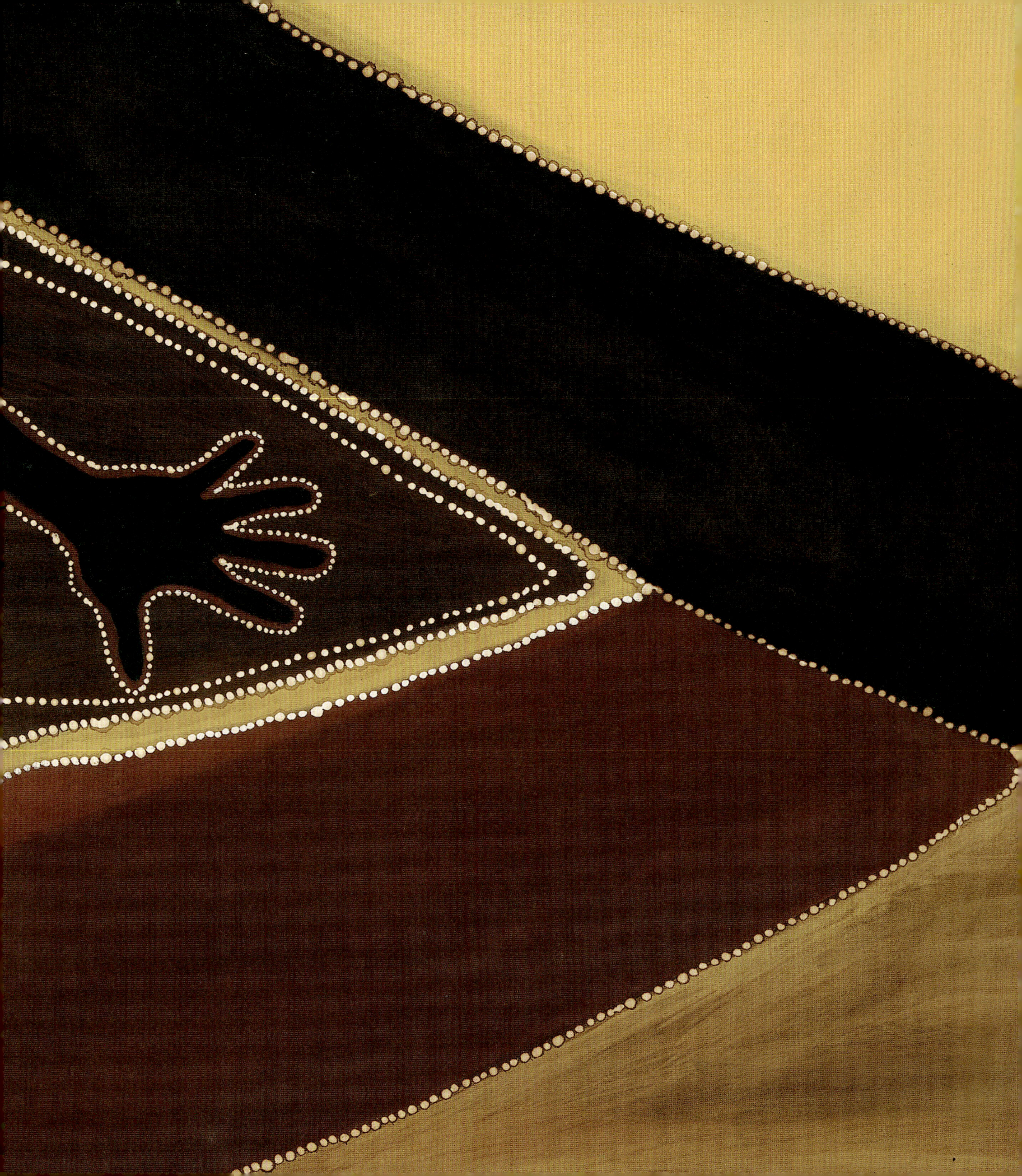

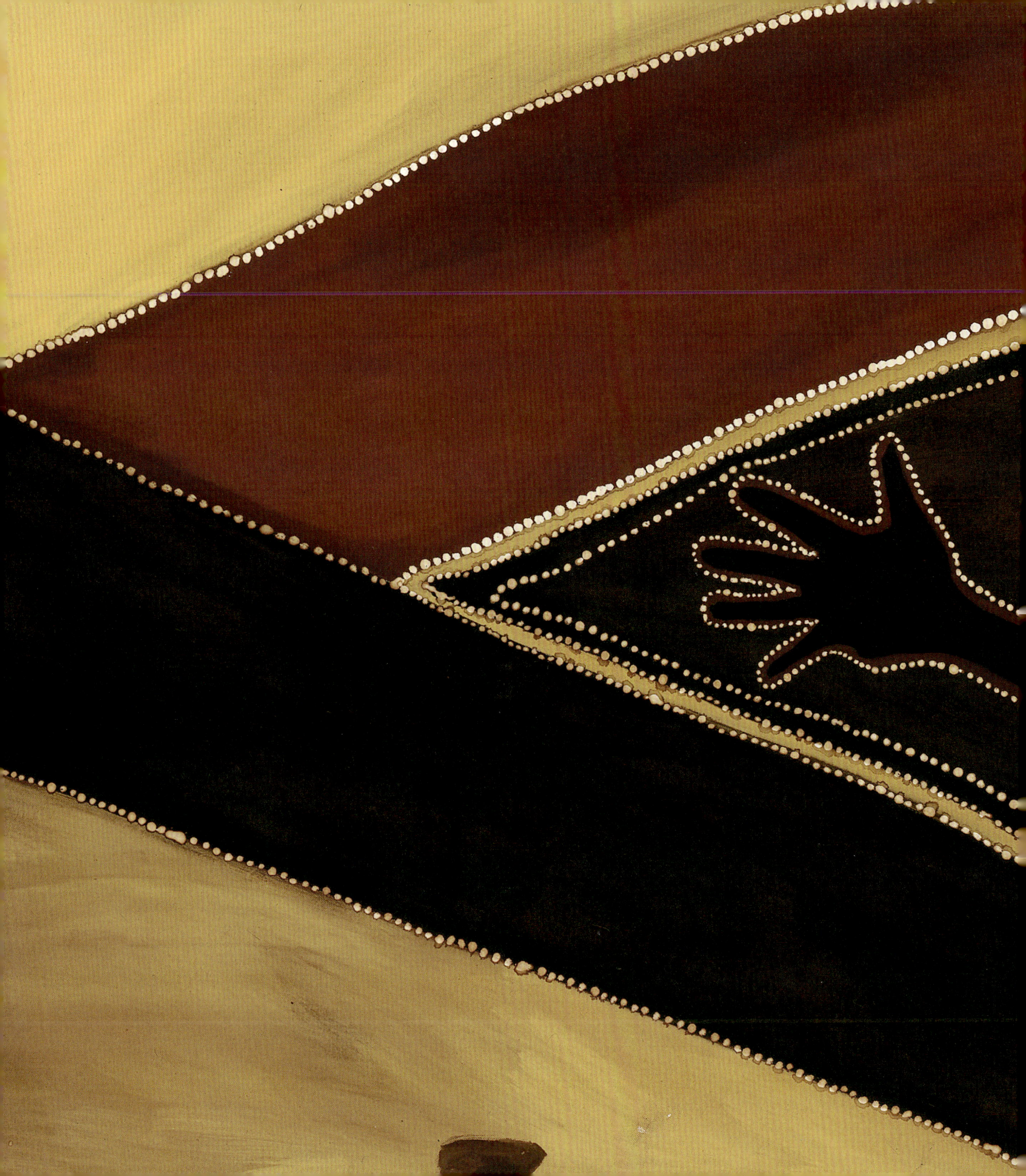

FOREWORD
HRH THE PRINCE OF WALES
11

PRESIDENT'S FOREWORD
CHRISTOPHER LE BRUN PRA
12

CHAIRMAN'S FOREWORD
ALLAN MYERS AO QC
15

MAP
20

AUSTRALIA: AN INTRODUCTION
KATHLEEN SORIANO
22

DEAD HEART / LIVE HEART
THOMAS KENEALLY
30

CHRONOLOGY
36

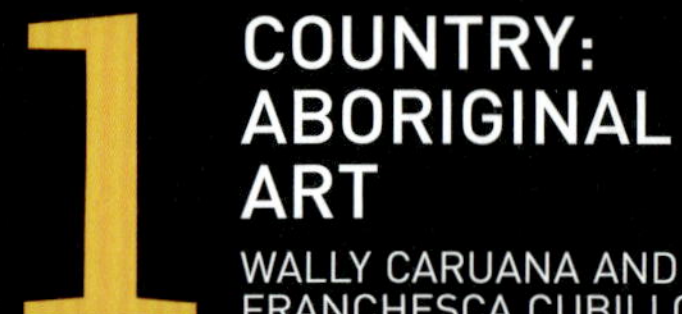
COUNTRY: ABORIGINAL ART
WALLY CARUANA AND FRANCHESCA CUBILLO
40

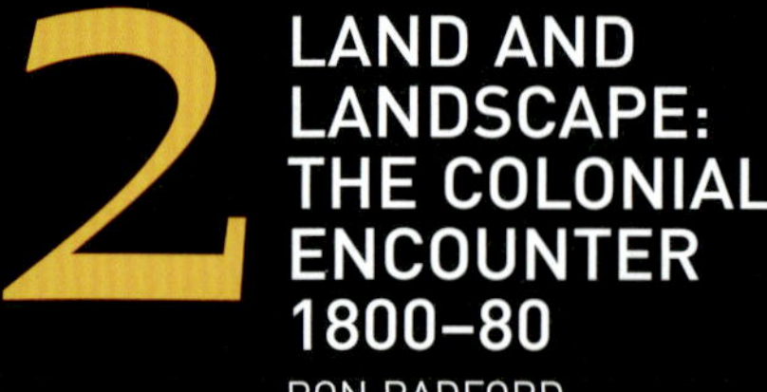
LAND AND LANDSCAPE: THE COLONIAL ENCOUNTER 1800–80
RON RADFORD
90

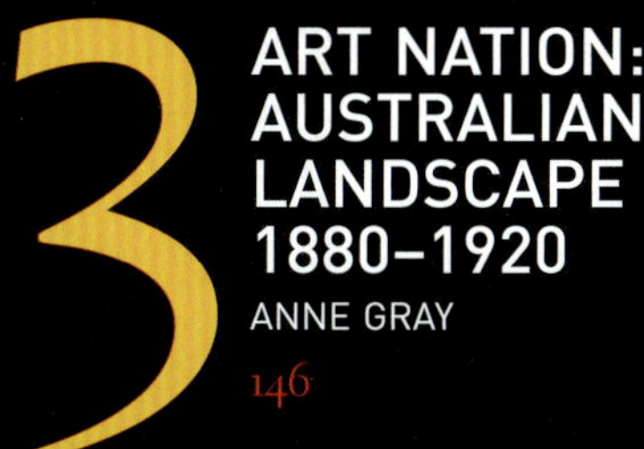
3 ART NATION: AUSTRALIAN LANDSCAPE 1880–1920
ANNE GRAY
146

4 AUSTRALIAN LANDSCAPE: PATHWAYS INTO THE MODERN WORLD 1920–50
DEBORAH HART
184

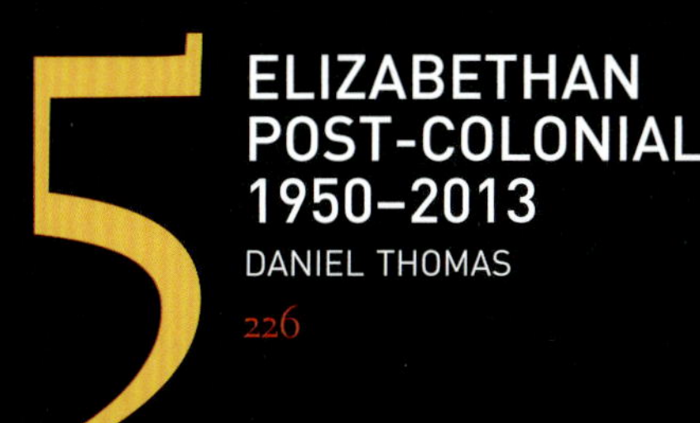
5 ELIZABETHAN POST-COLONIAL 1950–2013
DANIEL THOMAS
226

ARTISTS' BIOGRAPHIES
289

NOTES
305

SELECT BIBLIOGRAPHY
308

LENDERS TO THE EXHIBITION
313

PHOTOGRAPHIC ACKNOWLEDGEMENTS
314

INDEX
315

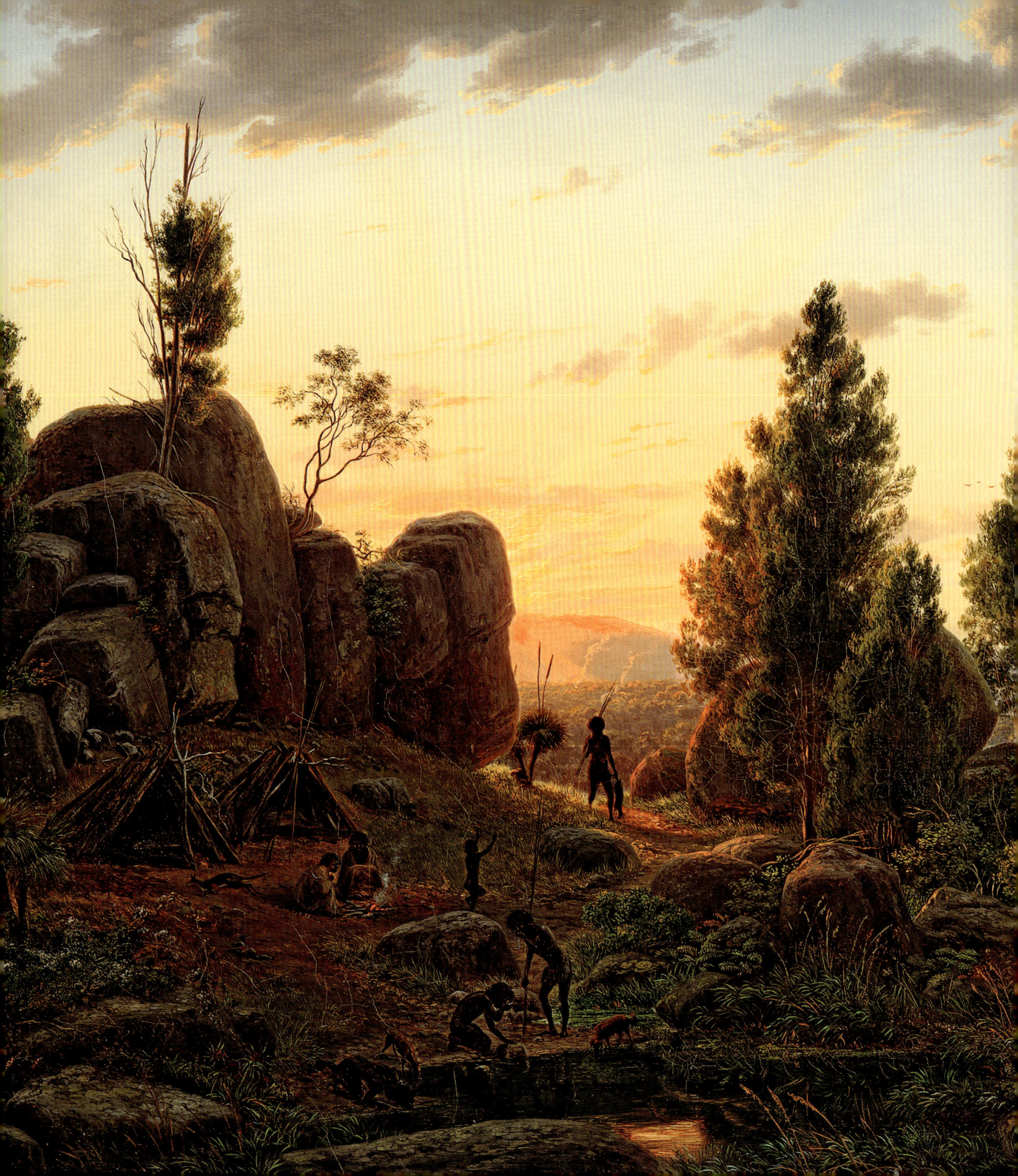

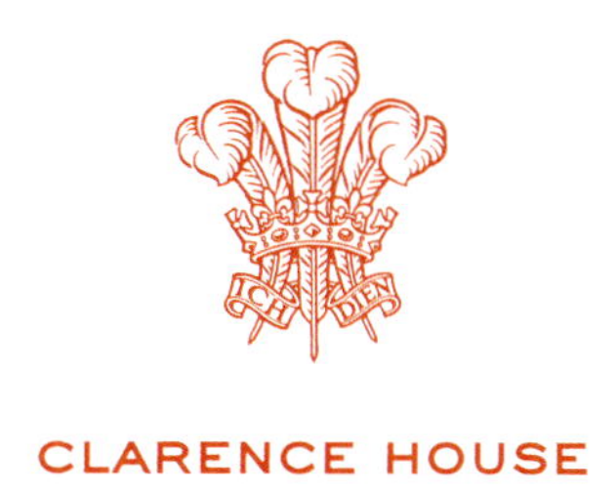

CLARENCE HOUSE

As Patron of this exhibition, I could not be more delighted that the Royal Academy of Arts and the National Gallery of Australia have joined together to present a truly remarkable collection of paintings that celebrates the story of Australian art from 1800 to the present day.

This exhibition highlights the close relationship between notions of land and landscape and the development of a unique visual arts tradition. It reminds us of the enduring truth of indigenous teachings about the land as a source of spiritual nourishment. It also demonstrates the powerful way in which art has served as an expression of knowledge for so many generations of Australians – from the powerful iconography of early and contemporary 'Dreaming' narratives to the sense of 'truth to Nature', which artists such as Frederick McCubbin and Tom Roberts sought to capture on canvas.

I can hardly believe that it is now almost fifty years since I first visited Australia. It was during that first stay that, like many before me, I was deeply struck by the distinctive colours and light of Mackellar's "sunburnt country" and came to love the diversity of its flora and fauna. It seems to me to be very easy to understand how such a rich natural palette has become indelibly linked with Australian national identity – and how it has inspired such diverse artistic responses.

Many of the works on display in the exhibition are illustrated in this magnificent catalogue. Each work is a deeply personal response to Australia's unique environment. As a collection, the works also provide a powerful visual narrative illustrating Australia's developing sense of nationhood. It is an extraordinary achievement that the Royal Academy of Arts and the National Gallery of Australia have been able to bring together so many important works for the first time outside Australia. I can only hope that you will be inspired, as I have been, by the depth and variety of the exhibition.

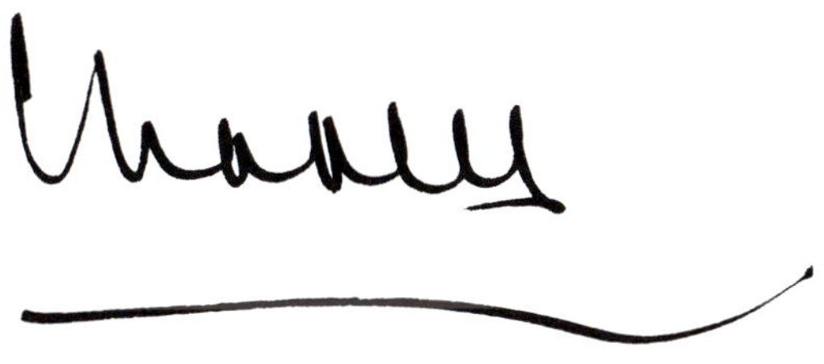

PRESIDENT'S FOREWORD

Only the scale of the Royal Academy's imposing main galleries could do justice to such a significant and long overdue exhibition as this. Encompassing over 200 years with more than 200 exhibits, 'Australia' allows the visitor to survey the full range of the island continent's art, with Indigenous alongside non-Indigenous artists, all of them profoundly connected by their response to Australian land and landscape. The great Australian Impressionist Tom Roberts studied at the Royal Academy Schools in the early 1880s, and many other non-Indigenous artists maintained links with the Academy long after they had left, some sending work back to the Annual Exhibitions. The royal links of our institution extend back to its foundation in 1768 with the support of King George III, and, as we share our royal family with the Commonwealth, I am delighted His Royal Highness The Prince of Wales has agreed to be the exhibition's patron.

It has long been the wish of Kathleen Soriano, our Director of Exhibitions and co-curator of this exhibition with Ron Radford and Anne Gray, to improve our knowledge and understanding of this tremendous body of artists. She first began to develop the idea with the art historians Rebecca Daniels and Michael Rosenthal, and we are grateful to them both for those early conversations; however, the exhibition that we see today has been developed in partnership with the National Gallery of Australia, Canberra. The determination of Ron Radford, its Director, to see a celebration of Australian art in Britain was fortuitous, and coincided with our own intentions. We owe him and his colleague Anne Gray an enormous debt of gratitude for their key role in furthering our Australian art education. Other members of the curatorial team at the National Gallery of Australia, among them Roger Butler, Franchesca Cubillo, Deborah Hart and Gael Newton, have been tireless in their enthusiasm for the project, and we have benefited enormously from their guidance and expertise.

Beyond this partnership, we extend our most sincere thanks to our many lenders, all of them public museums and institutions in Australia and in Britain. All have been supremely supportive of the project and have parted with their prized works so that we can enjoy this unique opportunity to see the greatest art treasures from across the Australian continent together at Burlington House. We also thank the many contemporary artists whose works are included here for their enthusiasm and their commitment to the show. The Australian Government's Department of Foreign Affairs, the Australia Council, and the Australian High Commission in London have championed the exhibition from its early stages and we are most grateful for their support throughout. The organisation of an Australian Season in London to coincide with the exhibition will greatly contribute to this Australian moment.

The home team has applied its usual hard-work ethic and expertise to the project: Idoya Beitia has brought her formidable organisational skills to the management of the project, ably supported by Elana Woodgate, with Kitty Corbet Milward on rights and reproductions, and Katia Pisvin on the curatorial front; Ivor Heal has created a marvellous setting for the exhibition, perfectly matched by the graphic design of Tim Harvey; Peter Sawbridge, Nick Tite and Rosalind Neely have devoted themselves to the lasting record of the exhibition, this catalogue, which has been elegantly designed by Isambard Thomas; and Andrea Tarsia has capably steered us through the four years during which *Australia* has been in the making.

None of this would have been possible without our supporters, of course. An independent institution, receiving no Government funds, the Royal Academy relies upon its sponsors, trusts and foundations, and its Friends and Patrons for their continued investment in our exhibition programme and many other activities. For 'Australia' we are extremely grateful for the generosity of the National Gallery of Australia Honorary Exhibition Circle, Qantas Airways, The Campaign for Wool, Westfield, the Simon Lee Gallery and Richard Nagy.

Christopher Le Brun PRA
President, Royal Academy of Arts

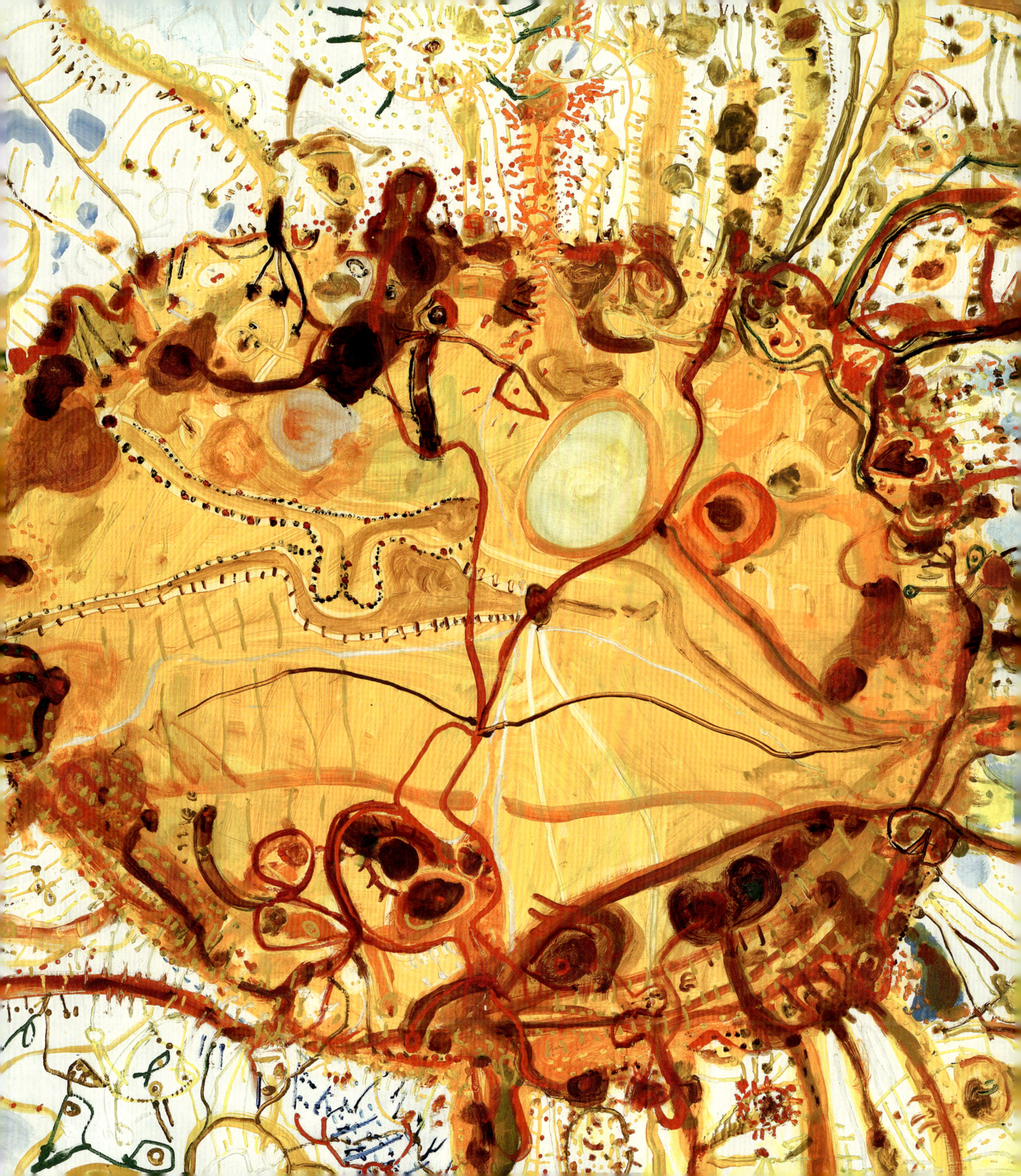

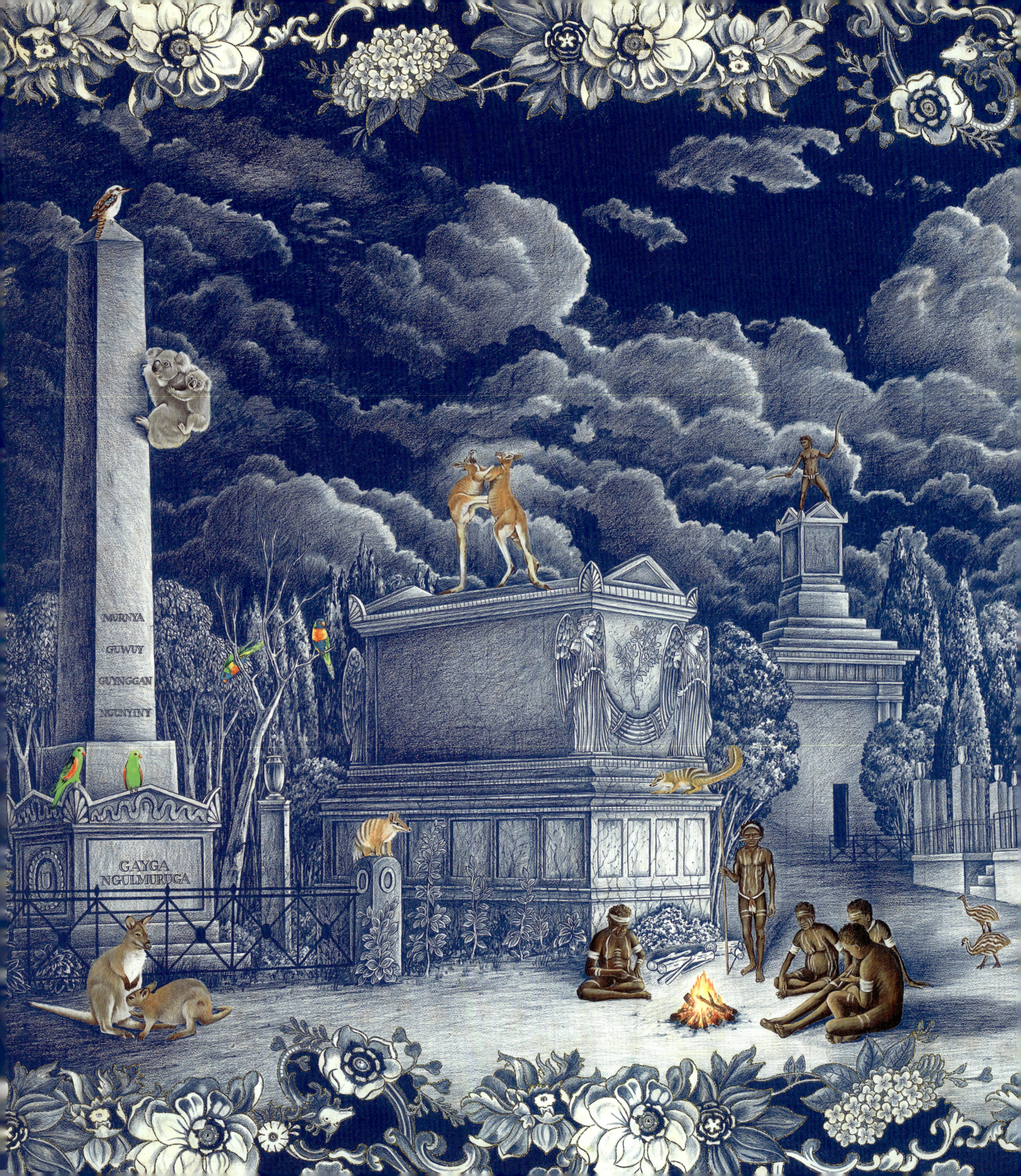
MURNYA
GUWUY
GUYNGGAN
NGUNYINY
GAYGA
NGULMURUGA

CHAIRMAN'S FOREWORD

We are honoured to be partners with the Royal Academy of Arts in this joint survey exhibition of Australian art. Beginning at 1800 and continuing until the present day, this exhibition shows more than 200 years of Australian art on the theme of land and landscape. It is the largest and most complete historical survey of Australian art ever to be displayed outside Australia.

Australians have a strong connection with their distinctive land and their landscape painting. This exhibition traces the development of Australian landscape art, which was the dominant focus of Australian art for more than 150 years. Although this is mainly a painting exhibition, it also includes prints, drawings, photography, video and some sculpture. It includes works by 38 living artists, both Indigenous and non-Indigenous. Aboriginal and Torres Strait Islander art makes up a quarter of the selection, with works ranging from one of the earliest surviving bark paintings to contemporary urban Aboriginal art. The theme of this exhibition reflects the importance of land and country to Aboriginal and Torres Strait Islander people, and its influence on their art practice.

All the works in the exhibition have come from public collections in Australia and Britain; half come from the collection of the National Gallery of Australia, Canberra. Other galleries, particularly the Australian state galleries, have been generous in lending their most iconic Australian works, some of which are usually never lent.

We are grateful to the National Gallery of Australia Honorary Exhibition Circle, whose patrons have been very generous in helping to sponsor the exhibition. They are Rupert and Annabel Myer, Philip Bacon, Tony and Carol Berg, Terry and Christine Campbell, Charles and Eva Curran, Ashley Dawson-Damer, Gordon and Marilyn Darling, James and Jacqui Erskine, Tim and Gina Fairfax, Lord Glendonbrook, John and Rosanna Hindmarsh, Wayne Kratzmann, Steven and Judy Lowy, Robyn and Mitchel Martin-Weber, Harold and Bevelly Mitchell, Roslyn Packer, Bruce Parncutt and Robin Campbell, Jeanne Pratt, Ray Wilson, and my wife and I. We are also grateful to Qantas Freight for transporting the works from Australia to London. And we thank the Department of Foreign Affairs and Trade for their grant towards this exhibition and the support of the Australian High Commissioner to the United Kingdom, the Hon. Mike Rann.

We are grateful to the Royal Academy of Arts and its President, Christopher Le Brun, its Secretary and Chief Executive, Charles Saumarez Smith, and its Director of Exhibitions, Kathleen Soriano, for enabling this large survey exhibition of Australian art to be mounted at Burlington House.

On behalf of the National Gallery of Australia, I would also like to thank our Director, Ron Radford, who has been pushing for such an exhibition for many years, and Anne Gray, Head of Australian Art, for her tireless efforts to bring this exhibition to fruition.

Visual art was the first art form that the Australian settlers developed, well before literature, music, dance and theatre. Aboriginal culture has always been highly visual and visual art remains the strongest art form in Australia. This exhibition provides the opportunity for the world to see Australians as the creative and visual people they are, and to appreciate the great diversity of the Indigenous and non-Indigenous art of our 'wilful lavish land'.

Allan Myers AO QC
Chairman, Council of the National Gallery of Australia

SUPPORTER'S STATEMENT

Qantas Airways, the Spirit of Australia and Major Partner of the National Gallery of Australia, is proud to be associated with the 'Australia' exhibition at the Royal Academy of Arts.

Flying from the United Kingdom for over sixty years, Qantas specialises in premium travel to Australia and has recently been voted Australia Pacific's Best Airline at the 2013 Skytrax World Airline Awards.

Our customers can enjoy the award-winning A380, operating daily from London Heathrow to both Sydney and Melbourne. On board, there is a choice of four cabins created by the award-winning designer Marc Newson and meals by the Australian restaurateur Neil Perry. First and Business customers can savour wines from the 'Best Overall Wine List', as awarded by the 2012 Cellars in the Sky Awards.

As the leading airline to and within Australia, Qantas offers an unrivalled network of over fifty destinations across the country to explore.

We look forward to welcoming you onboard and showcasing the best of Australia.

Eric Jelinek
Regional General Manager, UK and Ireland

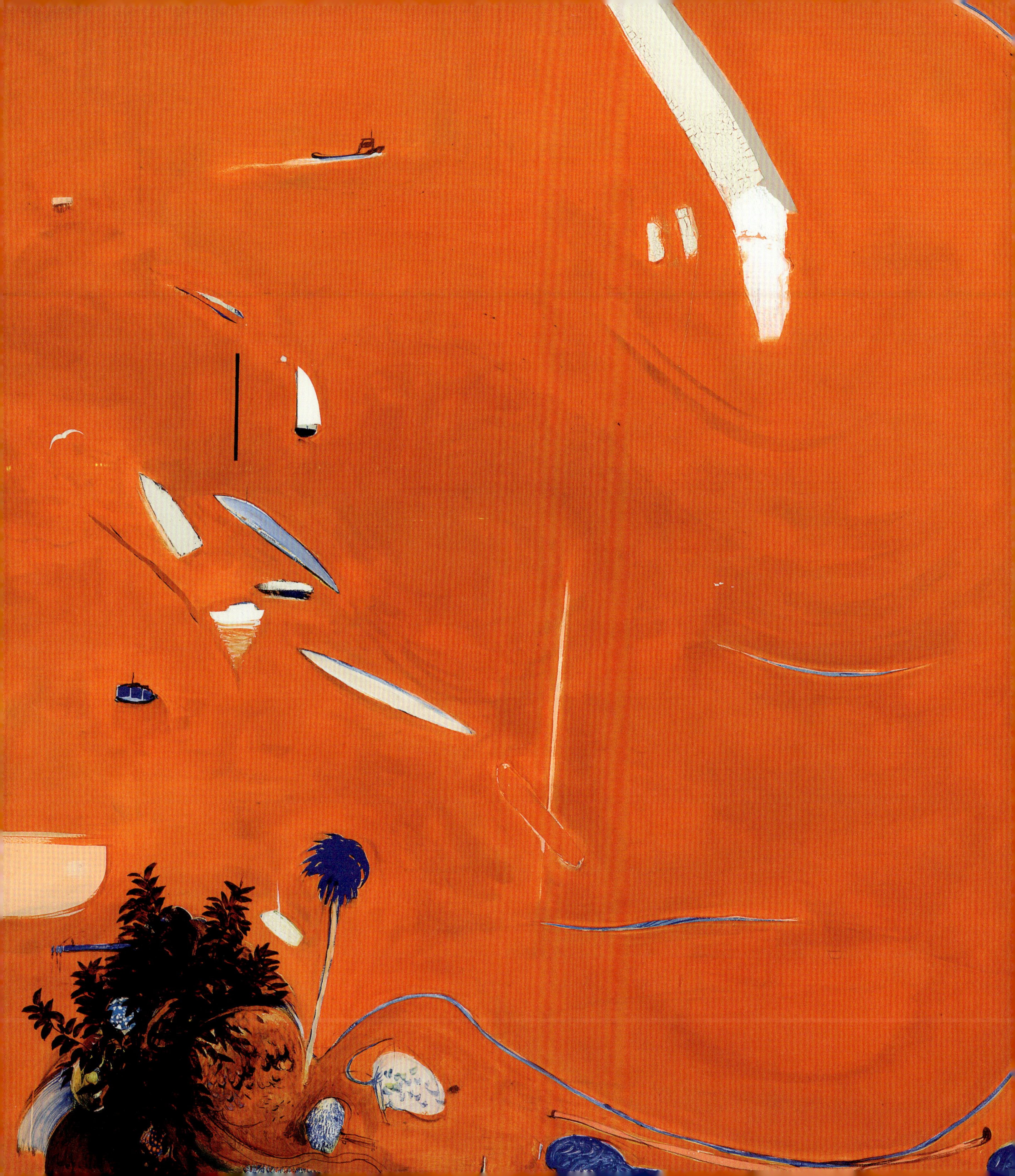

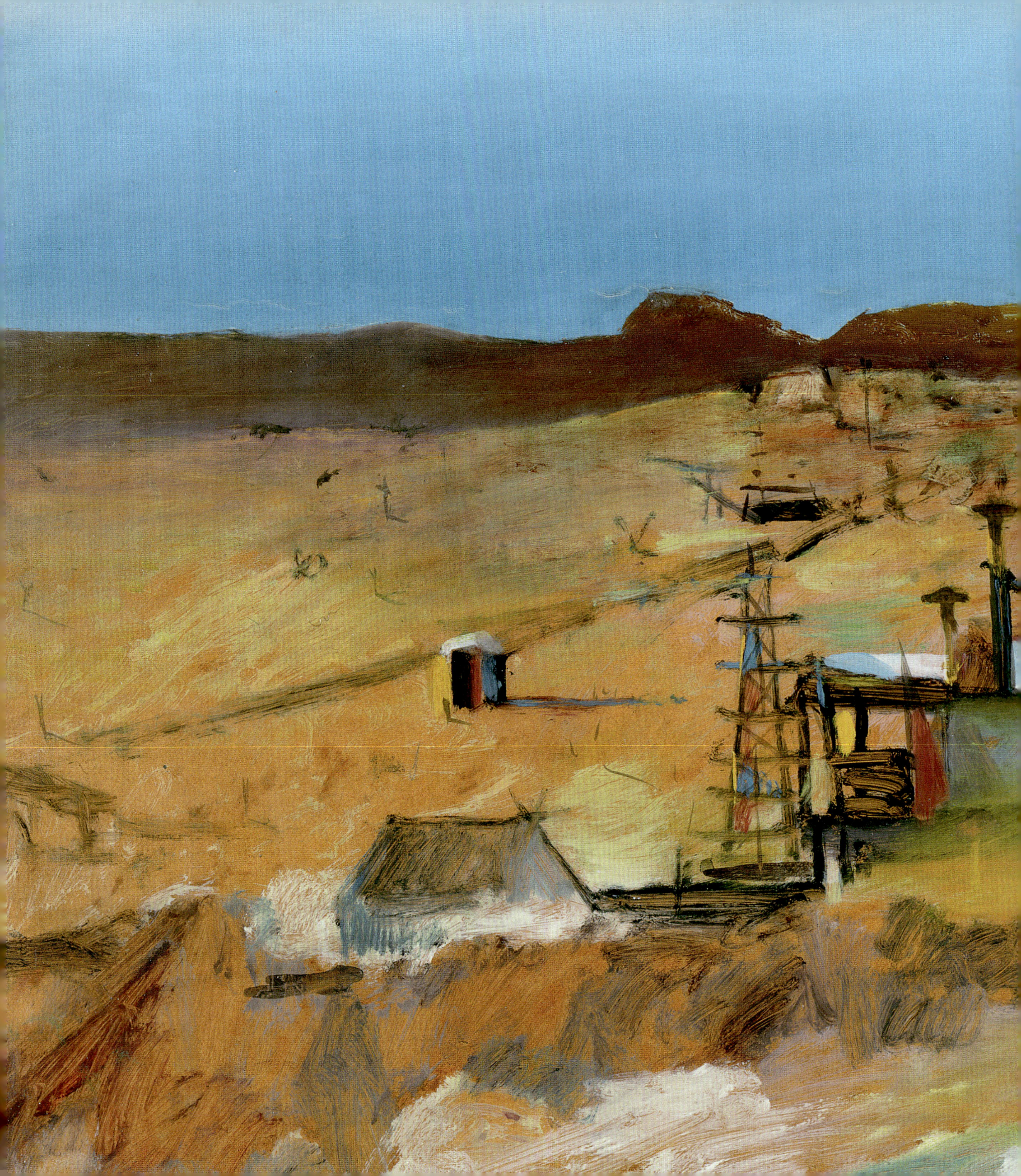

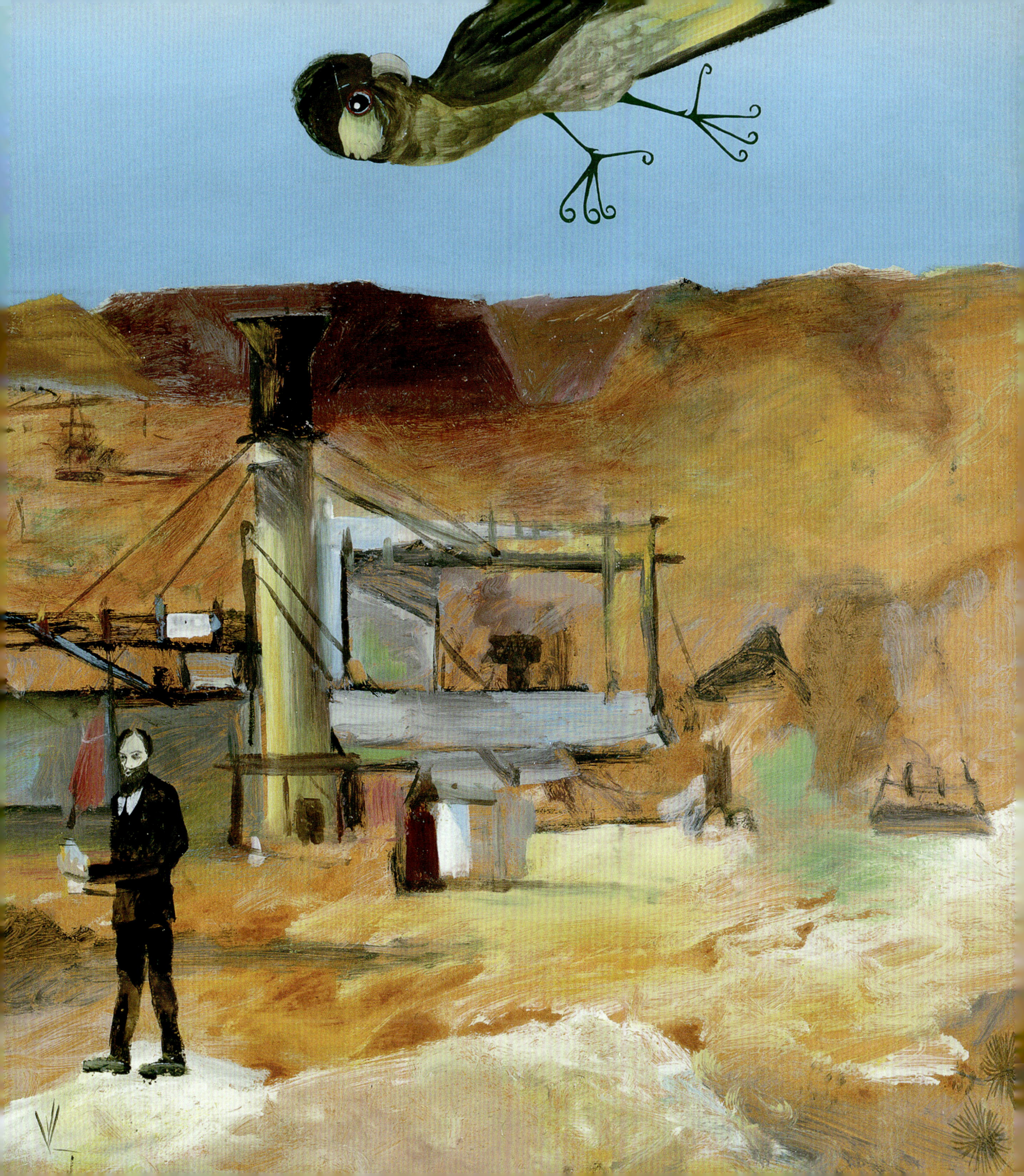

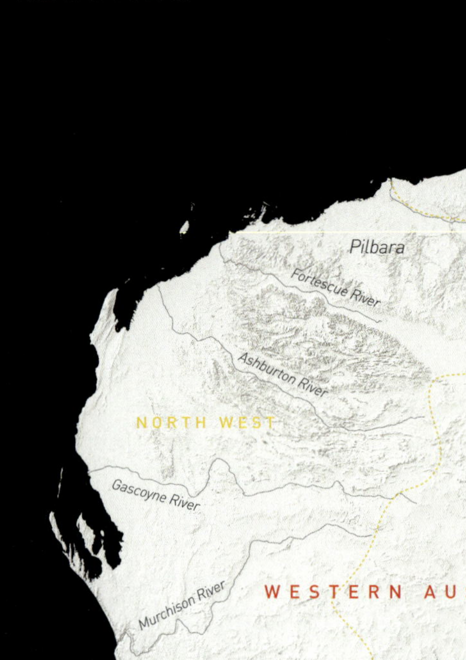

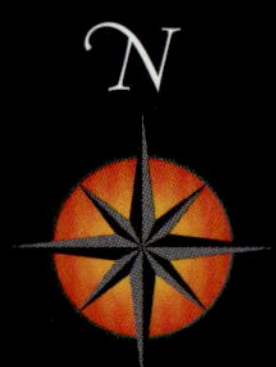

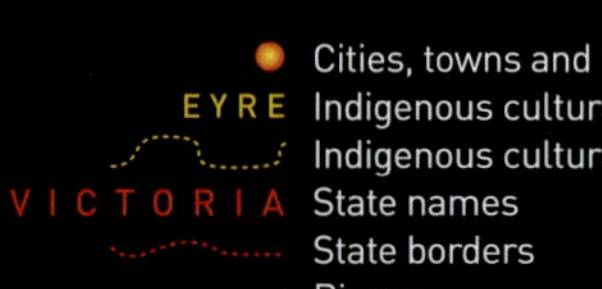

1 Gunbalanya
2 Maningrida
3 Kabulwarnamyo
4 Milingimbi
5 Yathalamarra
6 Ramingining

TORRES STRAIT ISLANDS

7 Waiben (Thursday) Island
8 Badu (Mulgrave) Island
9 Moa
10 Saibai Island
11 Masig (Yorke) Island
12 Erub (Darnley) Island
13 Mer (Murray) Island

0 — 500 — 1000 *miles*

800 — 1600 *km*

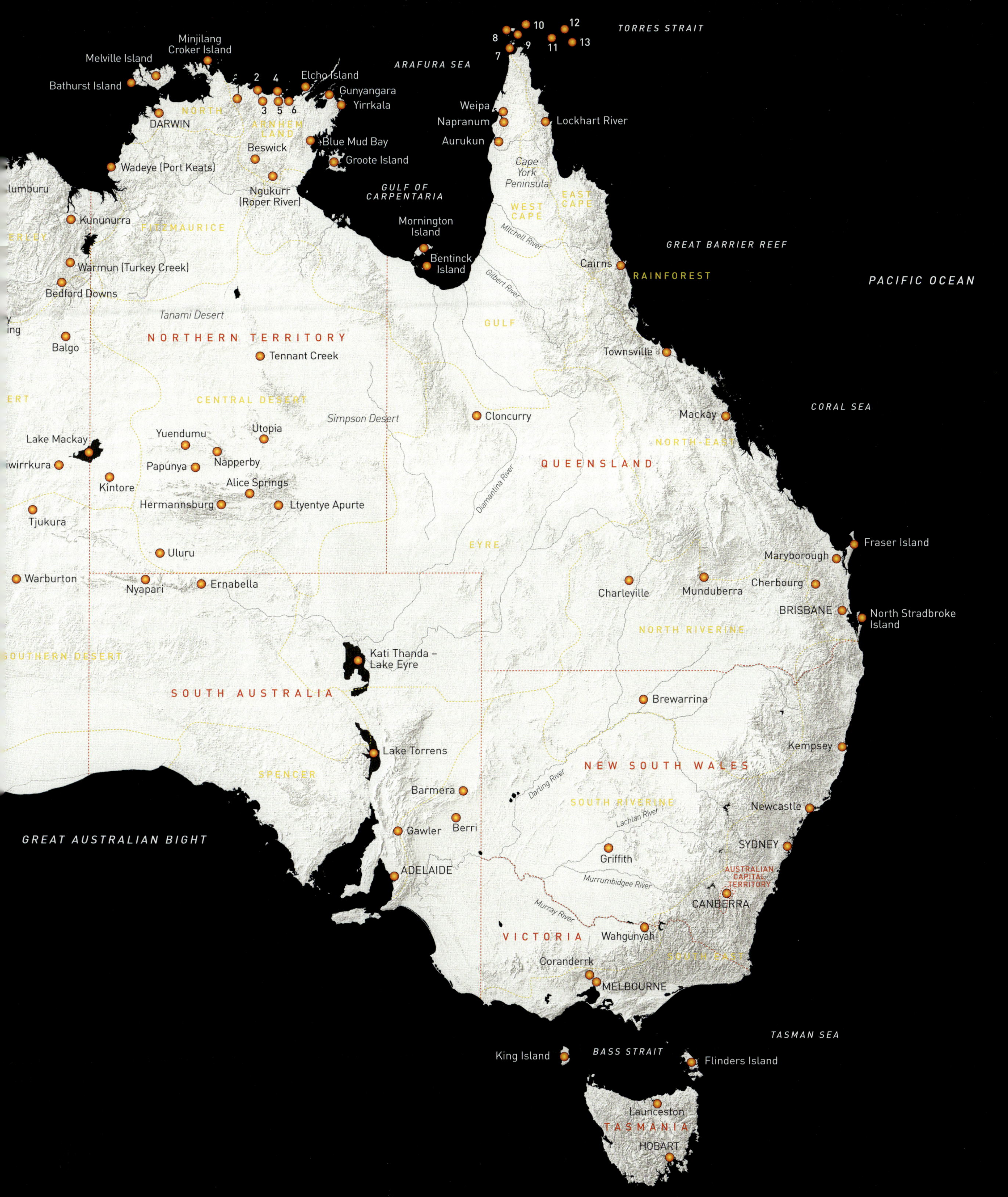

TORRES STRAIT
ARAFURA SEA
Minjilang
Croker Island
Melville Island
Bathurst Island
DARWIN
NORTH
ARNHEM LAND
Elcho Island
Gunyangara
Yirrkala
Beswick
Blue Mud Bay
Groote Island
Wadeye (Port Keats)
Ngukurr
(Roper River)
GULF OF CARPENTARIA
Weipa
Napranum
Aurukun
Lockhart River
Cape York Peninsula
WEST CAPE
EAST CAPE
Mitchell River
Mornington Island
Bentinck Island
Gilbert River
Cairns
RAINFOREST
GREAT BARRIER REEF
PACIFIC OCEAN
Kununurra
FITZMAURICE
Warmun (Turkey Creek)
Bedford Downs
Tanami Desert
NORTHERN TERRITORY
Balgo
Tennant Creek
GULF
Townsville
CENTRAL DESERT
Simpson Desert
Cloncurry
Mackay
CORAL SEA
NORTH EAST
Lake Mackay
Yuendumu
Utopia
Papunya
Napperby
Kintore
Alice Springs
Hermannsburg
Ltyentye Apurte
Tjukura
Diamantina River
QUEENSLAND
EYRE
Uluru
Warburton
Nyapari
Ernabella
Fraser Island
Maryborough
Charleville
Munduberra
Cherbourg
BRISBANE
North Stradbroke Island
NORTH RIVERINE
SOUTHERN DESERT
Kati Thanda – Lake Eyre
SOUTH AUSTRALIA
Brewarrina
Kempsey
Lake Torrens
NEW SOUTH WALES
SPENCER
Darling River
Barmera
SOUTH RIVERINE
Newcastle
Lachlan River
Gawler
Berri
GREAT AUSTRALIAN BIGHT
Griffith
SYDNEY
ADELAIDE
Murrumbidgee River
AUSTRALIAN CAPITAL TERRITORY
CANBERRA
Murray River
VICTORIA
Wahgunyah
SOUTH EAST
Coranderrk
MELBOURNE
TASMAN SEA
King Island
BASS STRAIT
Flinders Island
Launceston
TASMANIA
HOBART

AUSTRALIA: AN INTRODUCTION

KATHLEEN SORIANO

'In Australian landscape painting, as in all great landscape painting, the scenery is not painted for its own sake, but as the background of a legend and a reflection of human values.'[1]

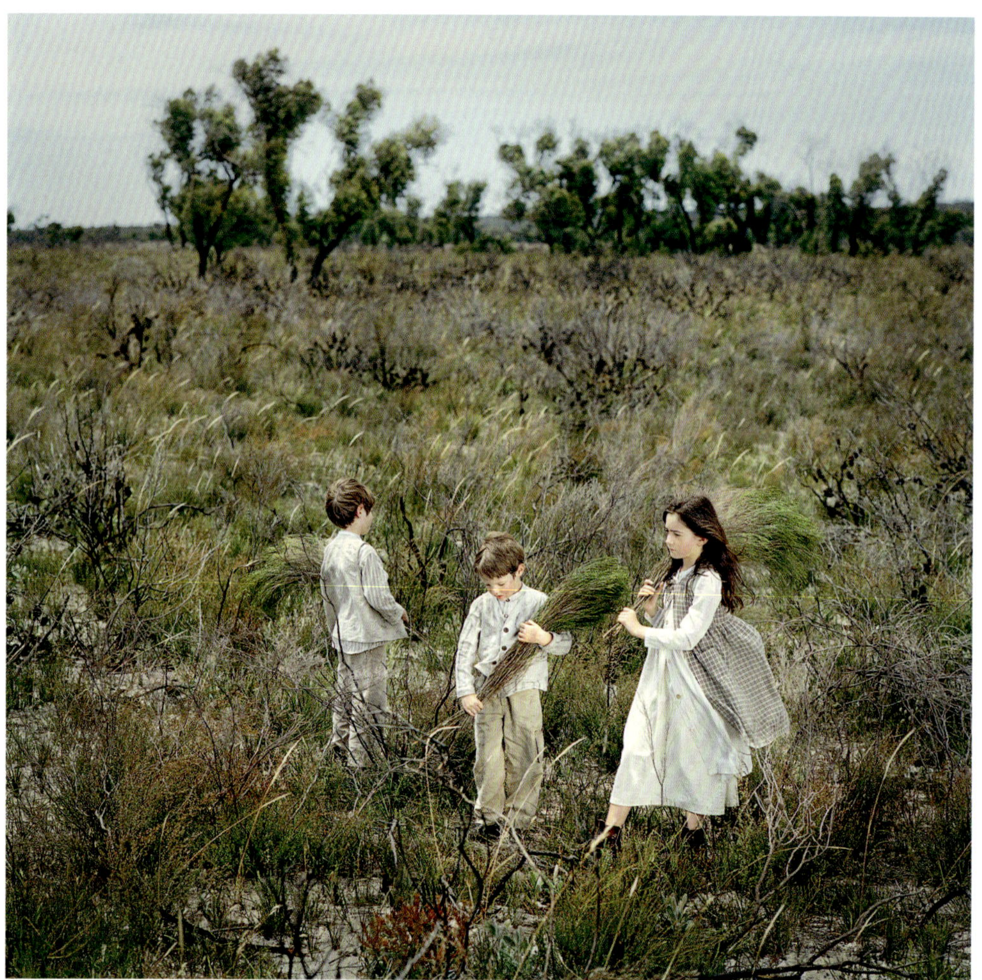

Fig. 1
POLIXENI PAPAPETROU,
The Wimmera 1864 #1, 2006, from the series *Haunted Country*, 2006.
Colour inkjet print, 105 × 105 cm
National Gallery of Australia, Canberra. Purchased 2011

It could be argued that Kenneth Clark's observations are as relevant today as they were in 1961, as some of the works of art in this book reveal. *Australia* takes us through two centuries of Australian art, from the time of the colonial settlers of 1800 to that of the well-travelled artists, Indigenous and non-Indigenous, of our own day. With the theme of land and landscape at its core, the selection conveys the drama and distinctiveness of Australian country, the complexity of its Indigenous and colonial history, the extremes and perceived dangers of nature, the mythologies of the land – such as the story of the child wandering into the bush to collect flowers, never to return (fig. 1) – and, above all, the history of Australian art that has been so clearly defined by its terrain.

Although the twentieth century afforded British audiences occasional opportunities to encounter Australian art, exhibitions were mainly focused on precise periods or movements; a very large survey show including Indigenous art has not been attempted in Britain before. The seminal exhibitions of the 1960s – 'Recent Australian Painting' at the Whitechapel Art Gallery in 1961 and 'Australian Painting: Colonial, Impressionist, Contemporary' at the Tate Gallery in 1963 – were criticised for their view of Australian art as a product of such national characteristics as the climate, the quality of light and the harshness of the landscape. This was considered a misconception at the time, but, as the present selection asserts, it is indeed a truth confirmed by a number of Australian artists, including contemporary practitioners' continued fascination with these subjects.

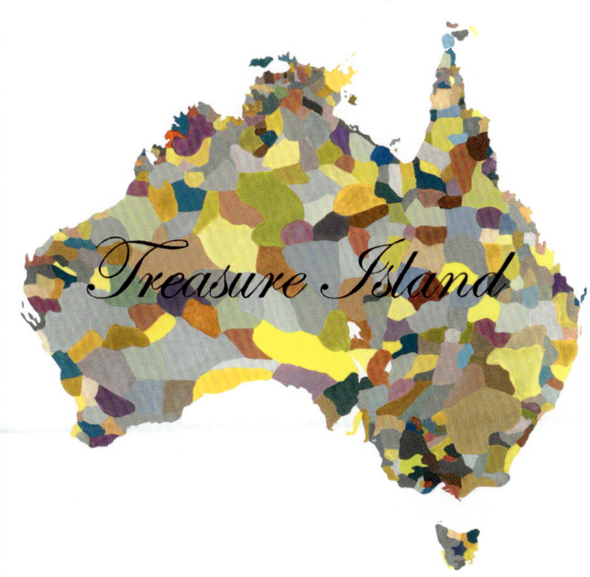

Fig. 2
DANIEL BOYD, **Treasure Island**, 2005. Oil on canvas, 192.5 × 220 cm

National Gallery of Australia, Canberra. Purchased 2006

In 'Australian Visions', the 1984 exhibition of Australian art at the Solomon R. Guggenheim Museum in New York, Thomas M. Messer, director of the Solomon R. Guggenheim Foundation at the time, wrote that 'artists speak for themselves while at the same time carrying upon their shoulders, willingly, deliberately or not, a share of that collective identity that is the mark of particular ethnic and cultural origins'.[2] In her essay for the same catalogue, the art historian Memory Holloway reflected: 'To trace the response to the landscape is to begin to understand how Australia's self-image has changed over time.'[3]

The Australian Indigenous peoples' relationship with the land, depicted in a rich language that varies considerably across the island continent, is embodied in the symbolic iconography of their 'Dreaming' or 'creation' narratives. This distinctive imagery, which constitutes the world's oldest unbroken art tradition, can be traced back some 50,000 to 60,000 years. Present-day Aboriginal painting has become a significant source of Australian national pride, partly for the antiquity associated with its iconography, partly for its aesthetics, but in some instances as much for its forceful and sometimes satirical political content (fig.2).

The notion of landscape as a second skin, your country as an extension of your body, is central to every Aboriginal art form. Country is heart, mind and soul, not property; if anything it owns the people. Conflicts over land sit at the centre of the debate, not only in terms of ownership and occupation, but also more importantly in relation to what land means. For Aboriginal people, land is the foundation of their spiritual being; for some non-Indigenous Australians it represents security and status, a source of wealth and authority. The Indigenous relationship with the land is concerned with an environmental consciousness in which theology and ecology are fused. By contrast, the story of Samuel Terry, who was sentenced in 1800 to seven years for stealing 400 pairs of stockings and transported to Australia in 1801, is a familiar one. On his death in 1838 he owned 19,000 acres, more than the greatest aristocratic landowner in England.

Some Australian myths and legends have emanated from the land and most particularly from the bush. The Australian bush has exercised a considerable influence on how outsiders see Australia and Australians. This perception has been reinforced by the media, most notably film, which has drawn on the many colourful characters populating Australian literature. The bushranger Ned Kelly is perhaps the most famous of these and his legend lives on, with many seeing him as the embodiment of the rebellious, anti-authoritarianism associated with Australian identity.

After the term 'bush', the word 'park' was most used to describe forested land by the first settlers, who assumed that Australian landscapes were natural pastures.[4] On identifying the site for Adelaide as a place of settlement in 1836, William Light, surveyor-general of South Australia, commented: 'This parkland is a pleasant scene, and has much the appearance of English parks, being adorned in many places by large native trees growing in clumps, and having the river passing through the grounds, for some distance, with handsome trees lining its banks.'[5]

Some early pioneers recognised that active management of the land through fire had been practised by the Indigenous people but it was not until the 1960s that researchers began to perceive system and purpose in Aboriginal burning, a work of land management going back thousands of years (figs 3, 4). However, for many in Australia, fire equalled fear and in 1847 Western Australia passed an ordinance to flog or imprison Aboriginals for lighting fires.

In Britain by the 1820s, landscape painting, headed by the Royal Academy's Turner and Constable, had become the dominant art tradition. Given this energetic British background and the compelling presence of Australia's dramatic natural scenery and distinctive light, it is not surprising that landscape painting evolved so successfully there in the first years of the nineteenth century; by the mid-nineteenth century it had grown to become the central concern of Australian art. The twentieth-century artist Howard Taylor (cat.174) commented on that distinctive light: 'The sun is straight

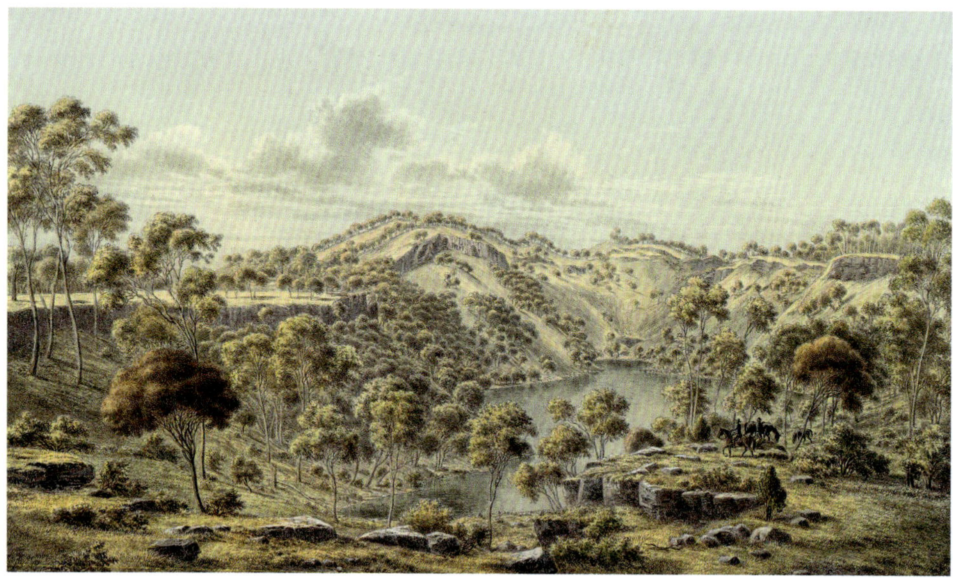

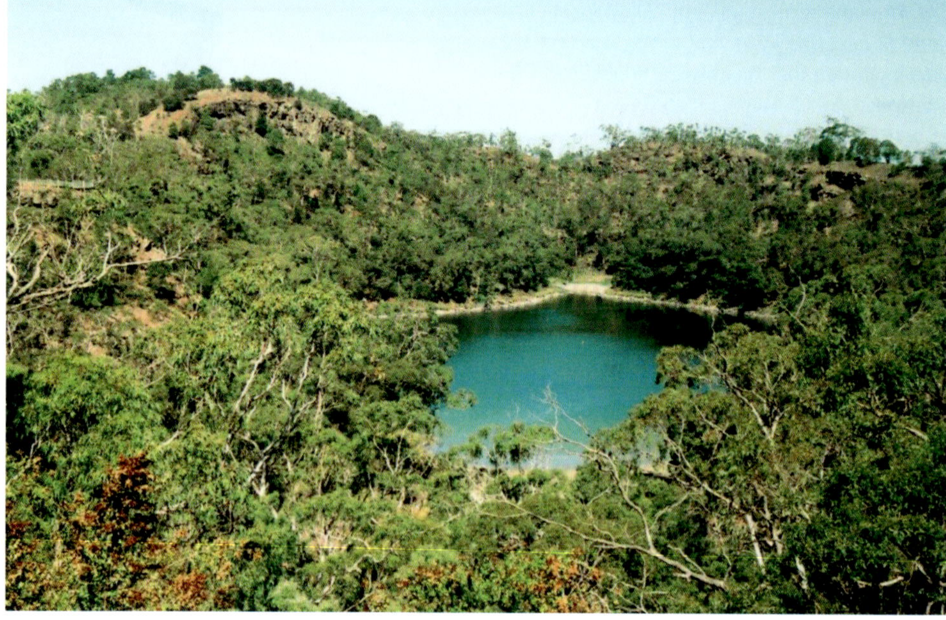

Fig. 3
EUGENE VON GUERARD,
The Crater of Mount Eccles, (Victoria), 1866–68. Lithograph, printed in colour, from multiple stones, 30.1 × 48.5 cm
National Gallery of Australia, Canberra. Purchased 1982

Fig. 4
The crater of Mount Eccles, Victoria, 18 March 2007. Photograph

up above you, it tends to flatten things out. You miss that half-covered sky or the diffused light you get in Europe.'[6]

It is true that some Australian artists, most particularly those of the early nineteenth century, were still inspired by the artists of the countries and cultures in which they had been trained and from which they had only recently arrived, be it the British landscape tradition, or German Romantic views or the outdoor scenes of the French Barbizon painters. But these same Australian artists, and those who followed them, quickly recognised the distinctive qualities and the diversity of the Australian landscape, its geology, flora and fauna, and very soon they were painting in a style that was authentic in conveying its Australianness.

The colonial artists were succeeded by a generation of energetic Australian Impressionists: Tom Roberts (previously a student at the Royal Academy Schools), Frederick McCubbin, Arthur Streeton and Charles Conder. In the tradition of *plein-air* painting, and keen to observe and capture the changing effects of light and weather, these Australian Impressionists promoted outdoor painting, often travelling out from the cities into the nearby countryside on the railway lines then being built.

Although Australia is the most urbanised nation on earth, with over 85 per cent of its population living in cities or on the coast, the bush has had a profound influence on the national psyche. Much as the western frontier shaped American self-perceptions, so the Australian natural environment has formed the Australian character. Bush legends are stereotypically male, tough and rugged, but most importantly their protagonists persevere against all odds. Roberts's depictions of livestock on properties in the late nineteenth century – *A Break Away!* (1891; cat.108) and *Shearing the Rams* (fig.5) – are a product of the romantic idealisation of rural Australia that accompanied the Depression of the 1890s.

Arthur Streeton is one of Australia's most celebrated Impressionist painters whose 'gold and blue' paintings have been a defining image of Australia (cats 101, 103, 109). Like other Australian artists at this time, Streeton regularly sent paintings to the Royal Academy's Annual Exhibitions.

The liberal interpretation of the term landscape throughout the selection allows us to consider the impact of urbanisation and the beachscape, and also permits us to examine the iconography of the presence, or the absence, of the human figure. The beach also provides a sub-theme, not only allowing for depictions of an idealised lifestyle to which people could aspire, but also encapsulating the myth of the healthy young nation. In much the same way, the construction and completion of the Sydney Harbour Bridge inspired many artists (particularly women) to redefine their visions of the city by incorporating into their work this new industrial structure that radiated optimism and energy in its celebration of modern engineering and the modern age.

Literature and painting of the Federation period, when at the turn of the twentieth century the six self-governing British colonies came together to form the Australian nation, reflects a new-found confidence and independence, most clearly expressed in terms of landscape. At the age of twenty-two, the third-generation Australian Dorothea Mackellar, homesick while visiting England from her family's inland cattle station at Gunnedah, wrote her classic Federation poem 'My Country' (published in 1908). Mackellar did not share the British 'Strong love of grey-blue distance / Brown streams and soft dim skies'. She preferred her own 'wilful, lavish land':

I love a sunburnt country,
A land of sweeping plains,
Of ragged mountain ranges,
Of droughts and flooding rains.
I love her far horizons,
I love her jewel-sea,
Her beauty and her terror –
The wide brown land for me![7]

Arthur Boyd and Sidney Nolan were of the generation of Australian artists of the 1950s and 1960s who spent a fair amount of time in London. Boyd was a master at translating visual and emotional experience into myth, often employing Biblical themes, influenced by his religious upbringing (cat. 147).

Nolan was an Associate of the Royal Academy for a number of years before becoming a full Royal Academician in 1991. As the defining figure of Australian art in the twentieth century (fig. 36), the artist who inserted human drama into the Australian landscape, Nolan claimed: 'We all took the policy of Paris on, there was nothing else to do, but always there was the thought that we would learn to tell our own story.'[8] In 1948 Nolan commented on his Ned Kelly series (cats 154, 155, 156, 157) that it was 'a story arising out of the bush and ending in the bush' and that 'the desire to paint the landscape involves a wish to hear more of the stories that take place in the landscape'.[9]

Humour – and a particular strain of irony – is an aspect of Australian art and can be found in the work of John Brack, Sidney Nolan, Russell Drysdale and Jeffrey Smart. John Brack's painting *The Car* (1955; cat. 160) is a good example of these artists' interest in life and the human condition, which is frequently reflected wryly with insight; the painting also illustrates another symbol-laden sub-theme within the selection, that of the long, straight road and the infinitely distant horizon.

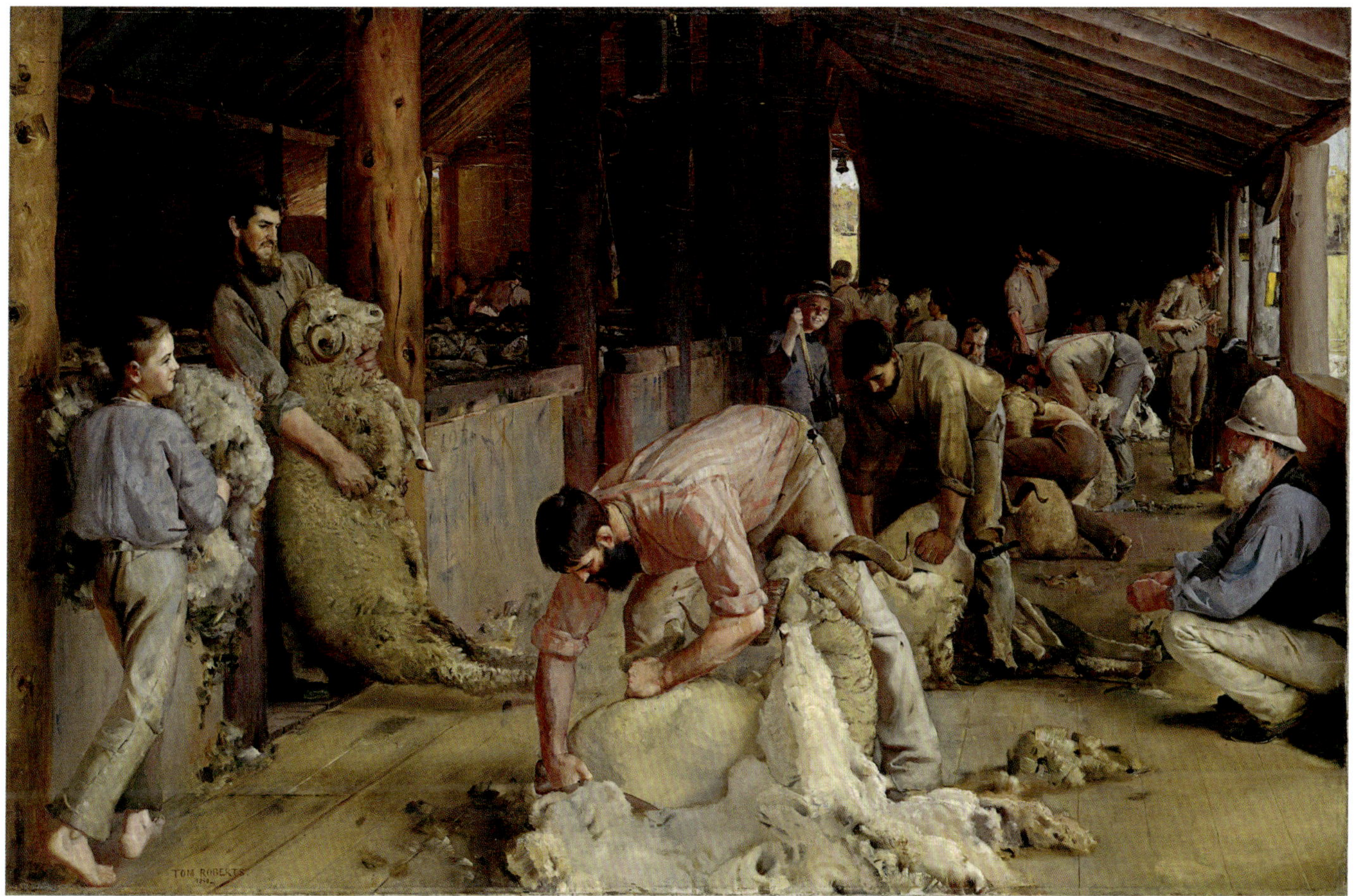

Fig. 5
TOM ROBERTS, **Shearing the Rams**, 1890. Oil on canvas on composition board, 122.4 × 183.3 cm
National Gallery of Victoria, Melbourne. Purchased through the Felton Bequest, 1932

Fig. 6
JULIE DOWLING (KALAAMAYA NATION), **Walyer**, 2006. Synthetic polymer paint and natural earth pigments on canvas, 200 × 150 cm
National Gallery of Australia, Canberra. Purchased 2007

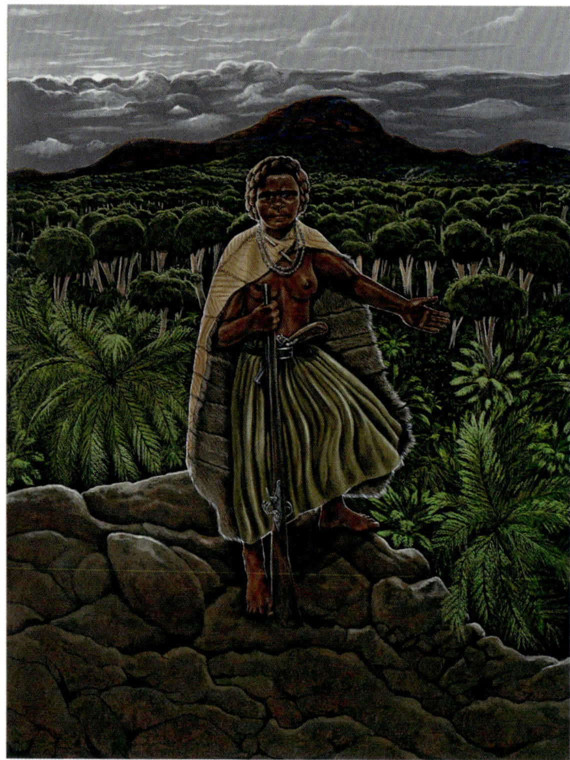

Non-Indigenous Australian artists of the mid- and late twentieth century absorbed traditions from many cultures, not only their own, more familiar European antecedents but also those of the Indigenous peoples. In the 1940s Margaret Preston reduced her palette to earth colours (cats 142, 143), reflecting the influence of Aboriginal art, but she also went on in her writings to express her hopes that Australians would not only be guided by the more familiar European influences but that they would also look to Asia for further inspiration.

In the late 1950s the painter Fred Williams became interested in finding a new aesthetic language with which to represent the very un-European Australian landscape. He established a pictorial equivalent to the overwhelmingly vast, primarily flat terrain in which the traditional European relationship of foreground to background breaks down, necessitating a complete reassessment of compositional space. He tilts the landscape up against the picture plane, so that often the only indicator of distance is the presence of a horizon line, or clumps of trees huddling closer together, suggesting recession.

In the 1960s John Olsen introduced a freshness and vitality into Australian landscape art (cat.161). His work is informed by Zen philosophy, literature and poetry, and its focus on Sydney, where he lived, gives it a strong sense of place. Sydney also served as the inspiration for one of Australia's most extrovert artists of the late twentieth century: Brett Whiteley (cat.168). Bryan Robertson, director of the Whitechapel Art Gallery at the time of the 1961 Australian art exhibition there, introduced Whiteley to Francis Bacon, the artist who was to have the greatest influence on him. Robertson went on to say of the group of Australian artists in London in the 1950s and 1960s: 'The light, the atmosphere and the texture of the landscape fill Australian art and determine its colour, tonality and density.... Australian painters are still much nearer their own landscape than European artists, still excited about it and often passionately identified with it even when the images they make from it are entirely abstract.'[10]

From 1971 to 1972, the art teacher Geoffrey Bardon encouraged Aboriginal people gathered at Papunya, north-west of Alice Springs, to put their Dreamings onto boards (cats 15, 17). Bardon's actions created a significant movement in Indigenous art history, the Papunya Tula Artists' co-operative, whose success went on to inspire Indigenous communities all over Australia. Long Jack Phillipus Tjakamarra, Mick Namarari Tjapaltjarri, Johnny Warangkula Tjupurrula and Clifford Possum Tjapaltjarri were all instrumental in finding a balance between art in ceremony and the public domain, and it was they who opened up new ways of understanding the land.

In the 1980s a group of urban-based Aboriginal artists emerged, considering themselves the freedom-fighters of Aboriginal art. Artists such as Fiona Foley (cat.194) and Robert Campbell Jnr (cat.38) had grown up in an environment in which Indigenous people were striving for recognition of their human rights and sovereignty over their traditional lands, and were using their art to address the many challenges that faced them, such as racism, oppression, dispossession, deaths in police custody, alcohol abuse and violence (fig.6). Other artists emerging during this period, such as Gordon Bennett (cat.176), have been concerned with alternative histories and rejecting racial stereotypes. The son of an Indigenous Australian mother and an Anglo-Celtic father, Bennett explores issues of identity and Australian colonial and postcolonial racism and social injustice in his works. Emily Kame Kngwarreye (cat.23) was touted by dealers as a septuagenarian overnight sensation when her paintings first entered the market in 1989, despite the fact that her achievements were the outcome of five decades of painting on people's bodies and on the ground in the restricted circumstances of ceremony.

Rover Thomas (cats 29, 30) and Paddy Jaminji (cat.28) initiated a renewal of painting in the Eastern Kimberley by lifting the lid on the secret histories of Australia with paintings of country drenched with the blood of Aboriginal victims of massacres; in 1990, with Trevor Nickolls, Rover Thomas was the first Aboriginal artist to appear at the Venice Biennale. Djambawa Marawili (cat.8) and John Mawurndjul (cats 3, 6, 7), two of the most renowned contemporary Australian artists with a string of international contemporary art appearances to their names, have revolutionised bark painting to make us feel the hum of ancestral powers in the earth itself. And that is not even to mention Albert Namatjira, who beguiled a generation but whose life ended in tragedy.

The strong photographic and video component in the last part of the selection reflects the burgeoning of these media around the globe. Tracey Moffatt, one of the most internationally acclaimed contemporary Australian artists, came to prominence in the 1990s with her vibrant, quasi-narrative series of photographs (fig.7), and her film and video compilations looking at gender, popular culture, racial politics and stereotypes (cat.191). Simryn Gill, representing Australia at the 55th Venice Biennale in 2013, considers questions of place and history in her work (cat.188). The displacement of objects in her photographs echoes our modern-day journeys and migrations.

The Australian population, now 23 million, has more than quadrupled in size since 1918, much of that increase from immigration. Since 1945 more than 7 million people have settled in the country as new immigrants, including more than 800,000 refugees. Today one in two Australians were either born overseas, or have at least one parent born abroad. That diversity of origin, and thereby of influence, is reflected in the Australian artists working today (fig.8). Although their art may respond less to their sense of place, their visual representations of Australia continue to be informed – led even – by land and landscape.

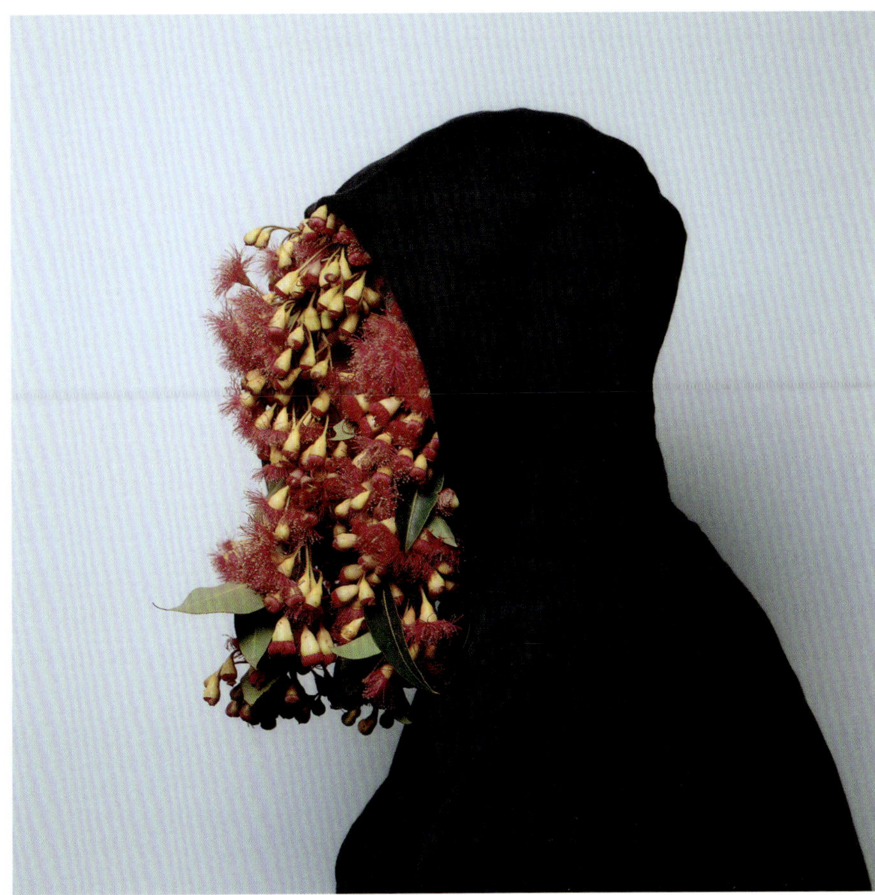

Fig. 8
CHRISTIAN THOMPSON, **Black Gum 1**, from the series *Australian Graffiti*, 2008. C-type colour photograph, 100 × 100 cm

National Gallery of Australia, Canberra. Purchased 2009

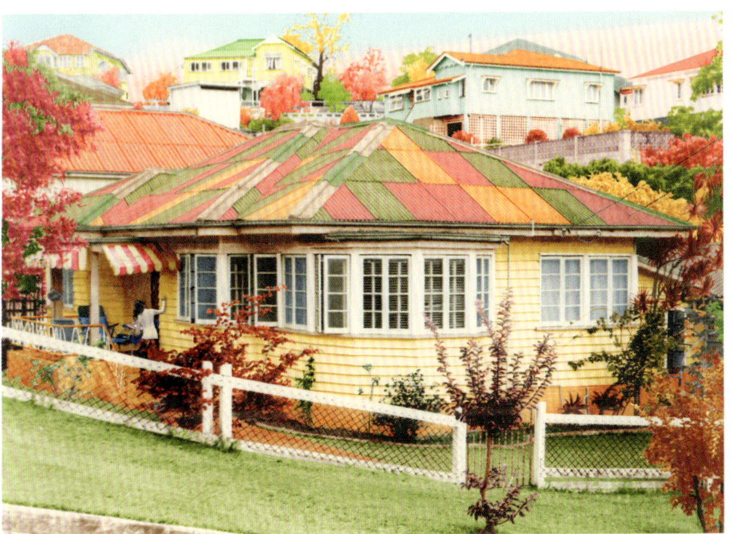

Fig. 7
TRACEY MOFFATT, **Selling Aluminium Siding 1978**, 2008. Digital colour photograph, 71 × 91.5 cm

National Gallery of Australia, Canberra. Gift of Rupert and Annabel Myer, 2008

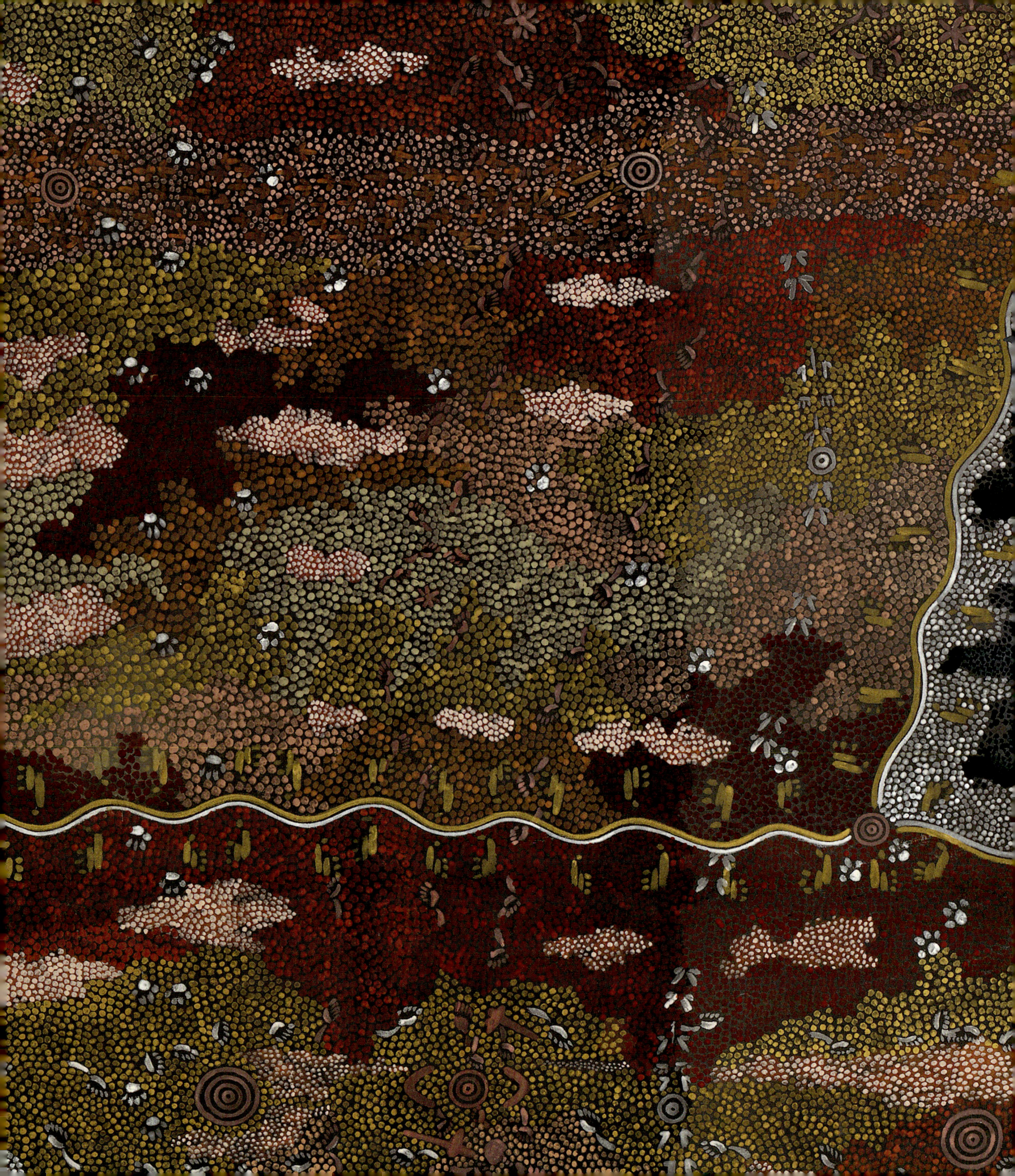

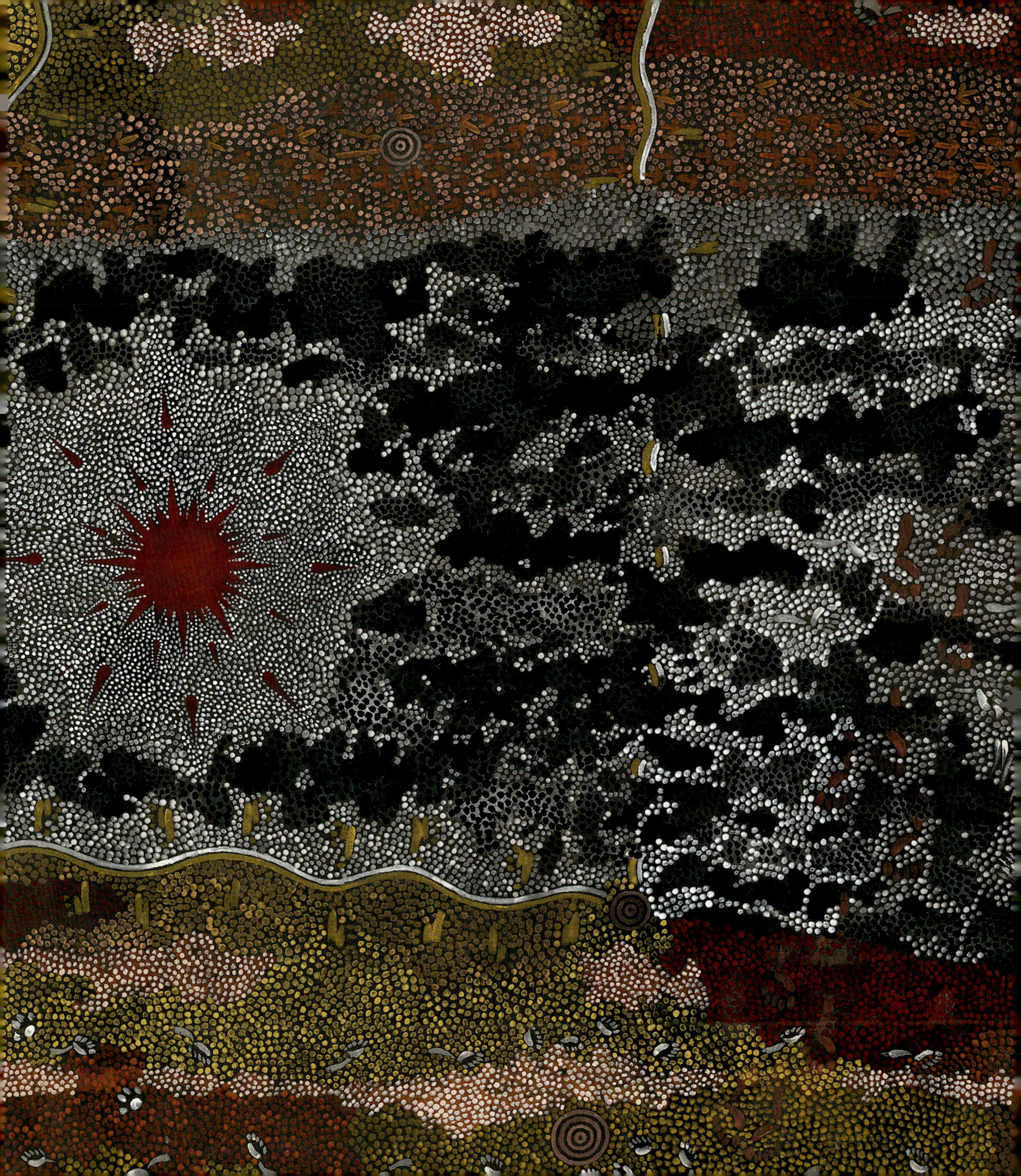

DEAD HEART / LIVE HEART

THOMAS KENEALLY

When Europeans first saw Australia, two reactions were evoked, one being the enthusiasm of the inquirers of the Enlightenment, the other a form of outrage at what a gross affront the place was to the sensibility of the Old World. Born in 1935, I was torn in my own heart between these two reactions. The poetry and novels I read at school had no relevance to the landscape I lived in. The landscape of art existed somewhere else. There were Australian benefits too. For a start, we had Don Bradman, and temperate seasons and, we told ourselves, sometimes deludedly, fuller plates at the dinner table. But also a sense of something missing, of not having discovered ourselves.

In a poem of 1819, the first Justice of the Supreme Court of New South Wales, Barron Field, looking on the same landscapes that had excited Captain James Cook and the lanky botanist Sir Joseph Banks nearly half a century before, demonstrated the aforesaid outrage and wondered whether Australia wasn't creation's mistake:

Kangaroo, Kangaroo!
Thou Spirit of Australia,
That redeems from utter failure,
From perfect desolation,
And warrants the creation
Of this fifth part of the Earth,
Which would seem an after-birth,
Not conceiv'd in the Beginning
(For GOD bless'd His work at first,
And saw that it was good),
But emerg'd at the first sinning,
When the ground was therefore curst; –
And hence this barren wood![1]

The truth was that Australian landscape has always been indifferent to the fact that Barron Field found it a 'barren wood' or an 'after-birth'. Its atmospherics existed always in their own right and went to no effort to offer comparisons. It was – as you see here – full of gods, but they were the gods of neither the ornamental nor social nor warlike passions of Europe. So Australia was not correctly the Antipodes at all. It was not interested in offering a counterbalance to Europe in any way. If anything it was the A-podes, not competing to be the polarity of the northern otherness. As you see in this exhibition, it was what it was, and could be interpreted only on its own terms.

Indeed, its indifference to European expectation was sometimes seen as malign. That's why it is a miracle of human ingenuity we have this exhibition of what is indeed 'this fifth part of the Earth', involving painters who could read the place in their own way. What you see here is what Australians have made of Australia, and it took some time, and above all some vision, to take us from Barron Field to today.

Over 1,200 miles west of Barron Field in 1819, and closer in still to the coast, there were people for whom this earth was no after-birth, but the mother, on whose bosom they found the delight of waterholes, the bounty of animals. There are particular icons in the Desert paintings representing trails, traditional campsites and food, such as in the case of Emily Kame Kngwarreye's painting in this exhibition (cat.23), the abundance of yams.

Just the same, for those of us of the immigrant or 'settler' tradition, a modified version of Barron Field afflicted us still. In 1906 an English geologist, J.W.Gregory, produced a book named *The Dead Heart of Australia*. Let me hasten to say that he wrote the book from within his own discipline and not out of any Pommy malice. But the phrase 'Dead Heart' dominated my childhood, and was a lamentation and an excuse. What, aesthetically, could be done with a country whose geographical 'Dead Heart' echoed what the great novelist Patrick White saw as a spiritual Dead Heart in our raw community? To pile on the self-loathing, a few years after I was born, towards the end of the Depression, a brilliant poet named A.D.(Alec) Hope wrote another influential indictment of Australia that was to resonate with Australians of his and further generations.

They call her a young country, but they lie:
She is the last of lands, the emptiest,
A woman beyond her change of life, a breast
Still tender but within the womb is dry.

Without songs, architecture, history:
The emotions and superstitions of younger lands,
Her rivers of water drown among inland sands,
The river of her immense stupidity

Floods her monotonous tribes from Cairns to Perth.[2]

If one gave the modern British backpacker heading for Cairns and Cape Tribulation that dolorous poem by A.D.Hope, he would not know what Hope's despair meant. But, as late as my childhood, we were still coming to terms in our heads with what Australia was: a venue of exaltation or one of melancholy.

Here, again, in this exhibition, one can see how artists were answering or battling with these propositions of Australian landscape, of bush and Dead Heart, of something immanent and crowded with significance there, or of great vacancy or nothingness. I am happy to say that the old melancholy argument over how to relate to Australia graphically means little to many of the younger generation of painters, whose agenda is less engaged by the Dead Heart–A.D.Hope propositions. And when I say younger I tend – like most of the elderly – to mean people younger than me – the tragic but exuberant Brett Whiteley (fig.9), for example.

But you will see in this exhibition many painters of the immigrant tradition, some of whom brought their techniques with them from northern Europe, who were trying to create a counterpoint to the pessimism of the poetry and of Australian strangeness, and the suspicion of backwardness that colonial and postcolonial life imposed on them. The 'monotonous tribes' were always generating their own images, and they made paintings far from lacking in songs.

Yet take a member of A.D.Hope's 'monotonous tribes' – the famous and unavoidable Sid Nolan, a Melbourne working-class child of the Dead Heart generations. Central Australia fascinated him, as if it gave the periphery of the continent, where most of us

Fig. 9
BRETT WHITELEY, **The Balcony 2**, 1975. Oil on canvas, 203.5 × 364.5 cm
Art Gallery of New South Wales, Sydney. Purchased 1981

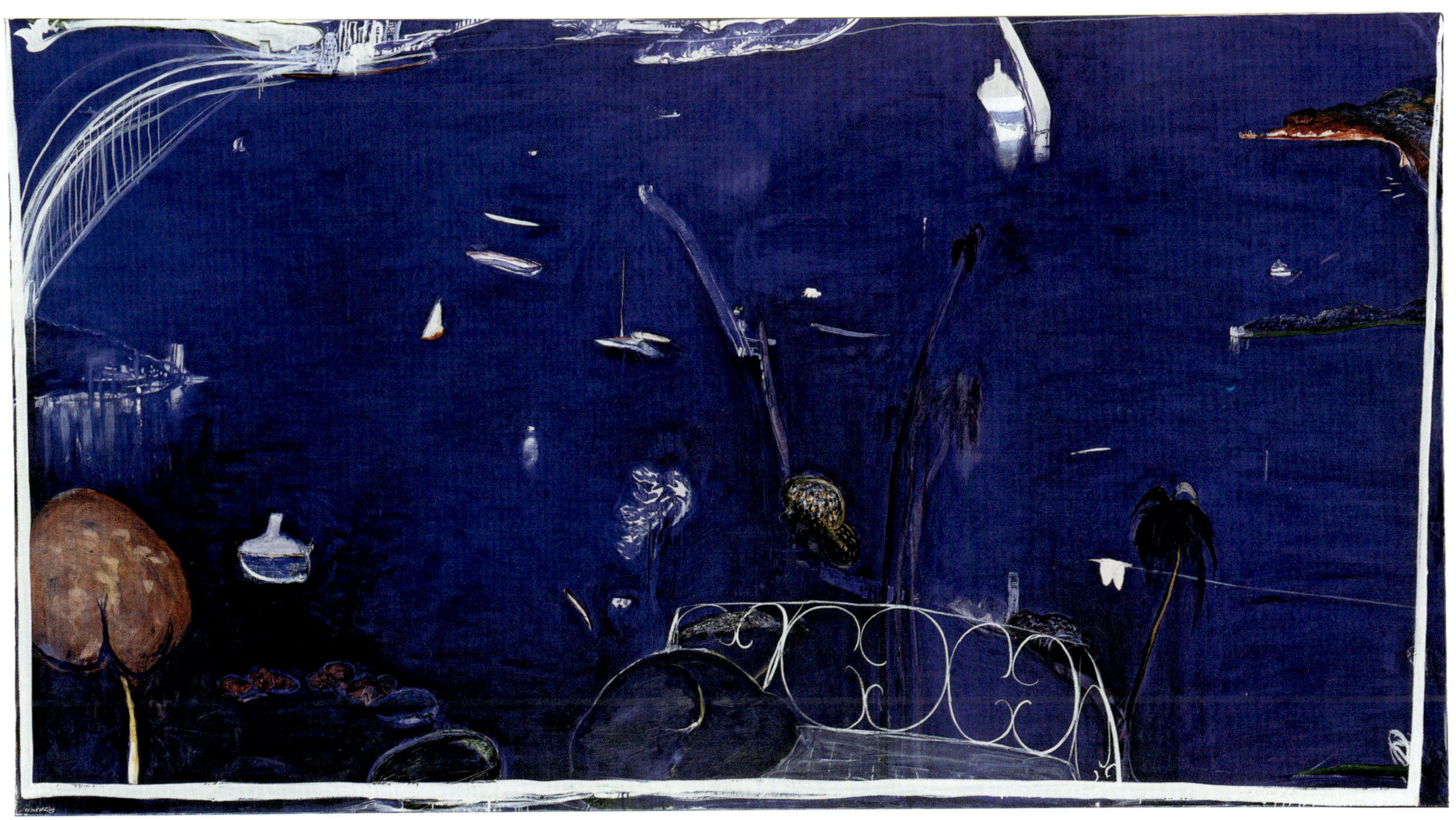

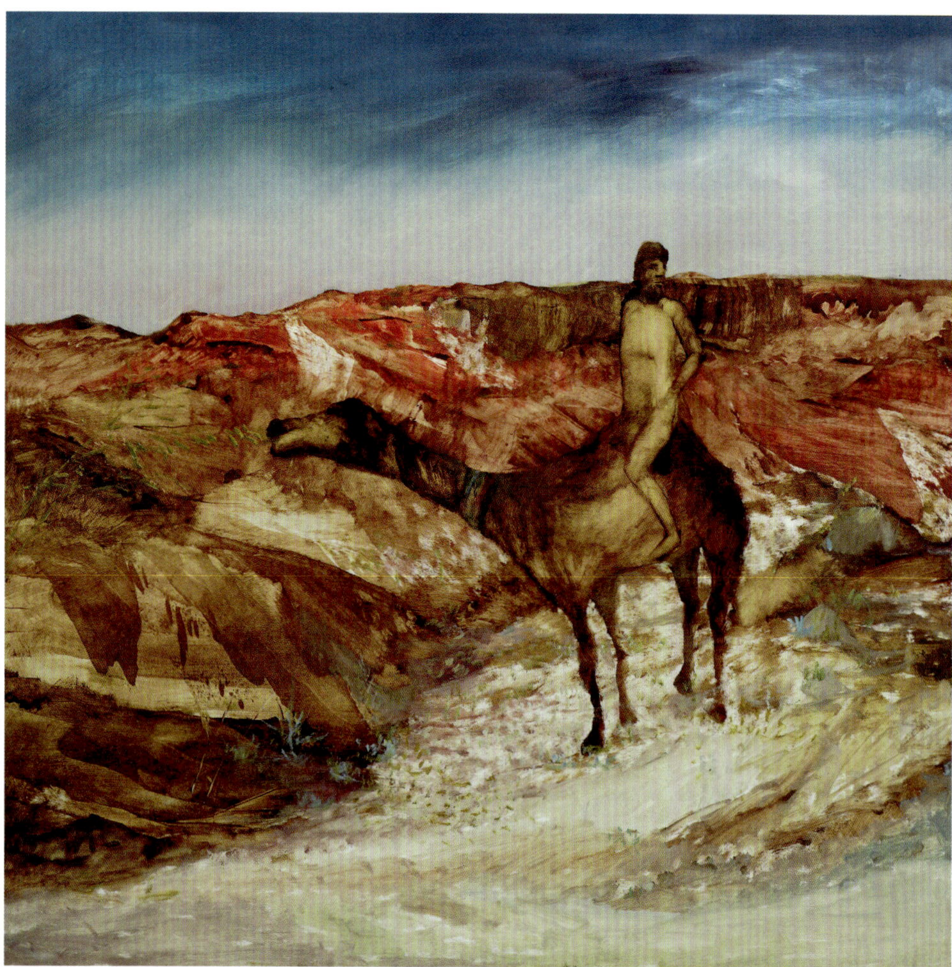

Fig. 10
SIDNEY NOLAN, **Burke**, *c.*1962.
Polyvinyl acetate and oil on hardboard, 122 × 122 cm
Art Gallery of New South Wales, Sydney. Gift of Godfrey Phillips International Pty Ltd, 1968

lived, its meaning. I was always fascinated in Nolan's Ned Kelly series that, although the outlaw family of Kellys lived in a region of Victoria heavy in vegetation, of wooded valleys and august mountains (after all, a terrain that contributed to the Kelly boys' success), in his renowned paintings Nolan narrated the story as if it had occurred in semi-desert. In one of the most magnificent of the Kelly series (cat.155), Ned rides off over a flat clay pan towards a distant fringe of scrubby trees, in a landscape that seems more marginal than the one that in strict truth he inhabited. The town of Mansfield is rendered in the same spirit, as if it were in dusty plains, which is not the geographic truth. In his series on the explorers Burke and Wills, Nolan paints each as he envisages them to have been before they embarked on their lethal, continent-crossing endeavours. In Nolan's version (fig.10) Burke is ultimately rendered naked, his nakedness blending with the body of the camel he rides, and all around an abominable desolation varying, in some of the paintings, only in changes in elevation.

This vision of Nolan's made sense when I heard the eminent Australian curator Patrick McCaughey argue that to the European sensibility Australia was the netherworld, and the seeking Orpheus, whether Ned Kelly or Burke, is meant to be the central and sole figure in a landscape of bewilderment, a Hades.

The Orphean view is there in literature too. In *David Copperfield* (1850) Dickens's Mr Micawber, failed Englishman, goes forth like tragi-comic Orpheus to become an Australian magistrate and thus a demi-redemption story. In *The Importance of Being Earnest* (first performed 1895) it is reported that Algernon must choose between 'this world, the next world, and Australia', Australia here cast, if one made the mistake of taking Oscar Wilde too literally (as one probably shouldn't), as Field's idea of a sort of addendum to the planned earth; a convenient netherworld for unsatisfactory Britons.

What I said about Nolan is not to accuse him of a flaw – for I, like all Australians, revere his work – but it is a matter of the time he inhabited. His painting still delights new generations and strikes to the heart because of the potency of imagery. It fills the Australian landscape with legends, and so it is fitting that the Australia he paints is not an egregiously pretty one. In any case, when it's a choice between verisimilitude and a divine lie that cuts to the heart of truth, we prefer the lie every time.

It is interesting what a high proportion of Australian landscape painting has involved itself with the interior, the bush – and gloriously so in the case of a painter like Fred Williams (fig.11). The more blatantly charming coast, within 125 miles of which most of us live, doesn't get the coverage you would expect. It's the Dead Heart that still grabs our attention. The coast is facilely wonderful. It's the centre that defined Australia by lacking a Mississippi, an amenable river system, and sinking all hope beneath the sand. Yet it's the wonder and not the horror that takes us in these days. Because there's a different sort of river flowing there, an omnipresent map and river of Dreamings. The relentlessly desolate landscape amidst which Burke sits astride his camel is the same sort of landscape, the late Clifford Possum Tjapaltjarri, for example, represented with such a mixture of traditional authority, myth and gusto (fig.12).

The oldest artworks still visible on earth are Australian Aboriginal ones. Where I live, near the great sandstone ledges of Sydney Harbour, it is common to come on areas where totemic animals – sharks, kangaroos, groupers – and human figures, male, female and hermaphrodite have been engraved. In the remote tropic north, around Ubirr Rock and Kakadu, and then westwards in the Kimberley Ranges, it is not extraordinarily difficult to encounter rock paintings of the Rainbow Serpent, the ancestor who provides rain and fertility, of totemic animals, of Gwion Gwion figures in the Kimberley and *mimih* spirits of Western Arnhem Land, dated at over 40,000 years. No, there is no displaced digit. Forty thousand – at least 1,500 human generations.

In the late 1930s an artist named Rex Battarbee met a desert Aboriginal named Albert Namatjira and provided him with the materials to paint landscape. Having done small landscapes on Aboriginal artefacts that he sold to passengers on the train to Darwin, Namatjira picked up painting in the European tradition with extraordinary speed, but always, he said, with 'country in mind'. The Australians were so gratified with his work that they freed him from the indignity of being a ward of the state.

Then, in about 1970, Geoffrey Bardon, a white schoolteacher on a demoralised Aboriginal settlement named Papunya, noticed that when people told stories of 'my country', a continually repeated phrase in conversations between whites and Indigenes, they drew narrative maps in the dust as they spoke. These maps involved a particular symbolism. Hills, water sources, stones, animals and humans were not depicted in a literal manner – if anything they were represented as if from the air. They also, by pure accident, echoed European abstract painting. Bardon also knew that Aboriginals occasionally cleared sandy areas and painted manifestations of the landscape on bare earth and with the range of desert pigments available to them. These sand paintings depicted holy places to do with the emergence and presence of the ancestor heroes, who had made the known world out of a void, and whose journeys and creation acts needed to be ceremonially

Fig. 11
FRED WILLIAMS, **Upwey Landscape**, 1965. Oil on canvas, 147.5 × 183.3 cm
National Gallery of Victoria, Melbourne. Purchased through the Felton Bequest, 1965

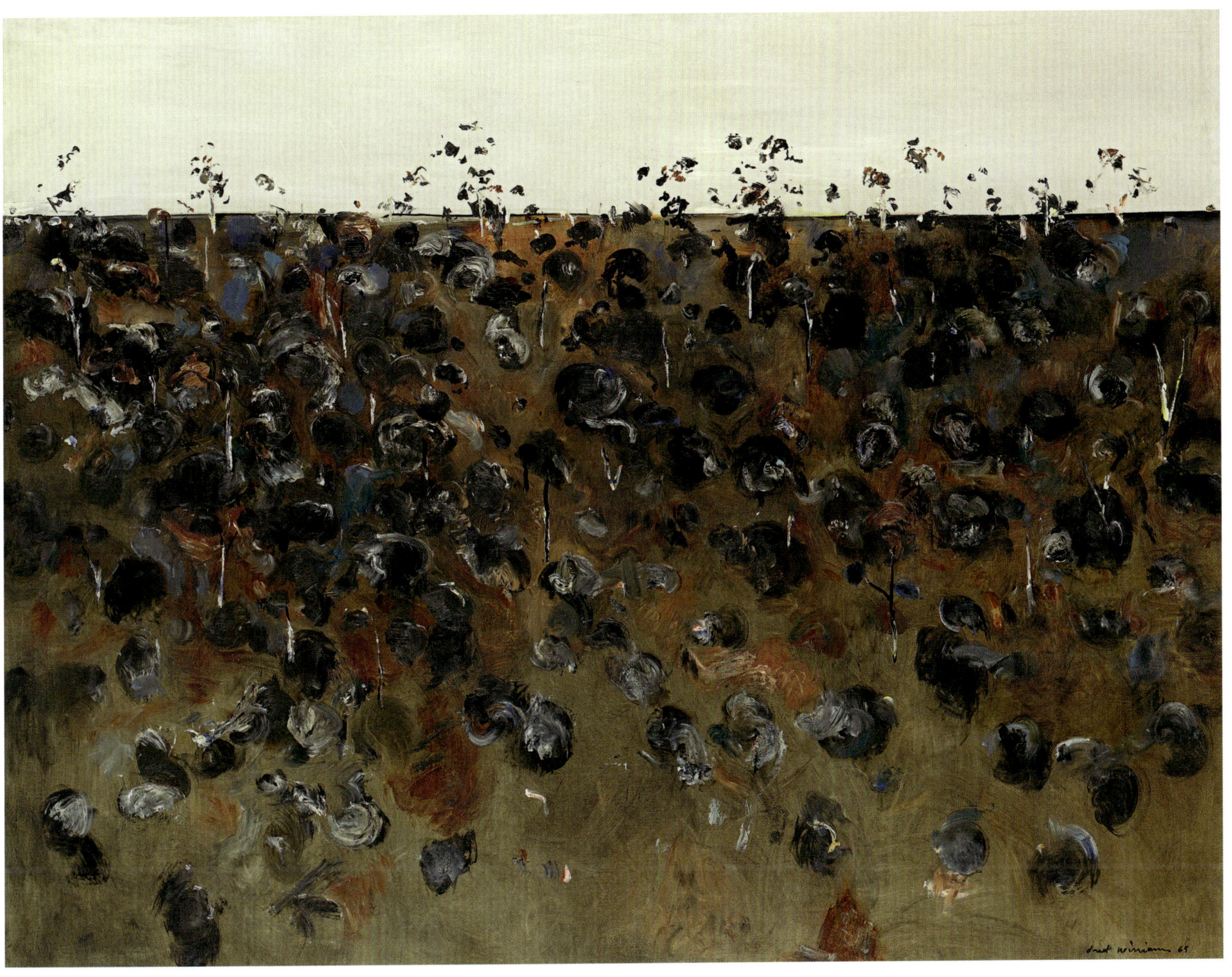

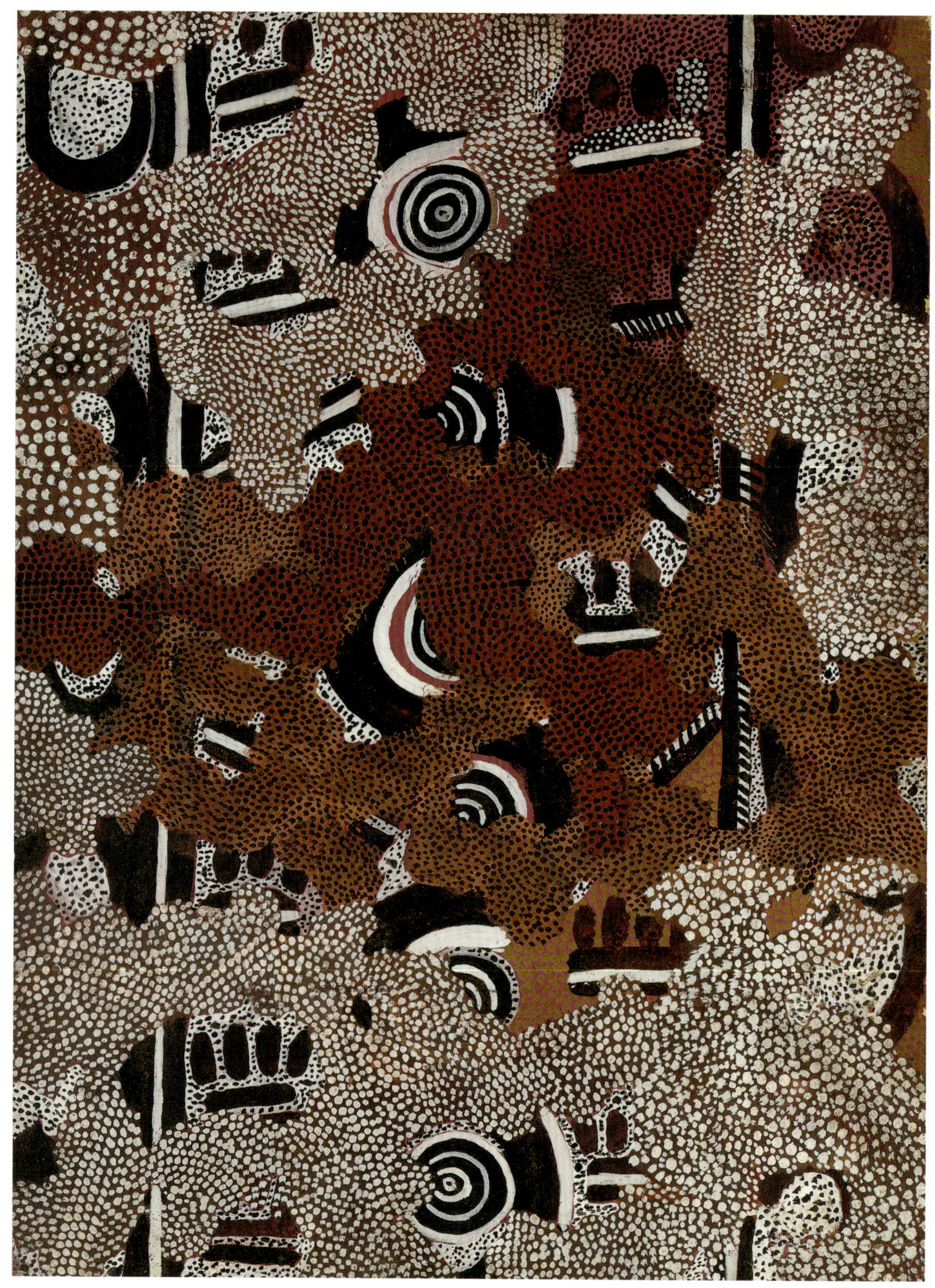

Fig. 12
CLIFFORD POSSUM TJAPALTJARRI, **Bushfire II**, 1972.
Synthetic polymer paint on composition board, 61 × 43 cm
National Gallery of Australia, Canberra. Purchased 1994

repeated at the places recorded in the design. In fact, this is an incomplete, but I hope not inexact, explanation of the word Dreaming. It narrates the creation of a region and shows which parts of the landscape are meaningful for sustenance, and for ceremonies by which the creation is maintained.

On top of everything else the paintings of the desert Aboriginals are also deeds of title – you could not know how to paint a Dreaming unless you had inherited it. These paintings are a variation of the first maps of the interior of Australia. Here are the spirits of the landscape that baffled many European settlers. Every man and woman in the desert retains an association, according to age, knowledge and kinship, in a range of Dreamings and in the ceremonies associated with them. All have a part in the great language-wide group ceremonies that take place at the right season in an area of plentiful food and water. So much for the Dead Heart.

In 1971 Bardon began to provide the community with paints and brushes, and in 1972 the Papunya Tula Artists' co-operative was founded. After the movement began at Papunya, other desert people began to paint using modern equipment. In northern Australia bark paintings of animals depicting their inner organs, wood carvings, wooden or tree-trunk casks for the bones of the deceased, grave-markers and other objects attracted equally intense interest, although these works had been collected by the earliest anthropologists and were considered objects of value long before Bardon gave the Papunya people modern pigments.

This sort of work does not arise from the sort of training undergone by, say, John Olsen and Arthur Boyd or Jeffrey Smart. Saying that is in no way to patronise those great artists. Their painting derives instruction from their elder kin. But the Indigenous visions were simply inherent. And since all desert dwellers know the map of their country, they can all paint it. Entire skin groups such as the Tjapaltjarri of Papunya and the Napangardi of Yuendumu do so.

I saw a very fine painting being done in the shade of a desert oak by two older women at Docker River (Aboriginal name Kaltukatjara), on the border of the Northern Territory and Western Australia in 1983. They worked on canvas – earlier, only wooden panels had been available. Occasionally the wind would blow dust across the canvas the women worked on, and sometimes a toddler would wander up without being warned about marring the canvas. A dog likewise stooged around as if he wanted to add something. The self-consciousness of European artistic endeavour was lacking from the scene. For all I know, that painting might be included in this exhibition.

The younger artists, of a very broad spectrum of origins, paint and make their artworks like artists everywhere, and do not fret about the same things their elders did. But to all the Australian artists represented here, those who struggled to read the heart and those for whom it had always been a torrent of subtleties, I and other Australians owe a debt. Because we have been expertly oriented by them.

They have shown us the track.

CHRONOLOGY

60,000–50,000 BC
Indigenous Australians are estimated to have arrived on the continent.

1606
The first undisputed sighting by Europeans (the Dutch) of the Australian mainland on western Cape York Peninsula, Queensland, home of the Wik people.

During the seventeenth century other Dutch navigators chart the whole of the north and west coasts of the continent, and the south coast as far as Ceduna, South Australia. They name the land New Holland.

1629
The first recorded images about Australia by a European are those illustrating the mutiny that followed the wreck of the Dutch East India Company ship the *Batavia* off the Western Australian coast. They are drawn from descriptions by the Commander Francisco Pelsaert and published in 1647 to illustrate his journal.

1642
Dutch explorer Abel Tasman sights the west coast of Tasmania, which he names Van Diemen's Land.

1688
Buccaneer William Dampier is the first Englishman to visit northern Western Australia (and again in 1699), producing the first-known detailed visual record of Australian flora and fauna.

1720s
The Macassans, from modern-day Sulawesi, commence their annual fishing visits to the shores of northern Australia, carried by the trade winds. They interact with local Aboriginal groups, but do not settle.

1770
Captain James Cook charts the east coast of New Holland, names it New South Wales, and claims it for Great Britain.

1788
18 January: the First Fleet of British convict and military colonists under Captain Arthur Phillip sails into Botany Bay.

26 January: the First Fleet arrives at Sydney Cove, establishing the first European settlement in Australia.

An estimate of the Australian Indigenous population at this time is 1 million.

1790
Pemulwuy (*c.*1750–1802), the first Aboriginal resistance fighter known by name, commences a guerrilla campaign against the new settlers at Parramatta and the Georges and Hawkesbury Rivers in the Sydney area.

1793
11 February: the first free settlers arrive in New South Wales.

1800
January: Australia's first resident professional artist, John Lewin, arrives in Sydney from London.

1801–03
Matthew Flinders circumnavigates New Holland. Flinders champions the name 'Australia' for the entire southern continent, rather than 'Terra Australis' or 'New Holland'. The Aboriginal Bungaree also participates in this voyage.

William Westall becomes the first professional landscape artist to work in Australia as part of Matthew Flinders's mapping voyage.

1802
French explorer Nicholas Baudin is the first European to record sighting paintings on sheets of bark, forming a shelter on Maria Island, Tasmania.

1803
Van Diemen's Land (now Tasmania) is colonised.

1804
A second convict settlement is established in Van Diemen's Land, at what is now Hobart.

1824
The British Admiralty agrees that New Holland should be officially known as Australia.

1825
Van Diemen's Land is proclaimed a separate colony from New South Wales.

1829
The colony of Swan River District (now Western Australia) is founded, formally making the entire continent a British territory.

1831
18 February: John Glover, a British landscape artist, arrives in Hobart from London, aged sixty-four, and becomes Australia's finest colonial artist in the 1830s and 1840s.

1835
Melbourne is settled, and in 1836 is named and declared the capital of the Port Phillip District of New South Wales (now Victoria).

Conrad Martens arrives in Sydney from London, becoming the leading landscape artist for over 40 years.

1836
27 August: W. C. Piguenit is born in Hobart, Australia's first locally born professional landscape artist.

28 December: the province of South Australia is founded.

1845
Ludwig Leichhardt is the first European to visit the Kakadu area in the Northern Territory. Aboriginal artists of the region capture this event in rock painting.

1850
1 June: the first convicts arrive in Western Australia, under the Comptroller-General, Edmund Henderson (who is also an artist).

1 October: the transportation of convicts to New South Wales is officially abolished.

1851
1 July: Port Phillip District separates from New South Wales and becomes the colony of Victoria.

Gold is discovered in New South Wales and soon afterwards more prolifically in Victoria.

1852
28 December: Eugene von Guérard arrives in Victoria and becomes Australia's most significant colonial landscape artist.

1855
Six Aboriginal bark paintings are shown at the Exposition Universelle, Paris.

1856
The name Tasmania, after the seventeenth-century Dutch navigator Abel Tasman, is officially adopted, replacing Van Diemen's Land.

1859
10 December: Queensland becomes a separate colony from New South Wales.

1861
A museum of art is established at the Public Library of Victoria, Melbourne, and in 1869 is named National Gallery of Victoria.

1868
The last convicts to be transported to Australia arrive at Fremantle, Western Australia.

1871
Art Gallery of New South Wales is established as the Academy of Art in Sydney.

1872
23 June: the first message on the Overland Telegraph is transmitted, connecting Adelaide via Darwin to Java; Australia is now in more rapid contact with the rest of the world.

1878
The earliest surviving bark paintings are collected from the Port Essington region, Northern Territory, and exhibited at a meeting of the Linnean Society of New South Wales in Sydney. The collection is now housed at the Macleay Museum, University of Sydney.

1880
Melbourne's first International Exhibition opens in the Royal Exhibition Building.

1881
Art Gallery of South Australia, Adelaide, is established.

1884
Art Gallery of Ballarat, Victoria, is founded.

Captain Frederick Carrington collects five bark paintings from a shelter on Field Island, at the mouth of the South Alligator River.

1885
Tasmanian Museum and Art Gallery, Hobart, is established.

1886
Warrnambool Art Gallery, Victoria, is established.

1887
Bendigo Art Gallery, Victoria, is founded.

1888
The centenary of European settlement is celebrated.

The Centennial International Exhibition, Melbourne, includes the first recognised exhibition of Aboriginal art.

1889
August: the groundbreaking '9 by 5 Impression Exhibition' in Melbourne includes works by Roberts, Streeton, Conder and McCubbin.

1890
One of Australia's worst economic Depressions begins.

1891
Victoria Museum and Art Gallery, Launceston (later Queen Victoria Museum and Art Gallery), is established.

A European, Joseph Bradshaw, first reports seeing the rock paintings in caves in the Kimberley region of Western Australia, formerly known as the Bradshaws and now known as the Gwion Gwion.

1893
Five works by Mickey of Ulladulla are awarded a medal at the Chicago World's Fair.

1894
South Australia extends the franchise to women, who vote for the first time in Australia in the 1896 South Australian House of Assembly election.

1895
Art Gallery of Western Australia, Perth, is established.

Queensland Art Gallery (later Queensland Art Gallery/Gallery of Modern Art), Brisbane, is founded.

1896
Geelong Gallery, Victoria, is established.

1897
The Art Gallery of New South Wales, Sydney, establishes the Wynne Prize for Australian landscape painting.

Art Gallery of South Australia, Adelaide, receives a bequest from Sir Thomas Elder, the first significant bequest to a major art museum in Australia.

1898
2 April–7 May: 'Exhibition of Australian Art in London' is held at the Grafton Galleries, London, the first major exhibition of Australian art to be shown overseas.

1900
17 September: Queen Victoria proclaims that the Commonwealth of Australia, comprising all six colonies, will come into existence on 1 January 1901.

1901
1 January: the six colonies of Australia become a federation, known as the Commonwealth of Australia. Melbourne is the temporary capital of Australia until

1927. Edmund Barton becomes the first prime minister.

29 March: the first Australian federal elections are held and Edmund Barton selects the first Federal Cabinet.

The national population of Australia is over 3.8 million. The minimum estimate of Australia's Indigenous population is 94,564.

1902
3 November: the empire cable, the submarine telegraph cable from Vancouver, Canada, to Southport, Queensland, is opened.

1904
The National Gallery of Victoria, Melbourne, receives the large Felton Bequest, from the businessman Alfred Felton.

1909
The Act establishing an Australian High Commission in London becomes law and Australia's first overseas office is established.

1912
Baldwin Spencer commissions and collects bark paintings from Oenpelli (Gunbalanya), Western Arnhem Land. The collection is housed at the Museum of Victoria.

1913
12 March: the capital of Australia is founded, and named Canberra.

1914
4 August: the First World War begins.

1915
25 April: the Australian and New Zealand Army Corps (ANZAC) land on the Gallipoli Peninsula, Turkey.

1918
11 November: peace is declared and the First World War ends.

25 May–22 June: 'Exhibition of Paintings by Australian War Artists' is shown at the Grafton Galleries, London.

The national population of Australia is over 5 million.

1922
George W. Lambert is elected an Associate of the Royal Academy.

1923
'An Exhibition of Australian Art' is held at Burlington House, London.

1927
9 May: the first Parliament House, Canberra, opens when the Federal Government relocates from Melbourne to Canberra.

1929
The economic crash known as the Great Depression begins.

1932
19 March: the Sydney Harbour Bridge is officially opened.

1934
William Moore's *The Story of Australian Art: From the Earliest Known Art of the Continent to the Art of To-day* is published.

1936
Australian painter Rex Battarbee teaches Aboriginal artist Albert Namatjira, along with other Aboriginal artists at the Hermannsburg mission in the Northern Territory, Western-style watercolour landscape painting. It becomes a popular style, known as the Hermannsburg School.

1939
3 September: Britain, France, Australia and New Zealand declare war on Germany.

Namatjira's *Illum-baura (Haasts Bluff), Central Australia* becomes the first work by an Aboriginal artist to be purchased by a major public art museum, the Art Gallery of South Australia, Adelaide.

The national population of Australia is around 7 million.

1941
The *Angry Penguins* literary and artistic magazine is first issued. It presents the work of Albert Tucker, Sidney Nolan and others and continues until 1946.

7 December: the Japanese attack Pearl Harbor in Hawaii, America declares war on Japan and the Pacific War begins.

The exhibition, 'Art of Australia, 1788–1941', opens at the National Gallery of Art, Washington DC. It includes eleven bark paintings from Oenpelli and two drawings by Tommy McRae, as well as works by Glover, McCubbin, Roberts, Streeton, Conder, Lambert, Drysdale, Preston and others.

1942
15 February: Singapore falls to the Japanese Army and the British abandon the people in the South Pacific; it is the beginning of the end of colonial rule in the region.

February: Japanese air raids begin on Darwin, Northern Territory, and in 1943 in Arnhem Land.

March: Japanese air raids start on Broome, Western Australia.

1945
8 May: the Second World War formally ends in Europe.

2 September: Japan unconditionally surrenders, ending the war in the Pacific.

1948
The American-Australian Scientific Expedition to Arnhem Land led by the ethnologist Charles Mountford is sponsored by the National Geographic Society and the Smithsonian Institution, Washington DC, and the Commonwealth of Australia. Some 600 works (paintings on bark and paper, along with several sculptures and artefacts) are collected, and eventually distributed among major public art museums in Australia and the Smithsonian.

1950
The national population of Australia is over 8.3 million.

Russell Drysdale's solo exhibition at the Leicester Galleries, London, convinces British critics that Australian artists have a distinctive vision of their own.

1956
22 November–8 December: the Olympic Games are held in Melbourne, the first to be staged in the southern hemisphere and the first to be hosted outside Europe and North America.

1957
28 August–14 September: the exhibition 'Aboriginal Art of Australia' is shown at the Institute of Contemporary Arts, London.

1961
June–July: the 'Recent Australian Painting' exhibition is shown at the Whitechapel Art Gallery, London.

1962
Australia becomes involved in the Vietnam War.

Bernard Smith's book *Australian Painting, 1788–1960* is published.

1963
January: 'Australian Painting' exhibition, the biggest survey of Australian painting to date in the city, is shown at the Tate Gallery, London.

The magazine *Art and Australia* is first published.

Yolngu artists of Yirrkala in Eastern Arnhem Land paint the Church Panels.

14 and 28 August: the Yolngu people present the Yirrkala Bark Petitions as title deeds to Parliament to recognise their rights to their traditional lands. Although unsuccessful at the time, these petitions led to constitutional reform.

1965

The exhibition 'Australian Aboriginal Bark Paintings 1921–1965', organised by the Australian Institute of Aboriginal Studies, Canberra, opens at the Walker Art Gallery, Liverpool, and is shown at the Commonwealth Institute, London.

1966

Robert Hughes's *The Art of Australia* is published.

1967

10 August: a referendum enables the Commonwealth Government to make legislation on behalf of the Indigenous Australians, a power that previously had rested with individual state governments, and to include Indigenous people in the national census.

1968

August: the National Gallery of Victoria, Melbourne, moves to its new quarters in St Kilda Road.

1971

A group of senior Aboriginal men at the government settlement at Papunya, west of Alice Springs, paint the first of a series of murals in traditional Desert designs on the walls of the local school. They are also encouraged to paint on movable supports. The event is the precursor of the Western Desert art movement.

1973

11 January: Australia's participation in the Vietnam War formally ends.

The Australia Council for the Arts is formed, the principal arts funding and advisory body in Australia.

Patrick White is awarded the Nobel Prize in Literature 'for an epic and psychological narrative art which has introduced a new continent into literature'.

20 October: the Sydney Opera House opens and is the first venue for the Biennale of Sydney, the international festival of contemporary visual arts.

1974–75

The 'Ten Australians' exhibition of contemporary Australian art, organised by the Visual Arts Board of the Australia Council for the Arts, tours to Paris, Stuttgart, Venice and Milan.

1976

The Aboriginal Land Rights (Northern Territory) Act, 1976 is passed in Federal Parliament. It is the first piece of Commonwealth legislation to acknowledge Aboriginal ownership of traditional or customary lands.

1982

12 October: the National Gallery of Australia, Canberra, opens.

The exhibition 'Eureka! Artists from Australia', organised by the Arts Council of Great Britain, is shown in London at the Serpentine Gallery and the Institute of Contemporary Arts.

1988

The Aboriginal Memorial, a monumental installation of 200 hollow log coffins representing 200 years of European invasion, is dedicated to all Indigenous Australians on the occasion of the bicentenary of European settlement. It is first shown at the Biennale of Sydney before moving to its permanent home at the National Gallery of Australia, Canberra.

31 March–29 May: 'Stories of Australian Art' is shown in London at the Commonwealth Institute, and later at the Usher Art Gallery, Lincoln.

12 June: the Barunga Statement, painted by seven Indigenous artists, is presented to the Prime Minister of Australia Bob Hawke, who promises to negotiate a treaty between the Commonwealth Government and Indigenous Australians.

1990

2 March–22 April: the first Adelaide Biennial is held at the Art Gallery of South Australia, Adelaide. It is the flagship visual arts event of the Adelaide Festival of arts and the nation's pre-eminent survey of contemporary Australian art.

Rover Thomas and Trevor Nickolls are the first Aboriginal artists to represent Australia at the Venice Biennale.

1991

26 June: Sidney Nolan is elected a Royal Academician.

November: the Museum of Contemporary Art, Sydney, opens.

1993

23 July–10 October: the exhibition 'Aratjara: The Art of the First Australians' opens at the Hayward Gallery, London.

17 September–5 December: the first Asia Pacific Triennial of Contemporary Art is held at Queensland Art Gallery, Brisbane.

2000

15 September–1 October: the Olympic Games is held in Sydney.

2002

25 November: the Ian Potter Centre of the National Gallery of Victoria opens in Federation Square, Melbourne, with the exhibition 'Fieldwork'. It is the world's first major art museum dedicated exclusively to Australian art.

2006

6 December: the Gallery of Modern Art (GOMA) opens. An adjunct to the Queensland Art Gallery, Brisbane, it is the largest gallery of modern and contemporary art from the twentieth and twenty-first centuries in Australia.

2007–08

13 October–10 February: the first Australian Indigenous Art Triennial, 'Culture Warriors', opens in Canberra at the National Gallery of Australia.

2008

13 February: in Parliament the Australian Prime Minister Kevin Rudd delivers his historic national apology to the Aboriginal and Torres Strait Islander people for the mistreatment of those from the 'Stolen Generations'.

2010

30 September: thirteen Aboriginal and Torres Strait Islander Australian galleries open at the National Gallery of Australia, Canberra. It is the world's largest space dedicated solely to Indigenous Australian art.

2011

21 January: the privately funded Museum of Old and New Art (MONA) opens in Hobart, Tasmania.

26 May–11 September: the exhibitions 'Out of Australia' and 'Baskets and Belonging' are held at the British Museum, London.

2012–13

9 October–20 January: the exhibition 'Aux Sources de la Peinture Aborigène – Australie Tjukurrtjanu' is shown at the Musée du Quai Branly, Paris.

2013

21 September–8 December: 'Australia' opens at the Royal Academy of Arts, London.

1

COUNTRY: ABORIGINAL ART

WALLY CARUANA AND
FRANCHESCA CUBILLO

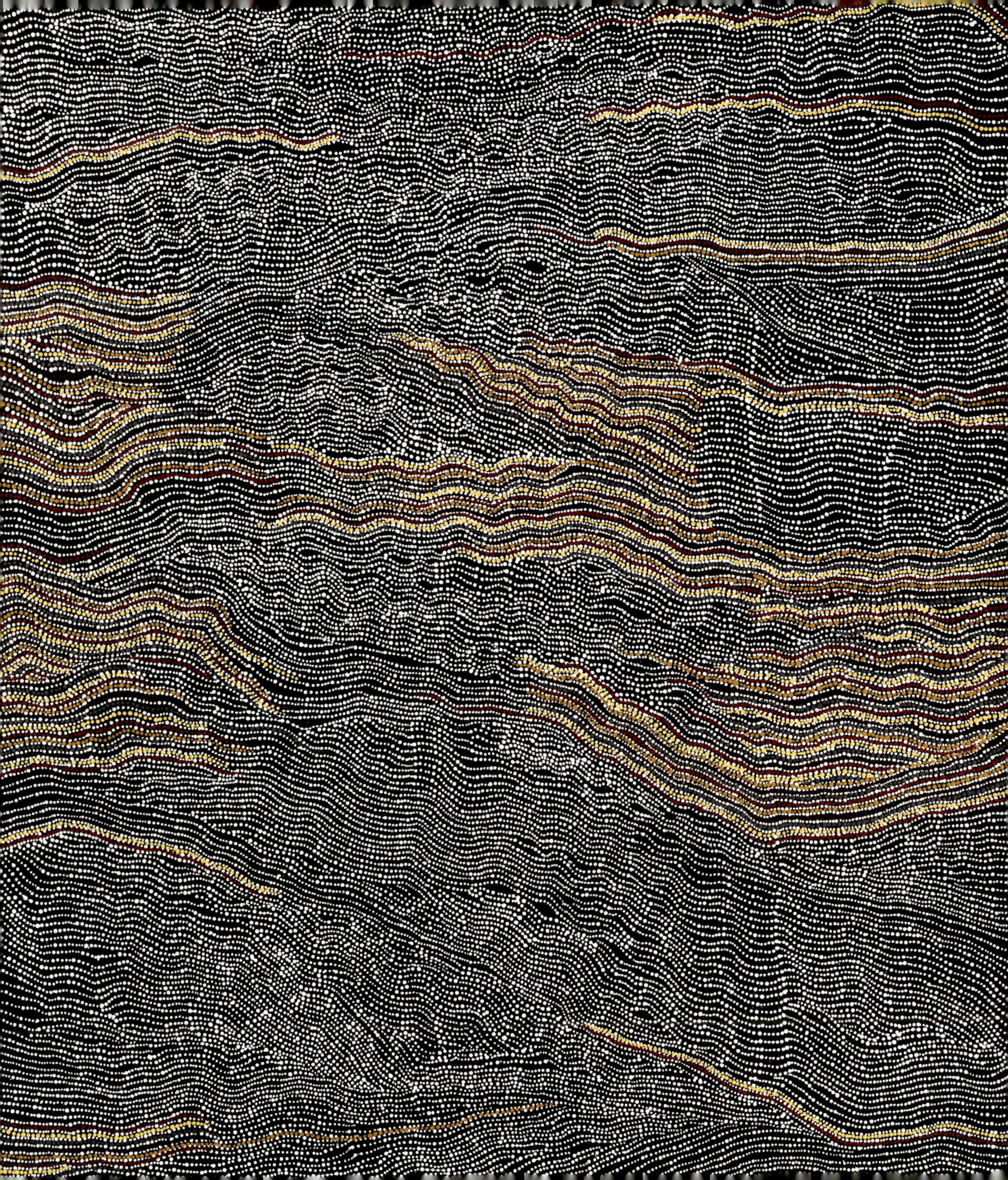

The second half of the twentieth century witnessed a revolution in Australian art. The paintings and sculptures of Aboriginal Australians were finally recognised as art and not artefact. Towards the end of the European Age of Enlightenment, the Aboriginal societies of the recently discovered continent of Australia were regarded as people with no art: where were the rectangular paintings in frames and sculptures on pedestals? Just as the continent of Australia had been misread, so too had Aboriginal culture. The land was considered a wilderness, empty or barely occupied, and of no economic benefit to its Aboriginal inhabitants: where were the ploughed fields and fences?[1] Yet the early explorers and settlers often described the coastal areas of the country as having the appearance of an English gentleman's park, with swards of grass surrounded by forests, and the first colonial artists painted it that way (cat.54; fig.13).[2] What the explorers and the early settlers failed to see were the ingenious ways in which Aboriginal Australians managed the land. Nor could they appreciate the intrinsic relationship between Indigenous people and the land that was and continues to be at the core of Aboriginal being: and at the core of Aboriginal art.

> English is incapable of describing our relationship to the land of our ancestors. We decided to ... [describe] it in a way we hoped non-Aboriginal people would understand: through pictures. If they wouldn't listen to our words, they might try and understand our paintings.[3]

Aboriginal art is about the land, made of materials gathered from the land, etched into its surfaces as rock engravings or ceremonial ground designs, and painted onto the bodies of the people who inhabit the country (figures in the landscape who carry the landscape on their bodies). The continent is the Aboriginal artist's canvas, fertile in natural and spiritual resources that are imperceptible to those with foreign eyes.

The land as we experience it today was shaped by the original creator-beings who transformed themselves into features of the landscape and who imbued the earth with their sacred forces (fig.15). The land is a spiritual entity, packed with symbolic meaning and totemic associations that are the subjects of an art that is fundamentally religious in character. Paintings about country are not mundane landscapes in the conventional sense of 'pictures of natural scenery',[4] nor do they represent 'physical form[s] of human emotion'.[5]

Paintings about the land are made with reference to the Ancestral Realm or, as it is commonly described today, the Dreaming.[6] The Dreaming is Aboriginal cosmology; it concerns the genesis of the universe, the creation period when the ancestors established the laws of nature, science, religion and society. But the Dreaming is not restricted to the past; rather it is a constant reality that governs, informs and sanctifies people's lives. It underpins people's identity and their relationship to the spiritual and physical worlds, and to their traditional lands. Thus, the idea of 'place' in Aboriginal Australia – where 'land', 'country', 'camp' and 'home' are synonymous – is a locus where the Dreaming is made manifest with specific relevance to the individual or the group.[7]

Traditionally, most art is made for ceremony (fig.14) in which neophytes gain ancestral knowledge through song cycles that bear comparison to Homer's *Odyssey*, *Beowulf* or the *Mahabharata* in their epic, episodic nature and complexity. Knowledge is also passed on through paintings. Paintings are not mere illustrations of episodes of the Dreaming; rather they are manifestations of ancestral agency and an

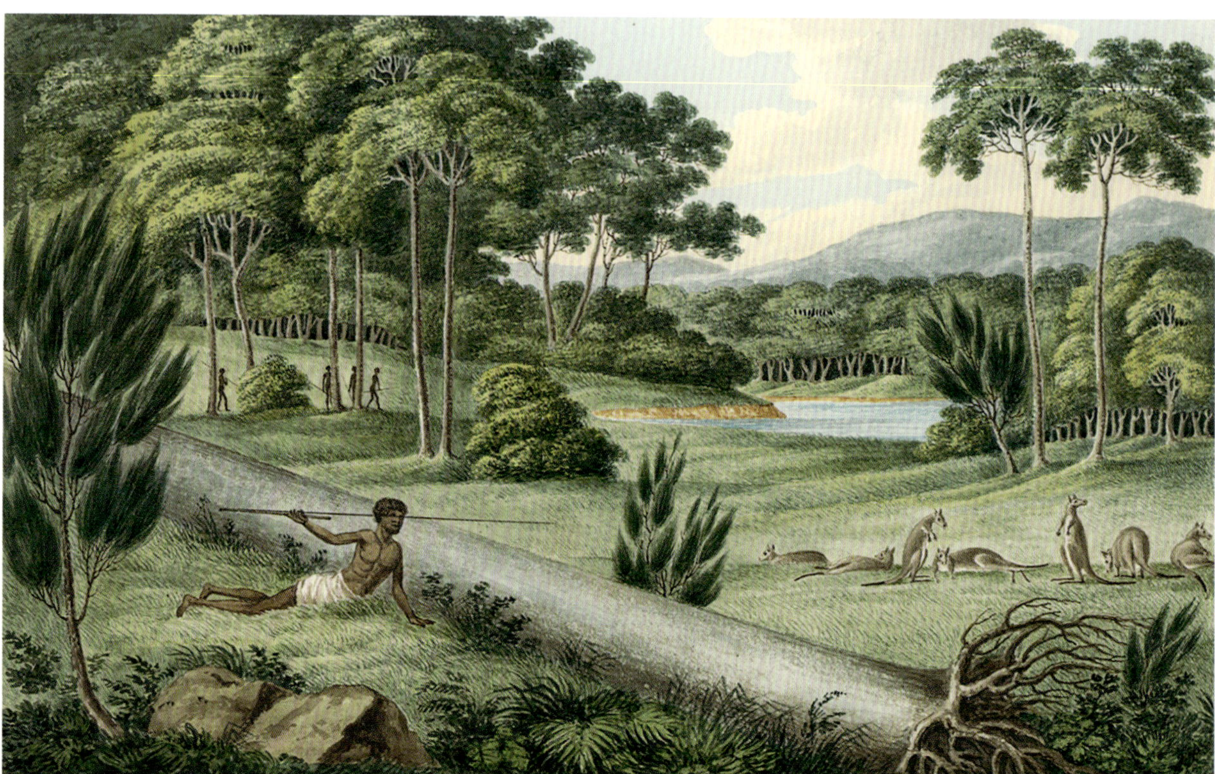

Fig. 13
JOSEPH LYCETT, **Aborigines Hunting Kangaroos** from **'The Lycett Album'. Drawings of the Aborigines and Scenery of New South Wales**, *c.*1820. Watercolour, 17.5 × 27.8 cm

National Library of Australia, Canberra. Purchased 1972

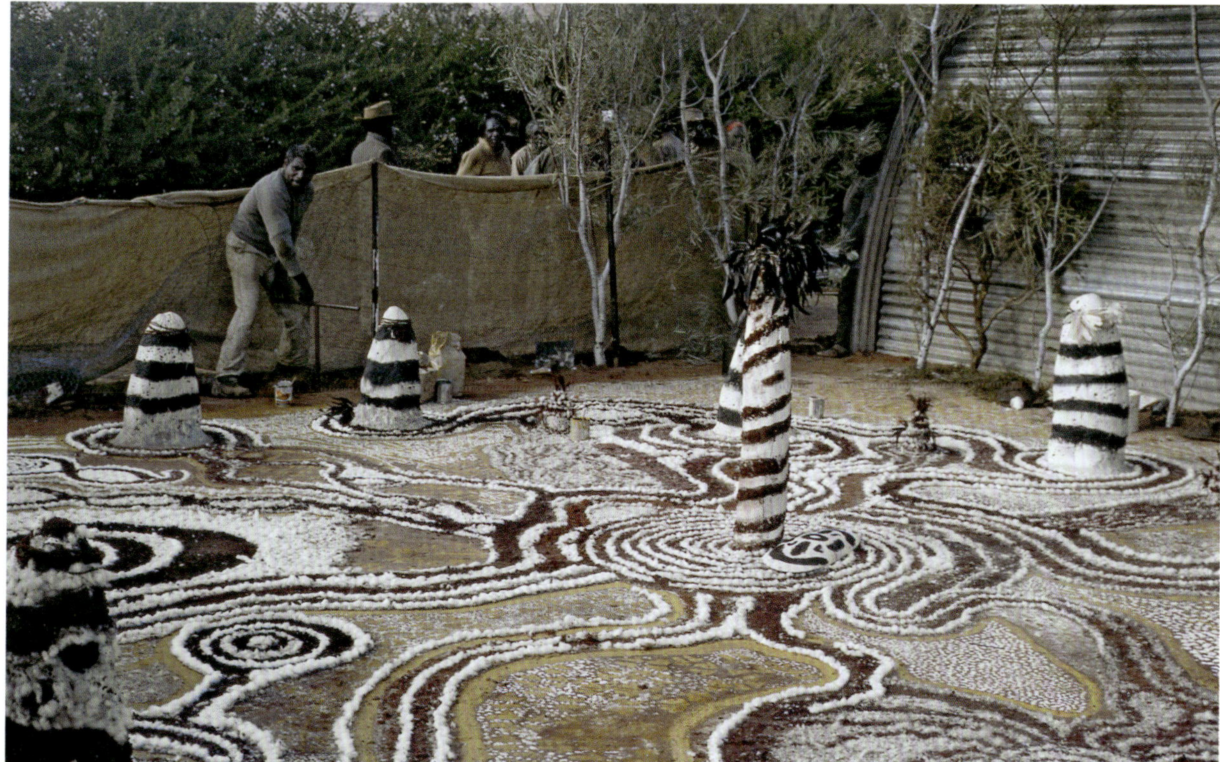

Fig. 14
Ground painting incorporating decorated termite mounds, made by Warlpiri men for exhibition at the Alice Springs Show, 1964
South Australian Museum, Adelaide. L.H.Leske Collection

affirmation of the artist's relationship to the ancestors and the land.

The lexicons of graphic symbols, icons and designs of Aboriginal art differ greatly from place to place; each group or clan owns sets of specific designs[8] that are painted onto people's bodies in ceremony, onto sacred objects, and, today, onto portable sheets of bark or canvas. Pictorial elements are composed along conventional templates that identify specific Dreamings.[9] Knowledge of these designs, the right to reproduce them and the act of making them are of greater significance than the surfaces to which designs are applied. In Aboriginal art, the emphasis is on iconography and compositional structures to reflect the esoteric nature of its themes, rather than on figurative accuracy. Authority over the levels of interpretation of designs allows for the protection of the cultural integrity of paintings in the public domain, as artists distinguish between the open interpretations of their work – the 'outside' stories – and those that prevail within the restricted circumstances of ceremony and the normal course of religious instruction – the 'inside' stories.

In 1788 some 250 distinct languages were spoken across the continent, each language group with its own set of traditions, kinship rules, laws, belief systems and styles of art.[10] Despite their individual identities, each Aboriginal clan or group is not an isolated unit. Neighbouring groups share several socio-cultural elements, allowing us to distinguish a number of cultural or regional blocs. And people are connected by an ancient web of trade routes that criss-cross the continent, allowing for the exchange of ceremonies, songs, words, objects and designs over vast distances.

The Indigenous artists represented here come from three of these regional blocs: Arnhem Land and its environs, the Western Deserts and the Kimberley. In addition, a number of artists hail from the eastern and southern seaboards where their ancestors experienced the initial force of colonisation at the cost of many lives, and of many cultural traits. But culture persists.
In the late nineteenth century, Mickey of Ulladulla, William Barak and Tommy McRae provided us with their impressions of a changing world. In modern times, their artist-descendants comment on their contemporary worlds, making us aware of Indigenous realities that slipped through the cracks left by the official histories written by the dominant society.

ARNHEM LAND, GROOTE EYLANDT AND TIWI ISLANDS

Painting in natural pigments on flattened sheets of eucalyptus bark is the archetypal art form in Arnhem

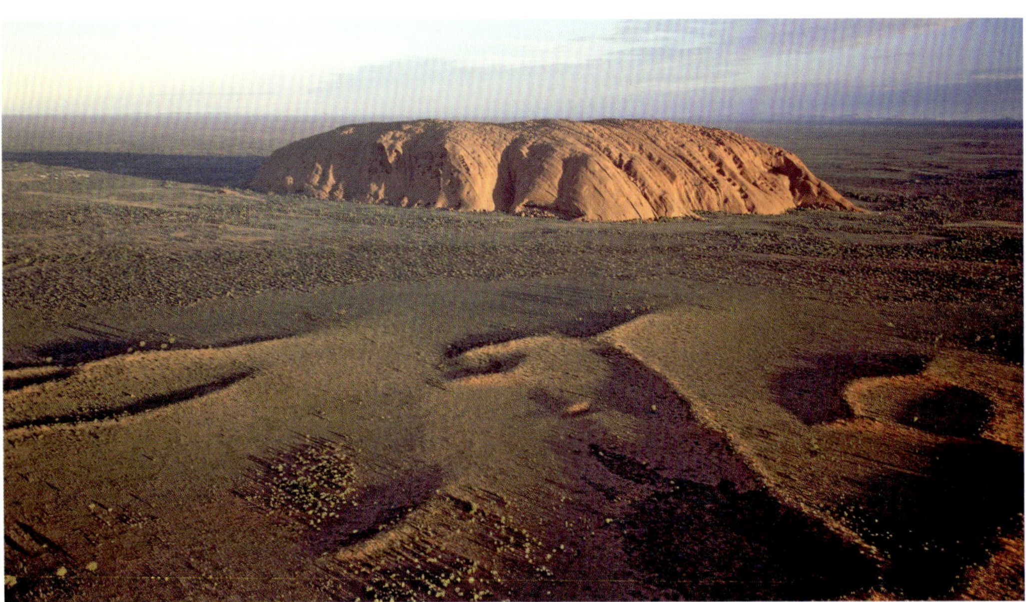

Fig. 15
Photograph of natural ancestral feature in landscape: **Uluru (Ayers Rock)**

Land and the surrounding regions, and, until the 1970s, was regarded as the only traditional form of portable Aboriginal painting. Bark paintings were first collected in the Western Arnhem Land region in the late nineteenth century.[11] Many were cut out from the walls of bark shelters and taken to public museums in southern Australia.[12] Stylistically figurative in nature, these bark paintings refer to the ancient paintings on rock surfaces and in caves throughout the region that date back some 35,000 years, and they introduced to a wider audience the first notions of an Aboriginal aesthetic. These early paintings depict ancestors in both human and animal form and refer to a time in the Dreaming when ancestors created, moved across, through and morphed into the landscape. The Field Island bark painting *Nadubi Spirit-Woman, with Possum, Magpie Goose and Fish* (*c.*1884; cat.1), collected about 1884, is a testament to such ancestors. It would have been used to instruct others about the spiritual and biological nature of these animal-ancestors, firmly associating them with their coastal riverine setting. In 1912 Baldwin Spencer (1860–1929) was the first anthropologist to commission bark paintings based on rock art.

The first bone-burial ceremony was performed for Kundaagi, the Red Plains Kangaroo, the subject of Yirawala's painting (cat.2), which epitomises the connectedness of paintings to the spiritual realm, to land, to ritual and to people. On another level, the painting depicts a hunter and his prey, with a component of the internal 'X-ray' to define the anatomical nature of these beings. However, Yirawala has given prominence to the resonating power of the sacred clan designs: the cross-hatched patterns known as *rarrk*.[13] These patterns represent the land belonging to Yirawala's clan and, significantly, they take the subject of the painting out of the realm of the mundane to that of the sacred. In the second mortuary ceremonies of Arnhem Land, the bones of the deceased are ritually put in a painted hollow log that is placed upright in the landscape to mark the safe arrival of the soul in the land of the dead.

Whereas the landscape is inferred in Yirawala's work, Bardayal Nadjamerrek sets out to render the latent power of the land in *The Artist's Country, Liverpool River* (1975; cat.5). Nadjamerrek captures the dominating magnitude of the escarpment country, the sheer escalation of the rock face, the gradient of different minerals and the vulnerability and fragility of the windswept plant life, to evoke the beauty, spiritual power and overwhelming drama of his country.

John Mawurndjul's painting style was influenced by Yirawala. Both artists are driven by a desire to capture the ancestral powers that imbue the land. In *Rainbow Serpent's Antilopine Kangaroo* (1991; cat.3), Mawurndjul's orchestrated rhythm of *rarrk* patterns subsumes the contorted figure of the Rainbow Serpent/Kangaroo ancestor giving birth. Redolent with suppressed energy, this image is an allegory for the creation of a sacred site, such as that referred to in *Mardayin Design at Dilebang* (2006; cat.6). Here, Mawurndjul has removed all figurative elements to focus purely on the manifestation of ancestral forces within the landscape and within the painting itself by creating a surface that radiates spiritual light, the light of revelation that finds a counterpart in a ceremony during which young boys, their bodies painted in similar designs, are transformed into men.

The modern painting movement in Eastern Arnhem Land commenced around the time of the establishment of a Christian mission in the region in 1935. A number of senior men recognised the need to teach *balanda* (white people) about Yolngu culture and the Yolngu people's intrinsic connection to the land.[14] And art was deemed to be the most effective means. By the early 1960s Yolngu society was under threat: although Christianity was largely accommodated within their cultural milieu, land rights became a major consideration as mining companies began to encroach upon traditional lands. In 1963, led by Mawalan Marika and Narritjin Maymuru (*c.*1914–1981), Yolngu artists painted two monumental panels featuring images of the major ancestors that were placed beside the altar in the local mission church, and, in legal proceedings against the miners, the Yolngu produced a series of bark paintings as title deeds to their land (fig.16).

Unlike the rock-art-inspired figurative style of Western Arnhem Land, that of Eastern Arnhem Land emphasises the use of clan patterns and compositional structures to render a narrative episodically in a series of frames. Munggurrawuy Yunupingu's *Fire Story at Caledon Bay* (*c.*1963; cat.9) relates the epic story of the creation of fire. Fire was to become the primary tool in managing the land.[15] In one frame the artist depicts Baru, the ancestral crocodile, before the fire burned the diamond pattern into his skin. The linked diamond design that features in several panels of the painting is the pattern of Yunupingu's clan, the Gumatj: it represents the flames, embers, smoke and ashes as *djirrikitj* (quail) carried burning twigs across the landscape, setting it on fire, and metaphorically linking a series of Yolngu clans.

Contemporary Yolngu artists such as Djambawa Marawili innovate and elaborate on traditional structures. Marawili's *Source of Fire* (2005; cat.8) depicts another episode in the story of Baru and the original fire. Here, the fire spreads out to sea, where it continues to burn beneath the surface. Unlike Yunupingu, who uses formal compartmentalisation in his painting, Marawili creates a highly evocative image as waves of linked diamond clan patterns at the top of picture, representing the fire on land (note the quail in the top-left corner), give way to an elongated, sinuous variation of the same pattern as it surges across the surface of the bark, as though swept along by the wind and waves, to the Fire Dreaming site in the lower right (note the dugong). Baru also features in Mawalan Marika's *The Milky Way* (*c.*1965; cat.10), which shows that the cosmos is an integral part of the spiritual and cultural landscape of the Yolngu. Marika vividly renders the Milky Way as a river in the sky filled with constellations of ancestral beings, animals and sea creatures.

The artistic styles and traditions of Groote Eylandt and the Tiwi people on Bathurst and Melville Islands differ significantly from each other and from those of Arnhem Land. Alice Wamba's *Coral* (1974; cat.13) depicts a coastal site that is the domain of Tiwi women, a place where they collect shellfish. It is also where the spirits of the yet-to-be-born reside among the coral and shallow waters. The formal regularity of Declan Apuatimi's *Pamijini* (*c.*1982; cat.14), depicting ceremonial armbands, echoes the structured nature of the Tiwi mourning ceremonies in which they are worn.

The traditions of painting in and around Arnhem Land also encompass subjects that are not part of the ancestral realm. Groote Eylandt has a rich rock-painting tradition that dates back some 2,700 years. It incorporates images of Macassan traders and fishermen from South Sulawesi in Indonesia who frequented the Arnhem Land coastline since before European settlement. They sailed on the annual trade winds to collect trepang (sea cucumbers). Although they did not settle, they had a marked influence on Aboriginal cultures. On Groote Eylandt, for example, the distinctive shape of the sails of their ships, seen in Nandabitta Maminyamandja's painting *Macassan Prau and Trepang Curing* (*c.*1974; cat.12), is now a symbol for the winds of the monsoon season.

PAPUNYA, THE DESERTS AND THE KIMBERLEY

The great revolution in modern Aboriginal art had its origins in the Western Desert, in the government settlement of Papunya, about 200 miles west of Alice Springs, that was built under an official policy to assimilate Aboriginal Australians into the dominant settler society. People belonging to several language groups covering an area approximately the size of England were taken off their ancestral lands to make way for the cattle industry, mining and testing of military weapons. For many, this was their first experience of contact with non-Aboriginal people. The apparent

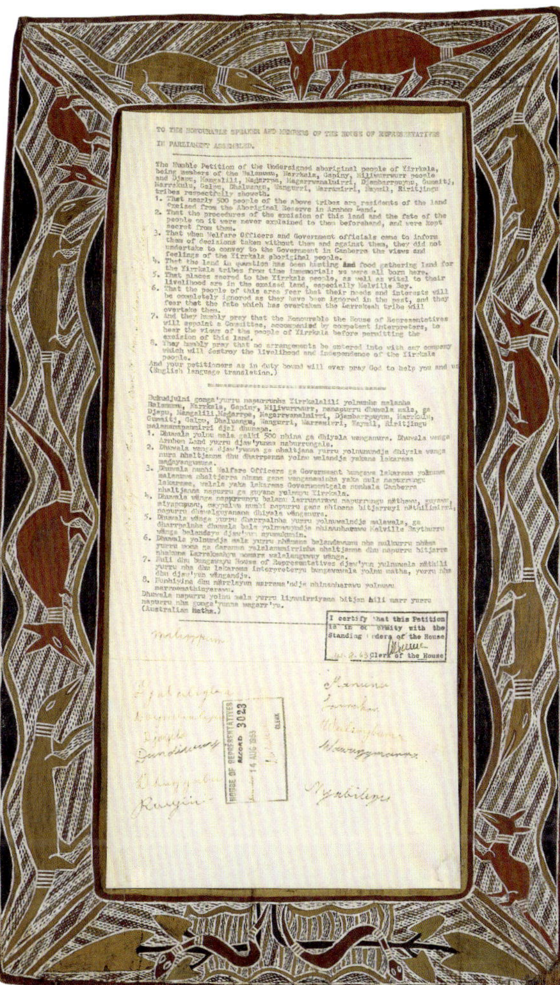

TO THE HONOURABLE SPEAKER AND MEMBERS OF THE HOUSE OF REPRESENTATIVES IN PARLIAMENT ASSEMBLED.

The Humble Petition of the Undersigned aboriginal people of Yirrkala, being members of the Balamumu, Narrkala, Gapiny, Miliwurrwurr people and Djapu, Mangalili, Madarrpa, Magarrwanalmirri, Djambarrpuyngu, Gumaitj, Marrakulu, Galpu, Dhaluangu, Wangurri, Warramirri, Maymil, Riritjingu tribes respectfully showeth.

1. That nearly 500 people of the above tribes are residents of the land excised from the Aboriginal Reserve in Arnhem Land.
2. That the procedures of the excision of this land and the fate of the people on it were never explained to them beforehand, and were kept secret from them.
3. That when Welfare Officers and Government officials came to inform them of decisions taken without them and against them, they did not undertake to convey to the Government in Canberra the views and feelings of the Yirrkala aboriginal people.
4. That the land in question has been hunting and food gathering land for the Yirrkala tribes from time immemorial: we were all born here.
5. That places sacred to the Yirrkala people, as well as vital to their livelihood are in the excised land, especially Melville Bay.
6. That the people of this area fear that their needs and interests will be completely ignored as they have been ignored in the past, and they fear that the fate which has overtaken the Larrakeah tribe will overtake them.
7. And they humbly pray that the Honourable the House of Representatives will appoint a Committee, accompanied by competent interpreters, to hear the views of the people of Yirrkala before permitting the excision of this land.
8. They humbly pray that no arrangements be entered into with any company which will destroy the livelihood and independence of the Yirrkala people.

And your petitioners as in duty bound will ever pray God to help you and us
(English language translation.)

I certify that this Petition is in conformity with the Standing Orders of the House
Clerk of the House

Fig. 16
Bark Petition presented to the Australian House of Representatives, Canberra, by the people of Yirrkala, Northern Territory, on 28 August 1963

effectiveness of the policy was epitomised in the previous decades by Albert Namatjira, from the nearby Lutheran mission of Hermannsburg. From the 1930s, Namatjira rose to prominence as a watercolour landscape painter in the European style and was fêted as a shining example of the success of assimilation: here was a black man who could paint as well as a white artist. Namatjira's paintings were so popular, especially in print form, that they created an image of Australia's desert centre in the minds of the vast majority of the population who had not visited the region. Yet Namatjira's watercolours depict sites of ancestral significance that allowed him to fulfil the customary obligation of honouring one's country – by painting it – just as the artists at Papunya were to do in the traditional visual language of the desert a dozen years after his tragic passing.

By 1971, disconnected from their homelands, the cultural life of Aboriginal people at Papunya was in disarray and a sense of hopelessness prevailed.[16] A catalyst for change came in the form of a non-Aboriginal outsider, Geoffrey Bardon, an art teacher at the local school, who invited the senior men of the community to paint a series of murals on the school walls in the Western Desert style (fig.17). Encouraged by the success of the mural, the men went on to produce portable paintings in acrylic and ochre on sections of board – usually discarded building materials (see cats 18, 19). Their subjects varied from images of the Dreaming to depictions of long-yearned-for ceremony; invariably, these themes reconnected artists to their ancestral lands. The forms and symbols within the paintings were the same as those used in large ceremonial ground mosaics – made of clusters of ochres, feather down and vegetable fibres – and body paintings, and the decoration of weapons and sacred objects (fig.19). Painting in acrylic on flat portable surfaces was now added to the Desert artists' repertoire.

Papunya paintings, however, were far from an overnight success. The Australian art world treated these apparently hybrid works with suspicion. The question of authenticity arose: in the public eye up until that time 'Aboriginal art' equated to paintings in natural pigments on sheets of eucalyptus bark; surely the use of introduced painting materials rendered these works 'inauthentic' as Aboriginal art? Controversy also arose at Papunya among the artists themselves who had little or no previous experience of the art market: some were wary of the consequences of revealing images of sacred Dreamings to an uninitiated audience. Moreover, figurative depictions of decorated sacred objects and ritual participants in full ceremonial regalia were deemed too sacred and secret to be shared in public. The dilemma facing the artists of Papunya was how to present their art publicly without loss of cultural integrity.

In response, the Papunya artists developed a number of pictorial strategies that included the elimination of figurative elements from their paintings, and an emphasis on the designs that decorate ceremonial objects rather than renditions of the objects themselves, as in Long Jack Phillipus Tjakamarra's *Kalipinypa Water Dreaming* (*c*.1972; cat.17). Here, the conventional iconograph for Rain or Water Dreamings – three sets of concentric circles joined by meandering lines – appears vertically in the centre of the composition. The masking of symbols is another strategy that is as painterly as it is conceptual. In Johnny Warangkula Tjupurrula's *A Bush Tucker Story* (1972; cat.15) graphic symbols denoting sacred sites and ancestral pathways are subsumed in an array of dots and dashes to suggest the abundant plant growth after rain. Dotting – as in the practice of applying paint to skin using the tips of one's fingers – is one of the Desert artist's techniques, and it replicates the process of placing clusters of ochre on the ground to create

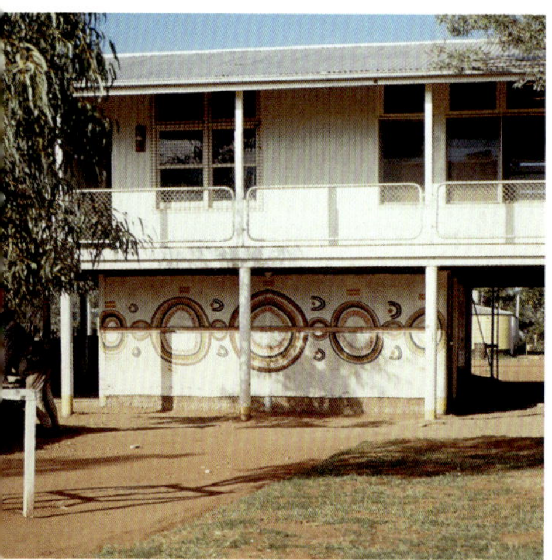

Fig. 17
Papunya school mural, painted by senior men of the community, 1971

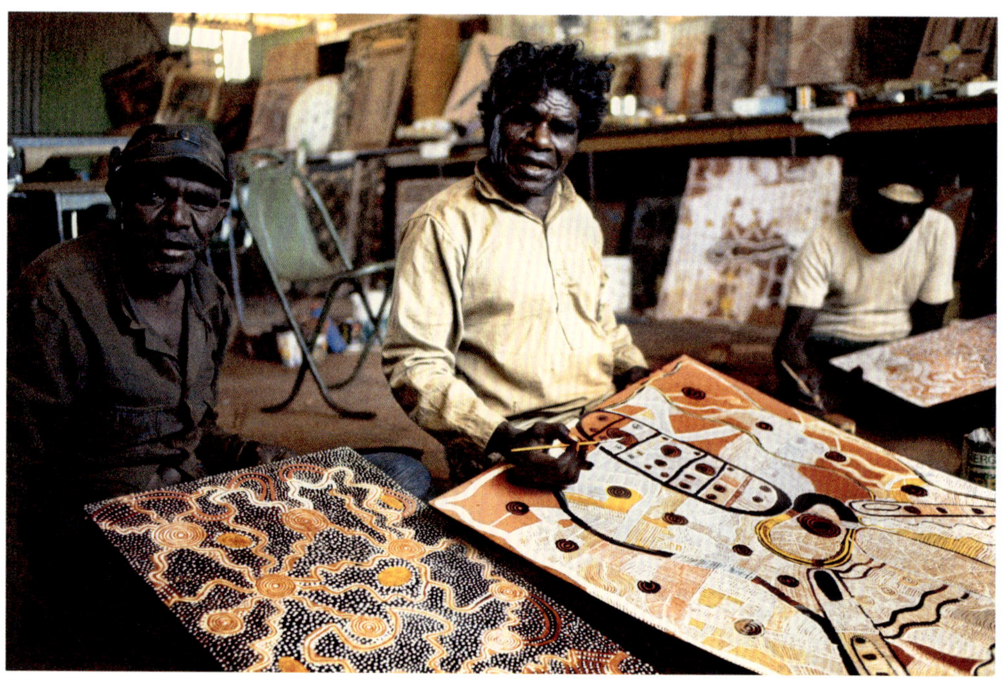

Fig. 18
Charlie Tarawa Tjungurrayi, Johnny Warangkula Tjupurrula and Timmy Payungka Tjapangati with their paintings in the Men's Painting Room at Papunya, 1972
National Library of Australia, Canberra

a mosaic design. Fields of dots and stippling may also create a visually animated surface of a kind that accords with Aboriginal aesthetics to express the presence of the shimmering forces of the ancestors within the land itself; Timmy Payungka Tjapangarti's *Sacred Sandhills* (1972; cat.19) is a good example.

By the end of the 1970s, Papunya painters had begun to paint on canvas rather than boards, allowing for the creation of large-scale works that relate to ceremonial practice in two ways: the increased size is akin to the scale of ritual ground paintings and these require artists to collaborate with others. Among the great monumental canvases of the period is Clifford Possum Tjapaltjarri's *Warlugulong* (1977; cat.21). In this work, the artist set out to map his ancestral lands and their Dreamings in a way that integrated the sacred diagrams of ground paintings and the topographical conventions of European maps. *Warlugulong* is a palimpsest of nine distinct Dreamings. The main subject is the first great desert bushfire created by Lungkata, the Blue-tongued Lizard Man, that chased his two ungrateful sons across the land until it engulfed them.[17] The orientation of the depiction of this Dreaming places the cardinal point of the east at the top edge of the canvas. The remaining Dreaming paths of the Dancing Women, Rock Wallaby, Possum and other ancestors are depicted so that the top edge points to the south. In effect, to marry the different orientations, Tjapaltjarri has turned the canvas through 90 degrees. Moreover, to produce a composition that satisfies the canons of Western Desert painting, he has located the main site of Warlugulong at the centre of the canvas, rather than placing it in its 'correct' geographical position.[18]

Uta Uta Tjangala often enlisted the assistance of others in the execution of his large canvases. With patrilineally inherited rights of ownership of a Dreaming and its associated designs, Tjangala worked with artists who had secondary or matrilineally inherited rights in the subject. Occasionally, in the making of canvas paintings, the collaborating group is extended to include other relatives such as wives, parents, siblings and children. In Tjangala's *Old Man's Dreaming* (1983; cat.20) the ground is constructed of a regular journey-site matrix of roundels linked by straight lines. On one level, the matrix may be regarded as a conceptualised map of the country in which the relative positions of the sites are more significant than their correct geographic orientations.[19]

The matrix is a feature of paintings by Pintupi artists who express themes related to the great Tingari ancestors. The song cycles of the Tingari constitute a body of esoteric and restricted knowledge that

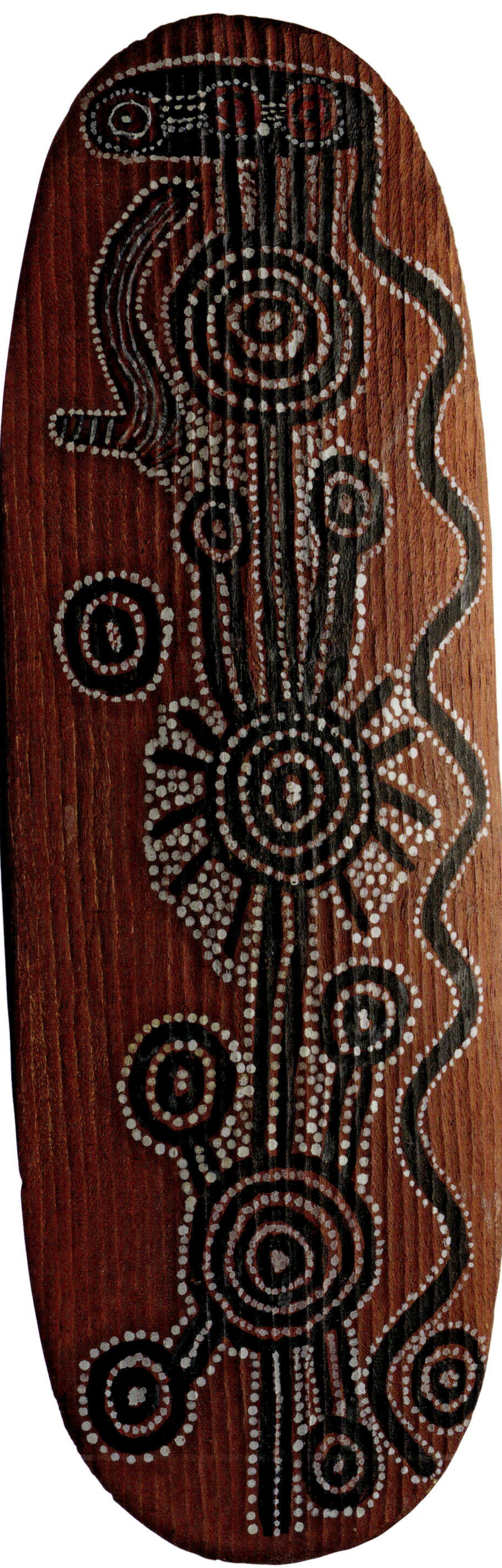

Fig. 19
Uta Uta Tjangala, **Old Man Dreaming shield**, 1972.
Pigment on wood, 65 × 21 × 7 cm
National Museum of Australia, Canberra

Fig. 20
PADDY JUPURRURLA NELSON,
Wardilykakurlu manu Yankirrikirlli – Bush Turkey and Emu (Yuendumu School Door no. 6), painted at Yuendumu, Northern Territory, early 1984, photographed after conservation, 1996. Acrylic on metal lined door, 203.6 × 91.2 × 4.5 cm
South Australian Museum, Adelaide

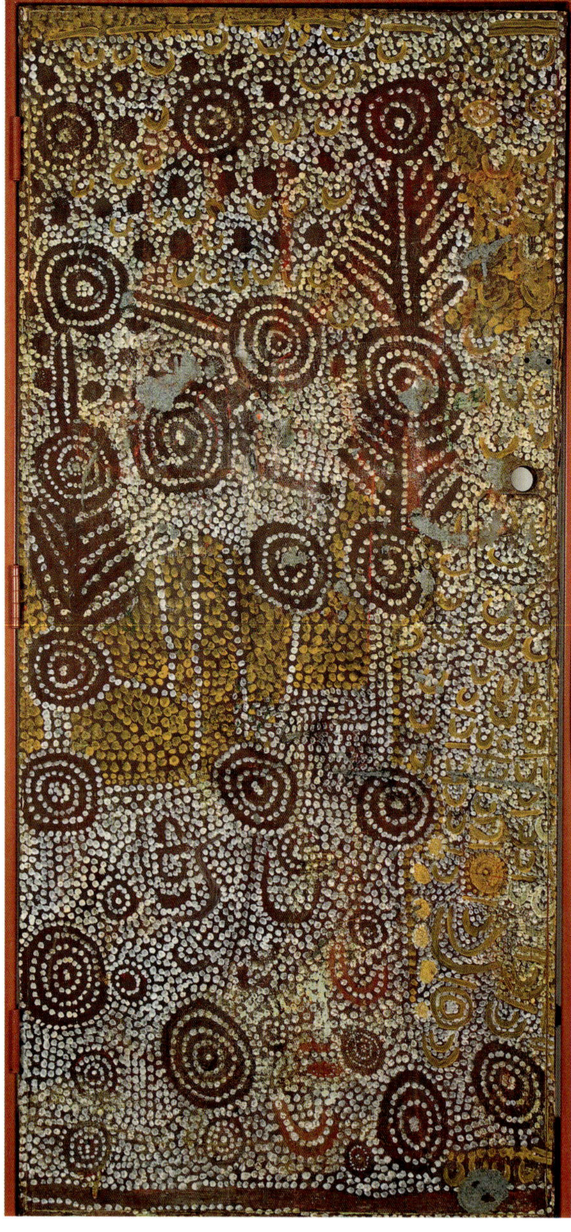

continues to inform the initiation ceremonies of the Pintupi, who were the last of the desert groups to make contact with European settlers. Tjangala's painting was created early on in a period when Pintupi artists were beginning to dispense with much of the desert symbolism and reduce their imagery to the barest minimum to reflect the sacred and secret nature of their subjects. By the early 1990s, Pintupi artists were elaborating on conventional geometric designs found on shields, body decoration and within the rhythms of the landscape itself to produce large-scale paintings of repeated lines of joined dots, as in Turkey Tolson Tjupurrula's *Straightening Spears at Ilyingaungau* (1990; cat.25). In Mick Namarari Tjapaltjarri's masterpiece *Rain Dreaming at Nyunmau* (1994; cat.24), the subtle shifts in tonality within the lateral lines lend this work a hypnotic, numinous quality that evokes the natural rhythms of sand hills and water; more significantly, the surface of the painting shimmers with ancestral light.

The Papunya artists' pioneering shift into the public art arena took time to be adopted by other desert communities. At Yuendumu, a nearby community made up entirely of Warlpiri people, elders were wary that the Papunya artists were trivialising their culture by painting small renditions of major ancestral epics. The change in attitude came after 1983 when a number of senior artists painted the doors of the local school with ancestral images in an act of cultural affirmation (fig. 20). Painting on such a large scale encouraged artists to create images like Paddy Jupurrurla Nelson, Paddy Japaljarri Sims and Larry Jungurrayi Spencer's *Yanjilypiri Jukurrpa (Star Dreaming)* (1985; cat.22),[20] which, in one reading, represents the earth surrounded by the constellations.

By the early 1990s the acrylic-painting technique had spread to communities in the Central and Western Deserts, each with its own inflections of the common Desert iconography. A number of individual artists who elaborated on these styles came to the fore. Chief among them was Emily Kame Kngwarreye (see cat.23) from the community of Utopia, who started painting on canvas as a septuagenarian. Within eight years, she had worked through a series of stylistic phases that adhered to the tenets of Desert painting but revealed a vigorous expression of the physical relationship between the painter, her canvas and her country. To the European eye, Kngwarreye's paintings seemed eminently modern and gestural in style, and she was promoted as an overnight sensation, a description that neglected the fact that for decades previously she had painted, and continued to paint, in the restricted setting of ceremony.

The Desert painting movement spread far to the west, to communities beyond the Canning Stock Route, which is a critical historical and cultural marker for the peoples of the region. Surveyed in the early 1900s, the route took cattle from the vast cattle stations in the Kimberley to markets in the south. It also took people from their desert homes in the region to government settlements, missions and into the Kimberley to the north in one of the great Australian diasporas of modern times.

As a boy Rover Thomas was taken to the Kimberley, where he was inculcated into the culture of the local Gija people. His revelation of the Kurirr Kurirr ceremonial cycle relating to Cyclone Tracy led directly to the development of a new painting movement in the Eastern Kimberley. In 1974 the cyclone flattened the city of Darwin and wreaked havoc over a wide area. Aboriginal elders across the Kimberley interpreted the cyclone as the work of an ancestral Rainbow Serpent that was warning people to retain their cultural practices in the face of the destabilising incursions of European presence.[21] The spirit of an aunt who had died as a result of injuries sustained in a car crash caused by floodwaters in the aftermath of the cyclone revealed to Thomas her posthumous journey across the Kimberley and her vision of the Rainbow Serpent destroying Darwin. Over a period of months, Thomas had had revealed to him the designs that were to be painted onto boards carried by performers in the Kurirr Kurirr ceremony, which, as a demonstration of cultural survival, was performed to both Aboriginal and non-Aboriginal audiences (cat.30).

By the early 1980s artists began to paint pictures of the Eastern Kimberley landscape independent of the imagery of the Kurirr Kurirr. In Thomas's paintings the landscape becomes a metaphor for ancestral and modern histories, marked and scarred by all those who traverse it. His paintings focus on sites of encounter, whether they be the massacres of Aboriginal people in the early decades of the twentieth century, as in *Ruby Plains Killing 2* (fig.21), or appeals for peaceful coexistence, as in *Roads Meeting* (1987; cat.29), which shows an ancestral red dirt track crossed by a bitumen road.

ABORIGINAL RESPONSES TO COLONIAL SETTLEMENT

The Aboriginal nations of the south-east regions of Australia were the first to experience the full impact of colonial settlement in the late 1700s. Foreign diseases spread far inland along traditional trade routes, decimating Indigenous populations. The land itself became a contested site: waterholes, rivers and sacred places became prime locations for settlement as black and white populations competed for access to essential resources such as water and food. As the non-Indigenous populations grew, Aboriginal people were displaced from their homelands and pushed to the outskirts of towns. Reserves and mission facilities were established some distance away from the new towns in an attempt to remove Indigenous people from public view in a form of apartheid.

In these small, heavily controlled government communities Aboriginal men emerged who used their artistic abilities to retain their cultural heritage in the face of major changes. In the late nineteenth century, artists such as William Barak, from what is now the Melbourne area, recorded traditional Aboriginal cultural life so that future generations would have a visual record of their unique heritage. Barak drew ceremonial scenes with participants painted with intricate body designs, others covered in possum-skin cloaks with clan patterns painted onto the leather (see cat.35), with song men orchestrating these events, while others (including women and children) look on and sing and dance. At the same time Tommy McRae (see cat.34) and Mickey of Ulladulla (see cat.36) also produced drawings that captured everyday events that occurred around them. Their work is a unique visual record of contact between the two cultures seen through Aboriginal eyes, and it is a testament to the cultural foresight of these artists. Equally, these artists destabilised the commonly held stereotype of the uncivilised savage: here were sophisticated Indigenous artists engaging effectively with their contemporary worlds.

The middle of the twentieth century marked a shift in direction as Aboriginal people began to unite and protest against the oppressive treatment that they experienced under government policies of segregation and assimilation. In most regions, Aboriginal people were controlled by official 'Aboriginal Protector(s)' who imposed strict curfews, determined who could travel outside their community, and who could enter into marriage. Out of this environment emerged the first generation of urban-based artists, including Trevor Nickolls (1949–2012), Lin Onus (1948–1996) and Robert Campbell Jnr. These artists, who had experienced at first hand the disastrous effects of

Fig. 21
ROVER THOMAS, **Ruby Plains Killing 2**, 1990. Natural pigments and binder on canvas, 90 × 110 cm
National Gallery of Australia, Canberra. Purchased 1990

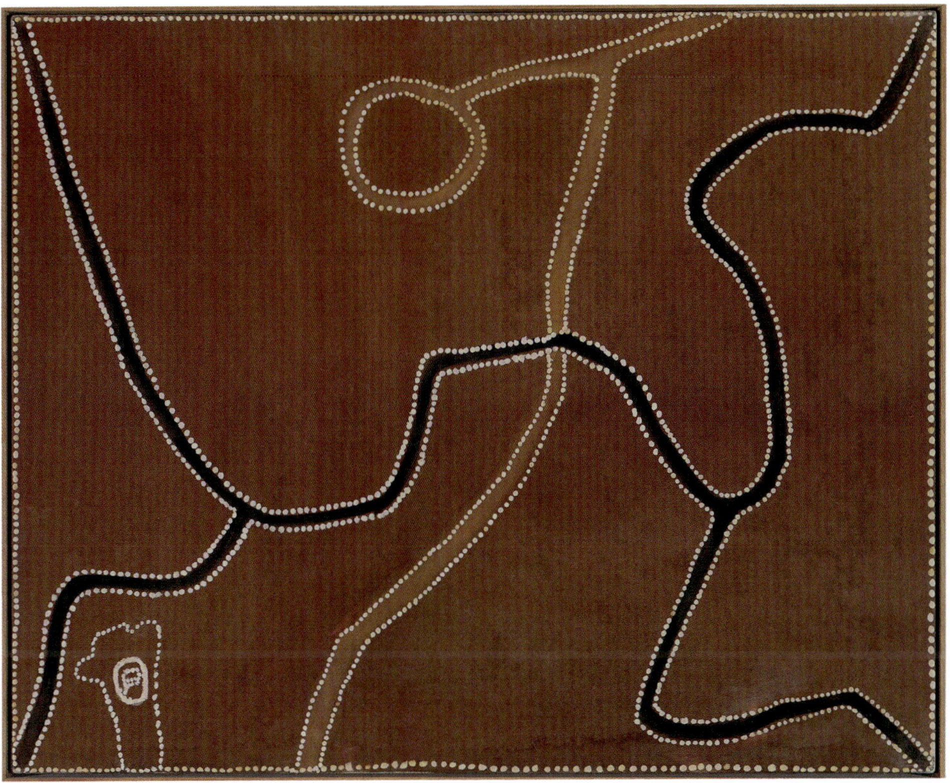

government-controlled life, discrimination and prejudice, became cultural freedom-fighters through their art. Their work is often provocative and political in nature. Campbell Jnr's *Abo History (Facts)* (1988; cat.38) is a confrontational piece that reinterprets the official history of black and white engagement over the last 200 years,[22] and alludes to the changing character of the Australian landscape.

The work of Fiona Foley is also concerned with unearthing and revisiting the past. She interrogates the archival records in her home state of Queensland to reveal hidden histories. *Bliss* (2006; cat.194) shows a field of poppies that sway hypnotically in the breeze. This seemingly meditative piece refers to an insidious practice of the mid- to late 1800s in which Aboriginal workers were enticed into opium addiction: they were paid not in cash but in opium dregs.[23]

The history of marginalisation and race relations are themes present in the photographic work of Ricky Maynard and Vernon Ah Kee. Maynard's *The Healing Garden, Wybalenna, Flinders Island, Tasmania* (2005; cat. 39), from *Portrait of a Distant Land*, a series of ten photographs taken on Flinders Island, where his people were exiled from the mainland of Tasmania in the nineteenth century, is an allegorical image of colonisation; figures in the landscape corralled within an English picket fence at the notorious concentration camp that was Wybalenna. The series is about the extreme nature of personal loss (dispossession) and connectedness (re-connectedness) to land, ancestry and cultural heritage. Ah Kee's political commentaries on current race relations within Australia are intentionally provocative. The title of the work *Can't Chant (wegrewhere) #2* (2009; cat.196) is derived from the slogan 'We grew here, you flew here', which was chanted by a group of white Australian males at Cronulla Beach, Sydney, during a confrontation with Muslim Australians in 2005. In Ah Kee's photograph, three defiant young warriors stand united, holding surfboards decorated with traditional clan designs of the Yidindji and Kuku Yalandji peoples. In this one act of solidarity Ah Kee reinterprets the cry of the Aboriginal land-rights movement: 'We grew here and this country is ours.'

In Nici Cumpston's photographs, images of desiccated and dead tree trunks stand as a metaphor for figures in the landscape and the treatment of her people. *Campsite V, Nookamka Lake* (2008; cat.40) is a lament and a memorial to her ancestors, who suffered under colonisation as their land, in the Lower Murray River region, was ravaged by excessive agriculture and mismanaged irrigation. The work responds to an iconic colonial image of the presumed demise of the Aboriginal race, set in the same landscape, H.J.Johnstone's *Evening Shadows, Backwater of the Murray, South Australia* (1880; cat.90). The disparate nature of Indigenous and non-Indigenous engagement with the land is interrogated in Danie Mellor's *An Elysian City (of Picturesque Landscapes and Memory)* (2010; cat.203): the built (non-Indigenous) environment versus the organic, self-sustaining, natural (Indigenous) environment. Mellor also alludes to the fact that the natural environment will ultimately reclaim the built landscape and encroach upon the buildings as they eventually crumble and decay.

Myth-making and constructed identity are explored by Christian Thompson in *Dead as a Door Nail* (2008; cat. 202). Operating in the realm of self-portraiture, Thompson dramatically references his spiritual, social and cultural connectedness to the Australian landscape – to his country. As an Indigenous artist who has spent many years abroad, he vividly portrays his longing for his homeland in his work. The security and protection of a typical Aboriginal camp with a temporary shelter (humpy) and the warmth and light of the fire convey a calming sense of hope and belonging. The work also parodies Frederick McCubbin's image of the settler in a foreign landscape, *Down on his Luck* (1889; State Art Collection, Art Gallery of Western Australia, Perth).

THE LAND OWNS US

'The land owns us',[24] a statement used by Aboriginal people to describe their relationship to the ancestrally created land, lies in polar opposition to European notions of land ownership. Whereas the physical landscapes of the continent of Australia may be seen as the common factor in the paintings of Aboriginal and non-Indigenous Australian artists, their pictorial treatment has been, historically, also diametrically opposed. Arthur Streeton, Tom Roberts, Russell Drysdale and Sidney Nolan were variously 'obsessed by the stillness and remoteness of the Australian landscape, its blinding light, and the contrast between its fertility and its ageless indifference to man'.[25] Through Aboriginal eyes, for 'stillness' read a landscape of animated totemic activity; for 'remoteness' read home or camp; for 'blinding light' see the dazzle of ancestral power; and for the land's 'ageless indifference' see the bounty and succour it offers and that is so richly celebrated in Aboriginal art.

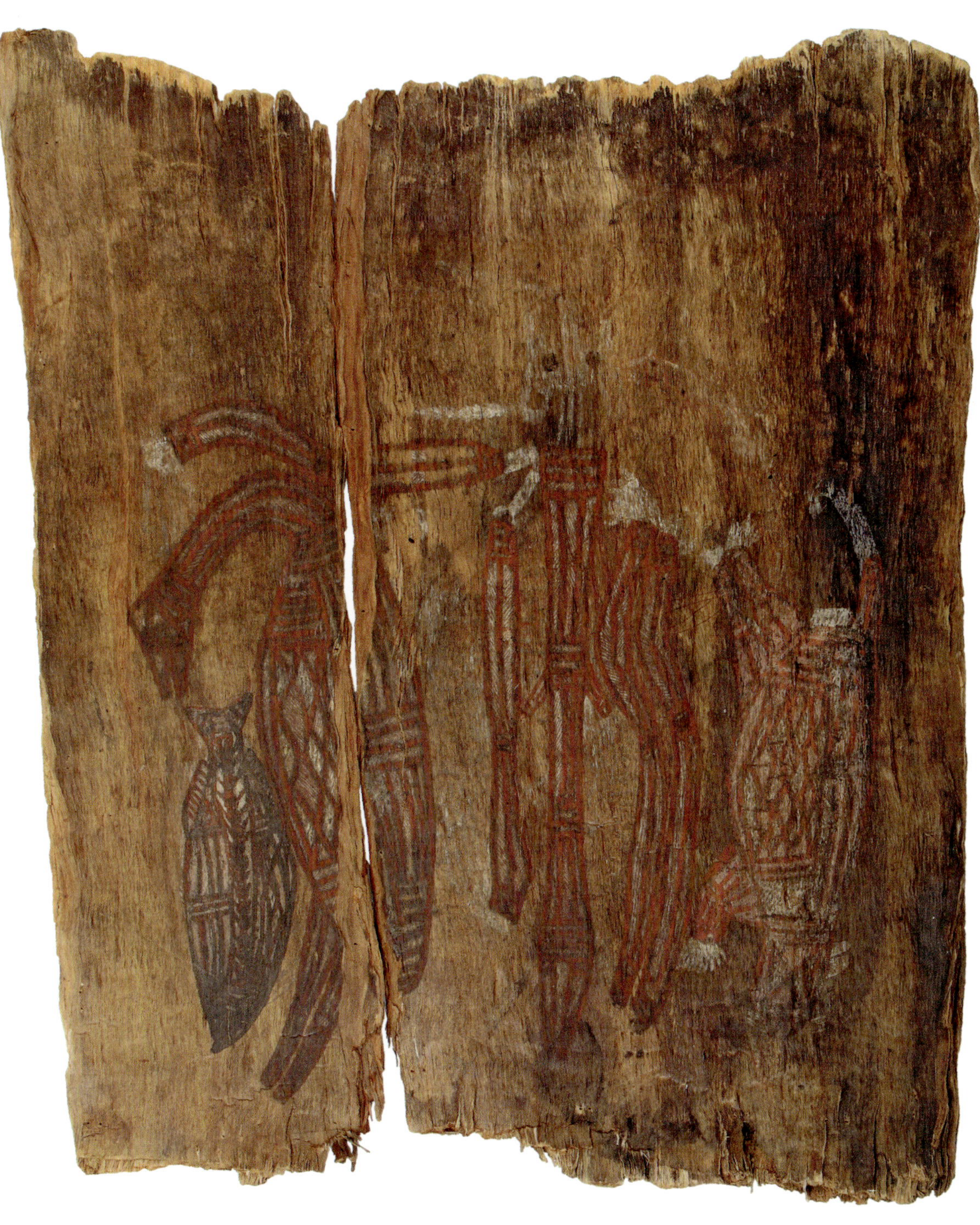

1

UNKNOWN Western Arnhem Land artist or artists
Nadubi Spirit-Woman, with Possum, Magpie Goose and Fish, *c.*1884
Ochres on bark, 83 × 63.5 cm

South Australian Museum, Adelaide. Collected by Captain Frederick Carrington, 1884, donated to the Royal Geographical Society of South Australia, Adelaide, 1890s, and thence to the South Australian Museum, Adelaide

2

YIRAWALA
Kundaagi – Red Plains, Kangaroo, 1962
Natural earth pigments on eucalyptus bark,
103 × 47 cm
National Gallery of Australia, Canberra. Masterpieces for the Nation Fund, 2012

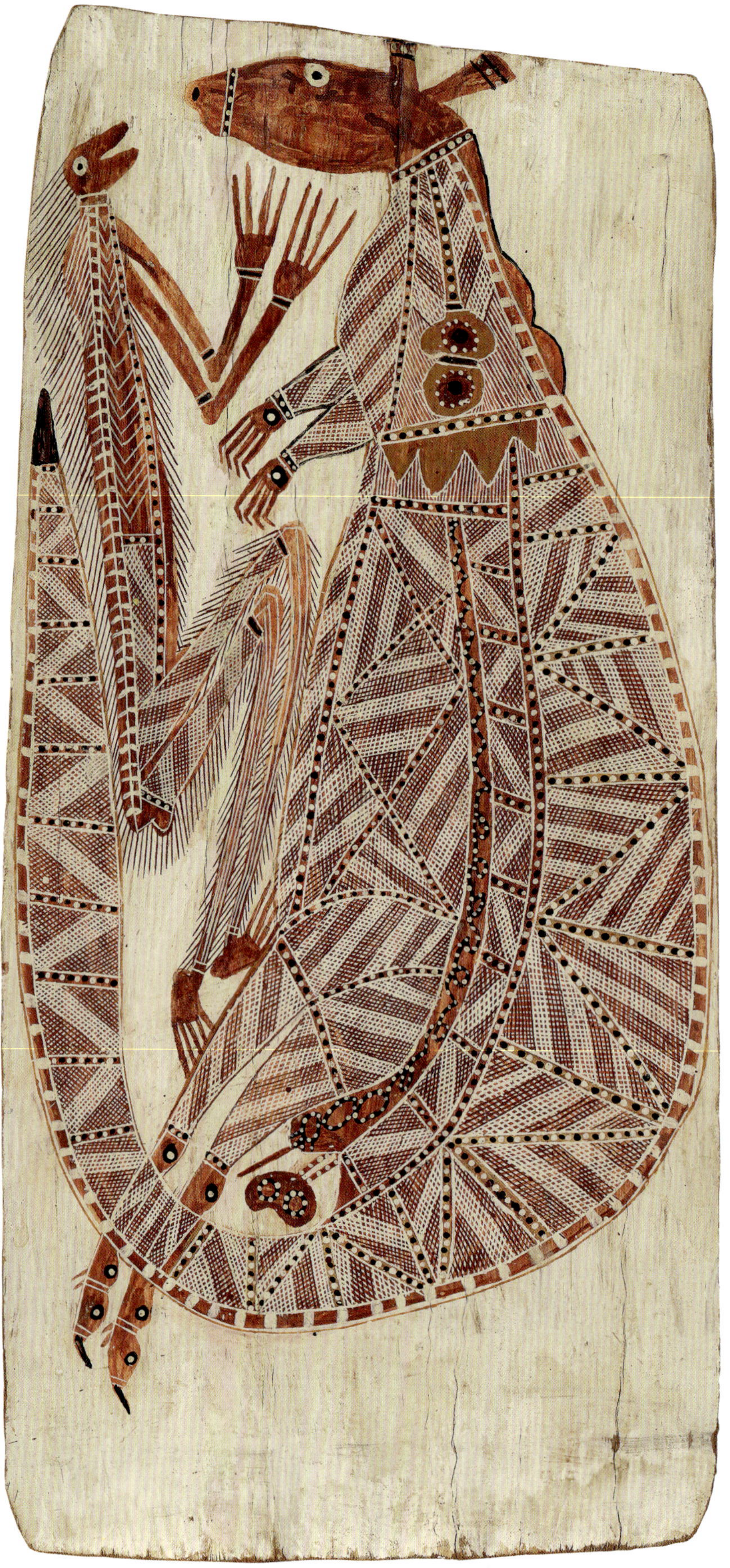

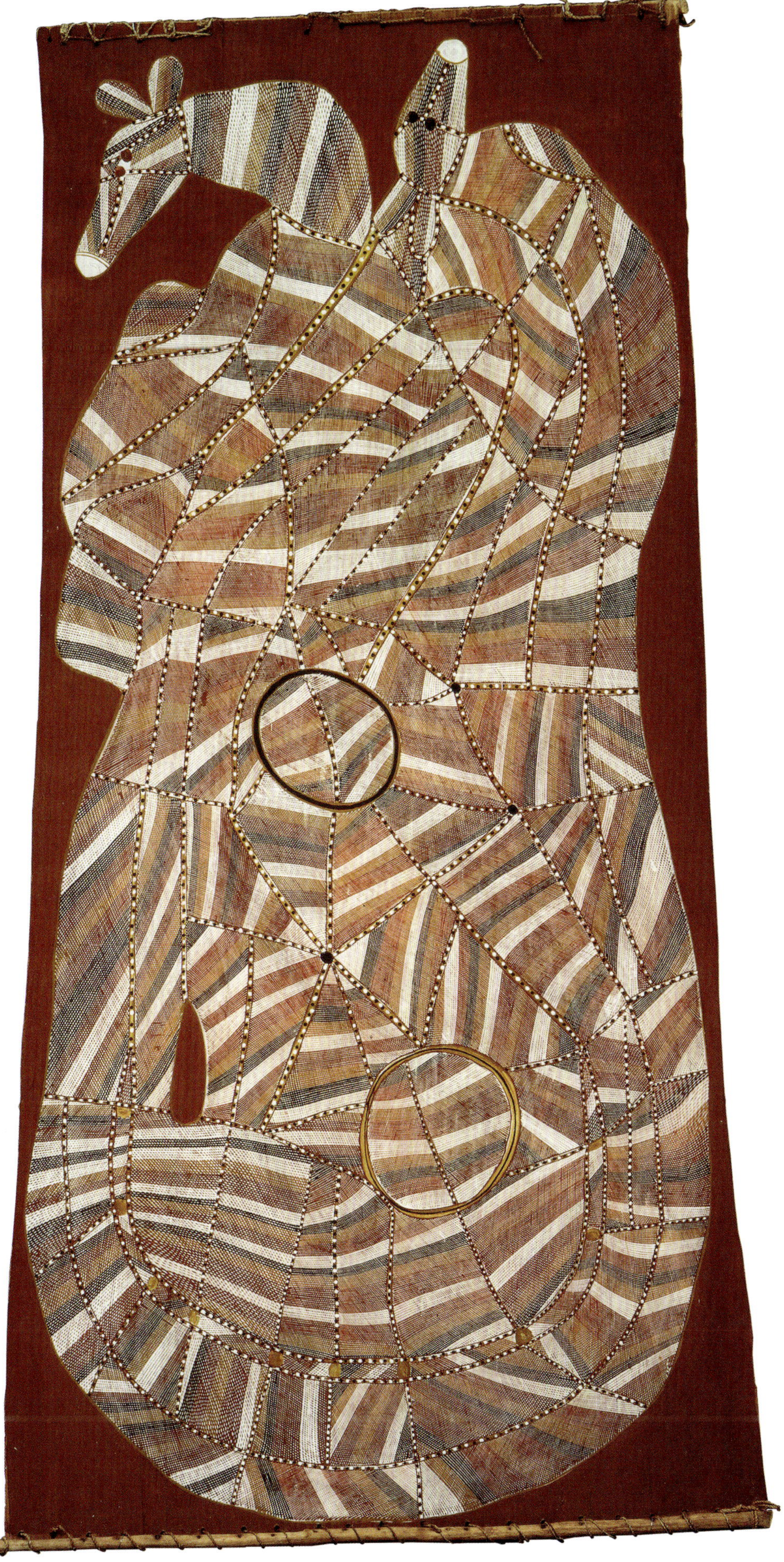

3
JOHN MAWURNDJUL
Rainbow Serpent's Antilopine Kangaroo, 1991
Natural earth pigments on eucalyptus bark, 192 × 99.5 cm
National Gallery of Australia, Canberra. Purchased 1991

BARDAYAL NADJAMERREK
Dead Man, *c.*1968
Natural earth pigments on eucalyptus bark, 60 × 30 cm
Art Gallery of South Australia, Adelaide.
South Australian Government Grant, 1969

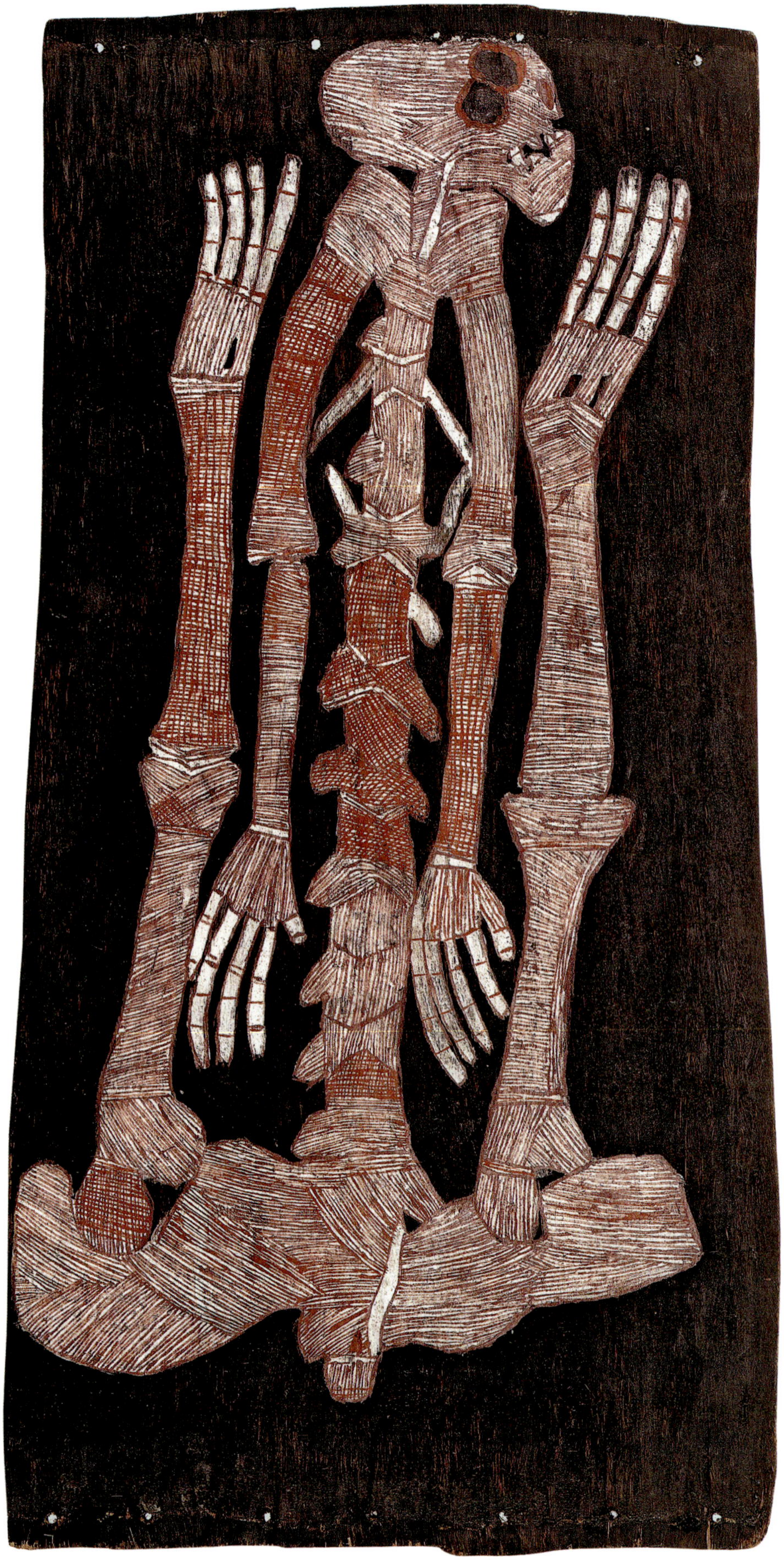

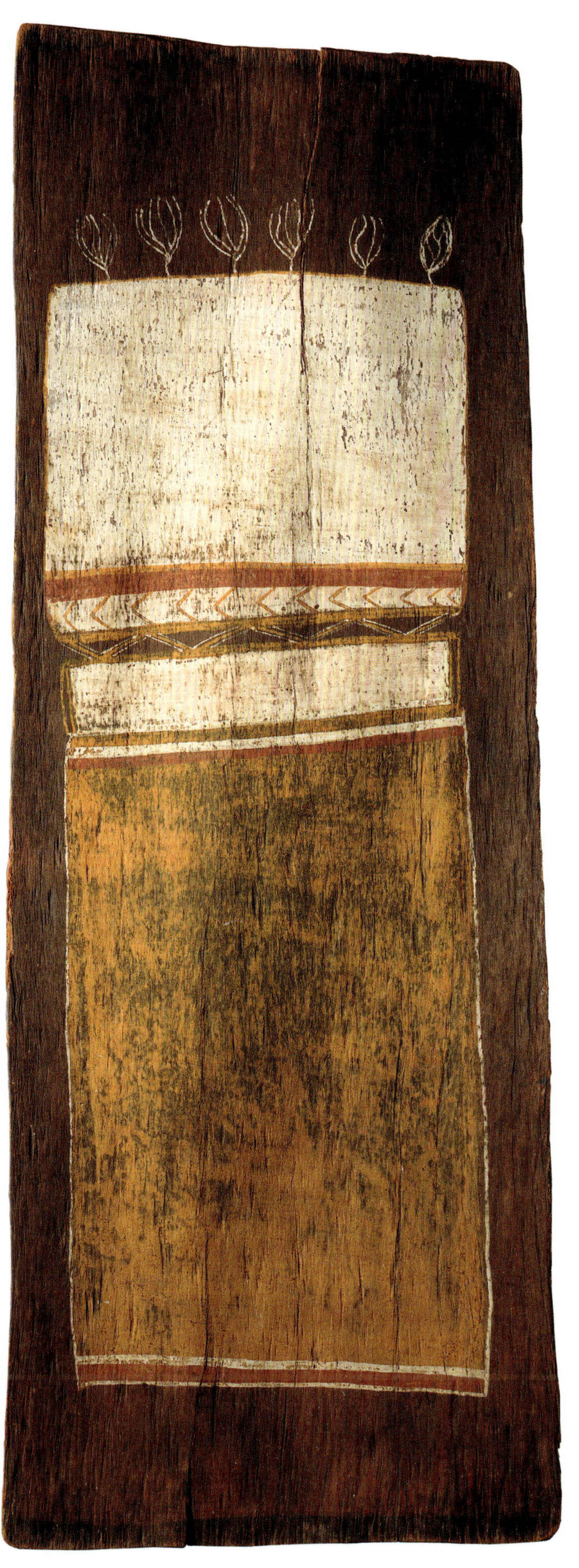

5
BARDAYAL NADJAMERREK
The Artist's Country, Liverpool River, 1975
Natural earth pigments on eucalyptus bark,
101 × 34.5 cm
National Gallery of Australia, Canberra. Masterpieces for the Nation Fund, 2010

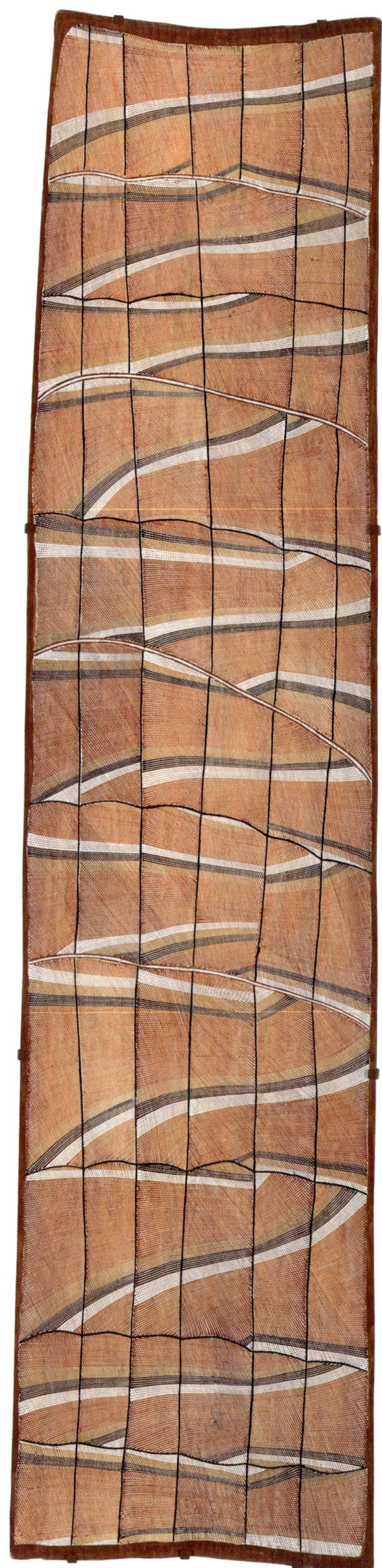

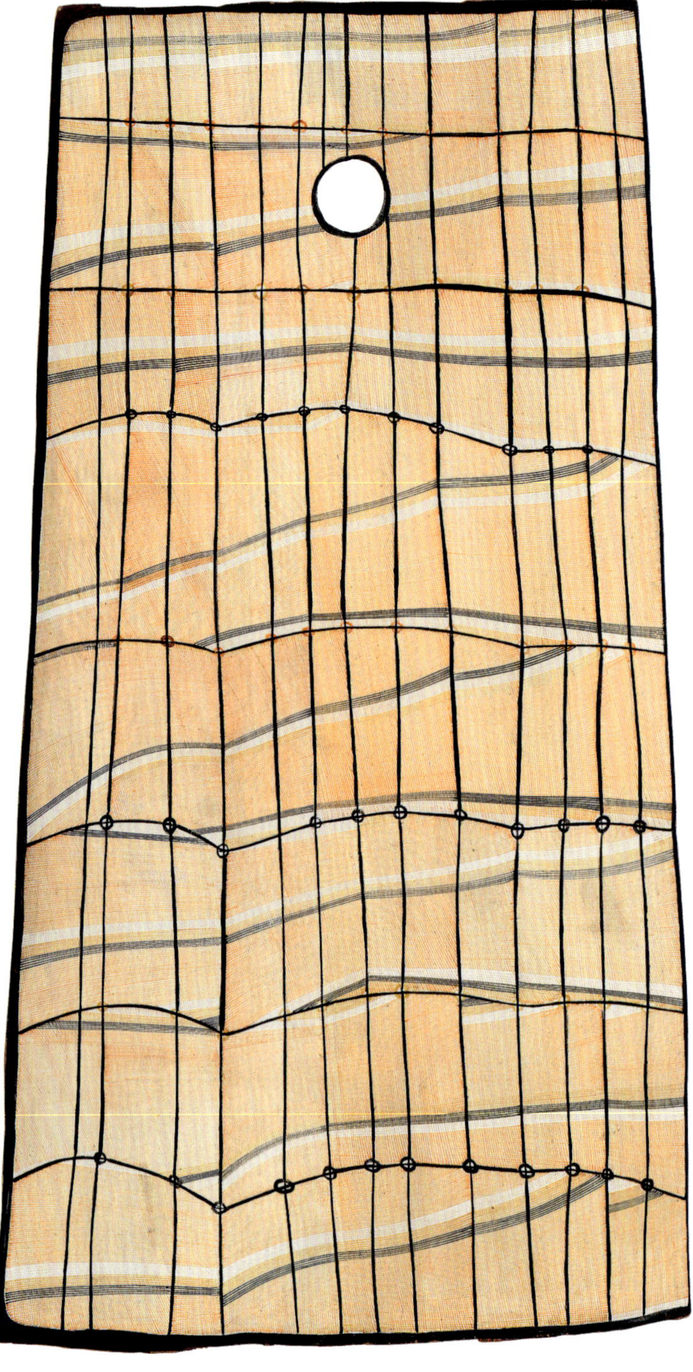

6

JOHN MAWURNDJUL
Mardayin Design at Dilebang, 2006
Natural earth pigments on eucalyptus bark, 200 × 47 cm
National Gallery of Australia, Canberra. Purchased 2007

7

JOHN MAWURNDJUL
Milmilngkan, 2008
Natural earth pigments on eucalyptus bark, 153 × 80.7 cm
National Gallery of Australia, Canberra. Purchased 2009

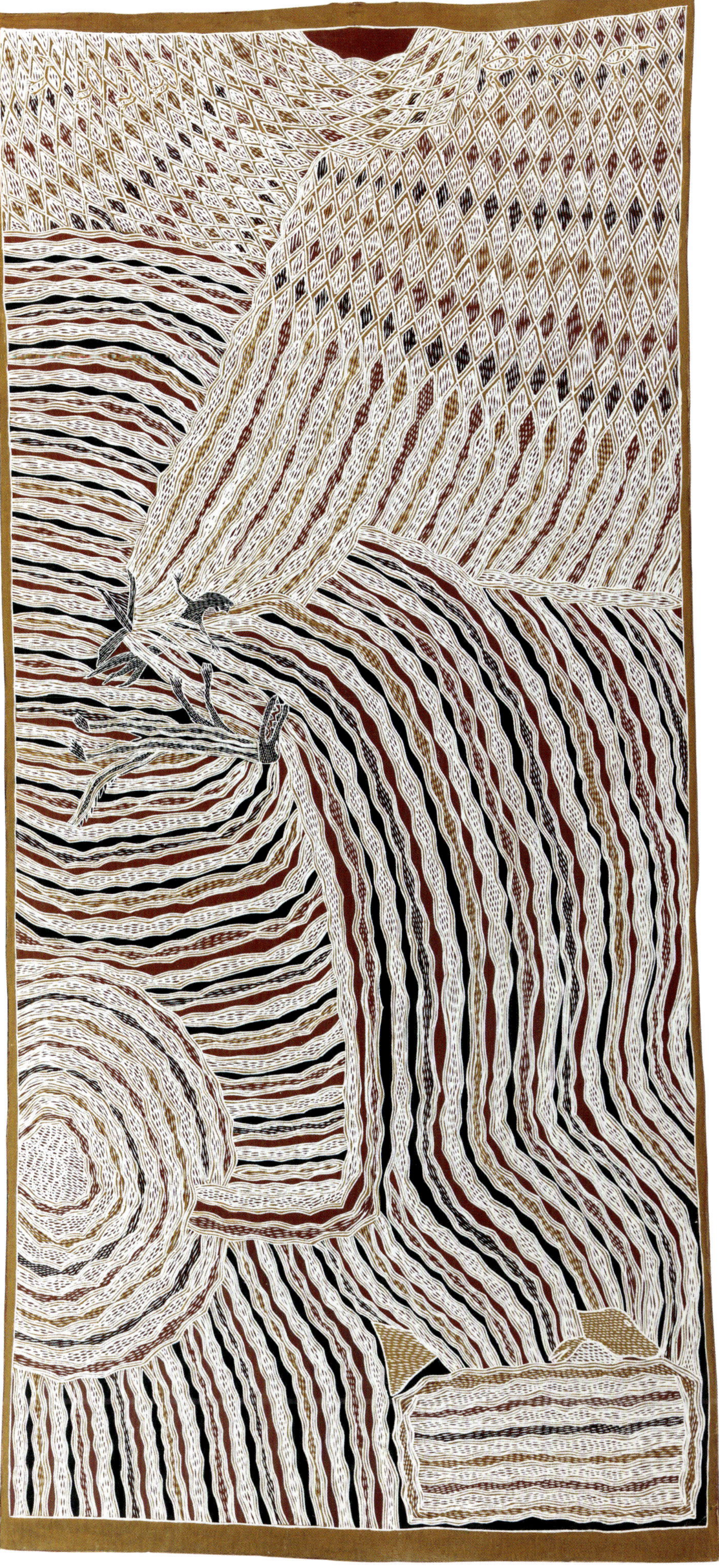

8

DJAMBAWA MARAWILI

Source of Fire, 2005

Natural earth pigments on eucalyptus bark, 191 × 84 cm

Art Gallery of New South Wales, Sydney. Purchased with funds provided by the Aboriginal Collection Benefactors' Group, 2005

9

MUNGGURRAWUY YUNUPINGU
Fire Story at Caledon Bay, *c.*1963
Natural earth pigments on eucalyptus bark, 114 × 52 cm
National Gallery of Australia, Canberra. Founding Donors' Fund, 1984

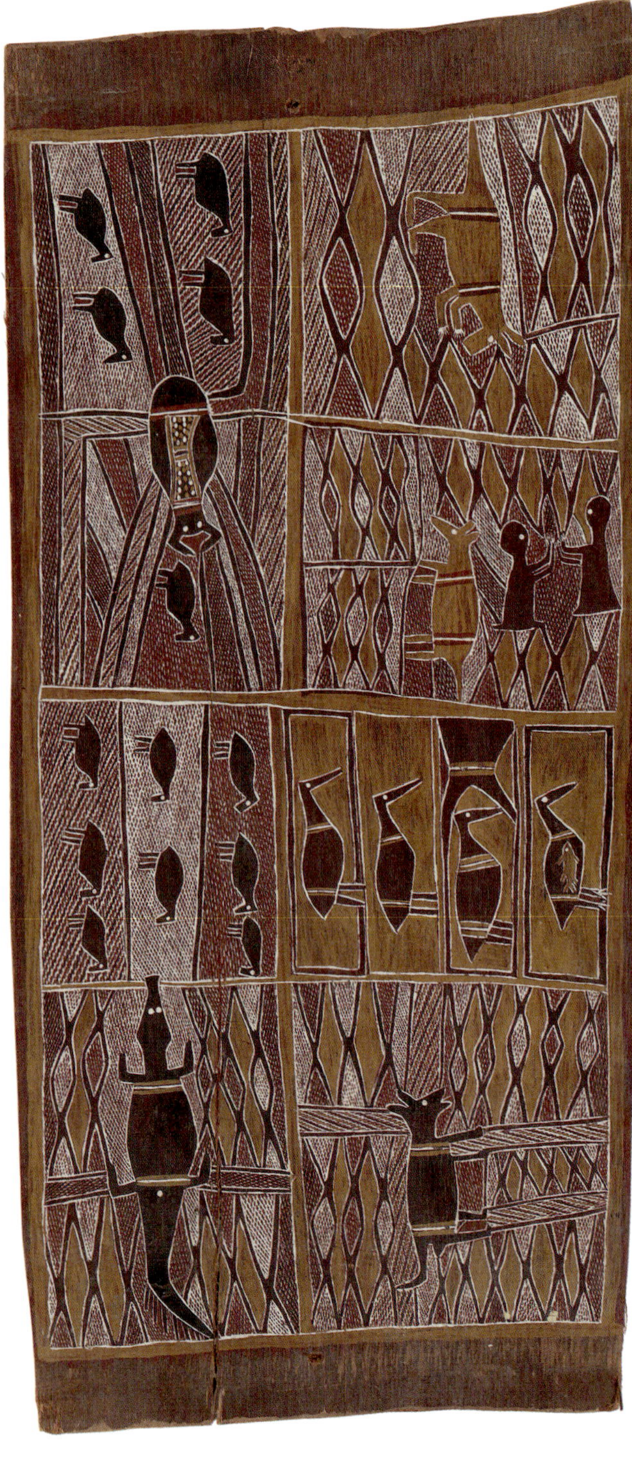

10

MAWALAN MARIKA
The Milky Way, *c.*1965
Natural earth pigments on eucalyptus bark, 177 × 68 cm
National Gallery of Australia, Canberra. Founding Donors' Fund, 2010

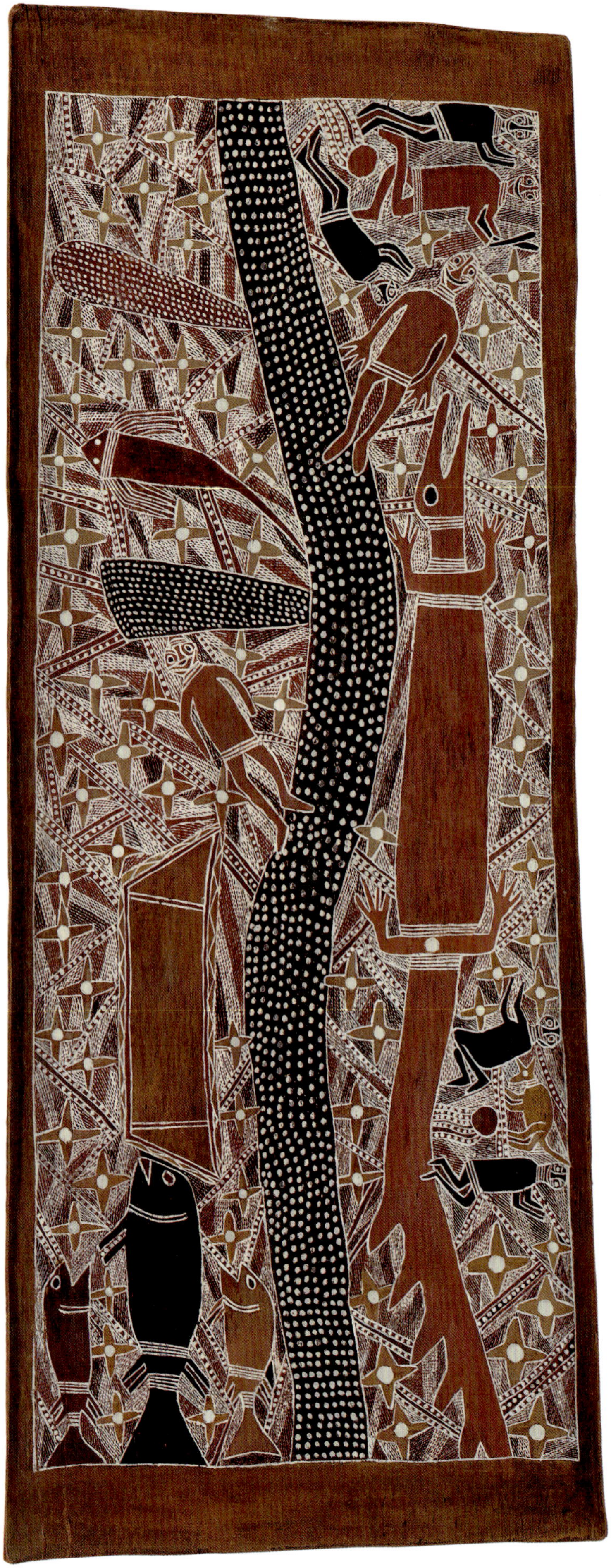

11

GULUMBU YUNUPINGU
Garak the Universe, 2007
Natural earth pigments on stringybark,
234 × 99.5 cm
National Gallery of Australia, Canberra. Purchased 2007

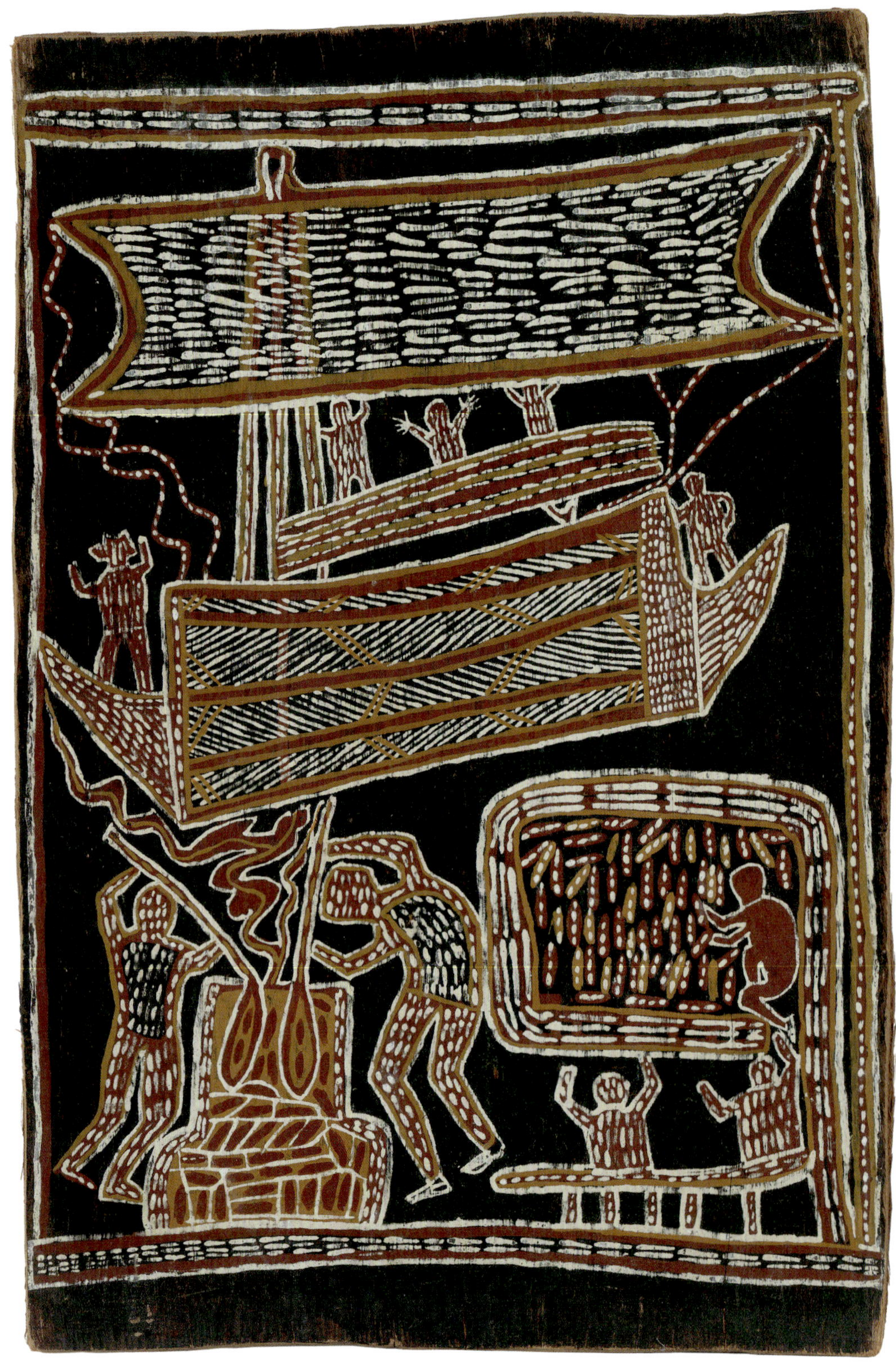

12

NANDABITTA MAMINYAMANDJA
Macassan Prau and Trepang Curing, *c.* 1974
Natural earth pigments on eucalyptus bark,
61.5 × 40 cm

National Gallery of Australia, Canberra.
Purchased from Gallery admission charges, 1984

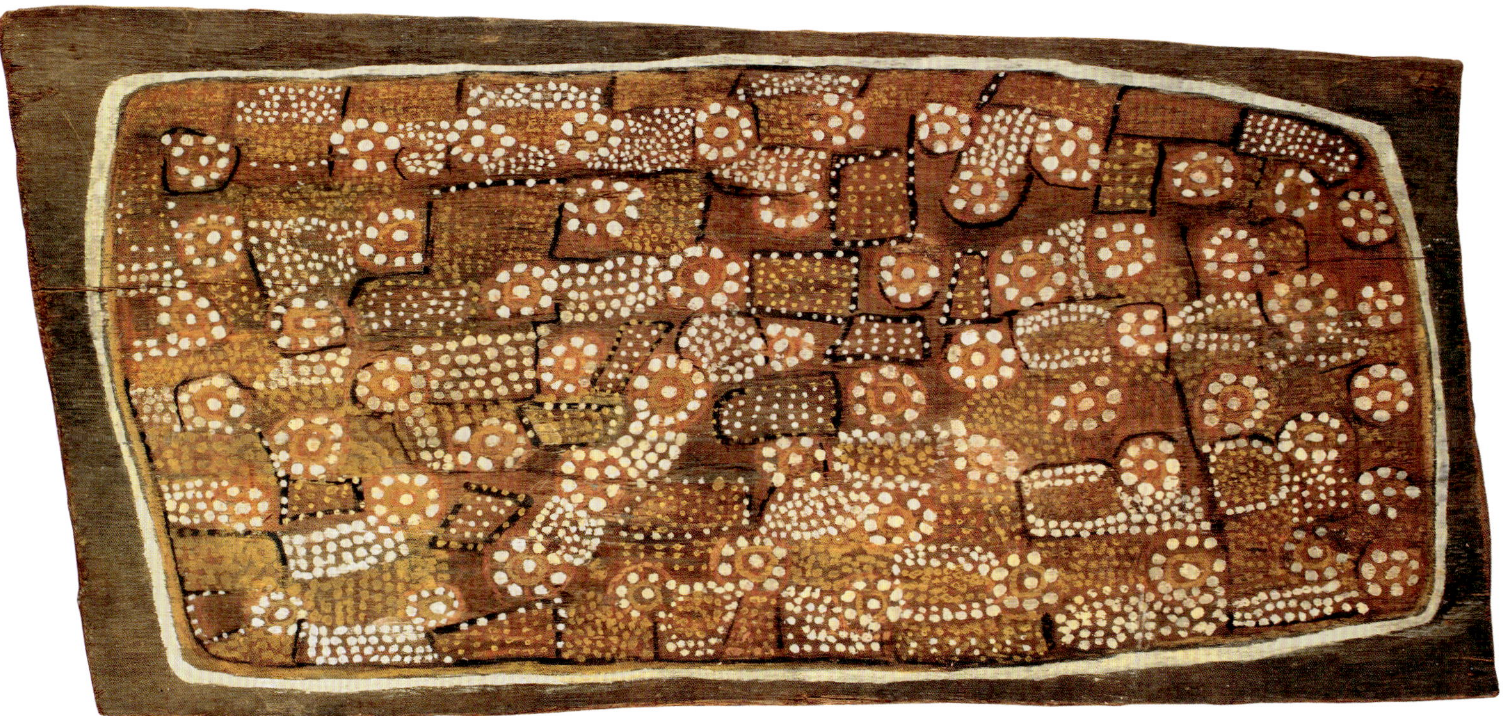

13
ALICE WAMBA
Coral, 1974
Natural earth pigments on eucalyptus bark, 42 × 84 cm
National Gallery of Australia, Canberra. Purchased 1984

14
DECLAN APUATIMI
Pamijini, *c.*1982
Natural earth pigments on eucalyptus bark, 48 × 93.3 cm
National Gallery of Australia, Canberra. Purchased 1992

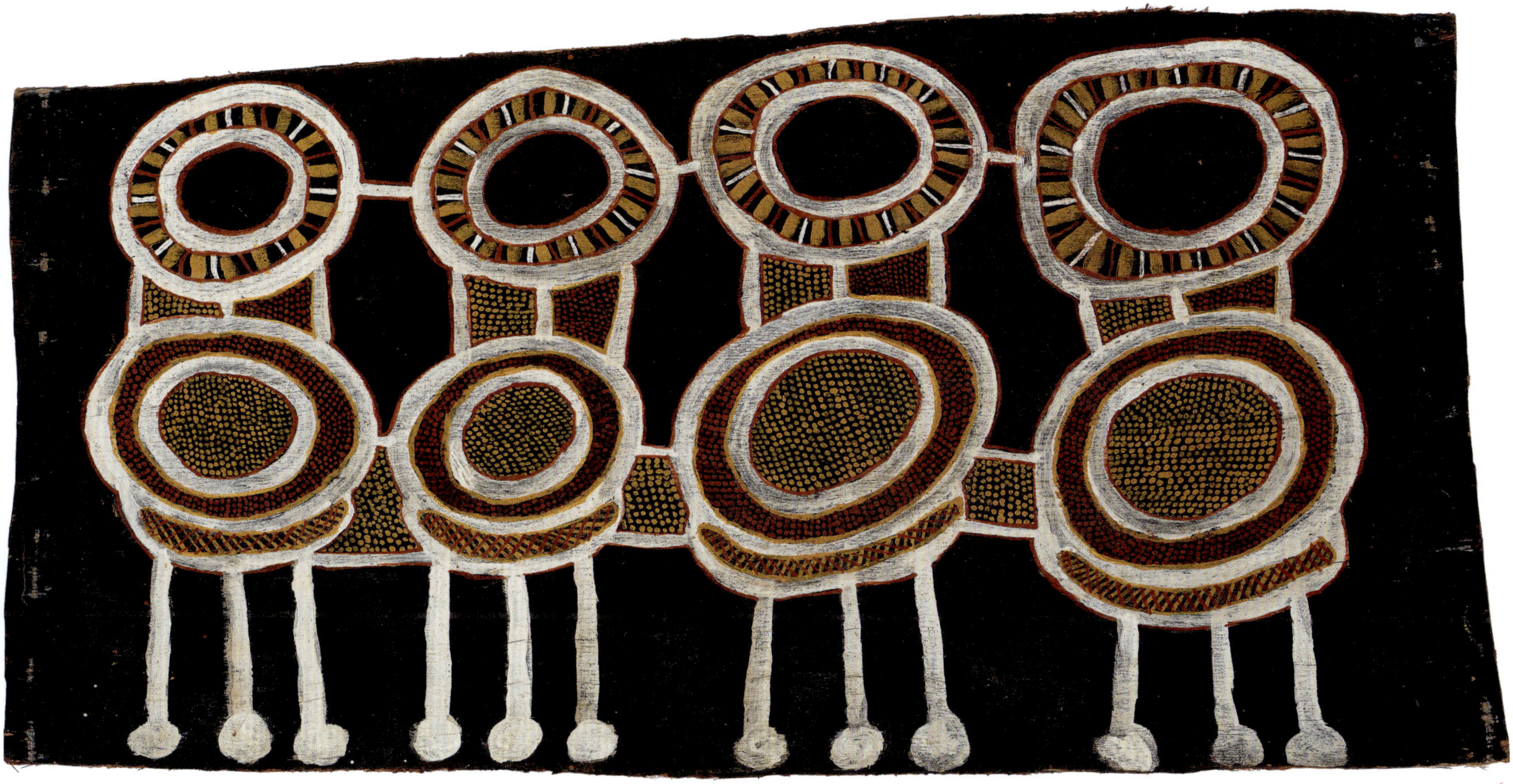

ANATJARI TJAMPITJINPA
Ceremonial Ground, 1981
Synthetic polymer paint on canvas, 182.5 × 182 cm
National Gallery of Australia, Canberra. Purchased 1992

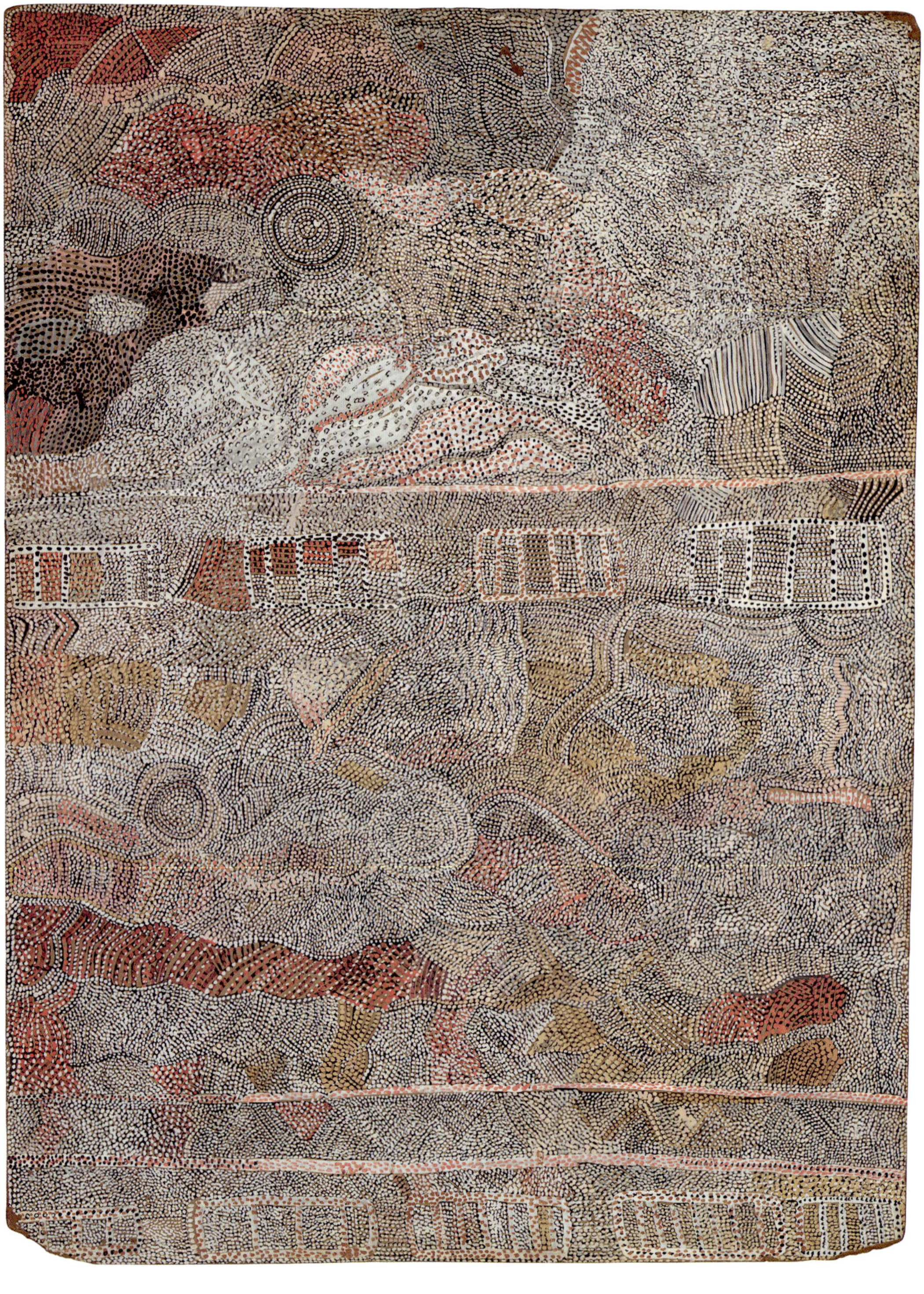

15
JOHNNY WARANGKULA TJUPURRULA
A Bush Tucker Story, 1972
Synthetic polymer paint on composition board, 91.4 × 66.2 cm
National Gallery of Victoria, Melbourne. Purchased through the Art Foundation of Victoria with the assistance of North Broken Hill Ltd, Fellow, 1987

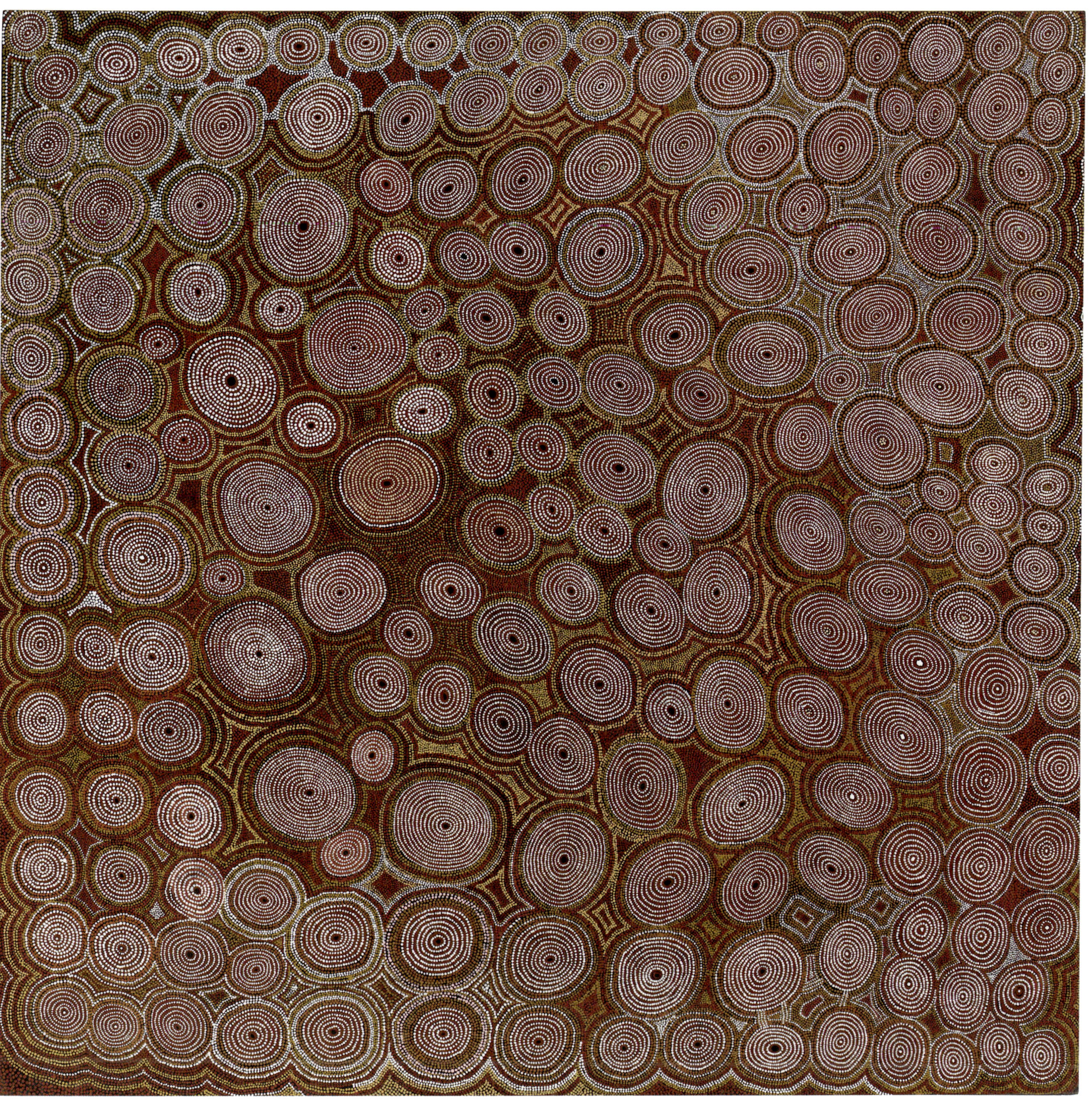

17
LONG JACK PHILLIPUS TJAKAMARRA
Kalipinypa Water Dreaming, *c.*1972
Synthetic polymer paint on composition board, 90 × 61.6 cm
National Gallery of Australia, Canberra. Purchased 1989

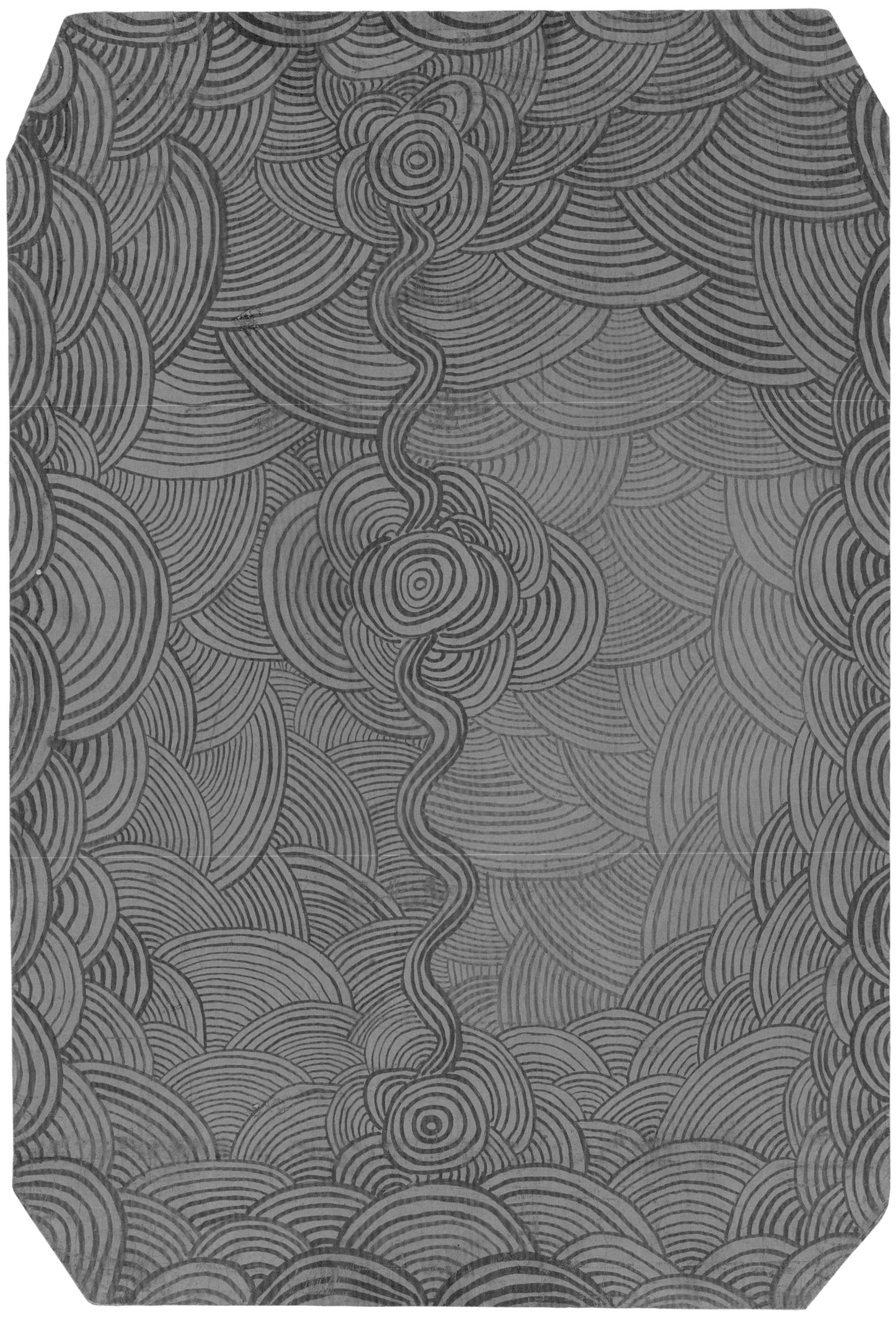

18

TIM LEURA TJAPALTJARRI

Fatal Love Dance, 1973

Synthetic polymer powder paint on composition board, 40 × 30 cm

National Gallery of Australia, Canberra. The Peter Fannin Collection of early Western Desert paintings, purchased 1998

19

TIMMY PAYUNGKA TJAPANGARTI

Sacred Sandhills, 1972

Synthetic polymer paint on composition board, 76 × 52 cm

National Gallery of Australia, Canberra. The Peter Fannin Collection of early Western Desert paintings, purchased 1998

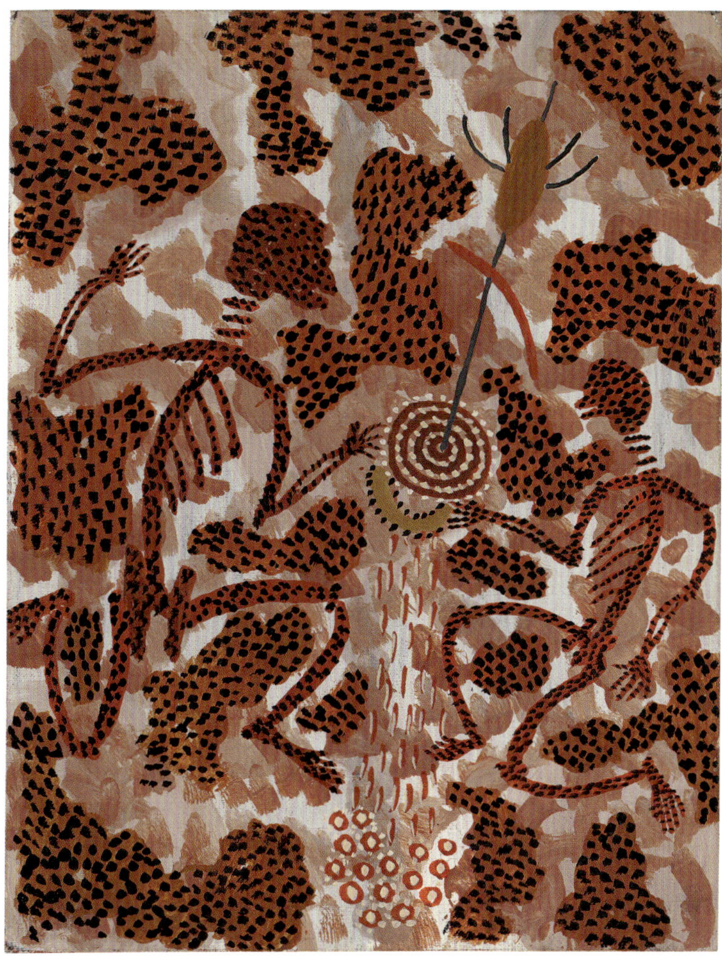

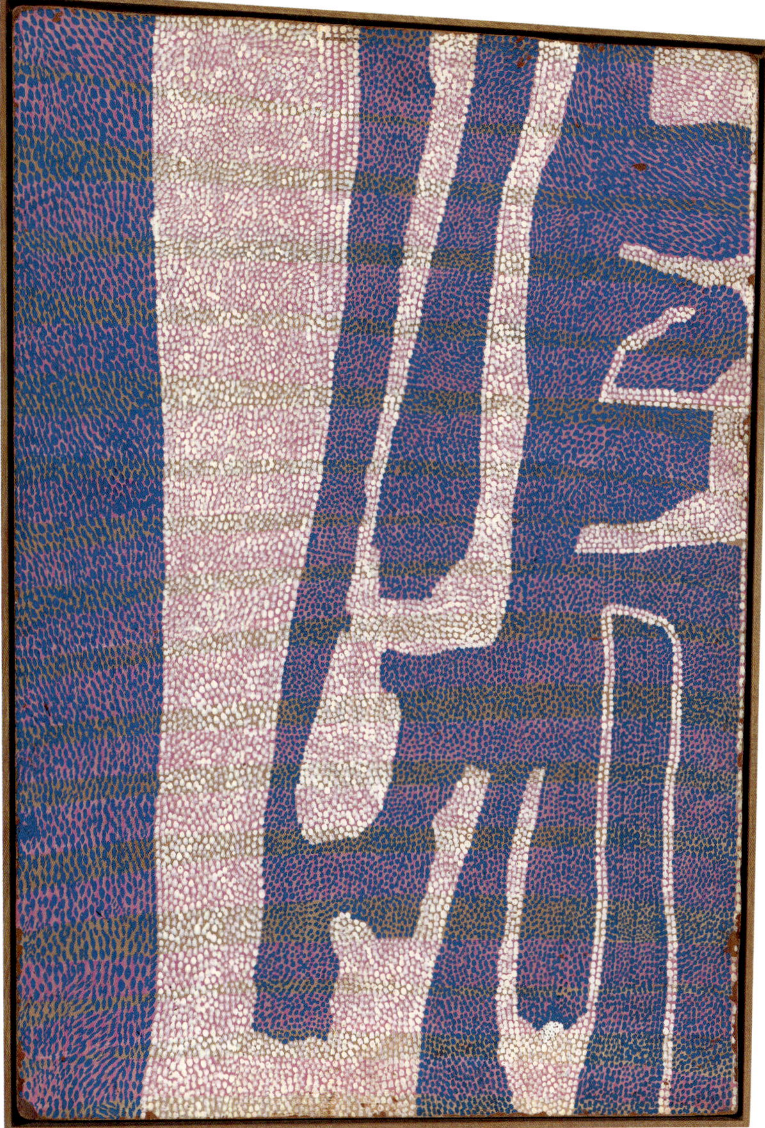

20

UTA UTA TJANGALA
Old Man's Dreaming, 1983
Synthetic polymer paint on canvas,
242 × 362 cm
Art Gallery of South Australia, Adelaide.
South Australian Government Grant, 1984

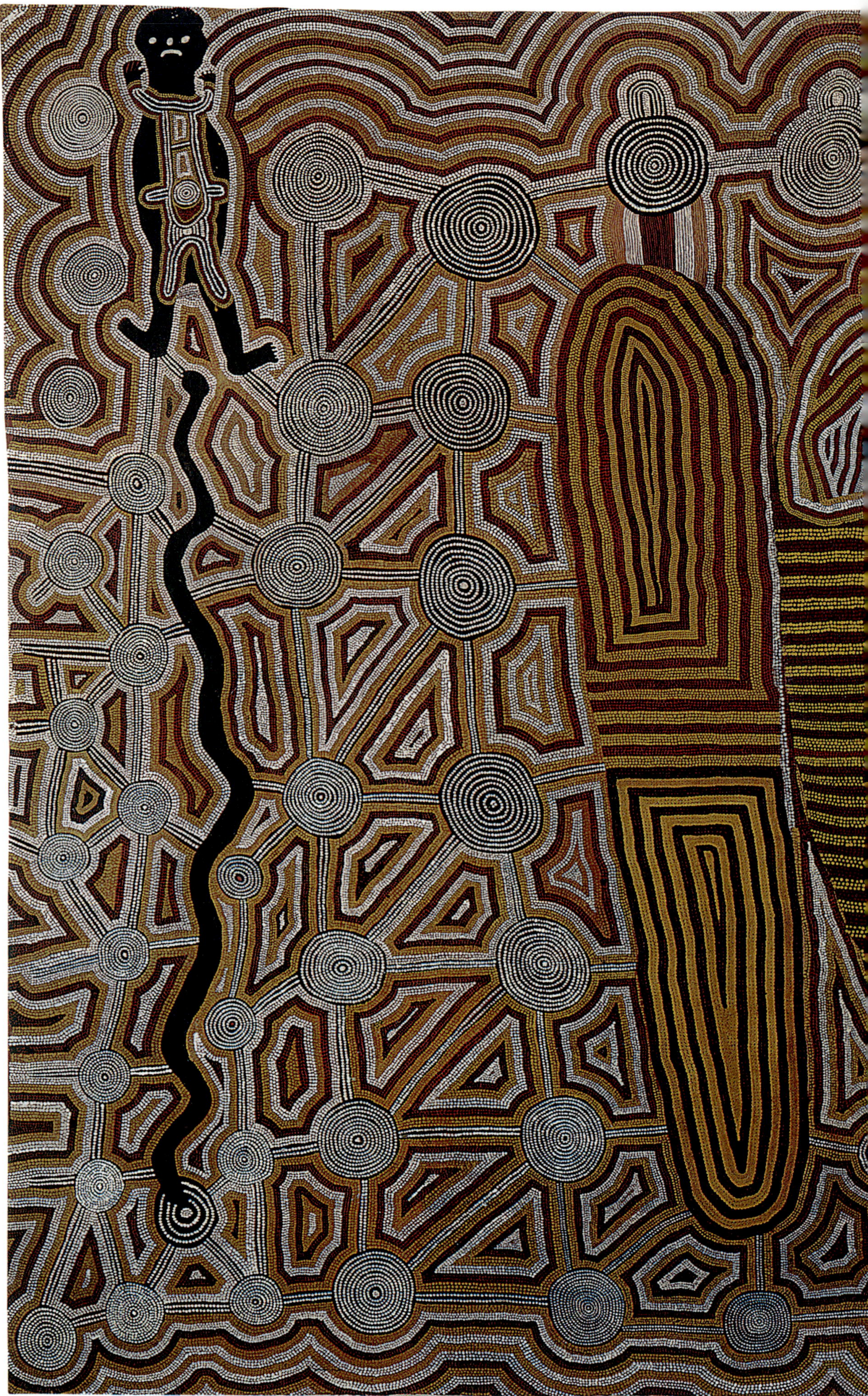

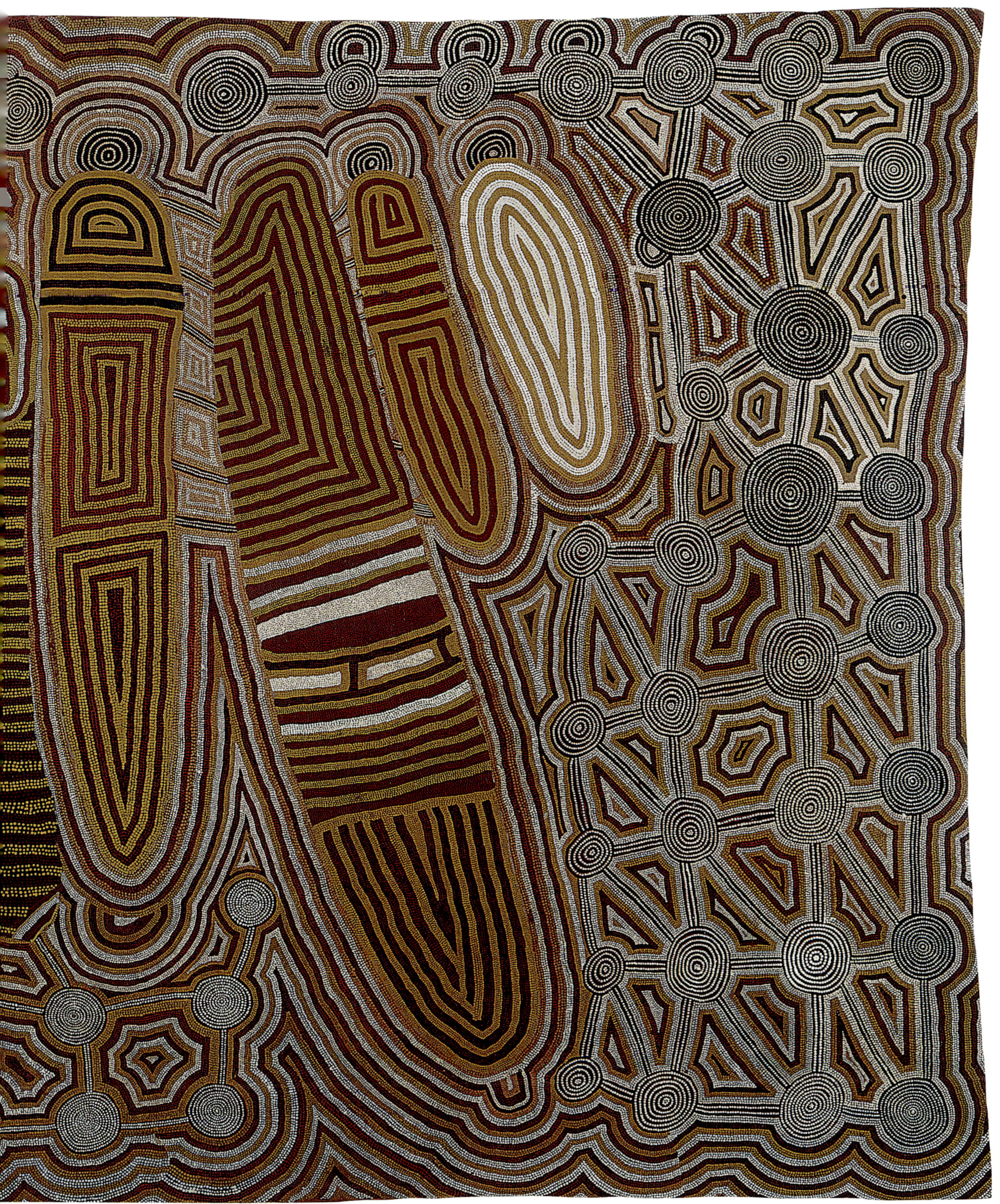

21

CLIFFORD POSSUM TJAPALTJARRI
Warlugulong, 1977
Synthetic polymer paint, oil and natural earth pigments on canvas, 202 × 337.5 cm

National Gallery of Australia, Canberra. Purchased with the generous assistance of Roslynne Bracher and the Paspaley family, David Coe and Michelle Coe, Charles Curran and Eva Curran, 2007

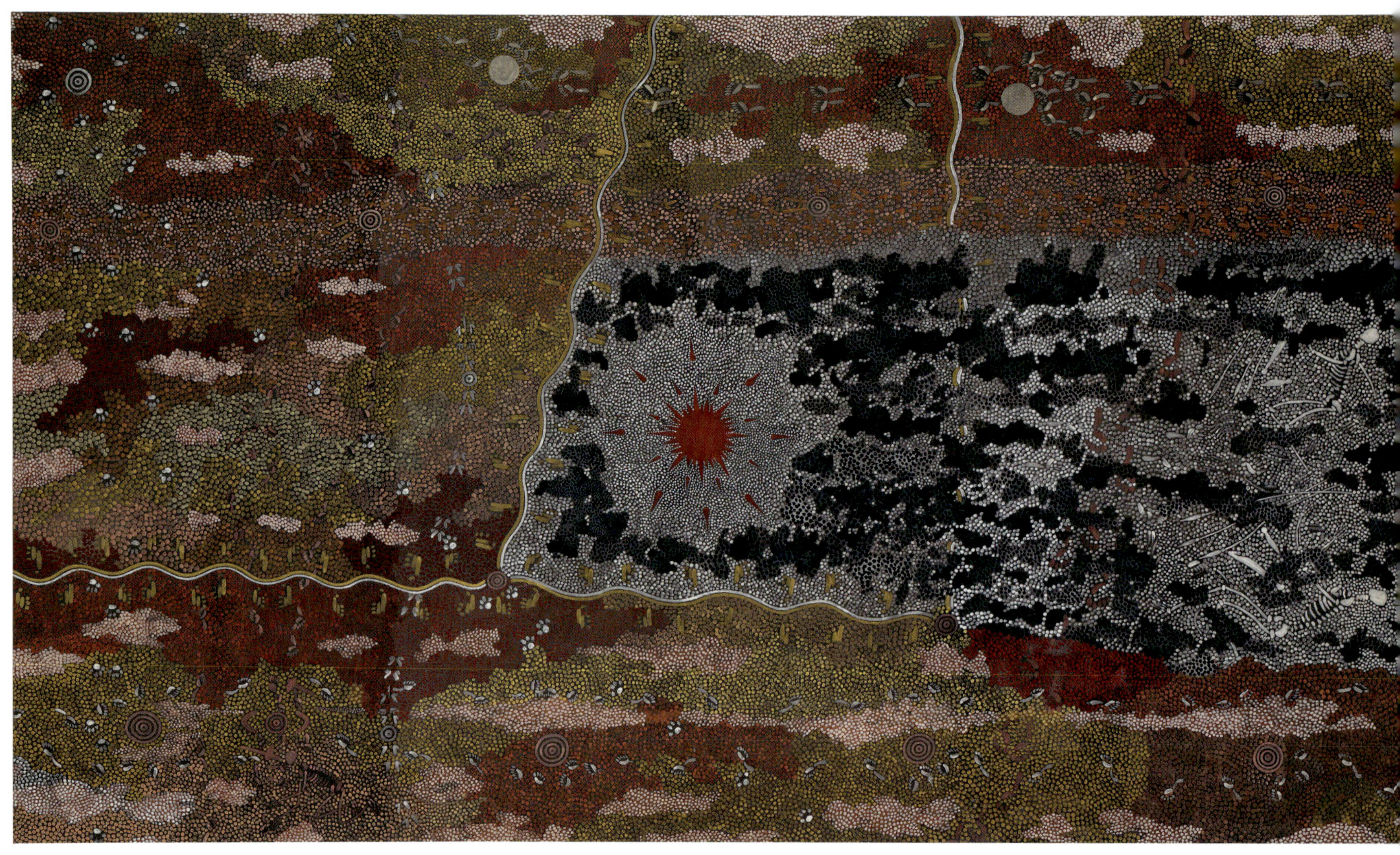

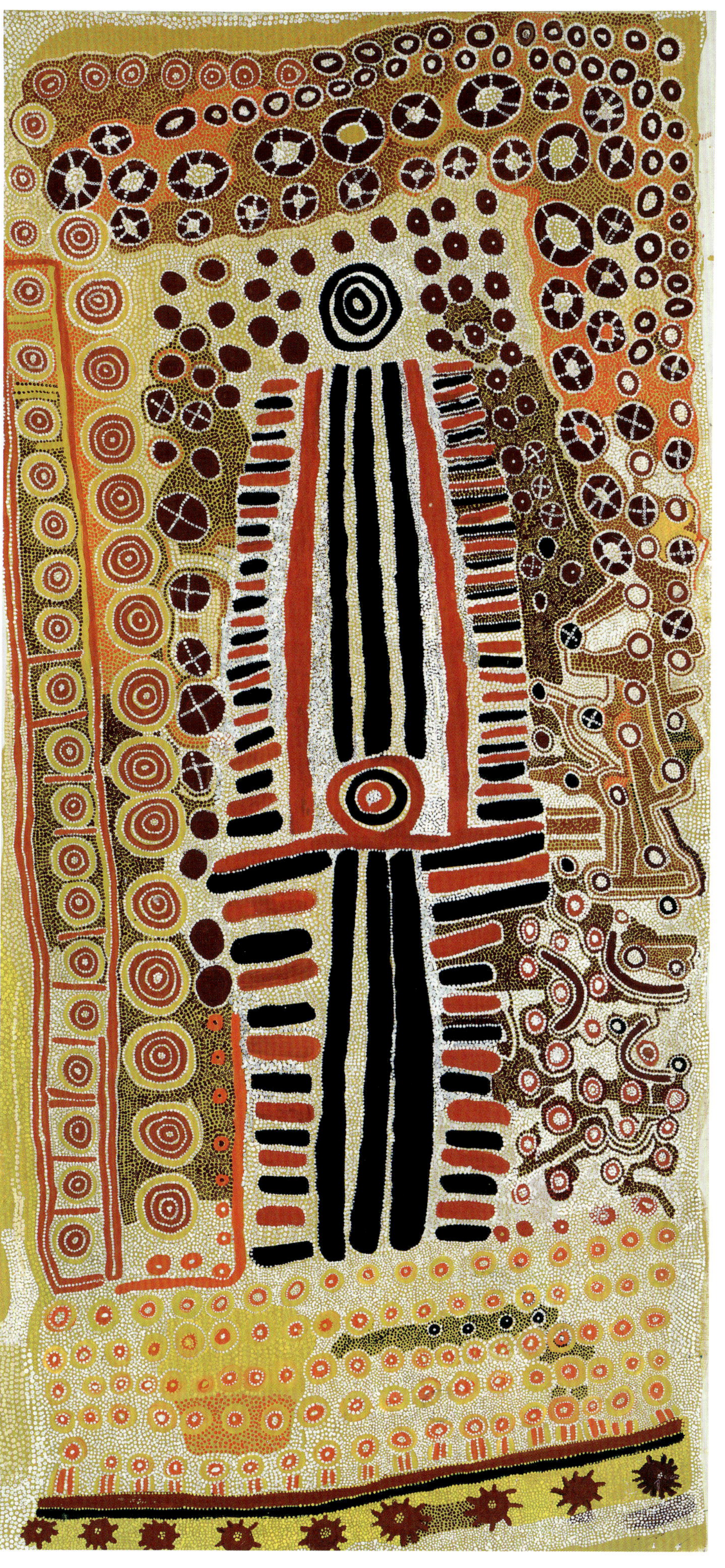

22

PADDY JUPURRURLA NELSON,
PADDY JAPALJARRI SIMS,
LARRY JUNGURRAYI SPENCER
Yanjilypiri Jukurrpa
(Star Dreaming), 1985
Synthetic polymer paint on canvas,
372 × 171.4 cm

National Gallery of Australia, Canberra.
Purchased 1986

23

EMILY KAME KNGWARREYE

Anwerlarr Anganenty (Big Yam Dreaming), 1995

Synthetic polymer paint on canvas, 291.1 × 801.8 cm

National Gallery of Victoria, Melbourne. Presented through the Art Foundation of Victoria by Donald and Janet Holt and family, Governors, 1995

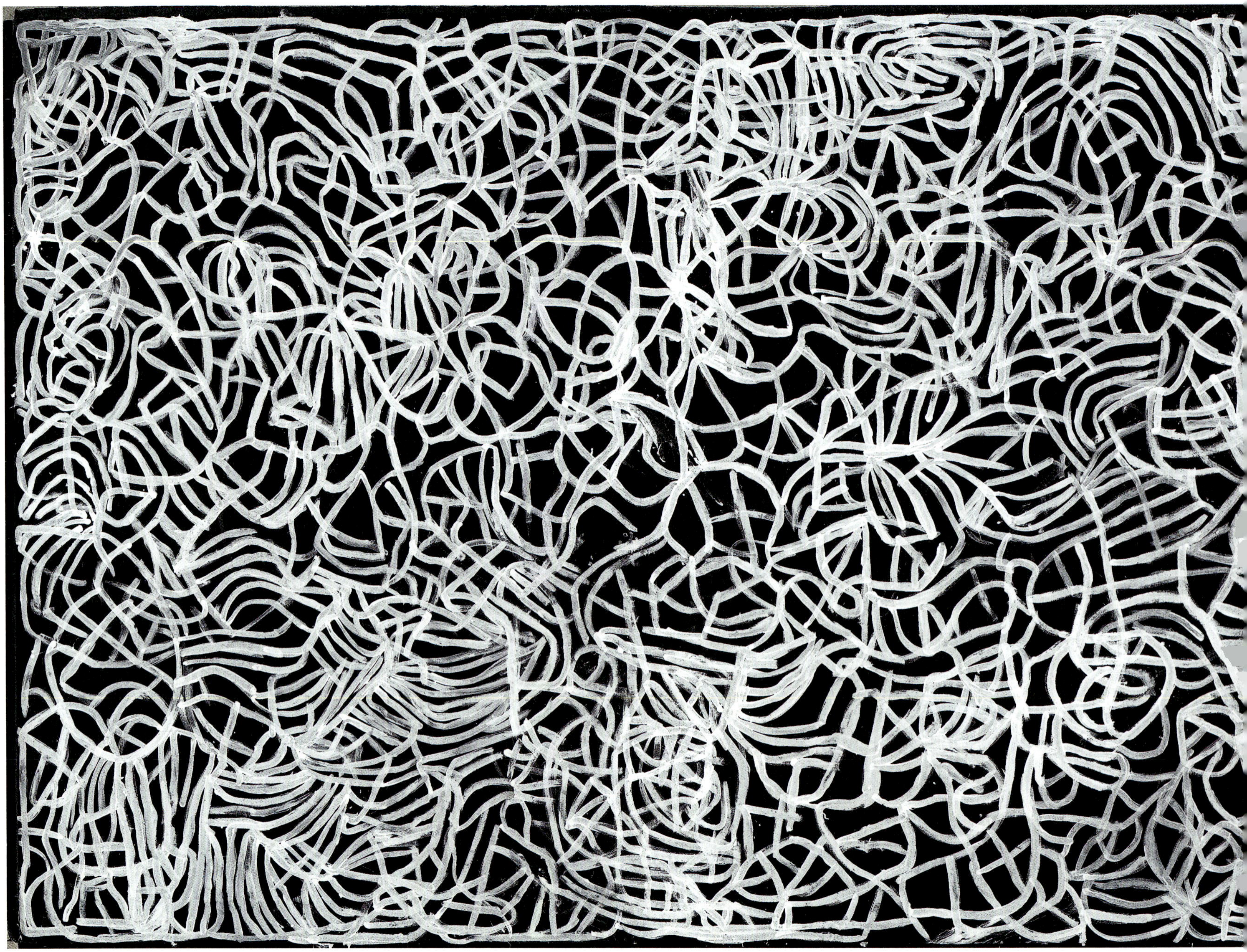

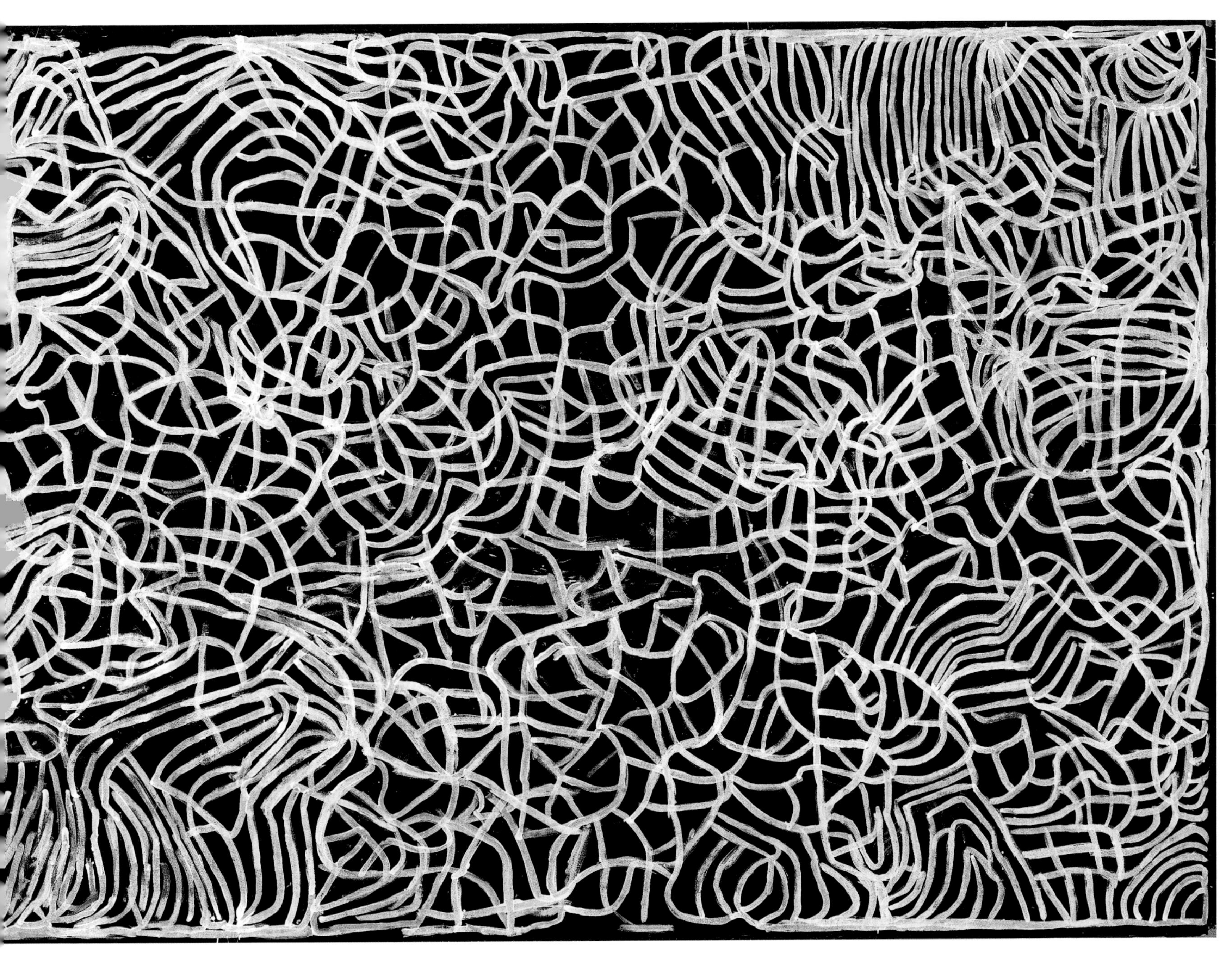

24

MICK NAMARARI TJAPALTJARRI

Rain Dreaming at Nyunmau, 1994

Synthetic polymer paint on linen, 152 × 183 cm

National Gallery of Australia, Canberra. Purchased with funds from the Honorary Exhibition Circle Patrons, 2013

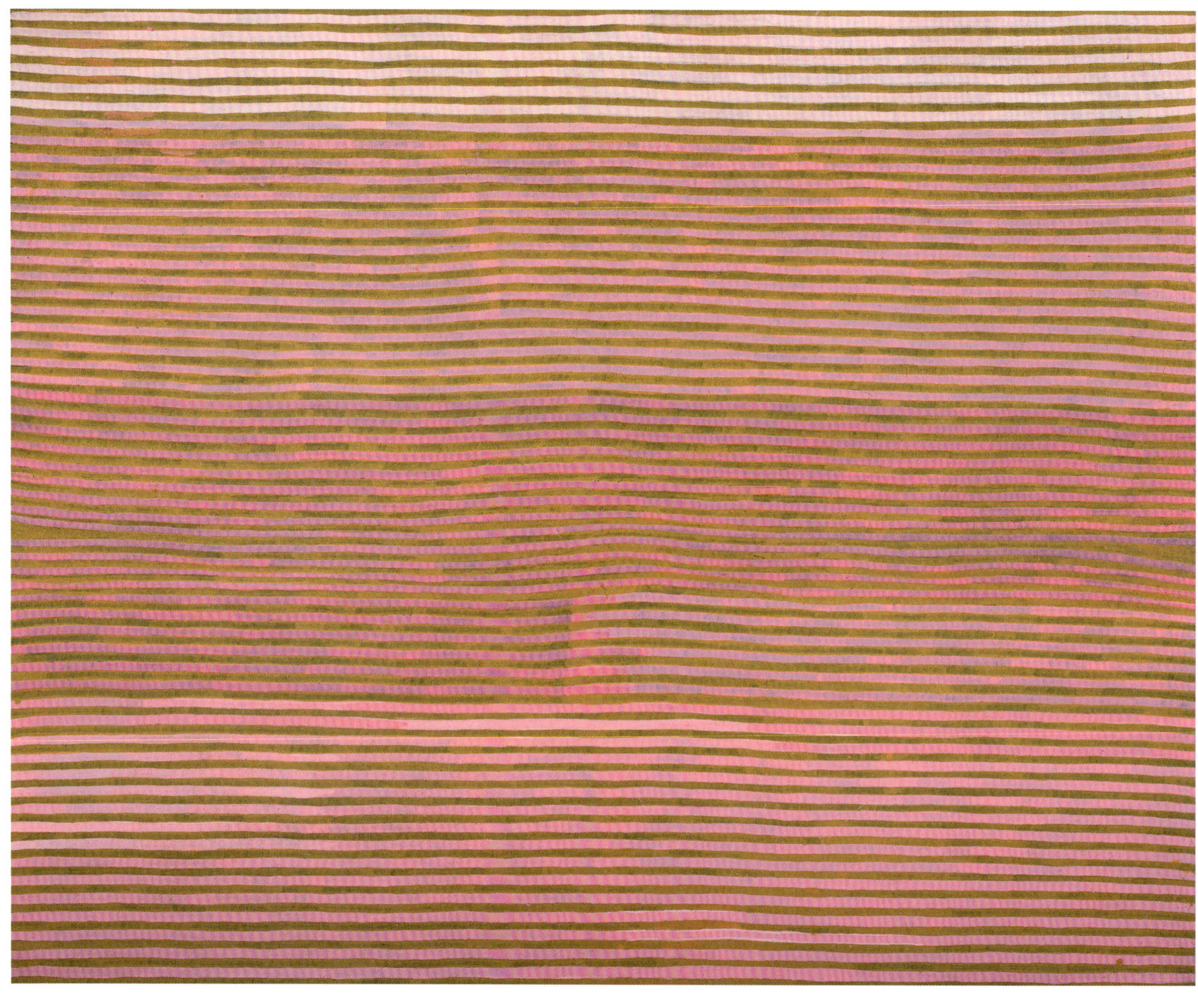

25

TURKEY TOLSON TJUPURRULA
Straightening Spears at Ilyingaungau, 1990
Synthetic polymer paint on canvas,
181.5 × 244 cm

Art Gallery of South Australia, Adelaide. Gift of the Friends of the Art Gallery of South Australia, 1990

26

JACK BRITTEN

Purnululu (Bull Creek Country), 1988

Natural earth pigments and natural binder on canvas, 160 × 200 cm

National Gallery of Australia, Canberra.
Purchased 1989

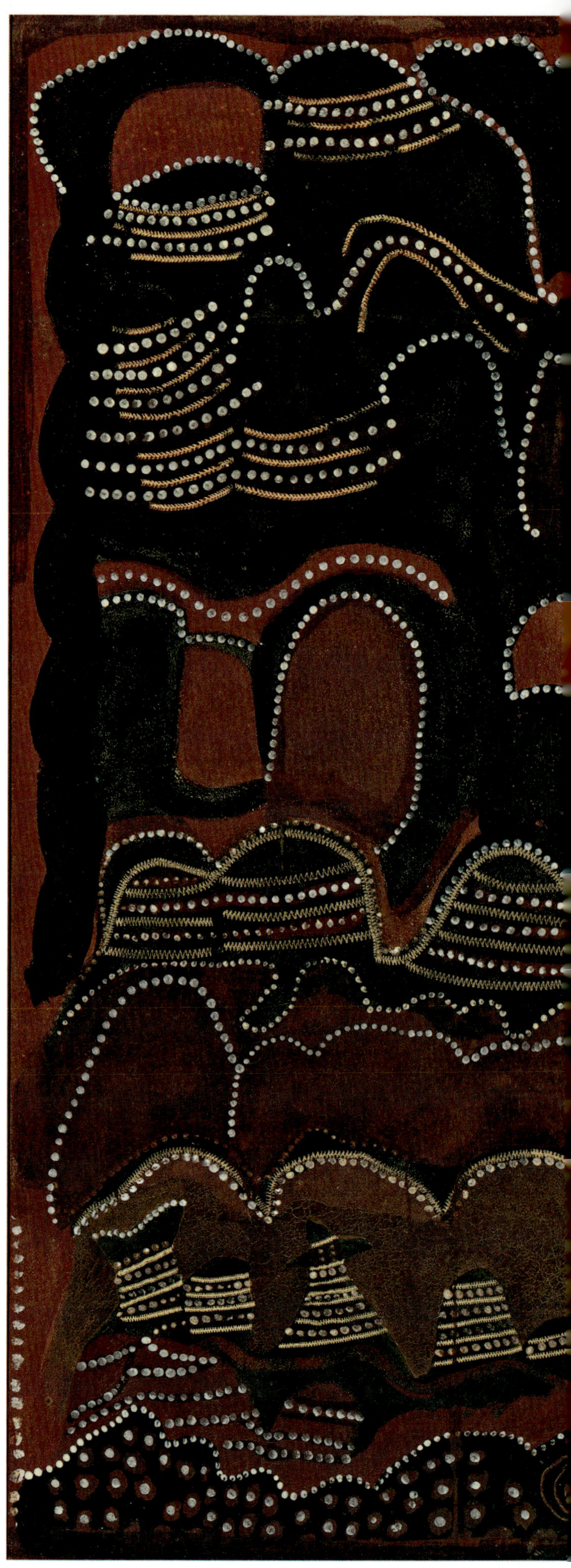

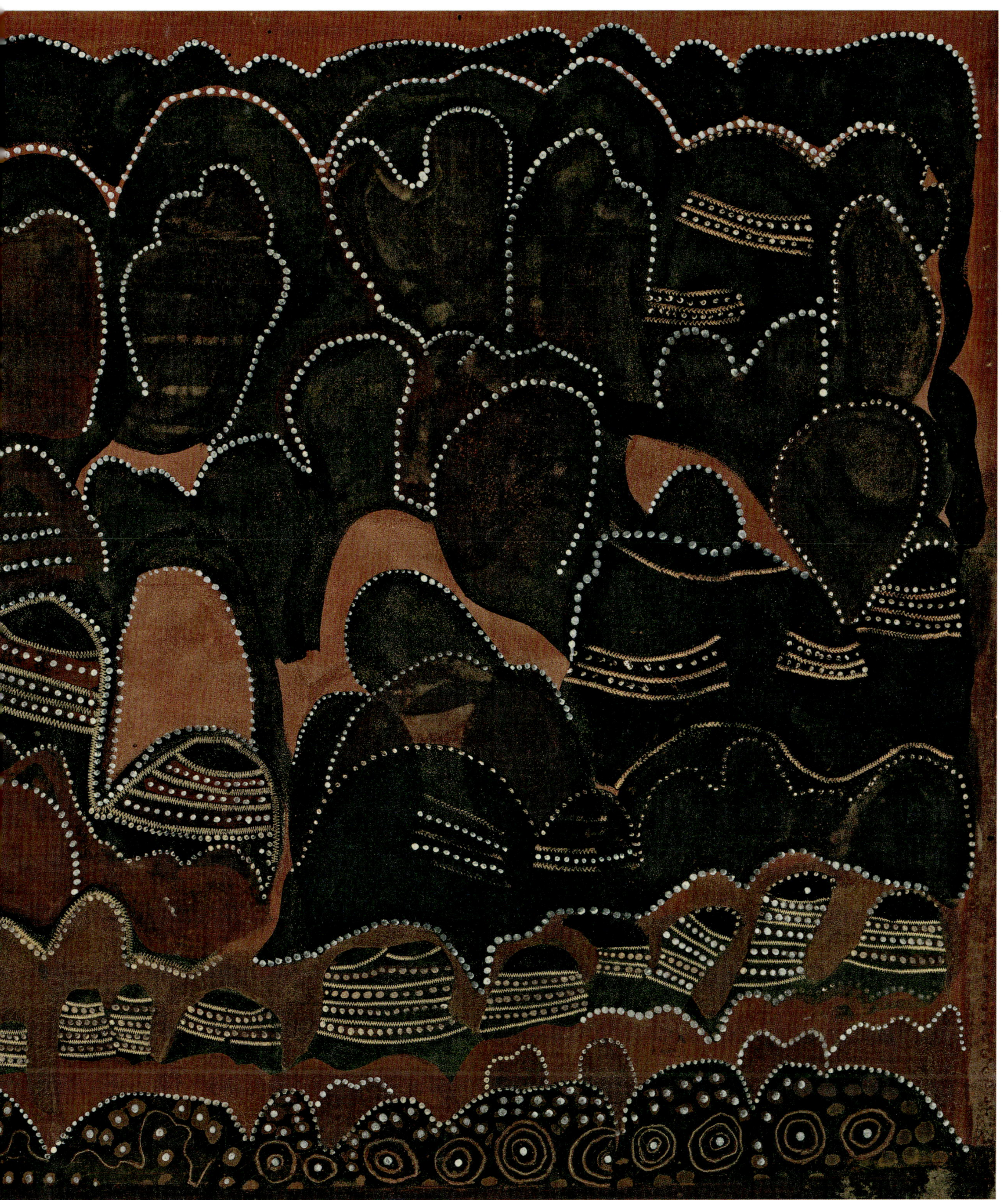

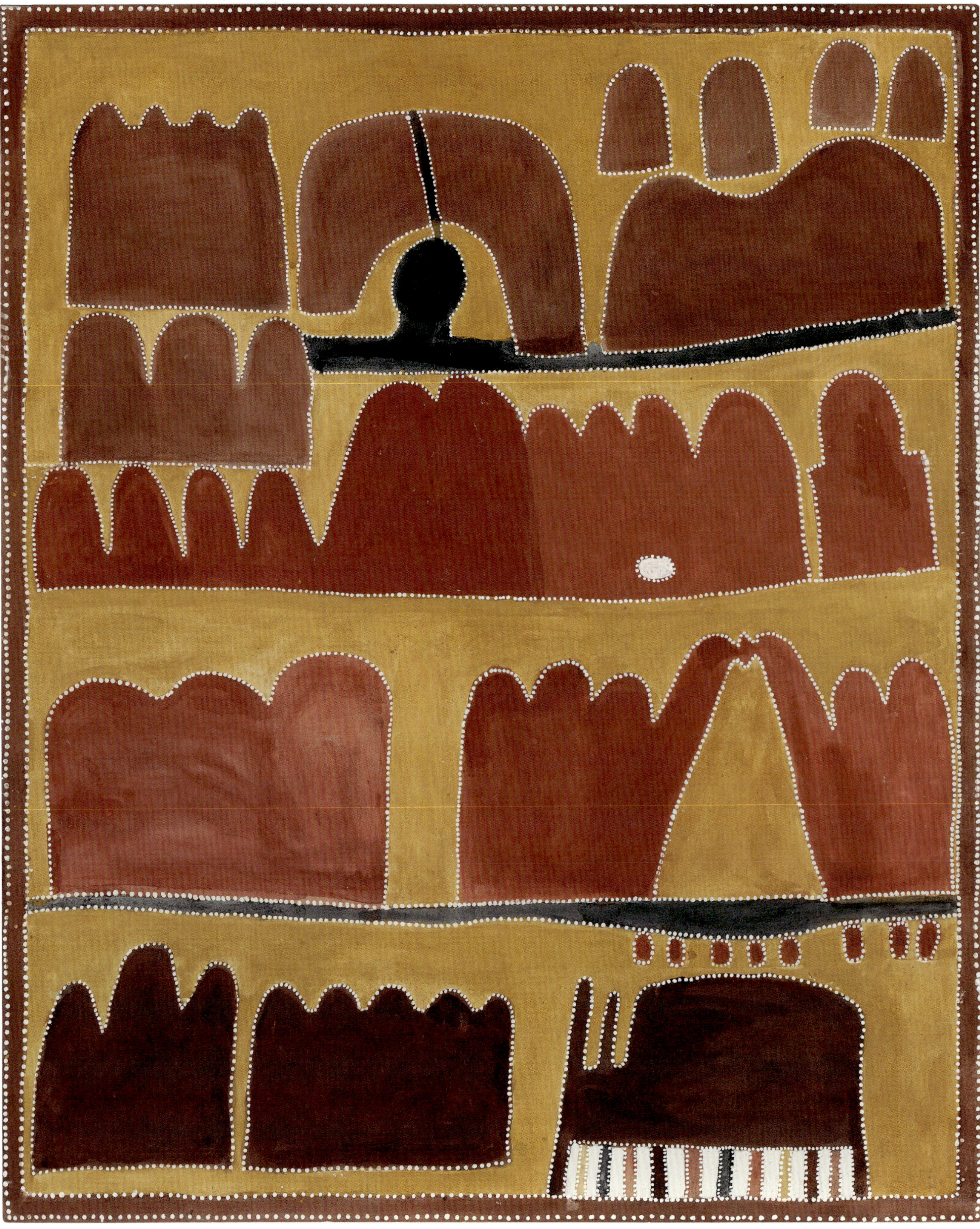

27

QUEENIE MCKENZIE
Gija Country, 1995
Natural earth pigments and binder on canvas, 200 × 160 cm
National Gallery of Australia, Canberra. Purchased 1996

28

PADDY JAMINJI
Kimberley Landscape, *c.*1984
Ochre on canvas, 195.8 × 270.3 cm
State Art Collection, Art Gallery of Western Australia, Perth. Purchased 1988

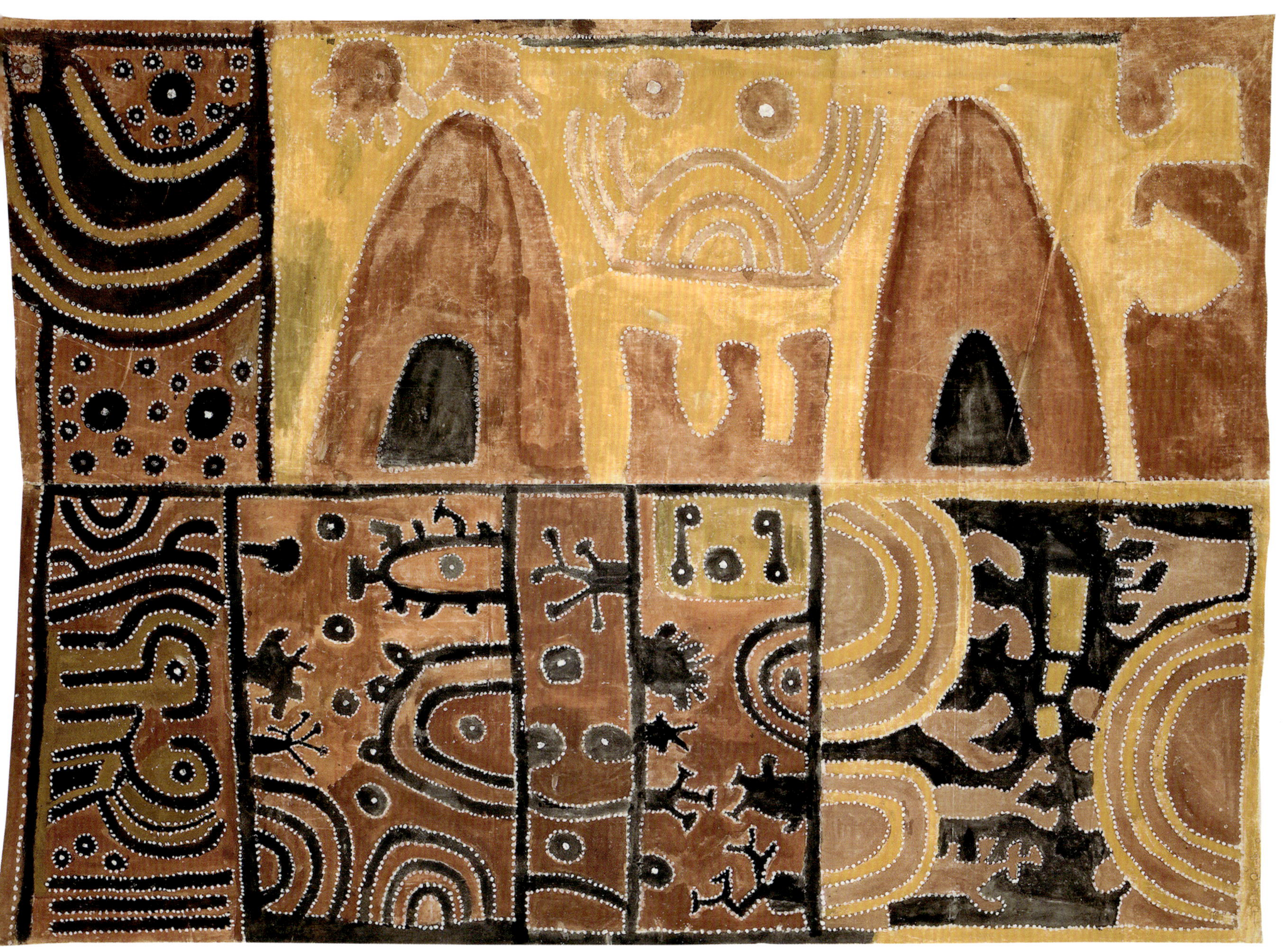

29

ROVER THOMAS
Roads Meeting, 1987
Natural earth pigments and binder on canvas, 90 × 180 cm
National Gallery of Australia, Canberra. Purchased 1988

30

ROVER THOMAS
Cyclone Tracy, 1991
Natural earth pigments and binder on canvas, 168 × 180 cm
National Gallery of Australia, Canberra. Purchased 1991

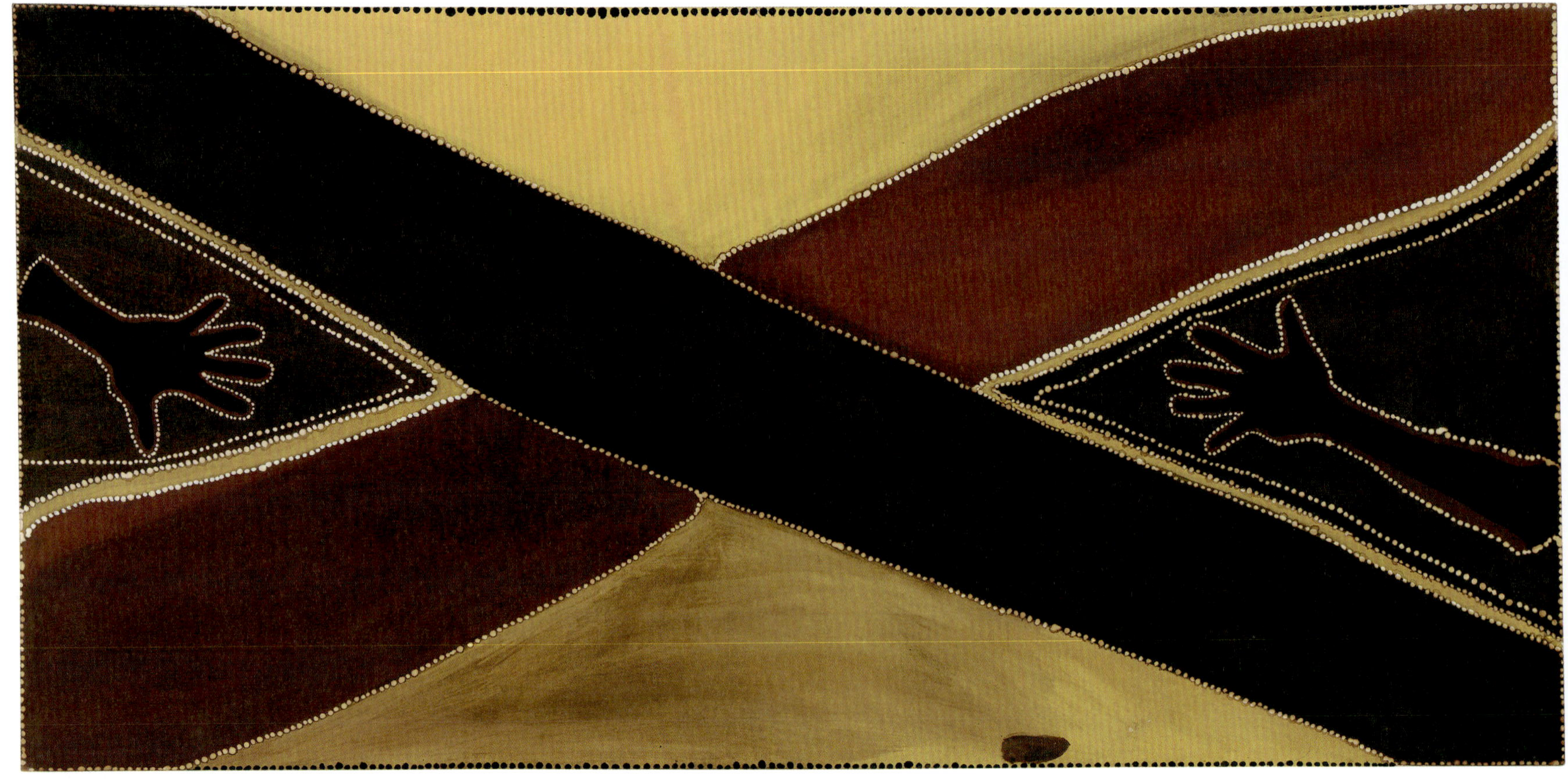

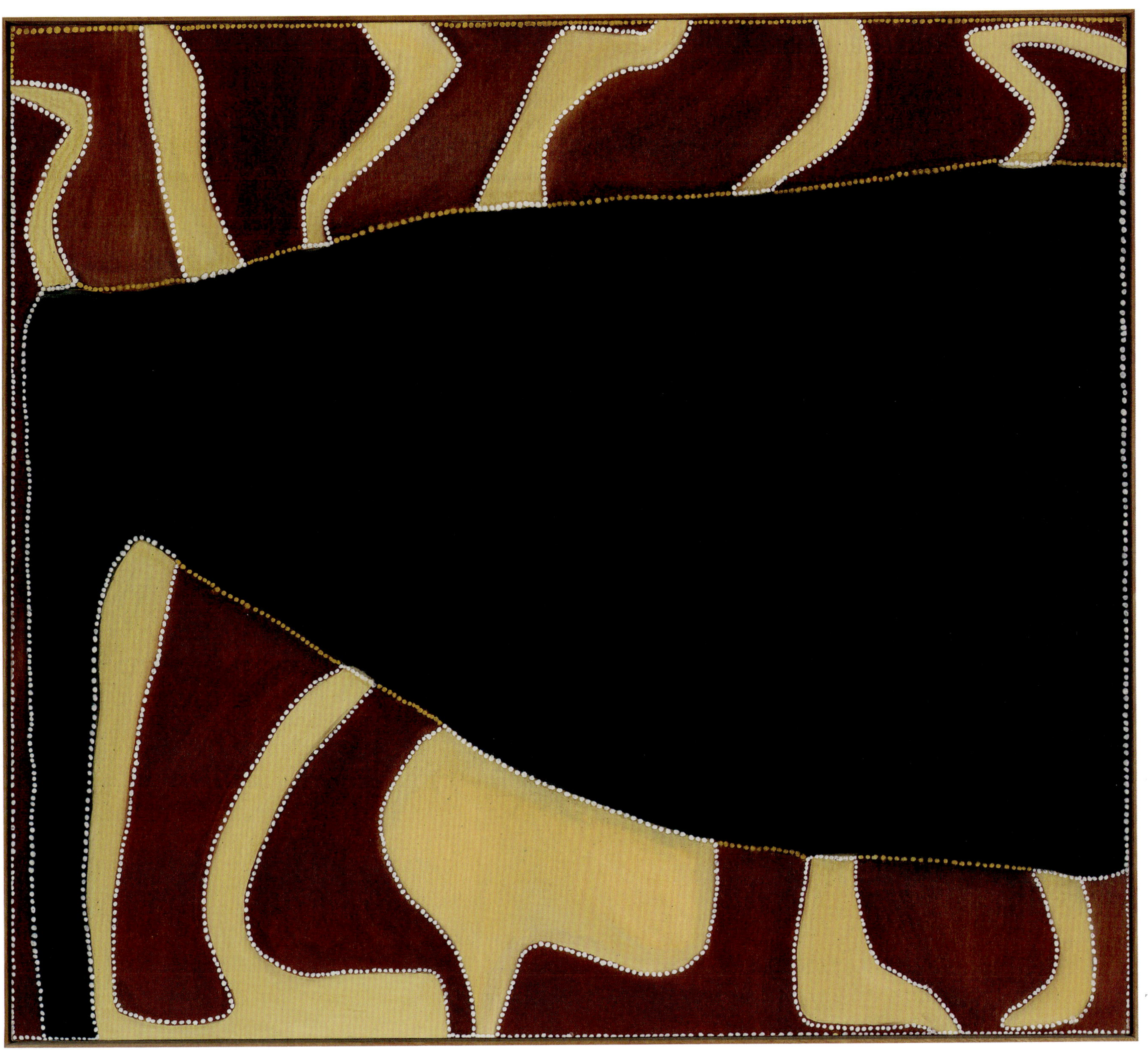

31

DOREEN REID NAKAMARRA
Untitled, 2007
Synthetic polymer paint on canvas, 183 × 244 cm
National Gallery of Australia, Canberra. Purchased 2007

32

DOROTHY NAPANGARDI
Sandhills of Mina Mina, 2000
Synthetic polymer paint on canvas, 198 × 122.7 cm
National Gallery of Australia, Canberra. Purchased 2

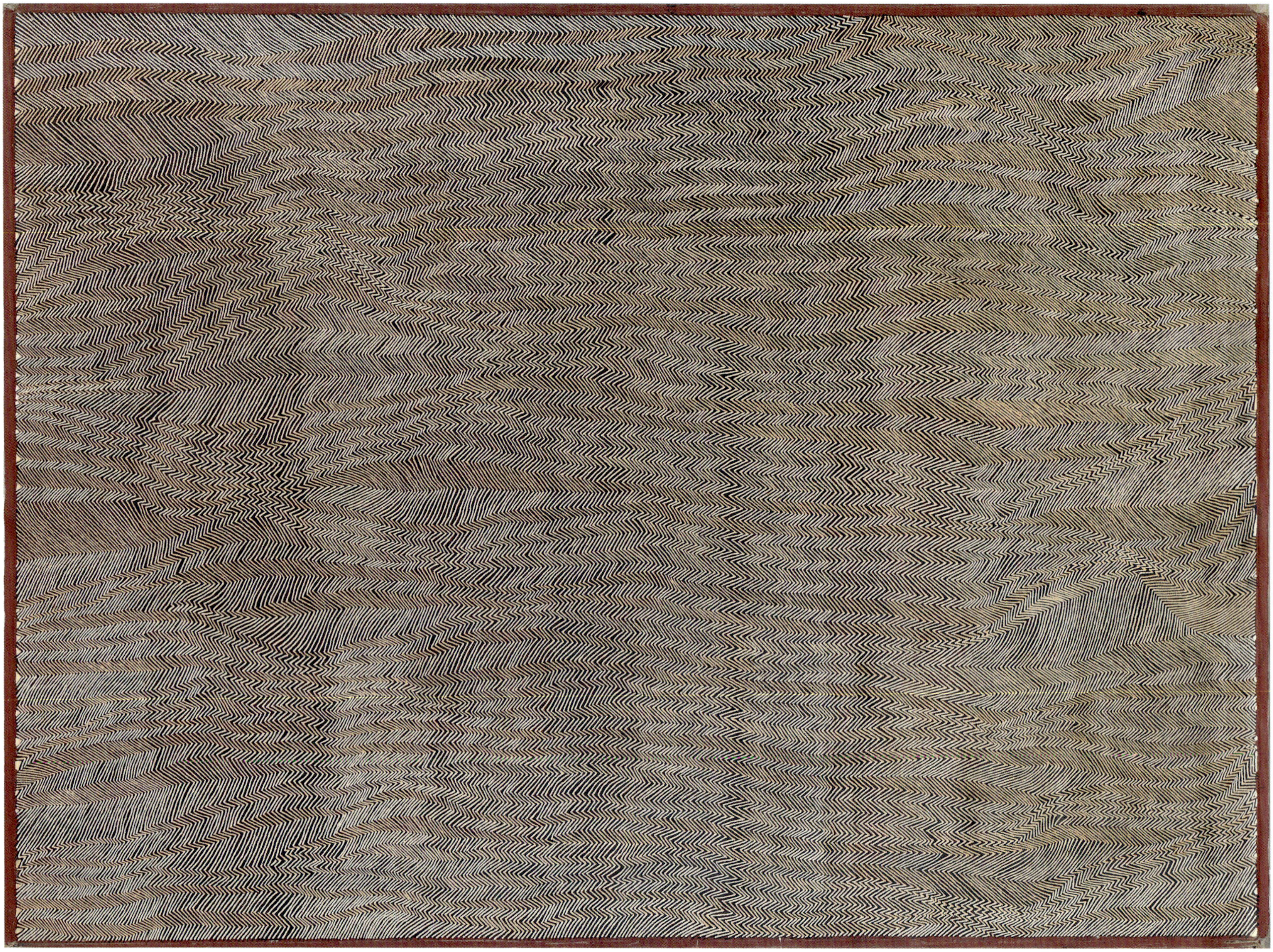

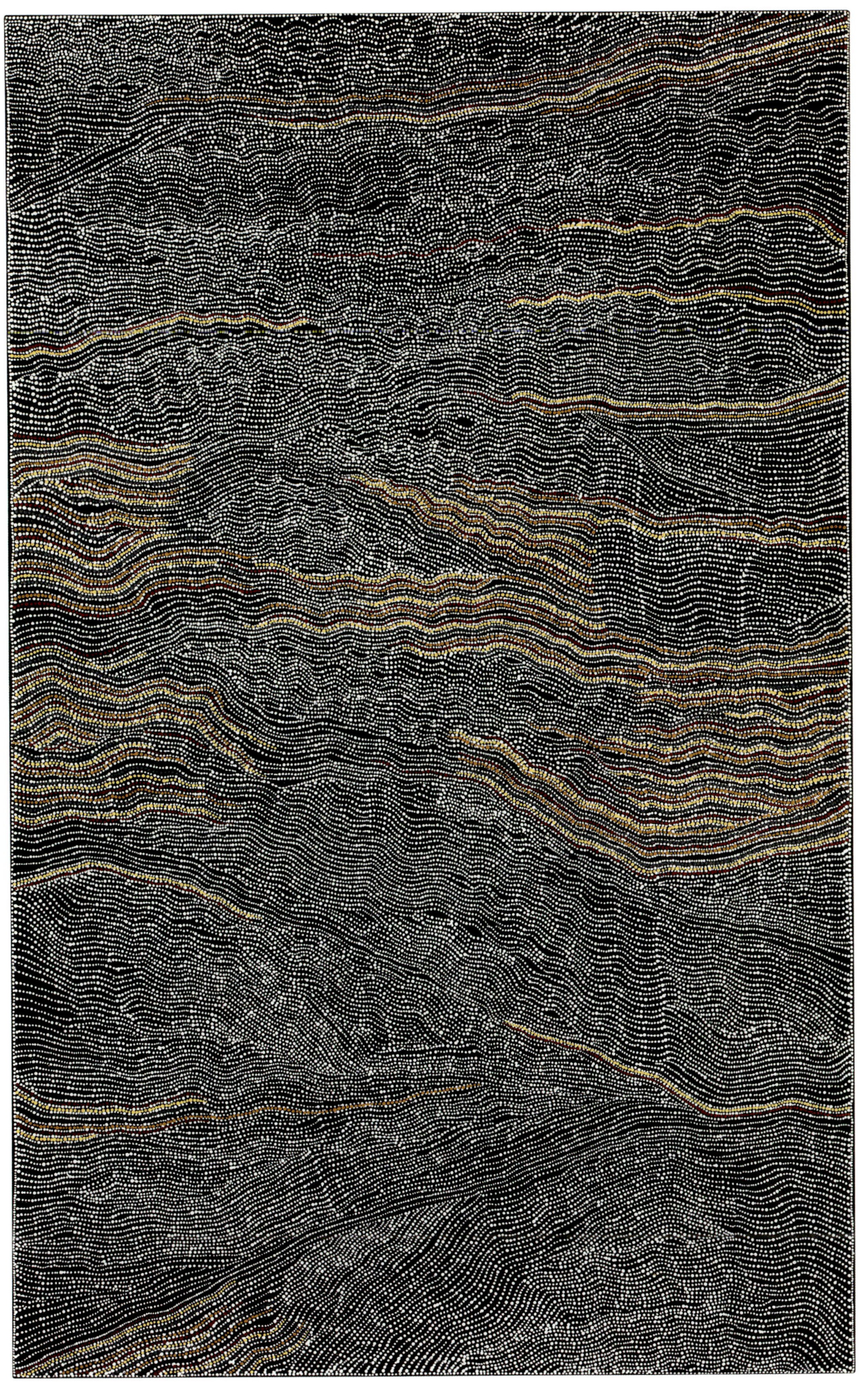

33

MARTUMILI ARTISTS
Ngayarta Kujarra, 2009
Synthetic polymer paint on canvas, 300.6 × 500.3 cm
National Gallery of Victoria, Melbourne. Purchased through the Felton Bequest, 2011

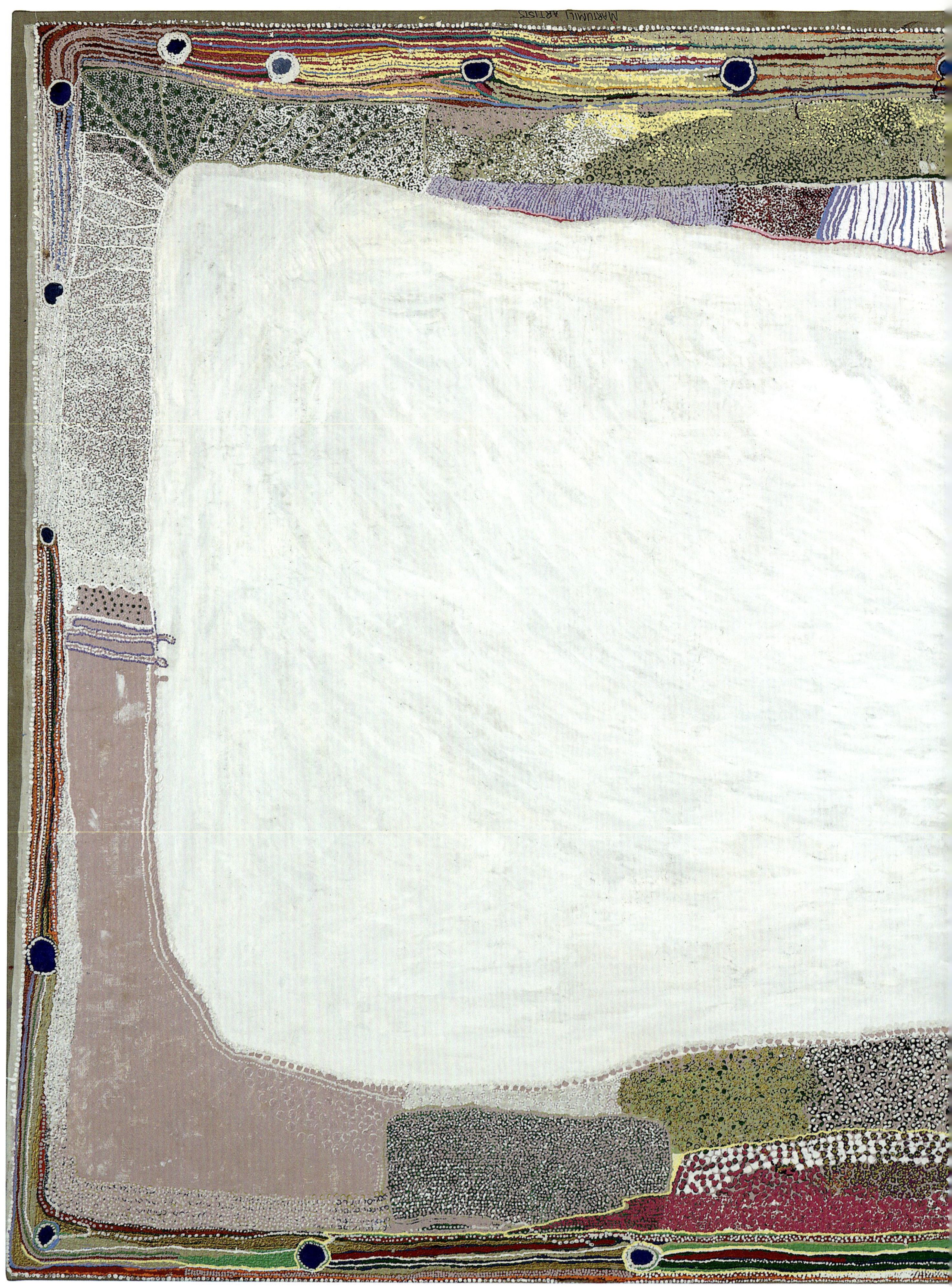

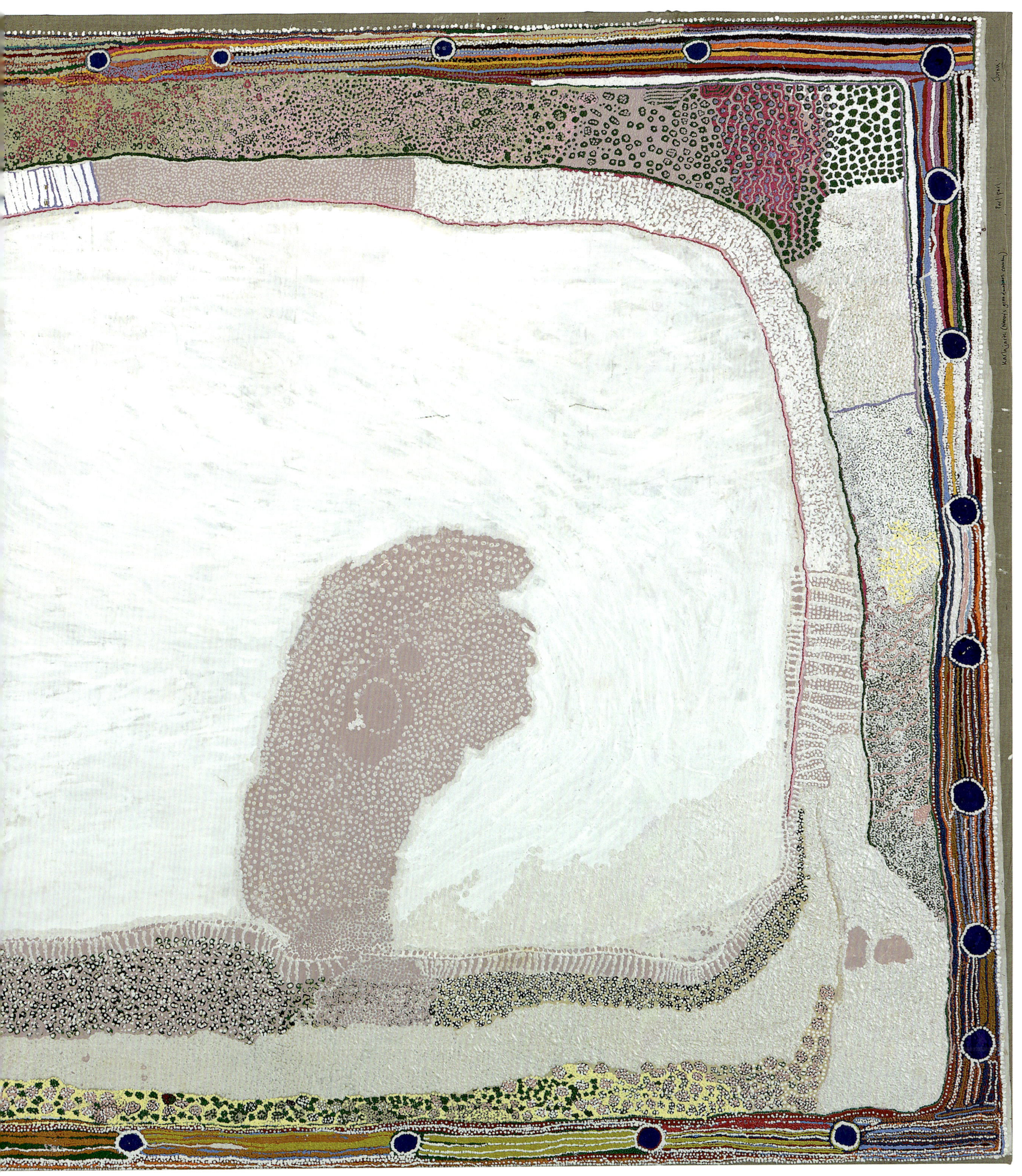

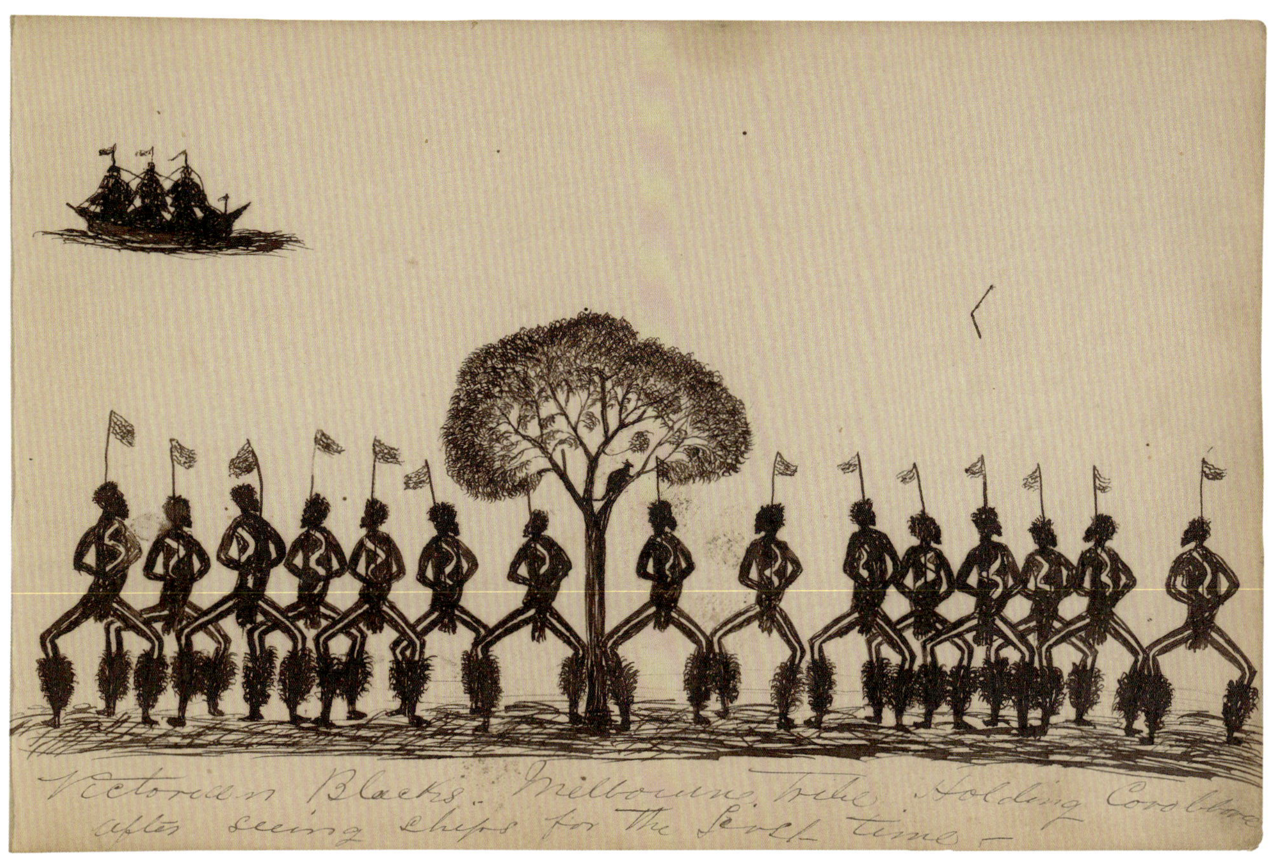

34
TOMMY MCRAE
Victorian Blacks — Melbourne Tribe Holding Corroboree after Seeing Ships for the First Time, 1890s
Pen and iron-gall ink, 23.8 × 36 cm
National Gallery of Australia, Canberra. Purchased 1994

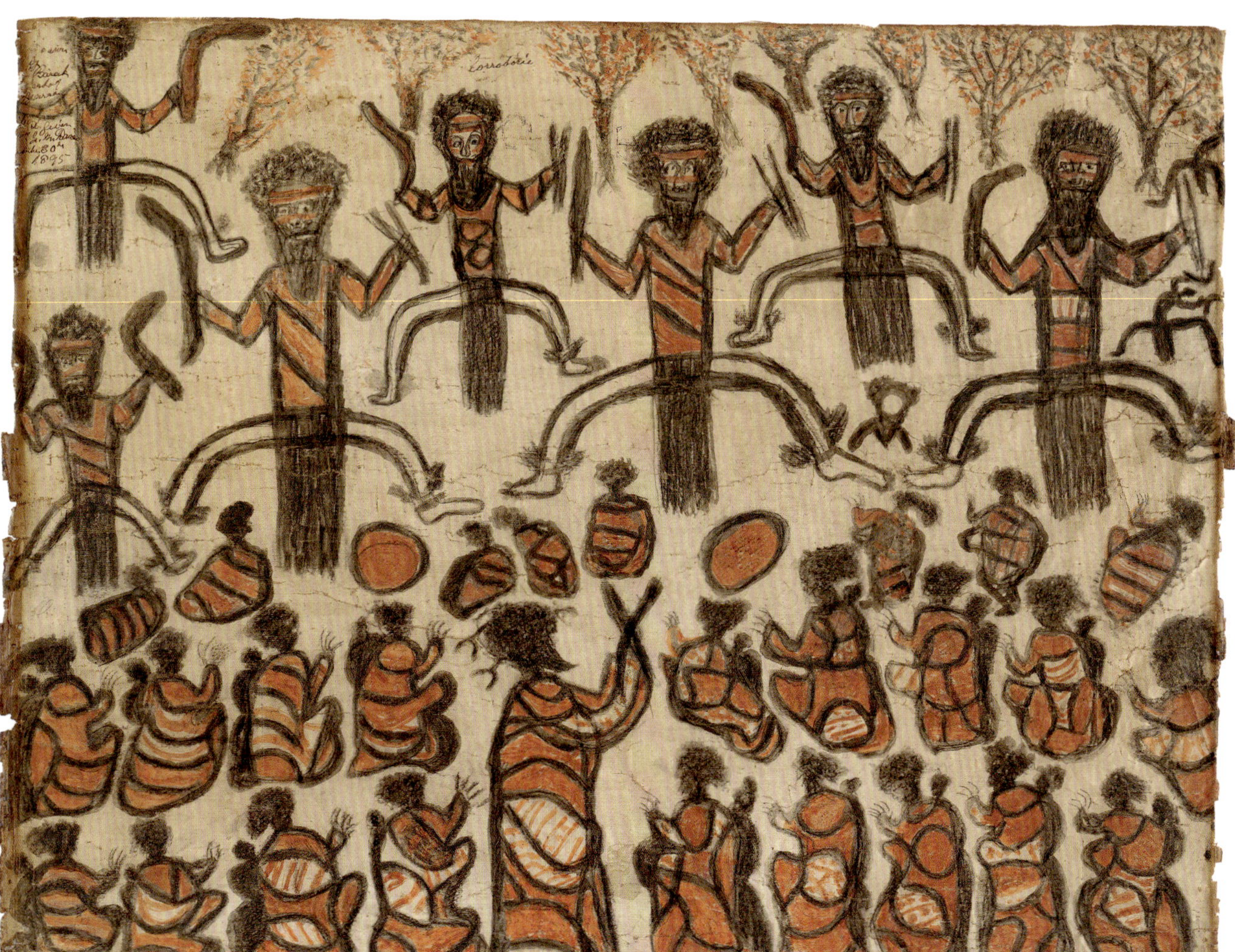

35
WILLIAM BARAK
Corroboree, 1895
Charcoal and natural earth pigments, over pencil on prepared linen, 60 × 76.4 cm
National Gallery of Australia, Canberra. Founding Donors' Fund, 2010

MICKEY OF ULLADULLA
Fishing, Native Flora and Fauna,
c. 1888
Gouache, watercolour, black ink and pastel over black pencil, 43 × 68 cm
National Gallery of Australia, Canberra. Purchased 1991

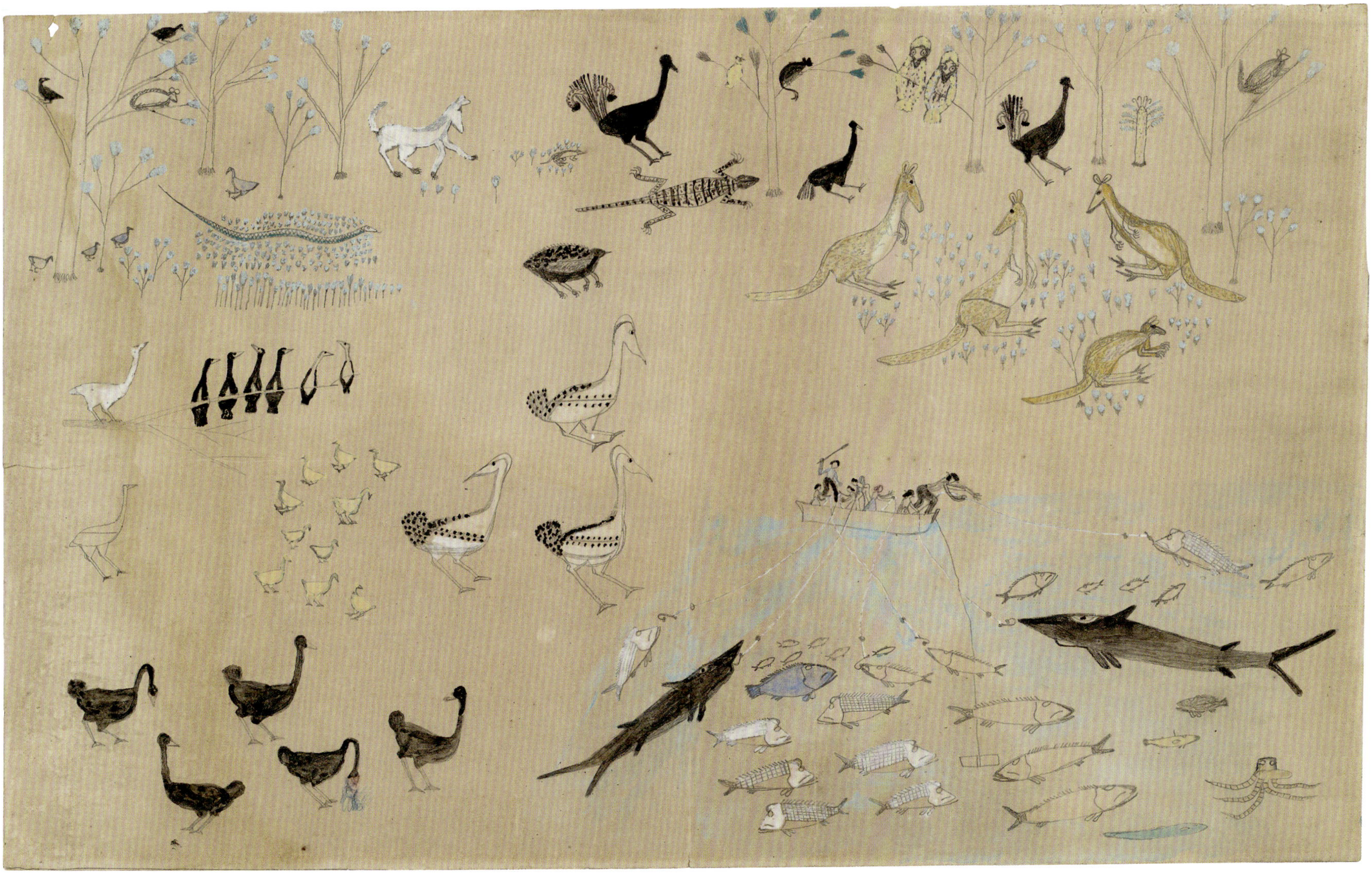

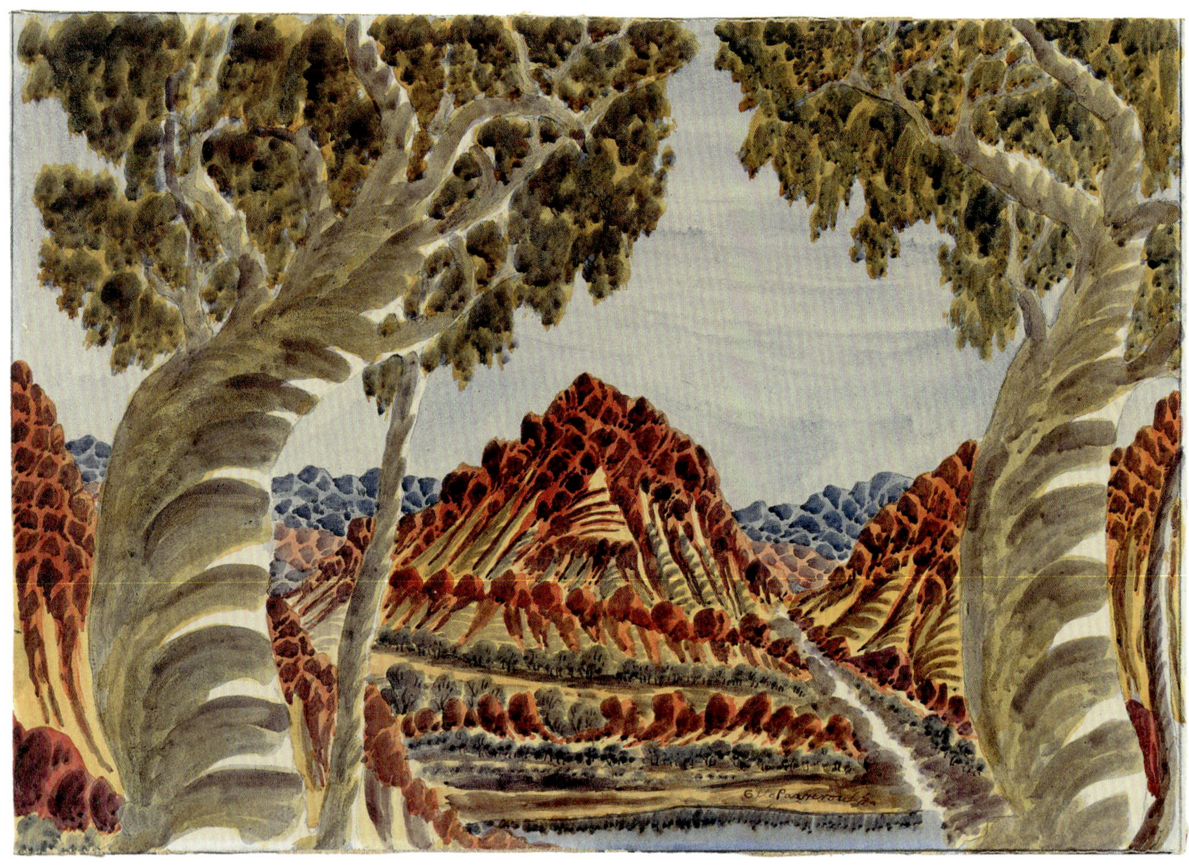

37
OTTO PAREROULTJA
Central Australian Landscape with Ghost Gums, *c.*1968
Watercolour, gouache over black pencil, 38.4 × 53.2 cm
National Gallery of Australia, Canberra. Purchased 2005

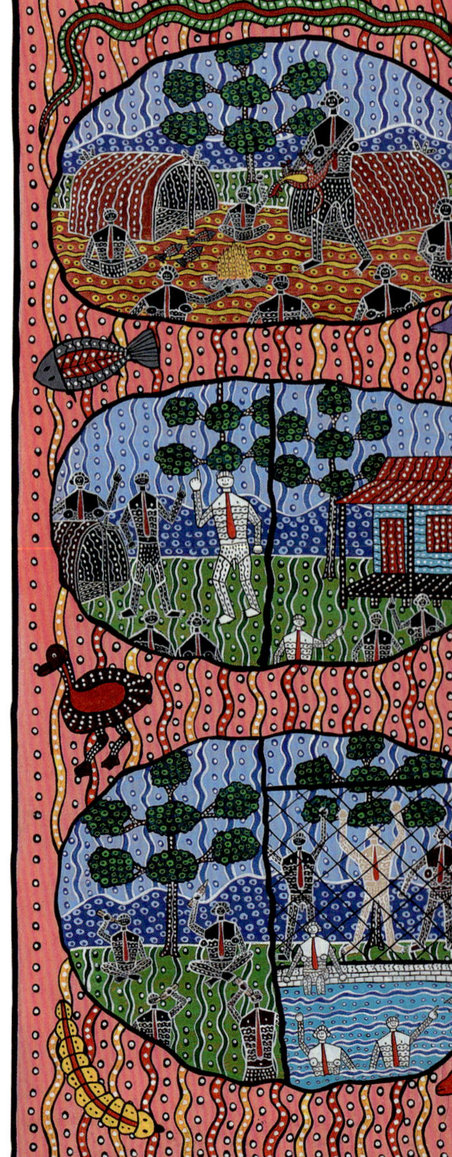

38

ROBERT CAMPBELL JNR

Abo History (Facts), 1988

Synthetic polymer paint on canvas, 130 × 200 cm

National Gallery of Australia, Canberra. Purchased 1988

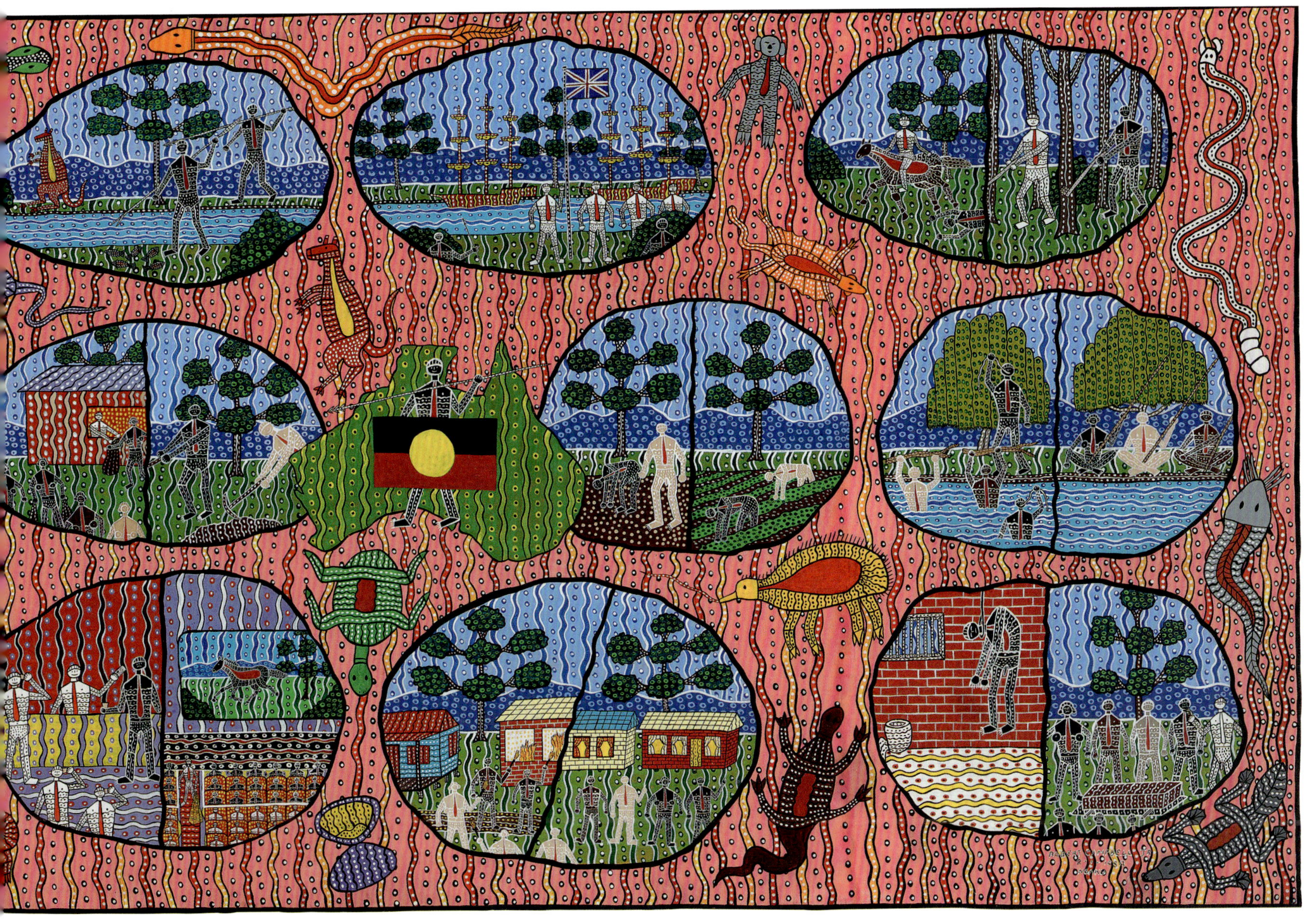

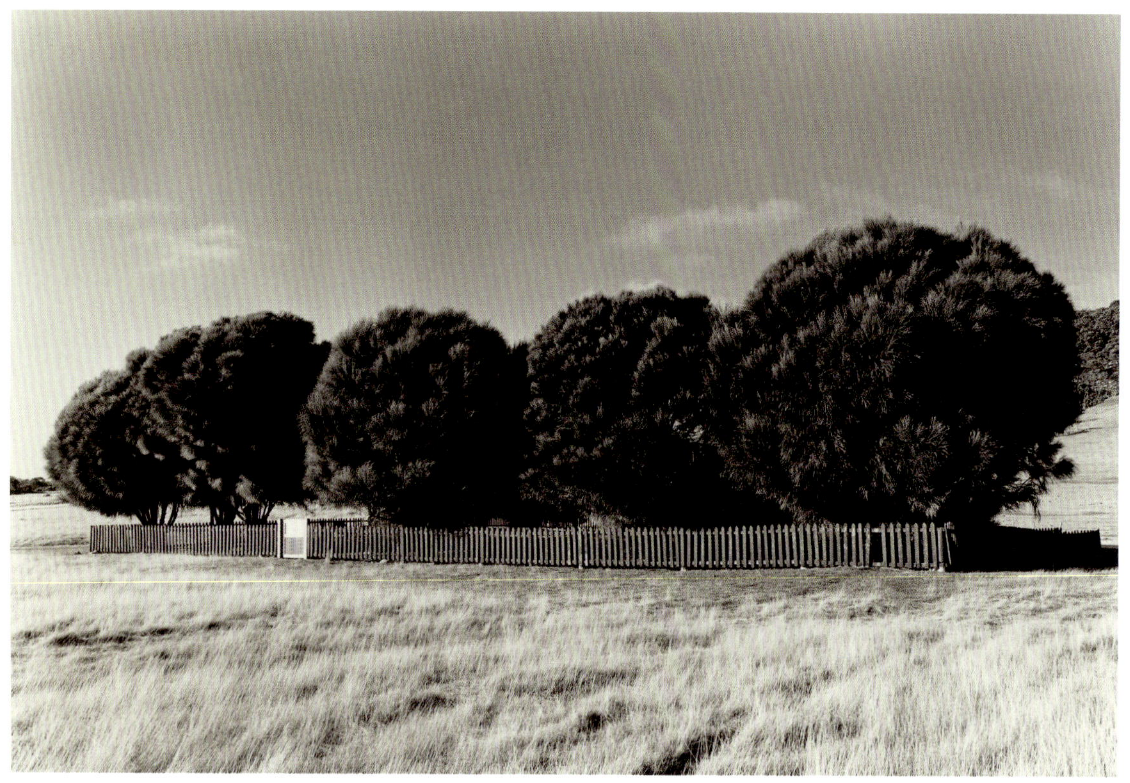

39
RICKY MAYNARD
The Healing Garden, Wybalenna, Flinders Island, Tasmania, 2005

One from a series of ten gelatin silver photographs, 40.7 × 58.2 cm

National Gallery of Australia, Canberra. Purchased 2009

40
NICI CUMPSTON
Campsite V, Nookamka Lake, 2008
Inkjet print on canvas, hand-coloured with pencil and watercolour, 77 × 206 cm

National Gallery of Australia, Canberra. Purchased 2011

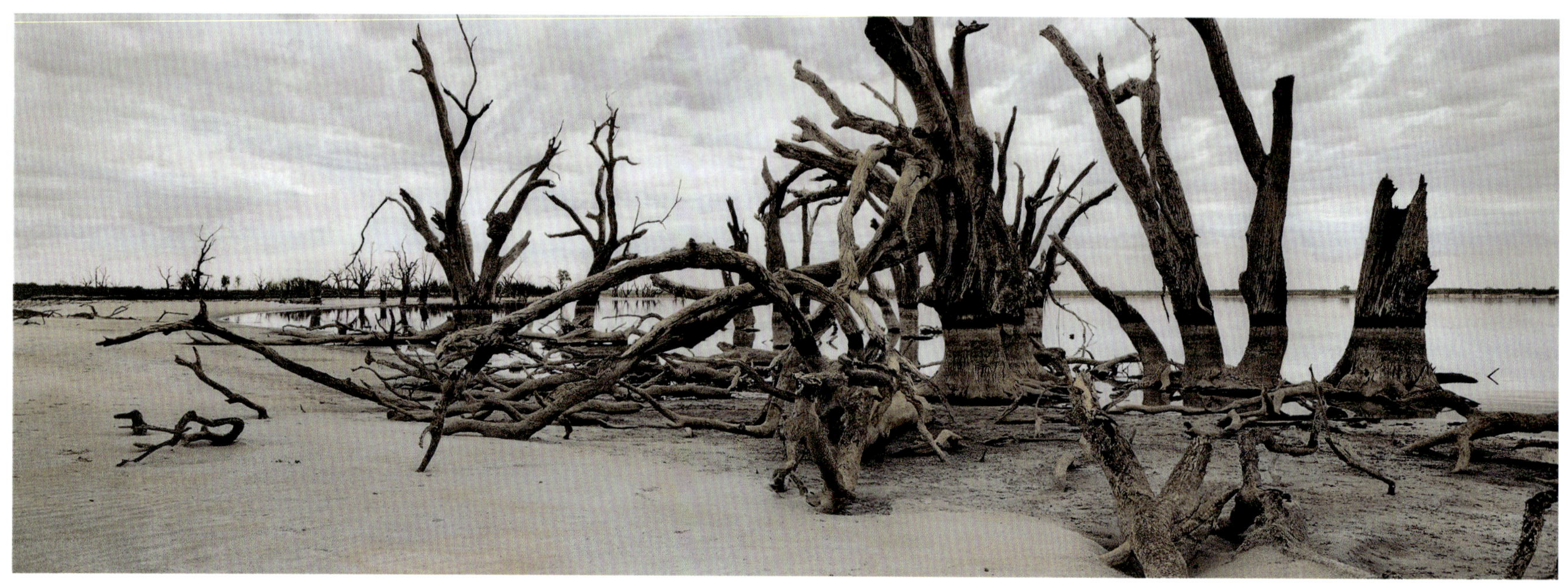

41

MIRDIDINGKINGATHI SALLY GABORI JUWARNDA
My Country, 2009
Synthetic polymer paint on canvas, 151 × 101 cm
National Gallery of Australia, Canberra. Founding Donors' Fund, 2010

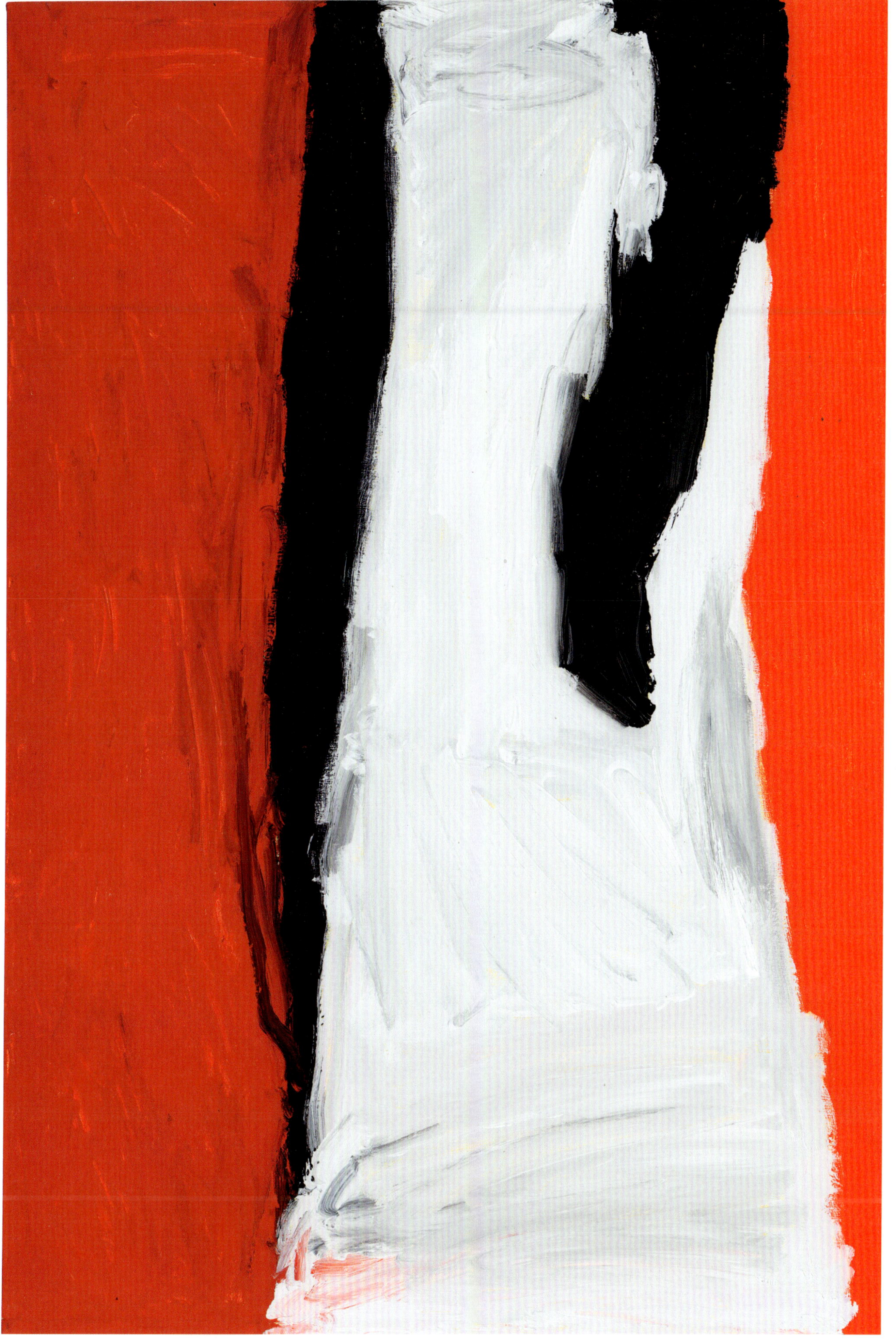

2

LAND AND LANDSCAPE: THE COLONIAL ENCOUNTER 1800–80

RON RADFORD

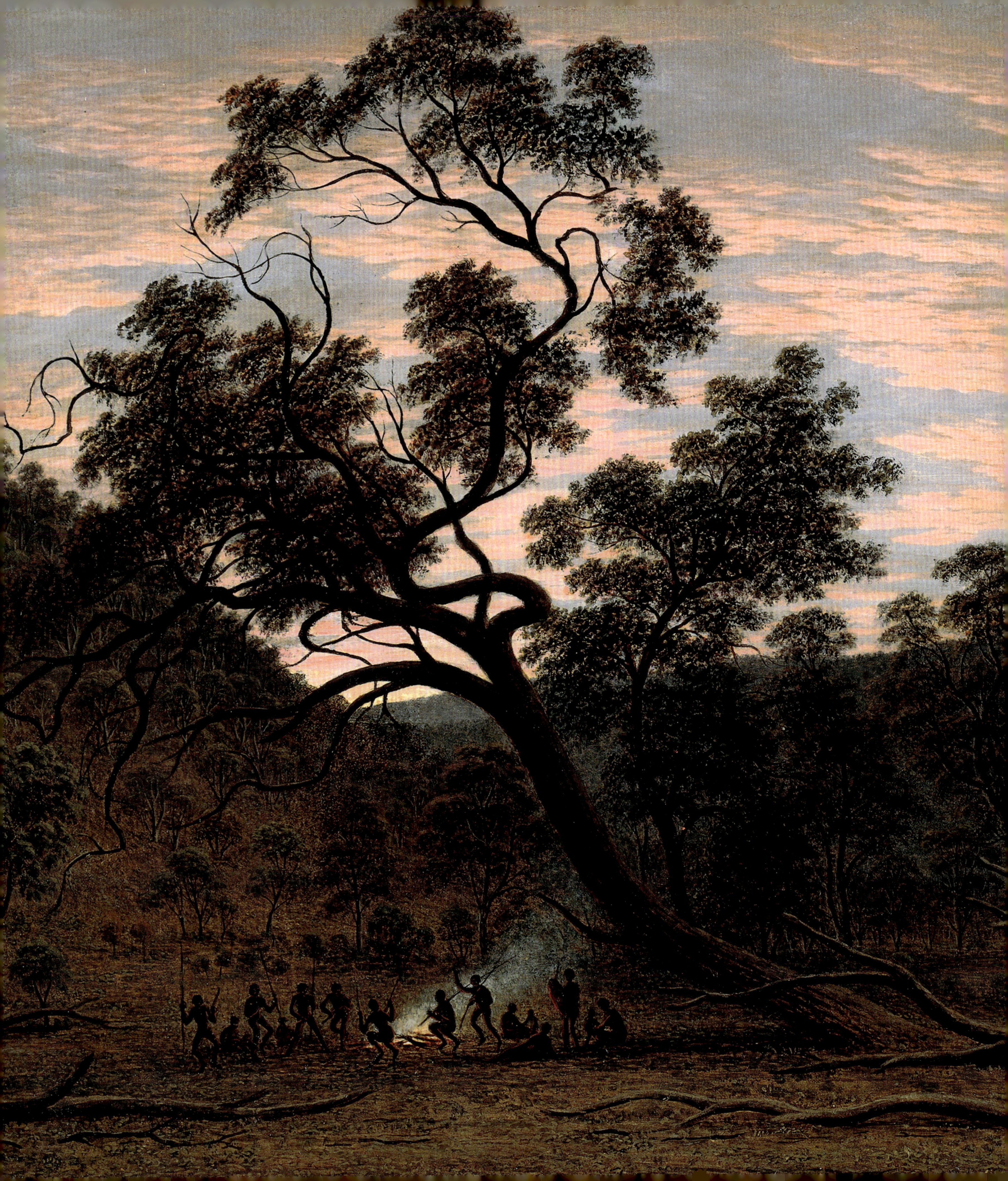

The first British settlers to arrive on the Great Southern Land in 1788 found it a strange, bewildering continent. The unique flora and fauna were enchanting, the native people intriguing, but the land itself appeared monotonous and frightening. The settlers feared being speared and, even more, being lost in the endless wilderness or bitten by venomous snakes or spiders. They soon found that the soils around Botany Bay and Sydney Harbour could not support crops. This new land seemed inhospitable.

The struggling penal settlement of New South Wales was not conducive to landscape painting. The colony's first semi-professional artist, the convict Thomas Watling, an illustrator, who arrived in 1792, described his and other settlers' responses to their new environment: 'The landscape painter, may in vain seek here for that beauty which arises from happy-opposed off-scapes ... The land, an immense forest, extended over a plain country ... trees, hoary with age, or torn with tempests.'[1] Watling, like almost all the earliest artists in Australia, was more interested in recording the wondrous native animals, birds, reptiles, fish and plants there, and the native people and the developing colonial settlement.

For decades, artists focused on views of the settlements rather than what was to them the more disturbing landscape that surrounded the enclaves. *View of the Town of Sydney in the Colony of New South Wales* (*c.*1799; cat.42) is one of a group of four oil paintings, the first made of Sydney. Painted in London, the canvas was probably based on Watling's drawings, or possibly painted by Watling himself after returning to Britain. At the end of the eighteenth century, the neat, rudimentary Georgian buildings of Sydney Town keep to a harbour shoreline backed by dark forest wilderness. This oil painting inspired an aquatint published in London by W.S.Blake in 1802, the first separate and frameable print of an Australian landscape. The print emphasises the sun rising over Sydney Harbour like a new beginning at the dawn of the nineteenth century (fig.22), but it is more a statement of British endurance and survival in this precarious foothold on the far side of the world than a celebration of a new land or landscape.

About a decade later, G.W.Evans, a surveyor and artist who arrived in the colony in 1802, painted *A View of Sydney New South Wales on Entering the Heads* (*c.*1809; cat.43), one of many watercolour views of the settlements made at this time by himself and others. Seen across the harbour at sunset, a light, almost heavenly civilisation rises from a dark abyss, encircling wilderness emphasised by a sombre foreground peopled with shadowy native figures.

Nearly ten years further on, settlements remained the main focus of Australian landscape painting. The convict artist Joseph Lycett, who arrived in 1814, was ordered by Captain James Wallis, Commandant of Newcastle, to produce a few oil paintings of that twenty-year-old convict town 90 miles north of Sydney. *Inner View of Newcastle* (*c.*1818; cat.50) accurately records Wallis's improvements, among them Christ Church, a hospital, gaol and barracks. Although it portrays a penal settlement, Wallis's commission maintains the primacy of civilisation over nature. He was not interested in a view of the local bush. The town sits on unproductive coastal land and Lycett can unleash a feeling for natural beauty only in his rendition of a vast Australian sky with whirling clouds.

Despite the settlers' initial reluctance to embrace the foreign beauty of their adopted land, landscape was soon to become the main stimulus for painting in Australia and would remain so for at least 150 years. Landscape is central to the culture of few other countries, but after 225 years of European occupation, Australian art still celebrates the diversity of terrain, vegetation, light and human settlement peculiar to the island continent.

When Australia was first colonised, the art of landscape painting was gaining greater strength in Britain than in other European countries. It was soon to surpass portraiture, which had dominated British art for the past three centuries. Not only were the British embracing views of their own countryside and tourist vistas of continental Europe, but they also wanted to see more distant 'New Worlds', especially the rapidly expanding British Empire. Demand grew for paintings and prints of these British-claimed lands. At the same time in Australia, free settlers, emancipated convicts and locally born colonials wanted images of the land for themselves and to send back with pride to curious relatives.

The first professionally trained landscape painter to travel to Australia was William Westall, a young student of the Royal Academy Schools and younger half-brother of the Royal Academician Richard Westall. He accompanied Matthew Flinders on his 1801–03 voyage to chart, for the first time, the entire coastline of the continent. Westall was required to draw coastal profiles, but he also executed meticulous and sensitive pencil drawings, and a few watercolours, of characteristic coastal scenery (fig.23). He commenced his drawings of the ship's first Australian landfall, Cape Leeuwin on the extreme southern tip of the western coast of Australia, on Monday, 7 December 1801 at 7.30 am; thus noting to the minute the birth of the venerable Euro-Australian

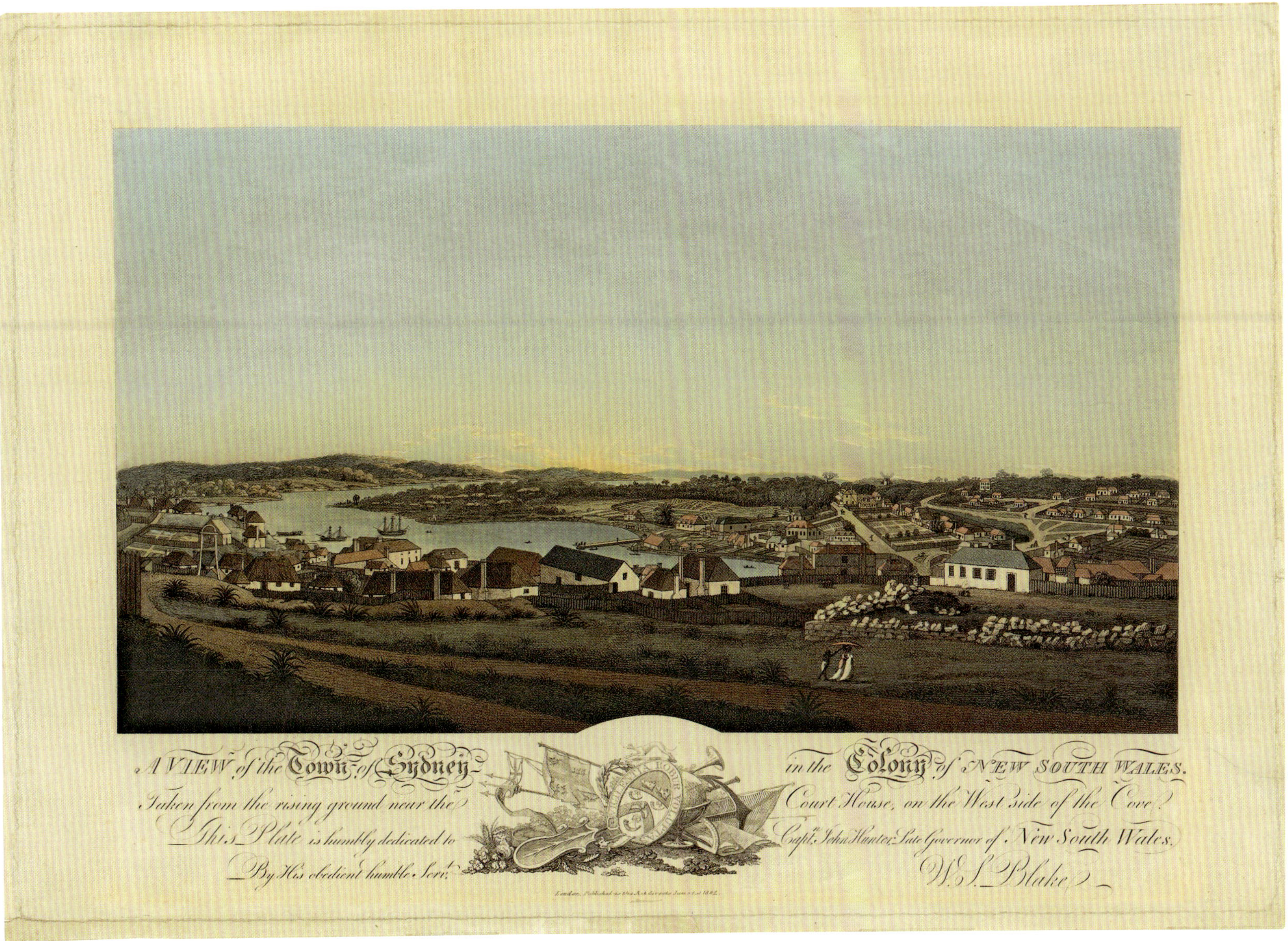

Fig. 22
W. S. BLAKE (engraver), **A View of the Town of Sydney in the Colony of New South Wales**, 1802.
Aquatint, printed in black ink, from one copper plate, hand-coloured, 23.6 × 41.4 cm
National Gallery of Australia, Canberra. Purchased 2000

landscape tradition. Back in Britain, the Admiralty, encouraged by Sir Joseph Banks, commissioned Westall to make finished oil paintings from his on-the-spot drawings.

Beautiful as his landscape drawings are, Westall, shortly after the Australian voyage, wrote to Banks from China complaining that he found the Australian landscape un-picturesque and the coast 'barren'. He claimed that his Australian subjects 'can neither afford pleasure ... nor curiosity from their singularity'.[2] Nevertheless, Australia inspired his finest works: after Westall exhibited his Admiralty canvases at the Royal Academy of Arts he was promoted to Associate of the Academy in 1812.

View in Sir E. Pellew's Group, Gulph of Carpentaria, Discovered by Captain Flinders, 1802 (c.1812; cat.46) has little precedent in the European tradition of landscape. Brighter than any previous painting of the South Seas, it shows a sandy island with rocks and palms off the northern coast of Australia, the beach and other distant islands bleached with sun-glare. A small bark shelter in the centre foreground contains an Aboriginal totemic ritual object, a rangga, of stone decorated with charcoal, feathers and down,[3] a reminder that this country was never *terra nullius*.[4] As well as this depiction of a sacred artefact, Westall sketched watercolours of rock art in a cave on Chasm Island (1803; cat.45), the first European visual records of Aboriginal paintings. A decade earlier, however, Watling had written in Sydney: 'The natives are extremely fond of painting, and often sit hours by me when at work. Several rocks round us have outré figures engraven in them.'[5]

By contrast, William Westall's *View of Cape Townsend and of the Islands in Shoal-Water Bay, Taken from Mount Westall, 1802* (*c.*1810; cat.47), painted in Britain, is a sub-tropical Queensland subject that – nevertheless – reminds us of J.M.W.Turner's Swiss alpine views. The rocky mountain-top foreground with its strange botany of hoop pines and other native trees, and its tall Aboriginal men, demonstrates that, despite Westall's earlier description of Australia's 'barren' landscape, it could be as dramatically sublime as any in Europe. When Westall exhibited these pictures at the Royal Academy in London in 1810 and 1812, it was the first time the British public had been able to see sizeable oil paintings of the Australian landscape and appreciate the beauty of the different coasts around the vast unknown land claimed by Great Britain.

Fittingly, this exhibition begins in 1800. In January of that year, Australia received its first free-settler resident professional artist, John Lewin. The British population in the colony after twelve years was only about 6,000, most of whom were convicts. Lewin was trained by his father in bird painting, not landscape painting, and, like all successful colonists, he became versatile. In Australia, he depicted not only the unique and exquisite native birds but also animals, insects, reptiles, fish, portraits of the Aborigines and of settlers, and, importantly for this exhibition, landscape. Like other artists, he recorded the growth of Sydney but he also painted what could be considered Australia's first pastoral landscape, *View from Governor Bligh's Farm, Hawkesbury, New South Wales* (*c.*1808; cat.44).

Numerous images of golden pastoral landscapes became conventional expressions of Australian nationalism in the late nineteenth and early twentieth centuries. Arthur Streeton's *Golden Summer, Eaglemont* (1889; cat.103) is a prime example of future imagery of

Fig. 23
WILLIAM WESTALL, **Hawkesbury River (View no. 7)**, *c.*1802.
Pencil on paper, 18.2 × 26.7 cm
National Library of Australia, Canberra.
Purchased 1969

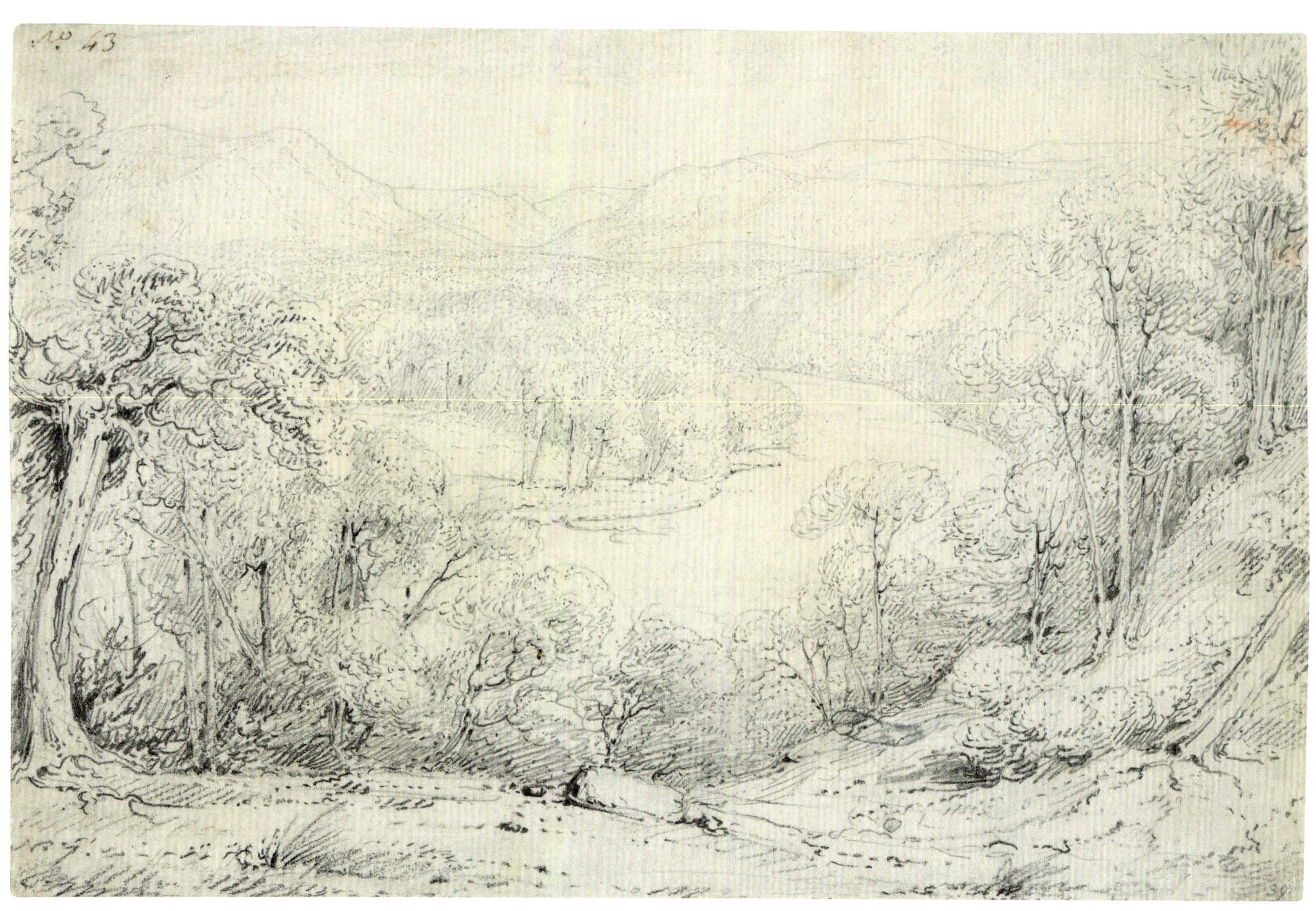

a land of abundance. Painted more than 80 years after Lewin's watercolour, it similarly captures a sun-filled pastoral panorama complete with river. However, Lewin's view, probably commissioned by Governor Bligh, is about the promise, at last, of secure food supply – of survival – not an early expression of nationalism. The farms at Parramatta and along the Hawkesbury River had become productive. The dead tree near the centre of the composition, and those in the distance, allude to successful clearing of the native bush for crops and pastures. But pastoral and agricultural expansion from the Sydney basin was halted by the Blue Mountains until explorers found a way through in 1813; and so too was imagery of the inner land.

Governor Macquarie ordered the surveyor-artist Evans to cut a rough pass across the mountains and in 1815 Macquarie made a historic procession through the Blue Mountains to the Bathurst Plains, where they saw potential for cultivation and pasture. Lewin volunteered to accompany the expedition and record the country. He made twenty on-the-spot watercolour landscapes,[6] the first pure landscapes to embrace a benign Australian wilderness. Rather than the threatening background to Evans's *View of Sydney* (cat.43), the setting for them consists of fresh, uncomposed views of attractive country by an artist who had already spent fifteen years familiarising himself with his new homeland. He had written to a friend in Britain in 1812 stating that his adopted country was 'the finest in the world'.[7]

From this expedition, Lewin's watercolour *Evans's Peak* (1815; cat.48) (named by and after the surveyor-artist) depicts a foreground of native pastures, with lightly forested open country in the middle distance, and more densely forested mountains in the distant background. What the settlers did not understand about the comparatively open landscape was that it had been tended by fire – systematically burnt by the Aboriginal people for thousands of years to clear space for native pastures in which kangaroos and wallabies would graze and become easier prey for hunters. Regular burning prevented the dense forest build-up that feeds large and devastating bushfires in the twenty-first century.[8] To Lewin and the first settlers, this was virgin country into which they could immediately introduce their livestock. *Evans's Peak* and other landscapes from this journey are the first paintings to perceive Australia's distinctive open bush country as both economically and visually attractive.

Lewin was also the first artist to experiment with oil painting in Australia. He taught himself the technique in 1812 and his *Fish Catch and Dawes Point, Sydney Harbour* (*c.*1813; cat.49) is the earliest-known oil painted in Australia.[9] It demonstrates his talent for both natural history and landscape, with a harbour fish catch on the foreshore of Kirribilli, and a distant view of Dawes Point, from which the Sydney Harbour Bridge now springs. The ambitious painting shows Lewin's inventiveness and ability to construct an engaging, original and powerful composition.

Lycett, the less talented convict artist, was Lewin's main rival in New South Wales. Already discussed is his painting of Newcastle, where he was confined. In about 1820, Lycett produced an album of twenty watercolours (cat.51) of the Aboriginal people in their natural landscape, and, in particular, the Awabakal people near Newcastle.[10] It shows them occupied in hunting, fishing, cooking and other survival activities and rituals. Concern was growing in Australia and Britain that expanding settlement had forced the local tribes out of their country, native traditions were consequently dying, and relations between the native people and settlers were thus deteriorating. Lycett intended to record the life of the Aboriginal people before they disappeared. In *Aborigines Using Fire to Hunt Kangaroos* (*c.*1820; cat.51) from *'The Lycett Album': Drawings of the Aborigines and Scenery of New South Wales*, he portrays a wooded gully set alight to smoke out kangaroos and catch them with spears or boomerangs as they flee, and thus illustrates both a successful hunting method and the use of fire to manage grazing land.

Lycett was not the only artist to record the Indigenous people in their natural environment. The most interesting and lively artist from Britain in the 1820s was Augustus Earle, who arrived in 1825 and stayed for less than four years. He painted Australia's first grand portraits in oil, and landscapes in watercolour and oil. His lithographs, the first made in Australia, and his watercolours included sympathetic portrayals of the plight of the Aboriginal people, and he was one of the few artists to draw attention to the infamous convict system.

In Earle's *A Native Camp of Australian Savages near Port Stevens, New South Wales* (*c.*1826; cat.53) Aborigines, warmed by evening campfires, settle into their bark shelters. They appear as an integral part of the natural bushland. By contrast, prisoners labouring on a new road through virgin forest are a strident element in his *View from the Summit of Mount York, Looking towards Bathurst Plains, Convicts Breaking Stones, New South Wales* (*c.*1826; cat.52).

By the 1830s, the Australian colonies had expanded well beyond New South Wales. The island of Van Diemen's Land (now Tasmania) was colonised in 1803, the Swan River District (now Western Australia) in 1829, the Port Phillip District (now Victoria) in 1835, South

Australia in 1836, and in 1859 Queensland separated from New South Wales. The respective capitals of the six colonies – Sydney, Hobart, Perth, Melbourne, Adelaide and Brisbane – were further in distance from each other than the capitals of European nations and therefore developed different art scenes. Free settlers now outnumbered convicts, and both Britain and the colonies were pushing for an increase in the free population. Attractive hand-coloured prints depicting (sometimes falsely) prospering settlements or available fertile land were produced to entice prospective immigrants.

The most impressive of these prints was a panorama almost three metres in length of one of the infant settlements in Western Australia, etched, hand-coloured and printed in London in 1834 (cat.54) after on-the-spot sketches made in 1830 by Robert Dale. It illustrates a vast, picturesque coastal land with exotic plants, and presents a harmonious relationship between settlers and native people around the small seaport of Albany. The view gives no hint of the then-precarious economic state of the colony in Western Australia.

Tasmania, the most fertile and productive of the colonies, produced the most interesting art in the 1830s and 1840s. John Glover, Australia's first and only already established successful landscape painter to arrive from Europe, settled in Tasmania in 1831, aged sixty-four, from Britain. A year later he secured a farm in northern Tasmania. Probably the first landscape he painted there was *A Corroboree of Natives in Mills Plains* (1832; cat.55). He could not have seen such a dance party on what was now his property, as the Aborigines had been driven from the district a year or so before. The first year in the colony he spent in Hobart and it was near there that he had seen Aborigines who had been rounded up by the colonial government. He had also seen corroborees there, just before the 200 or so remaining Aborigines were taken to be confined on Flinders Island, where it was thought they would no longer trouble the settlers and where most of them were eventually to die of disease and despondency. In this haunting evening corroboree, an imaginary performance on his land, probably painted while he was still living in a tent or temporary shelter, the farmer John Glover is perhaps feeling some guilt for his and his fellow settlers' role as land-takers.[11]

There is no evidence of guilt in the proud, sweeping view of his farm that he painted a year later. In *View of Mills Plains, Van Diemen's Land* (1833; cat.56) his newly completed house and farm buildings occupy the centre at middle distance, seen through native trees and bushes; contented cattle graze and water in the foreground creek; sparsely forested, Aboriginal fire-managed country fills the distance. A central gum tree dominates the composition, flanked by smaller native trees. The work is about pleasure in possession of the land. It is also a triumph of Australian landscape art, finer than anything Glover had painted in Britain. Free from the conventions of European landscape that dogged much of his British work, and with a heightened sense of wonderment, he has captured his new land's distinctive natural beauty. This is the finest Australian landscape painted to that date.

Glover's *A View of the Artist's House and Garden, in Mills Plains, Van Diemen's Land* (1835; cat.57) is even more obviously about pride of possession. He joyfully celebrates his new stone house and wooden studio, set amid his spectacular flowering garden on his new farm in his new, sunny country in the South Seas. The poignancy of the image is even greater when we understand that this was the final work completed for a shipment of paintings bound for his exhibition held in Bond Street, London, in August 1835.[12] In that exhibition, which included the three oils mentioned above, a British audience could appreciate the appearance of Australia more accurately than ever before.

Experienced exhibition-goers might also have observed that the elderly Glover in his newly colonised land had become a more remarkable and original landscape artist than he ever had been in Britain. His 1835 London exhibition can be regarded as the first major cultural exchange between Australia and Europe. A decade later, the Musée du Louvre in Paris, the greatest museum of Western art, acquired two 1840 Tasmanian landscapes by Glover for its collection.[13]

If Glover and Earle were the most significant Australian landscape painters before 1850, the next most interesting was Conrad Martens, who arrived in Sydney four years later than Glover, in 1835. Martens did not intend to stay but was soon commissioned by prosperous pastoralists and merchants of New South Wales to paint views of their homesteads and their picturesque seaport. He settled in Sydney, where he had a 43-year career, the longest and most successful of any Australian colonial artist. Trained in the English watercolour tradition, of which J.M.W.Turner was the greatest exponent and a major influence on Martens, he consequently produced works more atmospheric and light-filled than any of the landscapes painted by his Sydney predecessors. Like Glover, Martens was inspired by the new land to create work of greater quality. By the 1850s he was painting his finest watercolours. His most sublimely Romantic views were of Sydney Harbour, and occasionally of inland mountains. His dramatic *View of Sydney from Neutral Bay* (*c.*1857; cat.60) shows a rocky foreground with distant Sydney engulfed in a storm, recorded not just topographically but atmospherically. This tempestuous distant view contrasts with *Campbell's Wharf* (cat.59), painted the same year, a calm close-up of buildings and docked ships bathed in a Turneresque orange glow of the sun setting behind the city.

John Skinner Prout (nephew of the prominent British watercolourist Samuel Prout) arrived in 1840 and became one of Martens's few rivals in landscape painting in Sydney, albeit very briefly. His watercolour style was more up-to-date and freely painted than Martens's and he often finished his watercolours on the spot. He was also more entrepreneurial. He gave Sydney's first art lectures and made lithographic views for cheaper sale, either plain or coloured. Martens later imitated these initiatives. In 1844 Prout left Sydney for Hobart, where he perhaps expected better patronage, as Tasmania was less affected by the rural Depression at the time. In Hobart, Prout became the centre of a school of outdoor sketchers. Like those of Martens, his watercolours show the influence of Turner. Prout's *Shipwreck off Cape Pillar* (1846; cat.74) is full of the sublime drama of stormy weather and turbulent seas. His watercolours are always livelier than the few oils he produced in Australia, but his jewel-like *Maria Island from Little Swanport, Van Diemen's Land* (*c.*1846; cat.72) is full of thoroughly Australian light and atmosphere. After a brief spell travelling and sketching before the gold rush in Victoria, where he painted the light-filled *South Bank of the Yarra, near Melbourne* (1846; cat.73), he returned to England in 1848, leaving an artistic vacuum in landscape painting in Hobart.

Also influenced by Turner was the marine watercolourist Oswald Brierly, who exhibited at the Royal Academy before and after his time in New South Wales from 1839 to 1871. Many of his Australian watercolours dramatise the lucrative whaling industry in which he was involved, and which was a major part of the colony's economy before the gold rush. His *Amateur Whaling, or a Tale of the Pacific* (1847; cat.62) is a panorama of the dangers and heroism of whaling in small, vulnerable craft in big seas.

While Brierly and Martens were working in New South Wales, Prout in Tasmania and Edmund Henderson (cat.61) in Western Australia, a group of landscape painters was active in convict-free South Australia, which had numerous professional and amateur artists from its earliest years of settlement. In the 1840s, South Australia's economy was boosted by extensive copper mining, which helped to support a small but lively professional art community.

E.C.Frome, South Australia's Surveyor-General, was the first artist to portray the vast interior desert, which became a major theme for twentieth-century Australian landscape artists such as Hans Heysen, Jeffrey Smart, Sidney Nolan, Fred Williams and many art photographers. Frome's tiny but intensely evocative watercolour *First View of the Salt Desert – Called Lake Torrens* (1843; cat.66) depicts a lone explorer on a horse, telescope to his eye, insignificant in a frighteningly barren landscape below the Flinders Ranges, far inland from Adelaide and past the limits of pastoral settlement.

Only three years later, S.T.Gill (who arrived in Adelaide in 1839) was part of the 1846 Horrocks expedition to a different side of the Flinders Ranges in search of grazing land. Like Frome, Gill captured sparse desert landscapes but took more care to record the distinctive spiky qualities of the tough desert vegetation and the red colouring and the texture of stony ground. His *Looking SW from Table Land, August 22nd* (1846; cat. 64) shows featureless country stretching into infinite distance. In the foreground two dejected expedition horses, loaded but unattended, emphasise an eerie isolation.

Later, Ludwig Becker, who was the artist and scientific recorder on the ill-planned, ill-fated Burke and Wills 1860–61 expedition from Melbourne across the interior of the continent, made remarkable small-scale field sketches of the unfamiliar landscape that the explorers traversed. He was astonished by clear night skies glittering with stars and a flashing meteor (cat.69), deeply eroded sand cliffs and struggling vegetation (cat.70), and flat mud deserts shimmering in the searing heat (cat.71). Nothing in the European landscape tradition paralleled such works. This was new imagery.

George French Angas, son of the wealthy head of the South Australia Company, a founding pastoral enterprise of the Province of South Australia, was S.T.Gill's chief professional rival in landscape painting in Adelaide. Angas's landscapes always seem optimistic, as was his family's investment in the colony. Even his flat plain landscapes are more promising than Frome's or Gill's. *Scene Showing Emus in a Plain (Coorong)* (1844; cat.67) features these large flightless birds flourishing in a monotonous wilderness. Angas was interested in presenting the various kinds of land in South Australia, its distinct flora and fauna, and, more importantly, the original inhabitants of the country and their unique customs. Yet his *Port Lincoln from Winter's Hill* (1845; cat.68) shows no obvious evidence of Aboriginal occupation. Instead, the collection of huts in the distance represents the beginnings of the settlement of Port Lincoln, which was to become an important pastoral and fishing port. The open-treed landscape, no doubt tended by the Aborigines, accurately records in bright light the varying species of native trees and bushes with their characteristic faded olive-green colouration, entirely unlike the lettuce green of the English countryside.

South Australian settlers took pride in the convict-free origins of the colony. Their capital Adelaide was depicted more frequently, and by more artists, than other colonial capitals. S.T.Gill's genial and animated city views such as *North Terrace, Adelaide, Looking South-east from Government House Guardhouse* (1845; cat.63) showed not only the new buildings but also what the citizens wore, the way they walked, their different means of transport and the dogs they owned. His city views are like cinematic stills, capturing an Adelaide of individuals, free and democratic, with relatively little class distinction compared with the mother country. Although in this composition we see sentries in British uniforms guarding Government House, such formal official British presence was soon to become a thing of the past. Gill's later watercolours of the goldfields in the neighbouring colony of Victoria are even more democratic, with miners like working ants in the churned-up alluvial landscape (cat.65).

Before 1850, art in the Australian colonies understandably reflected directions in British art: the late-Georgian portrait tradition[14] and early nineteenth-century styles in landscape painting, particularly in watercolour painting. In 1851 gold was discovered, most of it in Victoria, which had recently separated from New South Wales to become an independent colony. The subsequent gold rush changed the course of Australian history and Australian art. The population of the colonies increased fourfold in the decade, from 250,000 to one million. Most of the increase was in Victoria and by the mid-1850s Melbourne had become the centre for Australian art, attracting artists from overseas and other colonies. It took over from Hobart, which had produced the liveliest art of the 1830s and 1840s,[15] and Adelaide, which had created the most interesting art from the mid-1840s to the mid-1850s.

During the gold rush, Australia's population, until then largely British, expanded to include immigrants from continental Europe – German, Swiss, French, Italian – and also from America and China. Many of the painters, silversmiths and other craftsmen who arrived in Australia during this period had German (and some Swiss) background and training. Australian landscape painting changed from the mainly British Romantic watercolour tradition to a German Romantic landscape tradition in oils.

Eugene von Guérard, who arrived in Victoria in 1852, was the greatest exponent of this new direction. Another German, Alexander Schramm, who painted Aborigines in distinctive Australian landscapes with straggly Australian eucalypts, was Adelaide's major artist of the 1850s and early 1860s. The German-born Ludwig Becker arrived a year before von Guérard. The Swiss-trained Nicholas Chevalier arrived at the end of 1854. In Melbourne, von Guérard strongly influenced Chevalier and later the Irish-born Isaac Whitehead. The Swiss artist Louis Buvelot arrived in Melbourne in 1865[16] and was the most influential painter for a younger generation of artists in the 1870s and early 1880s.

After an unsuccessful stint on the Ballarat goldfields, von Guérard settled in Melbourne and became Australia's leading landscape artist. He travelled widely with his sketchbook in Victoria and also undertook campaigns in Tasmania, South Australia, New South Wales and New Zealand. It took him time to grasp the breadth and spirit of the Antipodean landscape but by 1857 he had developed into the foremost Romantic landscape painter in the Southern Hemisphere. Although he was a mature artist of forty-one when he arrived in Australia, the surprising, ancient land and free society inspired and liberated his work – like that of all colonial landscapists – enabling it to reach new levels of excellence.

Some of von Guérard's paintings had symbolic intent. The most notable is *Stony Rises, Lake Corangamite* (1857; cat.76), which he originally and more appropriately named *An Australian Sunset*. Von Guérard was acutely aware of the displacement of the Aboriginal people, and the sun setting on a small Aboriginal tribe becomes a metaphor for the decline of a people. In this imaginary camp within a protective natural stone enclosure, we observe at the centre of the composition a lone Aboriginal child. One child does not raise hope for the survival of a race. In reality, at the time there were only sixteen survivors of the local Colac tribe, the Gulidjan people, which indeed included only one child. The young blackwood trees that surround the giant rocks are like vertical European cypresses, the trees of European graveyards. *Stony Rises* is the most symbolic and melancholy of all the artist's landscapes.[17]

The volcanic landform setting for this Aboriginal subject was part of the Manifold family's large land claim in the Western District of Victoria. They commissioned von Guérard to paint a pair of reciprocal views of the pastoral station to which they had given the Aboriginal name of Purrumbete. In faithful detail and with great clarity, von Guérard presented a view across Lake Purrumbete from the homestead verandah, which frames the view and emphasises European possession and civilisation. The companion painting looks back at Purrumbete homestead and farm buildings on the far side of the lake.

The long British tradition of estate and manor-house portraits dates from the late sixteenth century. It was introduced into Australia by the early 1820s, when pastoral homesteads begin to occur among Lycett's views, and in Martens's work from the 1830s to 1860s. From the mid-1850s to the 1870s von Guérard, Chevalier, Buvelot and others in Victoria derived much of their income from the commissions of wealthy pastoralists from well-established homesteads, mostly in the exceptionally fertile Western District, a region largely colonised in the mid-1830s and 1840s – before the gold rush – by Tasmanian pastoralists. By the 1860s – after the gold rush had subsided – Australia's economy settled down again to largely pastoral pursuits. The landholders' pride in their production of wool, beef and mutton inspired them to commission paintings that showed their rapid transformation of Aboriginal hunting grounds into pastoral stations. Von Guérard's homestead pictures were, however, always more than topographical recordings of property; he emphasised the particular geology and ecology of the region and often suggested Aboriginal displacement.

By the 1860s there was a growing demand in Australia for sizeable oil paintings of diverse picturesque landscapes. For Europeans now well settled into enjoyment and connoisseurship of Australia's unique natural features, von Guérard painted one of the most dramatic Australian landscapes, *North-east View from the Northern Top of Mount Kosciusko* (1863; cat.80). It is a breathtaking view from Australia's highest mountain. One of the small foreground explorer figures is shown with outstretched arms, as if to exclaim 'behold God's creation'; the panoramic expanse of the snow-capped Australian Alps is an ecstatic high point in Australian landscape.

Less benign is von Guérard's tragic nocturne *Bushfire* (1859; cat.81) in which an advancing wall of fire devastates the pastoral plains, from which rise extinct

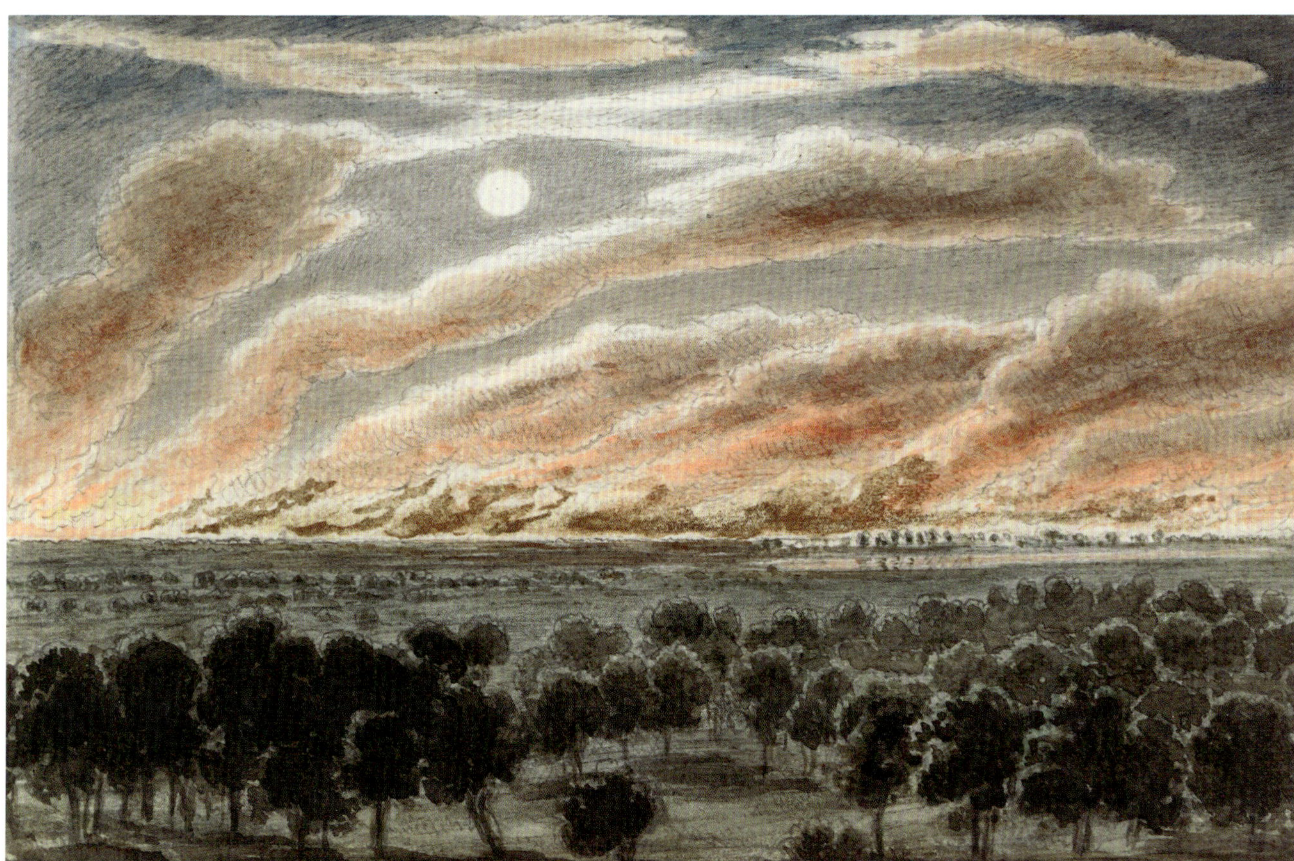

Fig. 24
EUGENE VON GUERARD,
Youyans (Sketch for Bushfire),
1857 in album *Views, Mainly of Victoria*, c.1859–63. Pen and ink, watercolour and gouache,
33.2 × 50.2 cm
State Library of New South Wales, Sydney

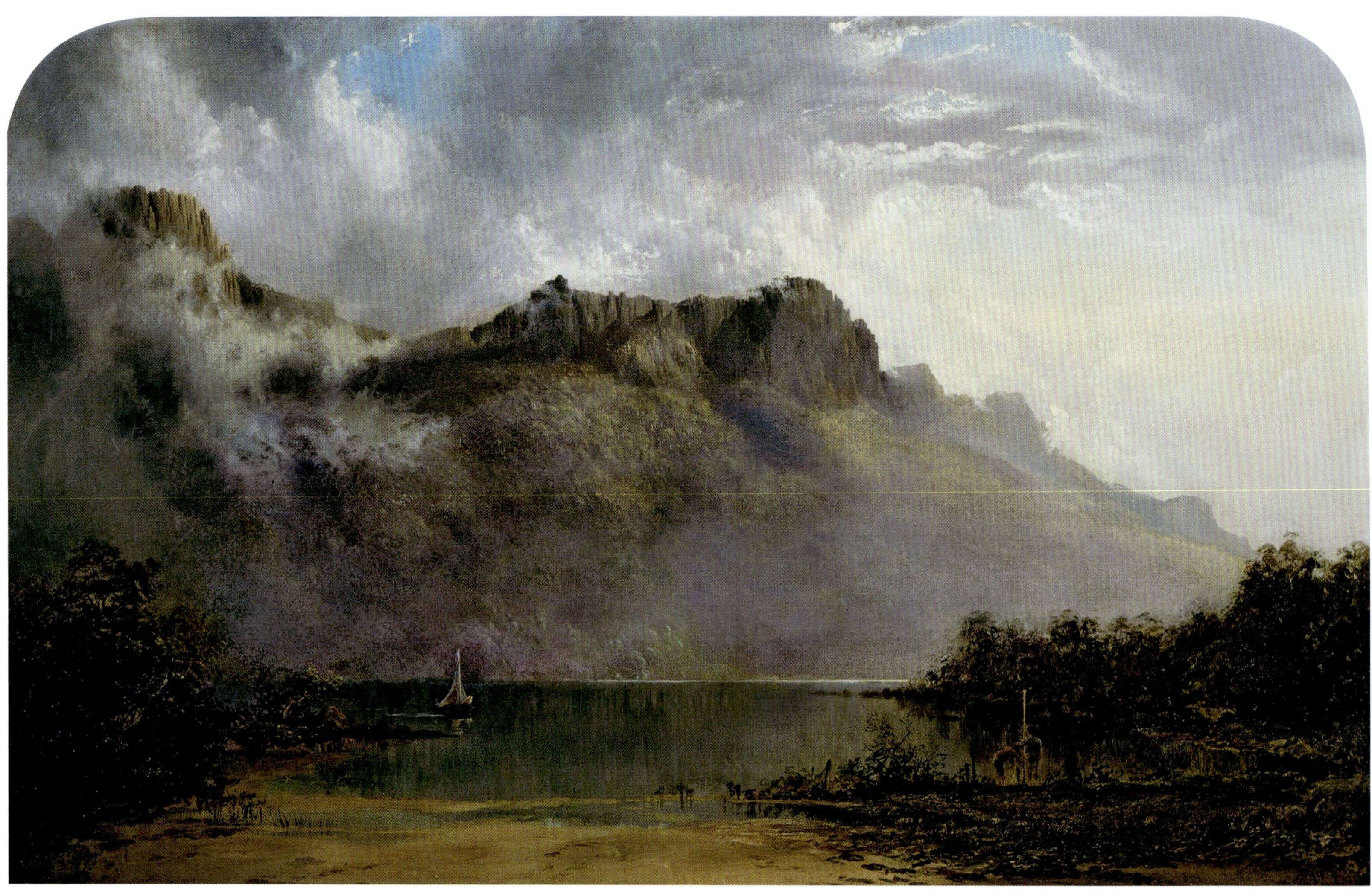

Fig. 25
W. C. PIGUENIT, **Mount Olympus, Lake St Clair, Tasmania, the Source of the Derwent**, 1875.
Oil on canvas, 69 × 107 cm
Art Gallery of New South Wales, Sydney.
Gift of 50 subscribers, 1875

volcanoes. The first oil painting of a bushfire in Australian art, the work was painted from a sketch made on the spot and thus contains the artist's direct experience of terror (fig.24). Grass and bushfires still strike fear into the hearts of Australians every summer and are now more severe than ever, partly through the lack of Aboriginal fire management that formerly controlled build-up of undergrowth, partly because of climate change.

This inferno on open plains is in direct contrast to the enclosed coolness of a damp *Ferntree Gully in the Dandenong Ranges* (1857; cat.77). One of the largest colonial landscape paintings, it celebrates a midsummer retreat to a secluded micro-ecology valley of ferns, much admired as exotic, prehistoric survivors.[18] The subject can also be seen as part of a worldwide phenomenon of 'fernmania': landscape paintings and photographs of fern-filled gullies were extremely popular. Nicholas Caire's *Fairy Scene at the Landslip, Blacks' Spur, Victoria* (1878; cat.89) is one of the most luxuriant examples of fernmania photography. Fern designs decorated furniture, women's clothing, napery, jewellery and, most prominently, commemorative table epergnes or candelabras such as the silver testimonial to John Ridley by German-trained Julius Schomburgk (1860; cat.83).

Von Guérard's *Ferntree Gully* inspired his follower Isaac Whitehead, who made a series of large paintings of forested fern valleys in the 1870s. His finest, *In the Sassafras Valley, Victoria* (1875; cat.88), shows not explorers in the damp luxuriant fern-glade but, by that date, bushwalkers. Vast eucalypt stands dwarf the figures and provide a protective canopy for ancient ferns to thrive, shielded from Australia's withering sun.

Nicholas Chevalier was von Guérard's closest follower. The most romantic of his many mountainscapes is *Mount Arapiles and the Mitre Rock* (1863; cat.85). Here he intensifies the red-tinged quartzite outcrop on the Wimmera plains with a sensational red sunset sky. More illustrative than von Guérard, he nonetheless extended the German Romantic landscape tradition in Australia.

Like Chevalier, Louis Buvelot was Swiss. However, he arrived in Melbourne in 1865 bearing not the Northern European Romantic tradition but instead the more up-to-date influence of French Barbizon painting. Whereas the landscapes of von Guérard and Chevalier were Romantic, extensive and detailed, Buvelot's outer-suburban Melbourne landscapes were intimate and casual. In *Winter Morning near Heidelberg* (1866; cat.87) we see across the Yarra River not explorers or even farmers but three picnickers, including a well-dressed woman, collecting firewood to build a warming midday fire for their outdoor repast. The presence of the woman signifies civilised landscape. Buvelot's motifs are always informal; here he shows the rough clay riverbank on the left and at the centre the exposed roots of a fallen tree, reflected in water. He captures the arbitrary growth of native trees on the embankment and the dead tree trunks.

Buvelot's brushwork is not tight and glassy in the style of German Romanticism, but loose and textured, as favoured in French art by the mid-nineteenth century. Subjects preferred by Buvelot, with figures at home in the Australian landscape, and his loose brushwork, greatly interested a new generation of painters, such as Tom Roberts and Frederick McCubbin, who were to pioneer outdoor Australian Impressionism in the 1880s and 1890s. Buvelot ceased painting in the early 1880s and died in 1888, the centenary year of European settlement, but his example and his works in the National Gallery of Victoria (including *Winter Morning near Heidelberg*) were a source of inspiration for these young nationalistic painters.

Over the past 100 years, Australian art history has traditionally concluded the colonial period around 1880, not in 1901 at Federation of the colonies and more independent constitutional rearrangements with Britain. One reason for this convention is that major colonial artists died or left Australia around 1880. For instance, Martens died in 1878 and Gill in 1880. Von Guérard returned to Europe in early 1882. Buvelot did not paint after the early 1880s. It was also a time when more up-to-date, influential teachers arrived, such as Julian Ashton in 1878, George Folingsby in 1880 and H.P.Gill in 1882. The colonial artists were succeeded by a new generation of Australian Impressionist painters, most of them born or trained in Australia, such as Tom Roberts, Frederick McCubbin, Arthur Streeton and Charles Conder. And in 1880, W.C.Piguenit, the first Australian-born and -trained professional landscape artist, moved from his birthplace, Hobart, where he had painted for almost a decade, to Sydney. In Hobart, he had painted dark Romantic landscapes with tight brushwork (fig.25). In Sydney from the 1880s onwards, influenced by Impressionism, his palette became lighter and his paint more viscous.[19]

As it happens, 1880 is also the date of a large and popular painting that does not fit easily into the chronological narrative of Australian landscape painting: H.J.Johnstone's *Evening Shadows, Backwater of the Murray, South Australia* (1880; cat.90). Johnstone was not only a painter but also a partner in a successful Melbourne photographic studio. The painting is rendered with the smoothness of an enlarged photograph, a regressive style compared with the painterly qualities of Buvelot's art at the time. It also has the distinction of being the first acquisition of the Art Gallery of South Australia, which opened in Adelaide in 1881. A quarter of a century later, the painting's giant river red gum trees, and unusually large canvas, inspired Hans Heysen in Adelaide to depict his more painterly gum trees as heroic symbols for the independent Australia of the early twentieth century. *Evening Shadows* became the most copied painting in Australian art, particularly in the Federation period.[20] The 'evening shadows' of the title do not refer to the giant gums reflected in the waters of Australia's longest river, the Murray, but to the Aboriginal figures and their bark shelter. Like von Guérard's *Stony Rises, Lake Corangamite* (cat.76) or Glover's *A Corroboree of Natives in Mills Plains* (cat.55), it was a valedictory homage to the Aboriginal people – the last major painting in the nineteenth century on that melancholy theme.

On the occasion of this Australian landscape exhibition in London, it might be noted that this most popular and most copied Australian landscape, with its glorification of great Australian river red gums and its nostalgia for the passing of an Aboriginal way of life, was in fact painted in London, from photographs.

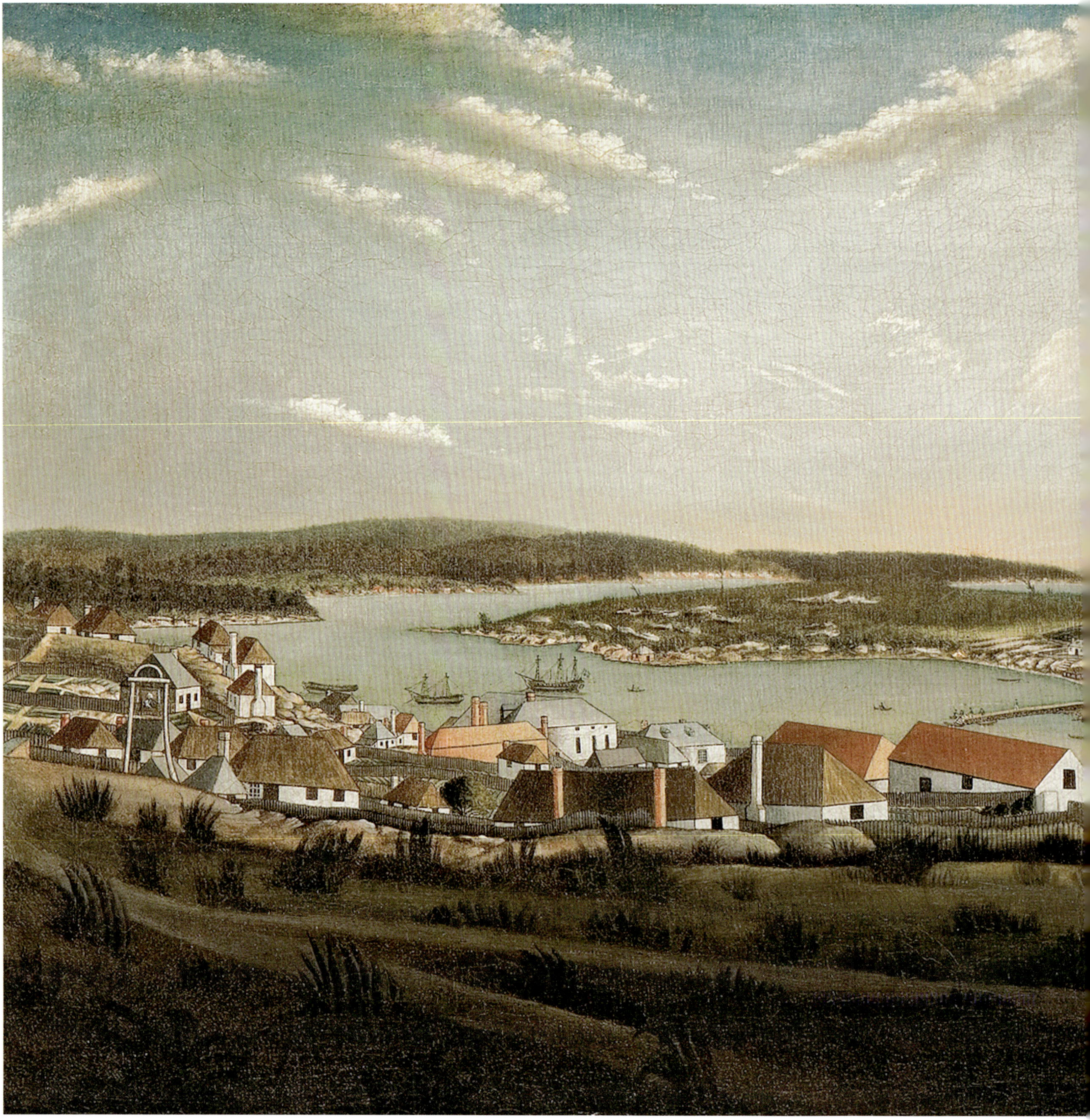

42

AFTER THOMAS WATLING

View of the Town of Sydney in the Colony of New South Wales, *c.*1799

Oil on canvas, 65 × 133 cm

Art Gallery of South Australia, Adelaide. M. J. M. Carter AO Collection

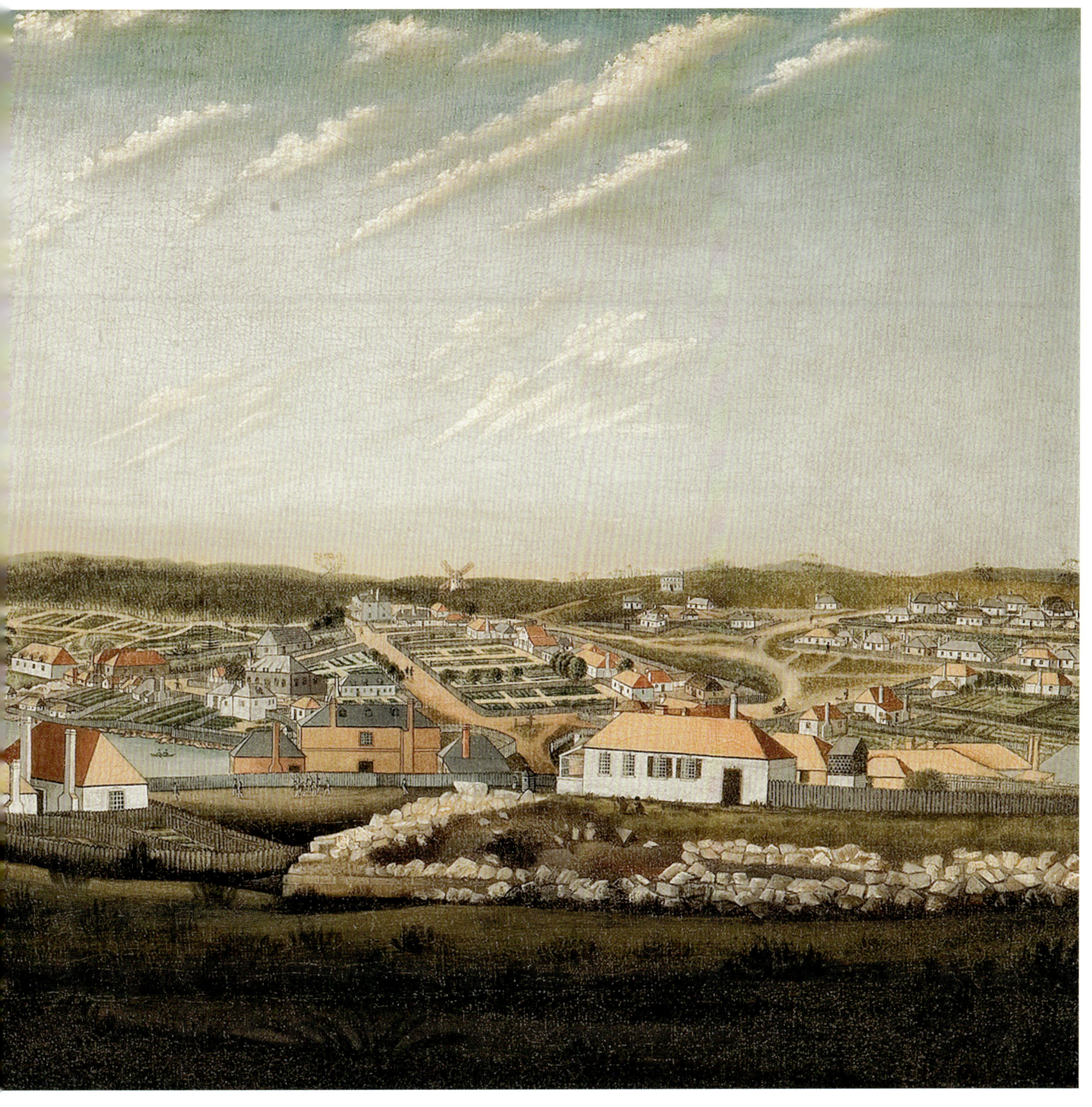

43
G. W. EVANS
A View of Sydney New South Wales on Entering the Heads, *c.* 1809
Watercolour, 22.5 × 36.1 cm
State Library of New South Wales, Sydney. Purchased 1950

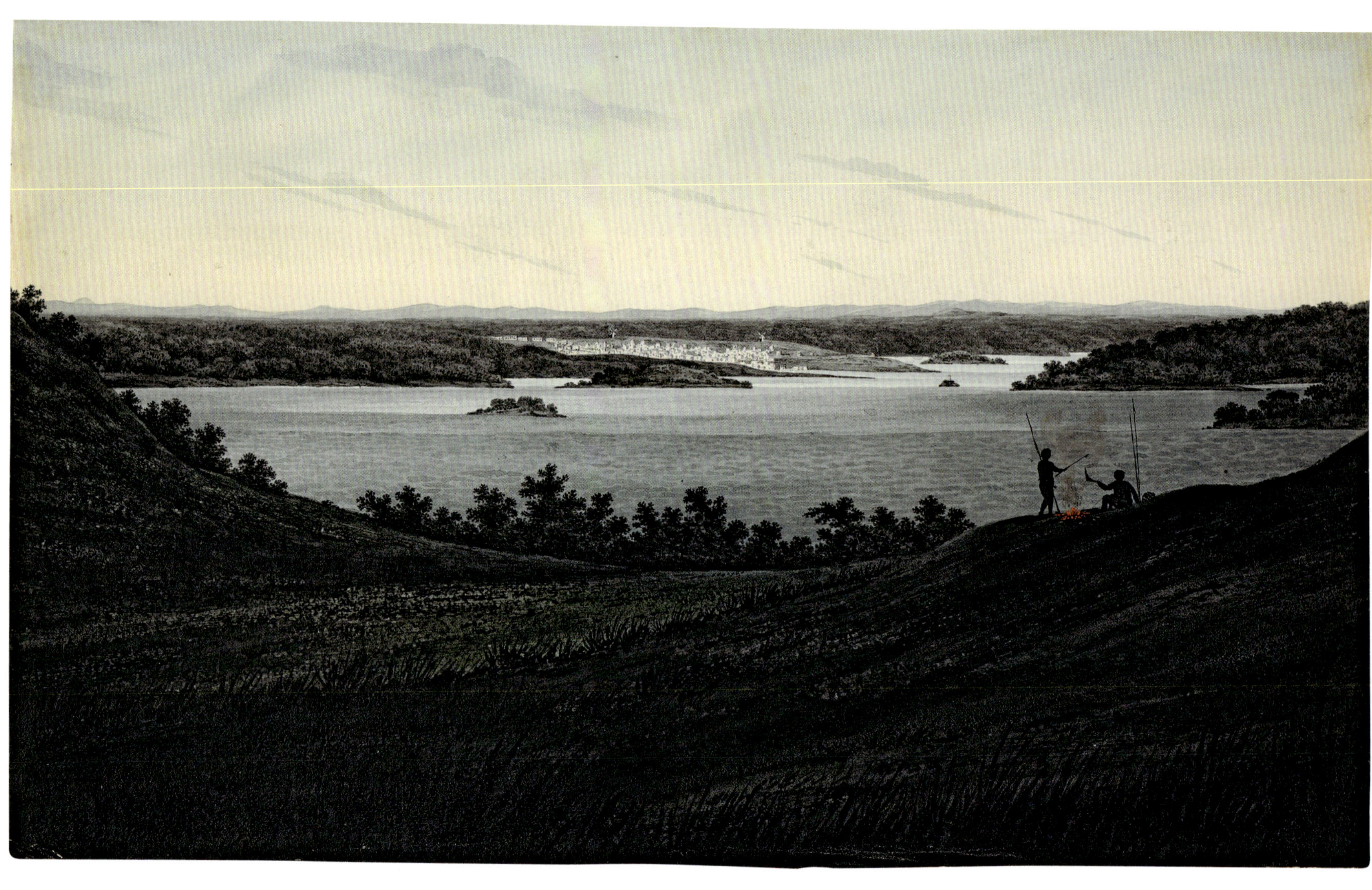

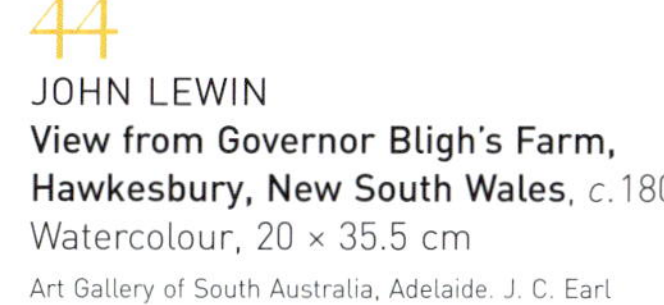

44
JOHN LEWIN
View from Governor Bligh's Farm, Hawkesbury, New South Wales, *c.* 1808
Watercolour, 20 × 35.5 cm
Art Gallery of South Australia, Adelaide. J. C. Earl Bequest and Elder Bequest Funds, 1989

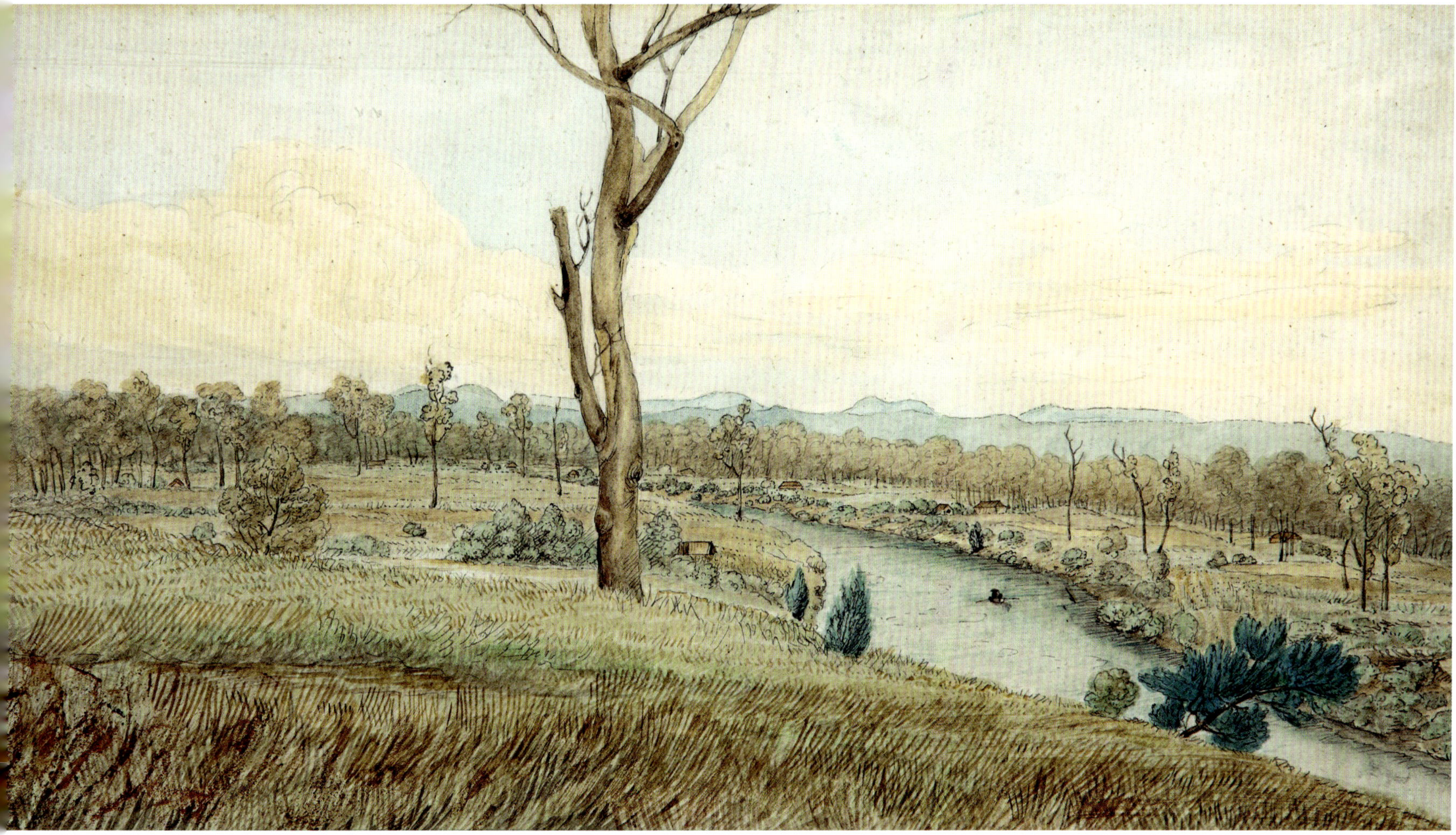

45
WILLIAM WESTALL
Chasm Island, Native Cave Painting, 1803
Watercolour, 26.7 × 37.2 cm
National Library of Australia, Canberra. Purchased 1969

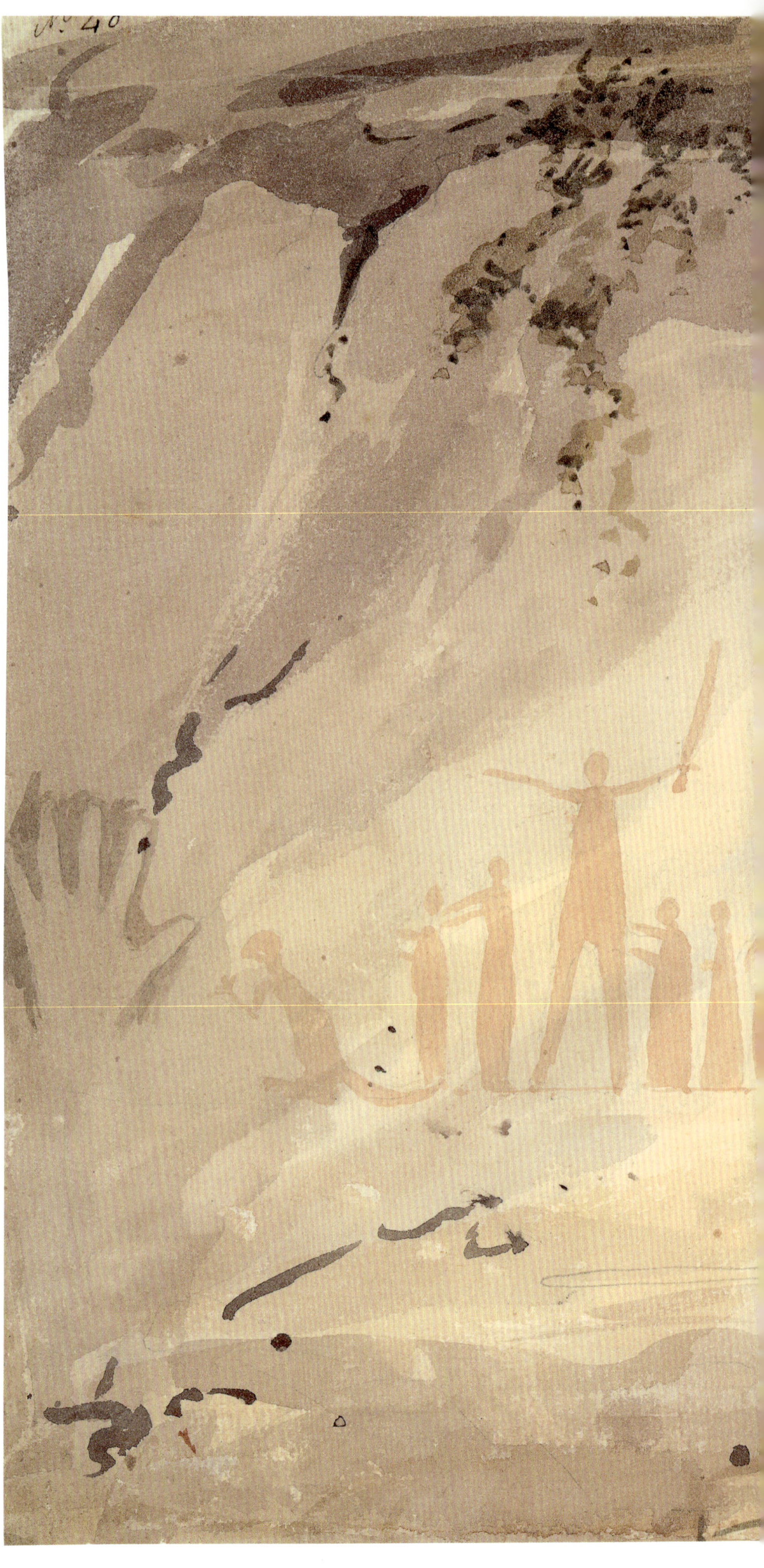

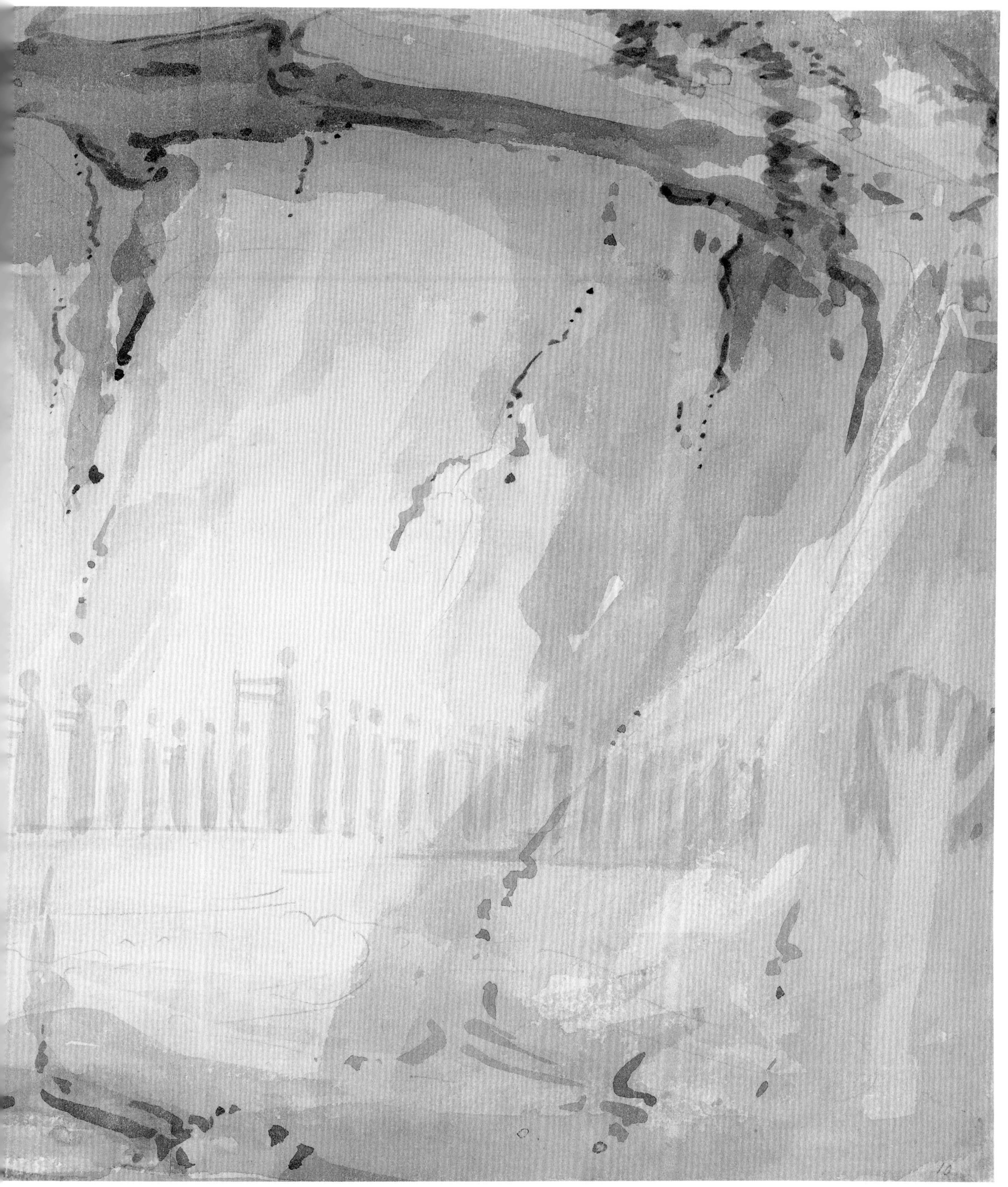

46

WILLIAM WESTALL

View in Sir E. Pellew's Group, Gulph of Carpentaria, Discovered by Captain Flinders, 1802, *c.* 1812

Oil on canvas, 61 × 88.5 cm

Ministry of Defence Art Collection, London

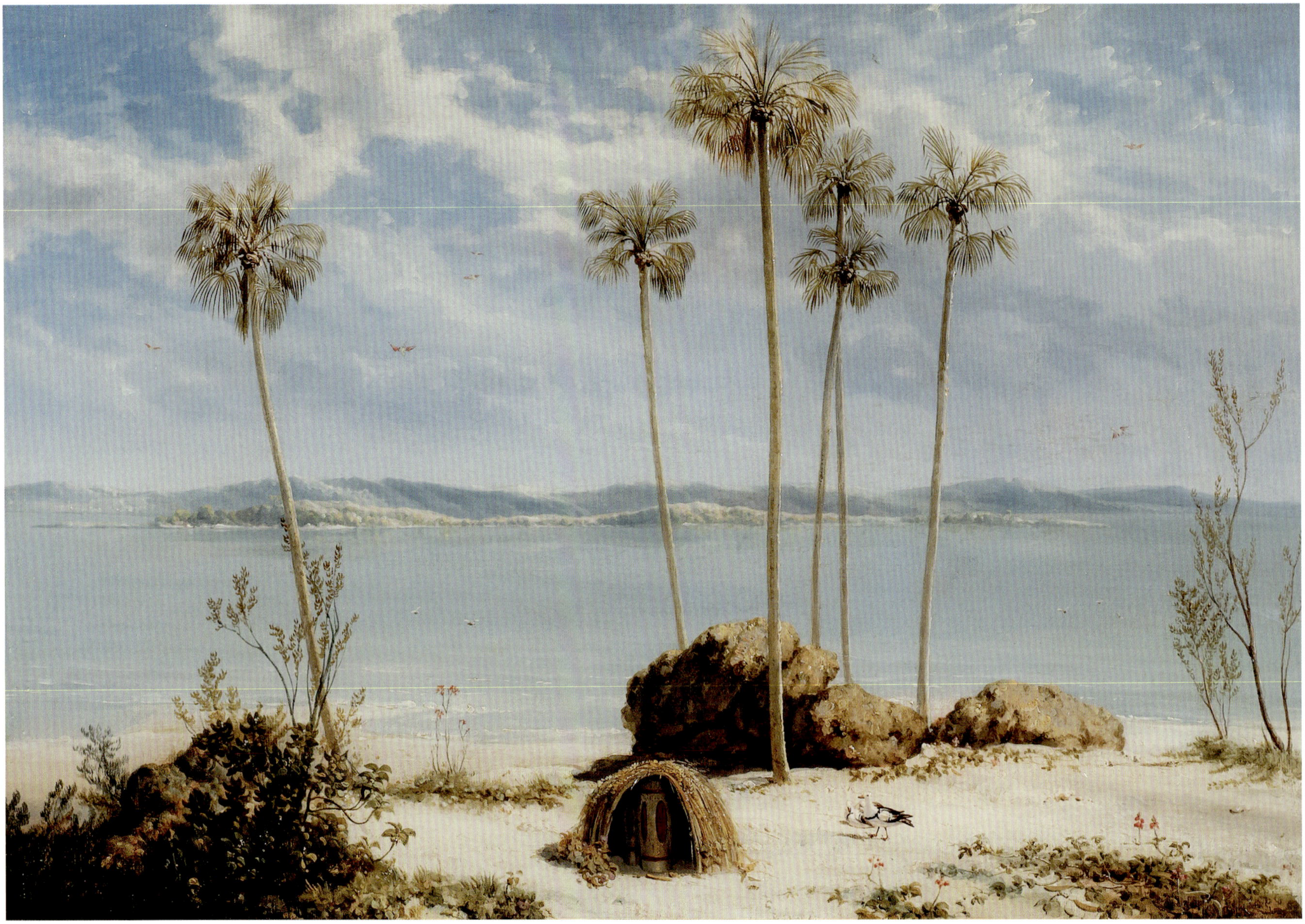

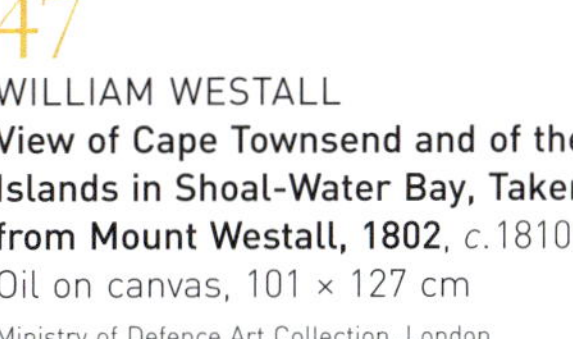

47
WILLIAM WESTALL
View of Cape Townsend and of the Islands in Shoal-Water Bay, Taken from Mount Westall, 1802, *c.*1810
Oil on canvas, 101 × 127 cm
Ministry of Defence Art Collection, London

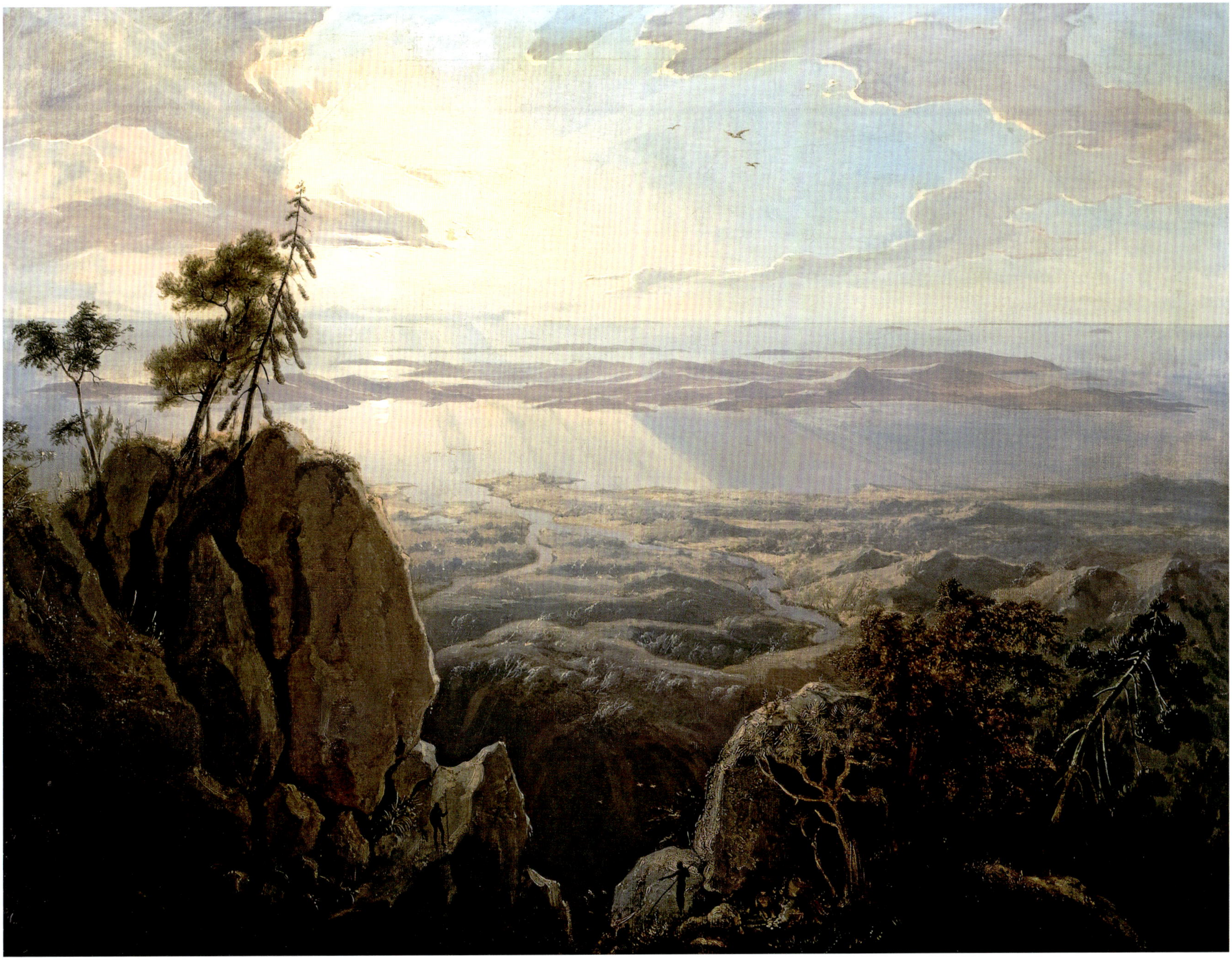

48

JOHN LEWIN

Evans's Peak, 1815

Watercolour, 22.8 × 27 cm

State Library of New South Wales, Sydney. Presented 1937

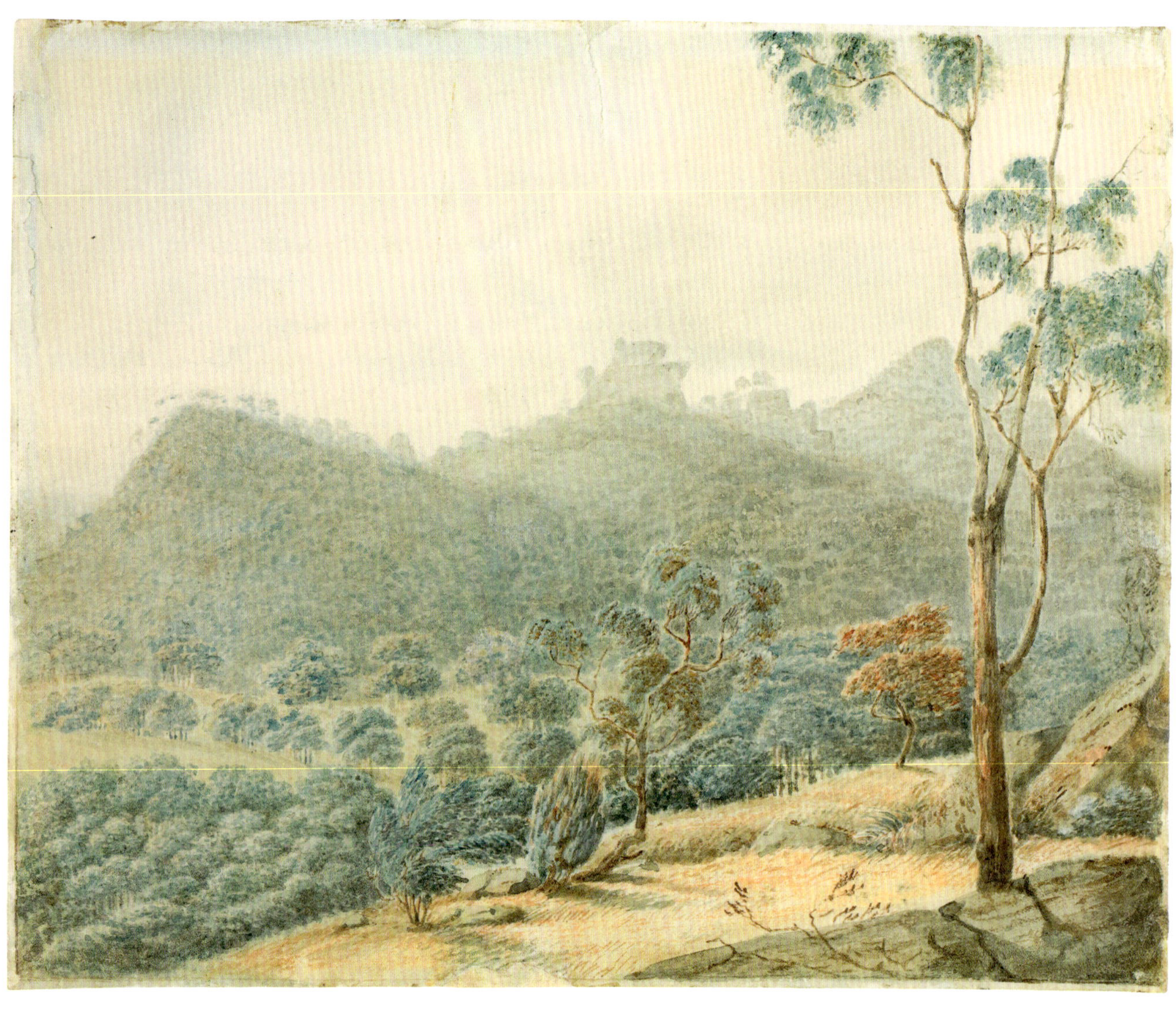

JOHN LEWIN

Fish Catch and Dawes Point, Sydney Harbour, *c.*1813

Oil on canvas, 86.5 × 113 cm

Art Gallery of South Australia, Adelaide. Gift of the Art Gallery of South Australia Foundation and South Australian Brewing Holdings Limited, 1989. Given to mark the occasion of the Company's 1988 Centenary

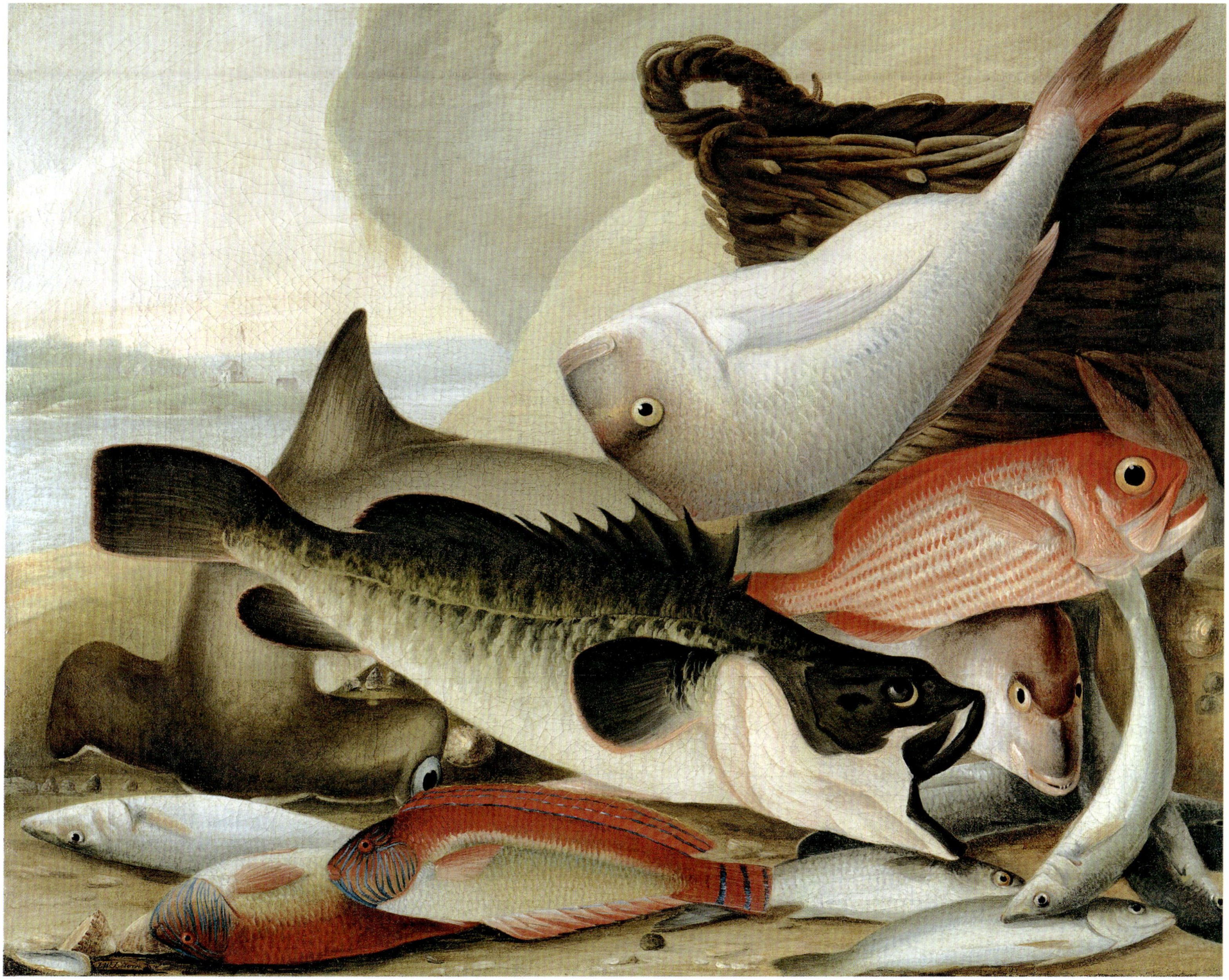

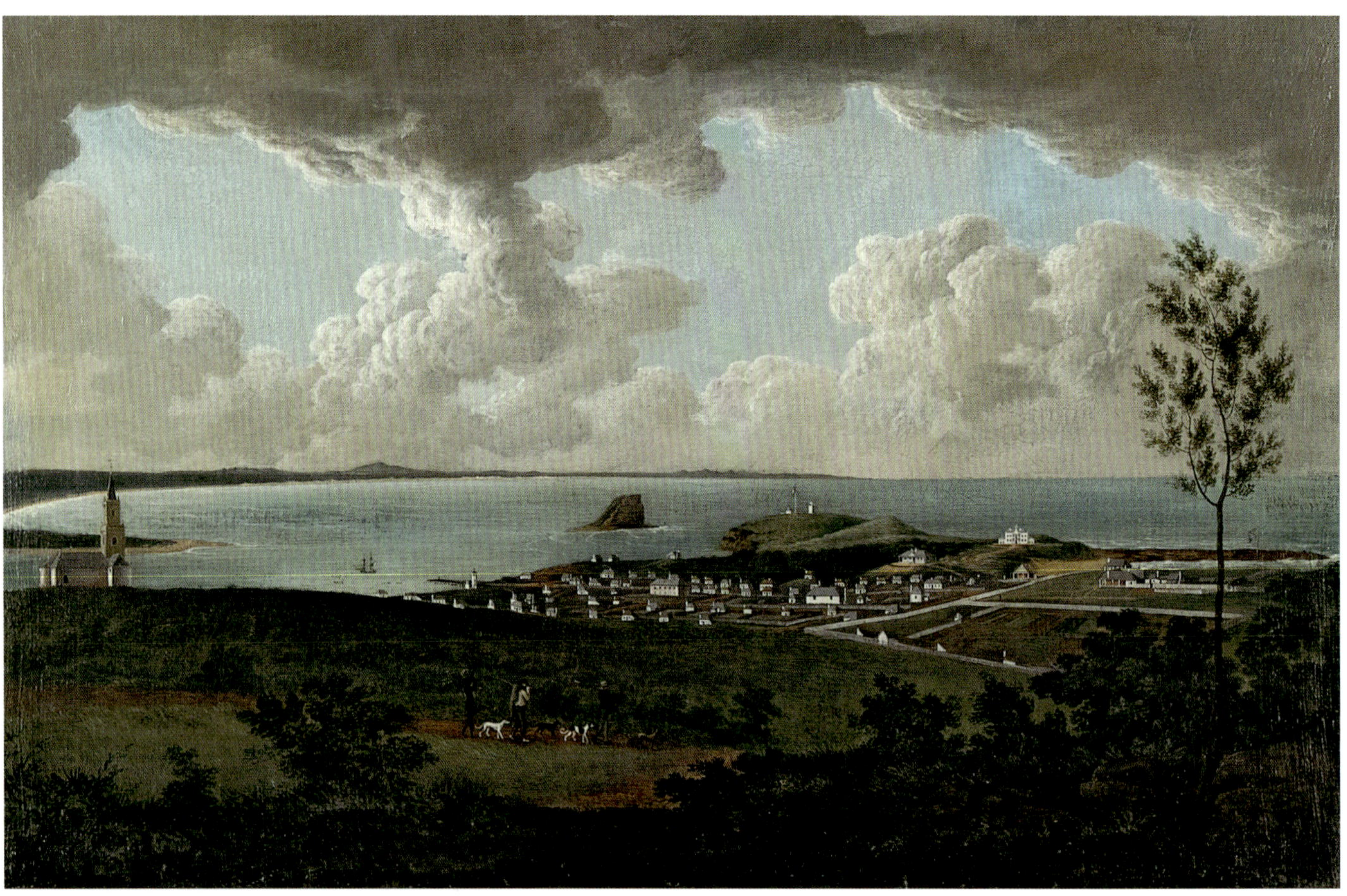

50
JOSEPH LYCETT
Inner View of Newcastle, *c.* 1818
Oil on canvas, 61 × 91.4 cm

Newcastle Art Gallery, New South Wales. Purchased with assistance from the National Art Collections Fund, London, 1961

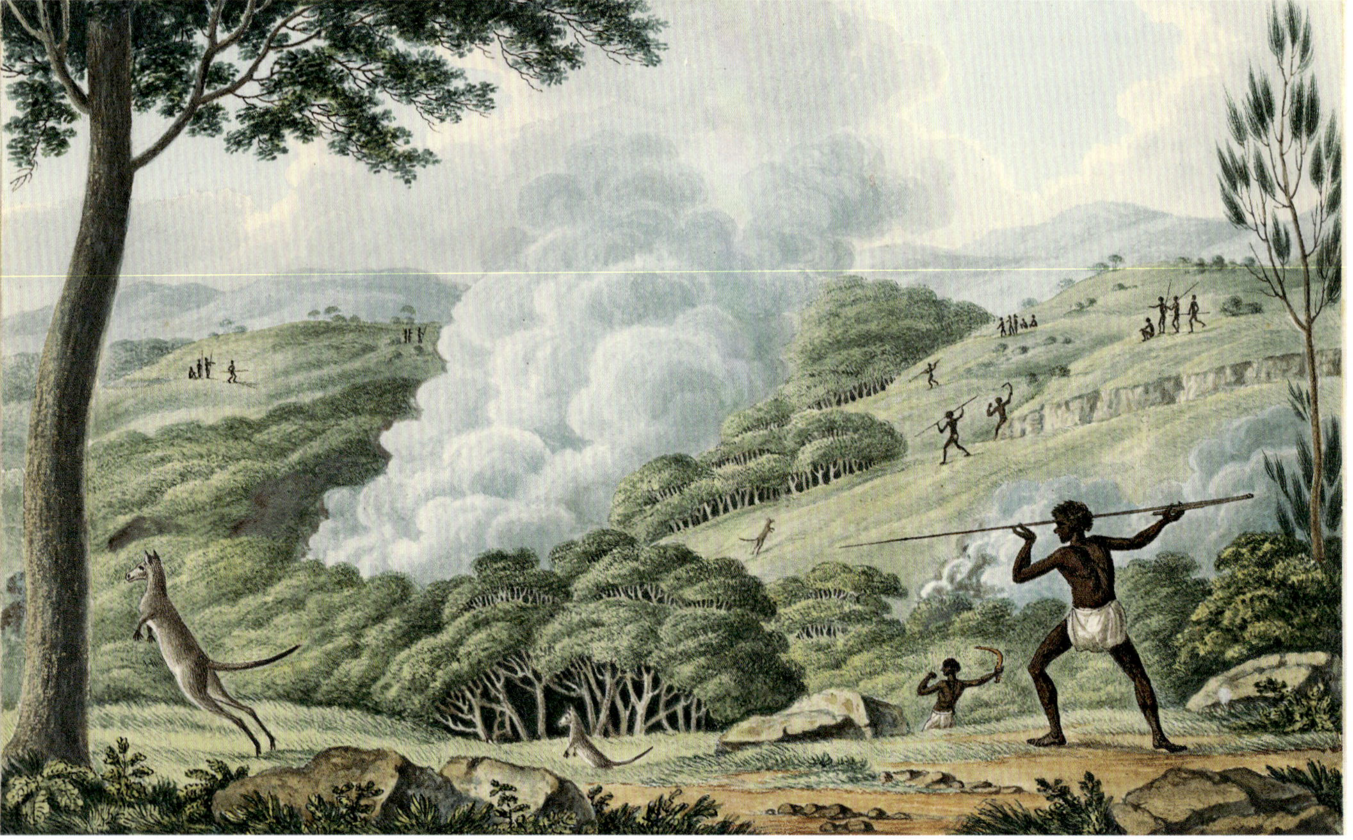

51
JOSEPH LYCETT
Aborigines Using Fire to Hunt Kangaroos from **'The Lycett Album'. Drawings of the Aborigines and Scenery of New South Wales**, *c.* 1820
Watercolour, 17.5 × 27.8 cm

National Library of Australia, Canberra. Purchased 1972

52
AUGUSTUS EARLE
View from the Summit of Mount York, Looking towards Bathurst Plains, Convicts Breaking Stones, New South Wales, *c.*1826
Watercolour, 22.5 × 33 cm
National Library of Australia, Canberra. Rex Nan Kivell Collection, 1959

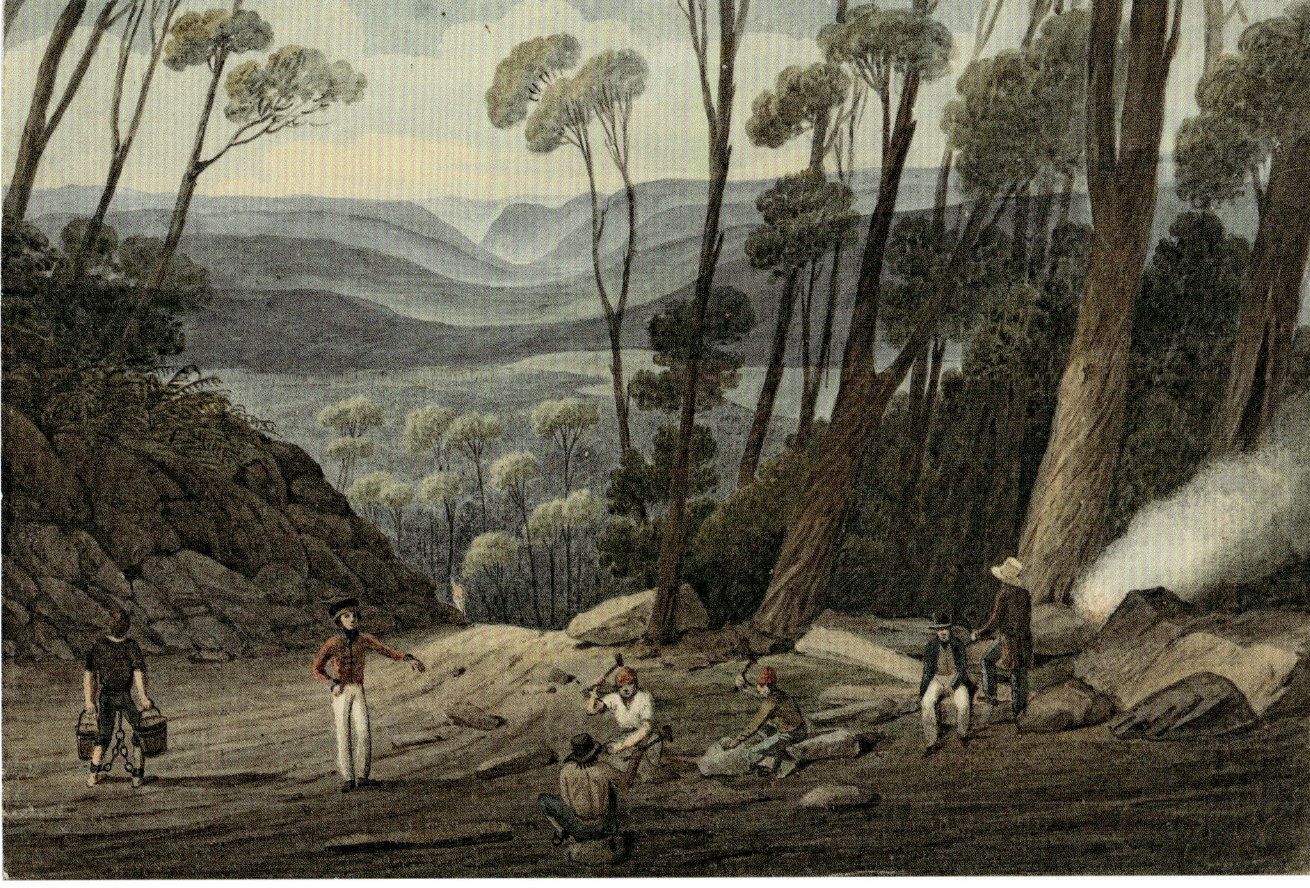

53
AUGUSTUS EARLE
A Native Camp of Australian Savages near Port Stevens, New South Wales, *c.*1826
Watercolour, 25.1 × 43.8 cm
National Library of Australia, Canberra. Rex Nan Kivell Collection, 1959

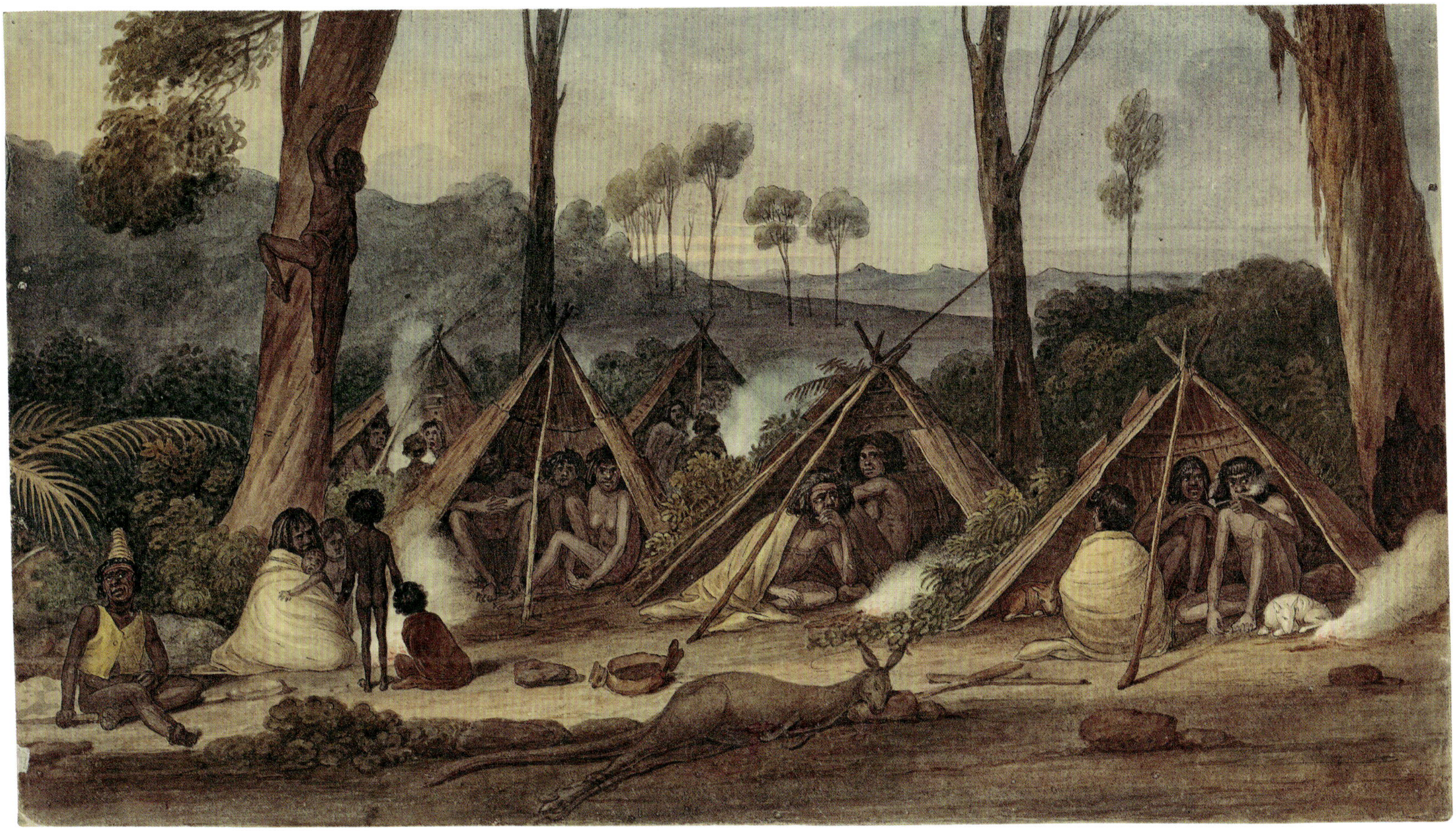

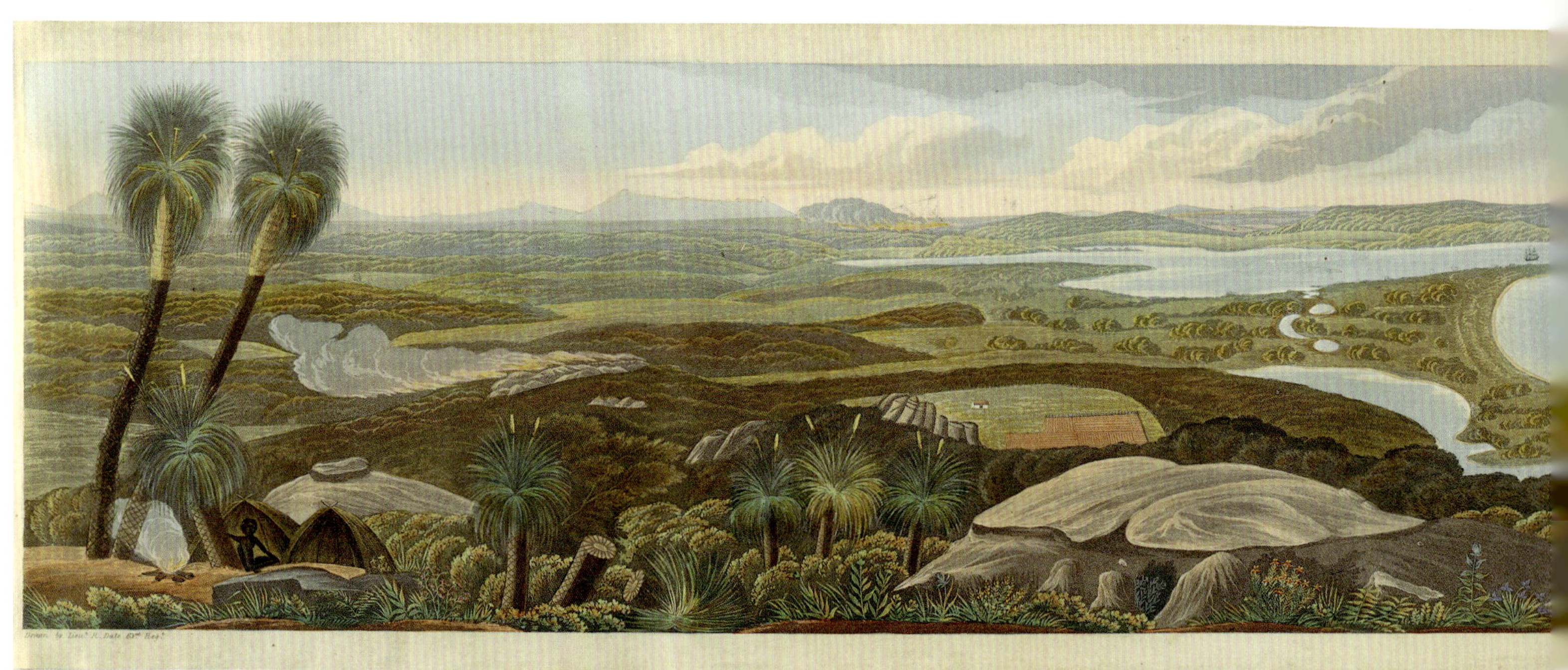

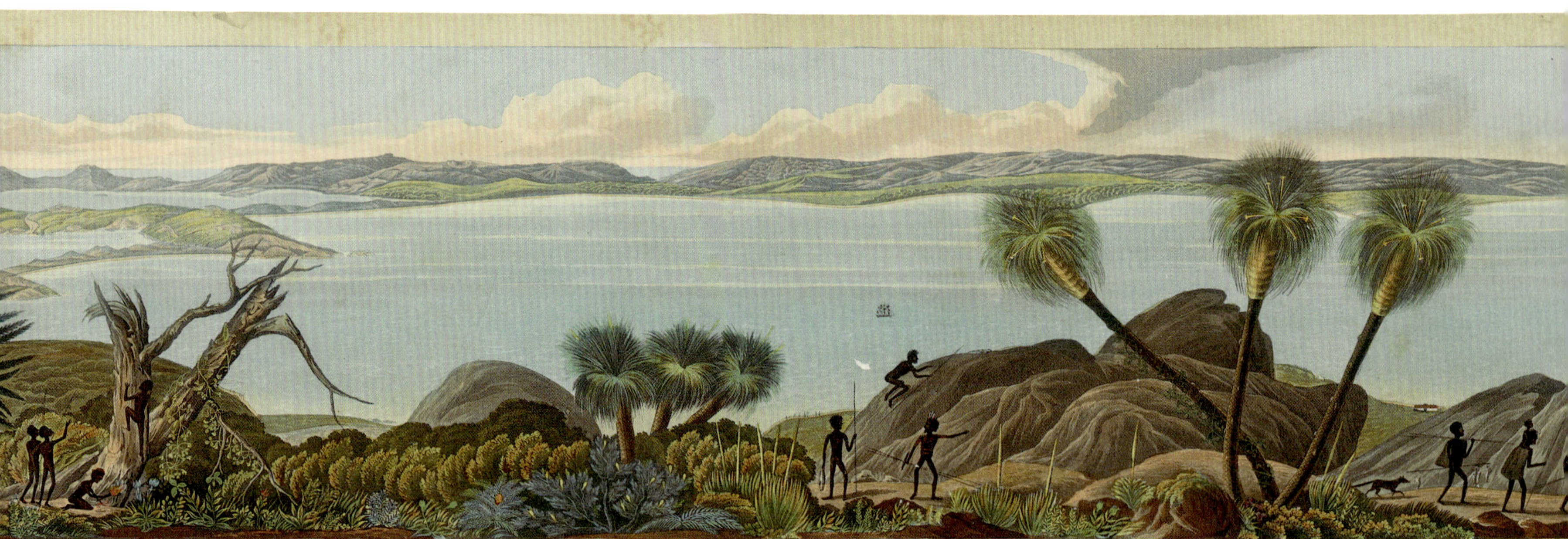

Panoramic view of King Georges Sound part of the colony of Swan River

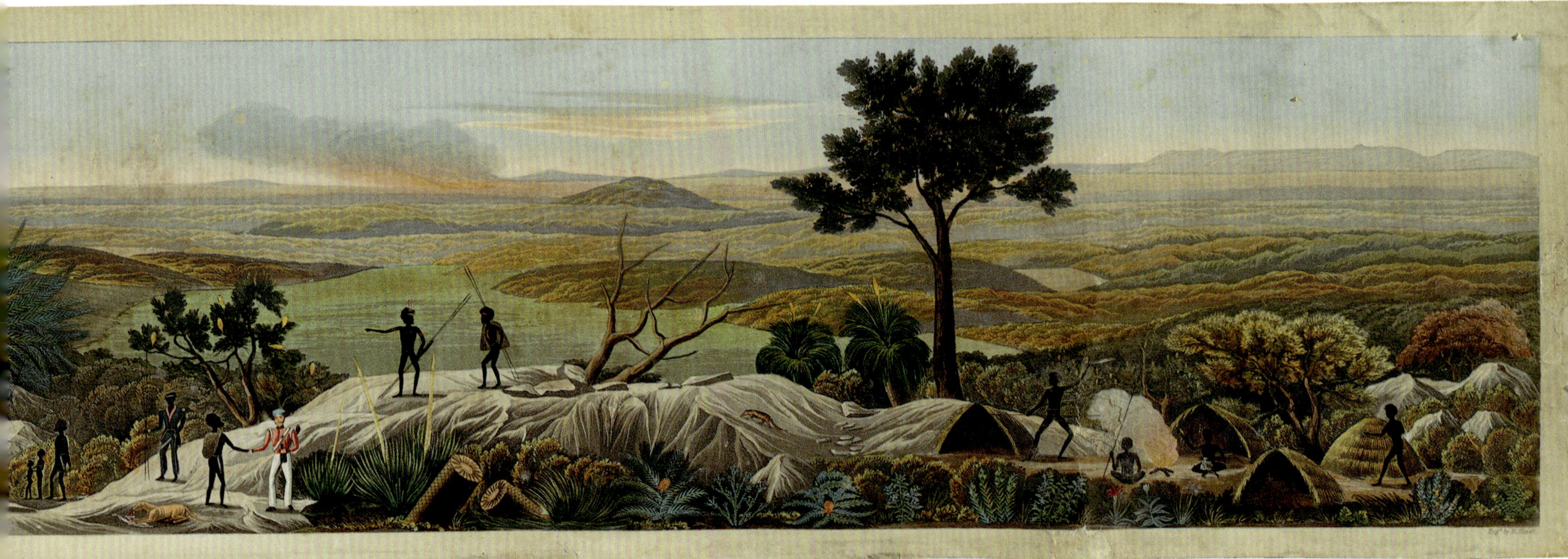

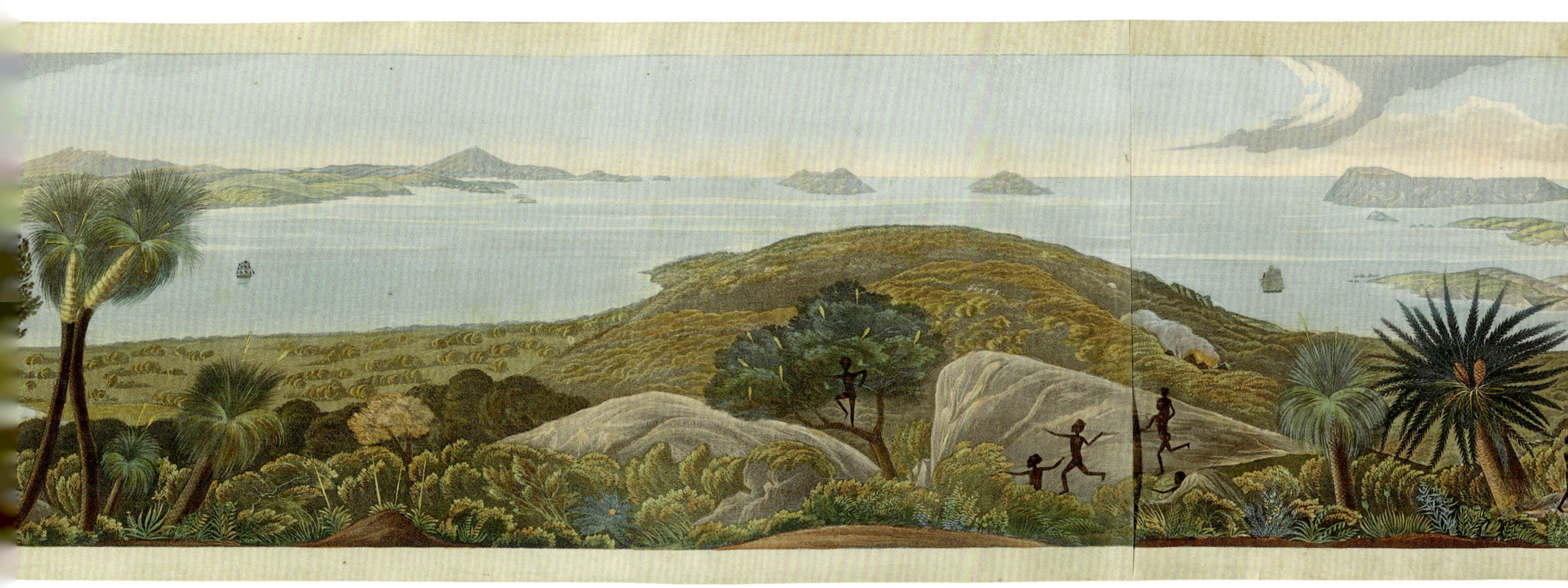

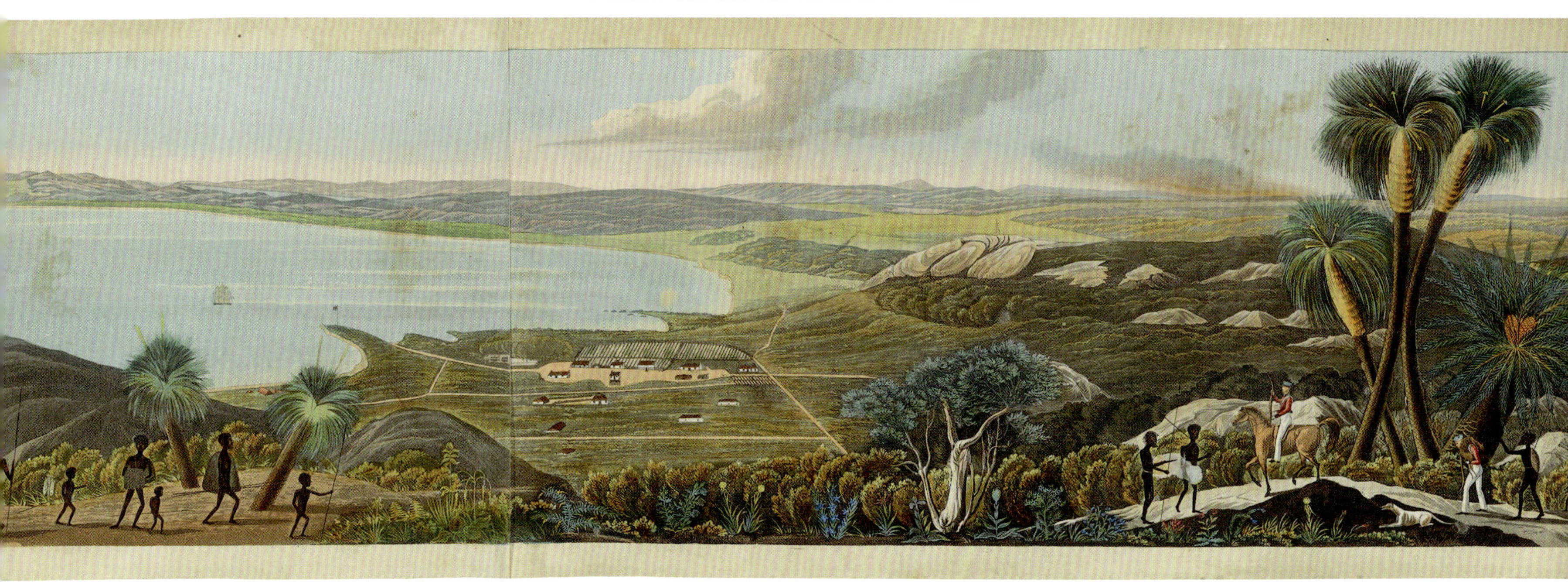

54

ROBERT DALE, print after; ROBERT HAVELL JNR, etcher and publisher

Panoramic View of King Georges Sound, Part of the Colony of Swan River, 1834

Etching and aquatint, printed in black ink from three plates on three joined sheets, hand-coloured in watercolour, 18 × 274.2 cm (overall)

National Gallery of Australia, Canberra.
The Wordsworth Collection, purchased 2010

55

JOHN GLOVER

A Corroboree of Natives in Mills Plains, 1832

Oil on canvas, 56.5 × 71.4 cm

Art Gallery of South Australia, Adelaide. Morgan Thomas Bequest Fund, 1951

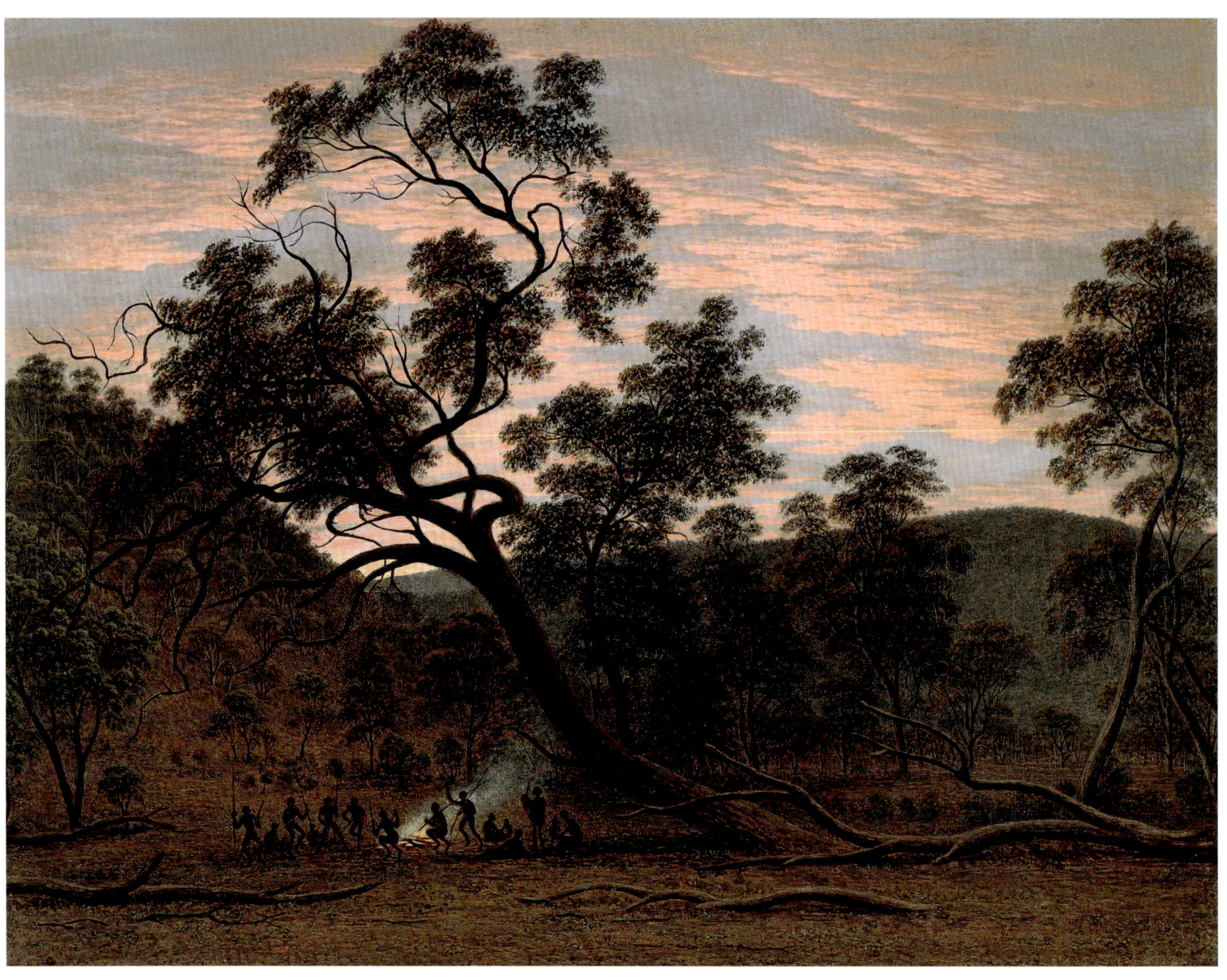

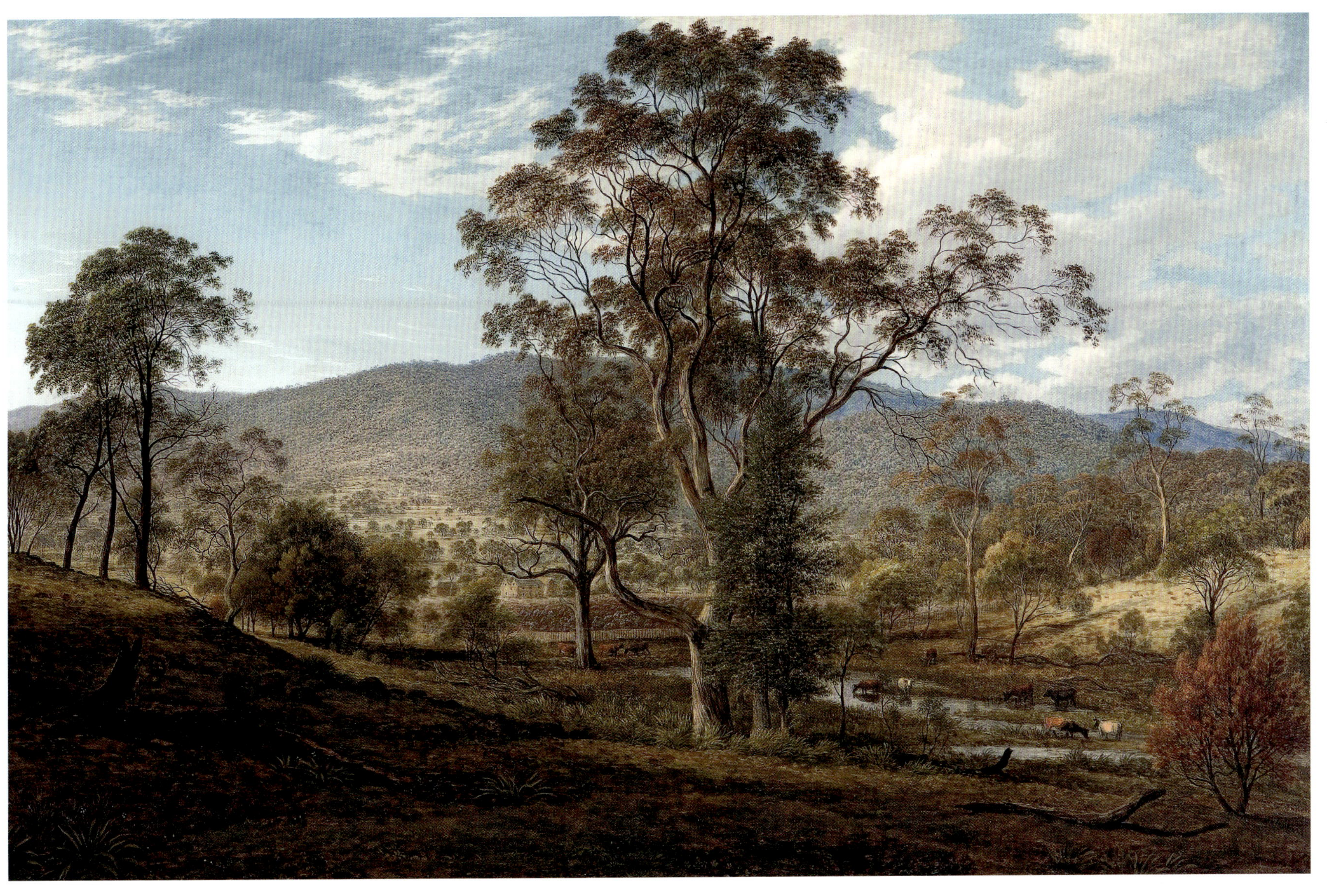

56
JOHN GLOVER
View of Mills Plains, Van Diemen's Land,
1833
Oil on canvas, 76.2 × 114.6 cm
Art Gallery of South Australia, Adelaide.
Morgan Thomas Bequest Fund, 1951

57

JOHN GLOVER

A View of the Artist's House and Garden, in Mills Plains, Van Diemen's Land, 1835

Oil on canvas, 76.4 × 114.4 cm

Art Gallery of South Australia, Adelaide. Morgan Thomas Bequest Fund, 1951

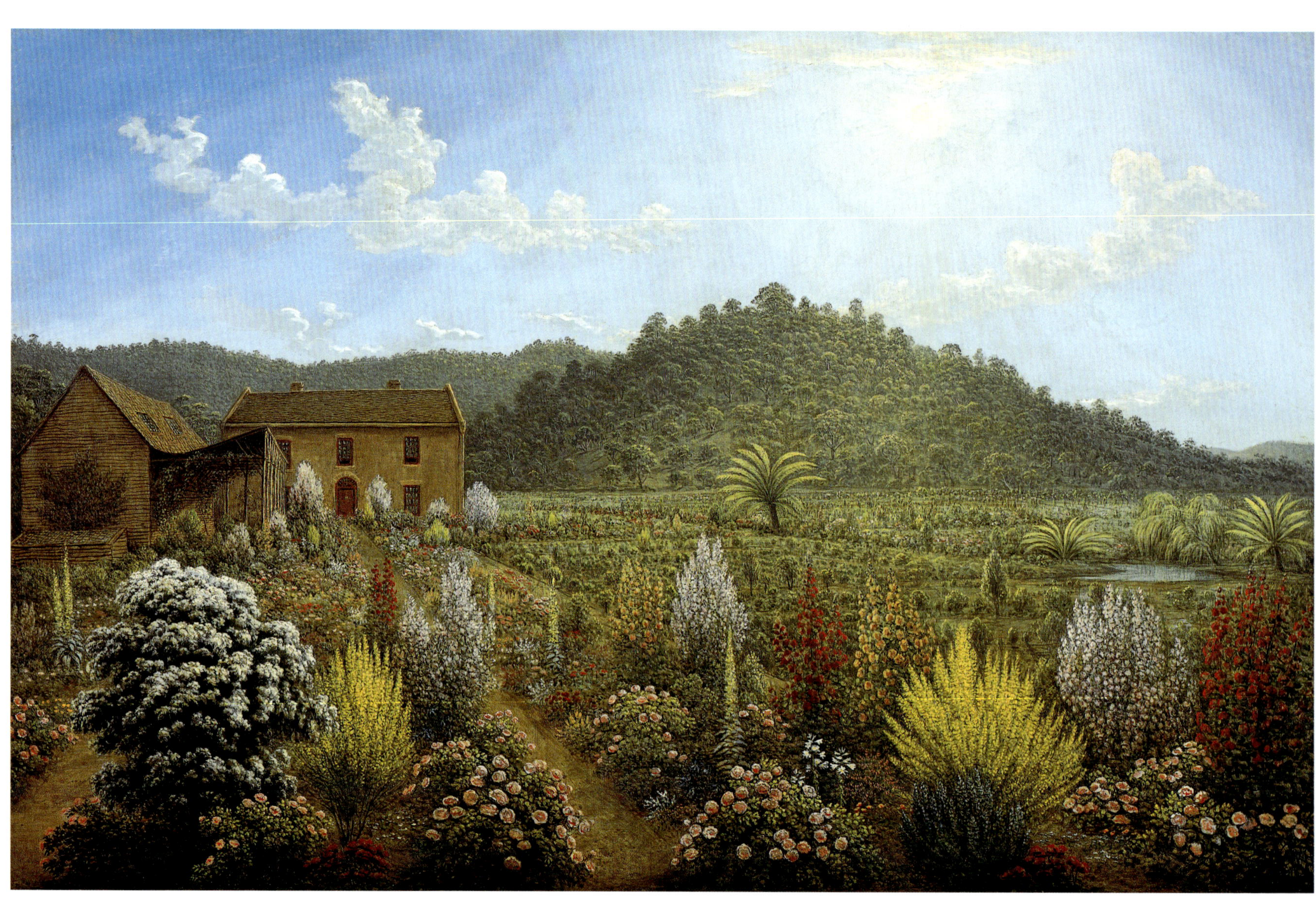

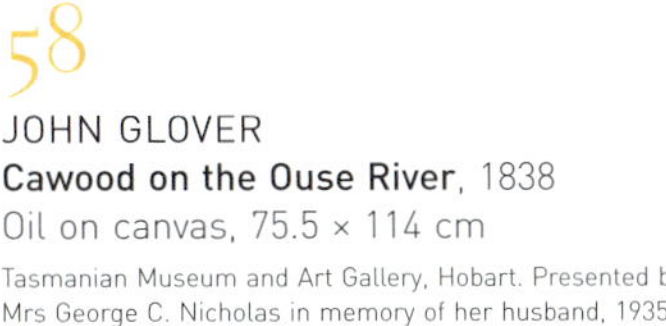

58

JOHN GLOVER

Cawood on the Ouse River, 1838

Oil on canvas, 75.5 × 114 cm

Tasmanian Museum and Art Gallery, Hobart. Presented by Mrs George C. Nicholas in memory of her husband, 1935

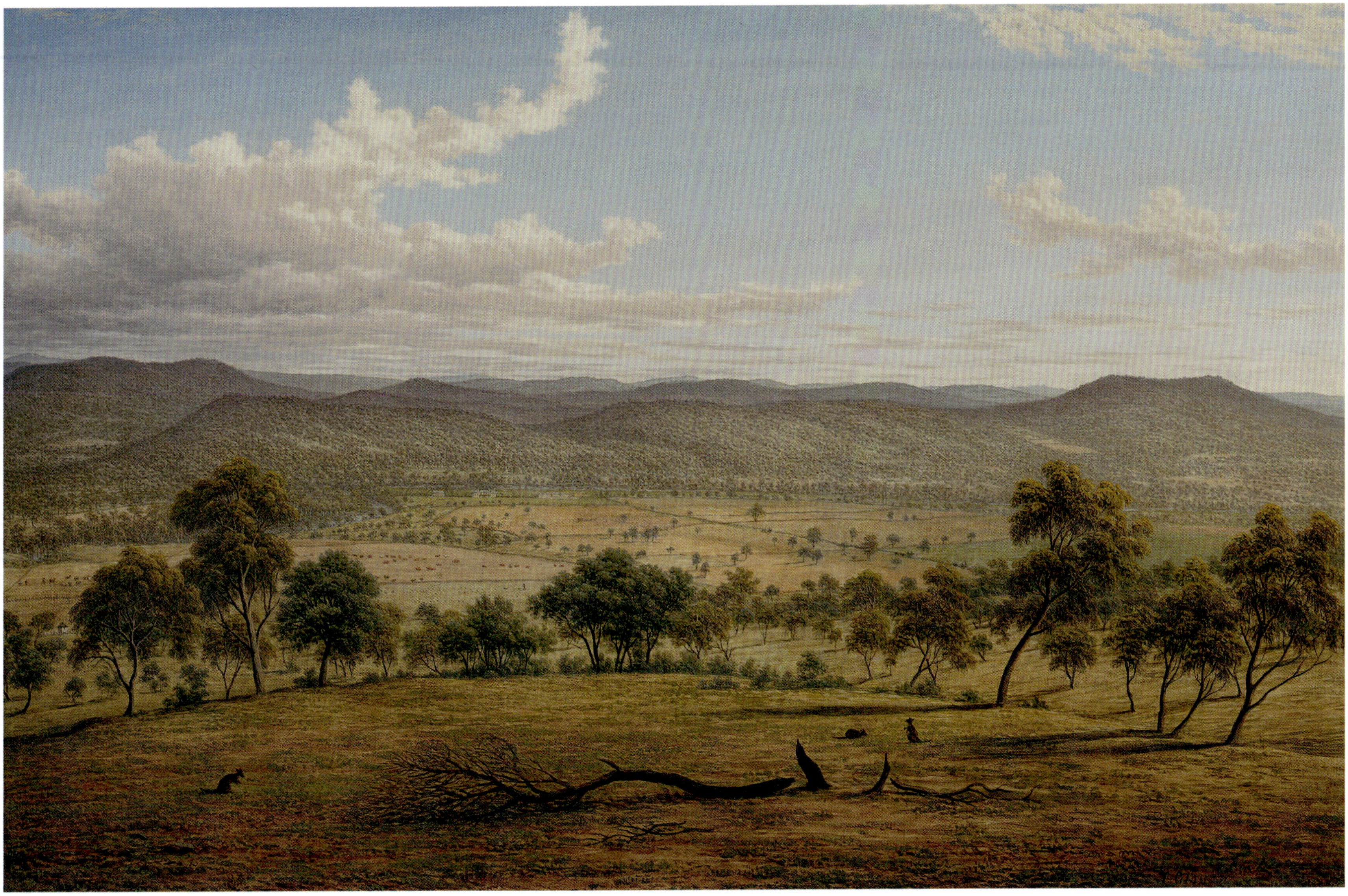

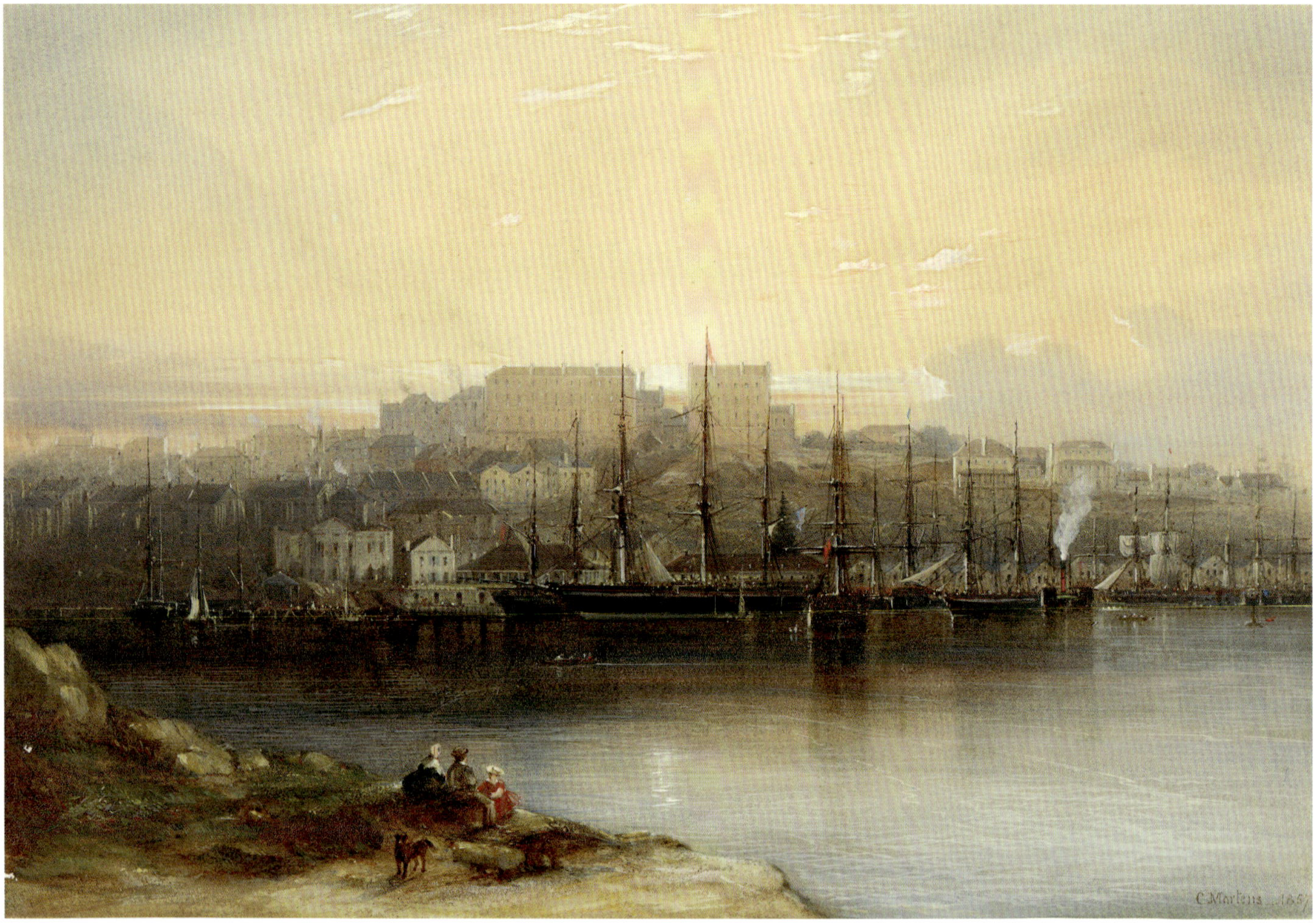

59
CONRAD MARTENS
Campbell's Wharf, 1857
Watercolour, with touches of gum arabic, 46 × 66 cm
National Gallery of Australia, Canberra.
Purchased with the assistance of the Members' Acquisition Fund, 2009

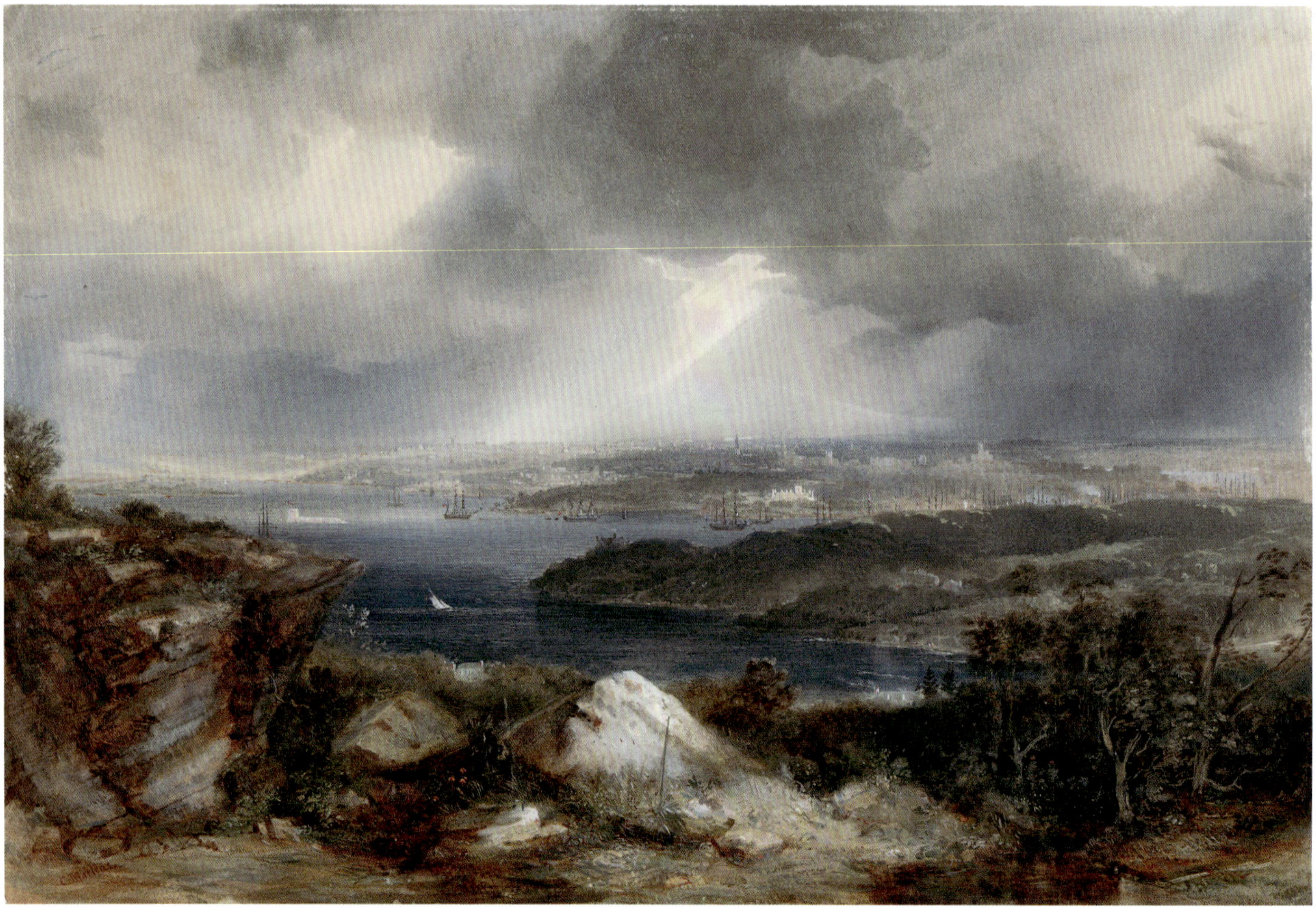

60
CONRAD MARTENS
View of Sydney from Neutral Bay, *c.*1857
Watercolour, gouache, black penc varnish, 45.1 × 65 cm
National Gallery of Australia, Canberra.
Purchased 1975

EDMUND HENDERSON
Perth, West Australia, 1862
Watercolour, 34.6 × 50.6 cm
National Gallery of Australia, Canberra.
The Wordsworth Collection, purchased 2010

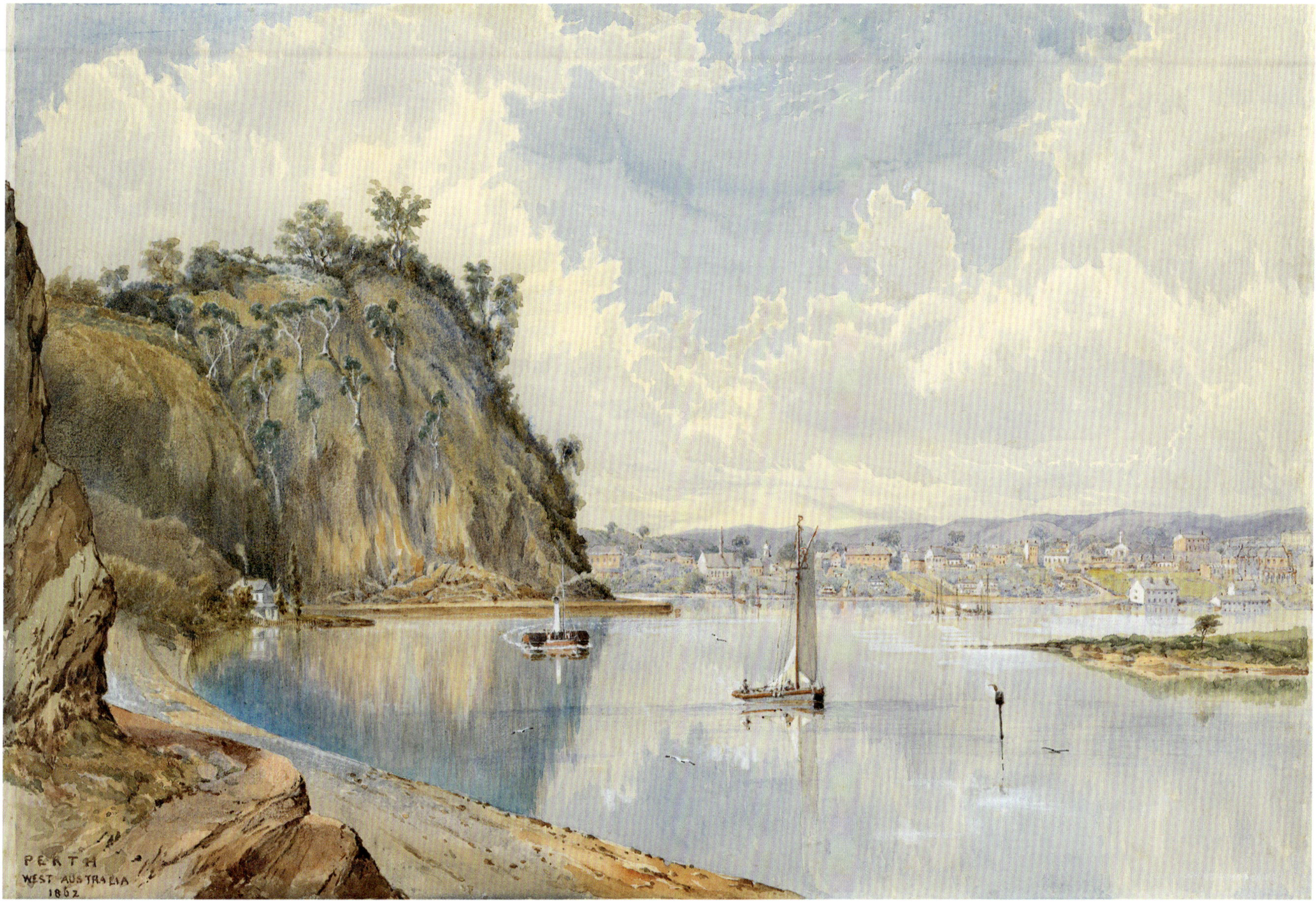

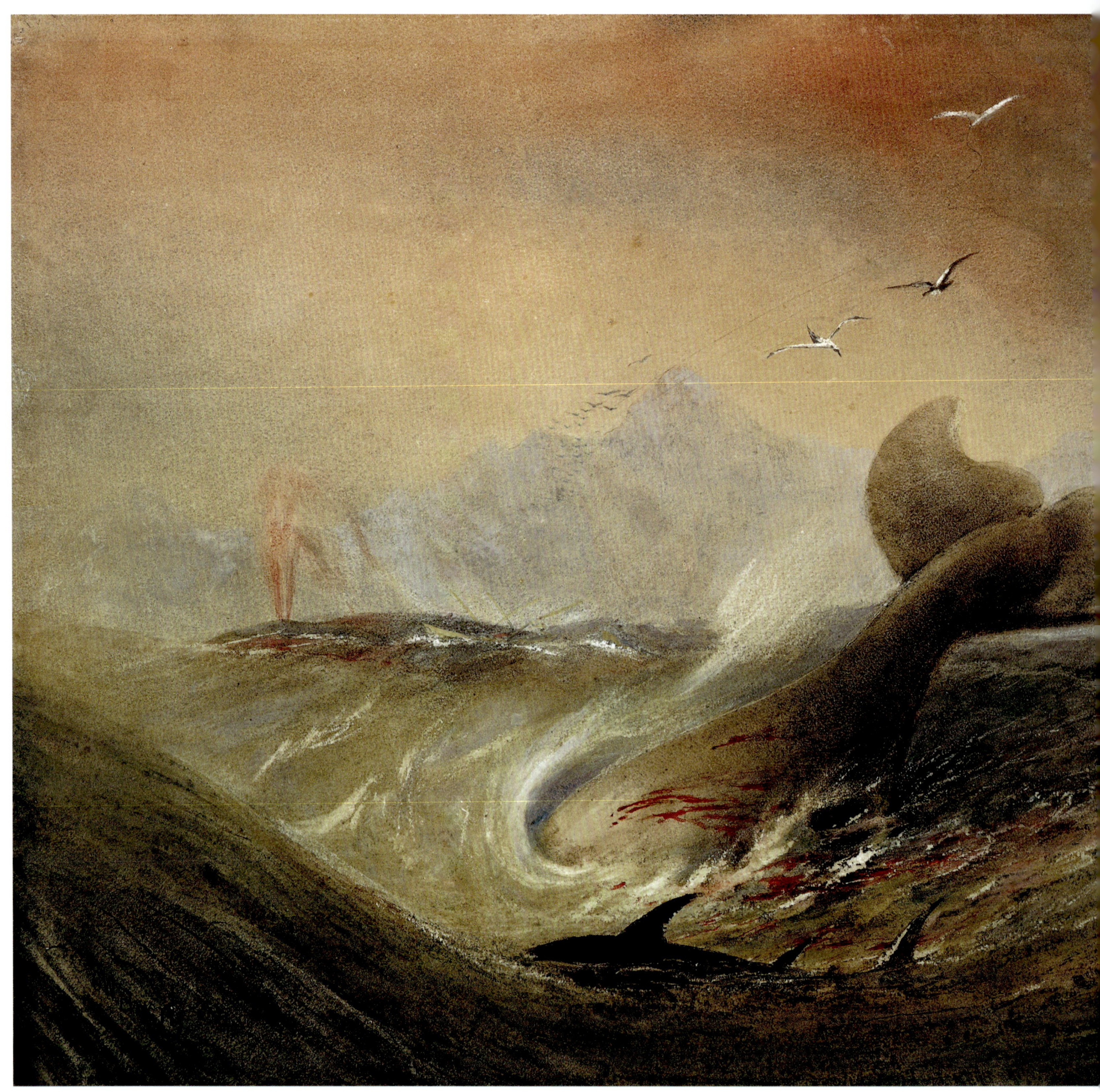

62

OSWALD BRIERLY
Amateur Whaling, or a Tale of the Pacific, 1847
Watercolour, 45.2 × 94 cm

Australian National Maritime Museum, Sydney. Purchased with funds from the USA Bicentennial Gift, 1989

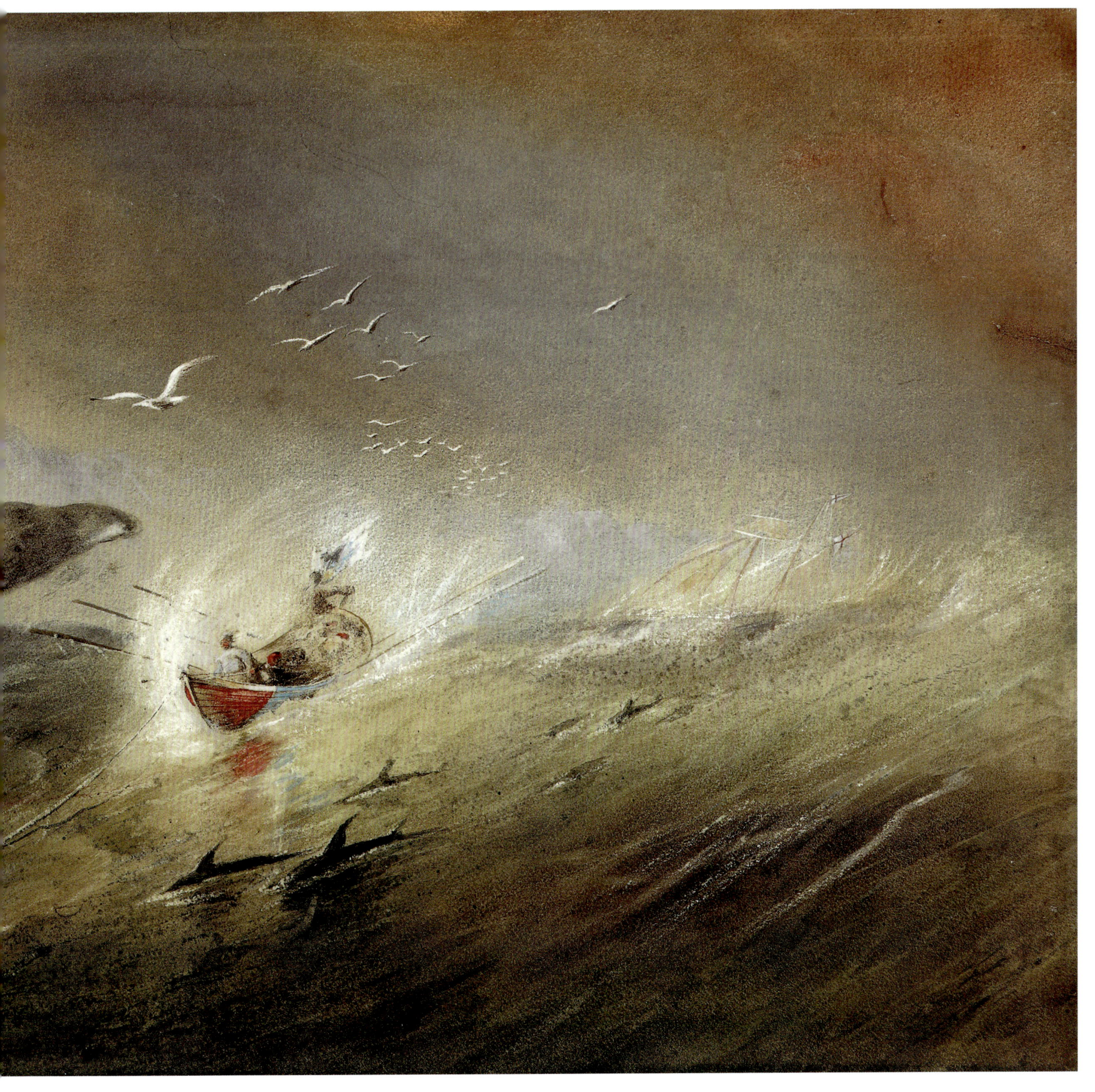

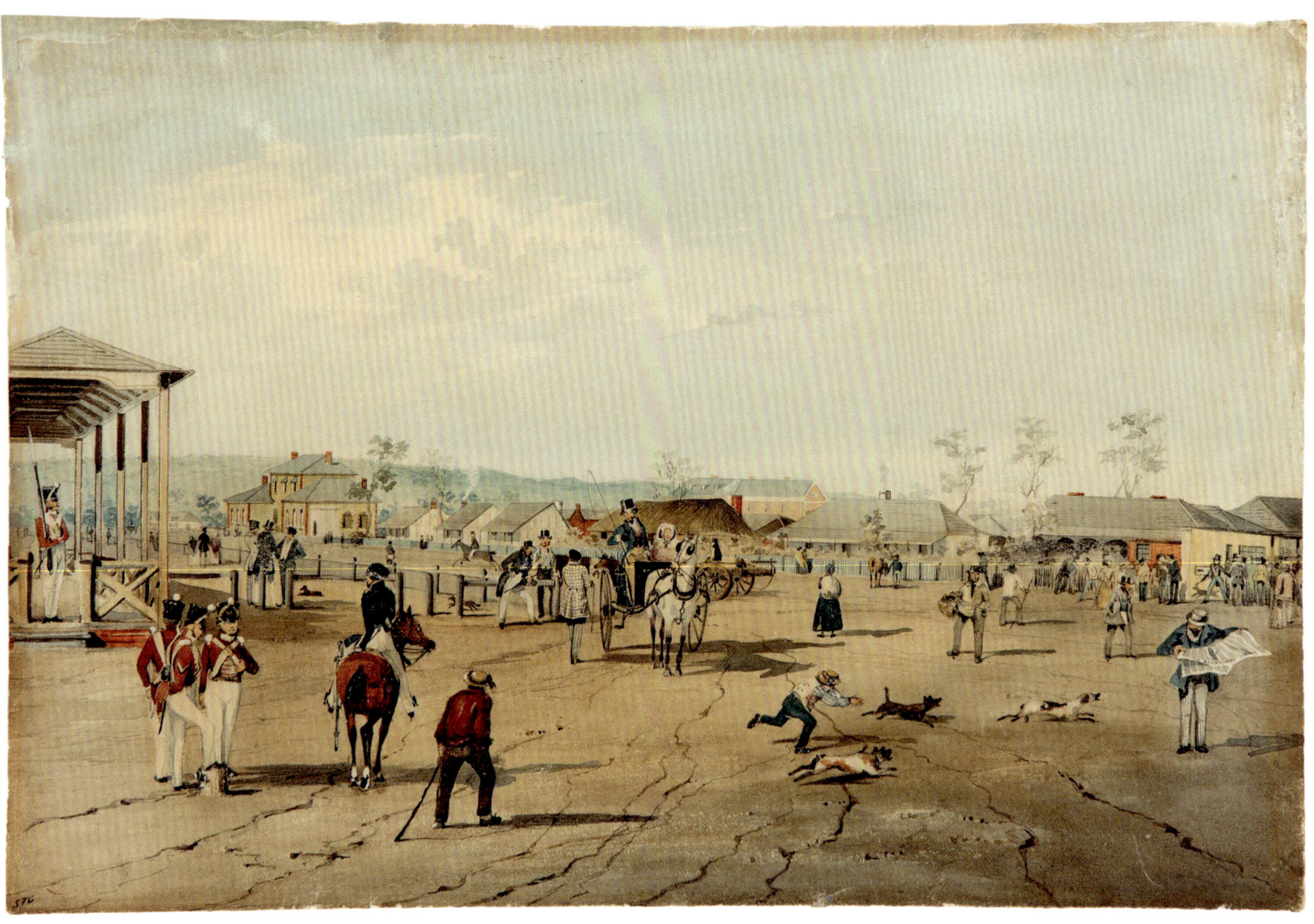

63
S.T. GILL
North Terrace, Adelaide, Looking South-east from Government House Guardhouse, 1845
Watercolour, 27.4 × 39.7 cm
Art Gallery of South Australia, Adelaide.
Gift of the South Australian Company, 1931

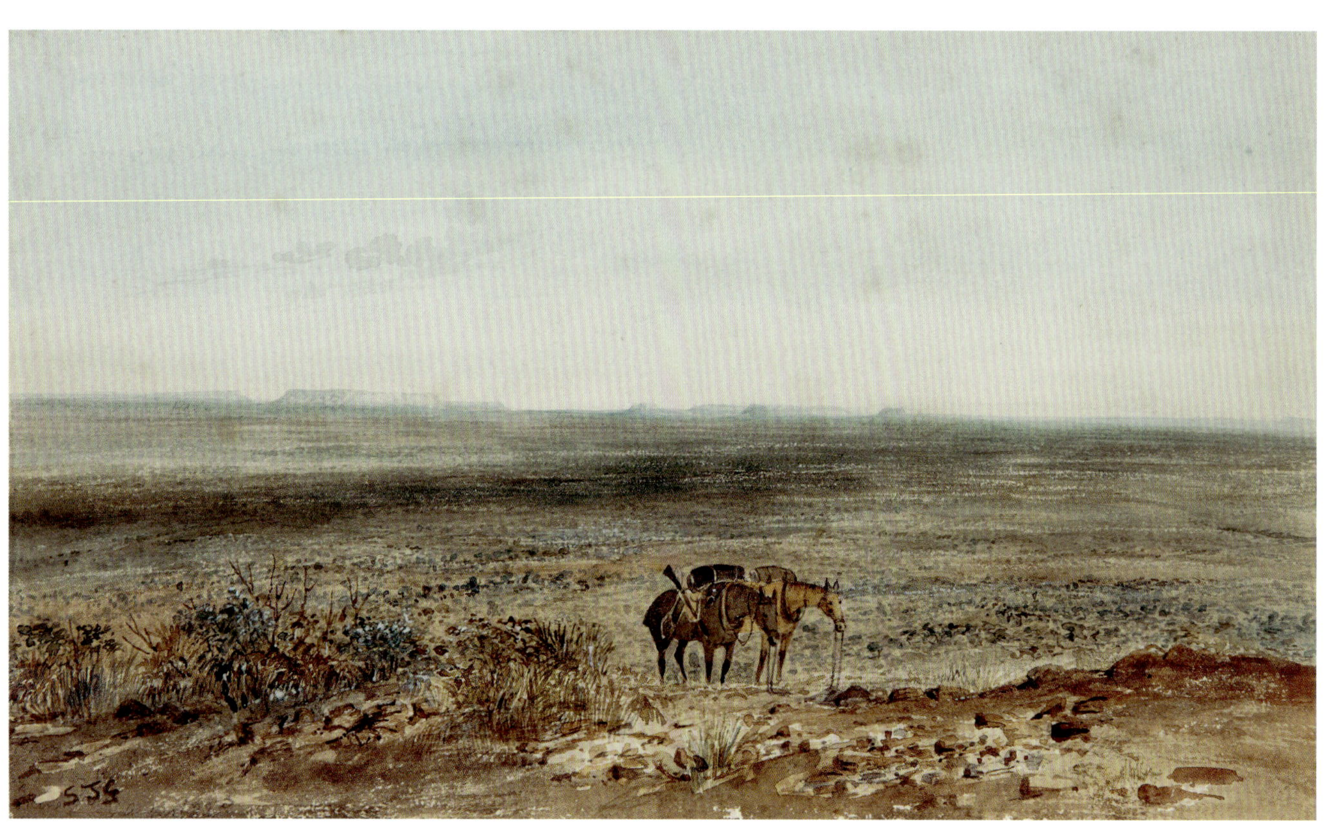

64
S.T. GILL
Looking SW from Table Land, August 22nd, 1846
Watercolour, 18.1 × 30.7 cm
Art Gallery of South Australia, Adelaide.
Gift of Douglas and Barbara Mullins, 1999

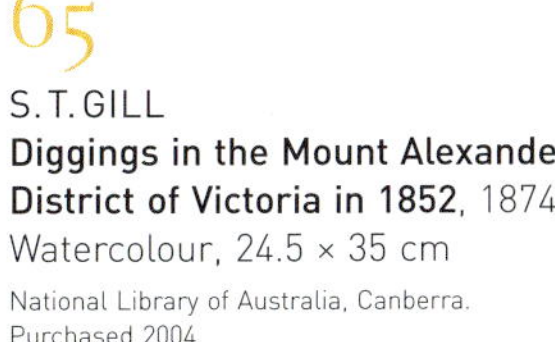

65

S.T.GILL

Diggings in the Mount Alexander District of Victoria in 1852, 1874

Watercolour, 24.5 × 35 cm

National Library of Australia, Canberra. Purchased 2004

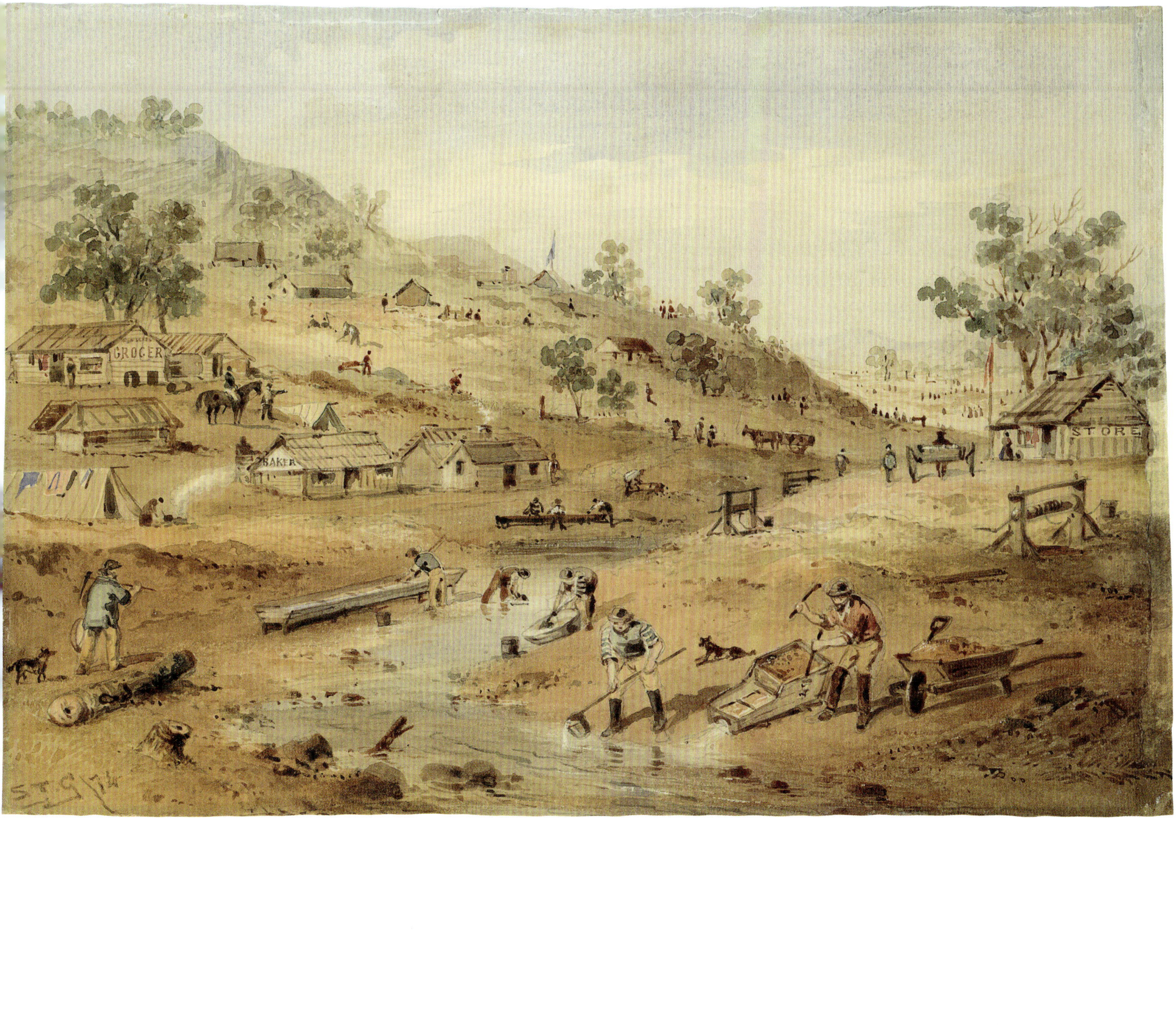

67
GEORGE FRENCH ANGAS
Scene Showing Emus in a Plain (Coorong), 1844
Watercolour, 23 × 32.5 cm
Art Gallery of South Australia, Adelaide. Gift of Miss E. M. Johnson, 1972

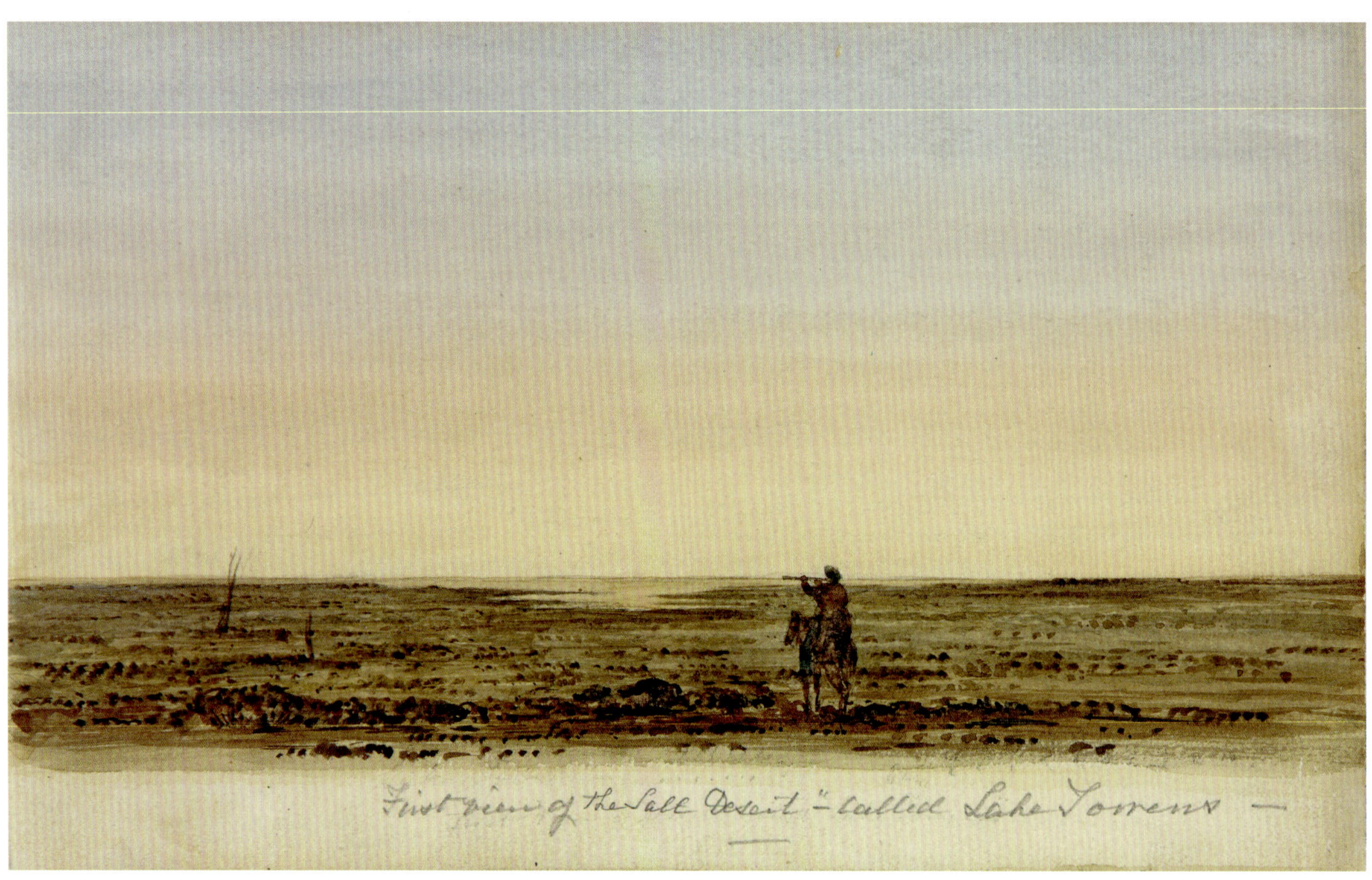

66
E.C.FROME
First View of the Salt Desert – Called Lake Torrens, 1843
Watercolour, 15.7 × 27.8 cm
Art Gallery of South Australia, Adelaide. South Australian Government Grant, Adelaide City Council and Public Donations, 1970

68
GEORGE FRENCH ANGAS
Port Lincoln from Winter's H
1845
Watercolour, 24.6 × 34.1 cm
Art Gallery of South Australia, Adelaide. Bequest of J. Angas Johnson, 1902

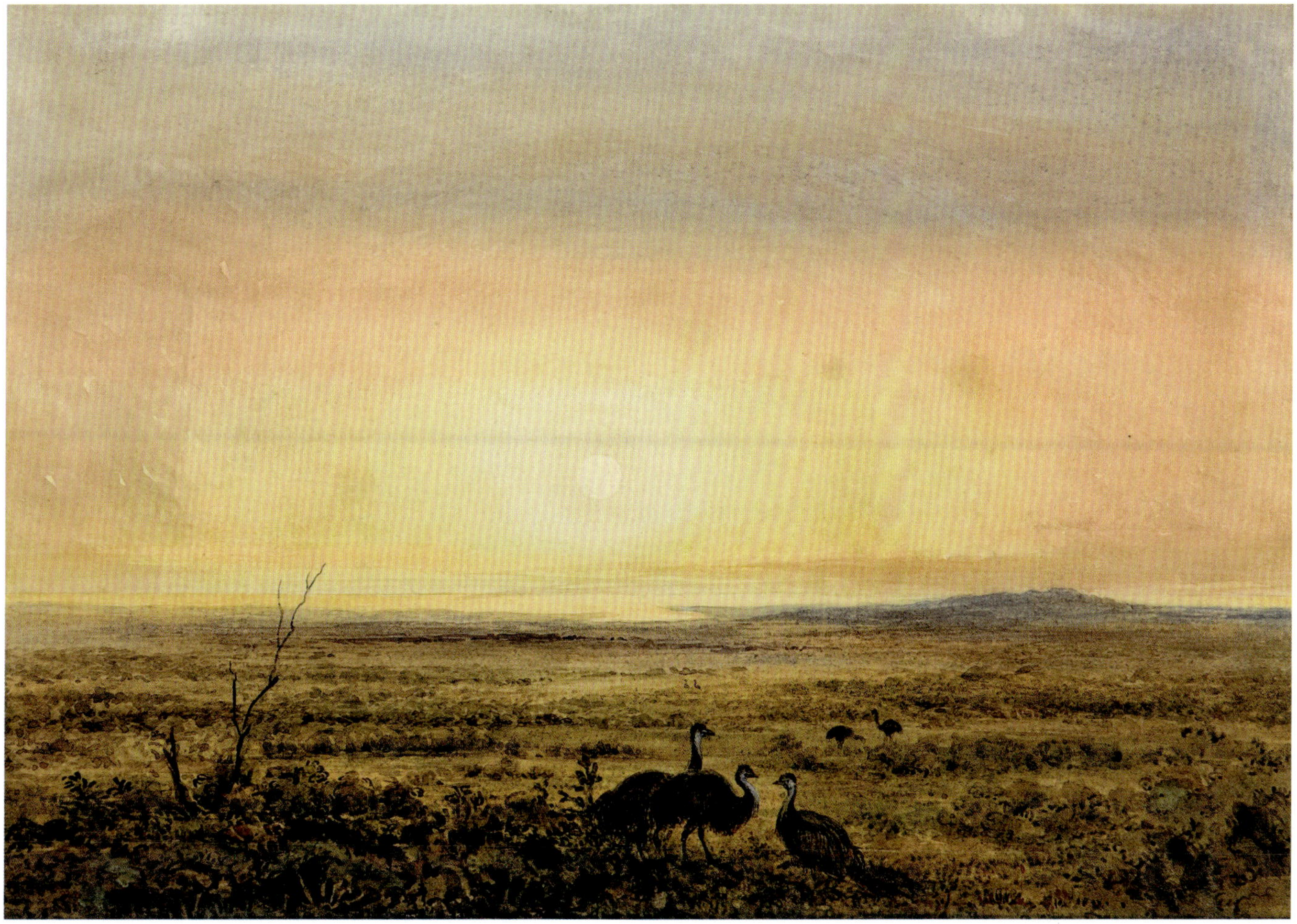

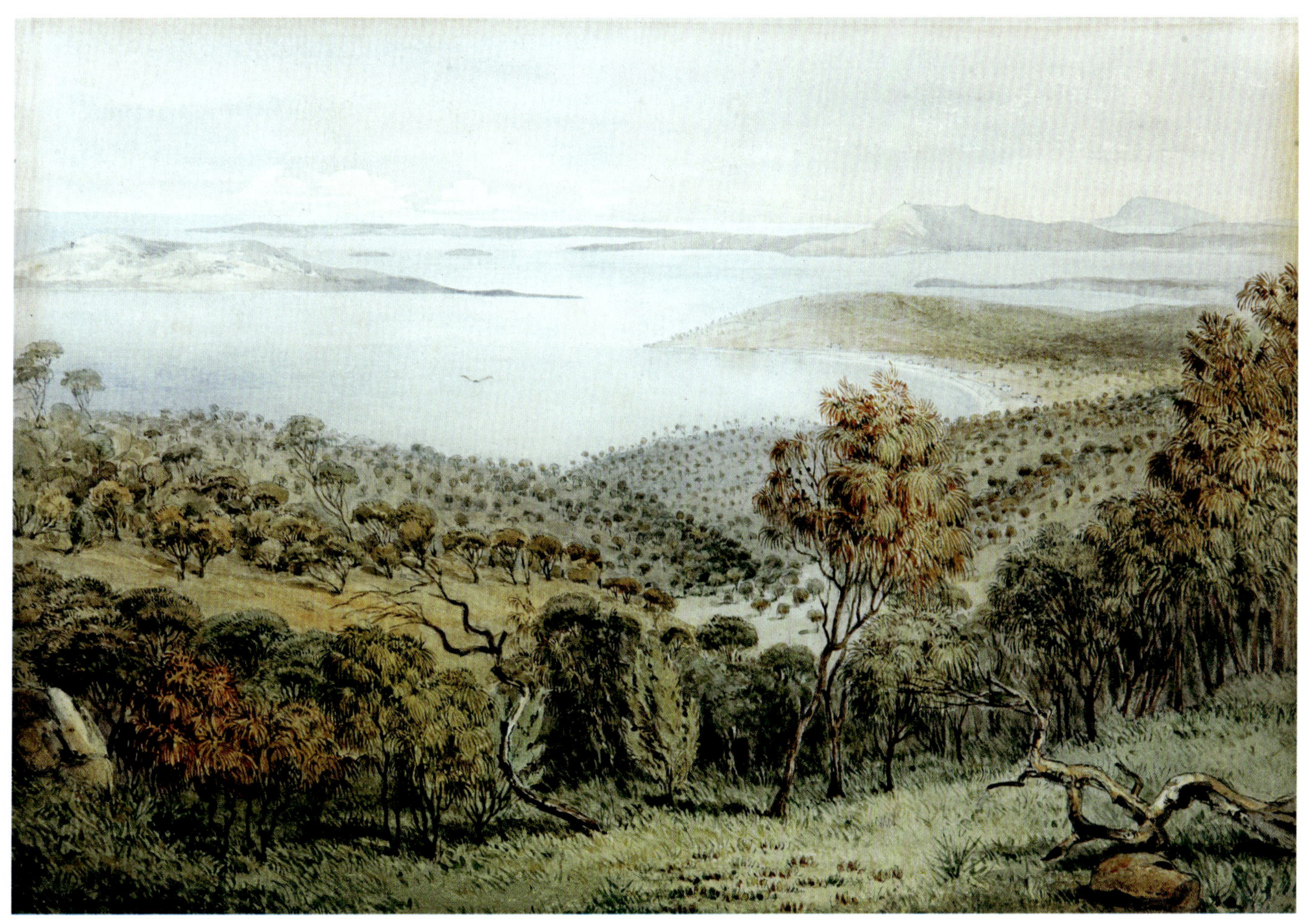

69

LUDWIG BECKER

Meteor Seen by Me on 11 October, 1860

Watercolour, 10.2 × 16.2 cm

State Library of Victoria, Melbourne

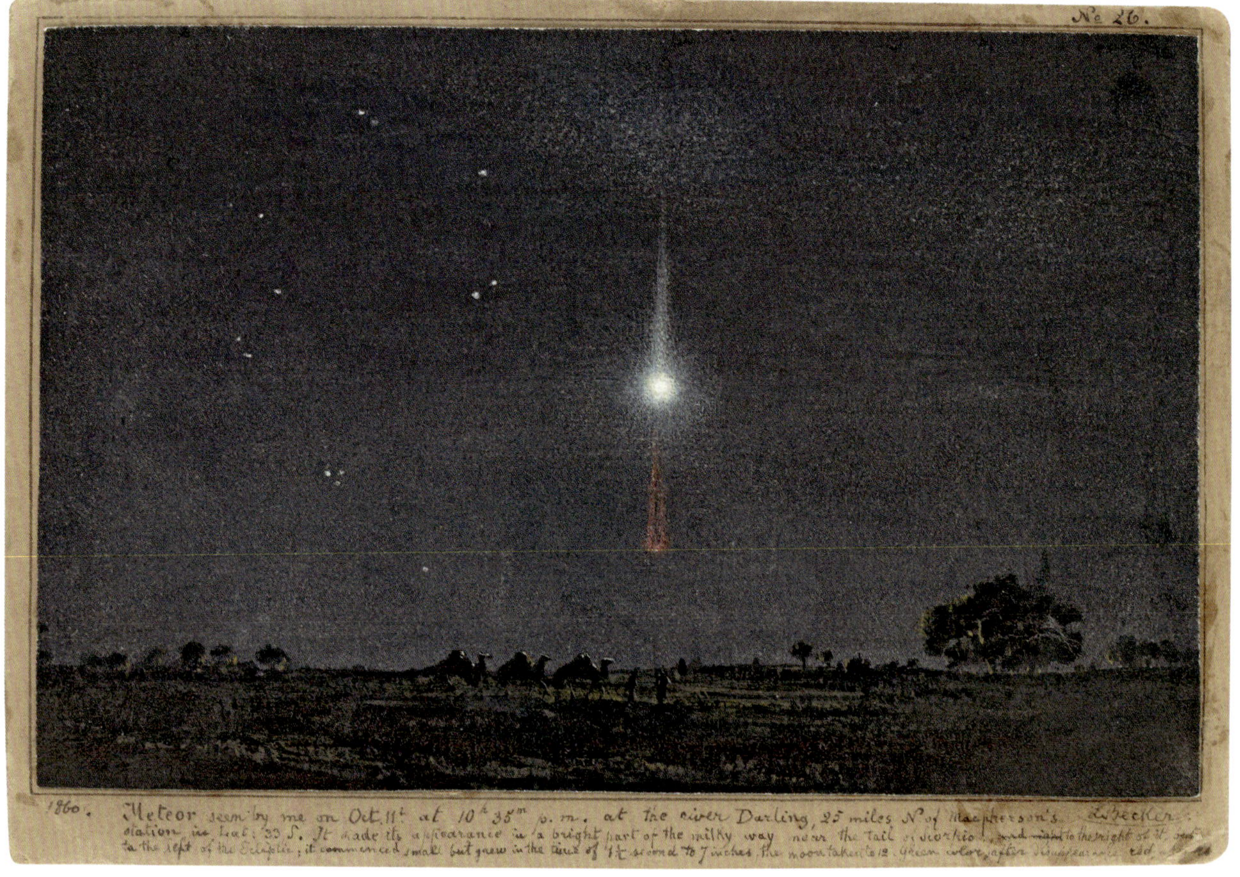

70

LUDWIG BECKER

Mallee Sand Cliffs at the Darling, 12 October, 1860

Watercolour and pencil, 12.1 × 16.1 cm

State Library of Victoria, Melbourne

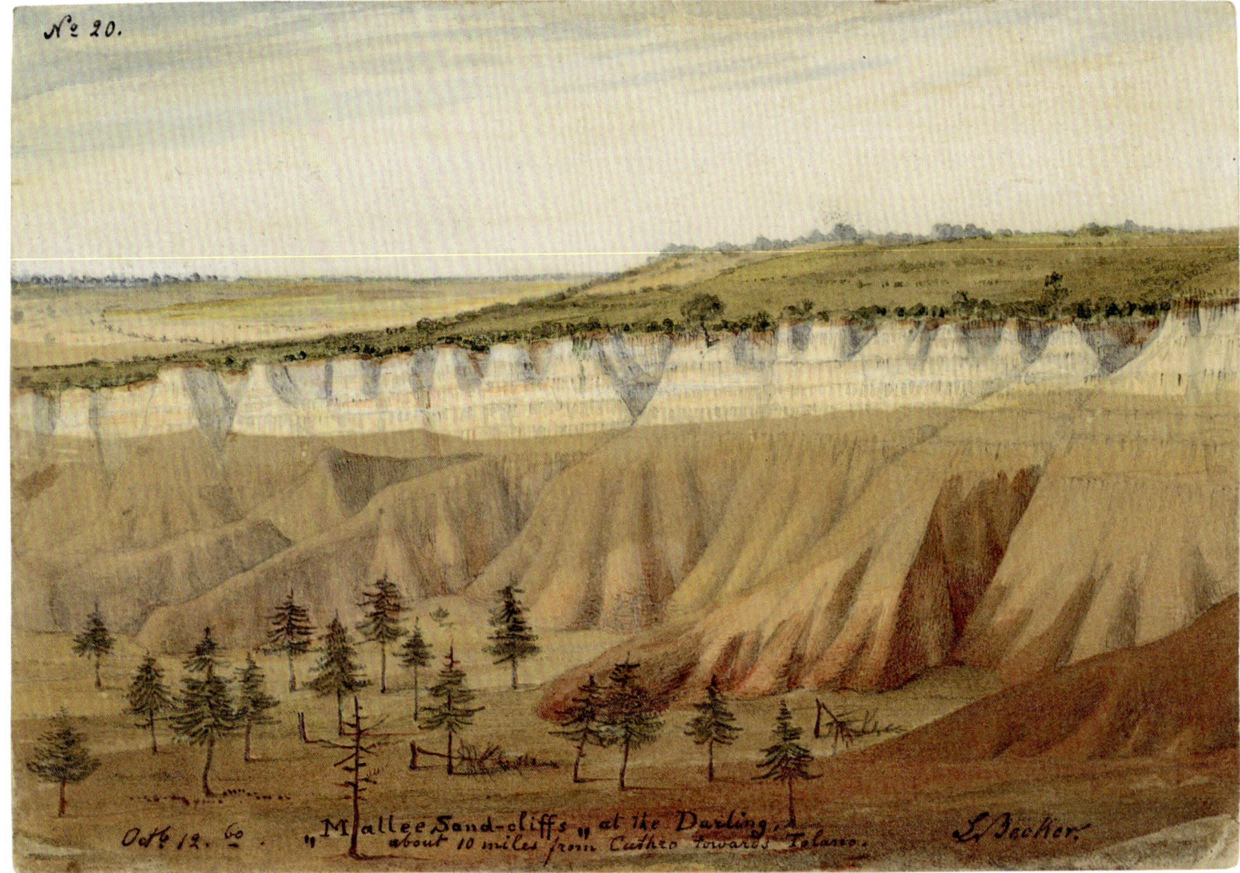

71

LUDWIG BECKER

Border of the Mud Desert near Desolation Camp, 9 March, 1861

Watercolour, 14 × 22.8 cm

State Library of Victoria, Melbourne

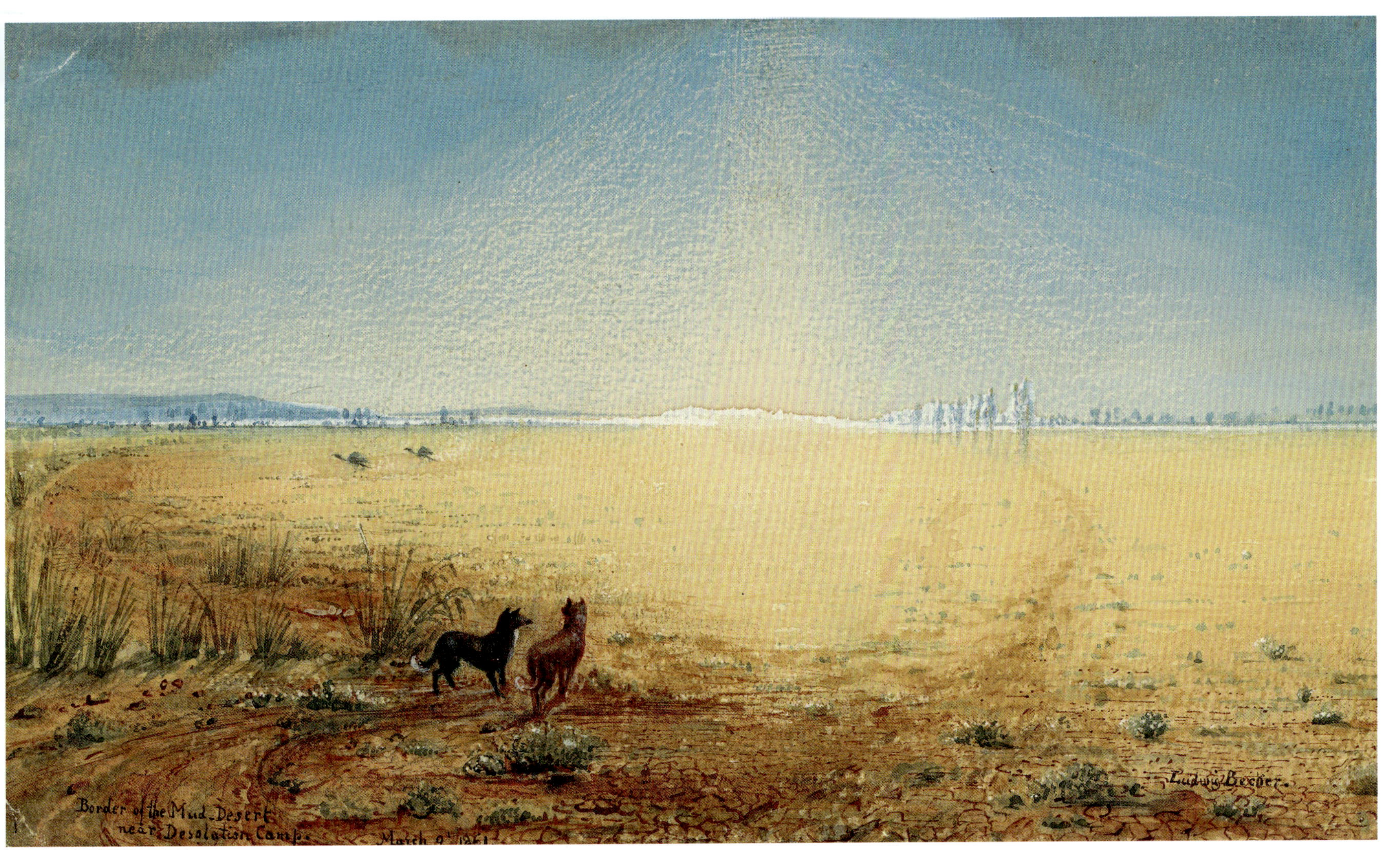

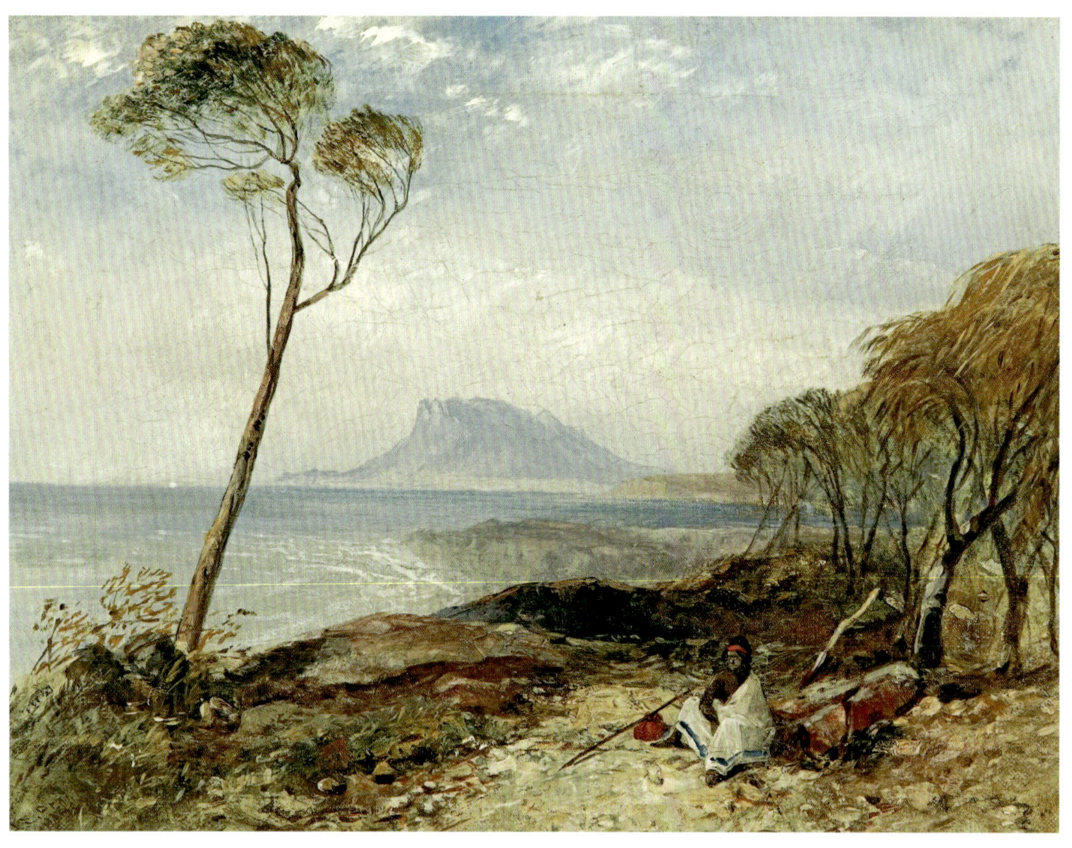

72
JOHN SKINNER PROUT
Maria Island from Little Swanport, Van Diemen's Land, *c.*1846
Oil on canvas, 29 × 35.5 cm
Art Gallery of South Australia, Adelaide. M. J. M. Carter AO Collection through the Art Gallery of South Australia Foundation, 1992

73
JOHN SKINNER PROUT
South Bank of the Yarra, near Melbourne, 1846
No. 7 in *Sketches in New South Wales, Victoria, Tasmania and Norfolk Island*, *c.*1841–47
Watercolour, Chinese white and scraping out, 37.5 × 40.5 cm
State Library of New South Wales, Sydney. Bequeathed by D. S. Mitchell, 1907

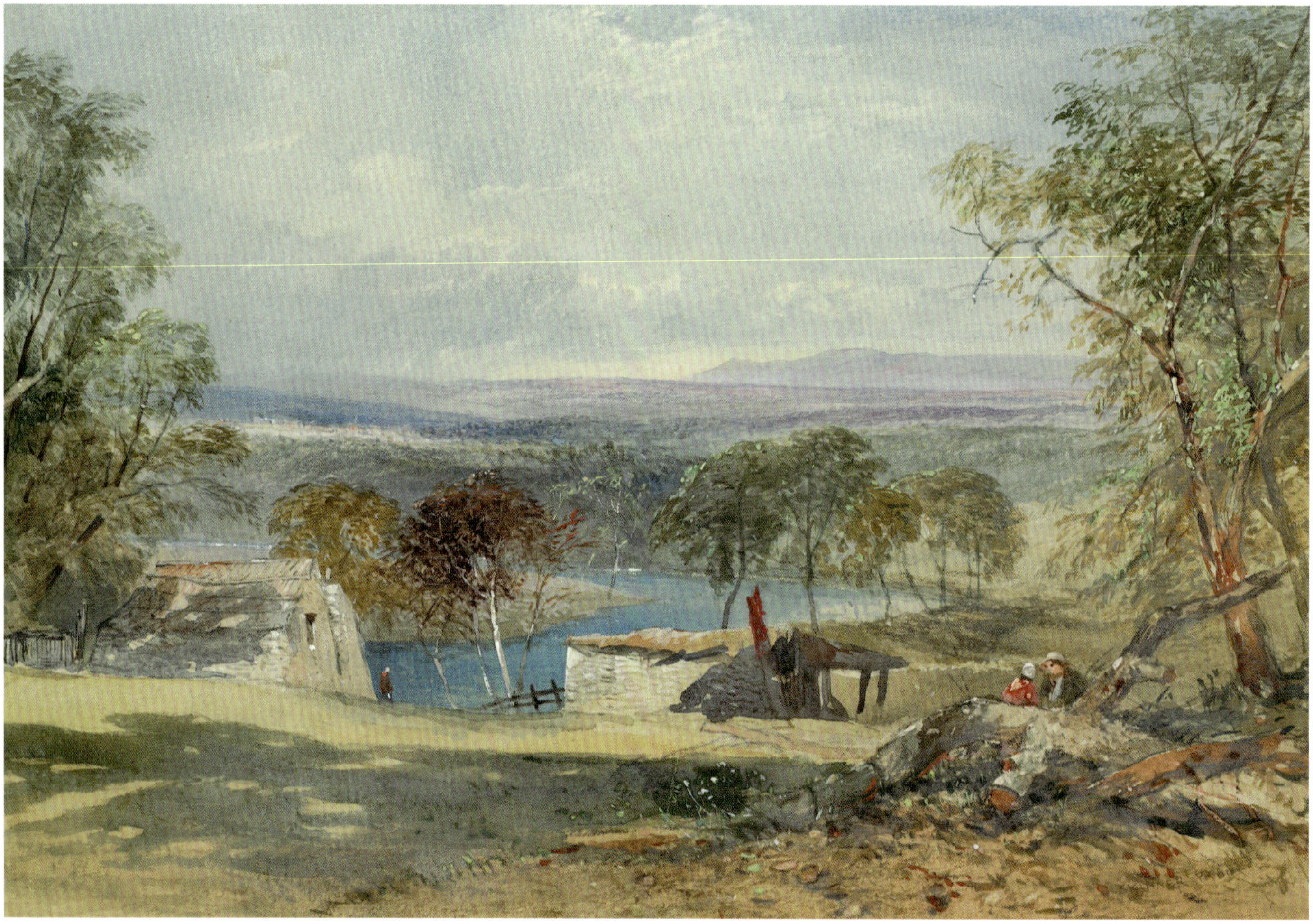

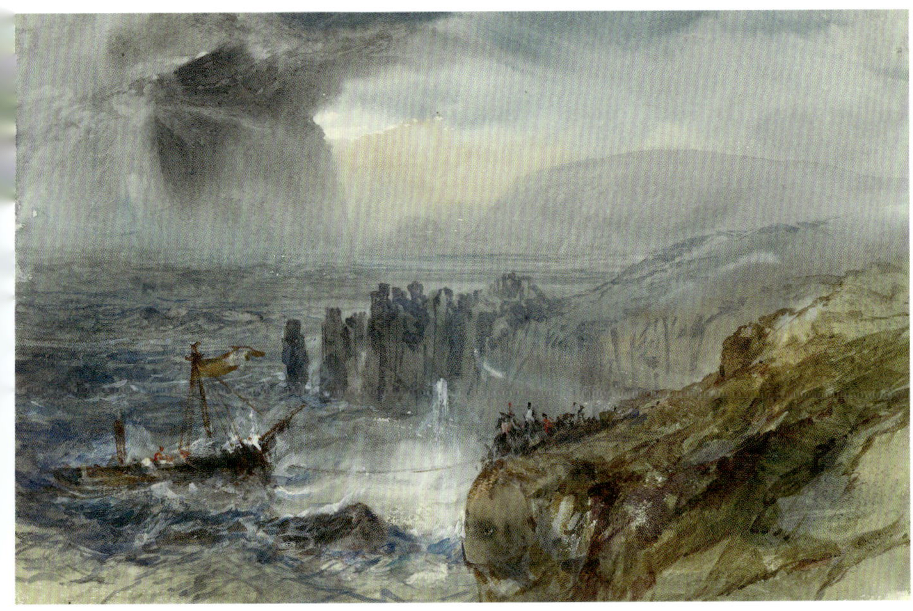

74
JOHN SKINNER PROUT
Shipwreck off Cape Pillar, 1846
Watercolour and gouache, 17 × 25.4 cm
National Gallery of Australia, Canberra. Purchased 1980

75
ALEXANDER SCHRAMM
Adelaide, A Tribe of Natives on the Banks of the River Torrens, 1850
Oil on canvas, 86.7 × 130.2 cm
National Gallery of Australia, Canberra. Purchased 2005

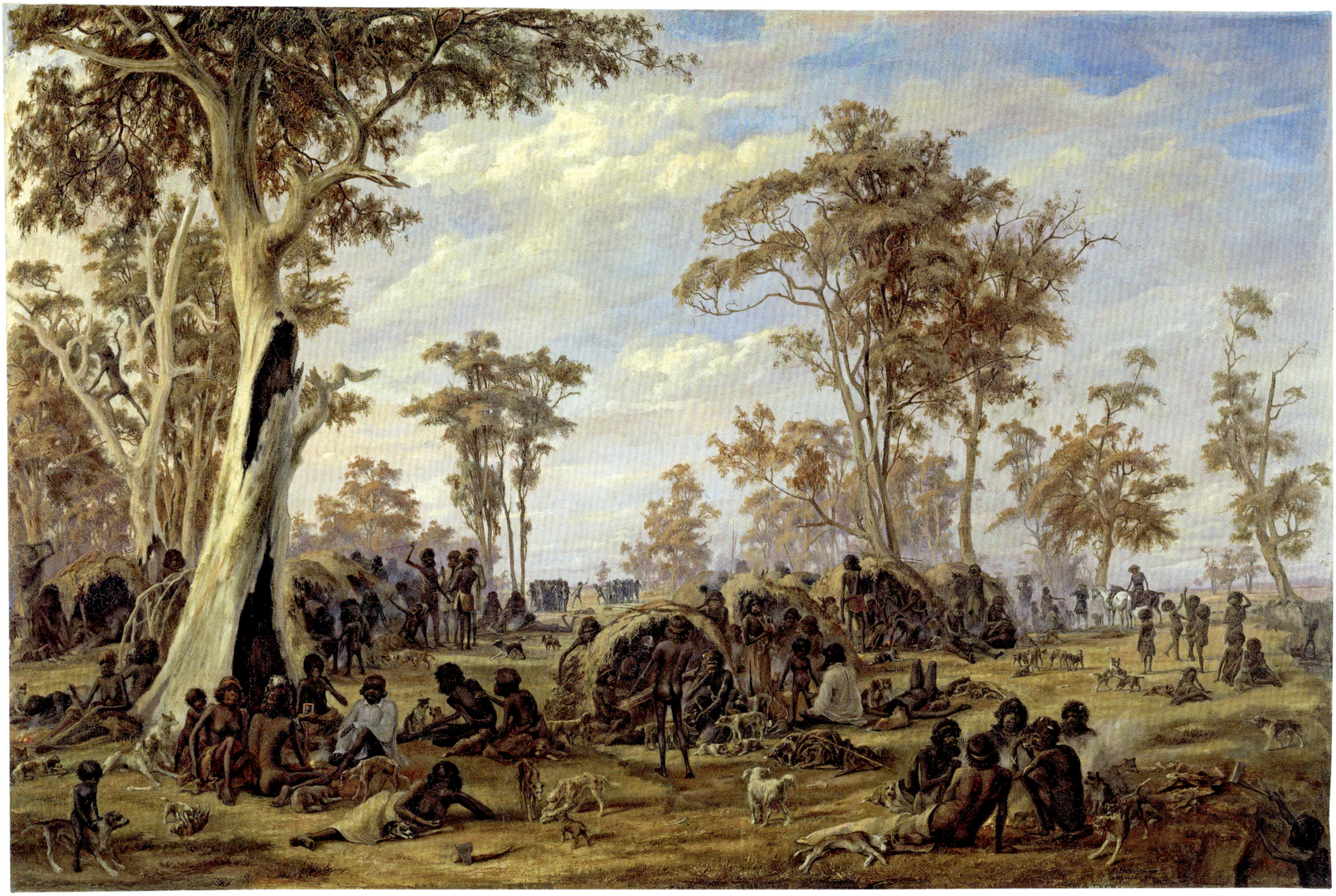

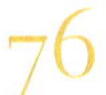

76

EUGENE VON GUERARD
Stony Rises, Lake Corangamite, 1857
Oil on canvas, 71.2 × 86.4 cm
Art Gallery of South Australia, Adelaide. Purchased with the assistance of the Utah Foundation through the Art Gallery of South Australia Foundation, 1981

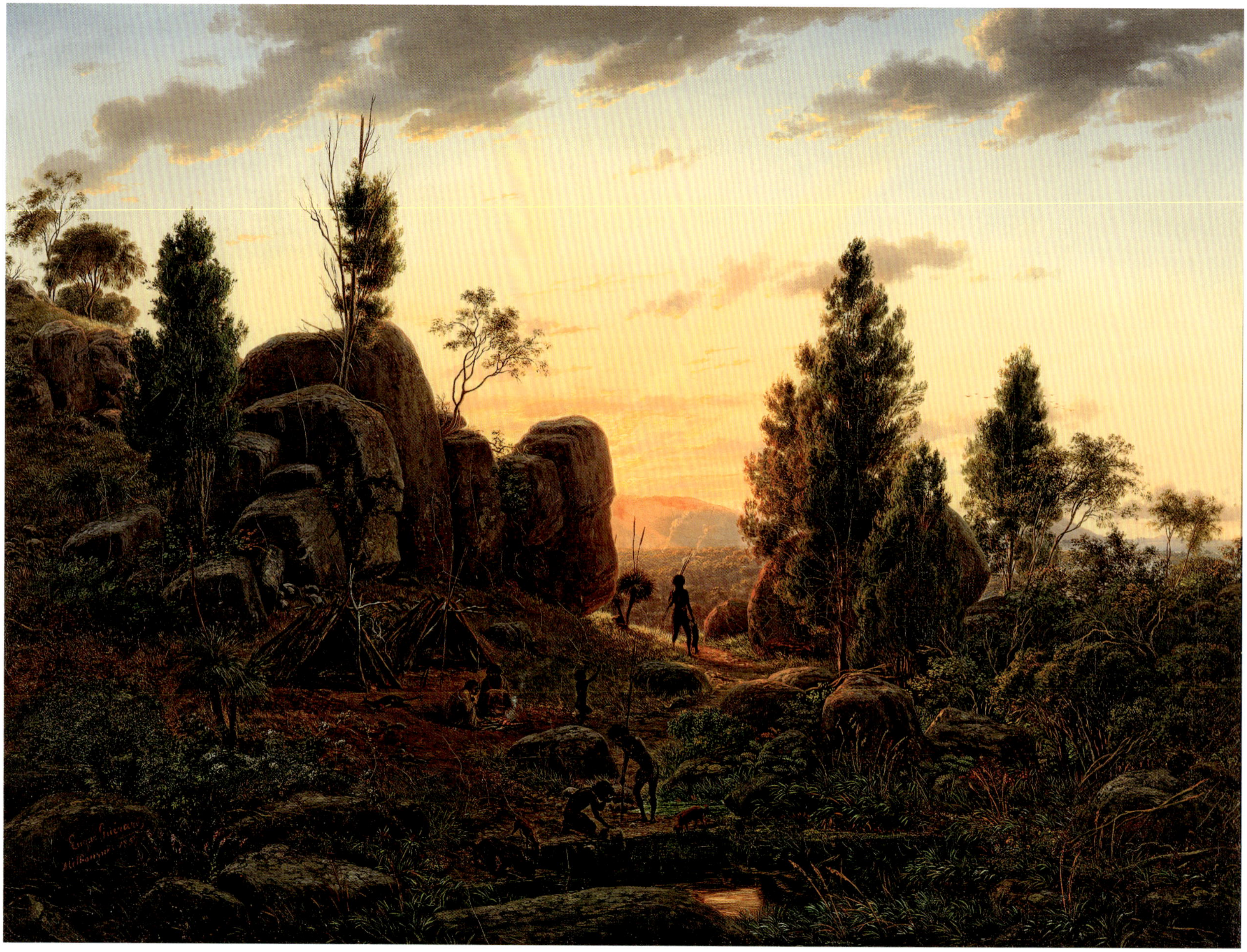

77
EUGENE VON GUERARD
Ferntree Gully in the Dandenong Ranges, 1857
Oil on canvas, 92 × 138 cm
National Gallery of Australia, Canberra. Gift of Dr Joseph Brown AO, OBE, 1975

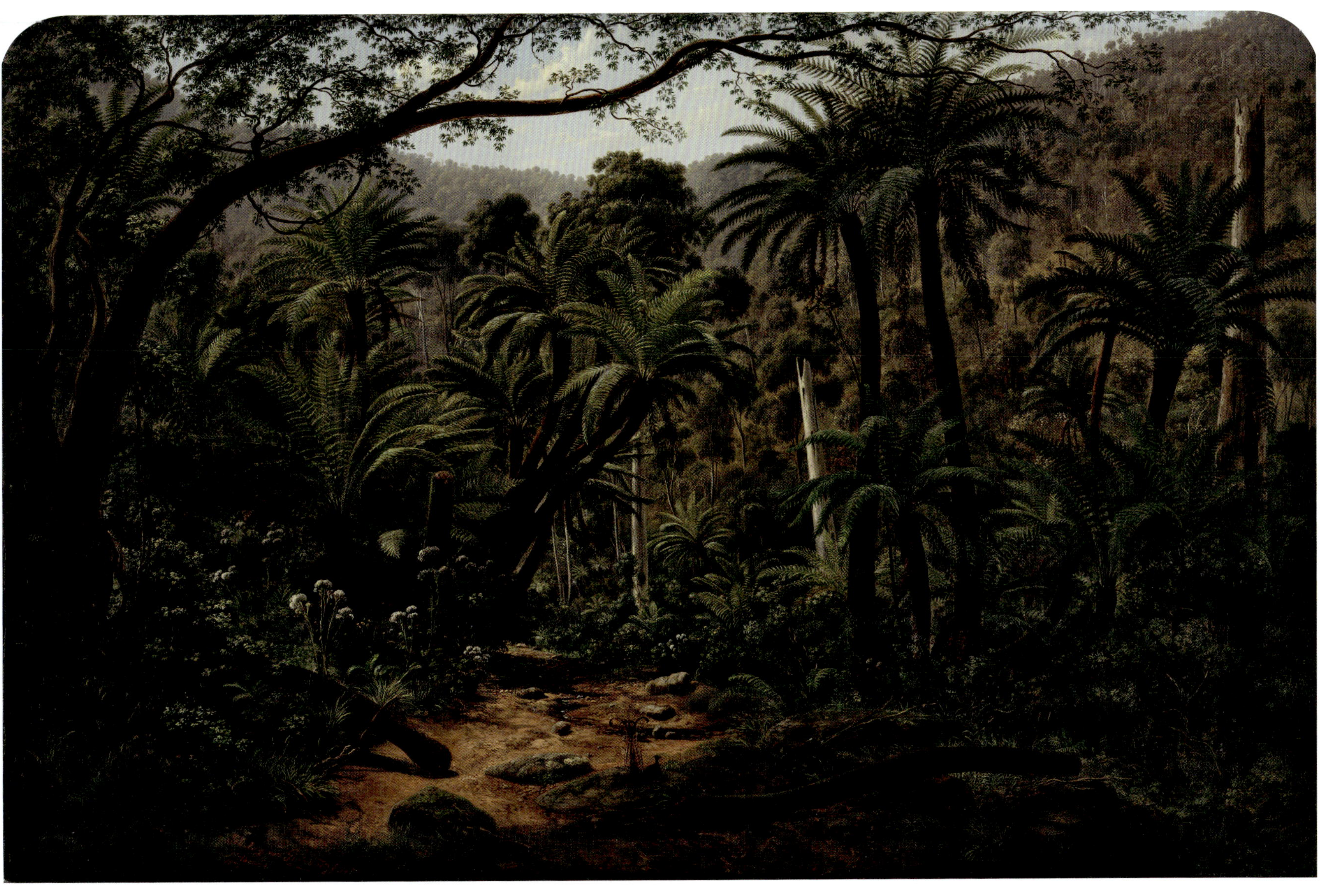

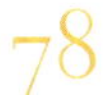

EUGENE VON GUERARD

Purrumbete from across the Lake, 1858

Oil on canvas, 51 × 85.5 cm

National Gallery of Australia, Canberra. Purchased with funds from the Nerissa Johnson Bequest, 1998

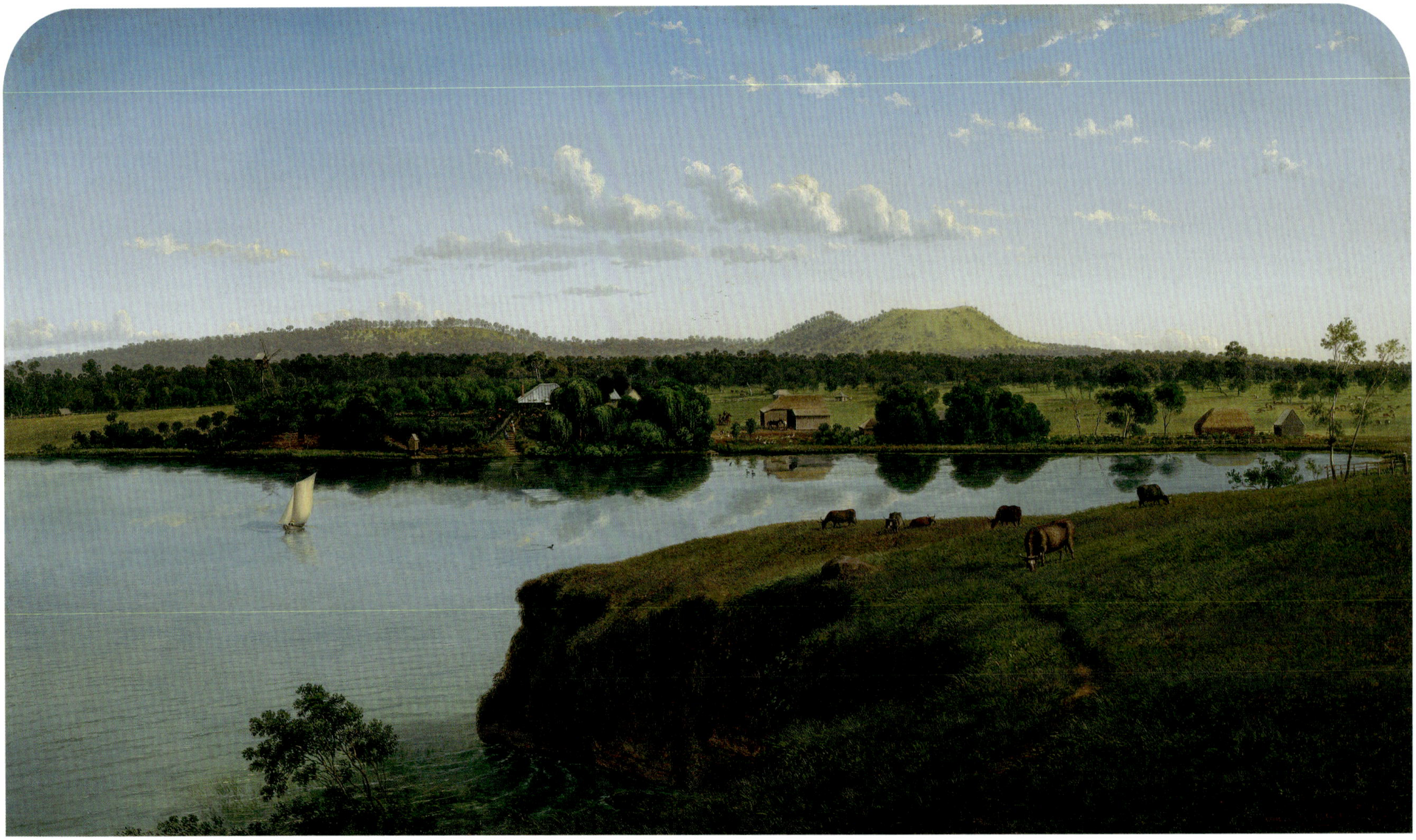

79
EUGENE VON GUERARD
From the Verandah of Purrumbete, 1858
Oil on canvas, 51.4 × 86.3 cm
National Gallery of Australia, Canberra. Purchased 1978

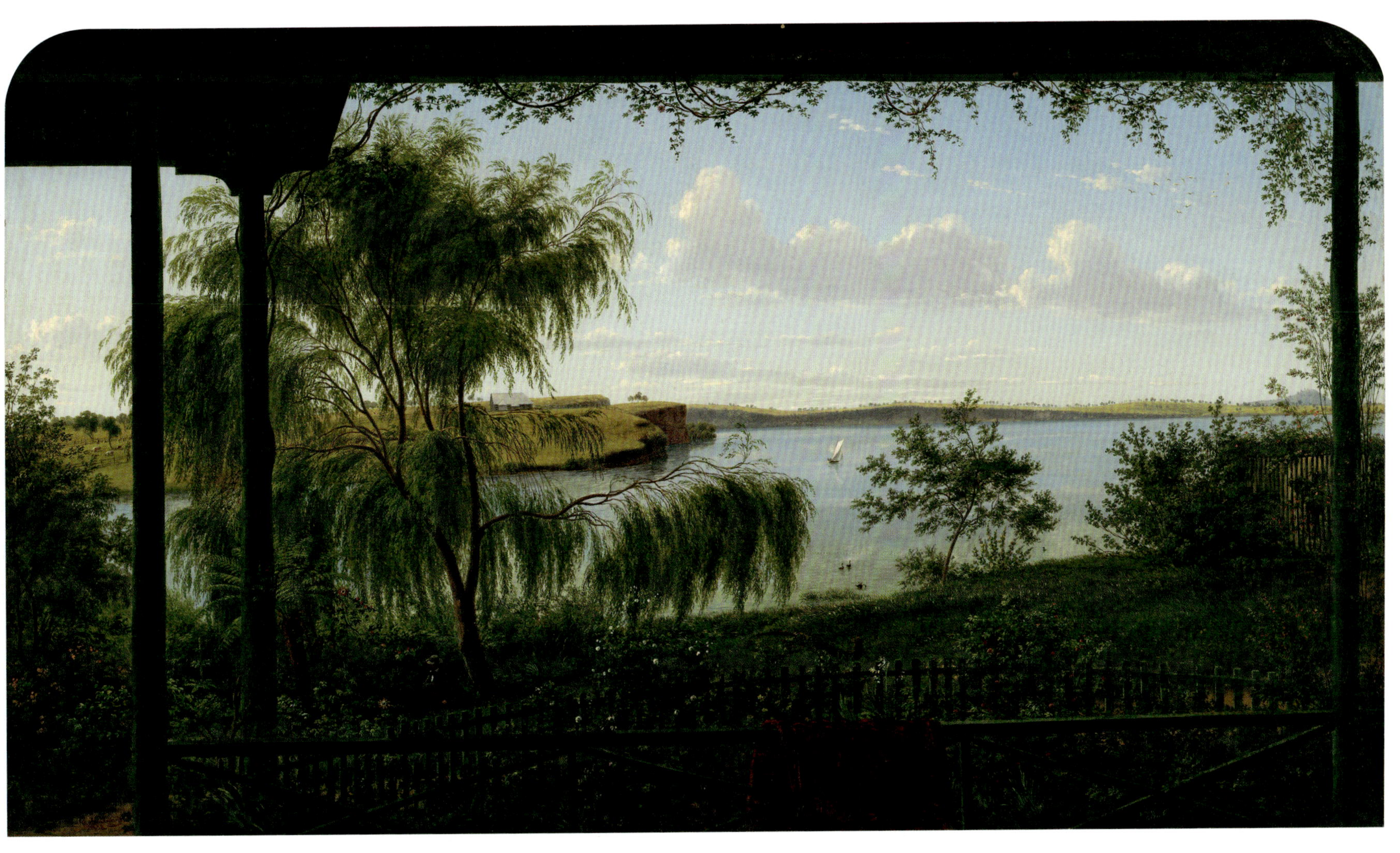

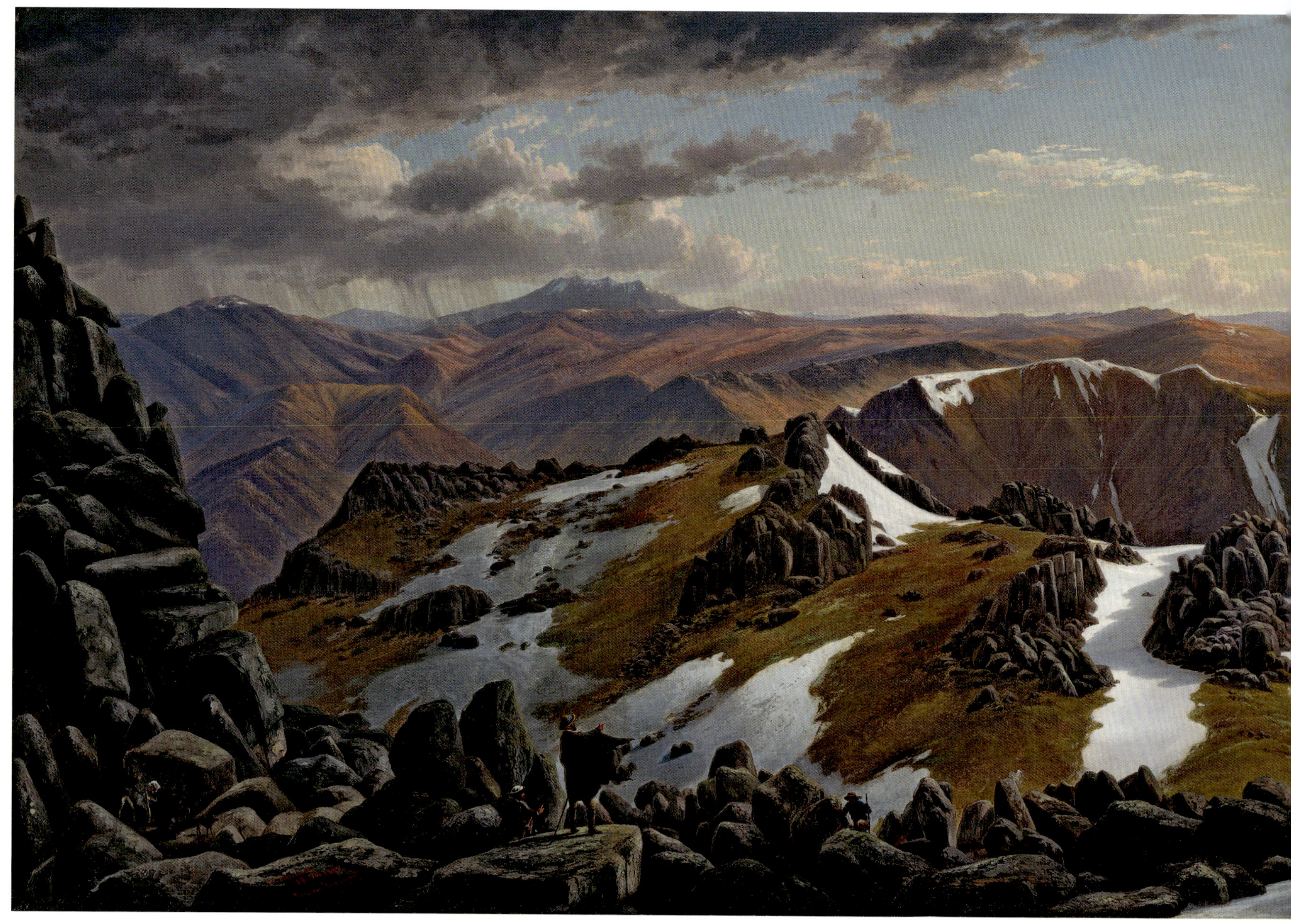

80

EUGENE VON GUERARD
North-east View from the Northern Top of Mount Kosciusko, 1863
Oil on canvas, 66.5 × 116.8 cm
National Gallery of Australia, Canberra. Purchased 1973

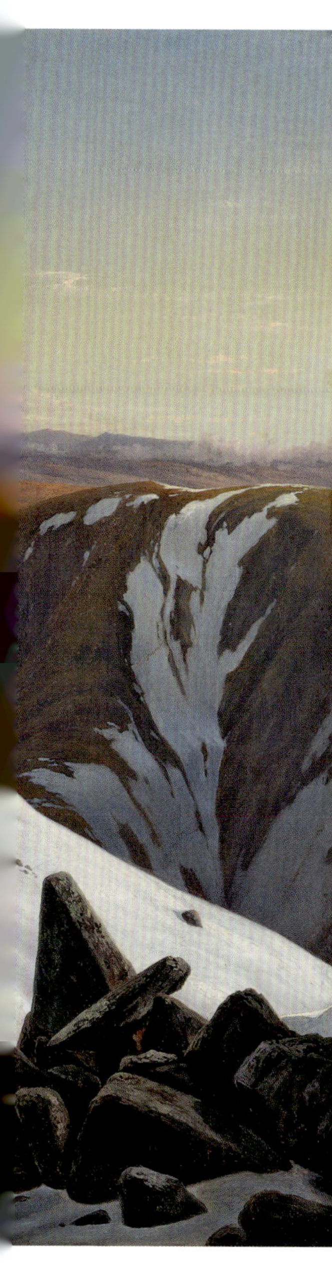

81

EUGENE VON GUERARD
Bushfire, 1859
Oil on canvas mounted on board,
34.8 × 56.3 cm

Art Gallery of Ballarat, Victoria. Gift of Lady Currie in memory of her husband, the late Sir Alan Currie, 1948

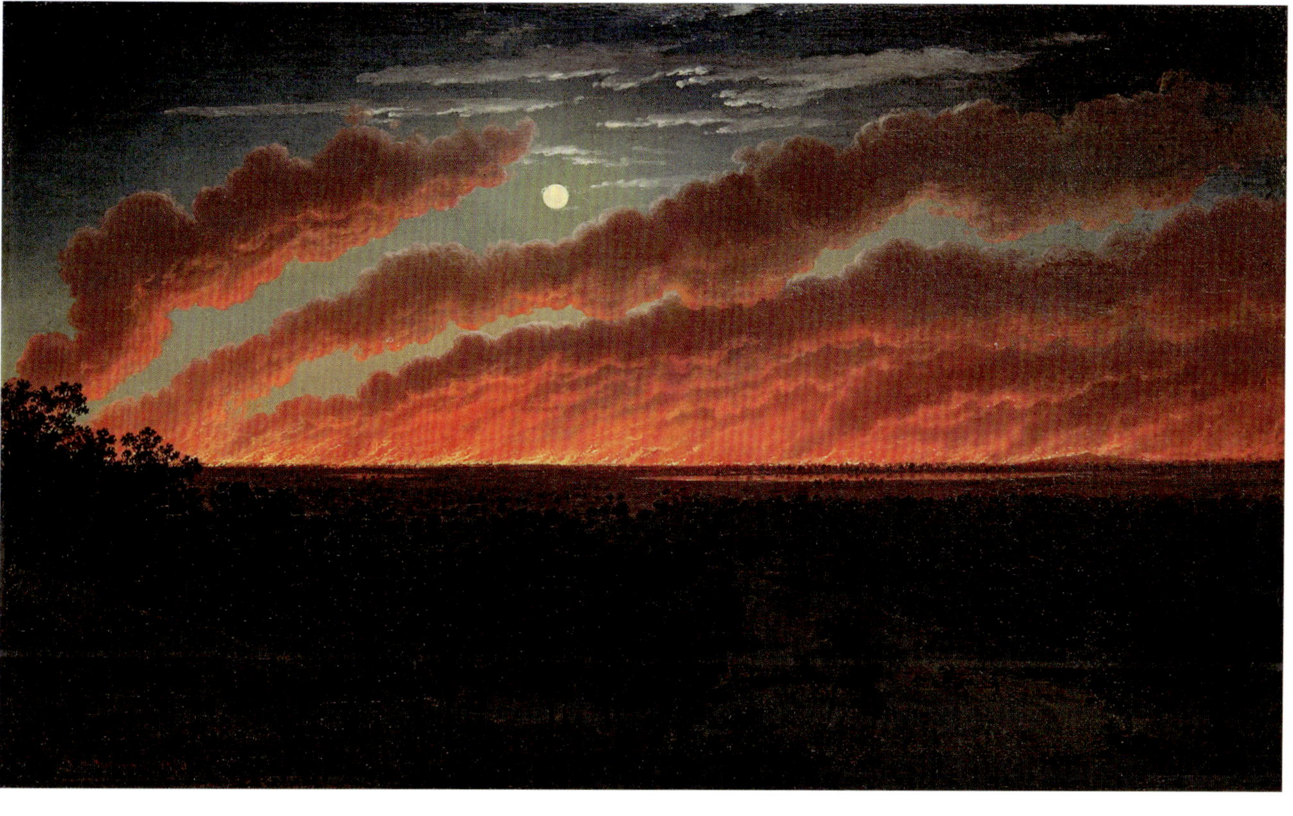

82

HENRY STEINER
Inkwell, *c.* 1870
Silver, emu egg, brass, blackwood,
29.1 × 28.6 × 19.8 cm

National Gallery of Victoria, Melbourne.
The Altmann Collection of Australian Silver, presented through the Art Foundation of Victoria by John and Jan Altmann, Founder Benefactors, 1986

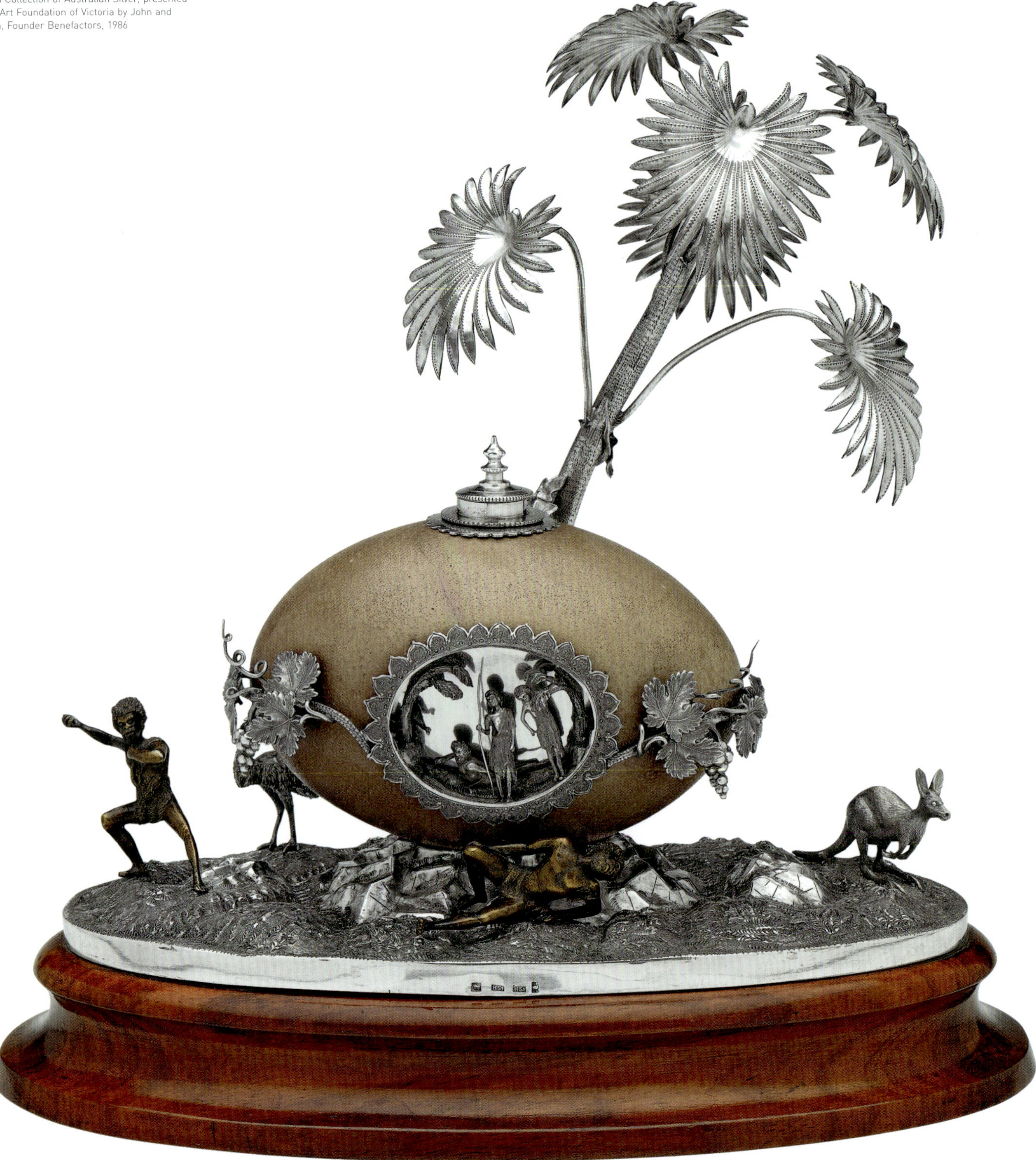

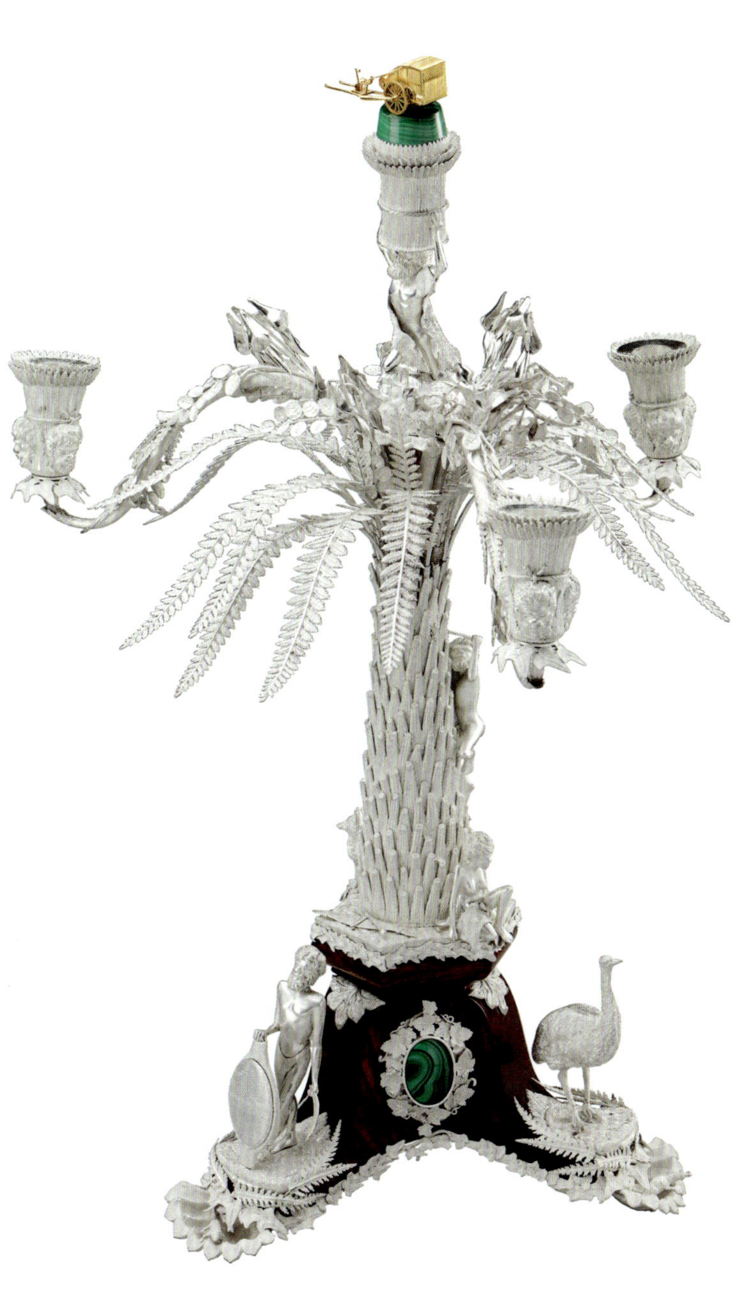

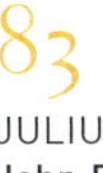

83

JULIUS SCHOMBURGK

John Ridley Testimonial Candelabrum, 1860

Silver, gold, malachite and blackwood, 64 × 42 cm

University of Adelaide Visual Art Collection. Gift of Miss J. T. Ridley, 1930

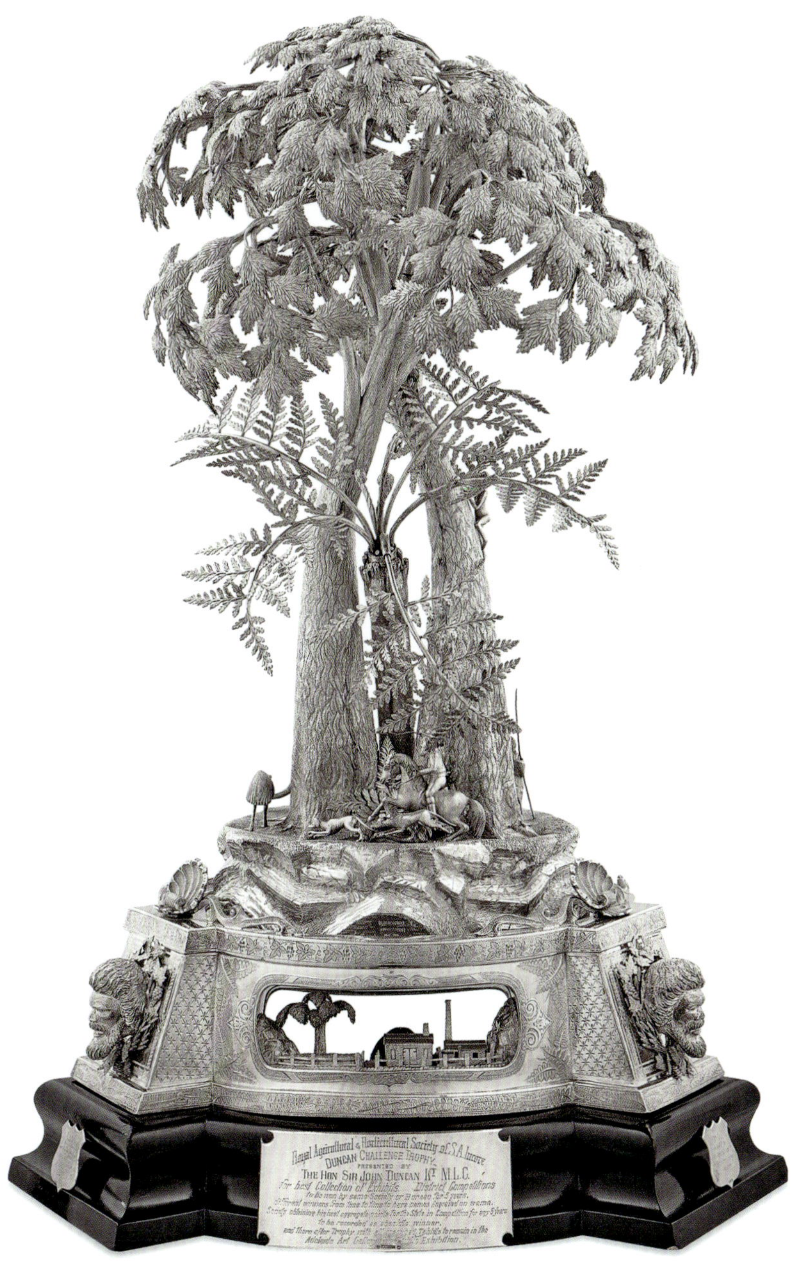

84

JULIUS SCHOMBURGK

Duncan Challenge Trophy, *c.* 1875

Silver, 66.5 × 37.5 cm

Royal Agricultural and Horticultural Society of South Australia, Adelaide. Awarded 1920

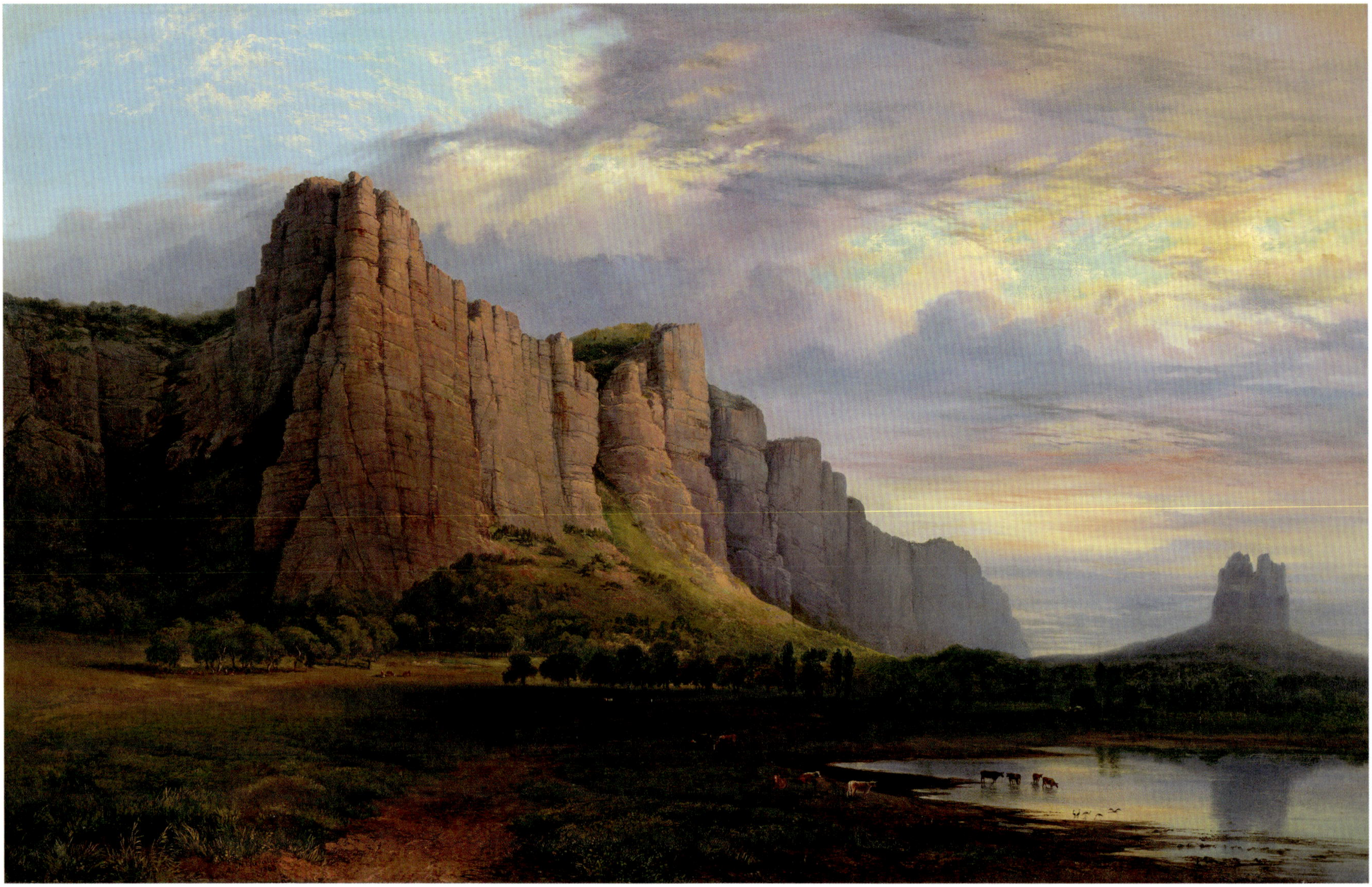

85

NICHOLAS CHEVALIER
Mount Arapiles and the Mitre Rock, 1863
Oil on canvas, 77.5 × 120.6 cm
National Gallery of Australia, Canberra. Gift of Dr Joseph Brown AO, OBE, 1979

86

RICHARD DAINTREE
Gold Diggers' Sale, Queensland, 1864–70
Albumen silver photograph, overpainted in oil, mounted on canvas, 39.2 × 60.7 cm
National Library of Australia, Canberra. Rex Nan Kivell Collection, 1959

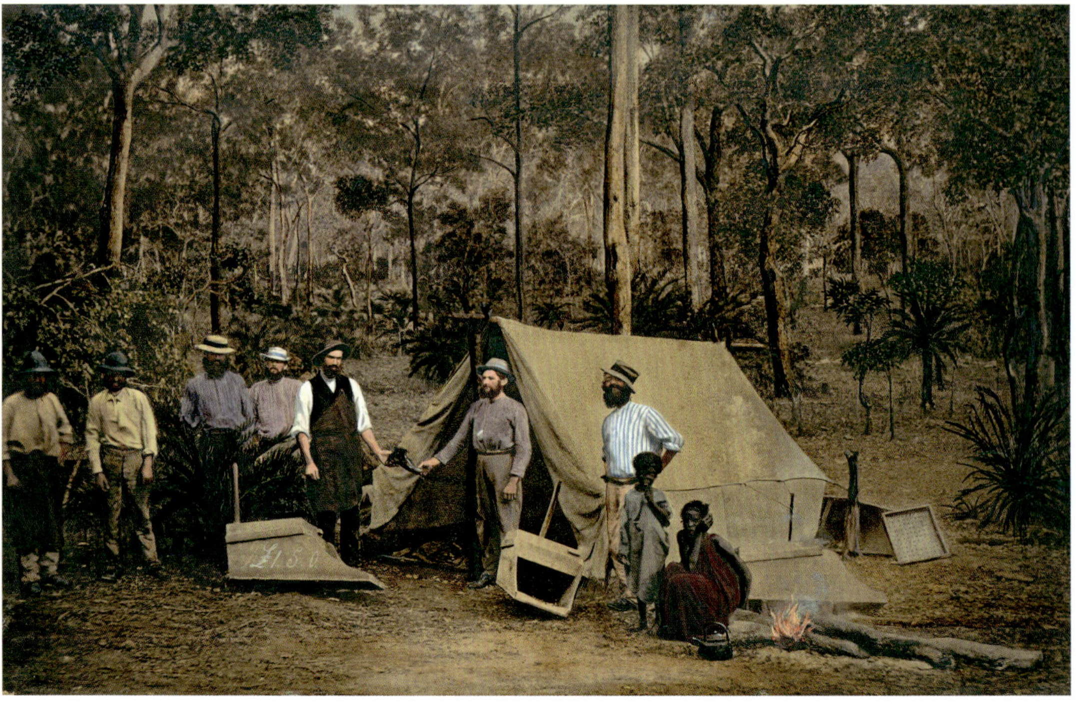

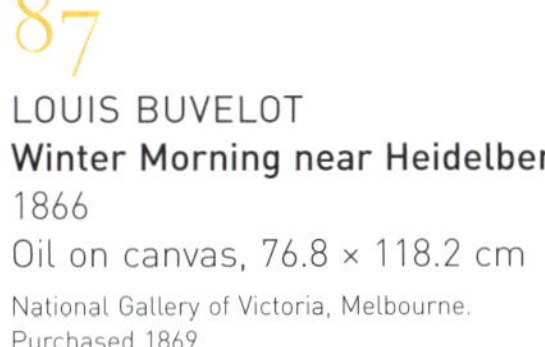

87

LOUIS BUVELOT

Winter Morning near Heidelberg, 1866

Oil on canvas, 76.8 × 118.2 cm

National Gallery of Victoria, Melbourne. Purchased 1869

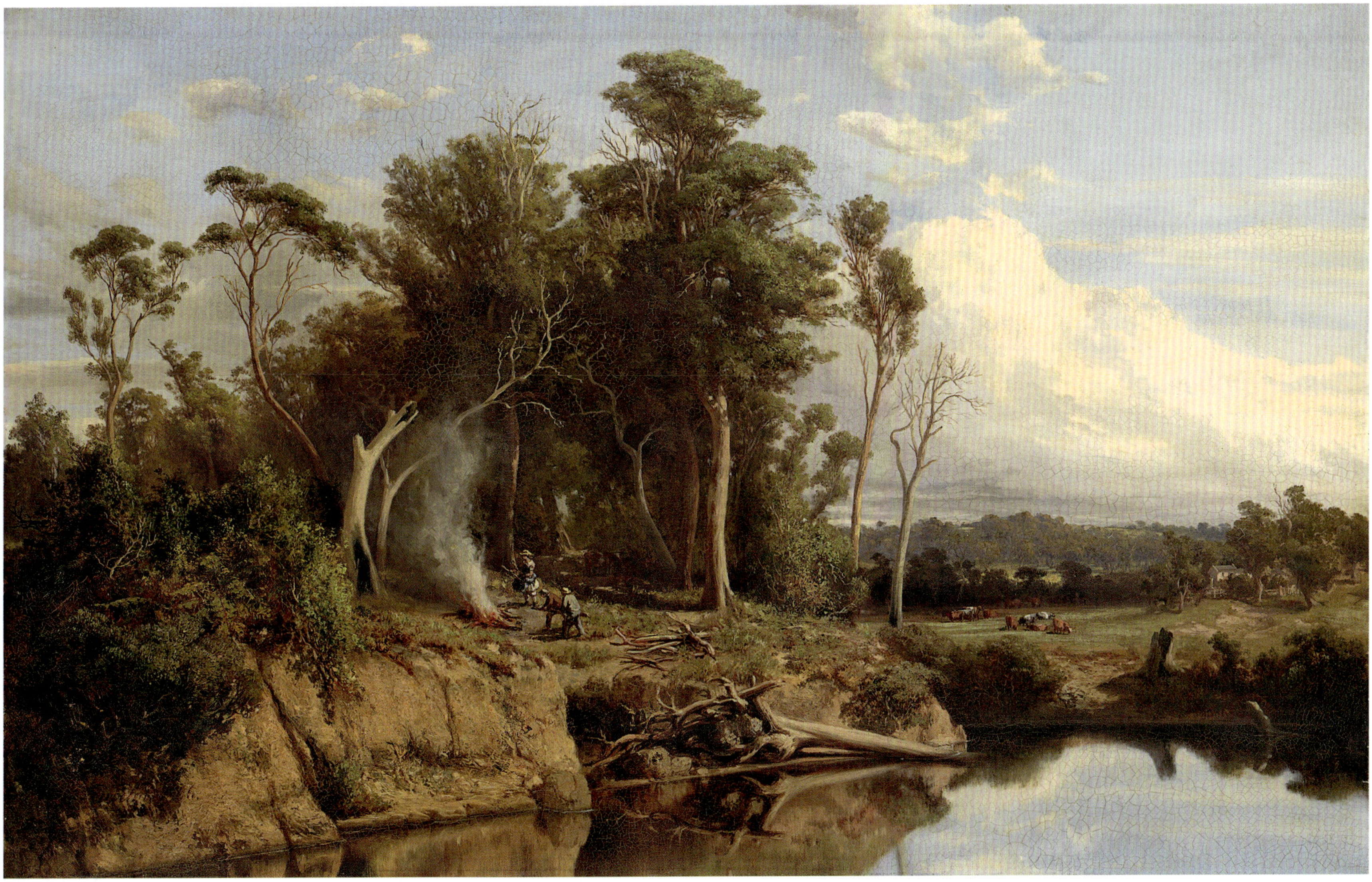

88

ISAAC WHITEHEAD

In the Sassafras Valley, Victoria, 1875

Oil on canvas, 99.2 × 132.9 cm

Art Gallery of South Australia, Adelaide. M. J. M. Carter AO Collection and the South Australian Government, 1996

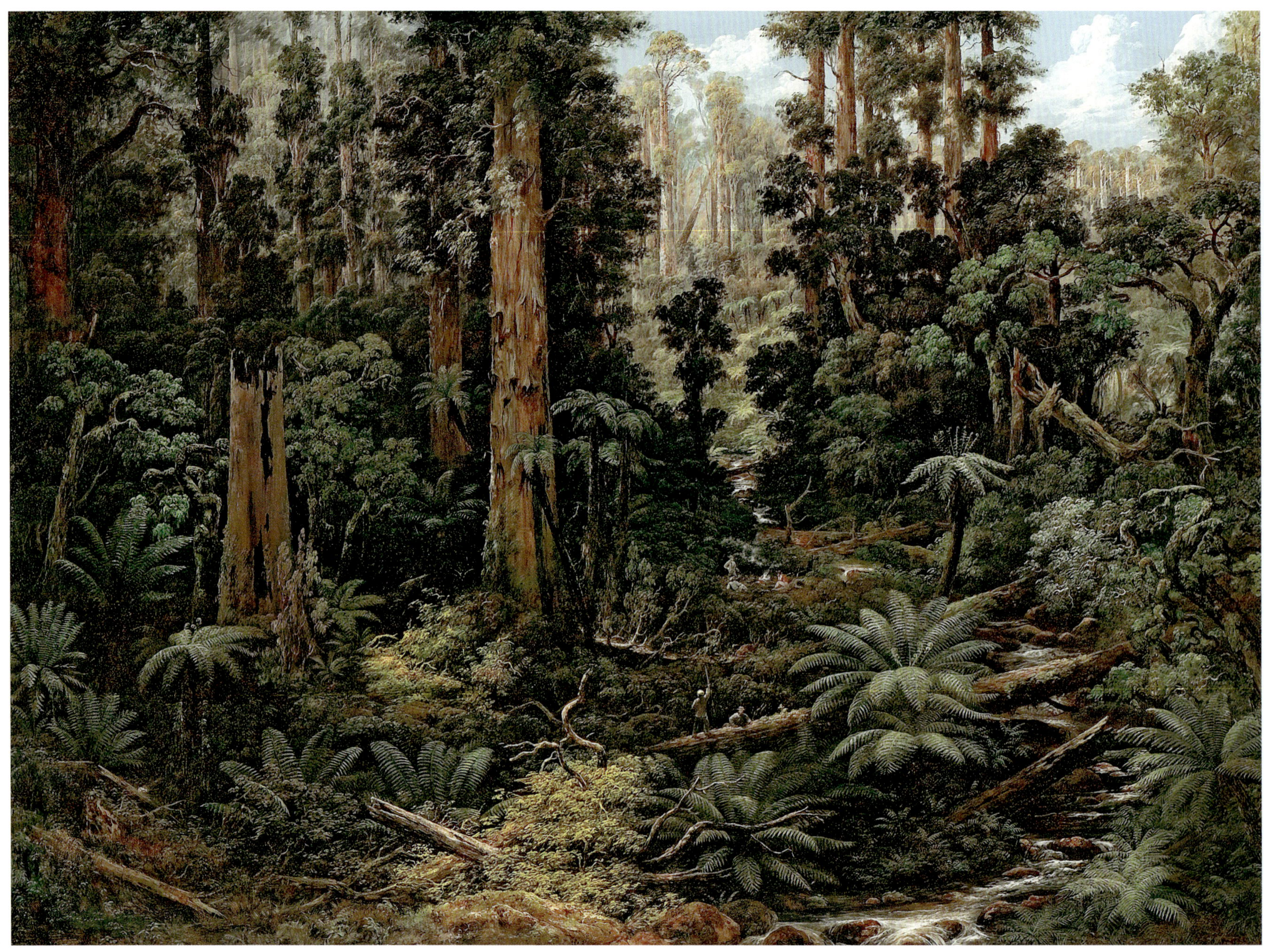

89

NICHOLAS CAIRE
Fairy Scene at the Landslip, Blacks' Spur, Victoria, 1878
Albumen silver photograph, 27.4 × 22.5 cm
National Gallery of Australia, Canberra. Joseph Brown Fund, 1981

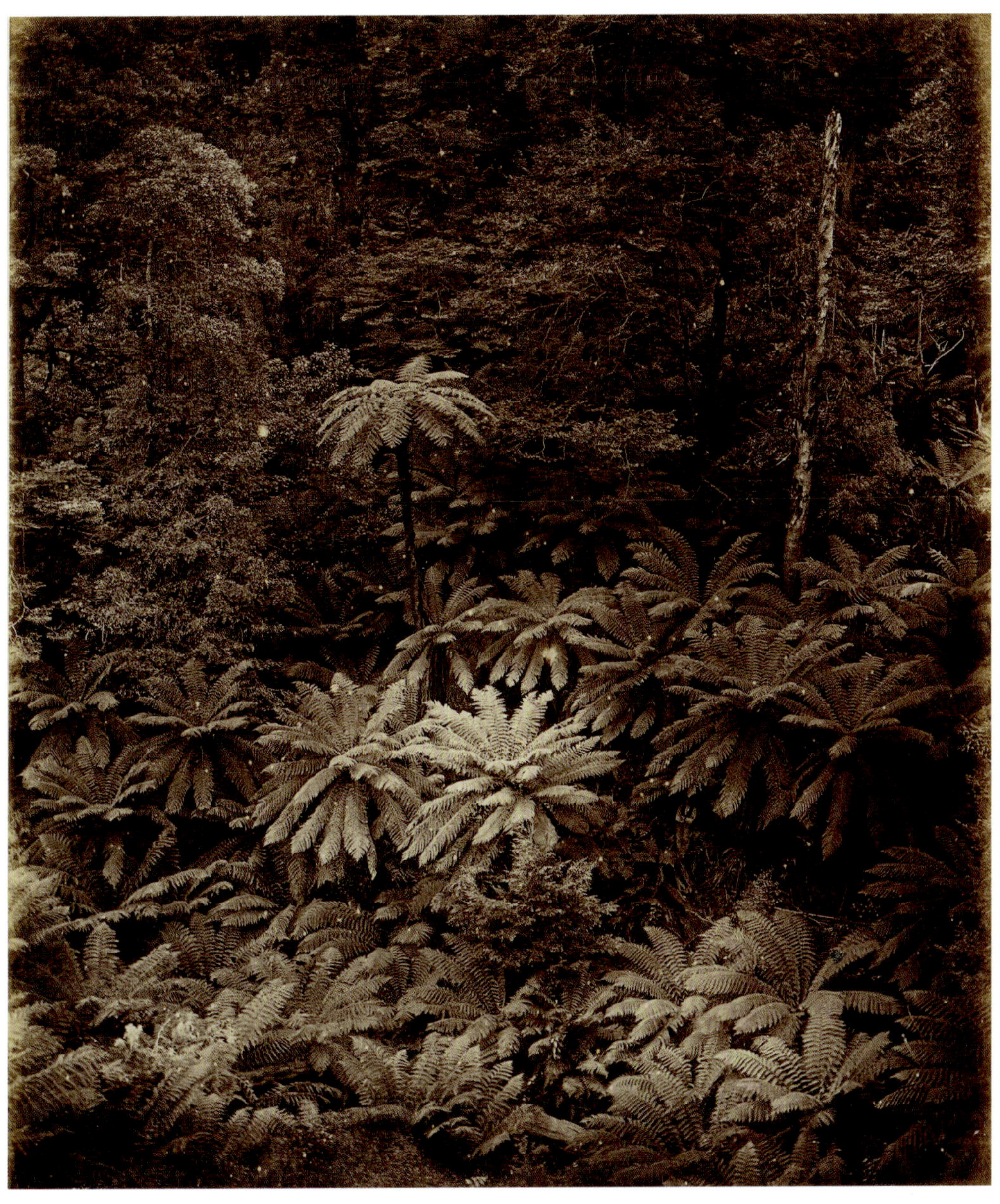

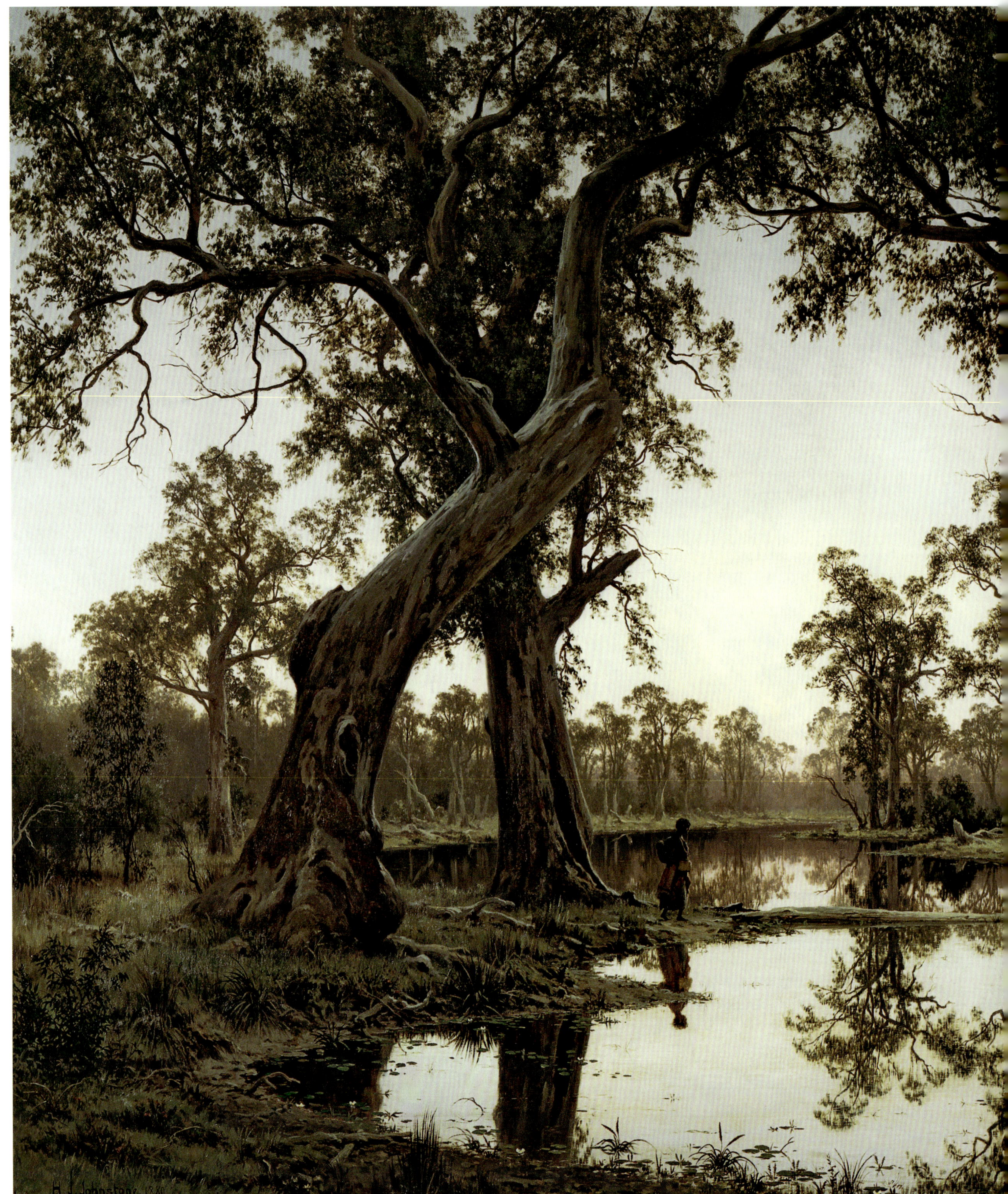
H. J. Johnstone. 1880.

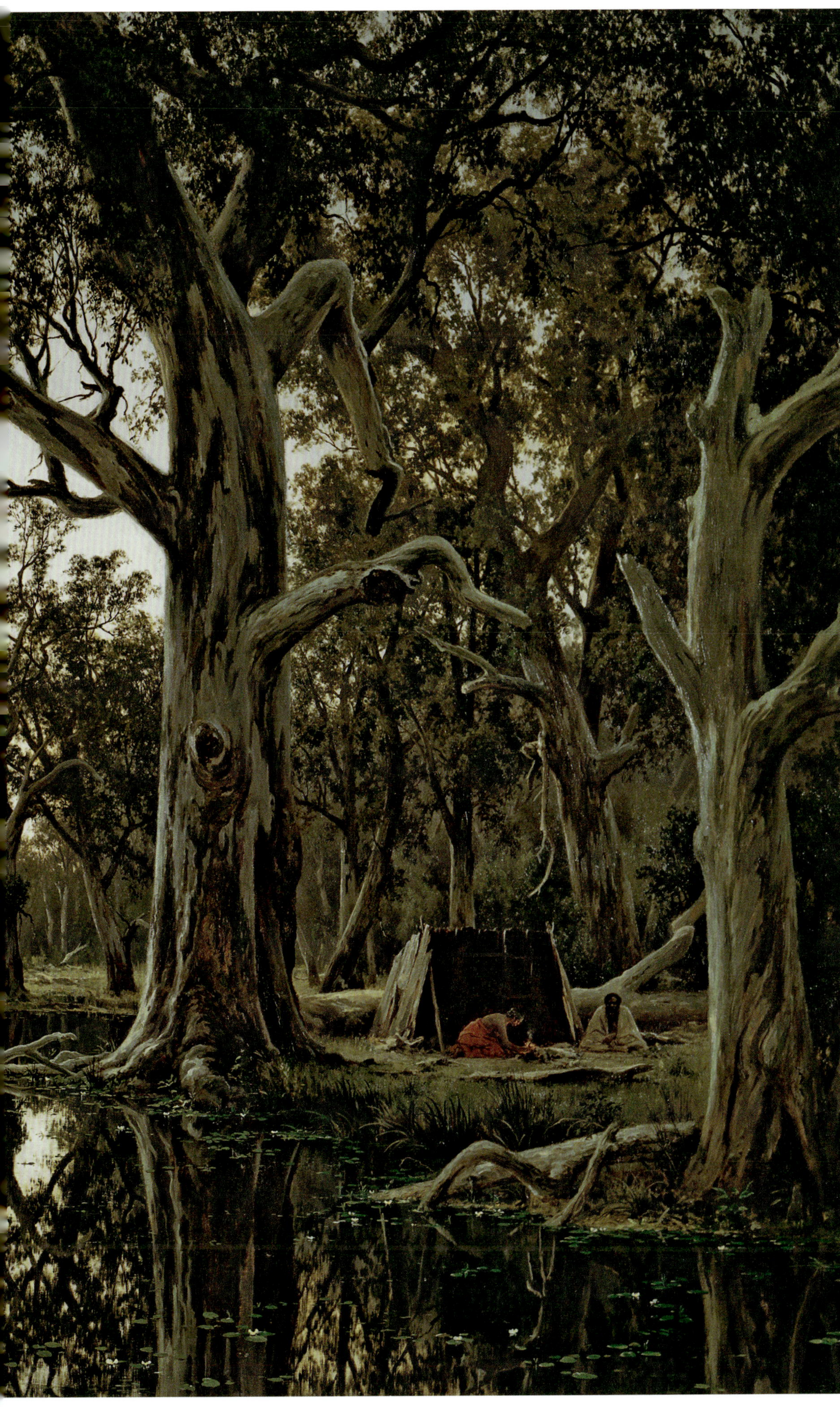

90

H. J. JOHNSTONE

Evening Shadows, Backwater of the Murray, South Australia, 1880

Oil on canvas, 120.6 × 184.1 cm

Art Gallery of South Australia, Adelaide.
Gift of Mr Henry Yorke Sparks, 1881

ART NATION: AUSTRALIAN LANDSCAPE 1880–1920

ANNE GRAY

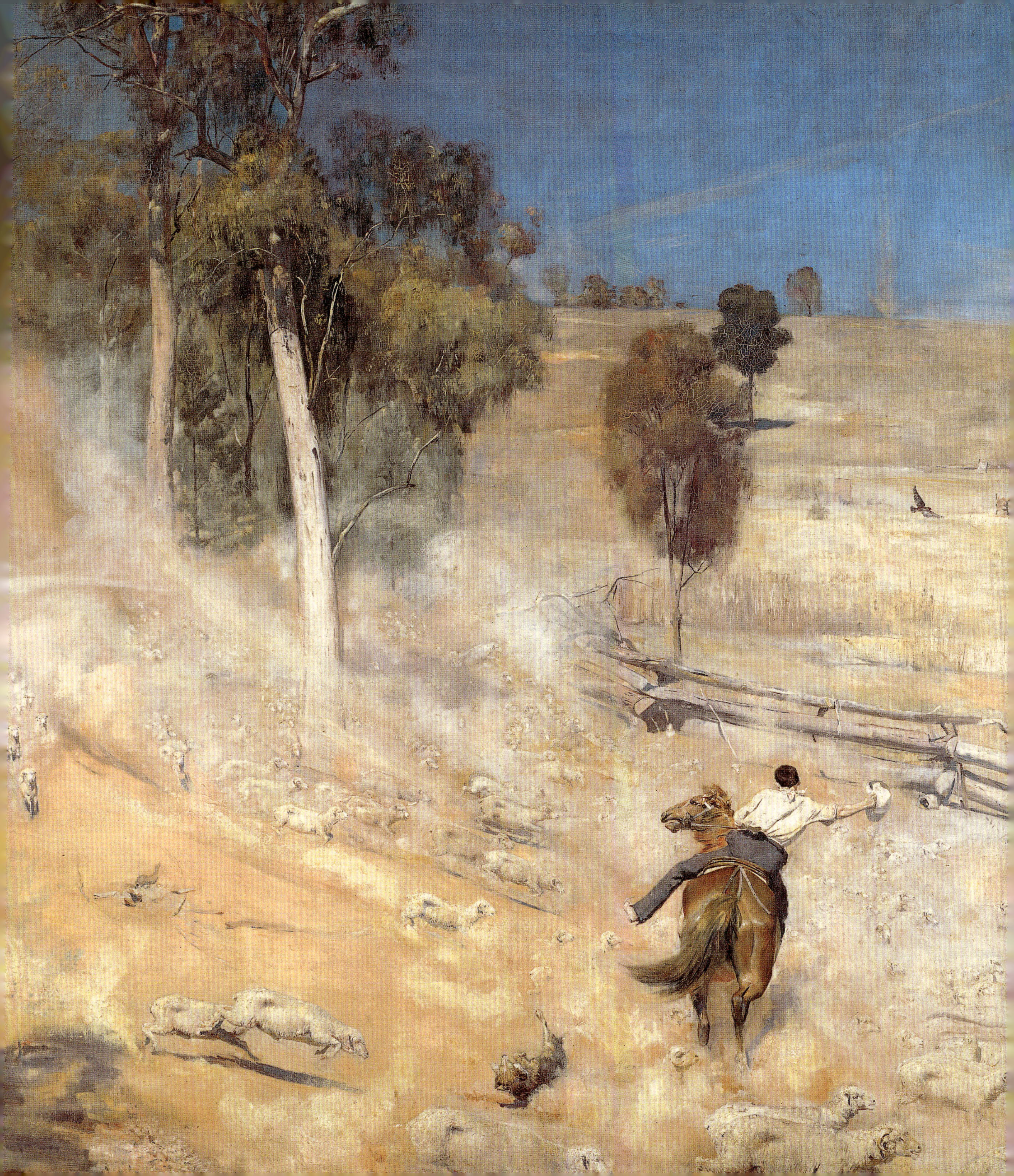

Fig. 26
TOM ROBERTS, **A Summer Morning Tiff**, 1886. Oil on canvas, 76.5 × 51.2 cm
Art Gallery of Ballarat, Victoria. The Pinkerton Bequest Fund, 1943

In the late nineteenth century some of Australia's best-known and most loved artists, the so-called Australian Impressionists – Tom Roberts, Frederick McCubbin, Arthur Streeton and Charles Conder – came into prominence. This was a period of excitement and change in Australian art, and in particular in landscape art, and it was a time when artists began to talk about an Australian tradition. Indeed, in the 1880s there was a self-conscious desire to create a national school and to develop a local market for Australian art. This may partly have been because several of the artists – W. C. Piguenit, McCubbin, David Davies, Streeton, Sydney Long and J. J. Hilder – were Australian by birth. Certainly, Long (1905) and McCubbin (1916), and later Streeton (1934), set out their ideas about Australian art, emphasising the achievements of the artists of their own time.[1] The drive for a specifically Australian art and subject matter was one in general circulation at the time, with writers as diverse as the Sydney artist Julian Ashton, Henry Laurie, Professor of Mental and Moral Philosophy at the University of Melbourne, and the art critic and journalist Sidney Dickinson promoting the cause.[2] By 1895 the Editor of the Melbourne *Argus* could proudly claim that 'there can be no doubt that an Australian School of painting is in process of birth'.[3]

Such ideas were in part a consequence of the non-Indigenous Australians celebrating the centenary of European settlement in 1888, and the preparations for a federated national government in 1901. These events created an increased public interest in Australian history and the country's natural environment, and fostered a desire to assert a particularly Australian culture. Banjo Paterson and Henry Lawson told stories of Australian life in their writing and artists deliberately introduced a local narrative into many of their landscape paintings.

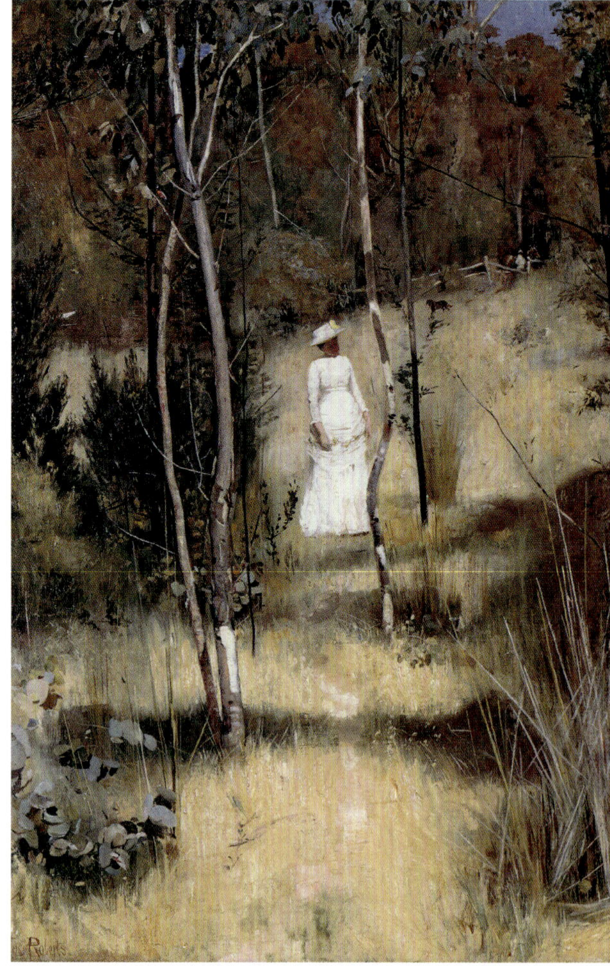

IMPRESSIONS

Tom Roberts was Australia's foremost artist of the late nineteenth century. He promoted outdoor landscape painting, choosing to depict important rural subjects of a national character, as well as being Australia's leading portrait painter. While studying at the Royal Academy Schools in London from 1881 to 1884, he saw Whistler's evocative 'Nocturnes' and Constable's small seascapes and cloud studies, and also looked at Corot's landscape sketches in Paris.[4] In 1885 he returned to Australia, where he began regularly to paint outdoors.

In the first major work he painted after his return, *Allegro con brio, Bourke Street West* (*c.*1885–86, reworked 1890; cat.93), Roberts created a new vision of urban Australia; instead of the panoramic cityscapes of earlier artists, he depicted a busy thriving Melbourne street viewed from a first-floor window. He captured the hustle and bustle of modern city life, giving value to everyday events and showing the colony as a vibrant, urban trading centre. He also conveyed the glare of the midday sun and the dust rising from the unsealed street. And, like contemporary photographers, he depicted buildings and people cropped off at their edges to show that this was just a segment of a scene that continued outside the image; just a moment of perception.

During the weekends, from 1885 to 1886, Roberts worked alongside the Australian-born Impressionist Frederick McCubbin at a *plein-air* painting camp at Box Hill, near Heidelberg, on the outskirts of Melbourne. (The railway line that opened in 1882 had made Box Hill easily accessible to city-based artists.) There Roberts and McCubbin created landscapes radically different in composition and technique from the sweeping grandeur of many earlier Australian paintings. Roberts's *The*

Artists' Camp (1886; cat.94) and *A Summer Morning Tiff* (fig.26), and McCubbin's *Lost* (1886; cat.91), show small glimpses of the bush, depicting enclosed groves from near vantage points, the skies virtually absent. Using soft colours and low tonalities, the artists captured the distinctive texture of slender eucalypt saplings, grasses and twigs. In *Lost*, McCubbin visualised a true story: that of a child lost in the bush for three weeks in May 1885. And in his image of a small girl vulnerably trapped by saplings he created a metaphor for the unease that some white Australians still feel when contemplating the untamed land surrounding their cities.

Roberts's *'Evening, when the quiet east flushes faintly at the sun's last look'* (1887–88; cat.97), probably painted on the hillside above the Box Hill camp, is a panoramic image, but its view of the quiet stillness of dusk was something of a novelty in Melbourne at the time, foreshadowing the paintings of David Davies and Walter Withers in the 1890s. The work's poetic title also reflects the interest of Roberts and his associates in the wider world of English Romantic poetry.

In 1887 the two experienced artists rented a summer cottage near Beaumaris, a bayside suburb about twelve miles from the centre of Melbourne, where they painted lively seaside views. There they encountered the young Australian-born art student Arthur Streeton, who was later to become one of Australia's best-known Impressionist painters. They created landscapes concerned with leisure, with coastal city dwellers relaxing in the wholesome fresh air by the sea. In *The Sunny South* (*c.*1887; cat.96) Roberts showed healthy young men (Streeton, McCubbin and Louis Abrahams) bathing naked in the coastal bush, revelling in their freedom like young pagans in the sunshine; and in *Slumbering Sea, Mentone* (1887; cat.95) he depicted a genteel boating party at the nearby cliff-enclosed beach on a hot, windless midsummer day. In his choice of title Roberts may have been referring to verse by the English poet Percy Bysshe Shelley, in which he described the joyous spirit that arises when love, freedom and health come 'like the vague sighings of a wind at even / That wakes the wavelets of the slumbering sea'.[5] Above all else it is about the pleasures of the Australian seaside in summer, an Impressionist celebration of Australian light and leisure. Certainly, Roberts and his friends wanted, among other things, to create paintings that both expressed a mood and depicted what was before them, and to do this they often used poetic titles to contribute to the meaning of their works. Roberts's *Slumbering Sea, Mentone* also reveals that this place was once inhabited by Aboriginal people, with the remains of coastal shell midden exposed in the eroded bank.

The young British-born artist Charles Conder moved from Sydney to Melbourne in 1888 and joined the group, painting *A Holiday at Mentone* (1888; cat.100) in the vicinity of Beaumaris. He presented fashionable Melburnians promenading during a day trip to the sea, carefully arranged in a stylish Whistlerian *Japonisme* manner. Earlier, in Sydney, in his painting *Bronte Beach* (1888; cat.98), he had depicted a sensuous beach landscape with a pearly translucence and a specifically Australian sense of space.[6]

In 1888 Streeton took the train to Heidelberg on the outskirts of Melbourne to visit the site of Louis Buvelot's *Summer Afternoon, Templestowe* (fig.27), and he was offered the use of an old weatherboard

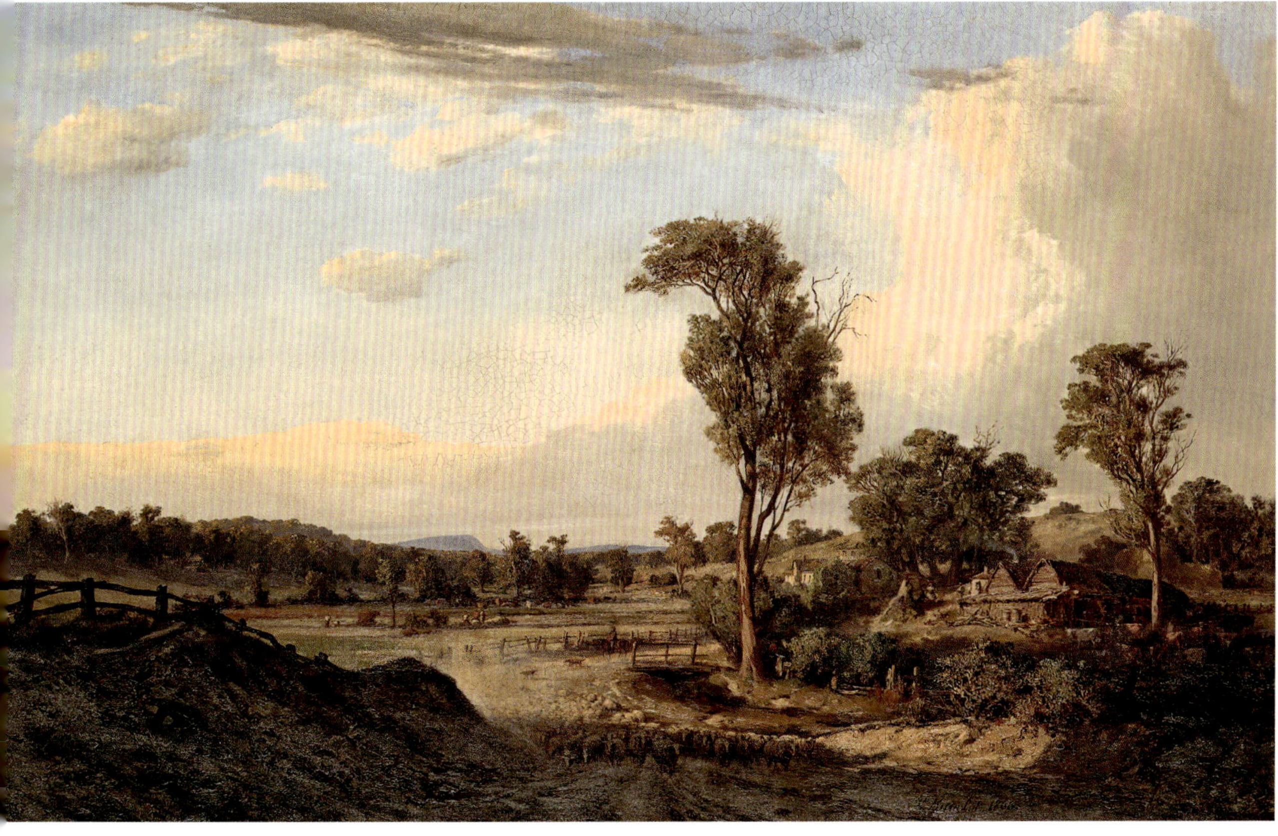

Fig. 27
LOUIS BUVELOT, **Summer Afternoon, Templestowe**, 1866.
Oil on canvas, 76.6 × 118.9 cm
National Gallery of Victoria, Melbourne. Purchased 1869

farmhouse on the nearby Mount Eagle estate (fig.28). Together with Conder and Roberts he spent two idyllic summers there from 1888 to 1890. 'Surrounded by the loveliness of the new landscape, with heat, drought, and flies', they worked hard and talked long into the night.[7] They were often joined by other colleagues, such as Walter Withers and Jane Sutherland (fig.29). And they painted many iconic Australian landscapes there, including Streeton's *Golden Summer, Eaglemont* (1889; cat.103), a large panoramic view showing shepherd and sheep moving slowly homeward at the end of the day, with 'the purple shadows ... fast creeping over the hills'.[8] Streeton captured the intense light, burning heat and dryness of many an Australian summer, using what was to become his characteristic 'blue and gold' palette. In 1891 *Golden Summer, Eaglemont* became the first painting by an Australian-born artist to hang in the galleries of the Royal Academy in London.

Streeton was a storyteller too, visualising narratives of past and present times. In *The Selector's Hut (Whelan on the Log)* (1890; cat.101), an Eaglemont landscape, he showed a selector resting on a felled log beside a tall, slender eucalypt, his axe beside him. The sky is charged with a hot summer wind blowing up the dust, and magpies whirl in the intense blue sky. The painting is a historical narrative of a hardy pioneer who has cleared this lonely patch of dry land (Jack Whelan, a tenant farmer on the Mount Eagle estate, was the model). Like *Golden Summer, Eaglemont*, this is an inhabited landscape, the figure suggesting a comfortable relationship between man and nature.

In August 1889 Roberts, McCubbin, Streeton and Conder held the now-legendary '9 by 5 Impression Exhibition' in Melbourne. They exhibited over 183 small panels measuring approximately 9 by 5 inches (many on cedar cigar-box lids) and depicting contemporary life and landscape. Conder's witty, eccentric *How We Lost Poor Flossie* (1889; cat.106) and Streeton's image of an Australian rules football match, *The National Game* (1889; cat.104), are typical of the charming, fresh paintings shown in the exhibition. Some works, such as Conder's joyous *Herrick's Blossoms* (*c.*1888; cat.107), were filled with light and colour, while others, such as Roberts's *Evening Train to Hawthorn* (*c.*1889; cat.105), conveyed the quieter moments of the day, the atmospheric effects of twilight. The artists presented their aims in the introduction to the catalogue, indicating that they sought to capture the fleeting effects of light, working directly from nature.[9] Their inspiration came from Whistler's evocative 'Nocturnes', rather than from the impasto paint and juxtaposed colours of Monet's French Impressionism. Their 'impressions' were accessible and affordable, and sold readily (often to the artists' friends).

Melbourne's economy crashed at the beginning of the 1890s. In September 1891, lured by new opportunities, Roberts and Streeton moved from Victoria to New South Wales. Streeton was captivated by the sparkling beauty of Sydney Harbour and it became the main focus for landscapes such as *Sirius Cove* (*c.*1895; cat.102). With his characteristically crisp brushwork he produced a radical view of the harbour, seen at close range and cut off at the edges. He created a sparkling image using a stylish blend of the spontaneity of Impressionism with the calligraphy and the long vertical format of a Japanese scroll painting; a modern view, quite distinct from the panoramic harbour landscapes of such earlier artists as Conrad Martens.

When Streeton ventured into the Blue Mountains, west of Sydney, in 1891 to paint *Fire's On* (1891; cat.109), he captured a radiant blue sky, quivering light, jagged rocks, sizzling summer heat and a tunnel that 'gapes like a great dragon's mouth'.[10] But he also depicted a

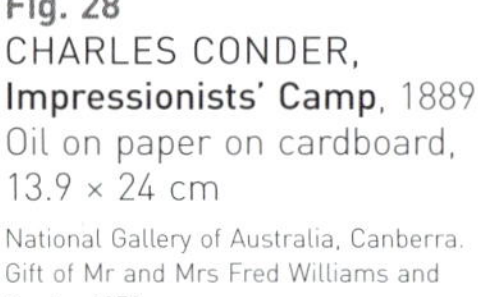

Fig. 28
CHARLES CONDER,
Impressionists' Camp, 1889.
Oil on paper on cardboard,
13.9 × 24 cm
National Gallery of Australia, Canberra.
Gift of Mr and Mrs Fred Williams and family, 1979

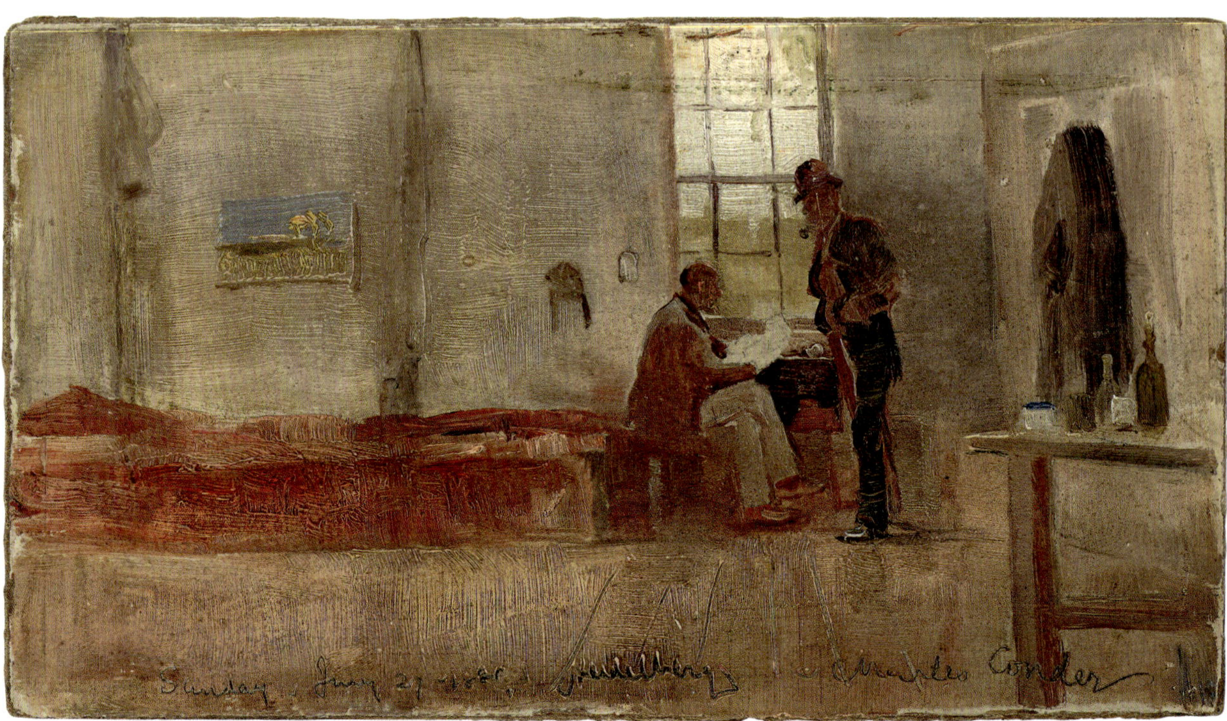

consciously nationalistic landscape, a painting described at the time as reflecting 'the contemporaneous life and activity of a new continent and a new race'.[11] The painting told the story of the blasting of the Lapstone tunnel during the construction of the railway line, with tumbling rocks and a dead miner being carried out on a stretcher. The image became an emblem of the pioneering spirit and of progress; but more importantly it expressed Streeton's 'sheer joy in the visual world'.[12]

Roberts too was interested in depicting Australian narratives, painting five large-scale heroic landscapes dramatising rural labour and showing the Australian male settler at work toiling on the land. He sought to portray 'a life different from any other country in the world'.[13] In *A Break Away!* (1891; cat.108) he presented a stampede of drought-stricken sheep in arid pastoral land, maddened by the scent of water. He conveyed the swirling dust blowing through the trees and covering the sheep, under the stark blue sky of a still, dry, hot day. And in his image of the heroic stockman straining to rein in his flock he visualised a distinctively Australian figure: strong, athletic, skilful and courageous.

With the Australian banking crisis of the 1890s and the coinciding worldwide Depression the sun went out of most Melbourne landscapes until about 1908. Artists such as the Victorian-born and -trained David Davies and the British-born and Royal Academy-trained Walter Withers worked in outer Melbourne, painting wistful landscapes, crepuscular and mysterious. Davies painted a series of unpeopled, aestheticised landscapes, such as *Moonrise* (1893; cat.111), in which he depicted the moon rising over empty paddocks of dried grasses.[14] He captured the quiet face of nature, the melancholic soul of the land. Using subtle, low-pitched colours and close-packed stippled paint he conveyed the solidity of the earth and evoked the lyrical quality of a warm Australian summer evening. Walter Withers often portrayed quiet village life, under a soft winter light or in stormy weather, in the early morning or evening. In *The Last of Summer* (1898; cat.112) he depicted a brave woman clasping her bundle as she makes her way home, a vulnerable figure under the dark clouds of a gathering storm heralding the end of summer and bringing welcome relief to the parched ground.

In Sydney in the late 1890s the Australian-born Symbolist Sydney Long also painted poetic moonrise subjects. Using an Art Nouveau approach in *The Spirit of the Plains* (1897; cat.110), he evoked something of the haunting spirit of the land. He depicted a nature sprite leading a group of elegantly dancing native birds before a stand of swaying eucalypts beneath a moonlit sky. This was a different image of Australia to that presented by Roberts and McCubbin: the spirit is female, and does not toil in the bush, but plays music and dances among the trees, in harmony with nature. As Robert Hughes observed, Long's nymphs were 'a natural outgrowth of the bush, an extension of its soul'.[15]

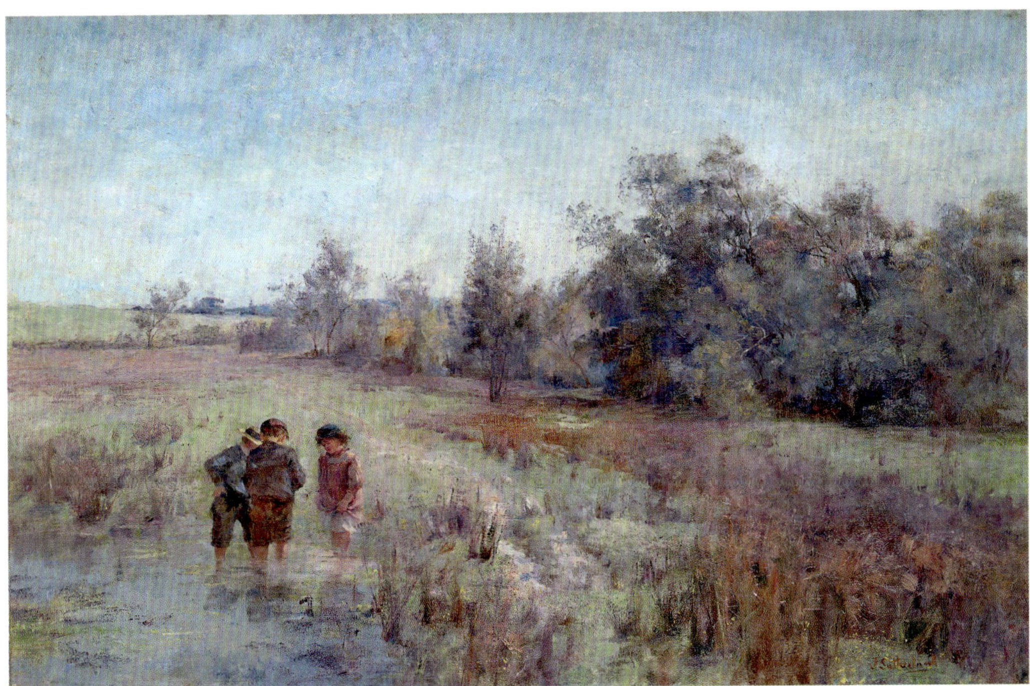

Fig. 29
JANE SUTHERLAND,
Field Naturalists, *c.*1896.
Oil on canvas, 80.9 × 121.3 cm
National Gallery of Victoria, Melbourne.
Gift of Mrs E. H. Shackell, 1962

Around the turn of the century, Conder, Streeton and Roberts left Australia, where the Depression of the 1890s had damaged the small local art market, seeking the bright lights of Paris and London and the colonial dream of European success. (This Conder certainly achieved: on his return to Europe in 1890, he gained a European reputation, becoming a friend of Toulouse-Lautrec and painting watercolours on silk with exquisite designs.) The artists departed at a time when the social order was changing in the Western world, and, although Australians still regarded themselves as British, the nation was beginning to assert itself as an entity.

FEDERATION LANDSCAPES

Australia became a Federation of states and territories in 1901. From this time until the 1920s, while figure painting was the focus of much British art, landscape continued to dominate Australian painting.[16] Pictures of giant gum trees, rugged hills, lively cities and expansive beaches gave Australians a sense of identity.

At Federation, Tommy McRae (who died in 1901) and William Barak (who died in 1903) were acknowledged as the senior artists of the Aboriginal people. They had a relationship with members of the European community, who provided materials and ensured the preservation of their works. However, as Ron Radford has noted, 'Aboriginal art as a concept was only just dawning on the colonisers' culture.'[17] Baldwin Spencer, Professor of Biology at the University of Melbourne and honorary Director of the National Museum of Victoria, was among those who recognised the significance of Aboriginal art. Between 1911 and 1912 he visited central and northern Australia and put together for the museum a large and important collection of Aboriginal art that he described as 'first-rate examples of first-rate artists'.[18]

A little earlier, in 1905, Sydney Long had suggested that Australian artists should develop a truly Australian mythology in which 'the lonely gullies will be wakened to life with graceful pastorals of native children. The Bell Birds chime, the Curlew's melancholy note will be pictured'.[19] This was a serious attempt to seek a new direction for Australian art, away from heroic masculine labour and national narratives, and to recognise the importance of Indigenous Australians and their understanding of the land. Indeed, just a year earlier, Long had painted *The Music Lesson* (fig.30), a pastoral with a young Aboriginal girl playing her flute to an audience of magpies, with the implication that she and the birds could teach us to understand the sounds and spirit of the Australian landscape.

For a few years after Federation McCubbin continued to craft imaginative images extolling the life of early settlers, such as his large triptych *The Pioneer* (1904; cat.113); but this was to be the last of his national, historical narratives. The work shows the struggle, resourcefulness, achievement and death of a settler and his wife, with a vision of the future, a prosperous city, rising in the background. But as Australia began to move into the twentieth century, and particularly after his only trip to Europe in 1907, when he was inspired by the works of Turner and Monet, McCubbin began to paint landscapes without a narrative, in a freer and more expressive manner, sometimes using rapidly applied dabs of juxtaposed colours. Indeed, some passages of these late paintings come much nearer to French Impressionism than anything in the works of his former colleagues. In *Violet and Gold* (1911; cat.121) McCubbin focused on a thicket of trees, capturing the distinctive green of the foliage and the dense tangle of the undergrowth. He showed the breadth of his vision and his deep understanding of the bush, conveying sparkling sensations of light and capturing some of the spiritual qualities of the Australian landscape.

McCubbin was fascinated by the Australian gum tree as a visual phenomenon, 'now faintly tinged with the early morning light; now glorious gold in the afternoon sun, each leaf and twig resplendent, and again softly flushed with the warm afterglow'.[20] The monumental gum tree was also central to the paintings of one of Australia's best-loved landscape painters, Hans Heysen. Australian trees had been depicted by earlier artists but Heysen was the first to portray individual species of eucalypt, distinguishing a river red gum tree from a white gum tree or a stringybark, making it a symbol of strong independent Australia. He became known for paintings with majestic eucalypts such as *Red Gold* (1913; cat.117). He captured the play of light and shadow on the gum trees' giant trunks, 'the tatters of loose bark hung to the wind, the stropping of mottled sunlight on leaves and limbs'.[21] At the same time he turned trees into semi-abstract sculptural forms ennobled by a golden light. In his watercolour *Midsummer Morning* (1908; cat.116) he captured the atmospheric effect of a warm early morning light shining through the trees and onto the dry golden grass. Heysen believed that light and atmosphere were the 'essence of Australian landscape',[22] and he used the translucence of watercolour to suffuse his scenes with luminosity.

There was a revival of interest in watercolour painting in Australia at the turn of the century: Heysen in Adelaide, J. J. Hilder and Sydney Long in Sydney, Blamire Young in Melbourne, James W. R. Linton (cat.126) in Perth, and, slightly later, Kenneth Macqueen in Brisbane. Their watercolours appealed directly to the domestic market, with the new middle class keen to purchase reasonably priced, small-scale images to decorate their living rooms. In *Dry Lagoon* (1911; cat.114) the Sydney artist Hilder created a mirage-like rural scene of lyrical beauty by using large areas of soft vibrating washes. In *Dry Weather* (*c.*1912; cat.115) the

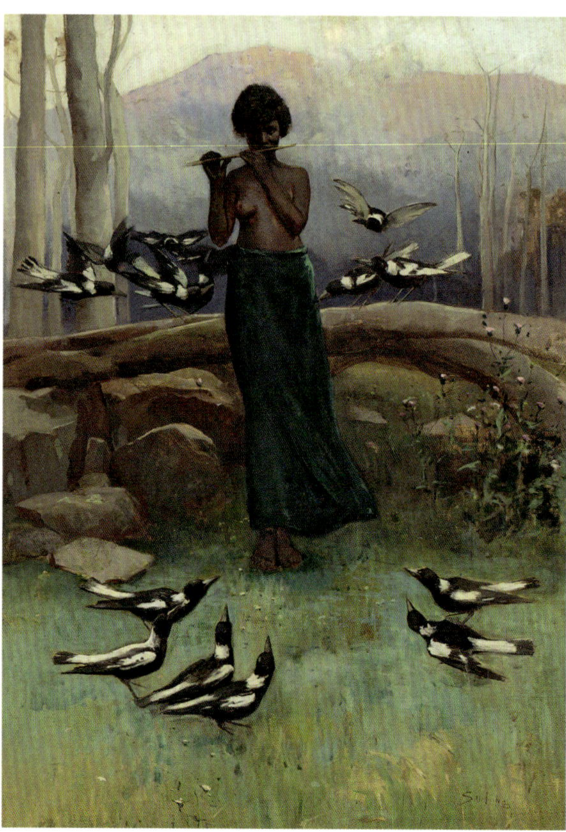

Fig. 30
SYDNEY LONG, **The Music Lesson**, 1904. Oil on canvas, 71.7 × 51.4 cm
Art Gallery of New South Wales, Sydney. Purchased 1969

British-born Blamire Young depicted the rhythmic contour of a parched, rugged hill counterbalanced by the sweep of its waterless veins, conveying the dry heat of a scorching Australian summer. It demonstrates Australia's bleached landscapes.

About this time McCubbin began to depict modern urban life: wharves, factories and Melbourne's city streets, such as *Collins Street* (*c.*1915; cat.120), which he painted from the back of his car. He delighted in capturing the dissolving, flickering forms of city life. Portraying his subjects in pure colour applied with a palette knife, he used paint in an almost abstract fashion, splattering it over the coarse canvas.

By Federation Australia had become a highly urbanised nation, with much of the population concentrated in the coastal capital cities and nearby beaches. Sea bathing increased in Sydney in 1906, after the regulation banning ocean bathing during daylight was rescinded.[23] In *Manly Beach – Summer Is Here* (1913; cat.119) the English-born and -trained artist Ethel Carrick depicted the hubbub of a summertime beach, with crowds clustering by the sea to bathe, parade and sit in the sun. Like many of her works, the painting celebrates a leisured but animated Australian life, in a colourful manner. By contrast, the Sydney artist Elioth Gruner depicted a lyrical, spare view of the beach in works such as *The Wave* (*c.*1913; cat.118). The gracefully dispersed figures are viewed from above and form bands of colour. The scene is generalised and could be almost anywhere – although the golden light and sense of space are typically Australian.

By the end of the war, Sydney had become the fastest-growing city in Australia and artists had become interested in developing a new approach to their art, using bold contrasting colours and strong forms. The leading modernist men, Roy de Maistre and Roland Wakelin, painted landscapes in a new fashion. Sydney artist De Maistre was one of the first Australian artists to adopt an abstract approach to painting (he later moved to London and became a friend of Francis Bacon). In *Forest Landscape* (*c.*1918; cat.122) he used the Australian gum tree to create a bold composition of verticals and diagonals; the play of warm advancing and cool receding colours is somewhat in the manner of Cézanne. The subject was similar to McCubbin's *Violet and Gold* (cat.121) but painted in a quite different – formalist – manner. From 1917 to 1919, with Roland Wakelin, De Maistre experimented with 'colour-music', examining the links between colour harmony and musical harmony. De Maistre suggested that colour brings 'the conscious realisation of the deepest underlying principles of nature ... it constitutes the very song of life and is, as it were, the spiritual speech of every living thing'.[24] These experiments with colour are visible in *Barn near Tuggerah* (1919; cat.123) and *Houses at Hunters Hill* (*c.*1919; cat.124) by the Sydney artist Roland Wakelin, in which trees, buildings, grass and fences are reduced to simplified coloured forms.

CONCLUSION

Between 1880 and 1920 Australian artists deliberately created an Australian national art. They celebrated their cities, beaches and bush, and sought to capture a characteristic Australian light – from the harsh midday glare to the gentle, subdued tones of early morning and evening at the turn of the century, to a sparkling golden light after about 1908. Although they sometimes adopted and adapted an international style in which to do this, their subjects were local. During the 1880s and 1890s artists frequently painted outdoors with spontaneity and freshness, bringing their subjects into a closer focus than had the panoramic views of much colonial art. And they peopled their landscapes with Australian men and women settlers who were comfortable in their surroundings, both at leisure and at work. They portray 'a life different from any other country in the world'.[25] From around 1900 artists ceased to tell narratives, and people appear less frequently in their landscapes. Instead they adopted strong landscape emblems: the sturdy eucalypt, redolent of masculine power; the city, suggestive of progress; and the beach, indicative of Australian egalitarianism and a healthy lifestyle.

These were the years too when Australia became more consciously cultural and supportive of creative pursuits.[26] Public art galleries were established around the nation and significant bequests were given to purchase art.[27] Galleries made major acquisitions of Australian art, such as Conder's *Departure of the Orient – Circular Quay* (1888; cat.99), Roberts's *A Break Away!* (cat.108), Streeton's *Fire's On* (cat.109) and McCubbin's *The Pioneer* (cat.113), as well as H.J.Johnstone's *Evening Shadows, Backwater of the Murray, South Australia* (1880; cat.90) and W.C.Piguenit's *The Flood in the Darling, 1890* (1895; cat.92). By this time Australia also had a number of established novelists, poets and film-makers.[28] Australia had become not only one united country, but also an art nation, and self-consciously so.

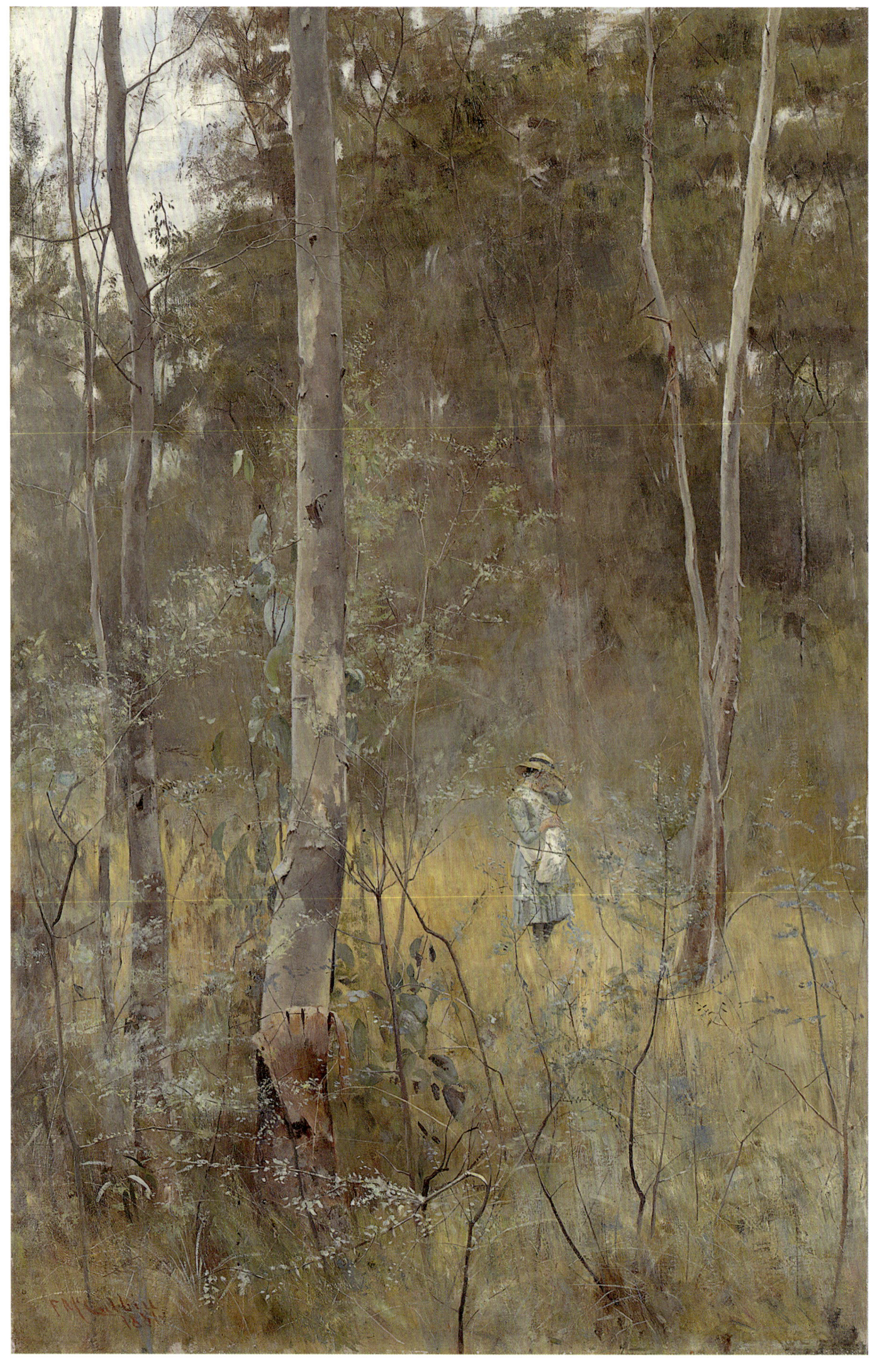

91

FREDERICK MCCUBBIN

Lost, 1886

Oil on canvas, 115.8 × 73.9 cm

National Gallery of Victoria, Melbourne. Purchased through the Felton Bequest, 1940

92

W.C. PIGUENIT

The Flood in the Darling, 1890, 1895

Oil on canvas, 122.5 × 199.3 cm

Art Gallery of New South Wales, Sydney. Purchased 1895

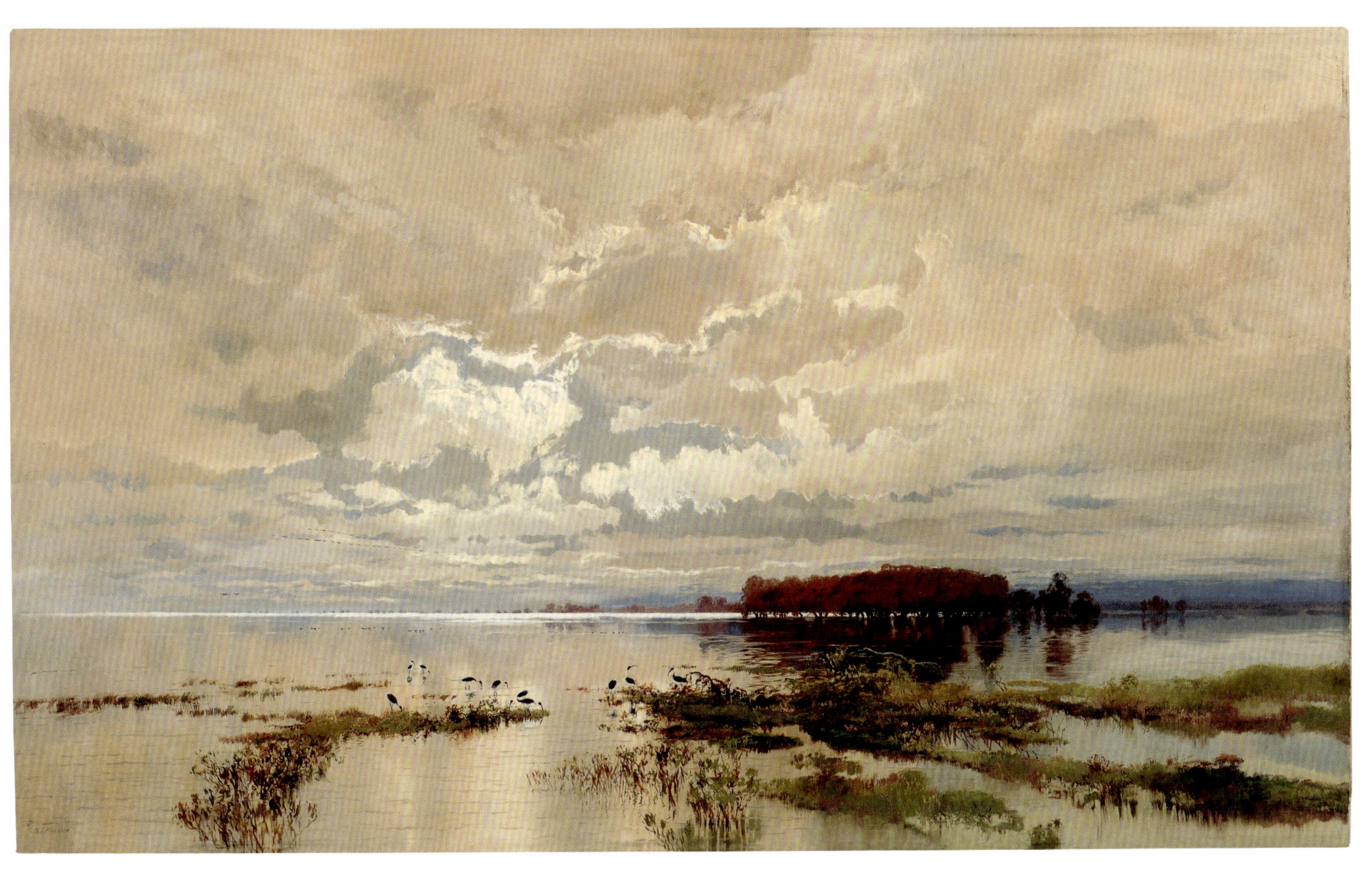

93
TOM ROBERTS
Allegro con brio: Bourke Street West,
*c.*1885–86, reworked 1890
Oil on canvas mounted on composition board, 51.2 × 76.7 cm
National Gallery of Australia, Canberra, and National Library of Australia, Canberra. Purchased 1918

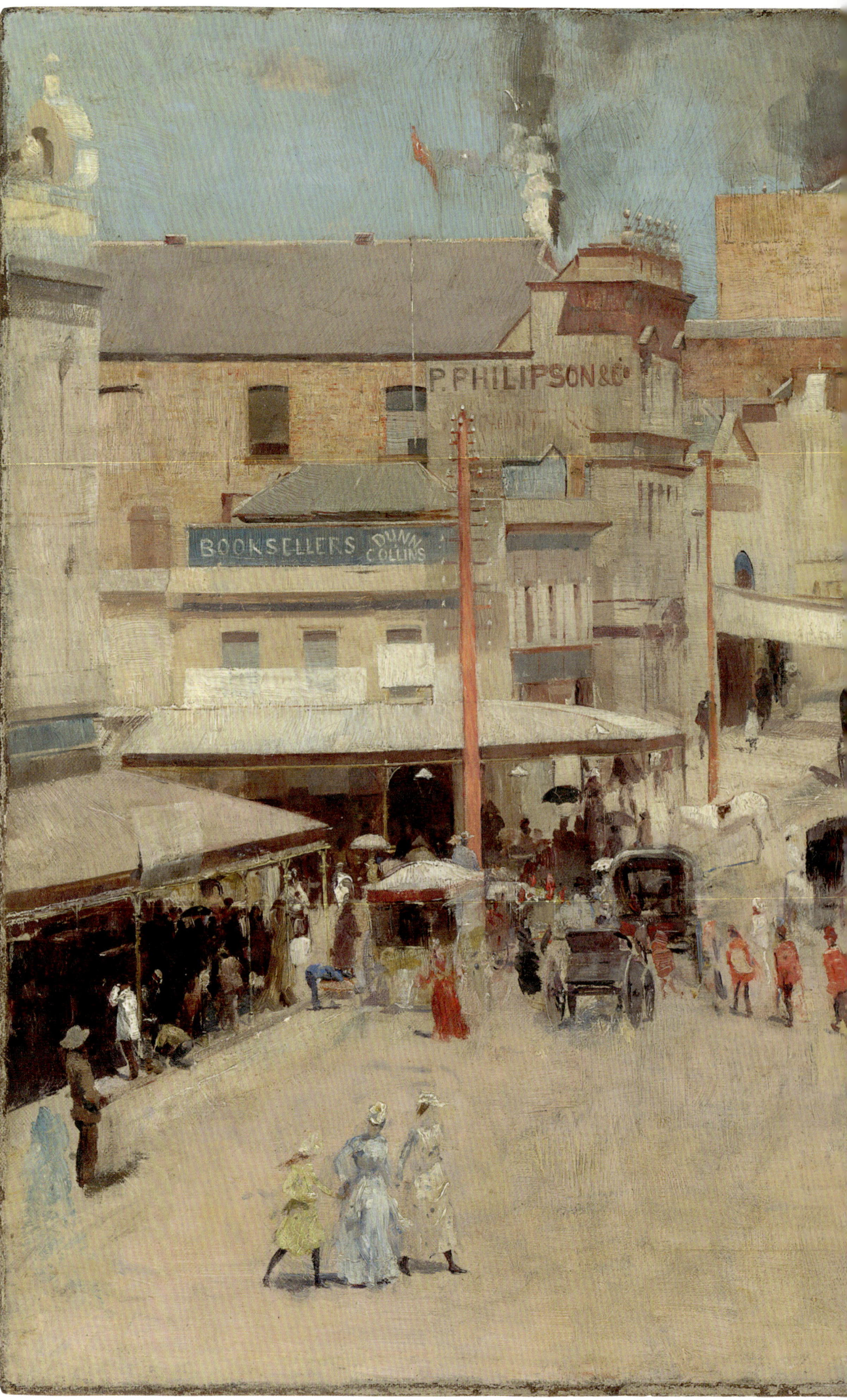

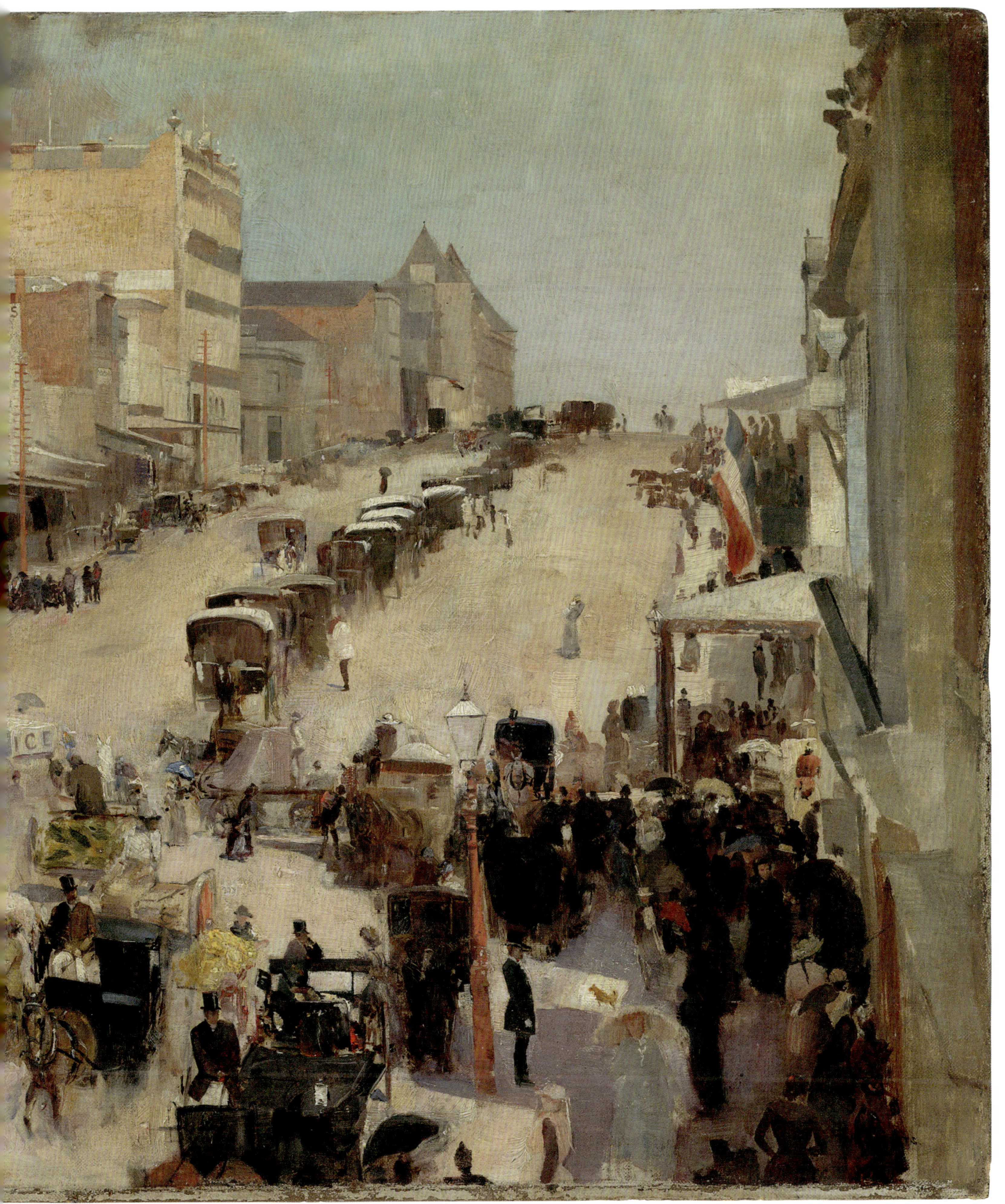
ICE

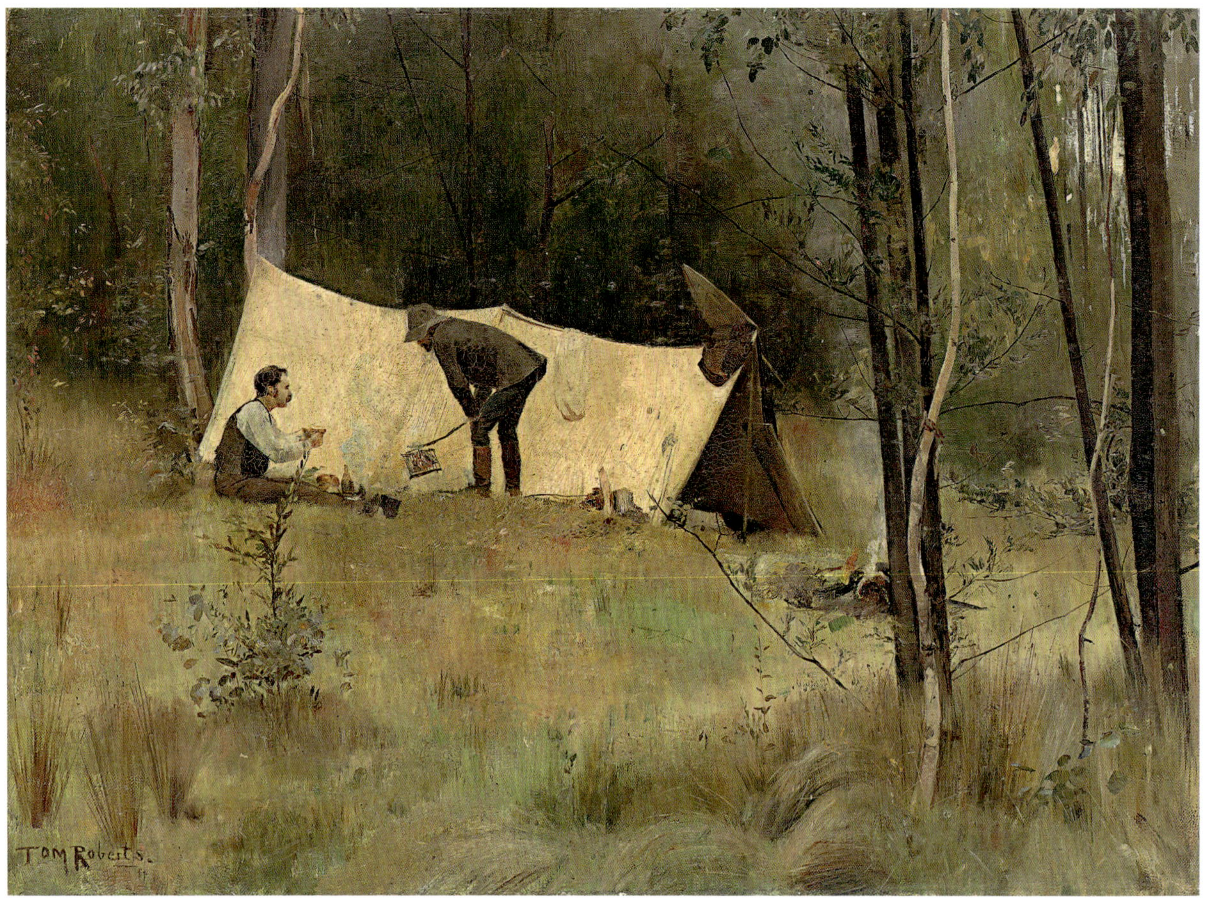

94
TOM ROBERTS
The Artists' Camp, 1886
Oil on canvas, 46 × 60.9 cm
National Gallery of Victoria, Melbourne. Purchased through the Felton Bequest, 1943

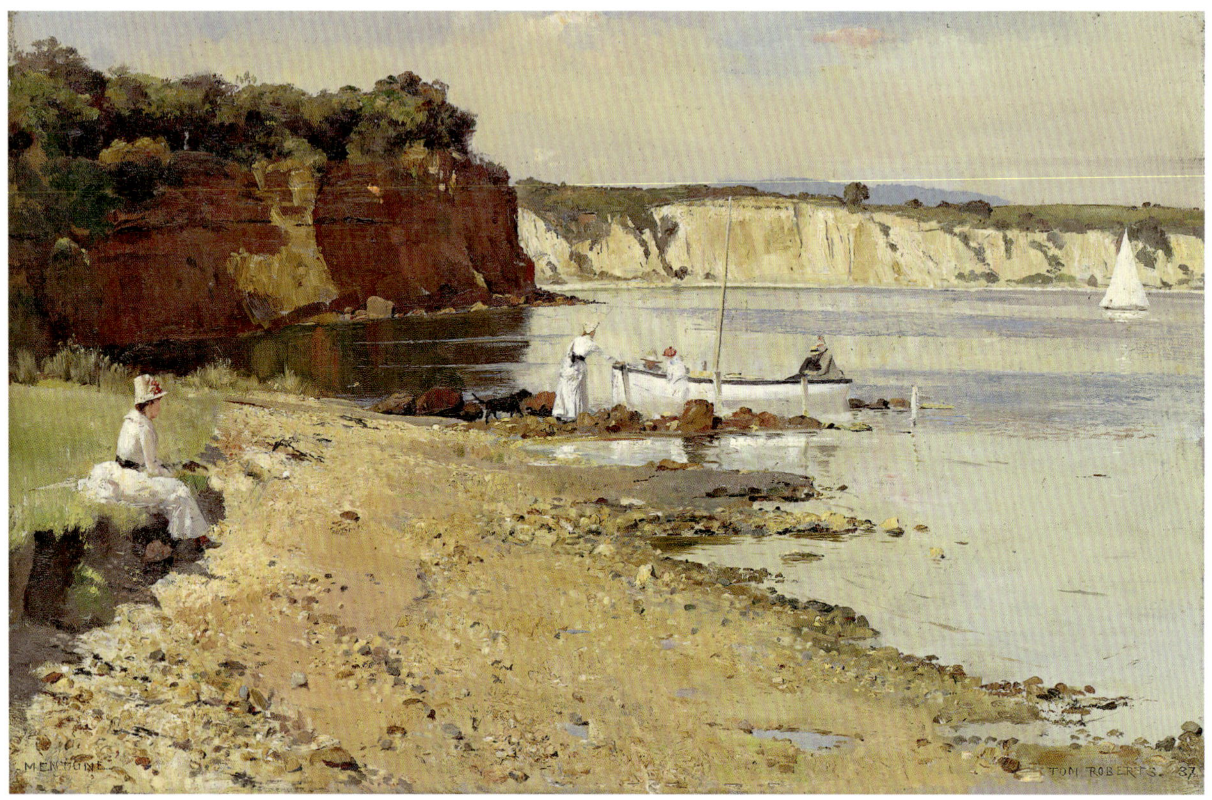

95
TOM ROBERTS
Slumbering Sea, Mentone, 1887
Oil on canvas, 51.3 × 76.5 cm
National Gallery of Victoria, Melbourne. Purchased with the assistance of a special grant from the Government of Victoria, 1979

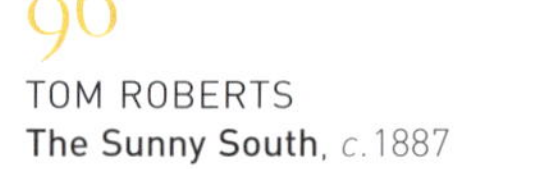

96
TOM ROBERTS
The Sunny South, *c.*1887
Oil on canvas, 30.8 × 61.4 cm
National Gallery of Victoria, Melbourne. Purch[...] through the Felton Bequest, 1940

97
TOM ROBERTS
'Evening, when the quiet east flushe[...] faintly at the sun's last look', 1887–8[...]
Oil on canvas, 50.8 × 76.4 cm
National Gallery of Victoria, Melbourne. W. H. Short Bequest, 1944

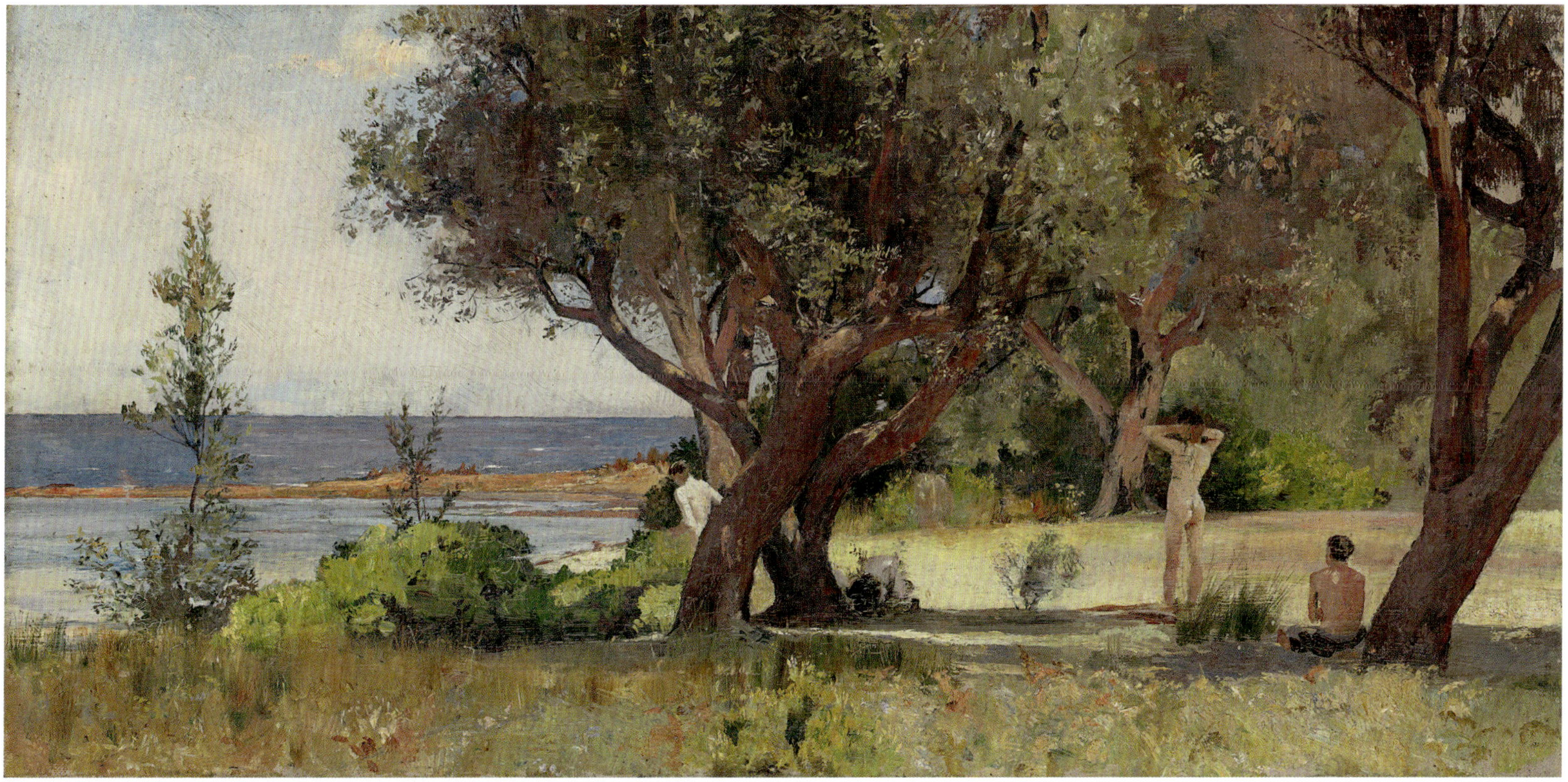

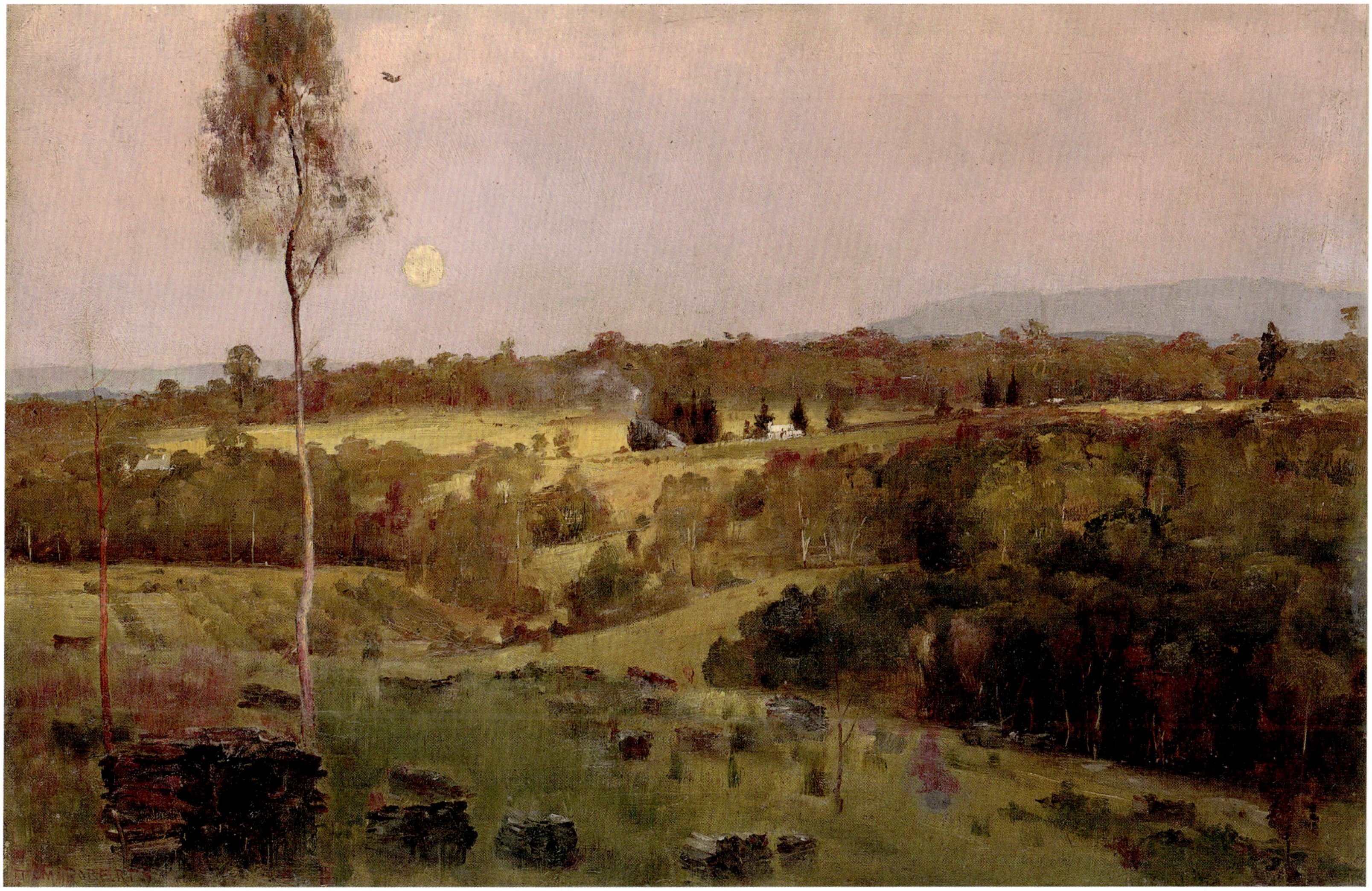

98

CHARLES CONDER
Bronte Beach, 1888
Oil on paper on cardboard,
22.6 × 33 cm

National Gallery of Australia, Canberra.
Purchased from Gallery admission charges, 1982

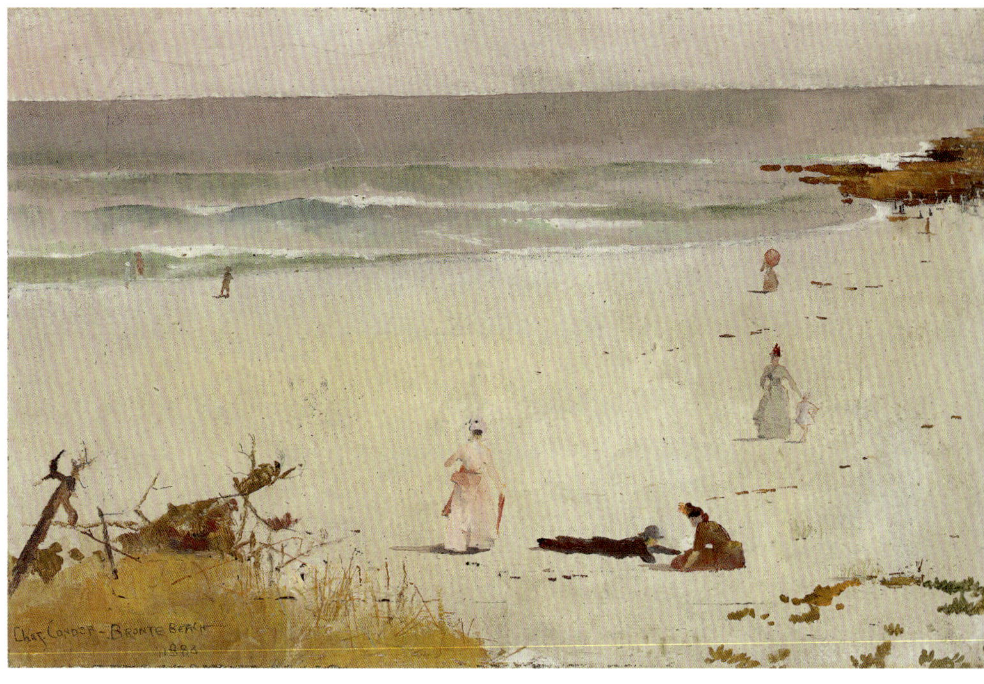

99

CHARLES CONDER
Departure of the Orient – Circular Quay, 1888
Oil on canvas, 45.1 × 50.1 cm

Art Gallery of New South Wales, Sydney.
Purchased 1888

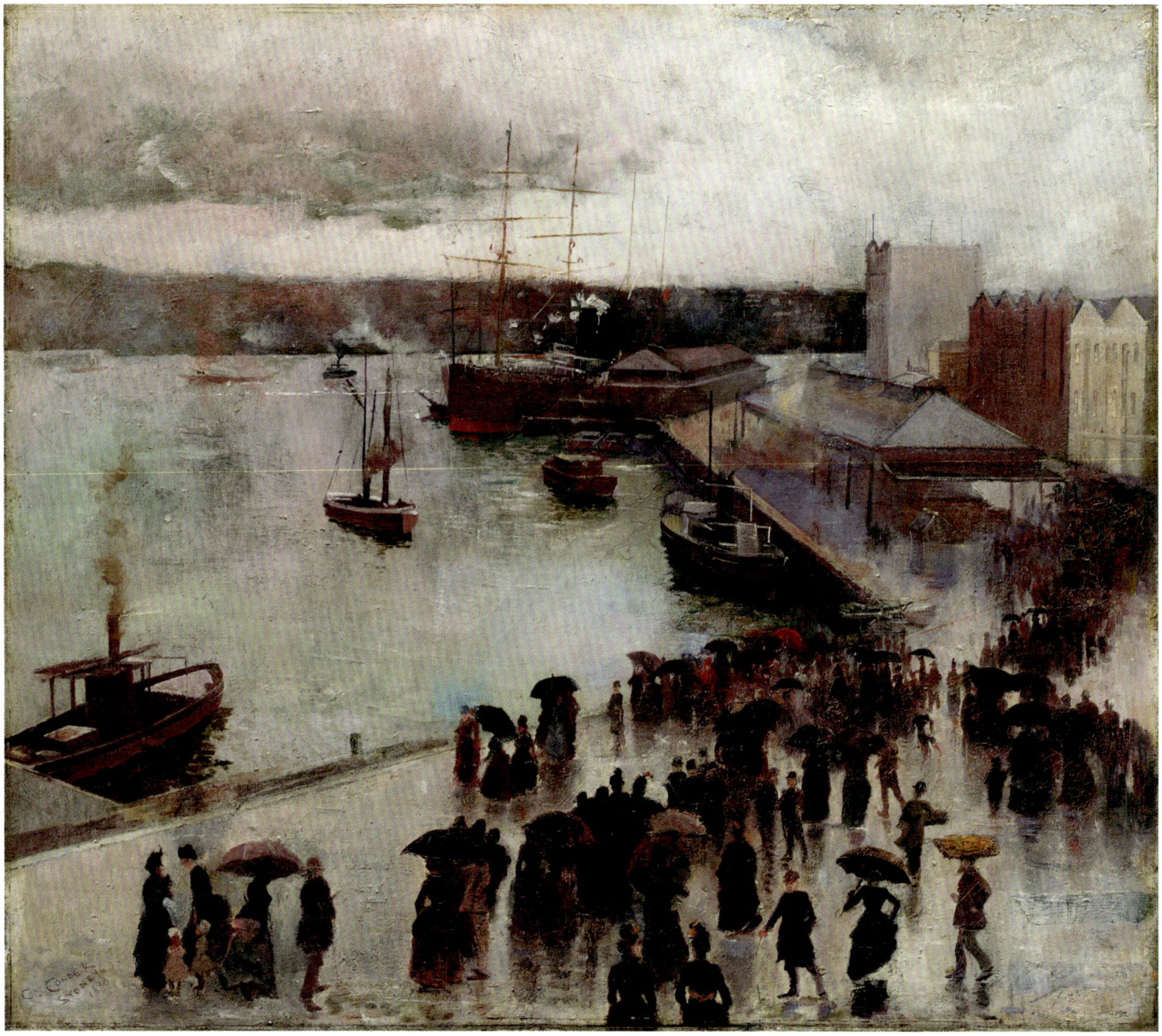

100

CHARLES CONDER
A Holiday at Mentone, 1888
Oil on canvas, 46.2 × 60.8 cm
Art Gallery of South Australia, Adelaide. South Australian Government Grant with the assistance of Bond Corporation Holdings Limited through the Art Gallery of South Australia Foundation to mark the Gallery's Centenary, 1981

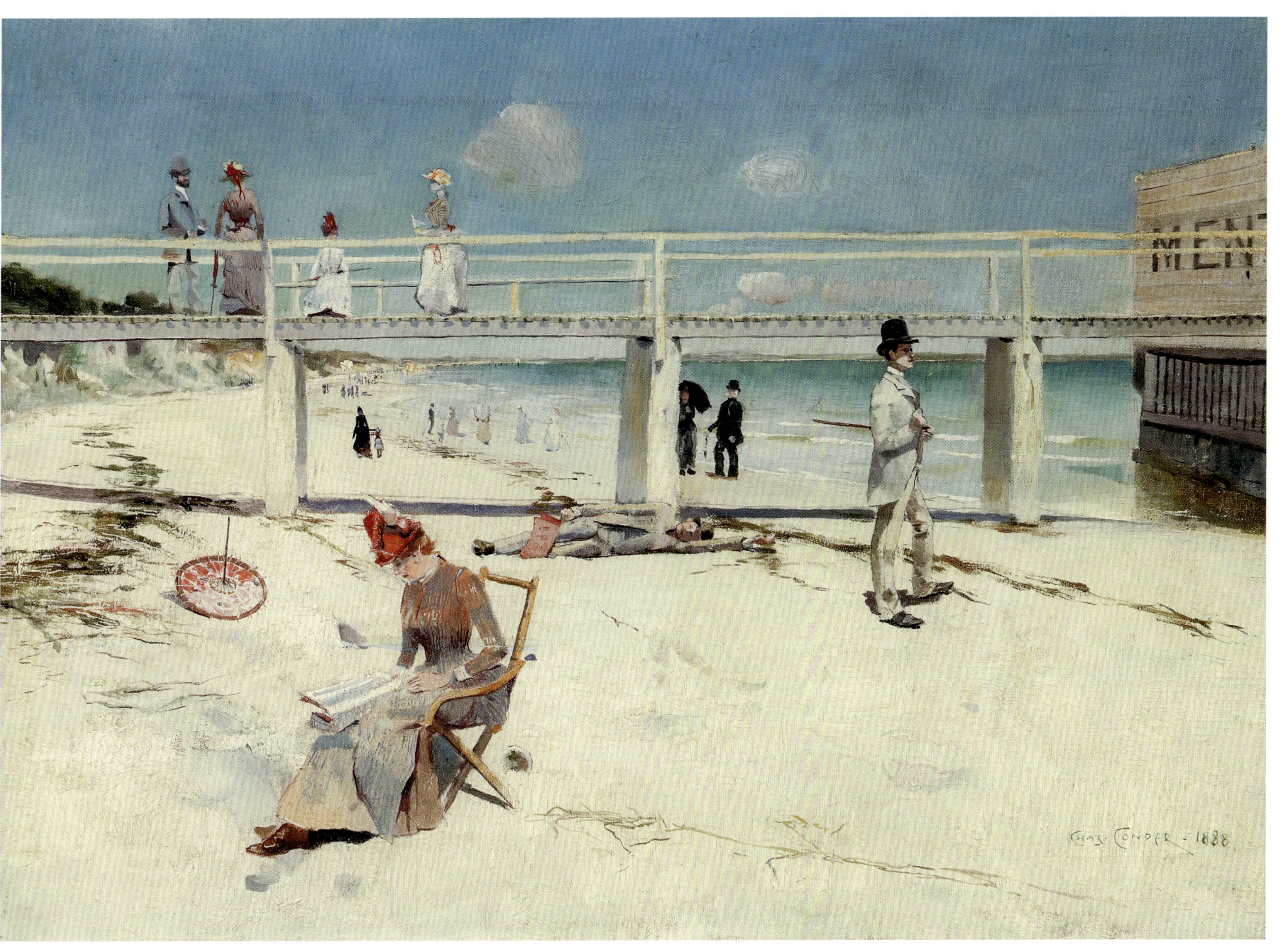

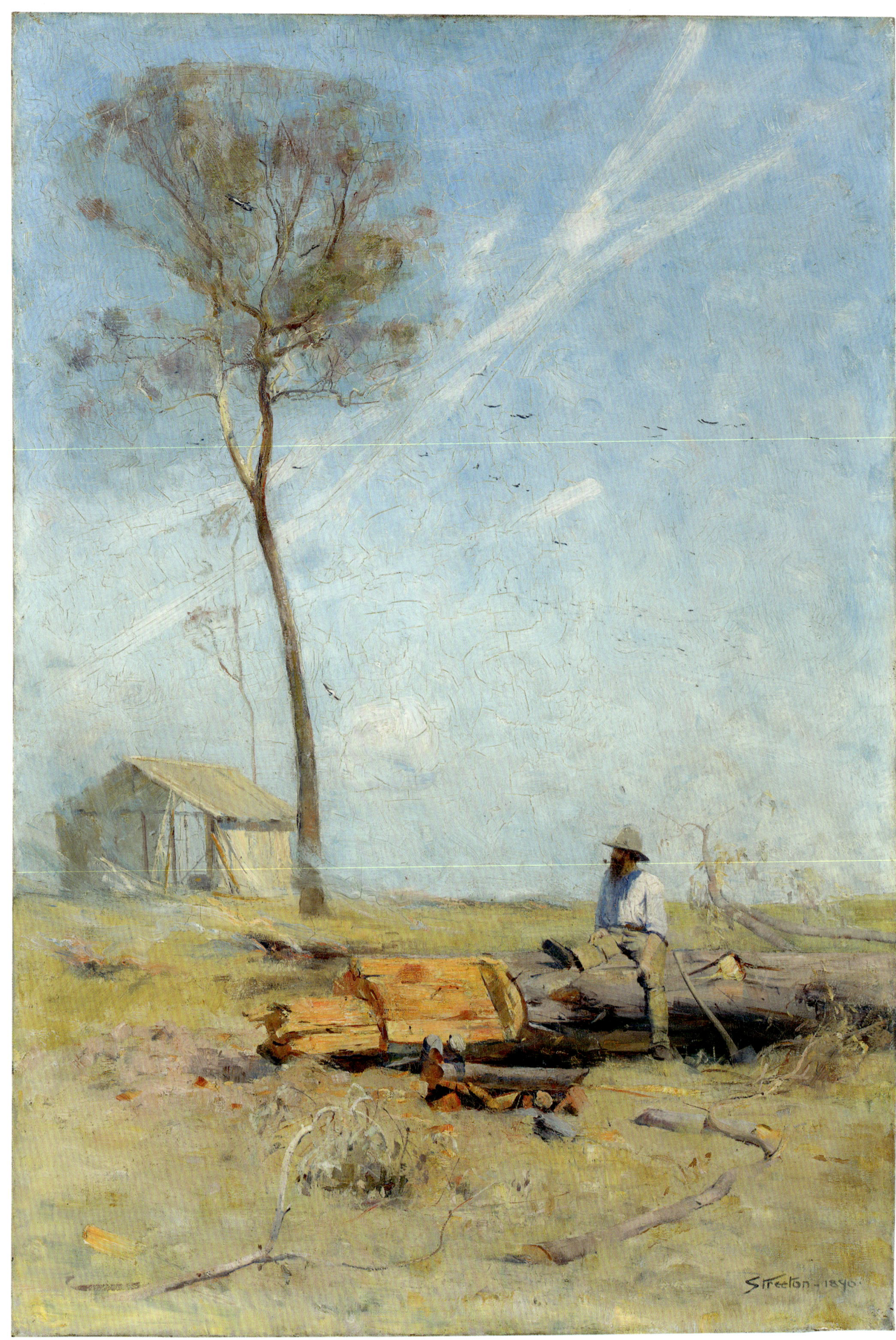
Streeton - 1890

101

ARTHUR STREETON
The Selector's Hut (Whelan on the Log), 1890
Oil on canvas, 76.7 × 51.2 cm
National Gallery of Australia, Canberra. Purchased 1961

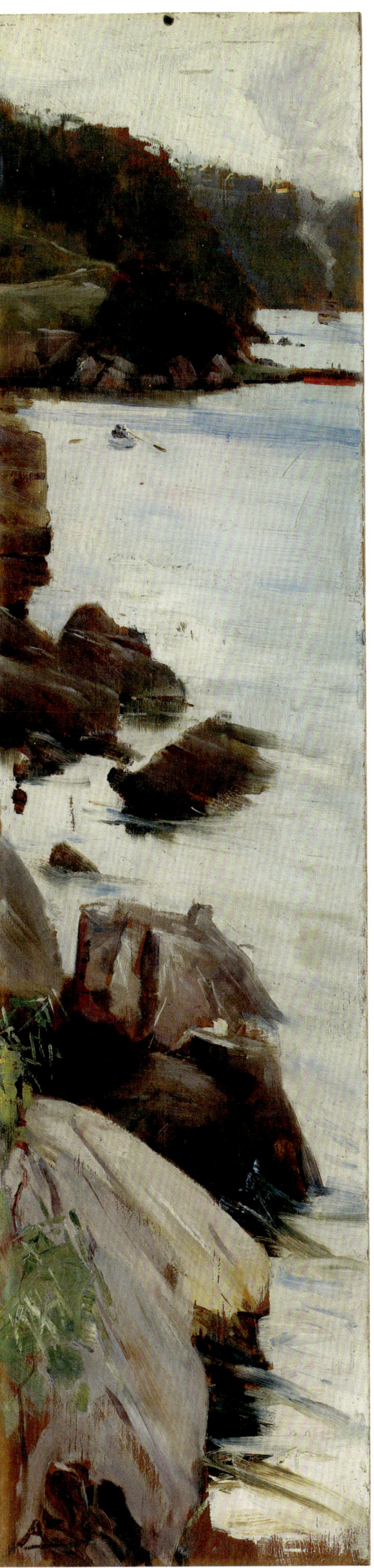

102

ARTHUR STREETON
Sirius Cove, *c.*1895
Oil on wood panel, 68.8 × 16.8 cm
National Gallery of Australia, Canberra. Purchased 1973

103 *overleaf*

ARTHUR STREETON
Golden Summer, Eaglemont, 1889
Oil on canvas, 81.3 × 152.6 cm
National Gallery of Australia, Canberra. Purchased 1995

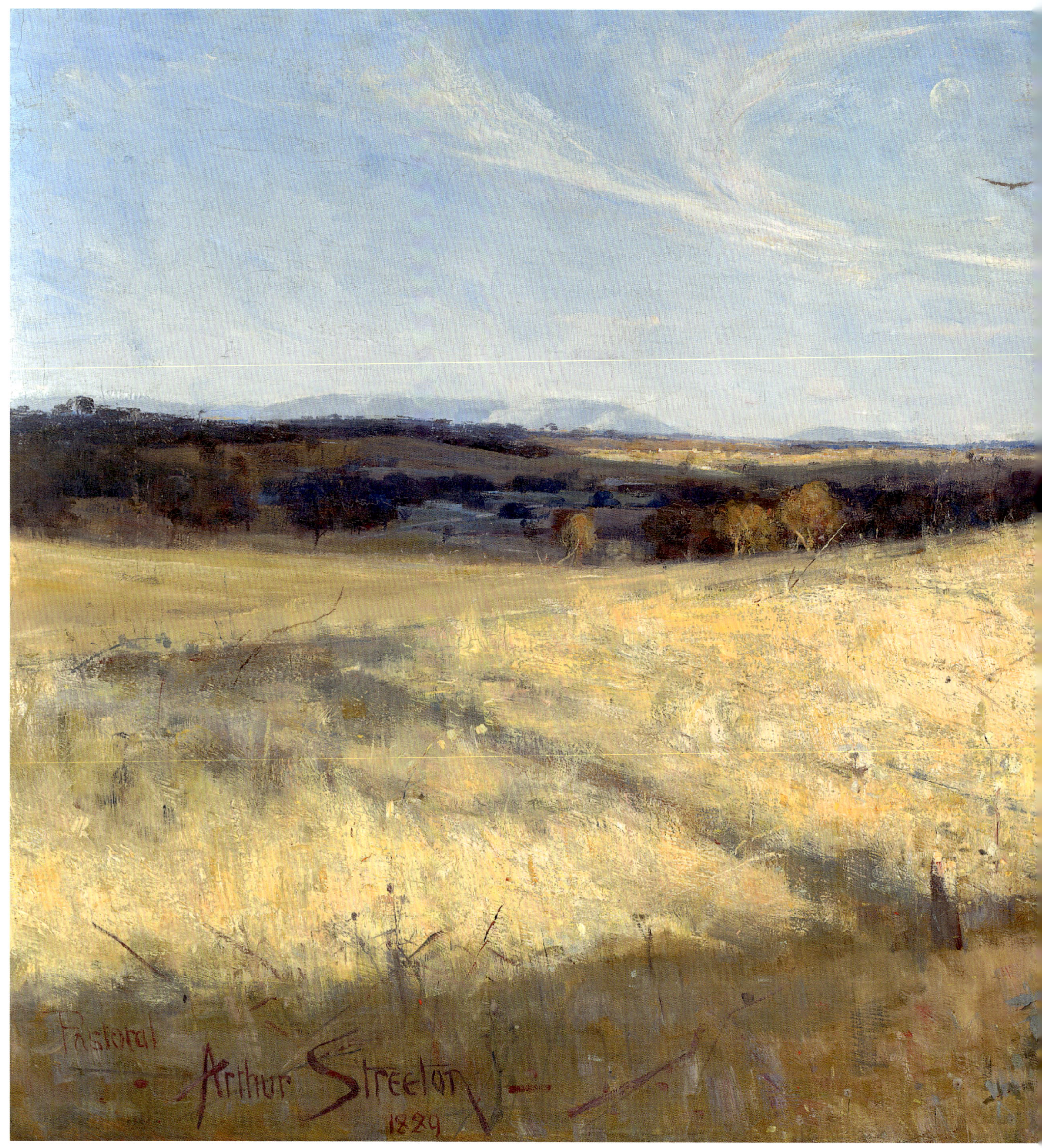
Pastoral
Arthur Streeton
1889

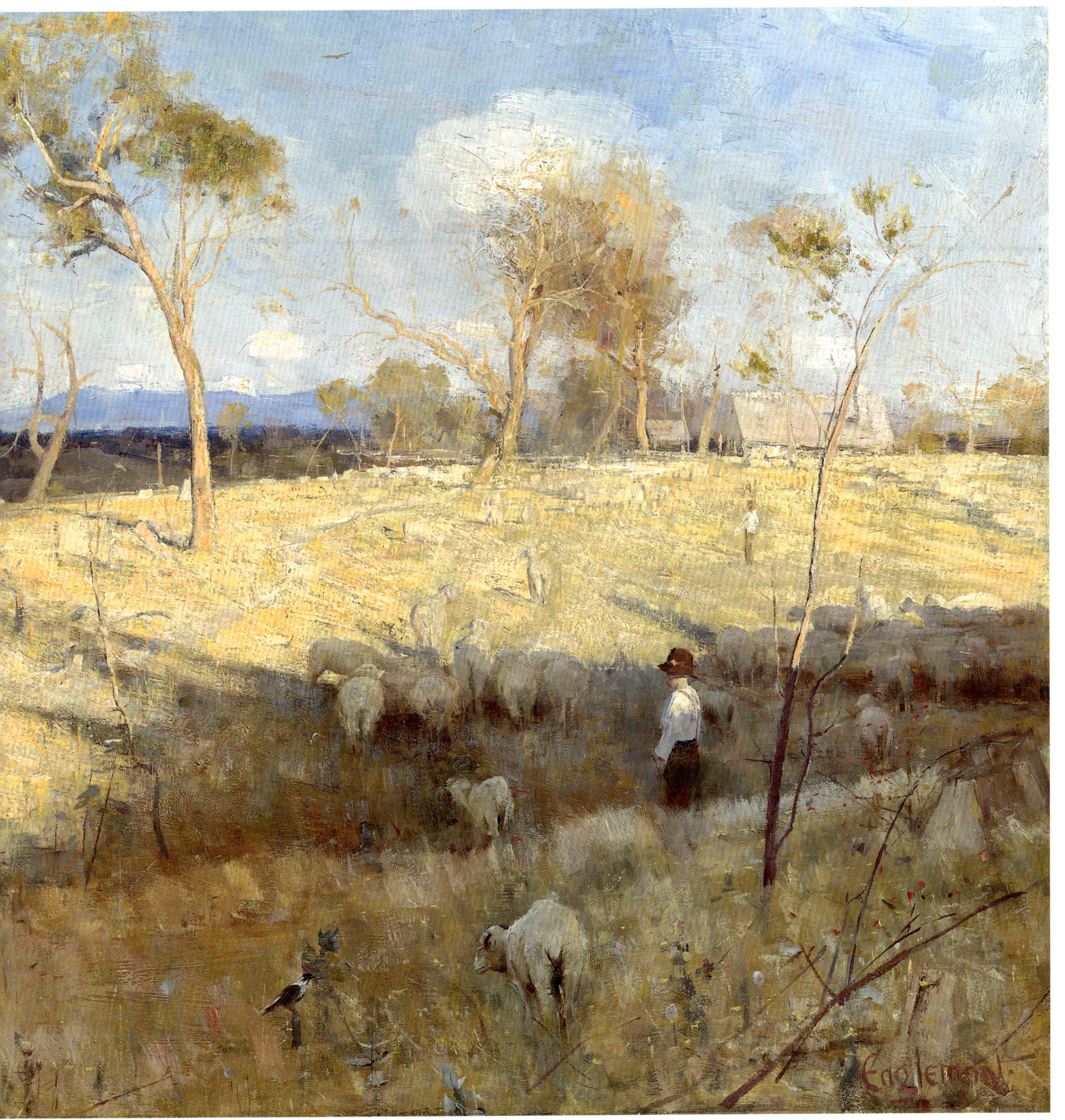

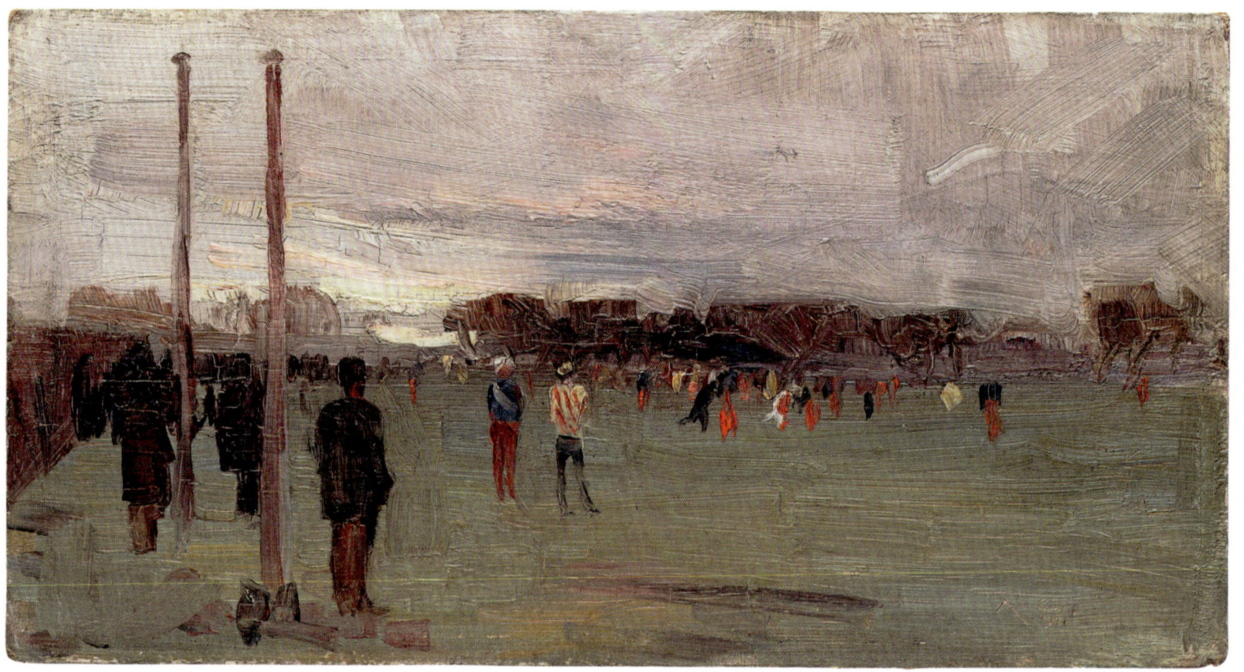

104
ARTHUR STREETON
The National Game, 1889
Oil on cardboard, 11.8 × 22.9 cm
Art Gallery of New South Wales, Sydney. Purchasec

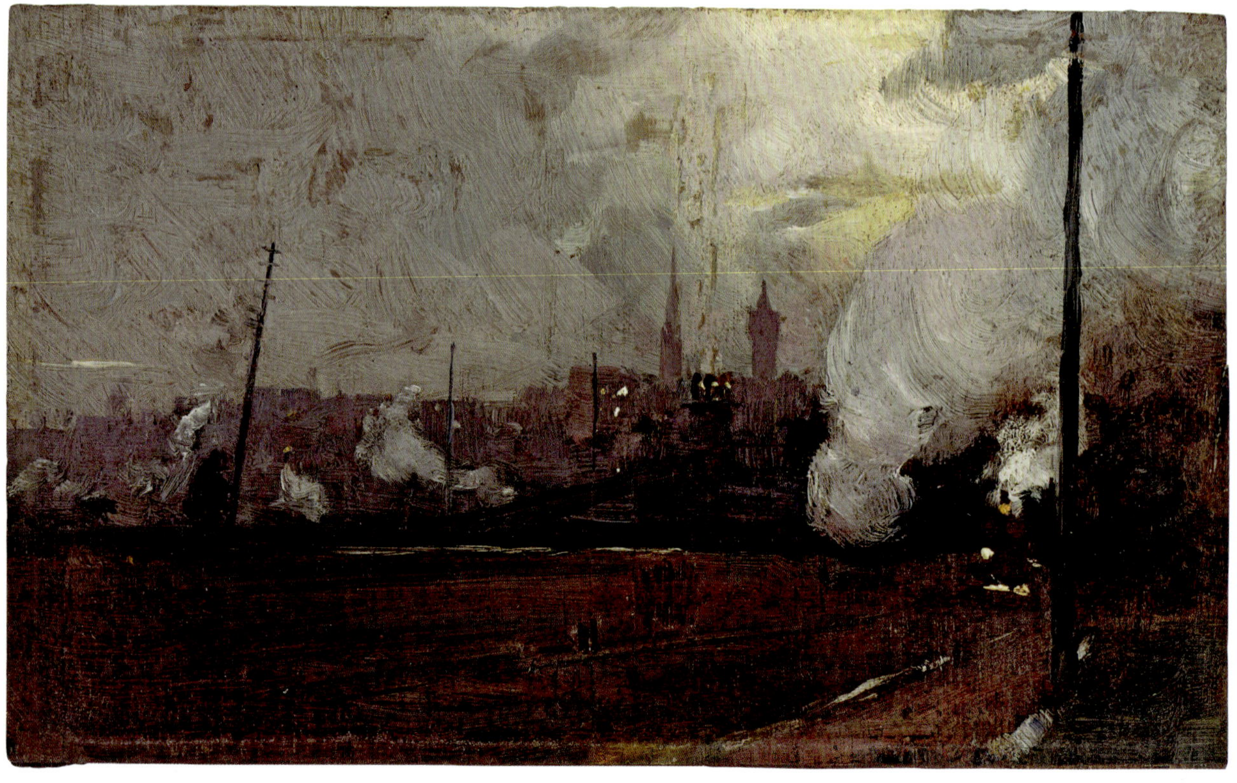

105
TOM ROBERTS
Evening Train to Hawthorn, *c.* 1889
Oil on cedar wood panel, 14 × 22.6
Art Gallery of New South Wales, Sydney. Edward Sti
Bequest Fund, 1991

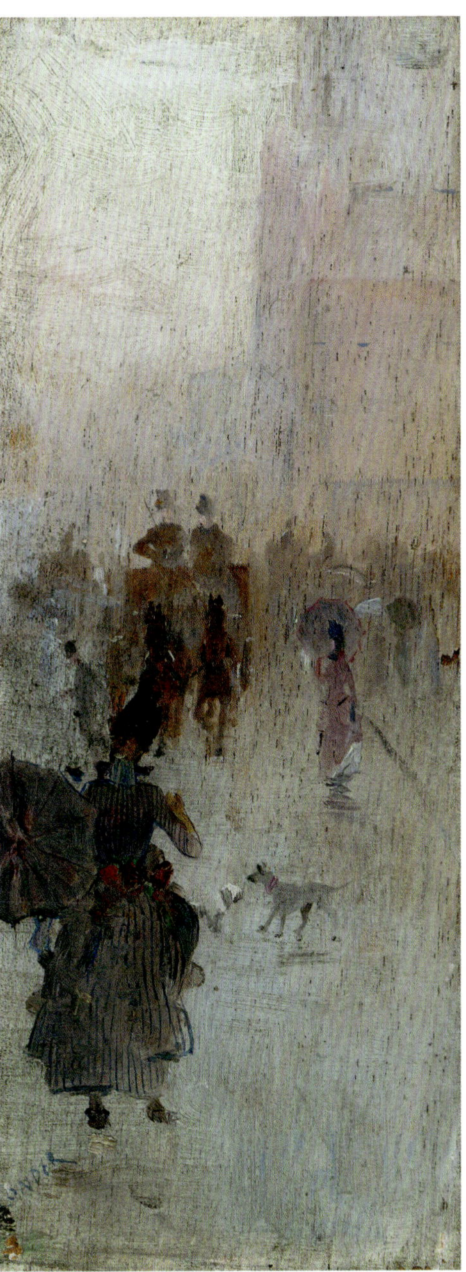

106

CHARLES CONDER
How We Lost Poor Flossie, 1889
Oil on cedar wood panel, 25 × 9.2 cm
Art Gallery of South Australia, Adelaide. Elder Bequest Fund, 1941

107

CHARLES CONDER
Herrick's Blossoms, *c.*1888
Oil on cardboard, 13.1 × 24 cm
National Gallery of Australia, Canberra. Purchased 1969

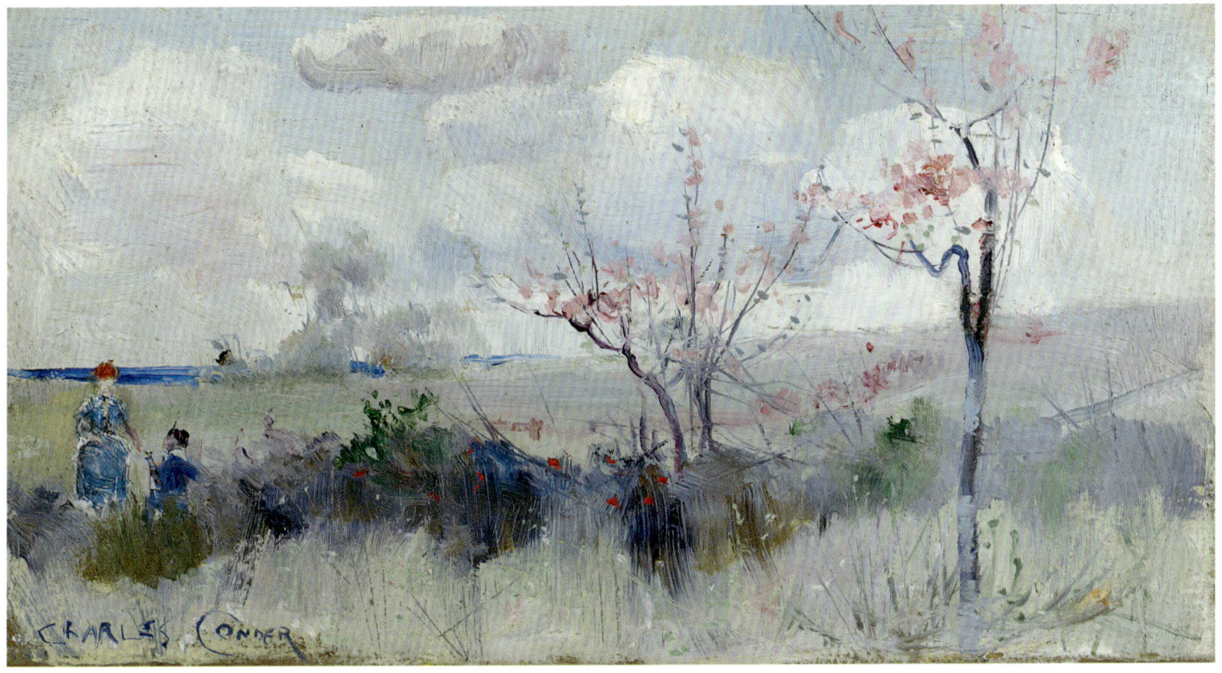

108

TOM ROBERTS
A Break Away!, 1891
Oil on canvas, 137.3 × 167.8 cm
Art Gallery of South Australia, Adelaide. Elder Bequest Fund, 1899

109

ARTHUR STREETON
Fire's On, 1891
Oil on canvas, 183.8 × 122.5 cm
Art Gallery of New South Wales, Sydney. Purchase
1893

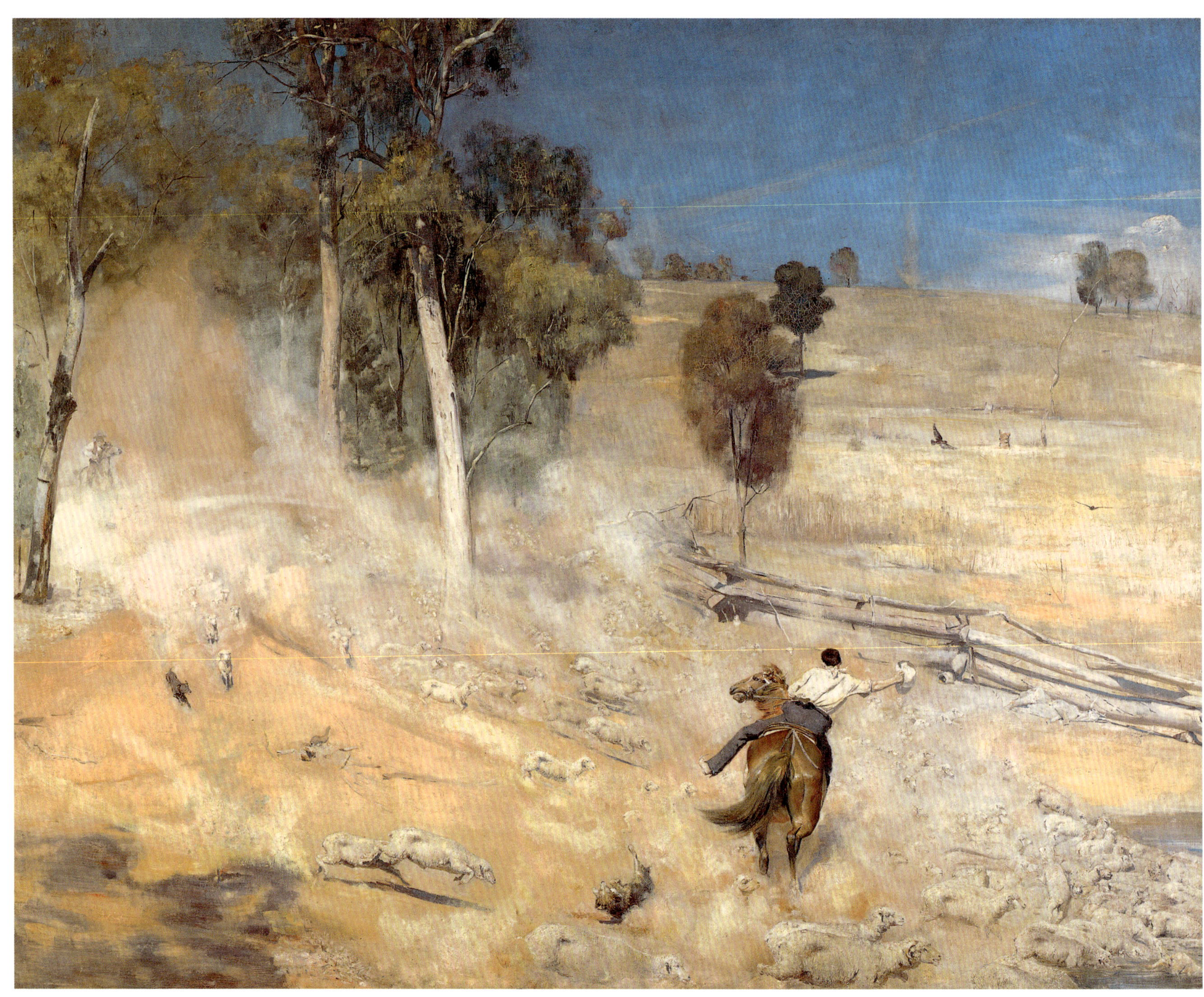

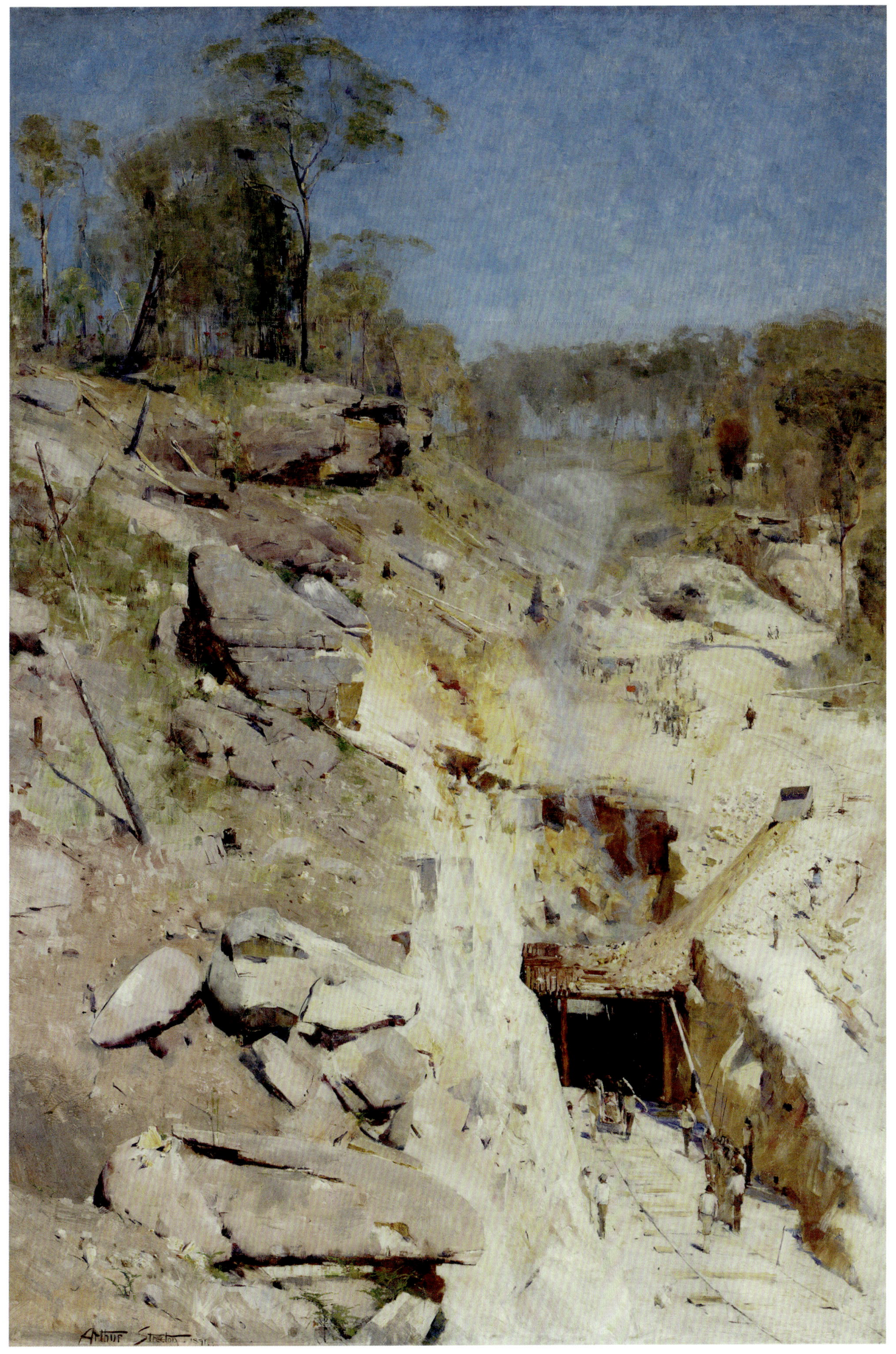
Arthur Streeton

110

SYDNEY LONG
The Spirit of the Plains, 1897
Oil on canvas on wood, 62 × 131.4 cm
Queensland Art Gallery, Brisbane. Gift of William Howard-Smith in memory of his grandfather, Ormond Charles Smith, 1940

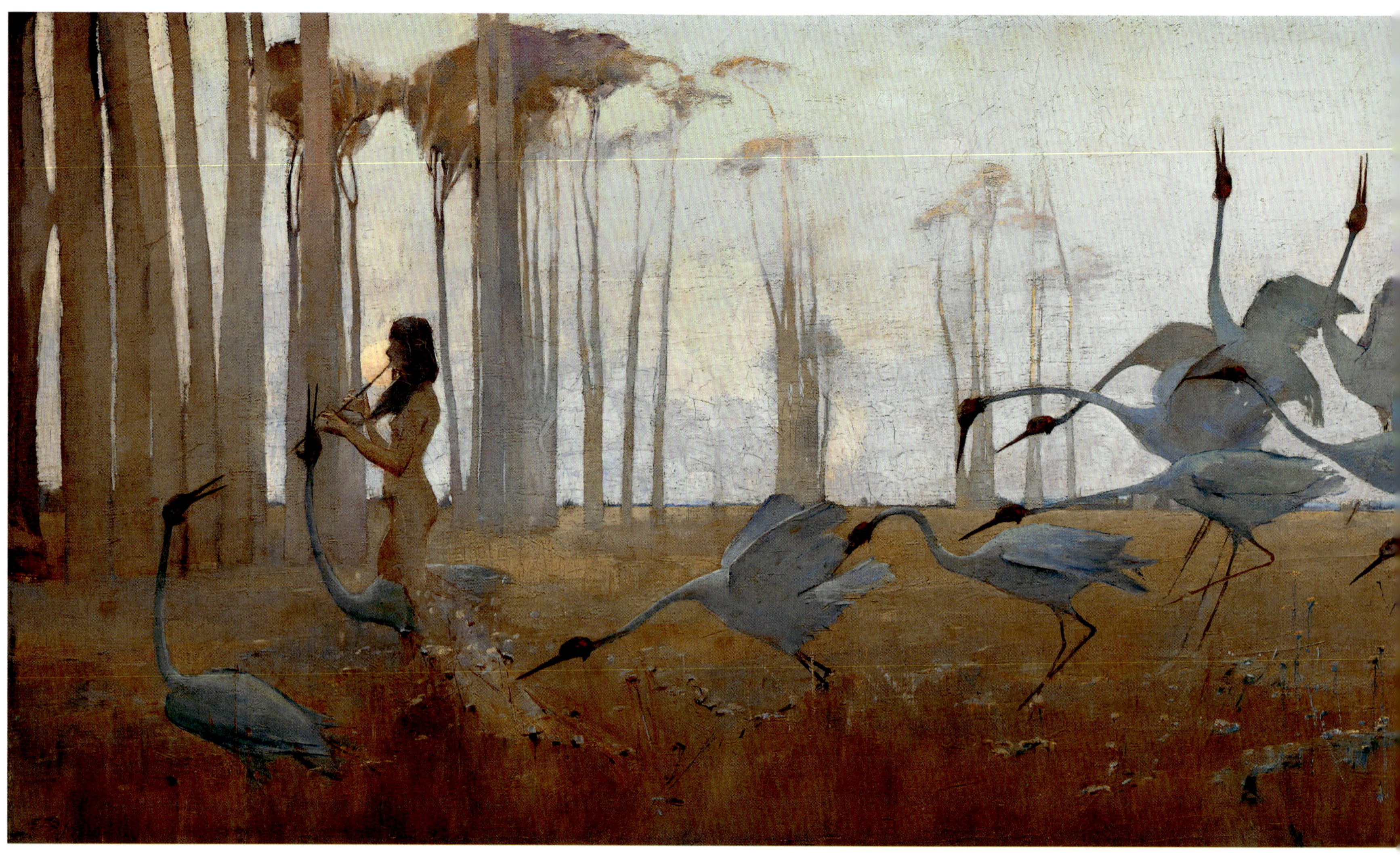

111

DAVID DAVIES
Moonrise, 1893
Oil on canvas, 50 × 60 cm
Art Gallery of South Australia, Adelaide. Elder Bequest Fund, 1947

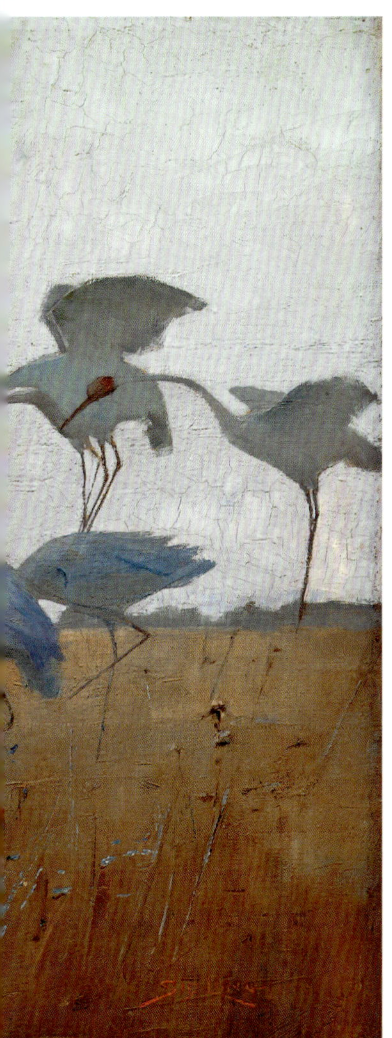

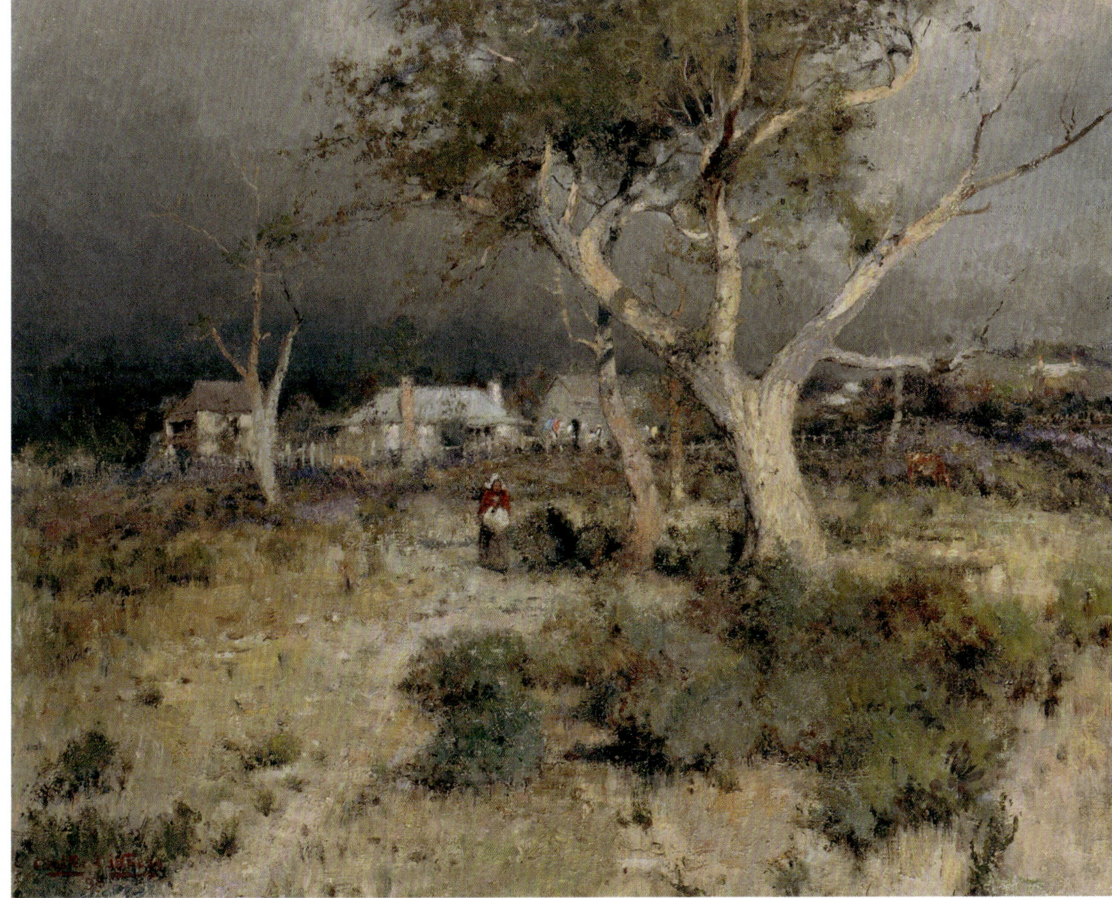

112

WALTER WITHERS
The Last of Summer, 1898
Oil on canvas, 77 × 92 cm
Art Gallery of Ballarat, Victoria.
Gift of Mrs I. Main-Rippin, 1932

113

FREDERICK McCUBBIN
The Pioneer, 1904
Oil on three canvases, 225 × 295.7 cm (overall)

National Gallery of Victoria, Melbourne.
Purchased through the Felton Bequest, 1906

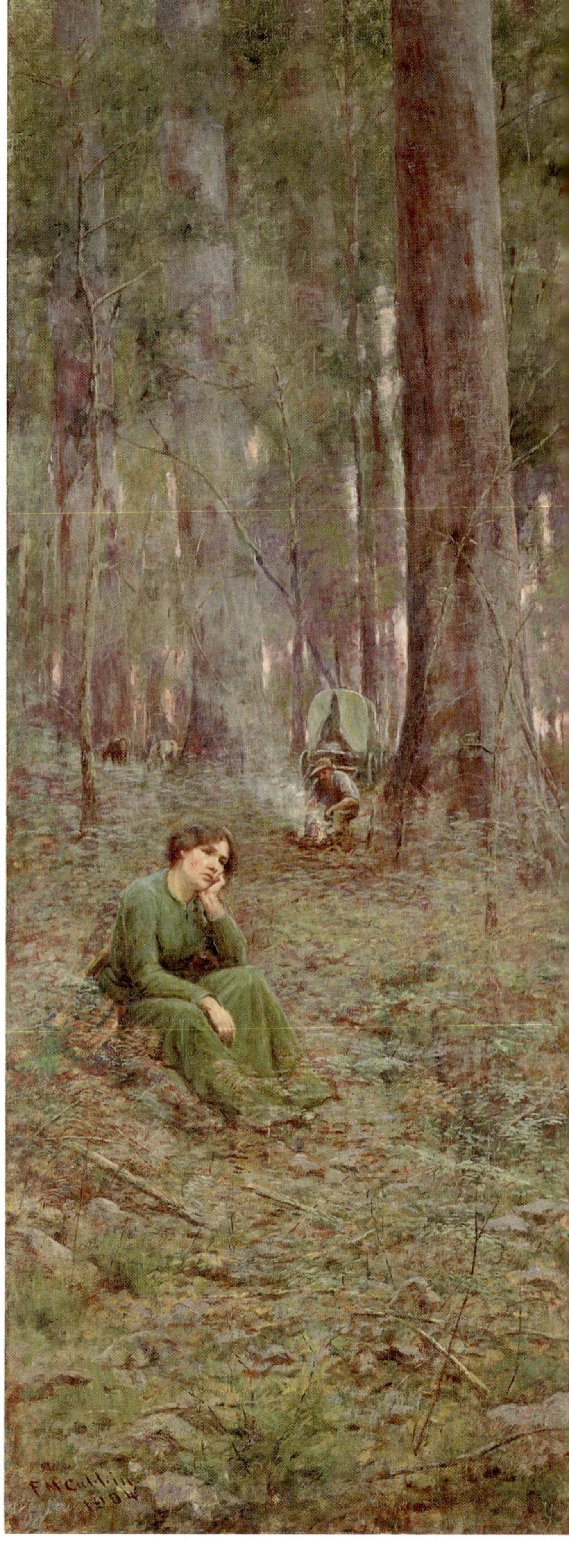

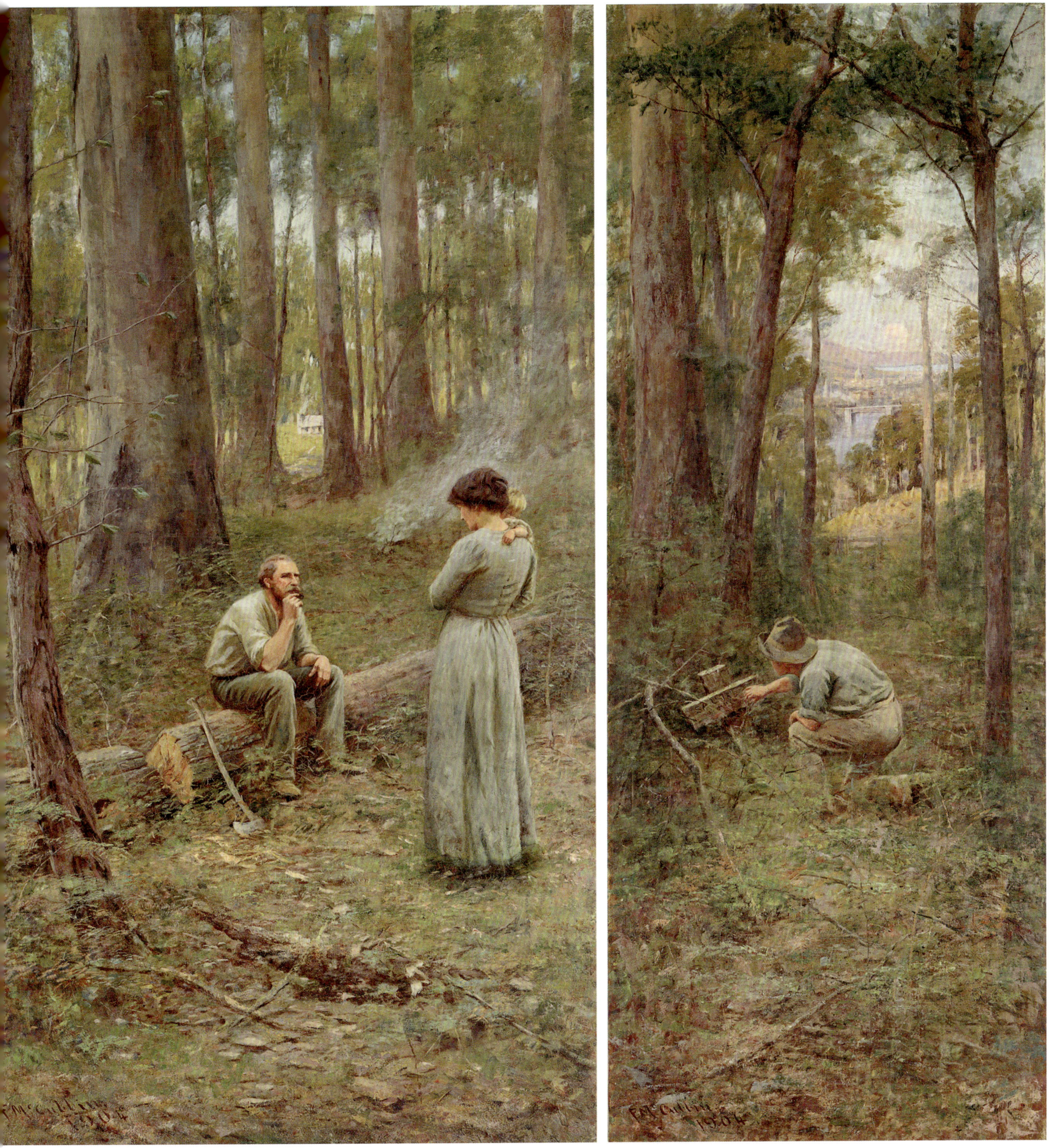

114

J. J. HILDER

Dry Lagoon, 1911

Watercolour and pencil, 66.2 × 99.1 cm

Art Gallery of New South Wales, Sydney. Purchased 1911

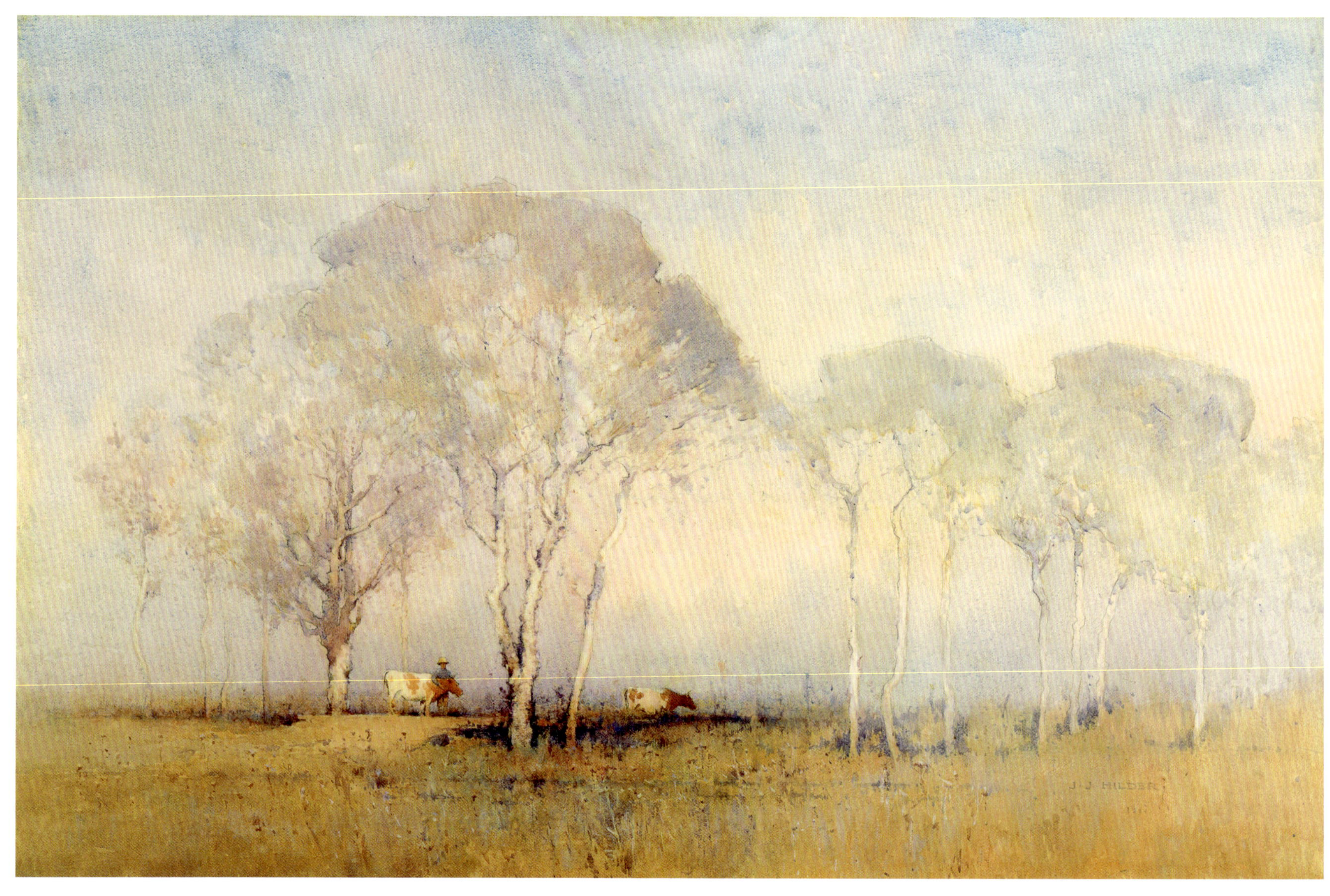

115

BLAMIRE YOUNG

Dry Weather, *c.* 1912

Watercolour, 56 × 76.8 cm

Art Gallery of New South Wales, Sydney. Purchased 1912

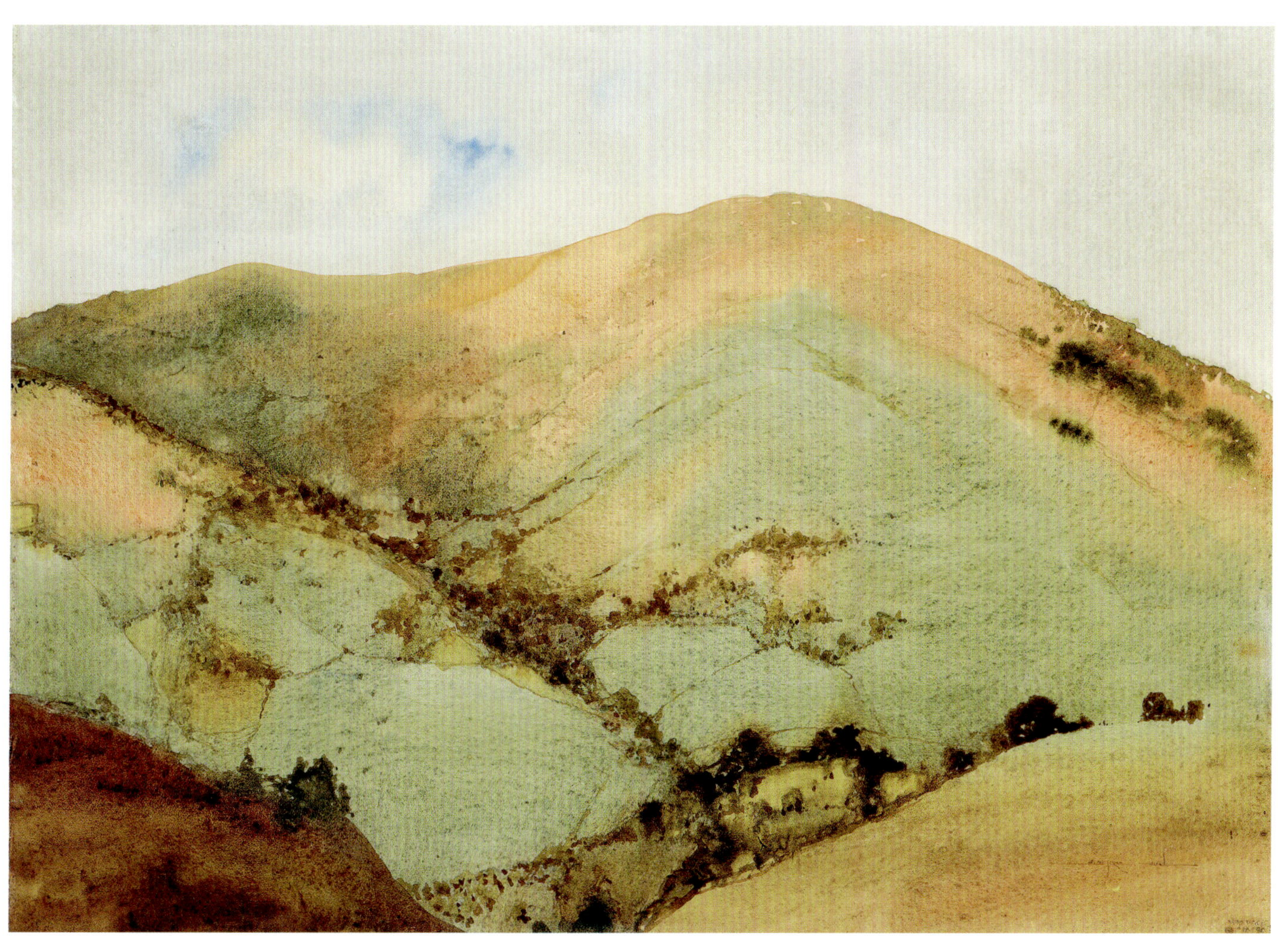

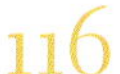

HANS HEYSEN
Midsummer Morning, 1908
Watercolour and pencil, 56 × 76.6 cm
National Gallery of Victoria, Melbourne. Purchased through the Felton Bequest, 1908

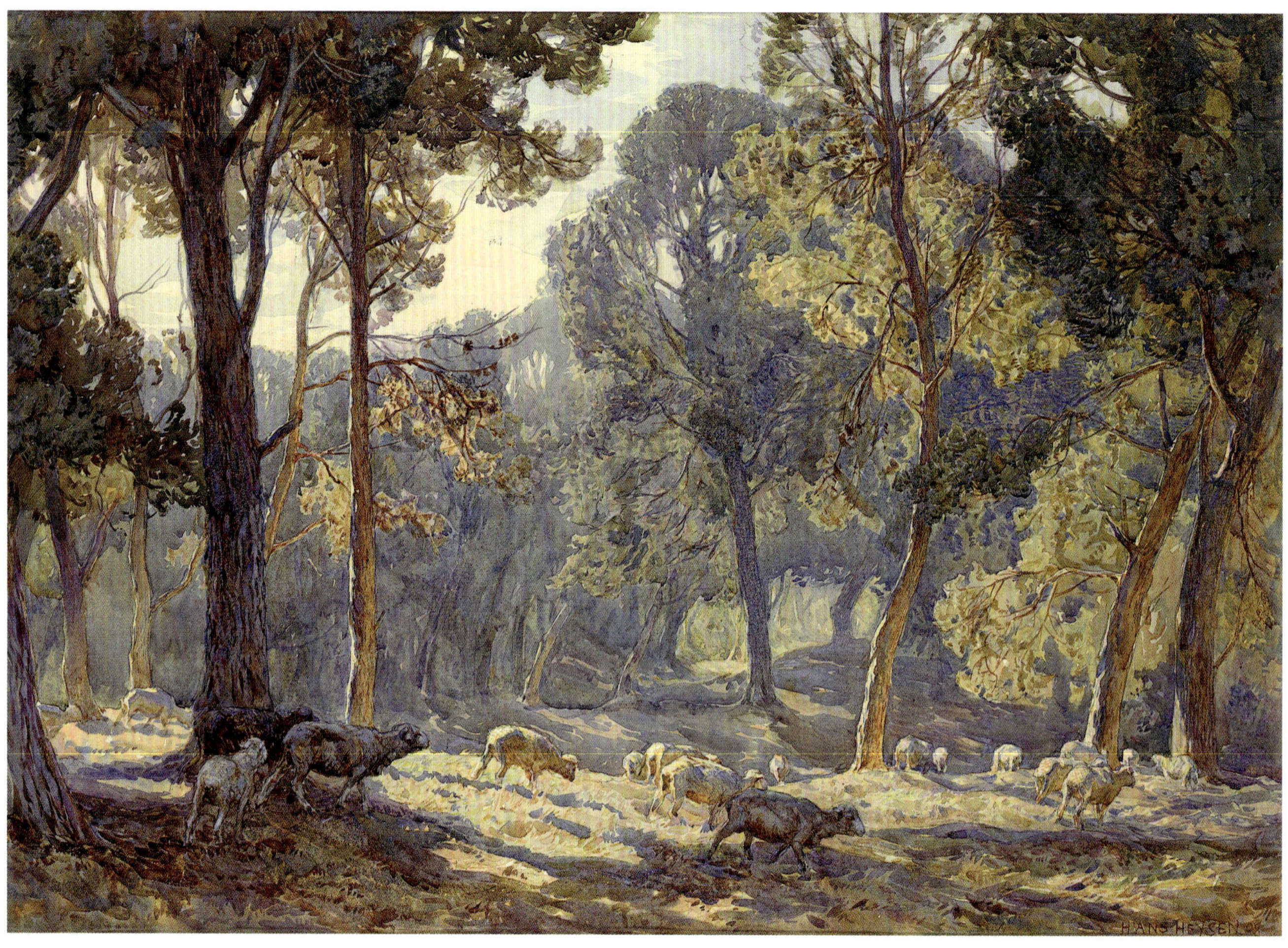

117

HANS HEYSEN

Red Gold, 1913

Oil on canvas, 129.5 × 174.5 cm

Art Gallery of South Australia, Adelaide.
Gift of the Rt Hon. Sir Charles Booth, 1913

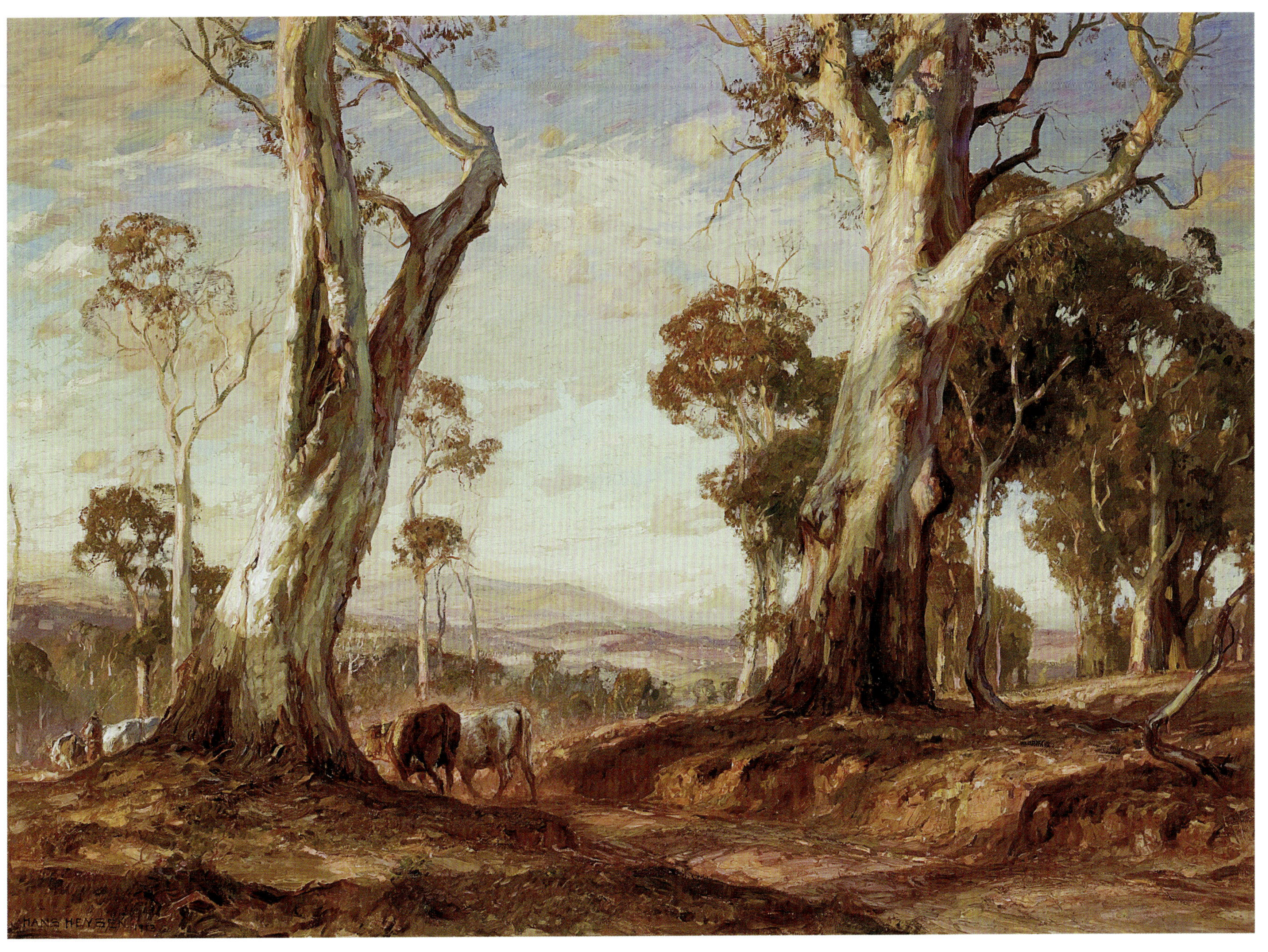

118

ELIOTH GRUNER
The Wave, *c.*1913
Oil on wood panel,
30.5 × 24.4 cm
Queensland Art Gallery, Brisbane. Gift of Lady Trout, 1978

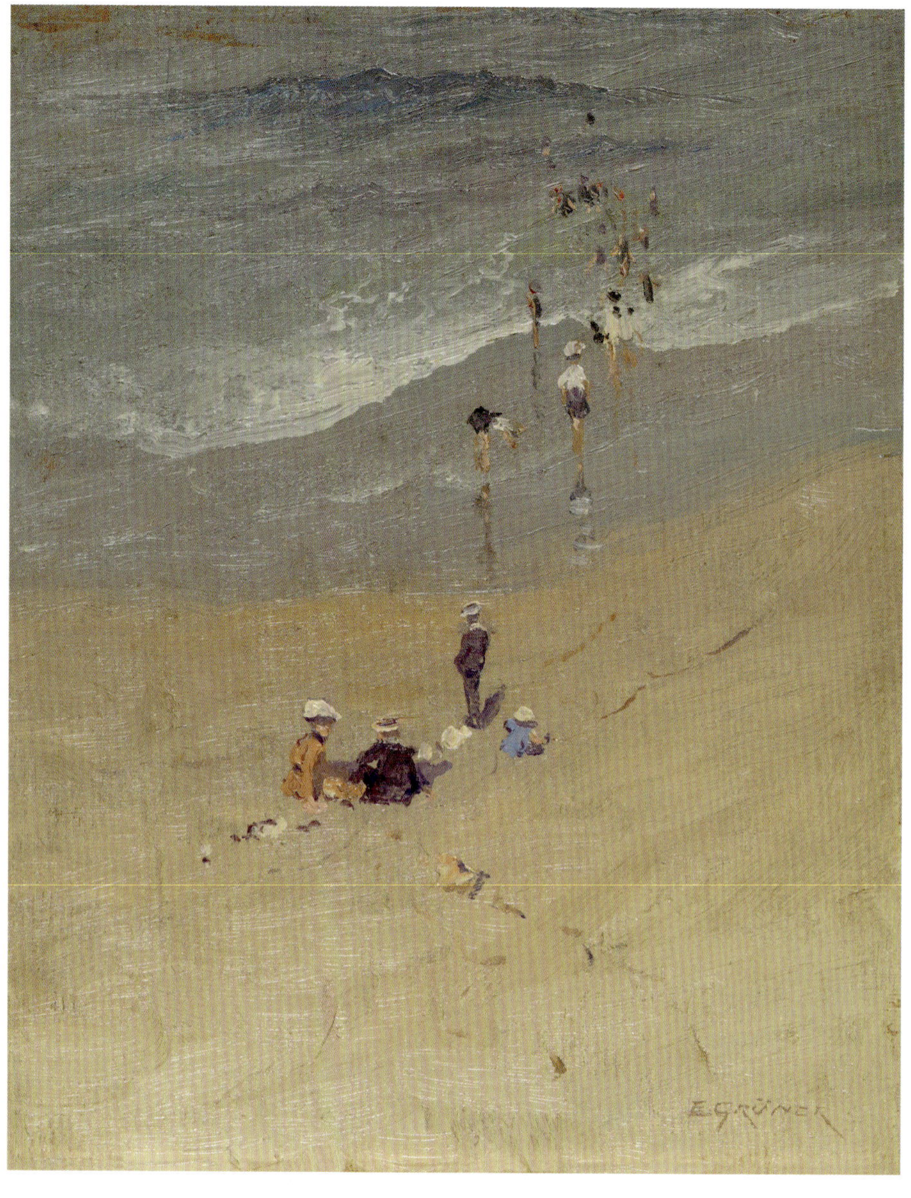

119

ETHEL CARRICK

Manly Beach – Summer Is Here, 1913

Oil on canvas, 81 × 102 cm

Manly Art Gallery and Museum, Sydney. Gift of the artist, 1934

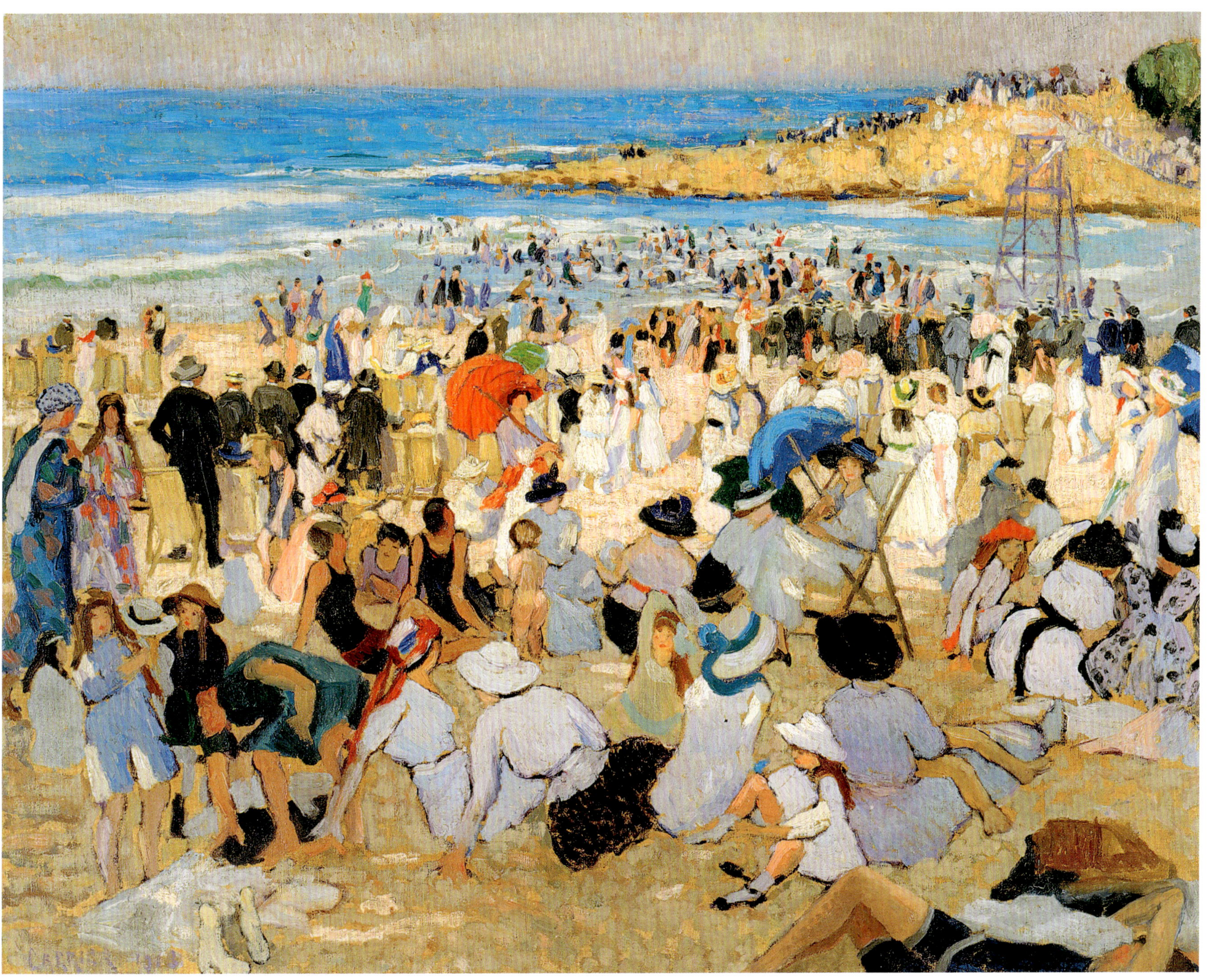

121

FREDERICK MCCUBBIN
Violet and Gold, 1911
Oil on canvas, 72 × 130 cm
National Gallery of Australia, Canberra. Purchased with the generous assistance of The Hon. Ashley Dawson-Damer and John Wylie AM and Myriam Wylie, 2008

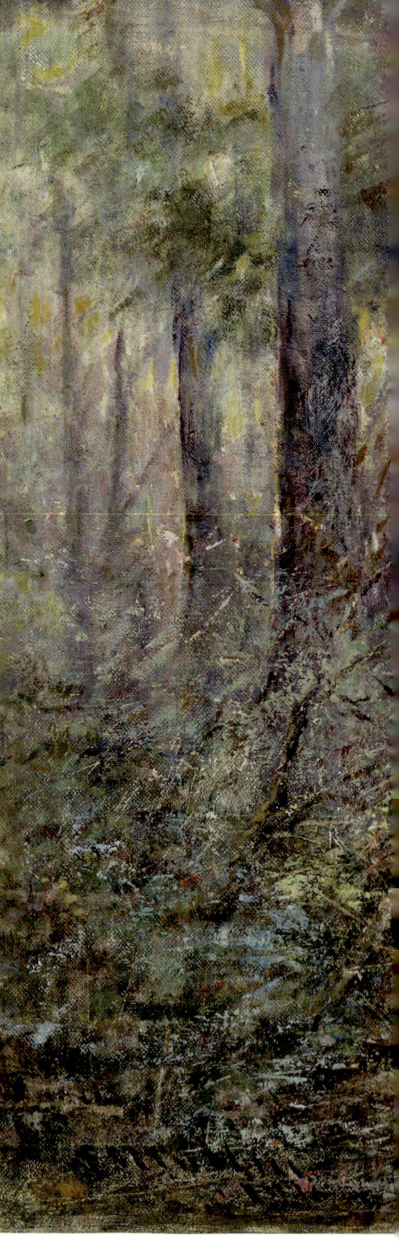

120

FREDERICK MCCUBBIN
Collins Street, *c.*1915
Oil on canvas on cardboard, 25 × 35.3 cm
Geelong Gallery, Victoria. H. P. Douglass Bequest Fund, 1945

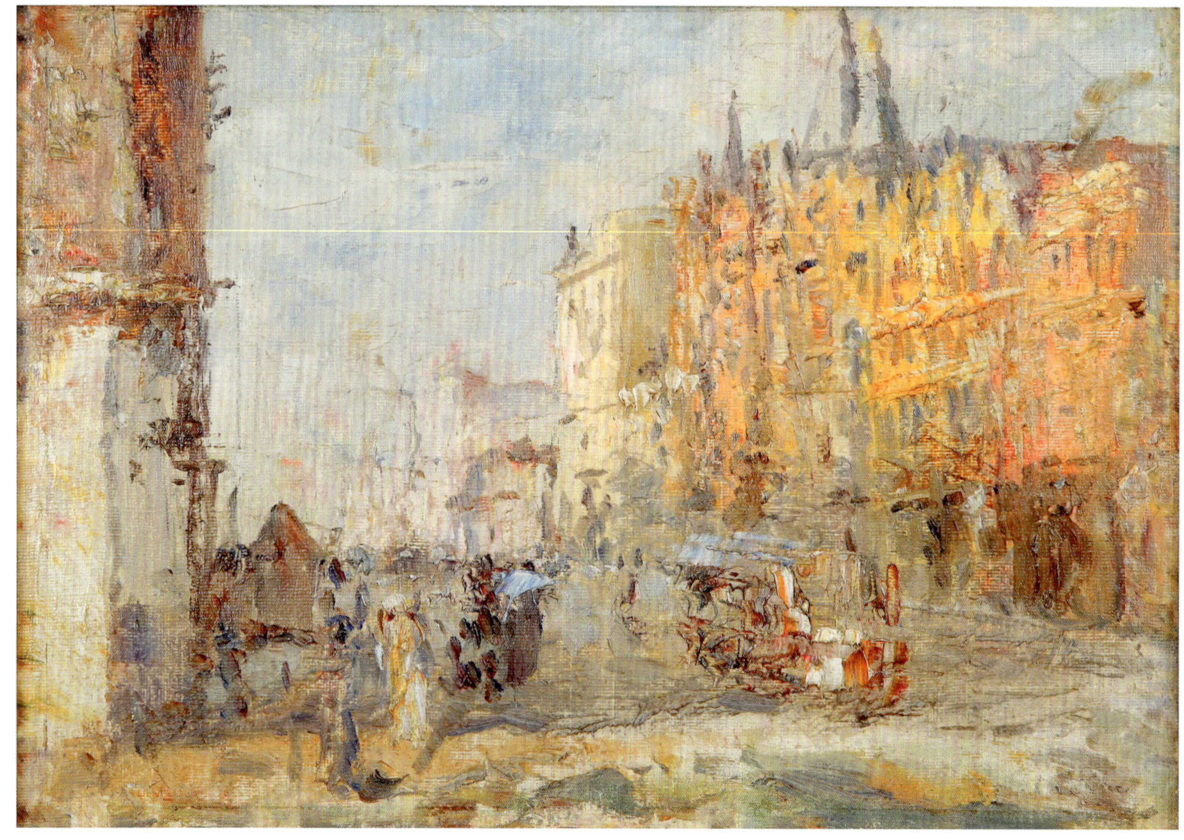

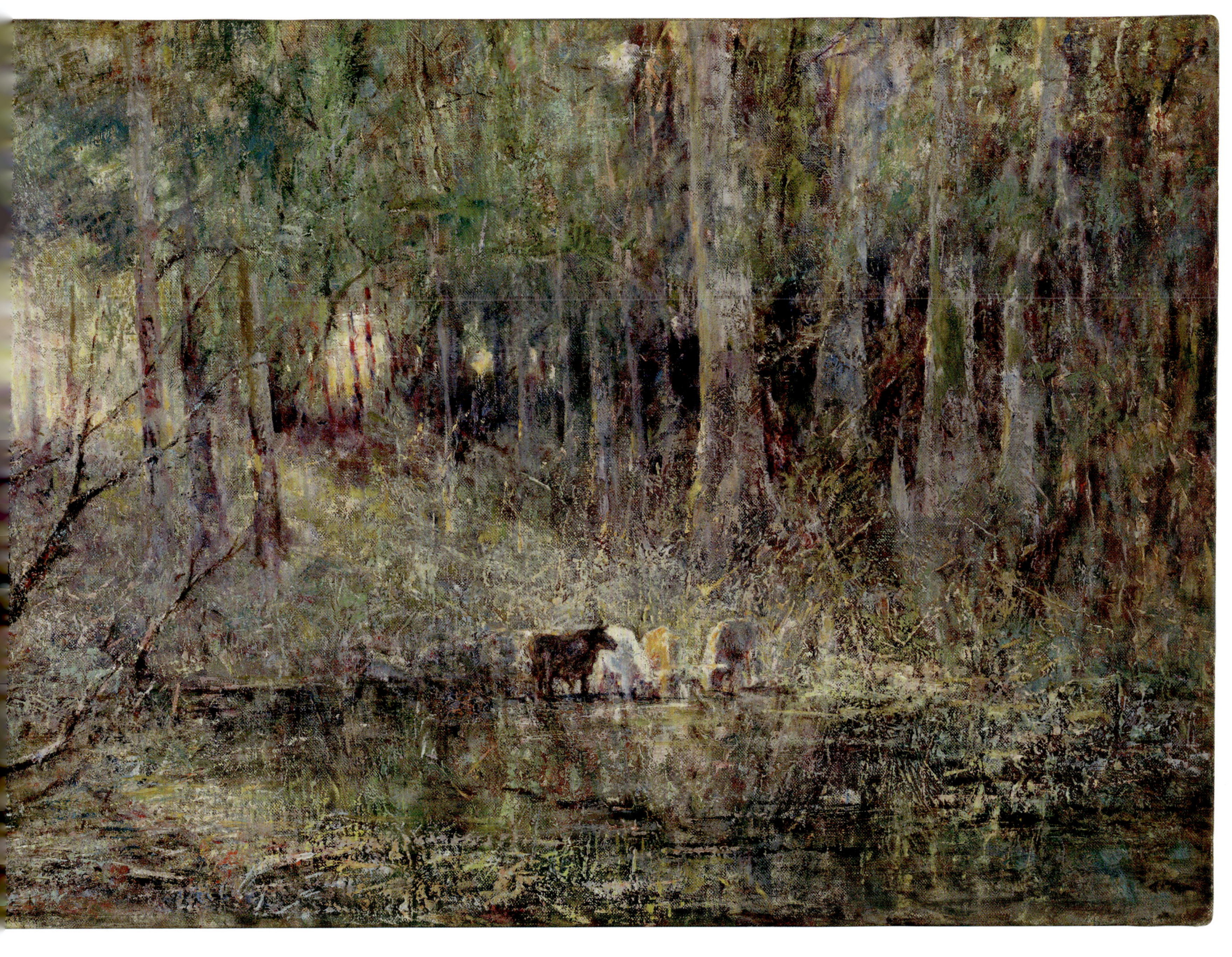

122

ROY DE MAISTRE

Forest Landscape, *c.*1918

Oil on cardboard, 35.4 × 40.6 cm

National Gallery of Australia, Canberra. Purchased 1971

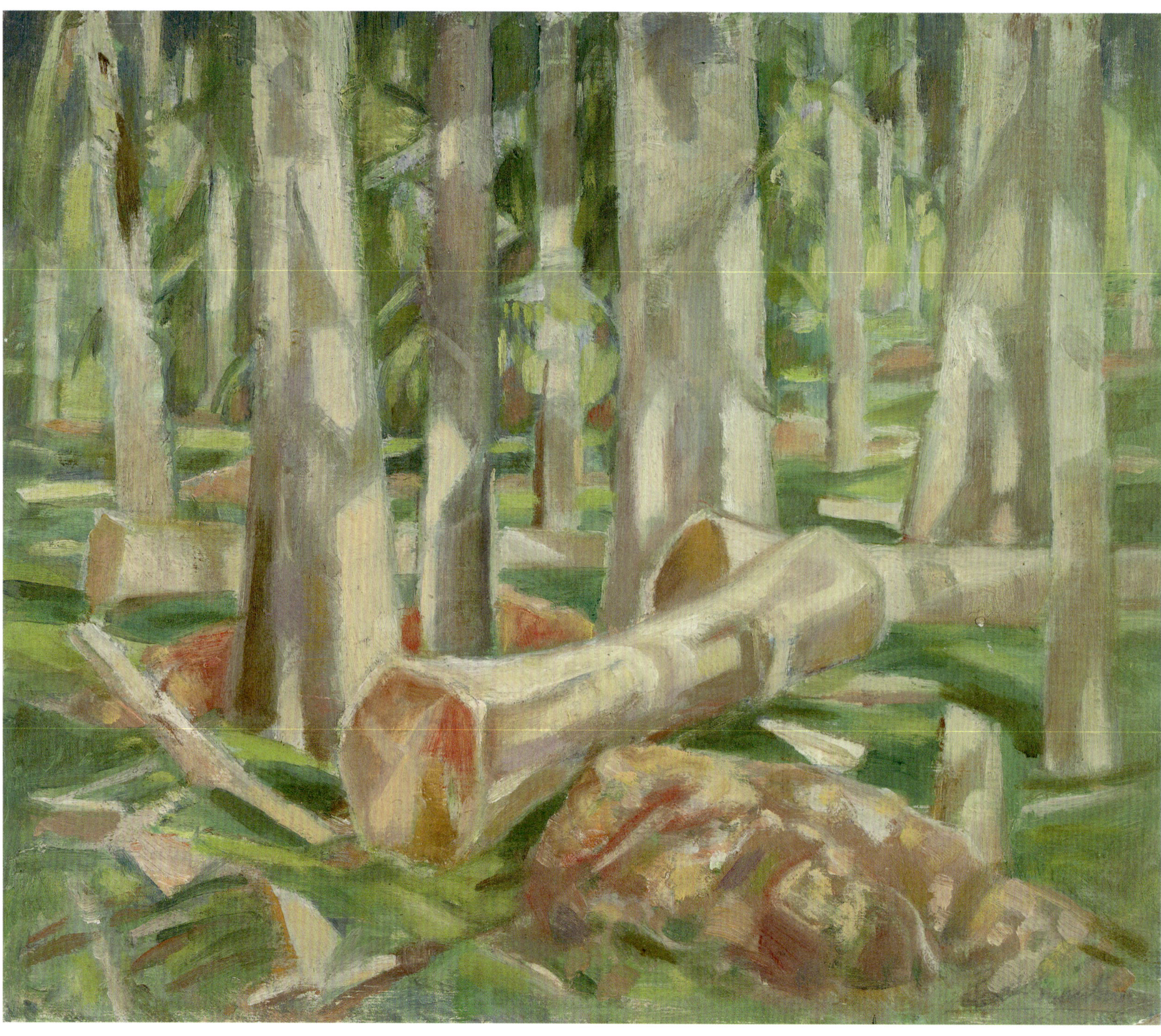

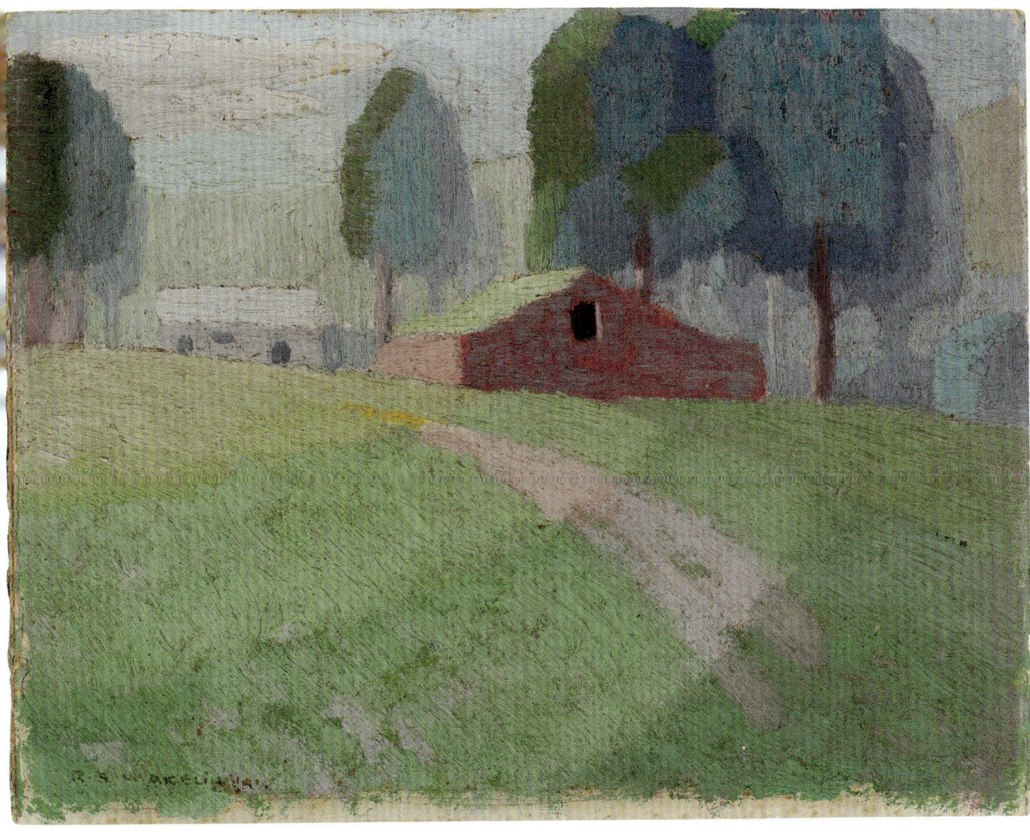

123

ROLAND WAKELIN
Barn near Tuggerah, 1919
Oil on composition board, 17.7 × 22 cm
National Gallery of Australia, Canberra. Gift of Daniel Thomas, 1981

124

ROLAND WAKELIN
Houses at Hunters Hill, *c.*1919
Oil on canvas on composition board, 24 × 20 cm
National Gallery of Australia, Canberra. Purchased 1963

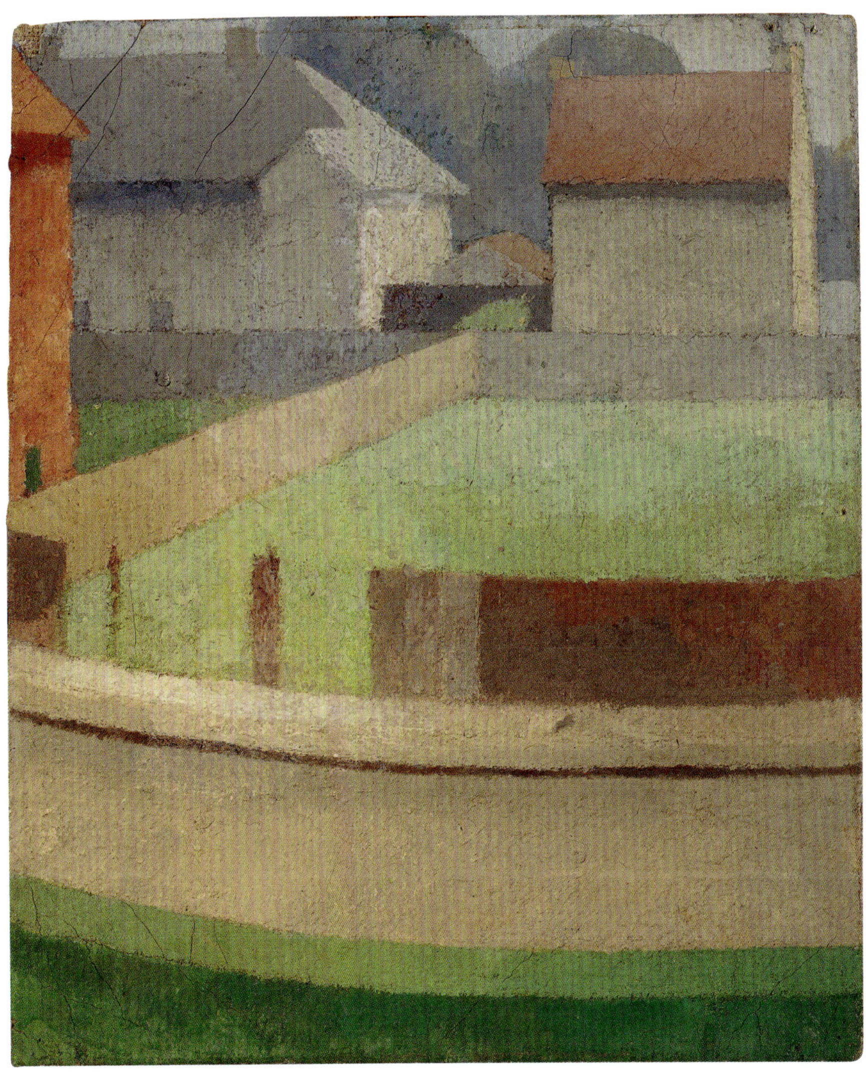

AUSTRALIAN LANDSCAPE: PATHWAYS INTO THE MODERN WORLD 1920–50

DEBORAH HART

4

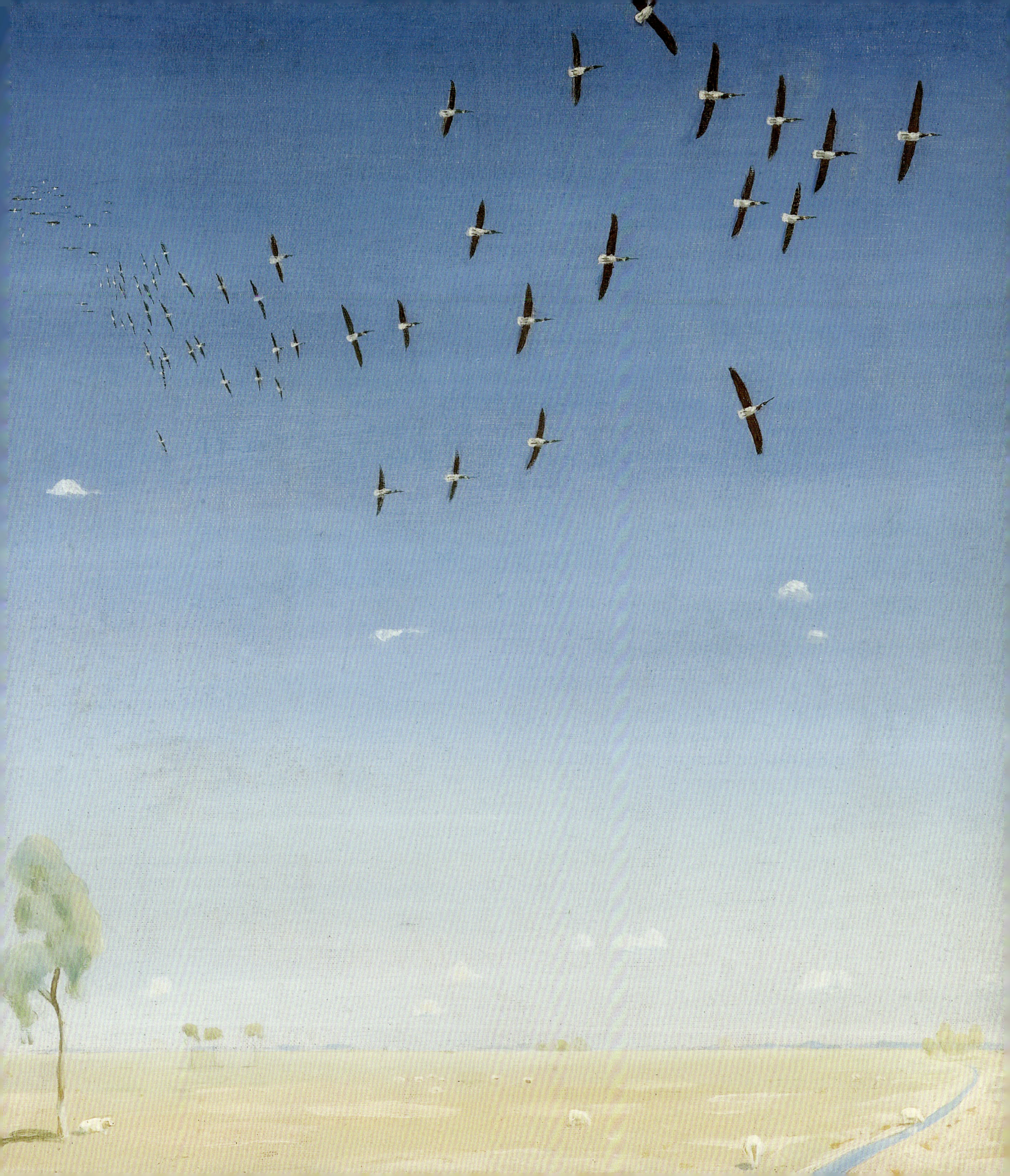

'There's no place like home.'
Dorothy, in L. Frank Baum, *The Wonderful Wizard of Oz* [1]

Home is a place to come back to. It is a state of mind and being, a place of belonging. It has been contested ground in the history of Australian landscape art for non-Indigenous peoples in a country in which British, European and Asian settlement is relatively recent. From the 1920s to the 1950s numerous Australian artists came from families who still considered Britain 'home' or 'the mother country'. In the young Commonwealth, echoes of Empire could still be felt through the period. Yet for many, like Grace Cossington Smith or Kenneth Macqueen, who had close ties with Britain, works undertaken abroad were never as strong as those painted in Australia, the place they very definitely felt to be home, where light, colour, plants and topography mattered. Over time, some like Macqueen, Sidney Nolan and Arthur Boyd expressed concern for wrongs inflicted by settlers on Indigenous people and saw landscape as something to be preserved, not pillaged or taken for granted.

Fig. 31
GEORGE W. LAMBERT,
A Sergeant of the Light Horse,
1920. Oil on canvas, 77 × 62 cm
National Gallery of Victoria, Melbourne. Purchased through the Felton Bequest, 1921

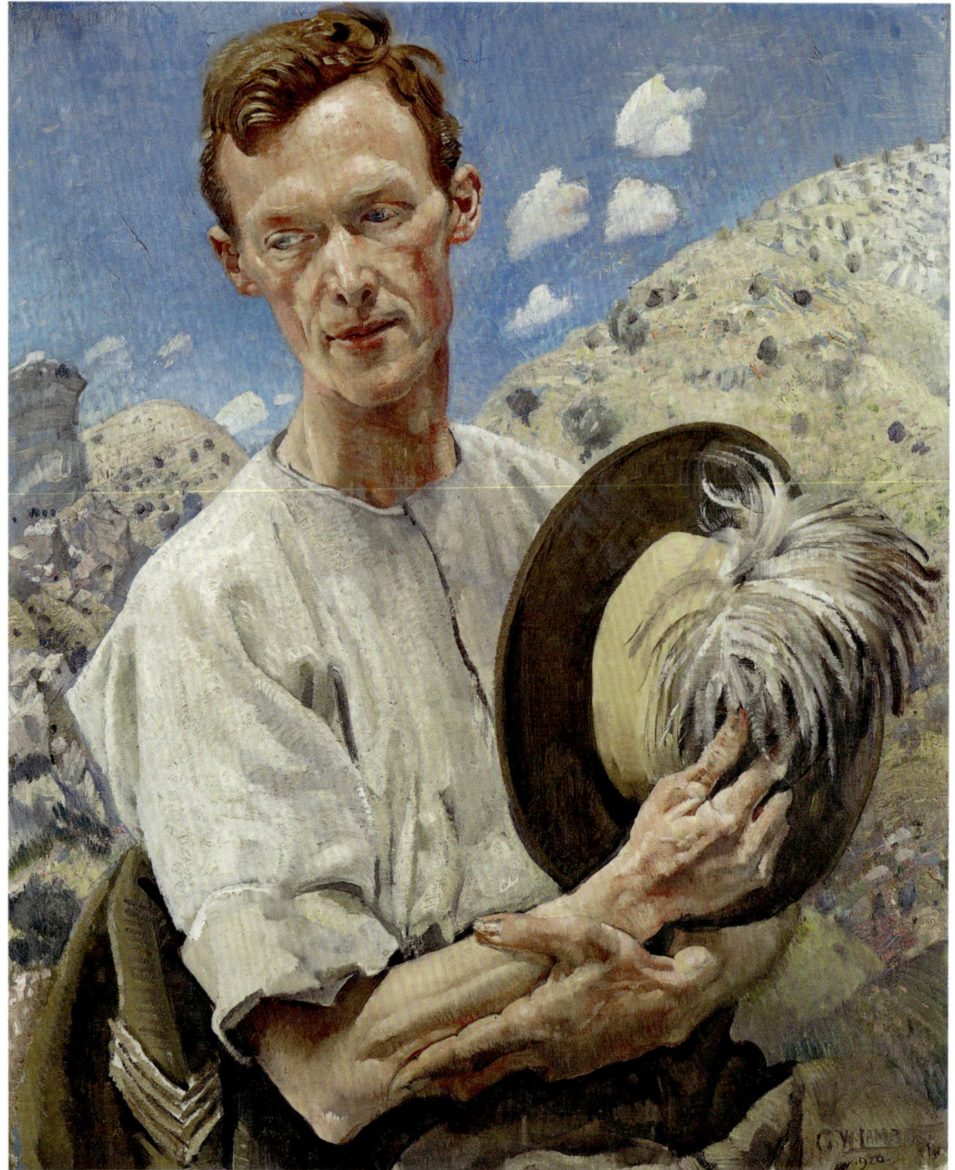

In the aftermath of the First World War there was a sense of relief that the conflict was over and also uncertainty as returning soldiers (including artists) struggled to re-establish normal lives back home. In the 1920s women artists were at the forefront of the modern movement, developing distinctive responses to their local environs. Modern artists were informed by an awareness of British and European art that they discovered in collections, in reproductions, on their travels and at such exhibitions as the 'Herald Exhibition of French and British Contemporary Art' that came to Australia in 1939.[2] Across the period, the French Post-Impressionists, particularly Cézanne, as well as exponents of Cubism, Surrealism and Expressionism directly informed artists' thinking. At the same time, many straddled the boundaries between Modernism and a more naturalistic response.

George W. Lambert spent his early adult life in London and returned to Australia in 1921. His painting *A Sergeant of the Light Horse* (fig.31) depicts a Digger with humility and dignity, perhaps recalling lost mates; some 60,000 young Australians were killed in the First World War. In *The Squatter's Daughter* (1923–24; cat.125), he reveals a more settled world of rural prosperity: a young modern woman walking her horse through the family property on the outskirts of Canberra at Michelago.[3] By the 1920s the area had become self-sufficient with income from wool, cattle and locally grown produce. Homesteads like this mirrored a way of life transferred from Britain: 'Horses, long rides, tennis, tea on the lawn ... farm workers to be visited.'[4] Lambert wrote a poem inspired by the dry grasses and light that at dusk appeared like 'Chinese silk of faded gold'. In the painting, lyricism is held in check by structure, the scene framed by gum trees, anchored by a pyramid hill. Hans Heysen observed that this work, in its 'search for character and form', was an object lesson for young landscape painters.[5]

Both Lambert and Heysen were supportive of a younger generation. By the 1920s Heysen's once innovative gum trees were at risk of over-exposure and he sought to reinvent his art in the ancient, expansive Flinders Ranges of outback South Australia. Ironically, it was there that Heysen saw a connection with modernity:

> Everything looks so old that it belongs to a different world. There are scenes ready made which seem to say 'here is the very thing you moderns are trying to paint'. Fine big simple forms against clear transparent skies – & a sense of spaciousness everywhere.[6]

In such paintings as *The Land of the Oratunga* (1932; cat.127), with its elemental forms that he described as 'the bones of the landscape laid bare', Heysen brought a radically new perspective to Australian landscape painting. The conical Patawarta Hill provides an anchor and counterpoint to the implied continuity of luminous, molten rock formations that flow into the viewer's space 'like arrested waves on the verge of breaking'.[7]

Harold Cazneaux was one of a number of artists who followed in Heysen's footsteps to the Flinders Ranges. In *The Spirit of Endurance* (fig.35), which Cazneaux considered his most Australian image, the towering eucalypt is set against distant ranges. A wounded specimen with part of its root system exposed, it has a hollowed-out centre. Nevertheless, it stands tall, enduring against the odds. The image was initially entitled *A Giant Gum Tree of the Arid North*, but was retitled in 1941, the same year that Cazneaux's only son died in the siege of Tobruk, North Africa.[8] He had already suffered greatly as a young man with the loss of friends in the First World War. Such human tragedy knows no bounds but the landscapes we inhabit physically and in our minds can offer some measure of solace and wonder.

Cazneaux was a founder of the Pictorialist movement that encompassed the 'sunshine school' of photographers; their manifesto of 1916 advocated close attention to the qualities of Australian sunlight. In the 1920s he was also official photographer for the thoroughly modern *Home* magazine, in which a number of his images of the Sydney Harbour Bridge first appeared. In *Arch of Steel* (1933; cat.132) Cazneaux combined Pictorialism with modernity in the contrasting patterns of light and shadow created by steel girders dramatically rising up like a contemporary cathedral. Before the Opera House, the Harbour Bridge was the icon of Sydney, making it one of the most distinctive Australian landscapes (fig.32).

During the Great Depression, which began in 1929, almost a third of Australians were out of work; others were receiving below the minimum wage. In this context, the building of the Harbour Bridge was a symbol of hope for many. Construction began in 1924 and was assiduously documented by numerous artists through to its completion in 1932. Jessie Traill's remarkable etchings celebrate and document the massive structure coming into being, taking account of the intricate complexities of specific tasks undertaken by members of a team. Although from Melbourne, she felt kinship with Sydney Harbour Bridge:

> In years to come when we dash across the Bridge in our taxi or take a walk across ... to see our harbour, we would have watched its progress and sketched and photographed its parts, [we] will feel with these workmen a sort of pride of possession, and it will be OUR BRIDGE too.[9]

By the time Grace Cossington Smith painted *The Bridge in Building* (1929; cat.131), construction was well underway. She returned often to the site, wearing a long skirt and hat, to make annotated drawings. In her daring, modernist painting, her viewpoint is from the ground near the triangular crane-base, pointing up to the sky. For her, the bridge was not only a feat of engineering but also a spiritual landscape; the latter is suggested by her radiant palette and auras mirroring the curve of the bridge reaching across the water, with a small crane far above like a spire.

Cossington Smith lived in the same house in Turramurra on Sydney's North Shore for most of her life. There she painted radical and more naturalistic works, such as *Four Panels for a Screen* (1929; cat.129), inspired by plants and birds in her garden – for example, a favourite yellow wattle visited by kookaburras – as well as a waterfall and rocky escarpments in the nearby bush. In her modernist *Eastern Road, Turramurra* (*c.*1926; cat.130) she conveys the meeting of old and new worlds. Looking down and up the long road, we can see suburban market gardens, and a horse and cart set against power lines and poles, signifiers of the modern world. Cossington Smith was a great colourist and her distinctive palette was informed by colour theory and Beatrice Irwin's publication *New Science of Colour* (1916).[10]

Kenneth Macqueen was inspired by the Pantheist writings of Richard Jeffries during the First World War. In Australia, his experience at Millmerran on the Darling Downs in Queensland, where he worked as a farmer and artist, shaped his contribution to landscape painting, his daily life bringing him close to the rhythms of nature. In *Birds and Sheep, Darling Downs* (*c.*1924; cat.128) freewheeling birds are suspended in a field of blue over a thin strip of grazing country. For Macqueen, the sky and clouds were inseparable from the land: 'Living on top of a mountain range, as I do, cloud formations offer a never-ending source of interest; very seldom is the sky devoid of cloud patterns sweeping into designs of lively beauty.'[11] Macqueen was mindful of environmental issues, setting aside some 'untouched forestry as a sanctuary'.[12]

A feeling for essentials in nature infused the art of Clarice Beckett, one of Melbourne's most significant modern artists, who moved to the bayside suburb of Beaumaris in 1918. Whereas Sydney is shaped by its harbour, Port Phillip Bay from Beaumaris to the Mornington Peninsula is a place to escape Melbourne's city life but still be within easy reach of it. Beckett came to know this area well, roaming clifftops, beaches and streets with her handmade painting cart, working

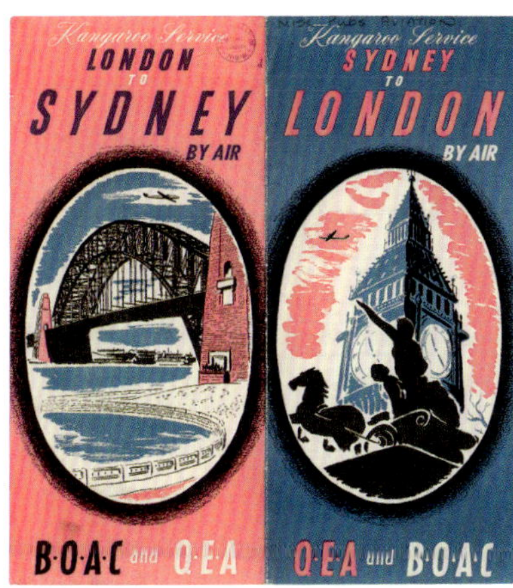

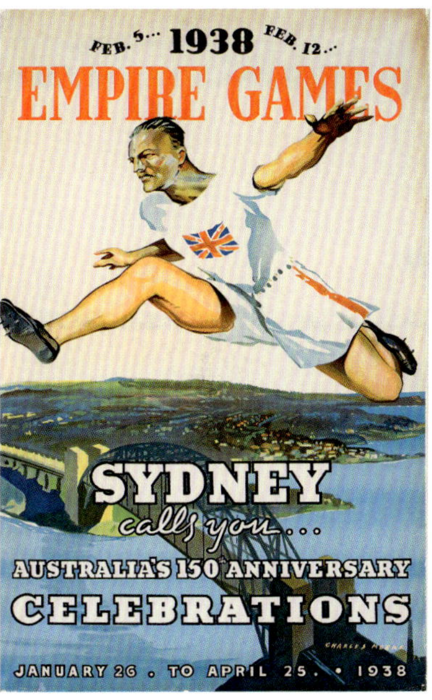

Fig. 32
UNKNOWN ARTIST, **Kangaroo Service: Sydney to London by Air/Q.E.A. and B.O.A.C.**, *c.*1948–50
State Library of New South Wales, Sydney

Sydney Harbour Bridge was used alongside London's Big Ben to promote flights by Qantas Empire Airlines and the British Overseas Airways Corporation.

Fig. 33
CHARLES MEERE, **1938 Empire Games poster**, 1938. Colour lithograph, 102.5 × 64 cm
Powerhouse Museum, Sydney. Gift of Pat Corrigan under the Commonwealth Cultural Gifts Program, 2009

outdoors in all weathers, often at dawn and dusk. Her personal vision emerged from Tonalism and Whistlerian distillation.[13] The strength of such luminous works as *Passing Trams* (*c.*1931; cat.136) derived from her capacity to combine presence and absence. In *Morning Shadows* (*c.*1932; cat.137) Beckett suggests a motorbike travelling unencumbered along the wide open road. Rich shadowy tones of dark and soft grey are enlivened by touches of luminous, vibrant colour in this world that is part of the everyday and yet quite dreamlike. In Beckett's art, as in Japanese *haiku*, every precise and delicate notation counts.

Compared with Beckett's atmospheric work, the beach and bush are graphically clear in Adrian Feint's *The Jetties, Palm Beach* (1942; cat.148), in which dominant trees with Art Deco-like interlacing branches provide a vertiginous view to jetties below. A highly stylised design also underpins Charles Meere's famous *Australian Beach Pattern* (1940; cat.139). Begun in 1938, the year of the Sydney Empire Games, the painting resembles a promotion for a land of eternal sunshine, health and prosperity. Meere designed a poster for the Games of an athlete leaping over the Harbour Bridge (fig.33), calling people to attend the celebrations coinciding with Australia's Sesquicentenary (the 150th anniversary of British settlement). In *Australian Beach Pattern* figures appear held in freeze-frame; swimmers wear up-to-the-minute swimming costumes showing off their athletic physiques; a bright ball balances high in the air. Ironically, London-born Meere did not much like the beach and the work was made in the studio. Emblematic of a uniform sense of place held in time, Meere's work provided the template for Anne Zahalka's *The Bathers* (fig.34), which presented a more diverse view of Australian society nearly 50 years later.

Max Dupain's iconic photograph *Sunbaker* (1937; cat.138) was of a friend resting on the beach after a swim; drops of water still glisten on his bronzed shoulders.[14] Yet through his skill and his great eye, he transformed the moment into a classic image of potent simplicity. Although *Sunbaker* is more natural than Meere's *Australian Beach Pattern*, in both works it is the figures *themselves* who stand in for the landscape, as though the environment has transmuted into their very beings.

The implicit relationship between the sensuality of body and landscape in Lloyd Rees's *The Road to Berry* (1947; cat.151) inspired younger artists, including John Olsen and Brett Whiteley. Rees's romantic temperament was nourished by the works of John Constable and by coastal Gerringong, south of Sydney, where his family had a holiday house at Werri Beach. He was inspired by the rolling hills and the curving road to Berry, which reminded him of the art and landscape that he had admired on a visit to Italy. In the shade of a tree outside Gerringong's scout hall, looking towards the road, he began to paint: 'When I put thin tones on it I began to feel the beauty of the canvas and form and rhythm drew into it. I realised I had achieved something that had new feelings coming.'[15]

One of Horace Trenerry's most modernist works is *The Road to Maslins* (1940; cat.140), its bold composition shaped by a road cutting directly across a curved hill. Trenerry was a member of Dorrit Black's Group 9 in Adelaide, which was formed to promote contemporary art. A committed modernist, Black studied with Claude Flight in London and with the Cubists André Lhote and Albert Gleizes in Paris. Lhote's principles of dynamic symmetry were also taught in relation to landscape when Black attended a summer school at Mirmande in the South of France. On her return to Australia she felt a strong desire to share her knowledge, first in Sydney and then in South Australia, where she set up a studio in her home at Magill in the Adelaide foothills. There she painted one of the great Australian modernist works, *The Olive Plantation* (1946; cat.141), in what was itself a transplanted idea of a Mediterranean landscape, the olive industry having thrived in that part of Australia since the nineteenth century. In Black's painting of the olive plantation echoes of lessons learnt in Europe are

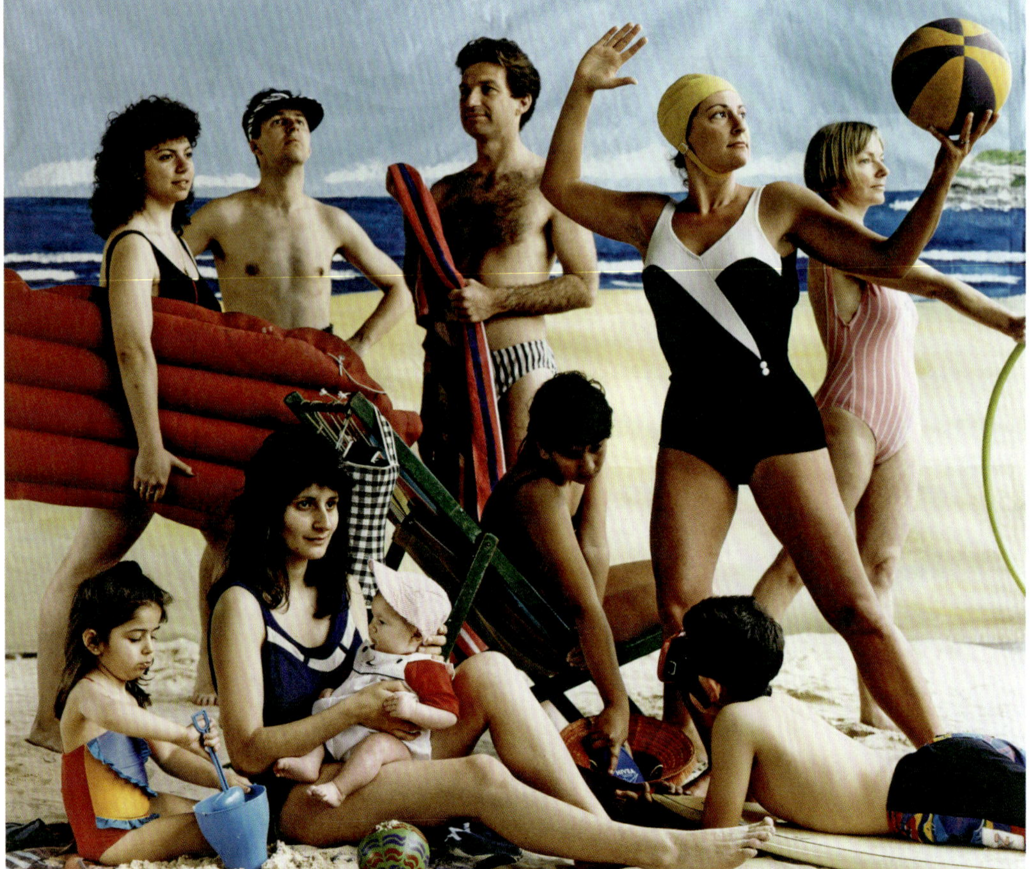

Fig. 34
ANNE ZAHALKA, **The Bathers**, from the series *Bondi: Playground of the Pacific*, 1989, printed 1990. C-type colour photograph, 72.4 × 83.5 cm
Art Gallery of New South Wales, Sydney. Hallmark Cards Australian Photography Collection Fund, 1990

combined with her intense feeling for place, conveyed in the dynamic energy of the rows and ridges of plantations like force-fields reaching forward from the high horizon into the viewer's space, as if to include us in the pulse of life. By implication, nature is not static but alive and gives life back to those who tend it. In the immediate aftermath of war the rounded hills also suggest the comfort of nurturing mother earth; the olive branch the symbol of peace.

Margaret Preston also painted robust modernist works. A prolific printmaker in the 1920s, she became a landscape painter in her sixties. A passionate advocate for an 'Australian ethos', Preston was an admirer of Heysen's paintings of the Flinders Ranges and felt strongly that Aboriginal art was central to an understanding of place (a view at odds with government policies of the day). Compared with her early appropriations of Aboriginal art, her work of the late 1930s took a new direction. By then she had travelled extensively to Indigenous communities and deepened her understandings with anthropologists.[16] She was also a keen supporter of Albert Namatjira's watercolours. By the time she painted *Aboriginal Landscape* (1941; cat.142), Preston was no longer adopting specific designs but conveying her experience of landscape rather more naturalistically, while acknowledging an indebtedness to Indigenous art in her palette, flat planes and aspects of mark-making. As Ian North has written, we might 'accept this bold little picture as an early gesture towards the idea of interculturalism, a developing paradigm for art today'.[17]

Preston's intercultural approach recurs in *Flying over the Shoalhaven River* (1942; cat.143), in which her depiction of the land and sinuous river viewed from the clouds draws on aspects of Chinese art and landscape that she had seen in Yunnan Province, on Japanese woodblock prints and Indigenous art, all brought together in her reconception of a regional landscape that was also to inspire Rees and Arthur Boyd.

In the 1940s Boyd and his peers were caught in the maelstrom of the Second World War. For the first time in its history Australia came under direct attack. The collective shock and fear were most keenly felt in Darwin and other parts of northern Australia, which were bombed by the Japanese in 1942.[18] Eric Thake's *Brownout* (1942; cat.144), painted from the Harp of Erin Hotel in the suburb of East Kew, depicts wartime partial blackouts that brought an eerie atmosphere to the night streets of Melbourne. An accomplished Surrealist, Thake combines movement in lines of lights that swing back into dark space, with an evocative stillness in larger luminous circles.

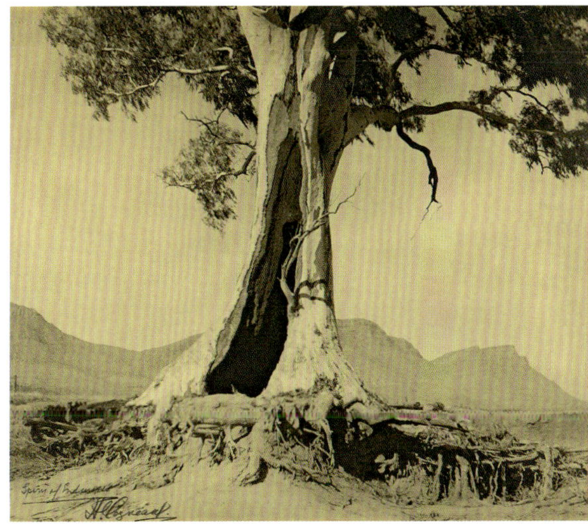

Fig. 35
HAROLD CAZNEAUX, **The Spirit of Endurance**, 1937. Gelatin silver photograph, 29.3 × 24.4 cm
National Gallery of Australia, Canberra. Purchased 2013

Time also stands still in Jeffrey Smart's unremittingly bleak *Holiday Resort* (1946; cat.150), like a Sunday afternoon stretching into oblivion. As in the world of Samuel Beckett, everything and nothing may be possible in the spaces between an abandoned pram and a man reading his newspaper. An existential feeling also pervades Albert Tucker's excoriating *Sunbathers* (1944; cat.145), which is about as far as it is possible to go from Meere's *Australian Beach Pattern* (cat.139). Tucker's beached, morphed figures on lurid yellow sand against a blue-black sky emerged from his anxieties about war and a loss of morality. Stranded on the furthest shores of the mind, with no place-markers, this is the psychological landscape of T. S. Eliot's *The Waste Land* (1922). In Australia, as in Britain, Eliot's poetry was a beacon that encapsulated a vivid consciousness of the inhumanity of war.

Arthur Boyd longed for an end to suffering and violence. Having been read Biblical stories as a child, he incorporated a New Testament theme into *The Mining Town (Casting the Money Lenders from the Temple)* (*c.*1946; cat.147), a morality tale of materialism and greed set in a composite landscape. The mine at the centre of the work recalls Bruegel's *Tower of Babel* (*c.*1563; Kunsthistorisches Museum, Vienna) and references a mine near Bendigo; a coffin falling from a hearse recalls an episode in James Joyce's *Ulysses* (1922) and the death of a miner; the local environment of Port Melbourne appears in the upper right of the composition, while in the foreground lovers sit in an enclosed garden where a gardener tends the roses.[19] This multifarious world is akin to the stories of Dylan Thomas that Boyd admired.

In Boyd's *The Hunter I* (1944; cat.146), the Victorian landscape is entangled with the artist's feeling of entrapment in the army and war. The figure of the hunter is also hunted. The man with his nemesis, a horned ram (a symbol of lust and corruption), may be seen either as the alien aggressor impinging on the land, hunting any native creature, or as vulnerably enmeshed in the bush, his arm reaching up in a gesture of supplication, a cry from the wilderness.

Russell Drysdale found another kind of devastation in remote areas of New South Wales in 1944, when he was invited by the *Sydney Morning Herald* to document one of the worst droughts in Australia's history. Likening what he saw to a war zone, he was appalled by the loss of homes, animals and trees. In the ensuing period he drew upon this direct experience, and on his knowledge of the art of Henry Moore and Graham Sutherland, who also created metamorphic landscapes. In the taut structure of *Emus in a Landscape* (1950; cat.153), twisted corrugated-iron wreckage represents the aftermath of bushfire heat fierce enough to make the real surreal, moulding weird sculptural shapes into a memorial to human loss, the strangeness of the atmosphere heightened by lone surviving emus wandering the vast, arid space.

On his travels to remote areas, Drysdale made a sketch of a drover's camp near Deniliquin. Since the nineteenth century drovers had moved livestock over vast tracts of land and were often away from home for long stretches of time.[20] In Drysdale's *The Drover's Wife* (*c.*1945; cat.152), the woman in a plain dress and hat, carrying a bag, has been left to fend for herself. Her feet planted firmly on the ground, she looks out with a stoic yet tender expression, trying to find her place against the odds in a world of stark realities. Drysdale saw precariousness in a largely inhospitable outback, but also witnessed 'a fighting spirit in the settlers, a faith that "it'll come good"'.[21]

A spirit of endurance underpins Axel Poignant's *Swagman on the Road to Wilcannia* (1954; cat.134), a moving image of a swagman encountered in the outback of New South Wales, pushing his bike with no chain or pedals and carrying his bedroll, pots, food, water and some books, making do with very little as he travels the long road of life.[22] Like the drover, the image of a swagman, an itinerant labourer who trudged the country, takes us back to the Depression and much earlier, immortalised in 'Waltzing Matilda', Australia's unofficial national anthem, written in 1895 by Banjo Paterson.

A child of inner-city Melbourne during the Depression, Sidney Nolan encountered the landscape of the Wimmera in north-west Victoria while travelling on the back of a lorry with fellow soldiers to Dimboola. Drawing upon his awareness of European Modernism, and his penchant for Henri 'Le Douanier' Rousseau, he painted *Kiata* (fig.36), emphasising the long, flat horizon. This paved the way for his famous Ned Kelly series (cats 154, 155, 156, 157), depicting the infamous nineteenth-century bushranger and his gang. The brilliance of the series resides in its fusion of legend and landscape, and the inclusion of a modernist black square for Kelly's armour, a powerful symbol of resistance to authority. Across the series Nolan provides diverse views of landscape, informed by visits to 'Kelly country', accounts of the day and his own imaginings. The background of *Quilting the Armour* (1947; cat.157) suggests the kind of rural backblock in which impoverished Irish settlers like the Kellys lived. The last painting set in landscape, *Glenrowan* (1946; cat.154), brings together an Aboriginal tracker, Irish and non-Irish police, and Kelly towering over them. As in a Shakespearian tragedy, his fate is sealed, yet his image was to endure. The iconic *Ned Kelly* painting (1946; cat.155) is a landscape of poetic imagination, the way Nolan thought Australia *should* look: sun-drenched, uncompromising, perfectly complementing its protagonist, both hero and anti-hero. A legend in its own right, this image was a backdrop in the opening ceremony of the Sydney Olympic Games in 2000.[23]

Between 1949 and 1950 Nolan was one of the first artists to fly vast distances across the country, discovering the red earth of the interior. On Australia Day, 26 January, in 1950 he wrote to Albert Tucker: 'We had a wonderful trip to the back of beyond, it is the proper Australia, old, dignified and coherent ... all told we just about covered the whole area of the inland.'[24] In his Central Australia paintings, such as *Inland Australia* (1950; cat.159), the patterns of rocks like waves meeting open country, stretching as far as the eye could see, recalled Heysen's images of the Flinders Ranges. Painted in delicate veils of oil and enamel, this work reveals Nolan's perceptions of the outback, which were partly informed by contact with Aboriginal people.

> They show you that the country is a gentle, dreaming one, the barrenness and harshness is all in our European eyes and demands. In fact one feels a barbarian at the gates.[25]

At the opening of Nolan's first exhibition of these works, James Gleeson wrote that it needed to be regarded as 'one of the most important events in Australian painting'. Cynthia Nolan also described 'old ladies from central Queensland carrying their string bags [who] come up with tears in their eyes and say it's so true, it's so real'.[26]

On a visit to Australia in 1949 Kenneth Clark had been greatly impressed by Nolan's works of deserted mining towns, such as the audacious *Pretty Polly Mine* (1948; cat.158). In this painting Nolan captures the absurdity of a mine manager who liked to feed the birds wearing a suit in the hot deserted landscape; the oversized parrot in the painting accentuating the poetic irrationality. Clark became a champion of Australian art in Britain, particularly of Nolan and Drysdale, whose reputations grew apace in the 1950s. In 1951, the year of Nolan's first London exhibition, the Tate acquired one of his Central Australian works, *Inland Australia*.

Nolan and Drysdale provided Australians (who mostly live on the coastal fringes) with distinctive new visions of the outback landscape. Their prominence in Britain and Australia meant that the continuing importance of the older generation of modernists, such as Grace Cossington Smith, Margaret Preston and Dorrit Black, was sometimes overlooked, along with the urban and suburban landscapes they often portrayed. In 1946, the same year that Nolan started his Ned Kelly series partly relating to Irish–Australian connections, Black painted *The Olive Plantation* (cat.141) that drew upon her own locality as well as aspects of European culture, offering the promise of hope after the war. This echoes the feeling of rebuilding confidence in artists' depictions of the Sydney Harbour Bridge in the wake of the First World War and the Depression.

Black's work also connects by implication with the idea of cultural exchange that would become increasingly significant after the Second World War, as migrations across the globe led to a mutable, complex sense of what 'home' might mean. After the traumas of war, many British and European migrants came to Australia to find a safe place to call home, often establishing bicultural identities. Artists like Nolan and Boyd would, conversely, spend long periods in Britain establishing two homes, often reflecting on their country of birth in landscapes of memory.

Between 1920 and 1950 many Australian artists had been evolving idiosyncratic responses to urban, suburban and regional landscapes, informed by local and international art, by the particularities of the environment and by the context of the times in which they were created. With wave upon wave of change since the First World War, artists continued to forge new pathways into the modern world, reminding us that responses to place in a settler society are not static but about states of *becoming*, open to new beginnings and cross-cultural meeting-places.

By the start of a new decade the scene was set for overlapping stories to unfold, including the reassertion of links with Britain under the Prime Ministership of Robert Menzies; a continuously deepening connection with Australia and its varied terrain facilitated by the greater ease of road, rail and air travel; a gradual recognition of Indigenous culture that still had a long way to go; and the influx of new migrants who were to enrich the cultural landscape for ever.

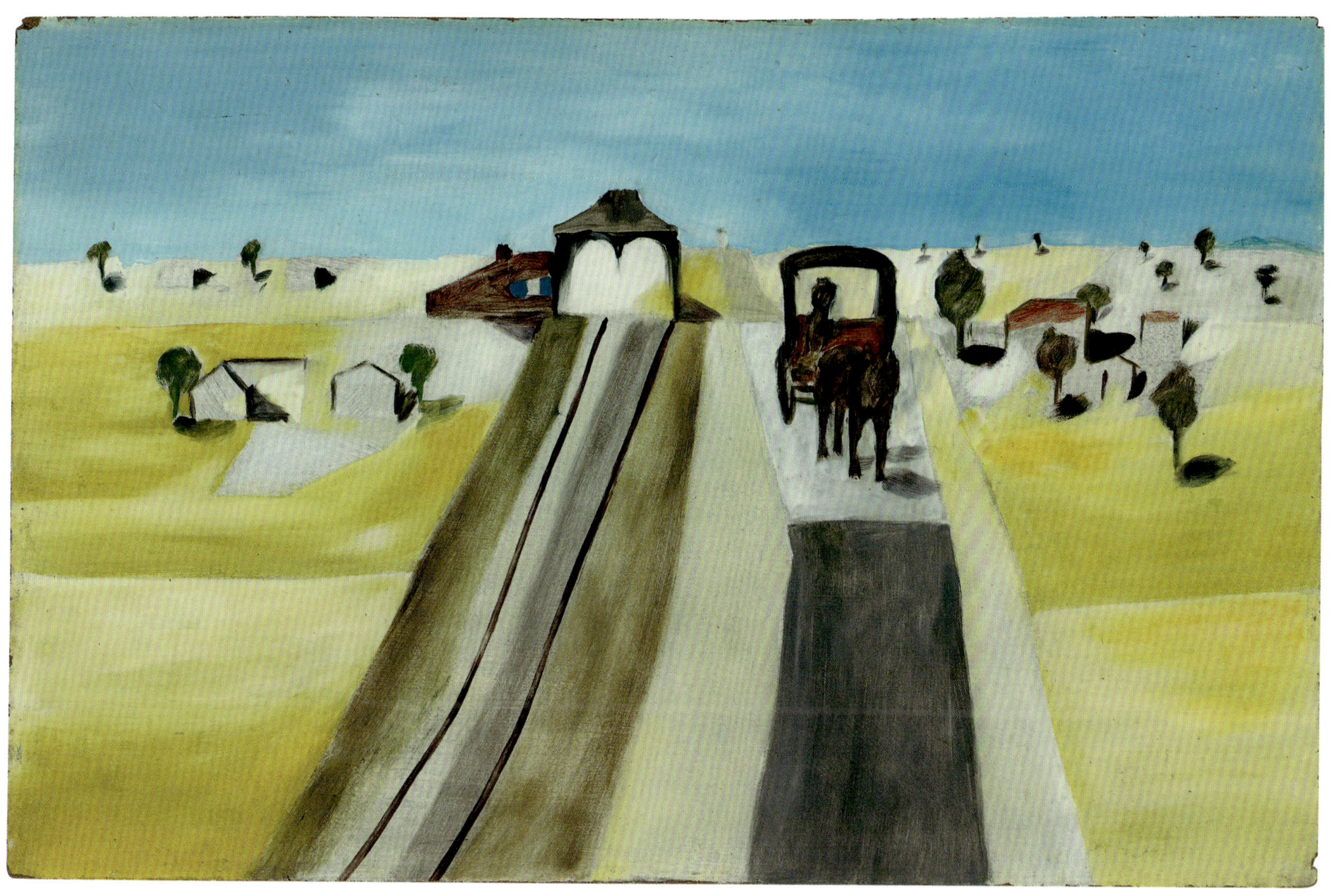

Fig. 36
SIDNEY NOLAN, **Kiata**, c.1943.
Enamel paint on composition board, 60.9 × 91.7 cm
National Gallery of Australia, Canberra. Purchased 1973

125

GEORGE W. LAMBERT

The Squatter's Daughter, 1923–24

Oil on canvas, 61.4 × 90.2 cm

National Gallery of Australia, Canberra.
Purchased with the generous assistance of James Fairfax AO and Philip Bacon AM and the people of Australia, 1991

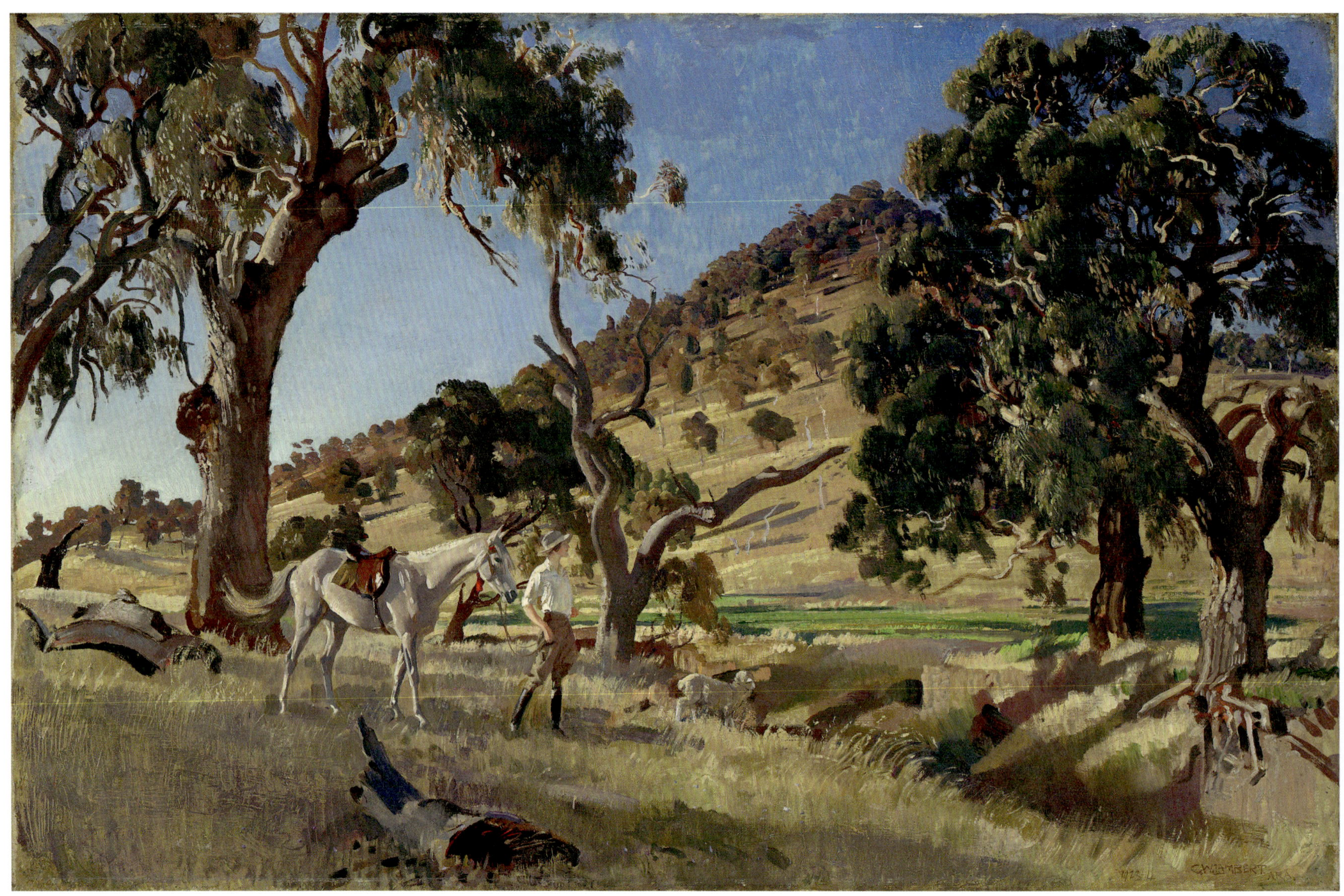

126

JAMES W. R. LINTON
Falls Road, Late Evening, 1926
Watercolour, 54.6 × 75.4 cm
National Gallery of Australia, Canberra.
Purchased 1980

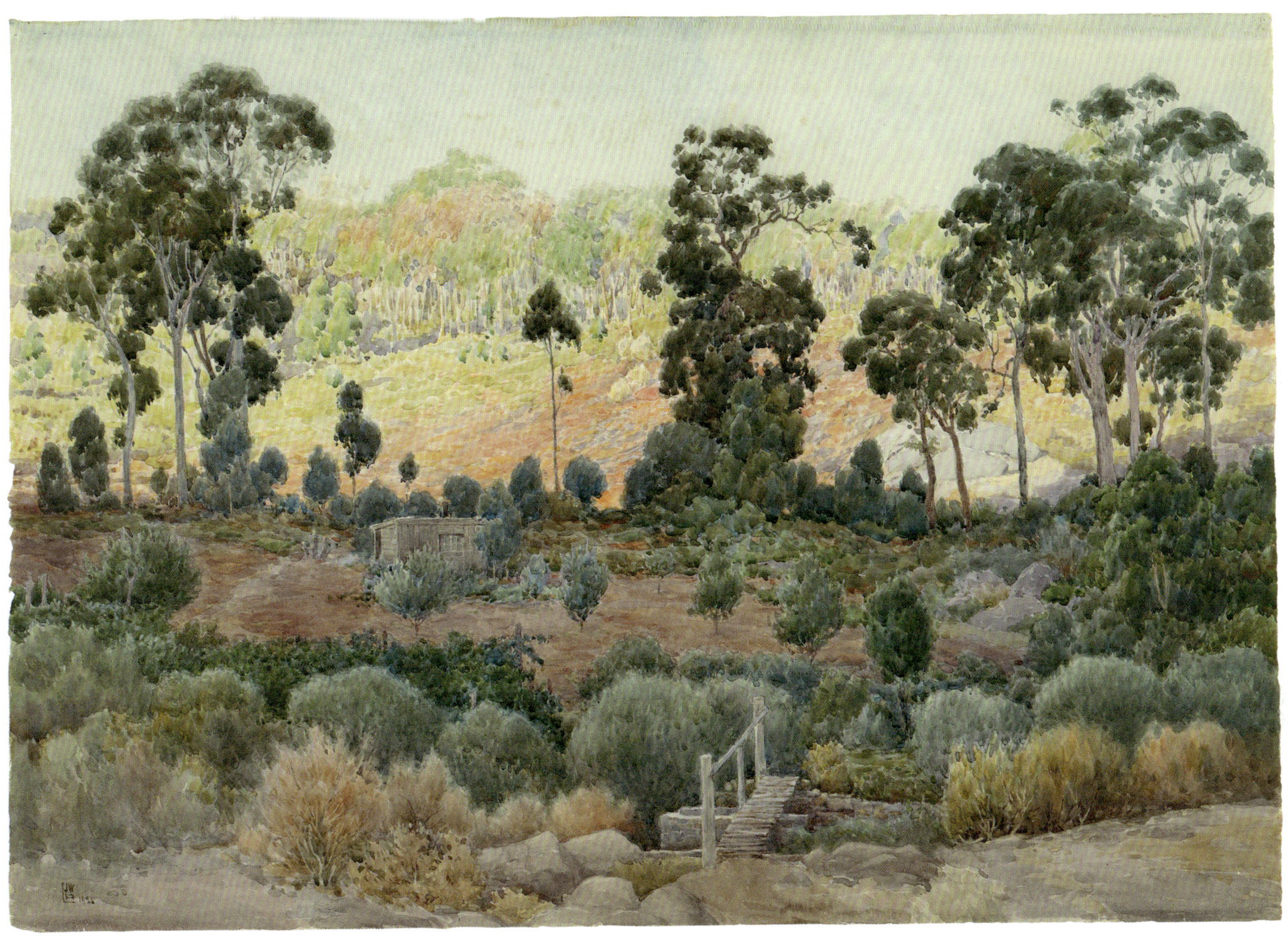

127

HANS HEYSEN

The Land of the Oratunga, 1932

Watercolour, 47.3 × 62.6 cm

Art Gallery of South Australia, Adelaide.
South Australian Government Grant, 1937

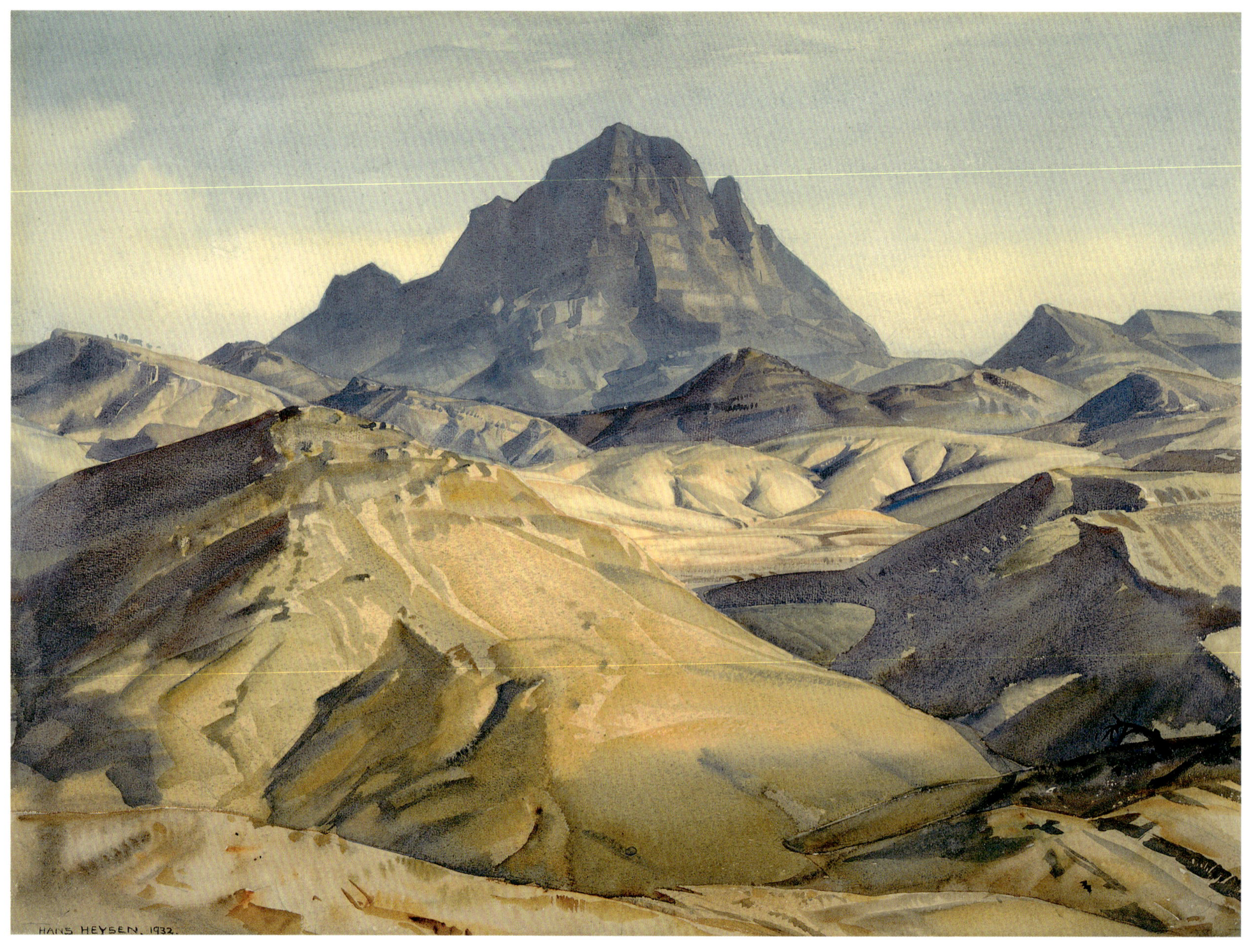

128

KENNFTH MACQUEEN
Birds and Sheep, Darling Downs, *c.*1924
Oil on board, 52.6 × 65.1 cm
Art Gallery of South Australia, Adelaide.
Ivor Francis Bequest Fund, 1995

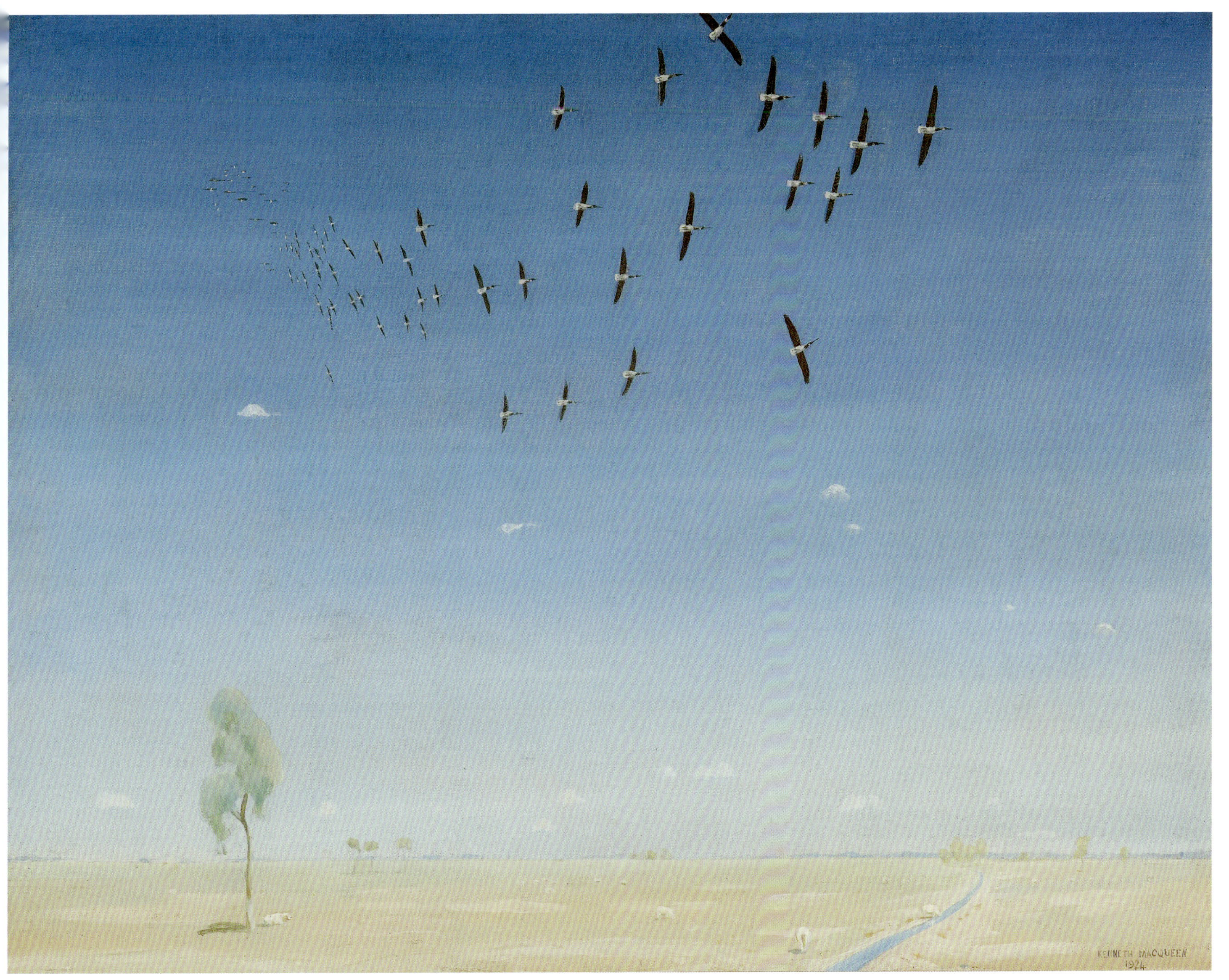

129

GRACE COSSINGTON SMITH
Four Panels for a Screen: Loquat Tree, Gum and Wattle Trees, Waterfall, Picnic in a Gully, 1929
Oil on cardboard,
144.2 × 53 cm (each)
National Gallery of Australia, Canberra. Purchased 1976

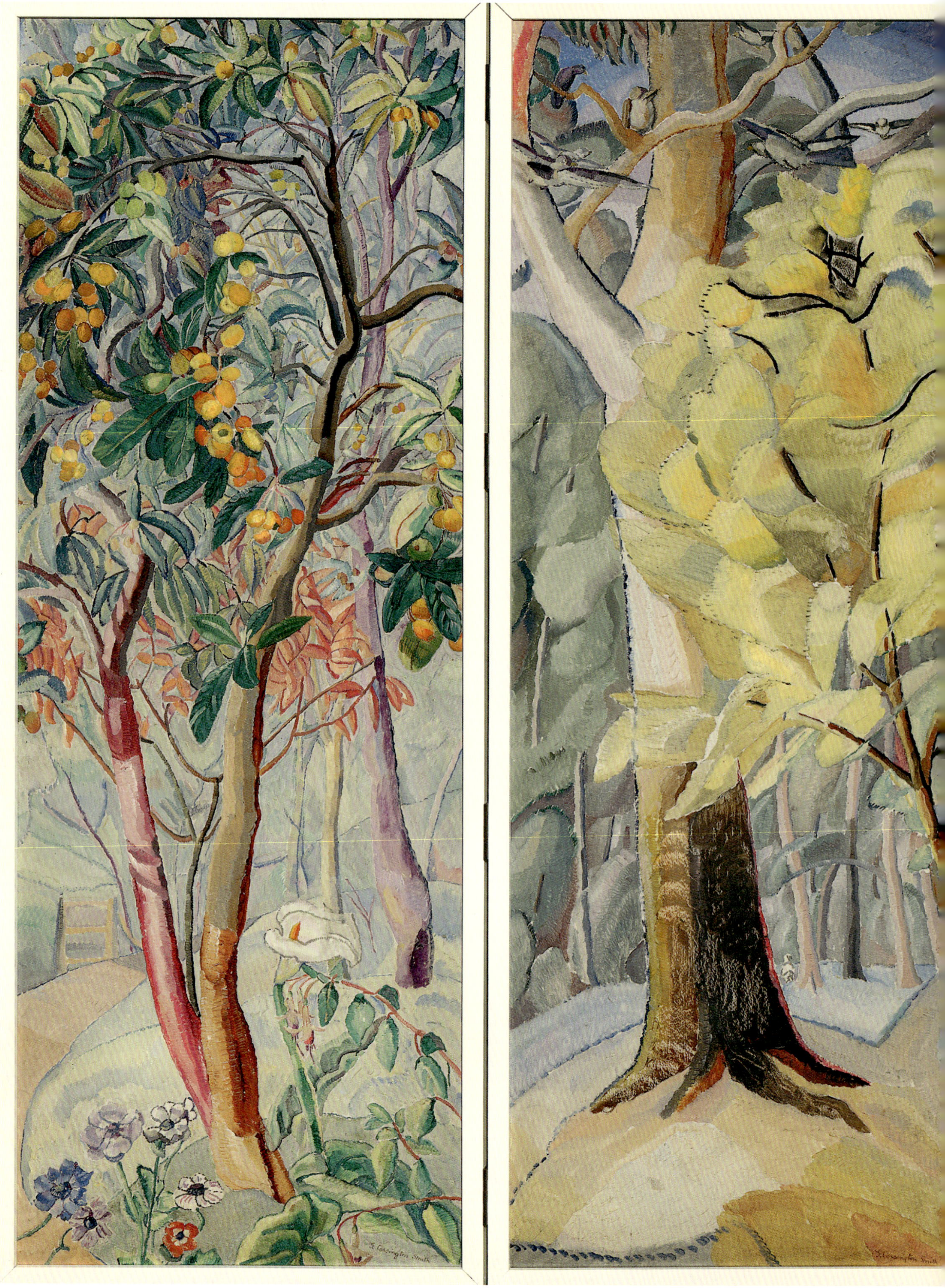

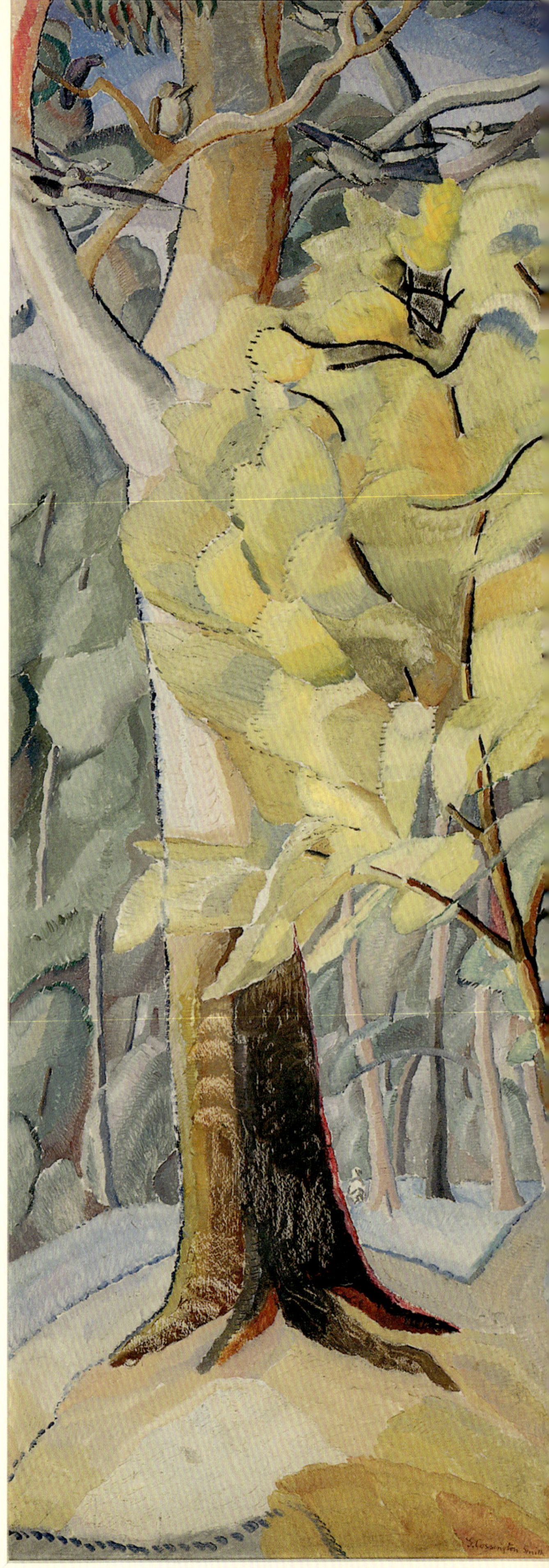

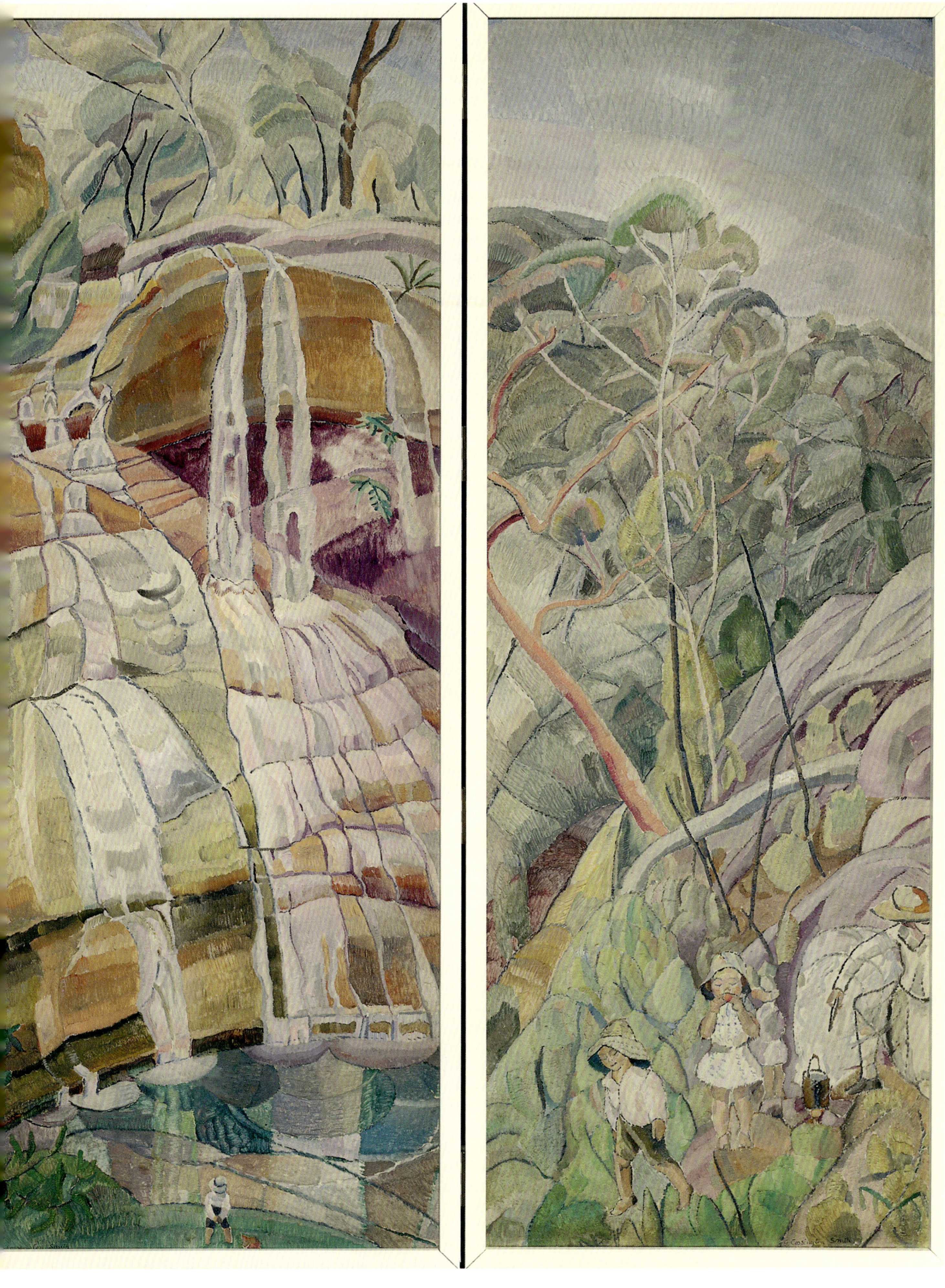

130

GRACE COSSINGTON SMITH
Eastern Road, Turramurra, *c.*1926
Watercolour and black pencil, 40.6 × 33 cm
National Gallery of Australia, Canberra.
Bequest of Mervyn Horton, 1984

131

GRACE COSSINGTON SMITH
The Bridge in Building, 1929
Oil on pulpboard, 75 × 53 cm
National Gallery of Australia, Canberra.
Gift of Ellen Waugh, 2005

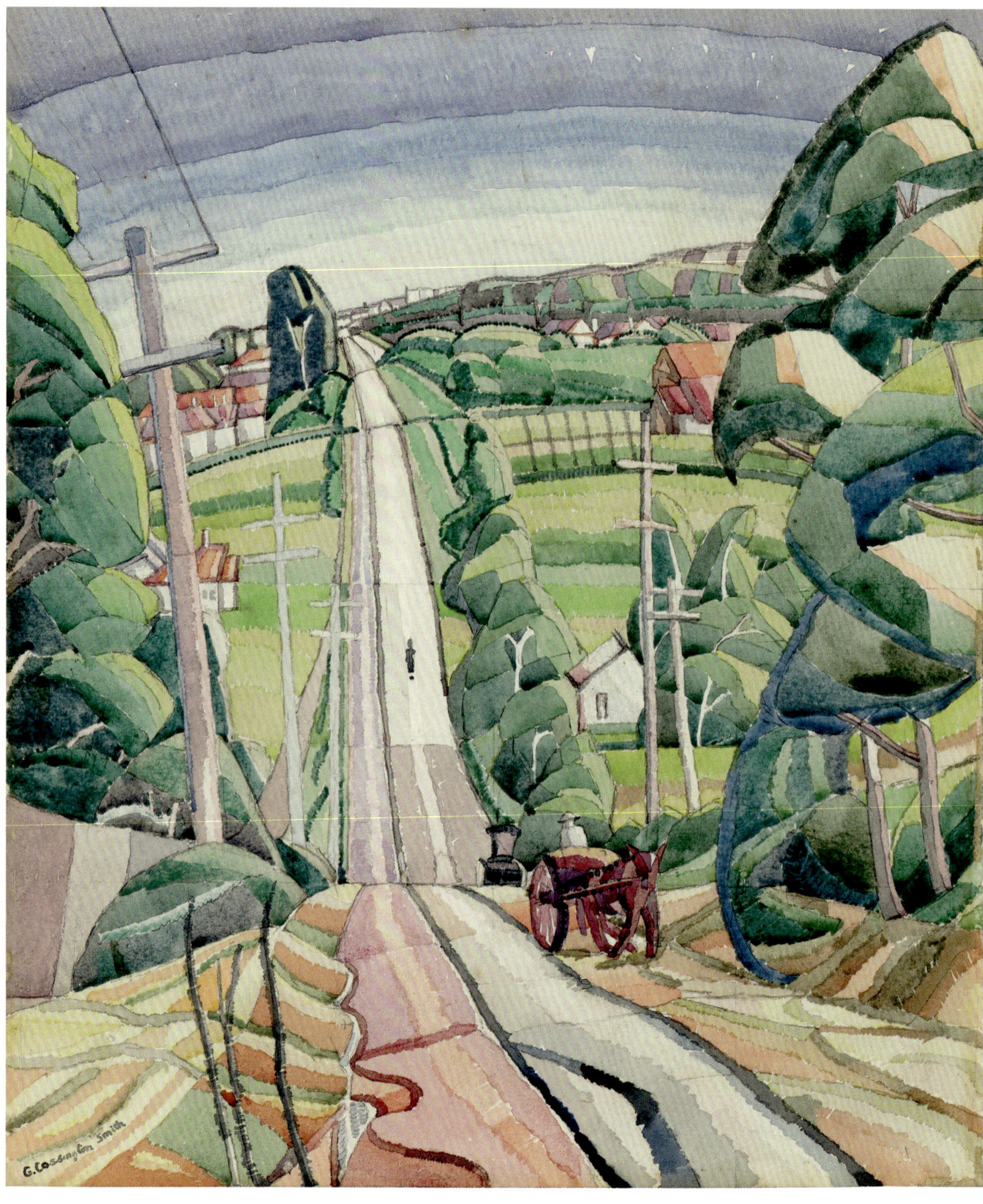

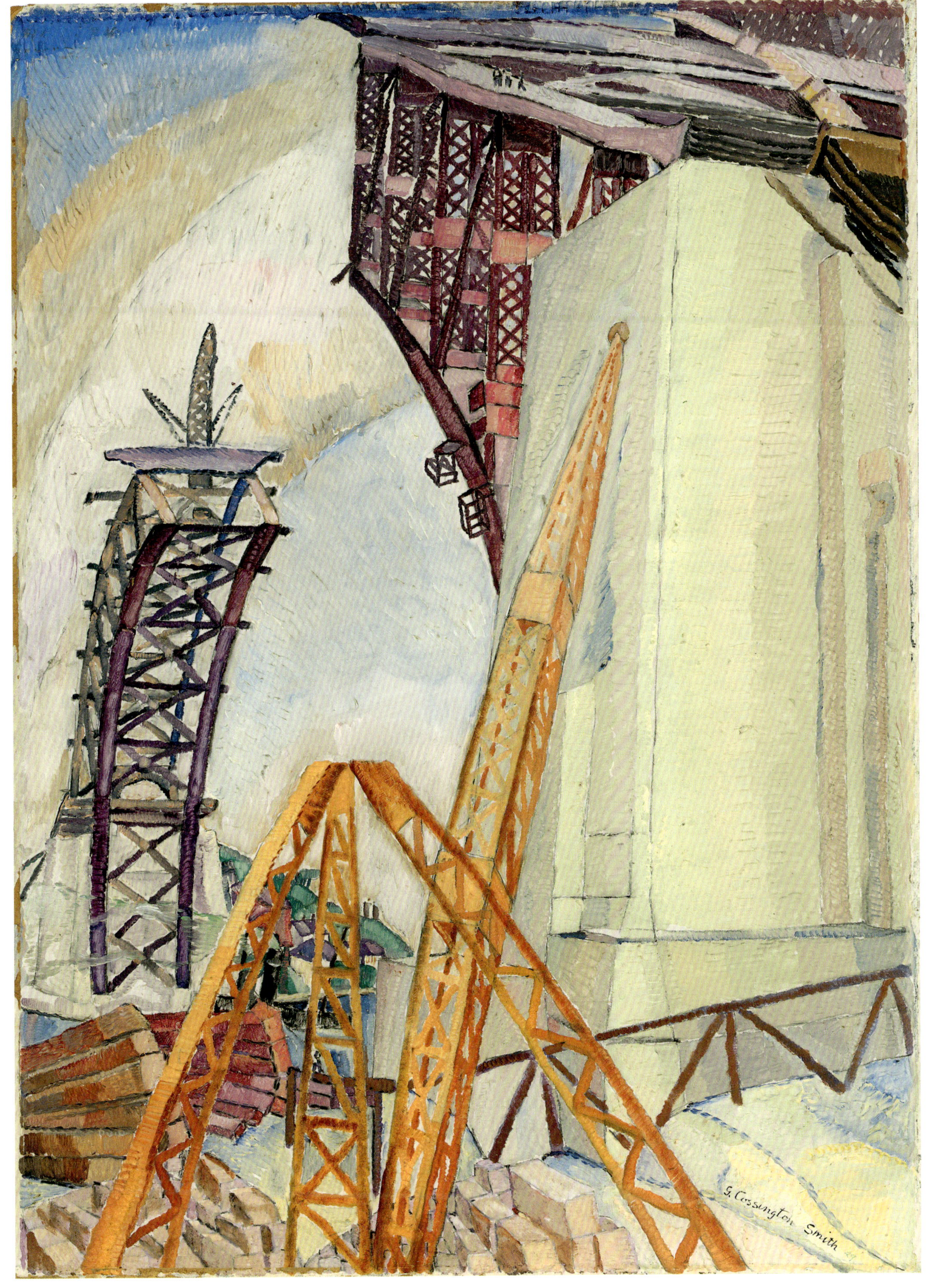
G. Cossington Smith

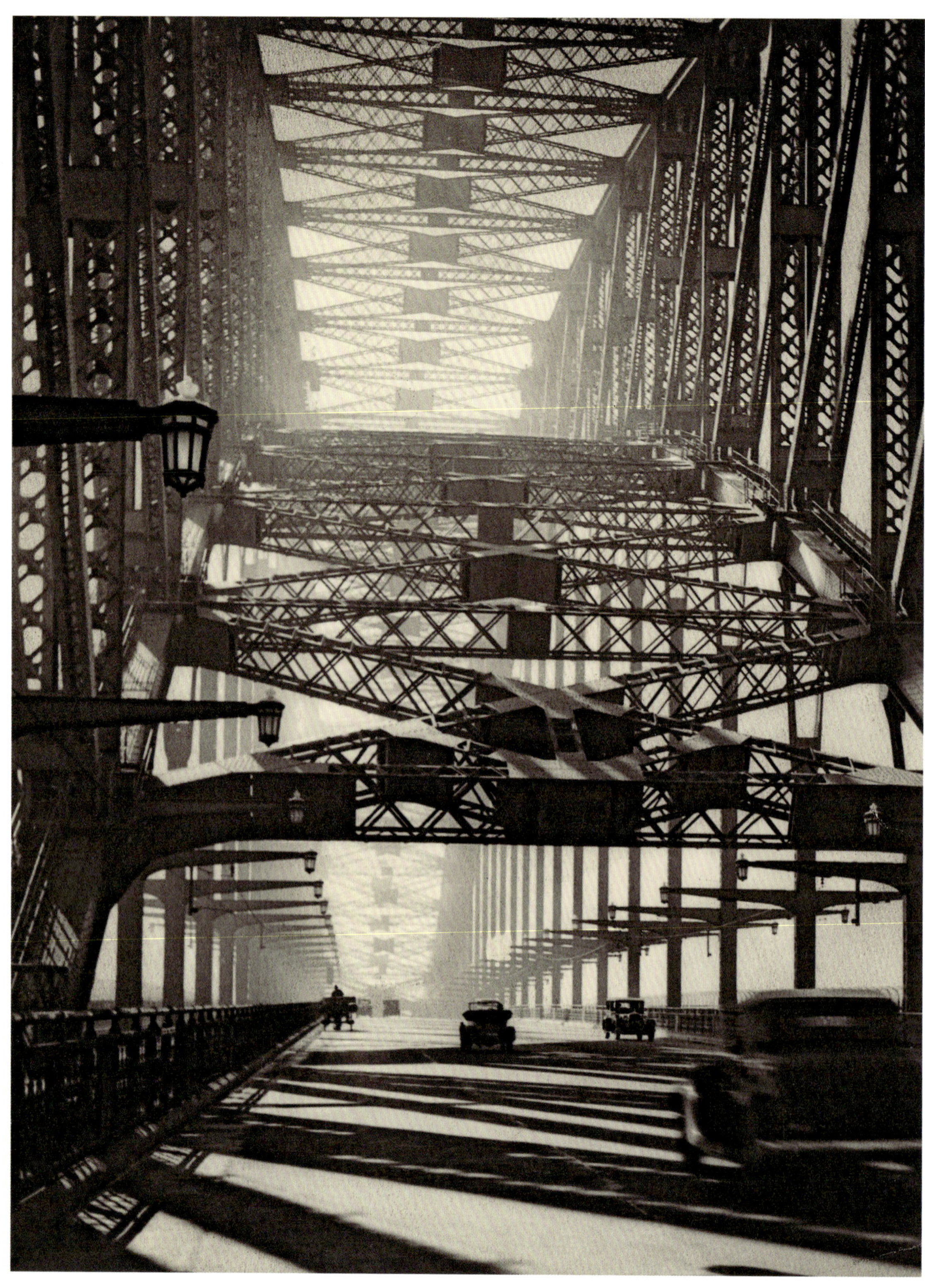

132

HAROLD CAZNEAUX
Arch of Steel, 1933
Gelatin silver photograph, 37.7 × 27.2 cm
National Library of Australia, Canberra. Cazneaux Collection 1974

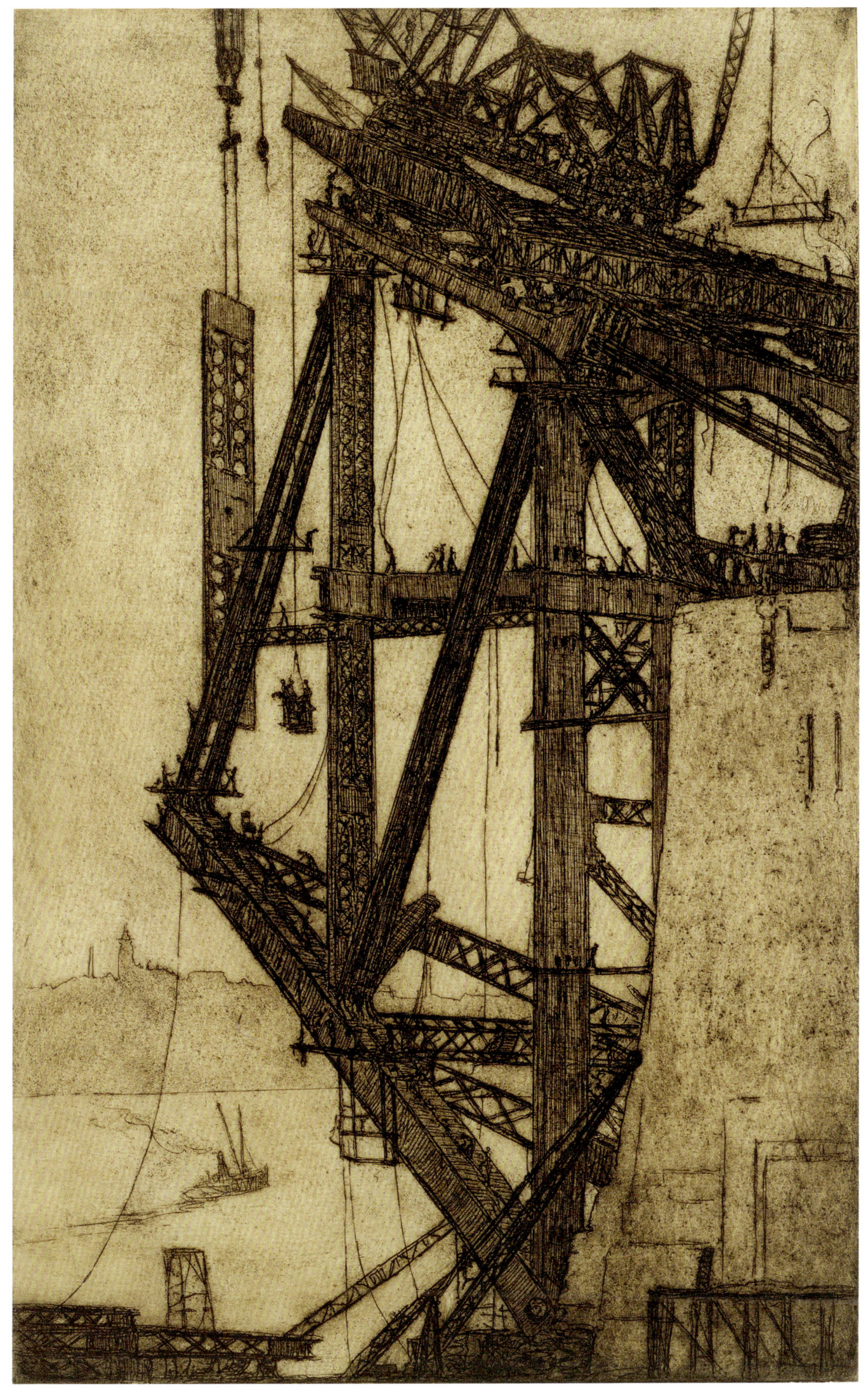

133
JESSIE TRAILL
Building the Harbour Bridge IV: The Ant's Progress, November 1929, *c.*1929
Etching, foul-biting, printed in brown ink with plate tone on paper, 40.3 × 24.8 cm
Art Gallery of South Australia, Adelaide. David Murray Bequest Fund, 1932

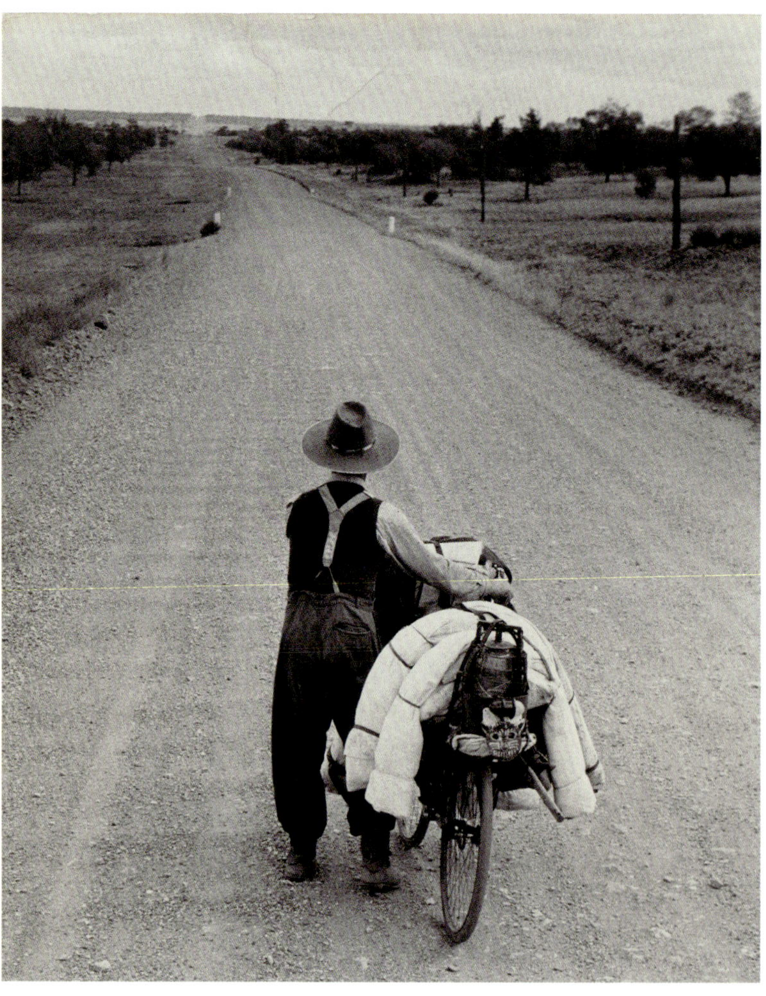

134
AXEL POIGNANT
Swagman on the Road to Wilcannia, 1954
Gelatin silver photograph, 50.4 × 40.1 cm
National Gallery of Australia, Canberra.
Purchased 1984

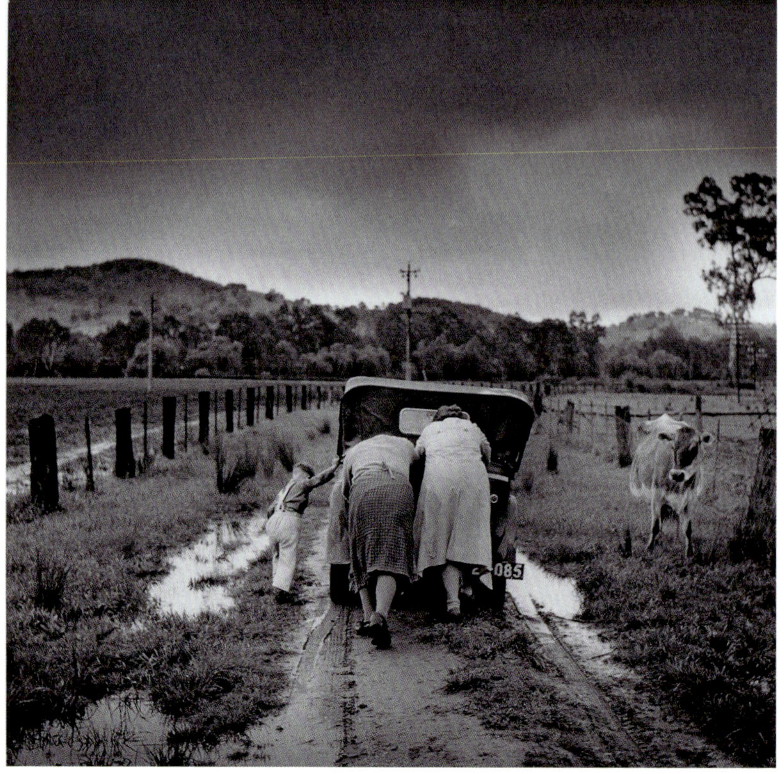

135
JEFF CARTER
Tobacco Road, Ovens Valley, 1956,
printed 2000
Gelatin silver photograph,
28.1 × 27.7 cm
National Gallery of Australia, Canberra.
Purchased 2000

136
CLARICE BECKETT
Passing Trams, *c.*1931
Oil on board, 48.6 × 44.2 cm
Art Gallery of South Australia, Adelaide. Edna Berniece Harrison Bequest Fund through the Friends of the Art Gallery of South Australia, 2001

137
CLARICE BECKETT
Morning Shadows, *c.*1932
Oil on canvas board, 49.5 × 60 cm
Art Gallery of South Australia, Adelaide. South Australian Government Grant, 1980

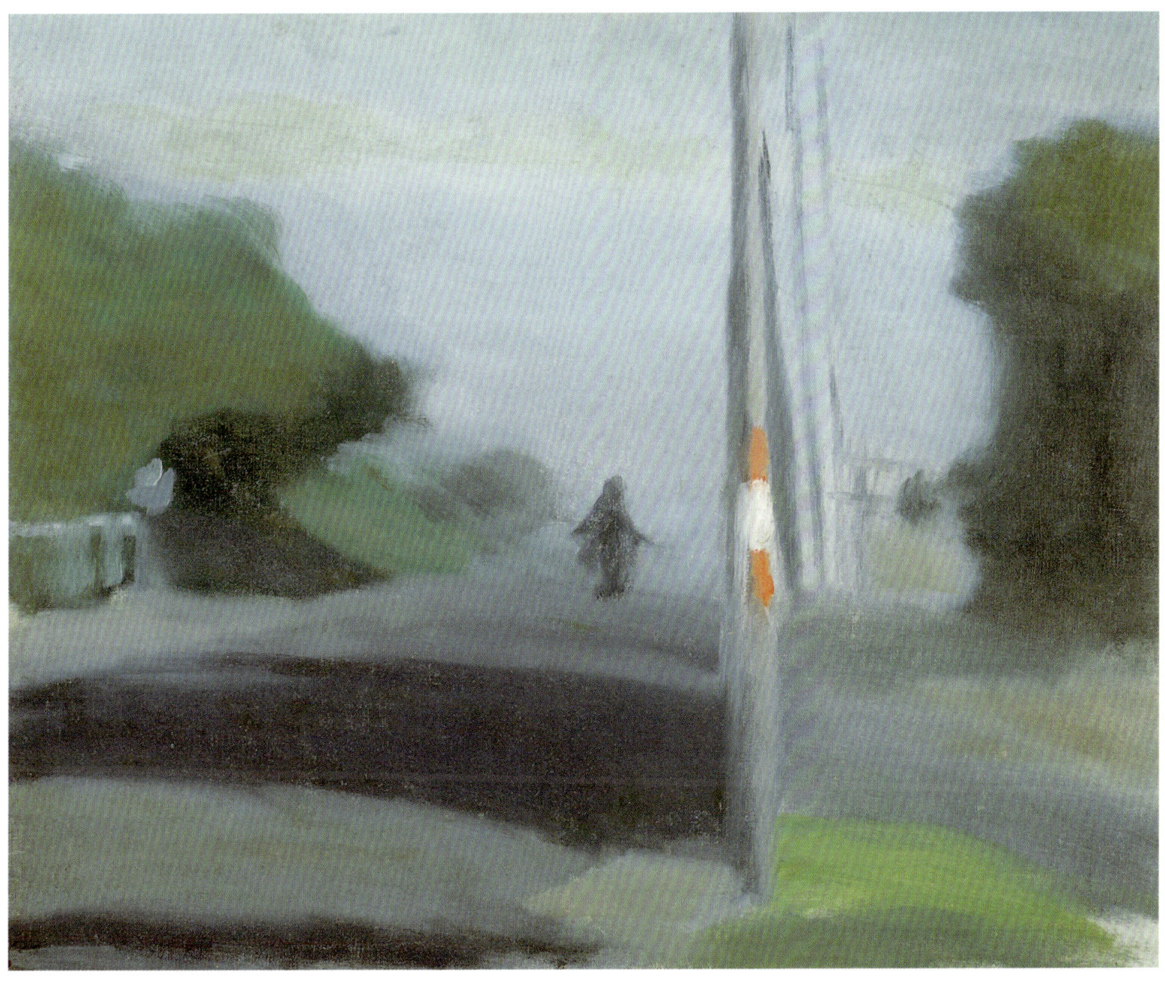

139
CHARLES MEERE
Australian Beach Pattern, 1940
Oil on canvas, 91.5 × 122 cm
Art Gallery of New South Wales, Sydney.
Purchased 1965

138
MAX DUPAIN
Sunbaker, 1937, printed 1975
Gelatin silver photograph, 38.6 × 43.4 cm
National Gallery of Australia, Canberra.
Purchased 1976

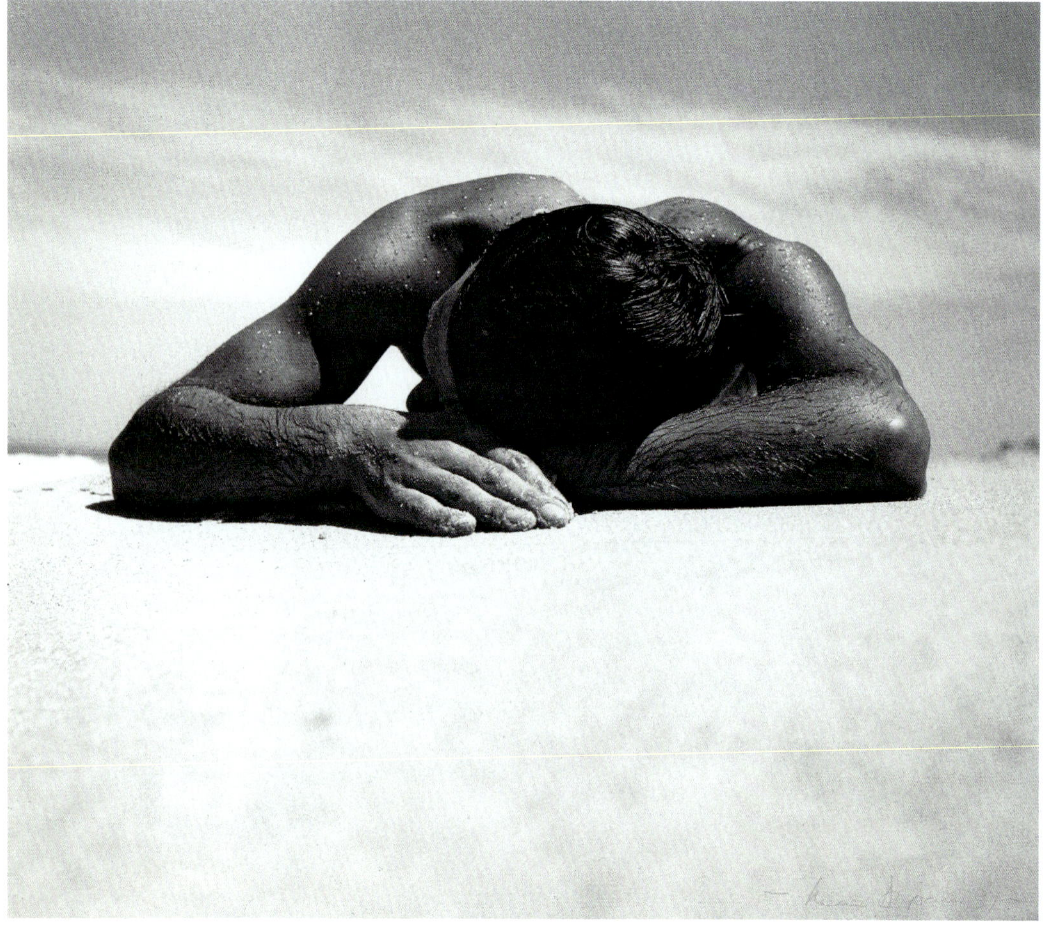

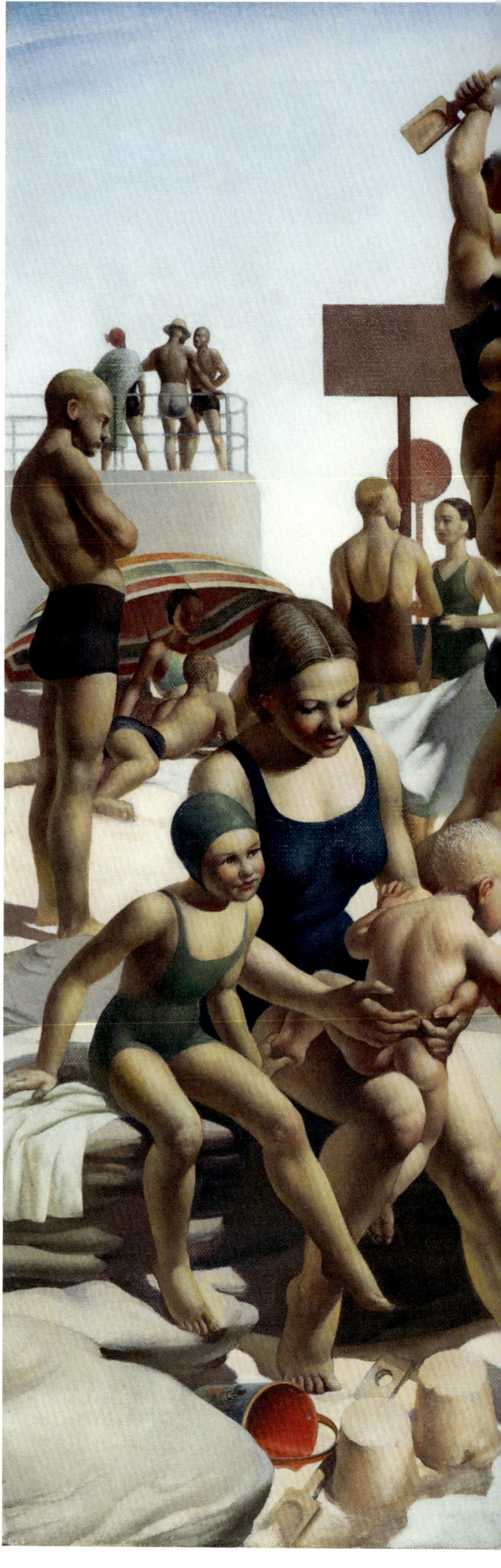

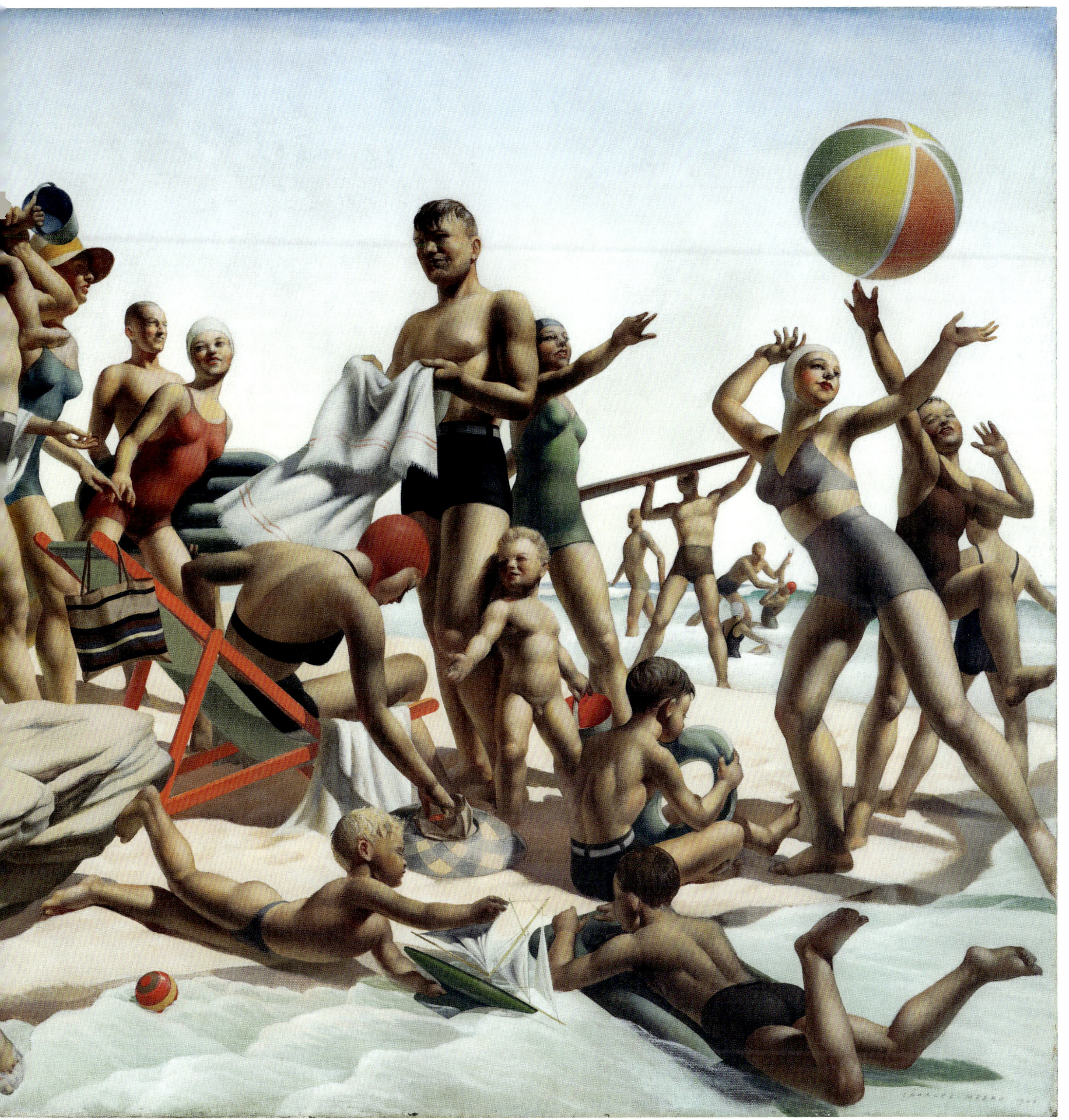

140

HORACE TRENERRY

The Road to Maslins, 1940

Oil on cardboard, 48.5 × 57 cm

Art Gallery of South Australia, Adelaide.
Gift of Douglas and Barbara Mullins, 2002

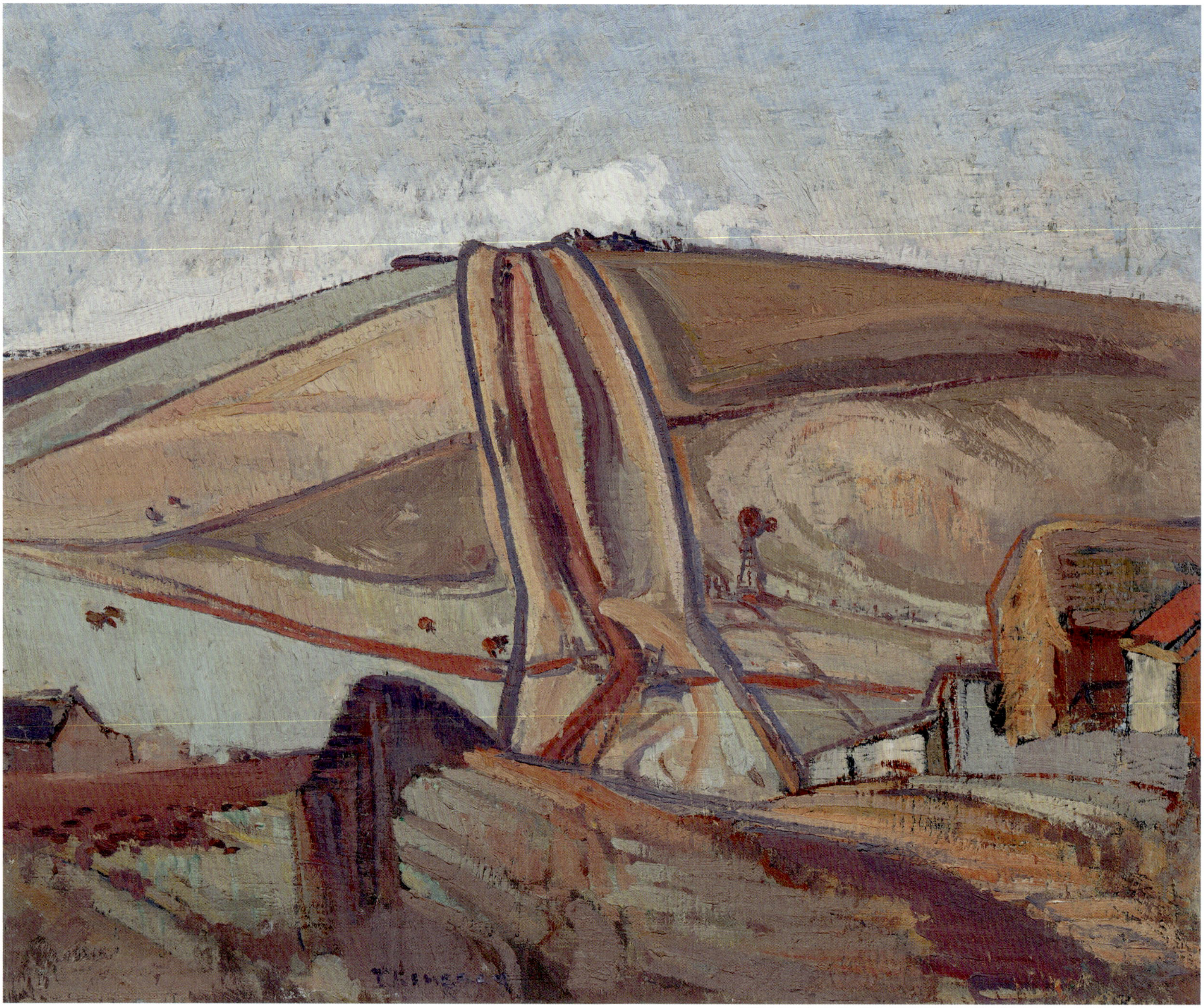

141

DORRIT BLACK

The Olive Plantation, 1946

Oil on canvas, 63.5 × 86.5 cm

Art Gallery of South Australia, Adelaide.
Bequest of the artist, 1951

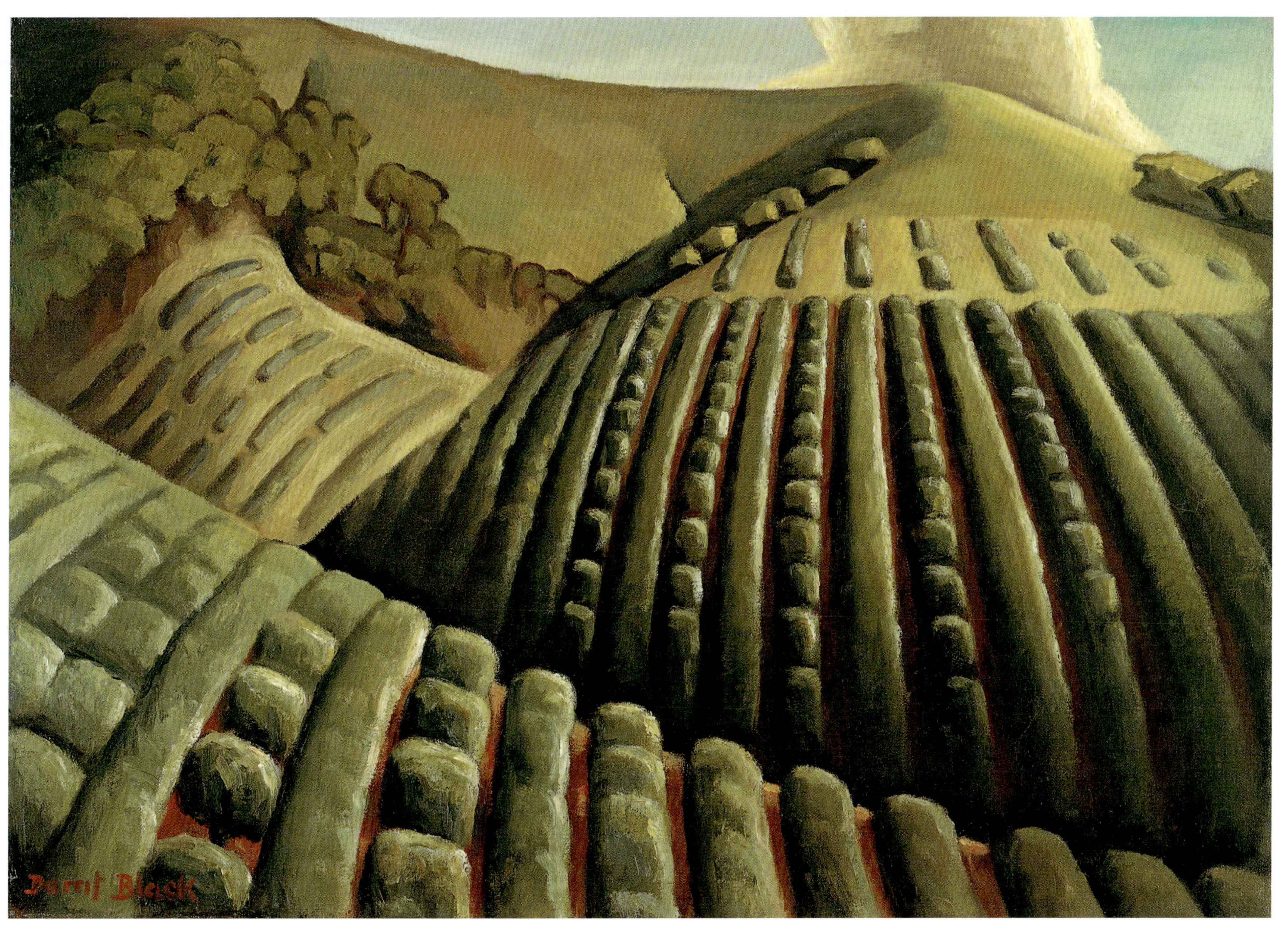

142

MARGARET PRESTON

Aboriginal Landscape, 1941

Oil on canvas, 40 × 52 cm

Art Gallery of South Australia, Adelaide.
D. & J. T. Mortlock Bequest Fund, 1982

143

MARGARET PRESTON

Flying over the Shoalhaven River, 1942

Oil on canvas, 50.6 × 50.6 cm

National Gallery of Australia, Canberra.
Purchased 1973

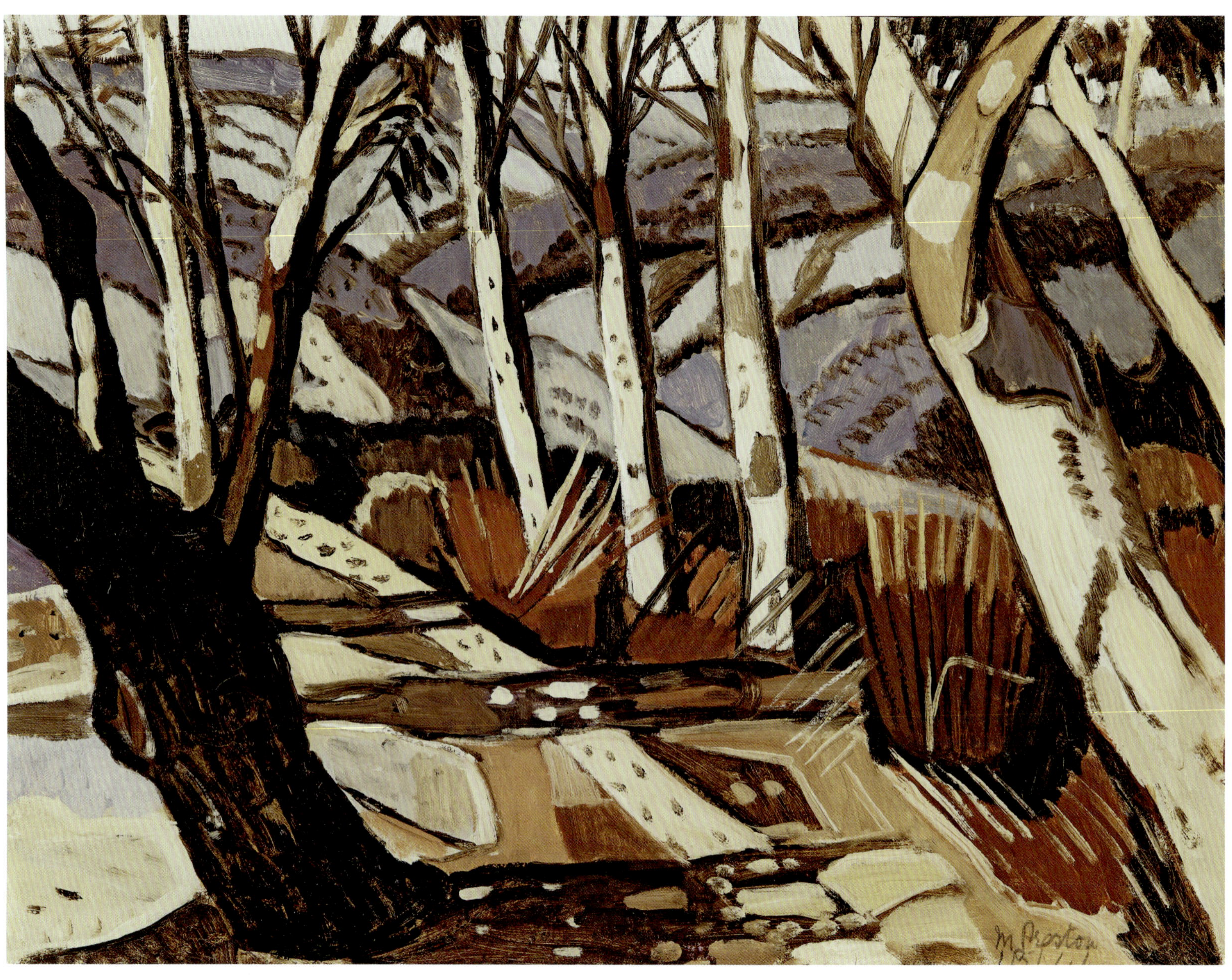

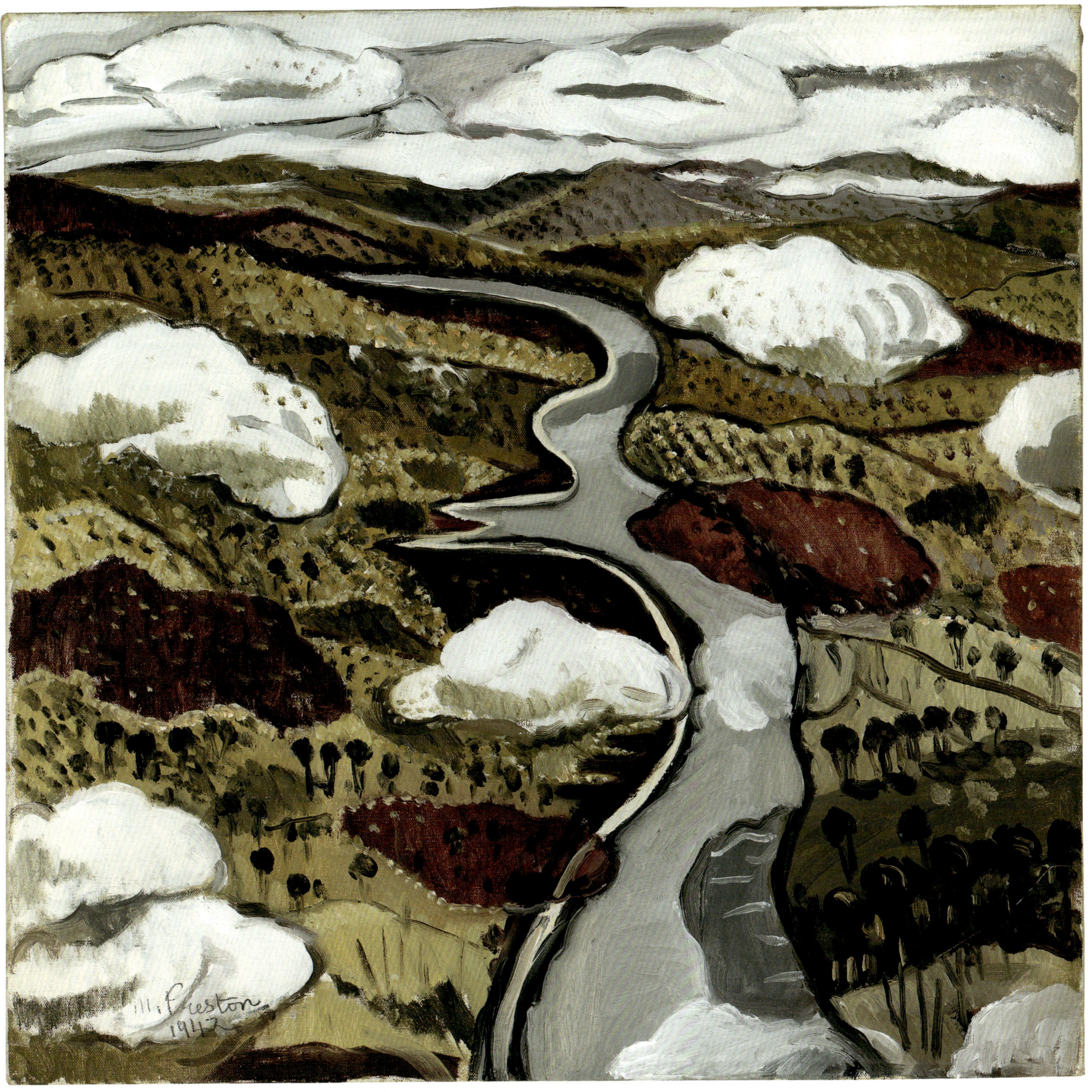
M. Preston
1942

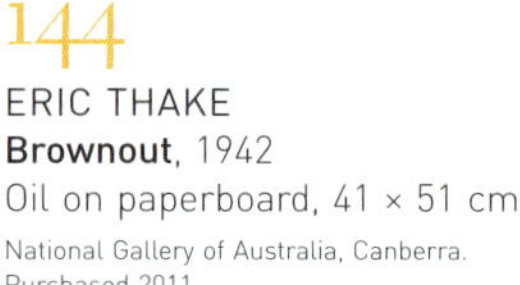

144

ERIC THAKE

Brownout, 1942

Oil on paperboard, 41 × 51 cm

National Gallery of Australia, Canberra.
Purchased 2011

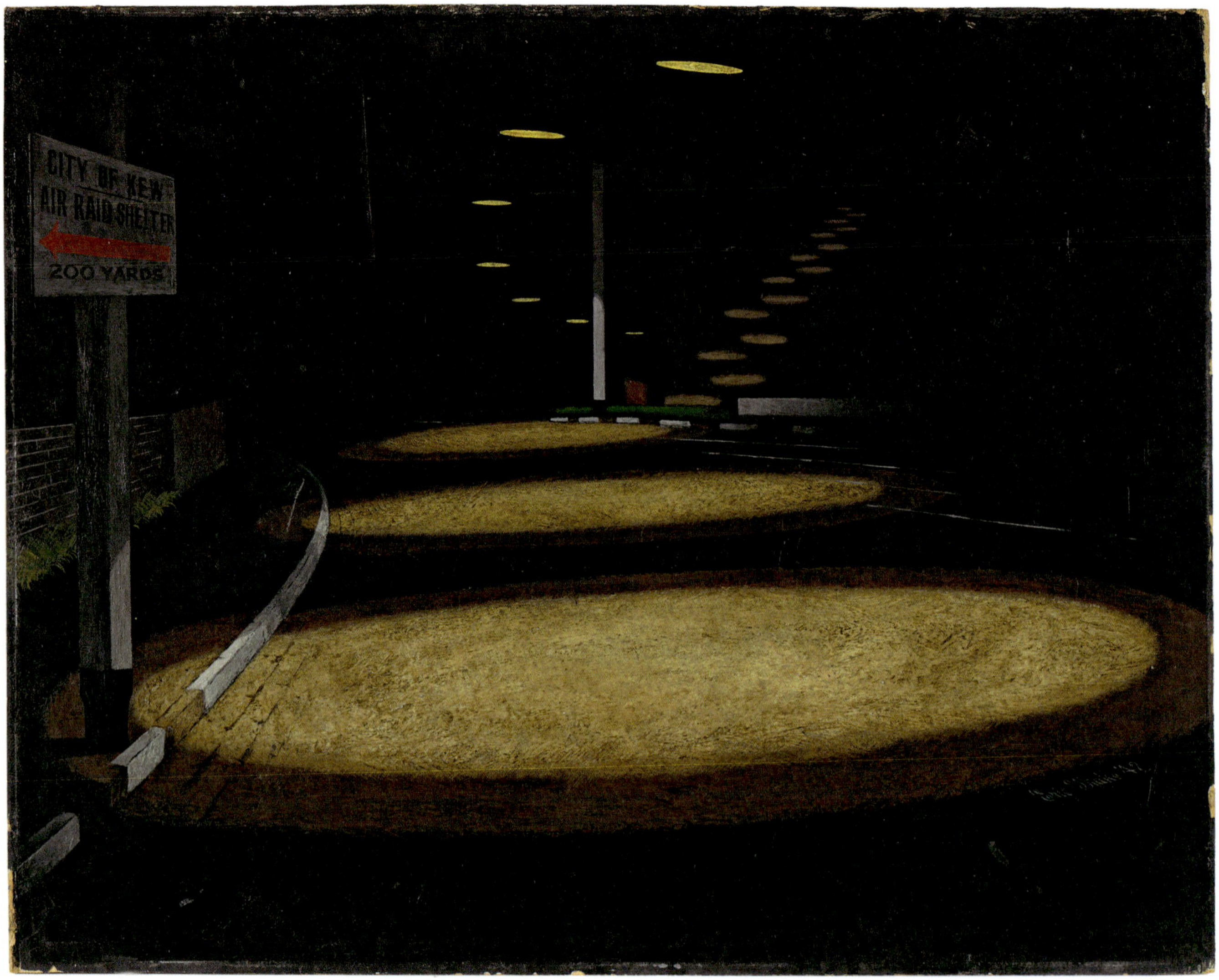

145

ALBERT TUCKER

Sunbathers, 1944

Oil on cardboard, 59.2 × 86 cm

National Gallery of Australia, Canberra.
Purchased 1981

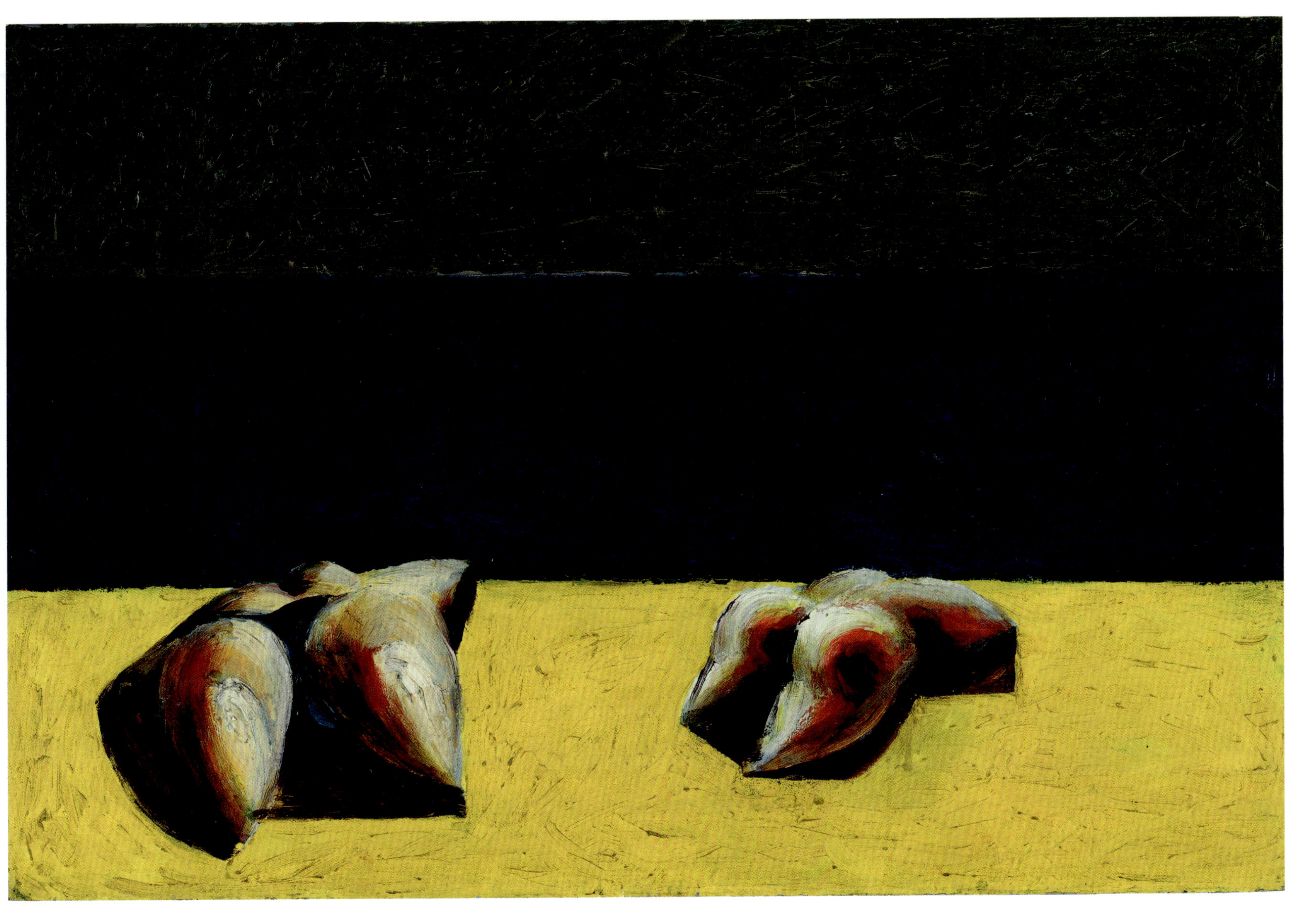

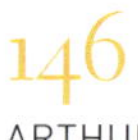

ARTHUR BOYD
The Hunter I, 1944
Oil on cotton gauze on cardboard,
63.6 × 75.8 cm

National Gallery of Australia, Canberra.
The Arthur Boyd Gift, 1975

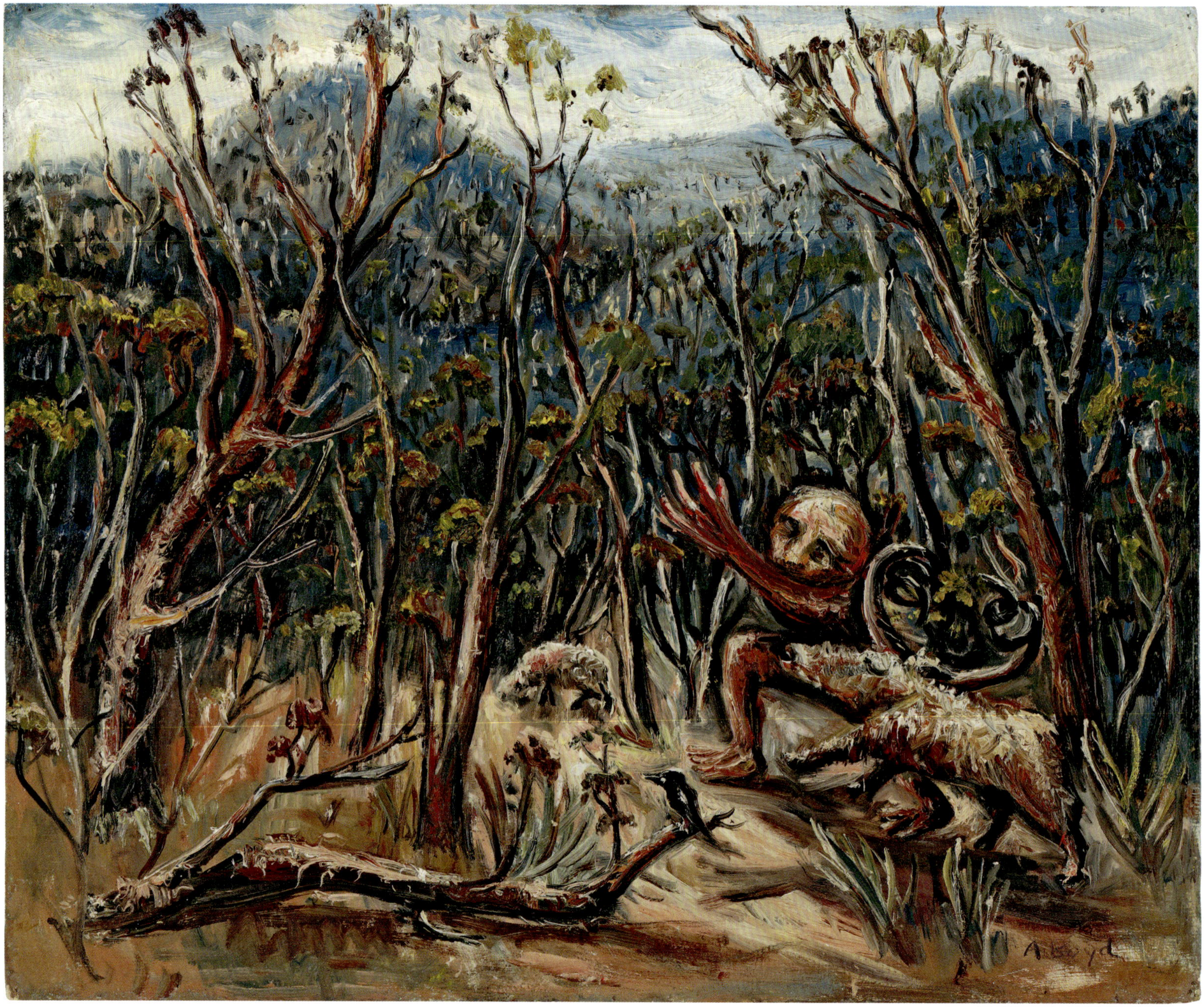

147
ARTHUR BOYD
The Mining Town (Casting the Money Lenders from the Temple), c.1946
Oil and tempera on composition board, 87.4 × 109.4 cm
National Gallery of Australia, Canberra. Purchased 1974

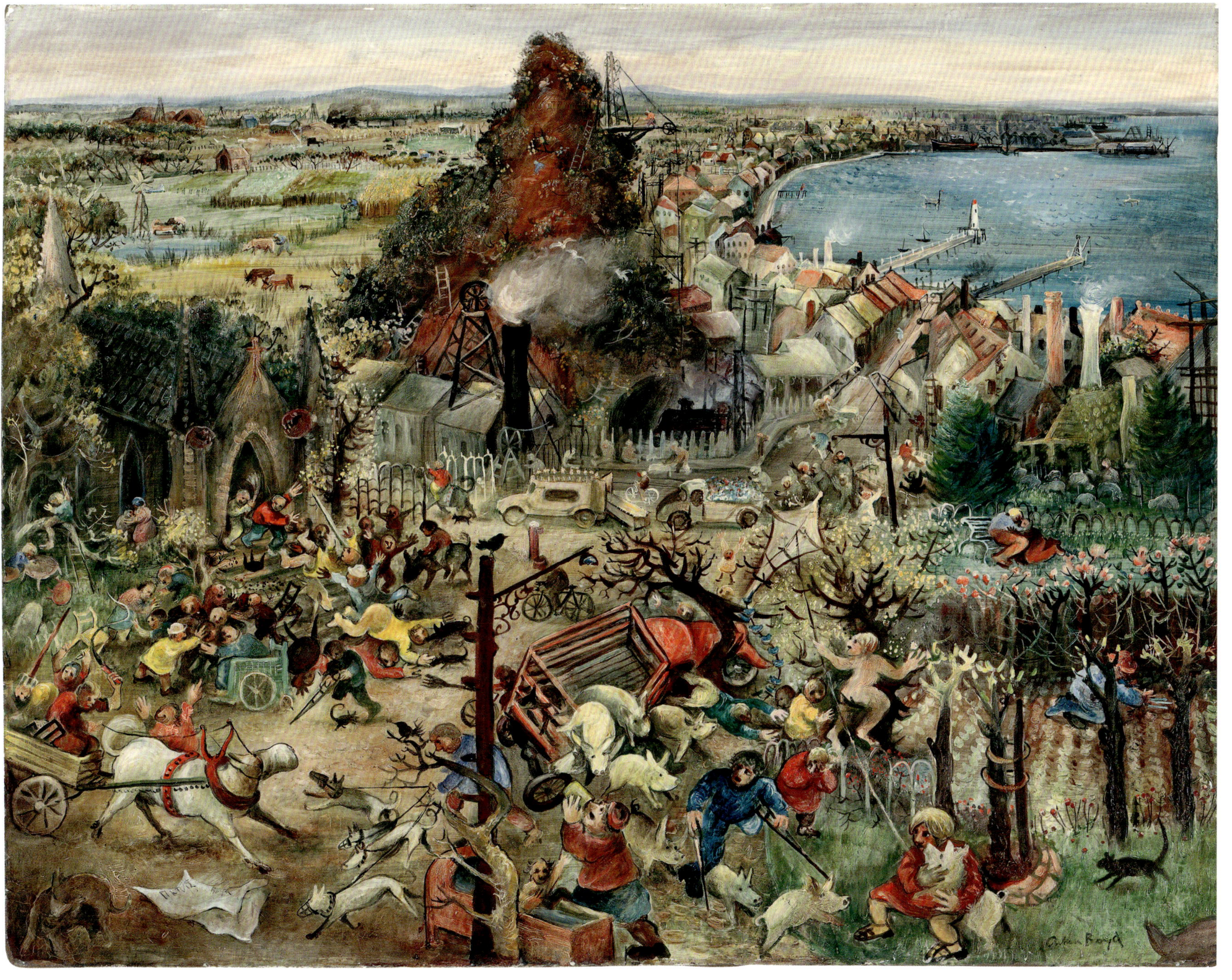

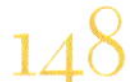

148

ADRIAN FEINT
The Jetties, Palm Beach, 1942
Oil on canvas, 50.7 × 45.6 cm
New England Regional Art Museum, Armidale, New South Wales. Howard Hinton Collection, 1942

149

MARGARET PRESTON
The Expulsion, 1952
Stencil print, printed in colour from one hand-cut paper stencil, on thin black card; hand-coloured with gouache, 64 × 51 cm
Art Gallery of New South Wales, Sydney. Gift of Mr W. G. Preston, the artist's widower, 1967

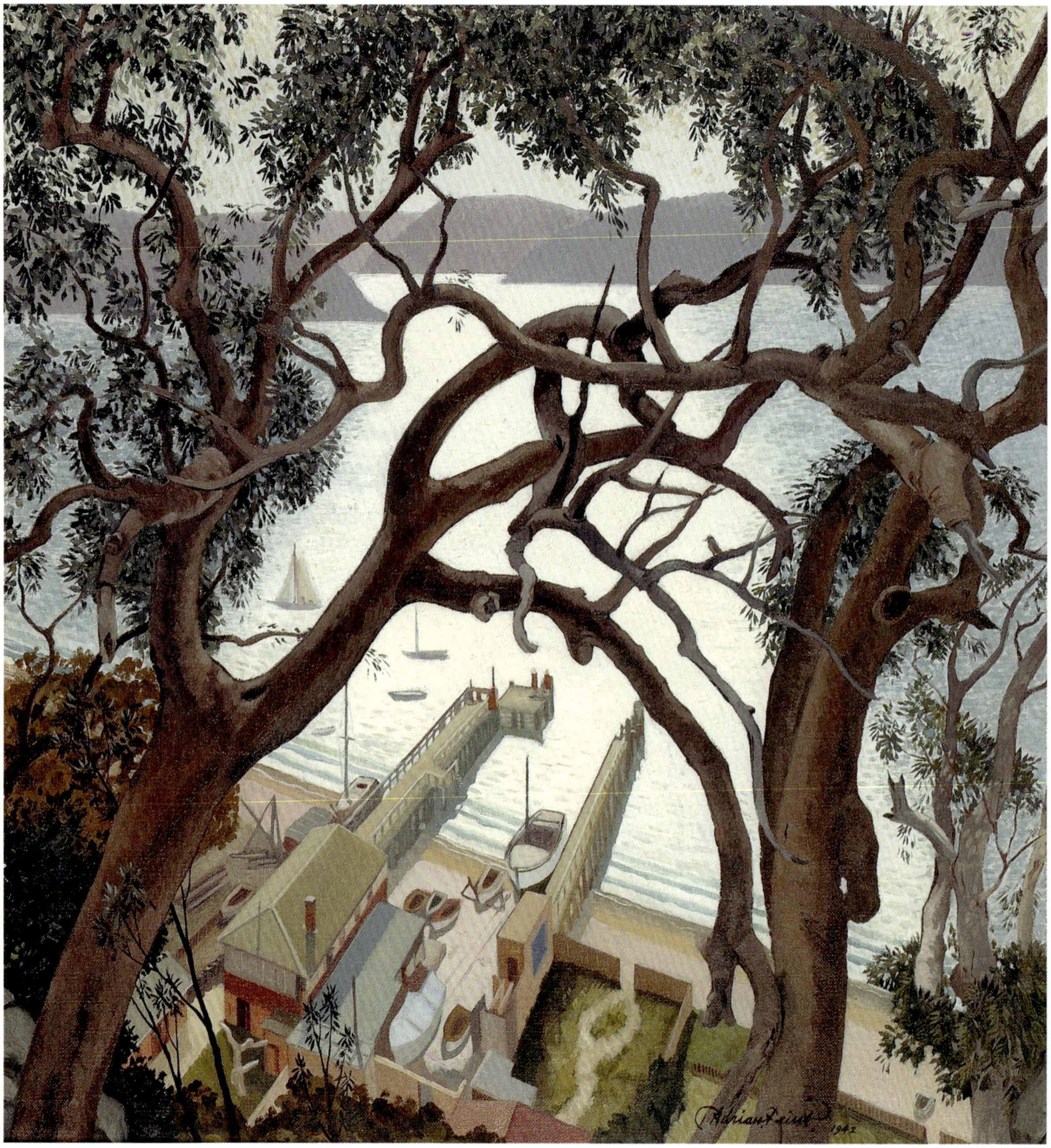

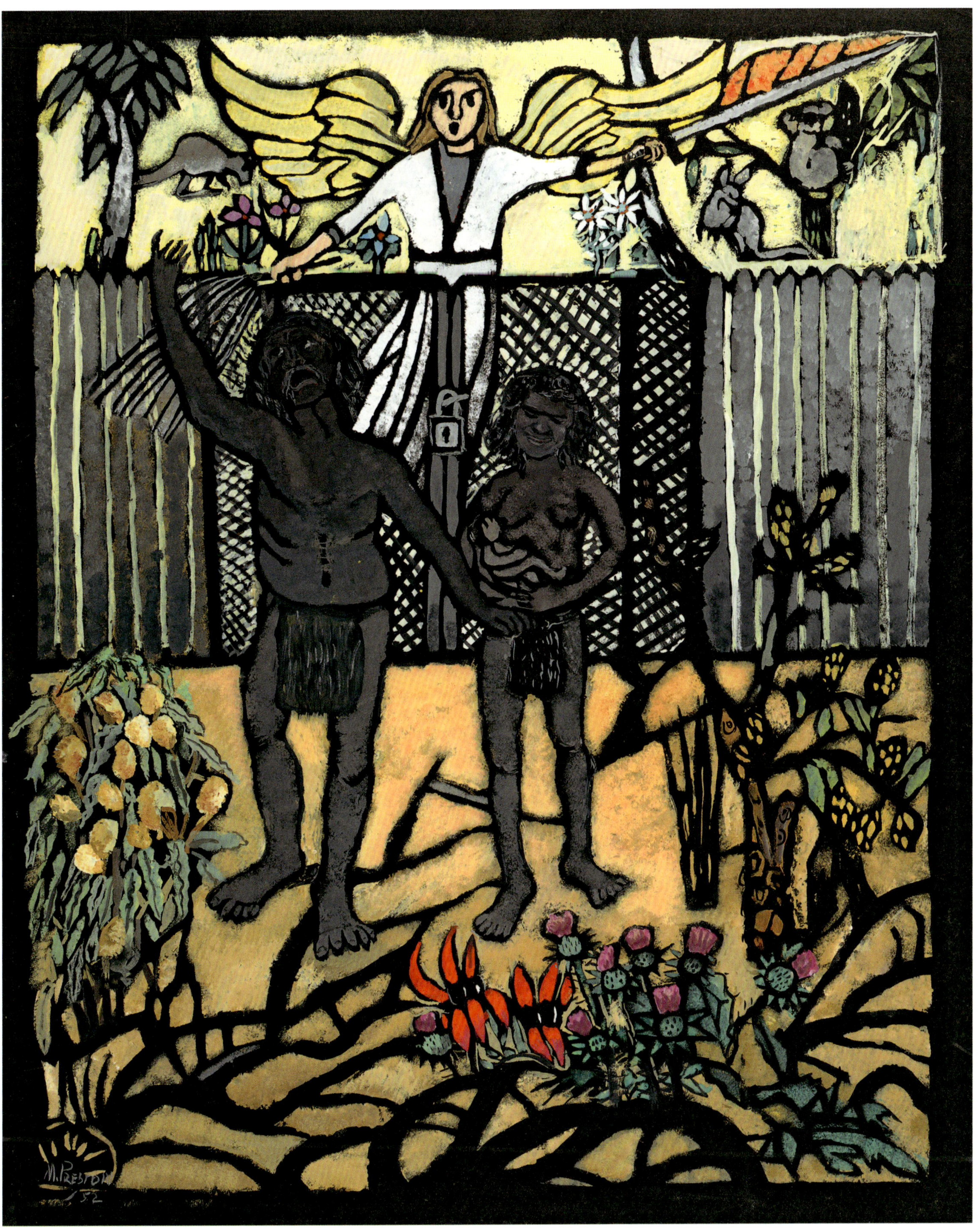
M.PRESTON
/52

150

JEFFREY SMART
Holiday Resort, 1946
Oil on canvas, 50.9 × 60.9 cm
Art Gallery of South Australia, Adelaide.
Gift of Douglas and Barbara Mullins to commemorate the Gallery's
125th anniversary, 2006

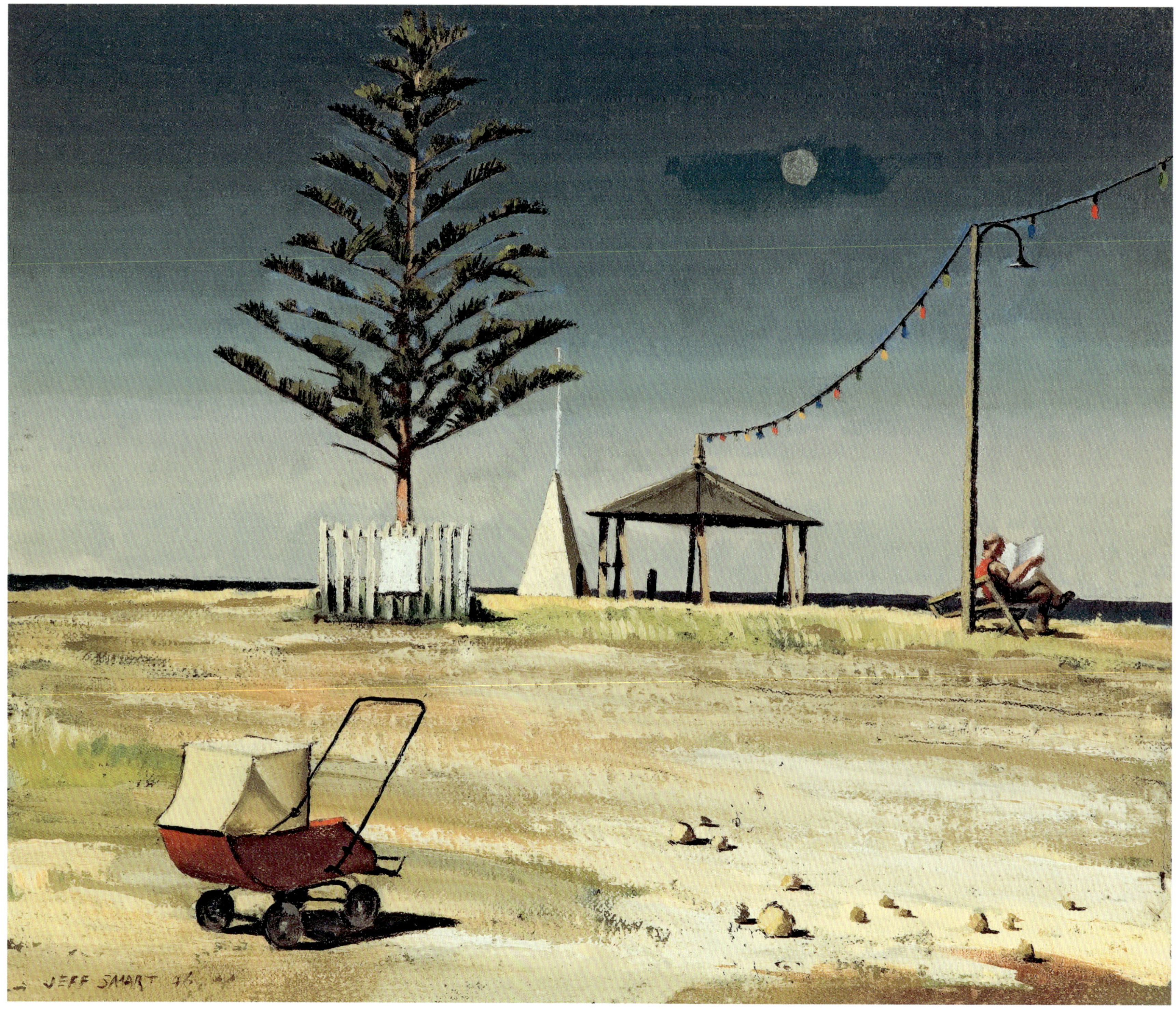

151
LLOYD REES
The Road to Berry, 1947
Oil on canvas on paperboard, 34.6 × 42.2 cm
Art Gallery of New South Wales, Sydney. Purchased 1947

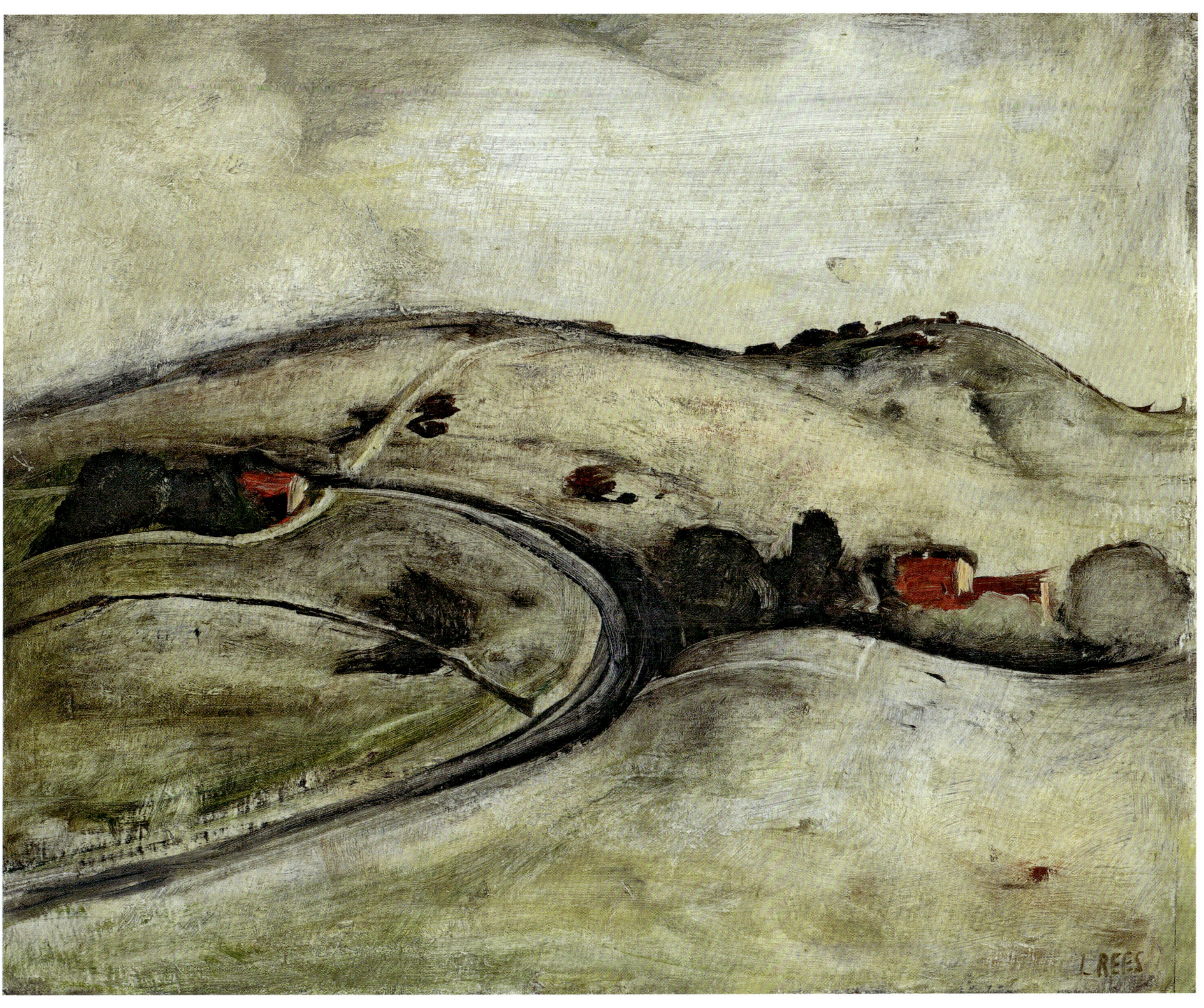

152

RUSSELL DRYSDALE

The Drover's Wife, *c.*1945

Oil on canvas, 51.5 × 61.5 cm

National Gallery of Australia, Canberra. Gift of American Friends of the National Gallery of Australia Inc., New York, NY, USA, made possible with the generous support of Mr and Mrs Benno Schmidt of New York and Esperance, Western Australia, 1987

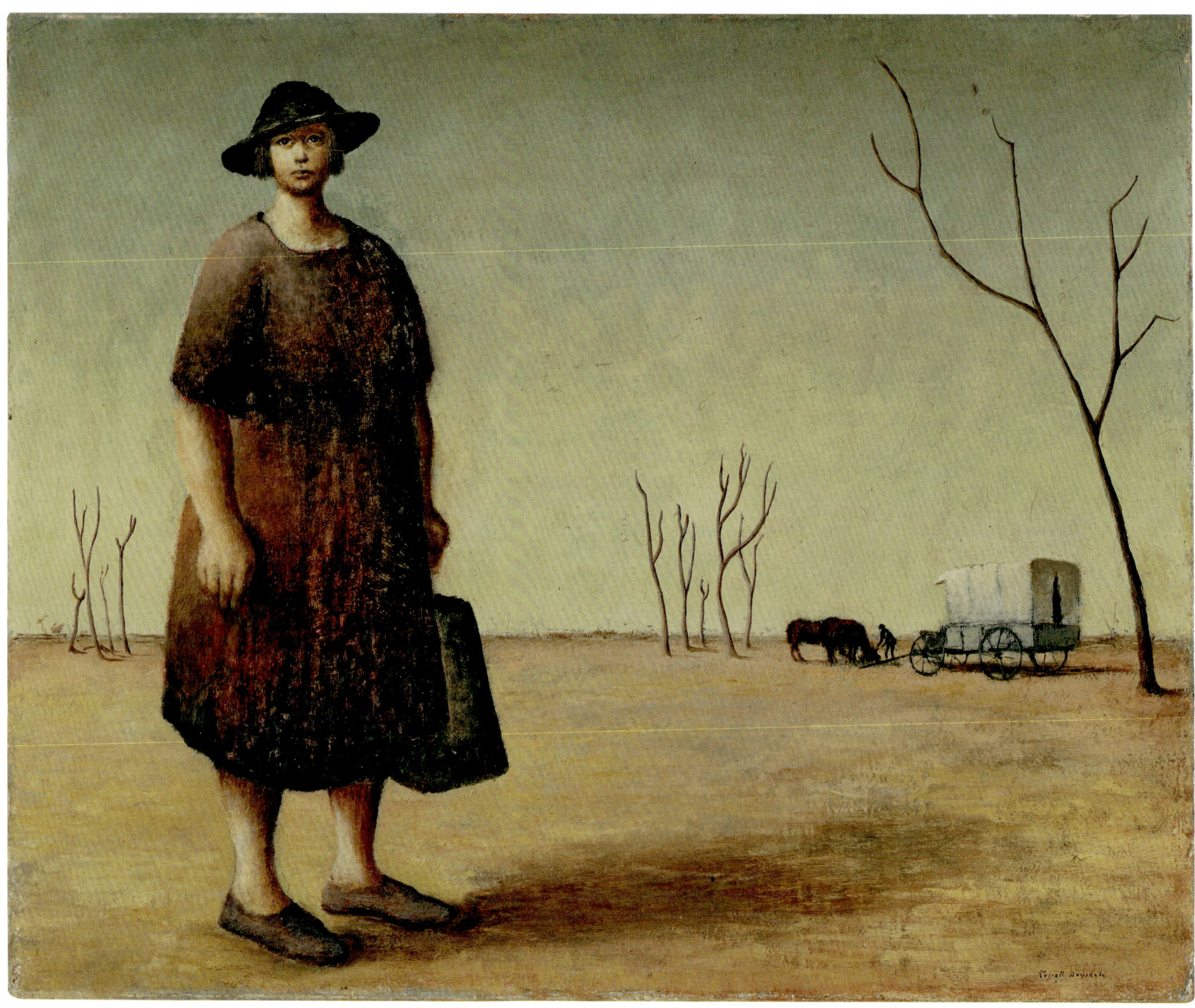

153
RUSSELL DRYSDALE
Emus in a Landscape, 1950
Oil on canvas, 101.6 × 127 cm
National Gallery of Australia, Canberra.
Purchased 1970

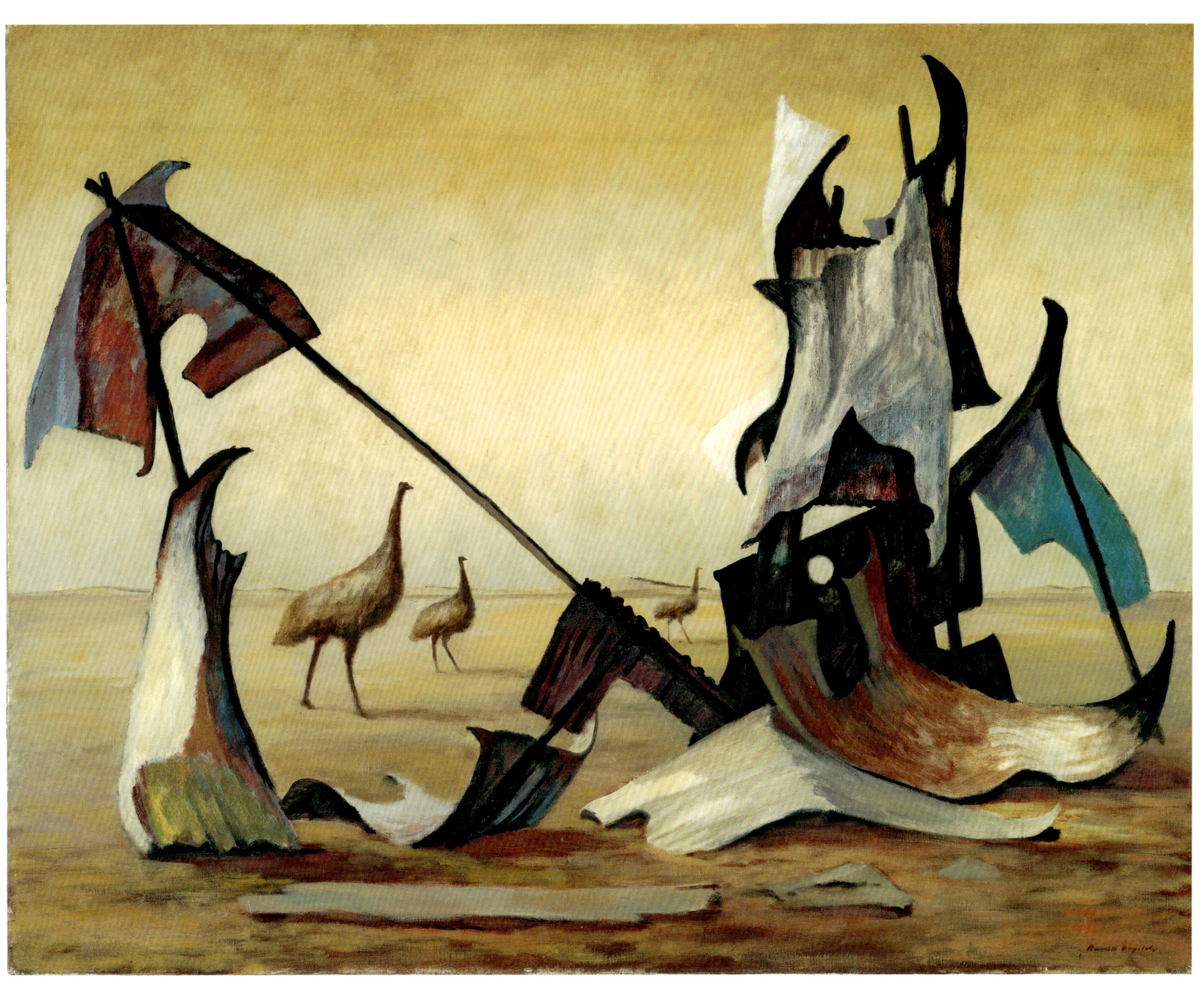

154

SIDNEY NOLAN

Glenrowan, 1946

Enamel paint on composition board,
90.9 × 121.2 cm

National Gallery of Australia, Canberra.
Gift of Sunday Reed, 1977

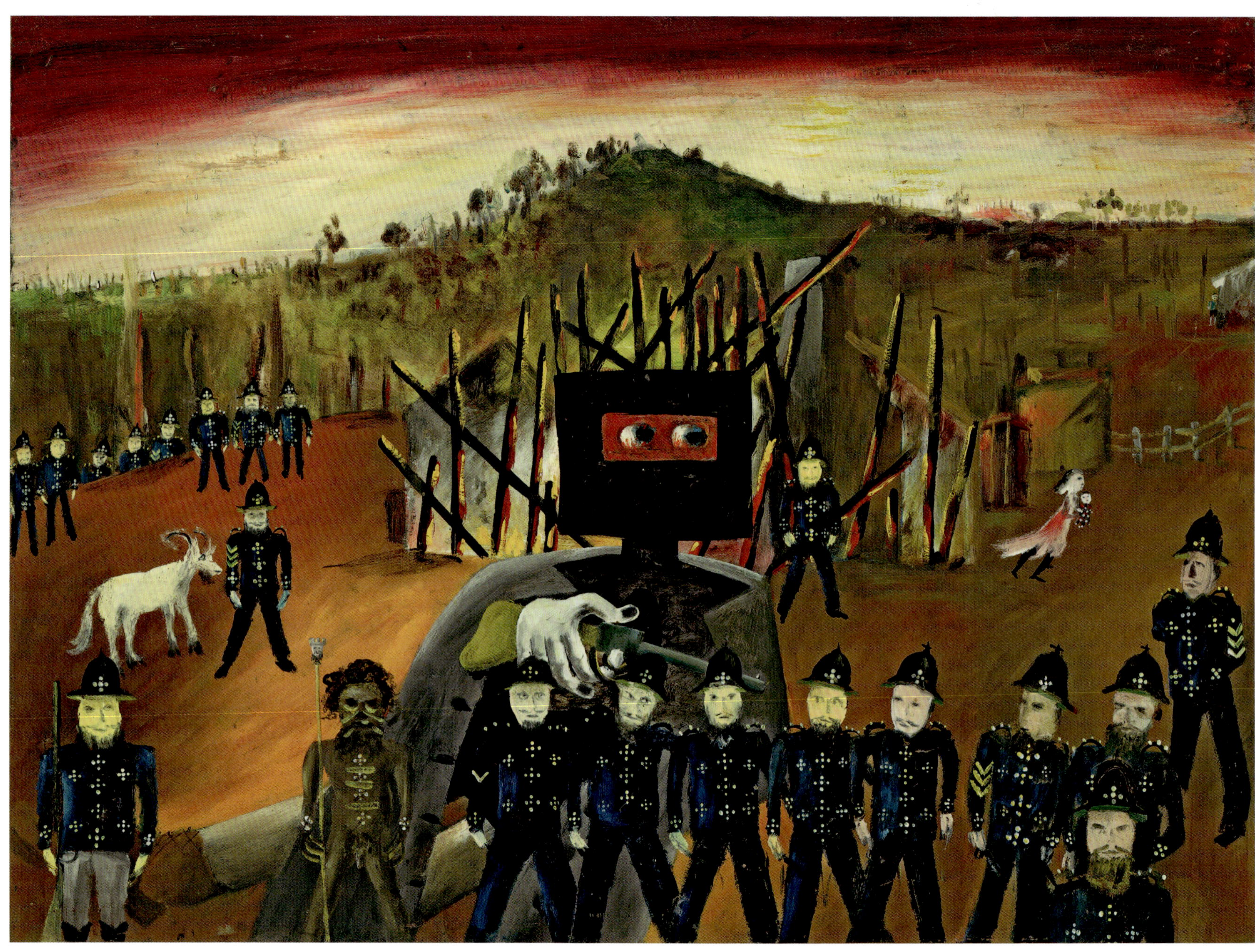

155

SIDNEY NOLAN

Ned Kelly, 1946

Enamel paint on composition board, 90.8 × 121.5 cm

National Gallery of Australia, Canberra. Gift of Sunday Reed, 1977

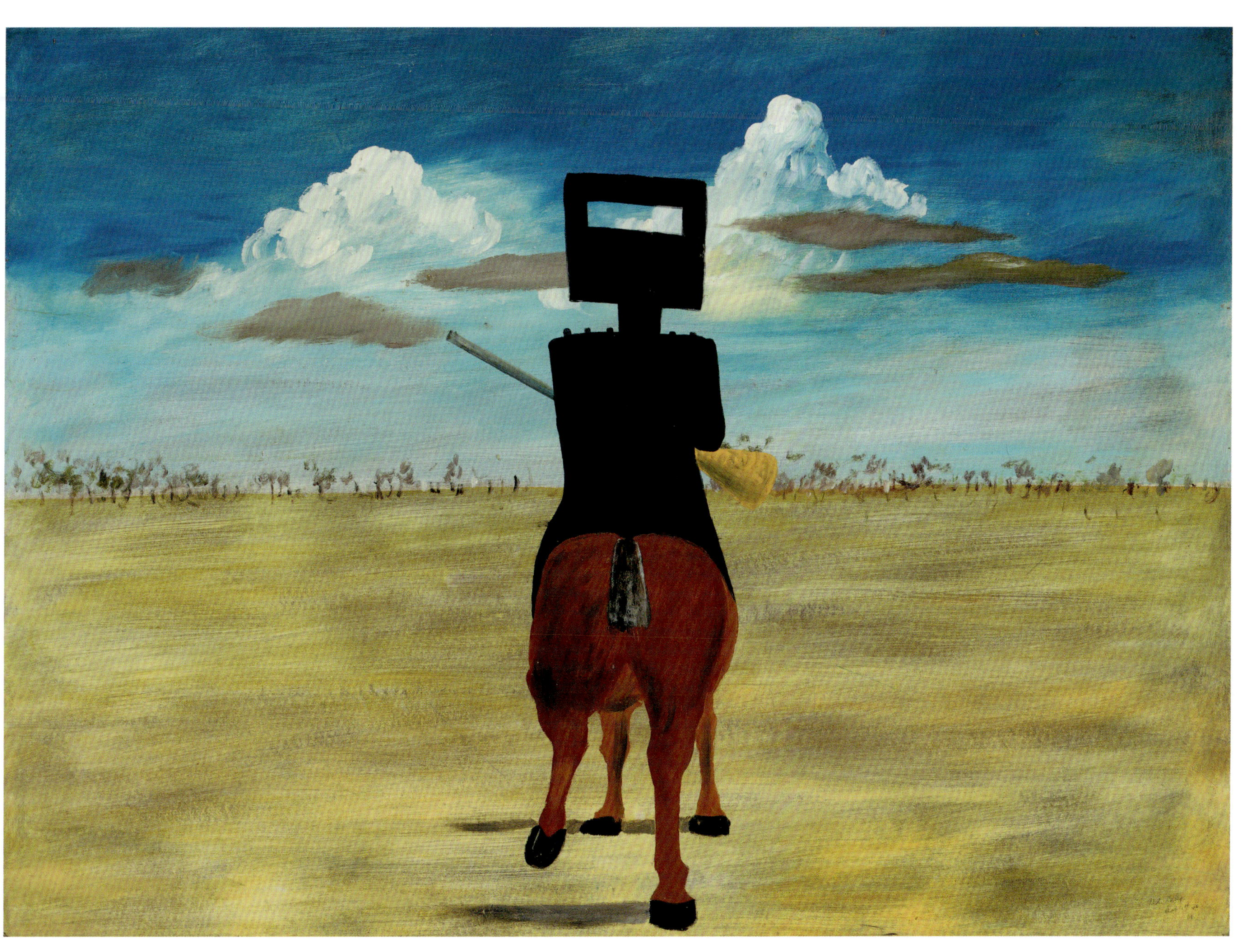

156

SIDNEY NOLAN
The Burning Tree, 1947
Enamel paint on composition board,
90.7 × 121.2 cm
National Gallery of Australia, Canberra.
Gift of Sunday Reed, 1977

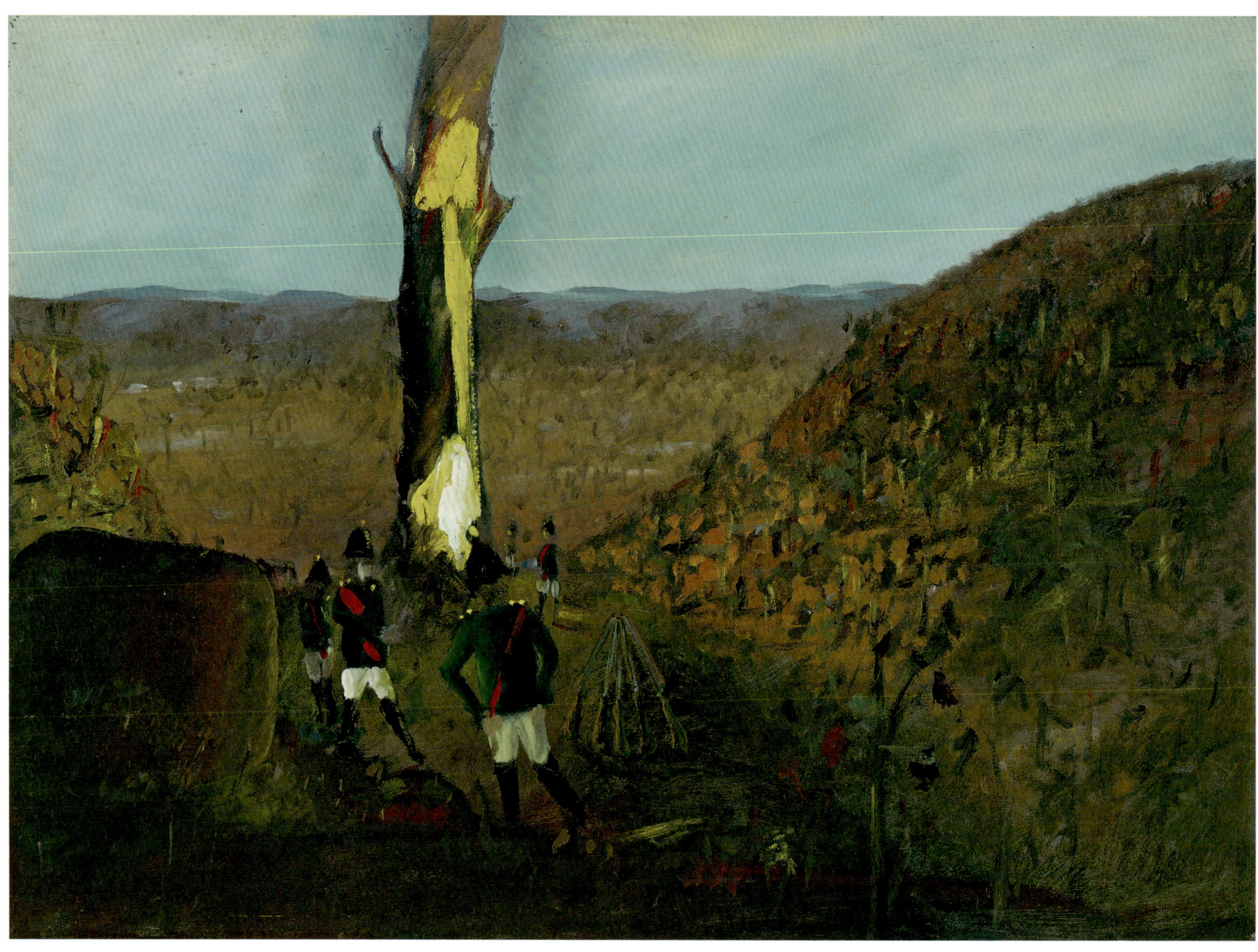

157
SIDNEY NOLAN
Quilting the Armour, 1947
Enamel paint on composition board,
90.4 × 121.2 cm
National Gallery of Australia, Canberra.
Gift of Sunday Reed, 1977

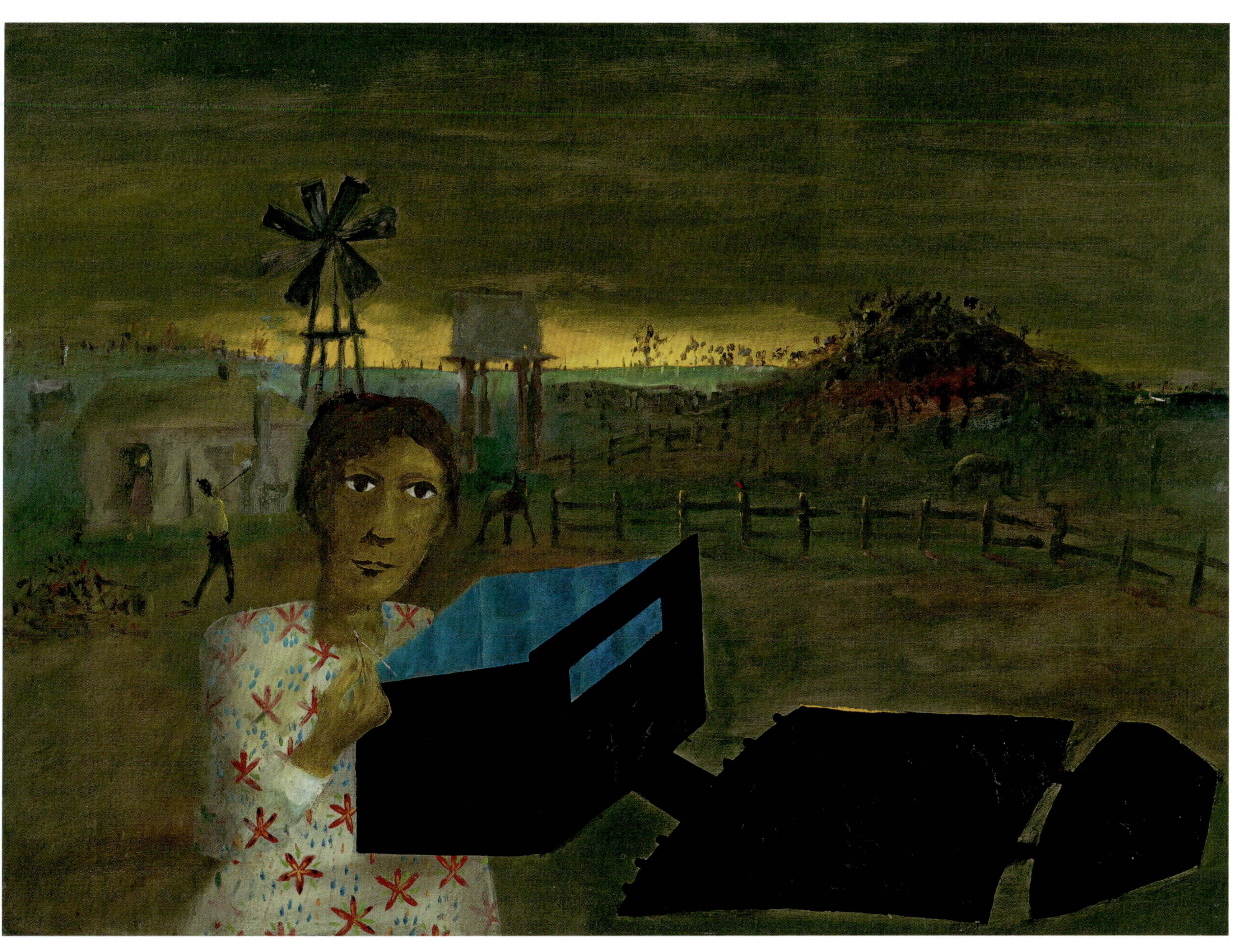

158

SIDNEY NOLAN

Pretty Polly Mine, 1948

Enamel paint on hardboard,
91 × 122.2 cm

Art Gallery of New South Wales, Sydney.
Purchased 1949

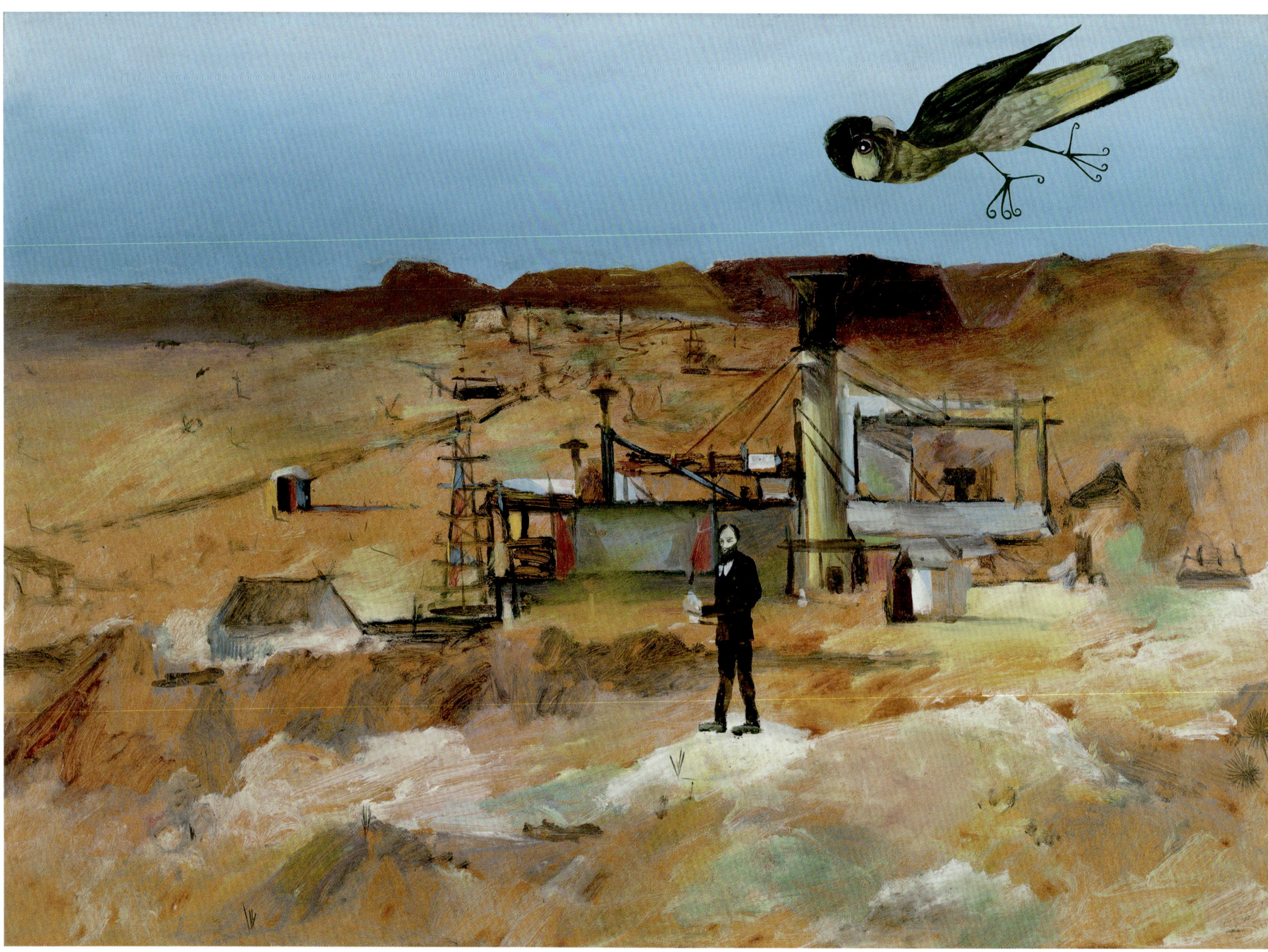

159
SIDNEY NOLAN
Inland Australia, 1950
Oil and enamel paint on composition board,
91.5 × 121 cm
National Gallery of Australia, Canberra.
Purchased 1961

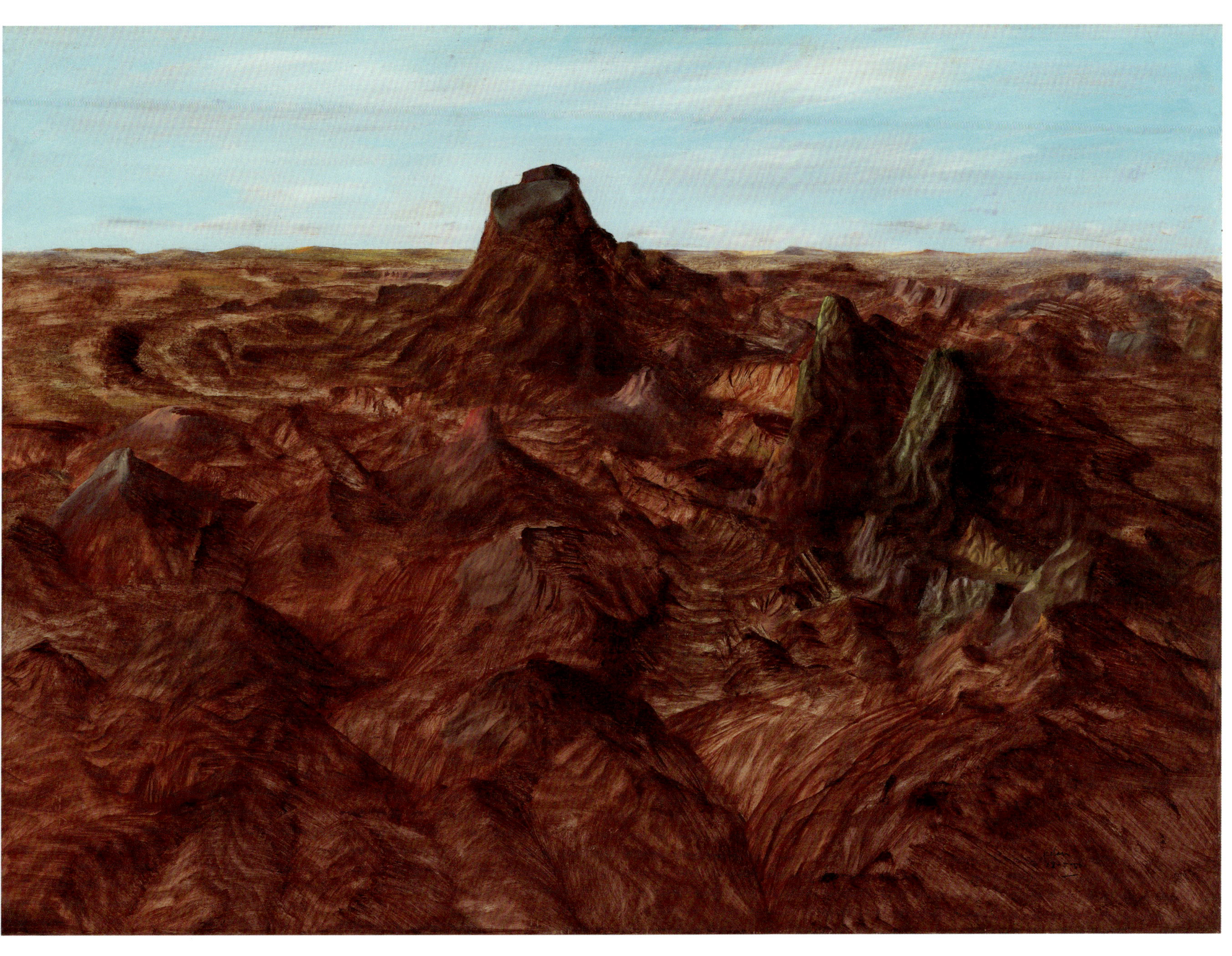

ELIZABETHAN POST-COLONIAL 1950–2013

DANIEL THOMAS

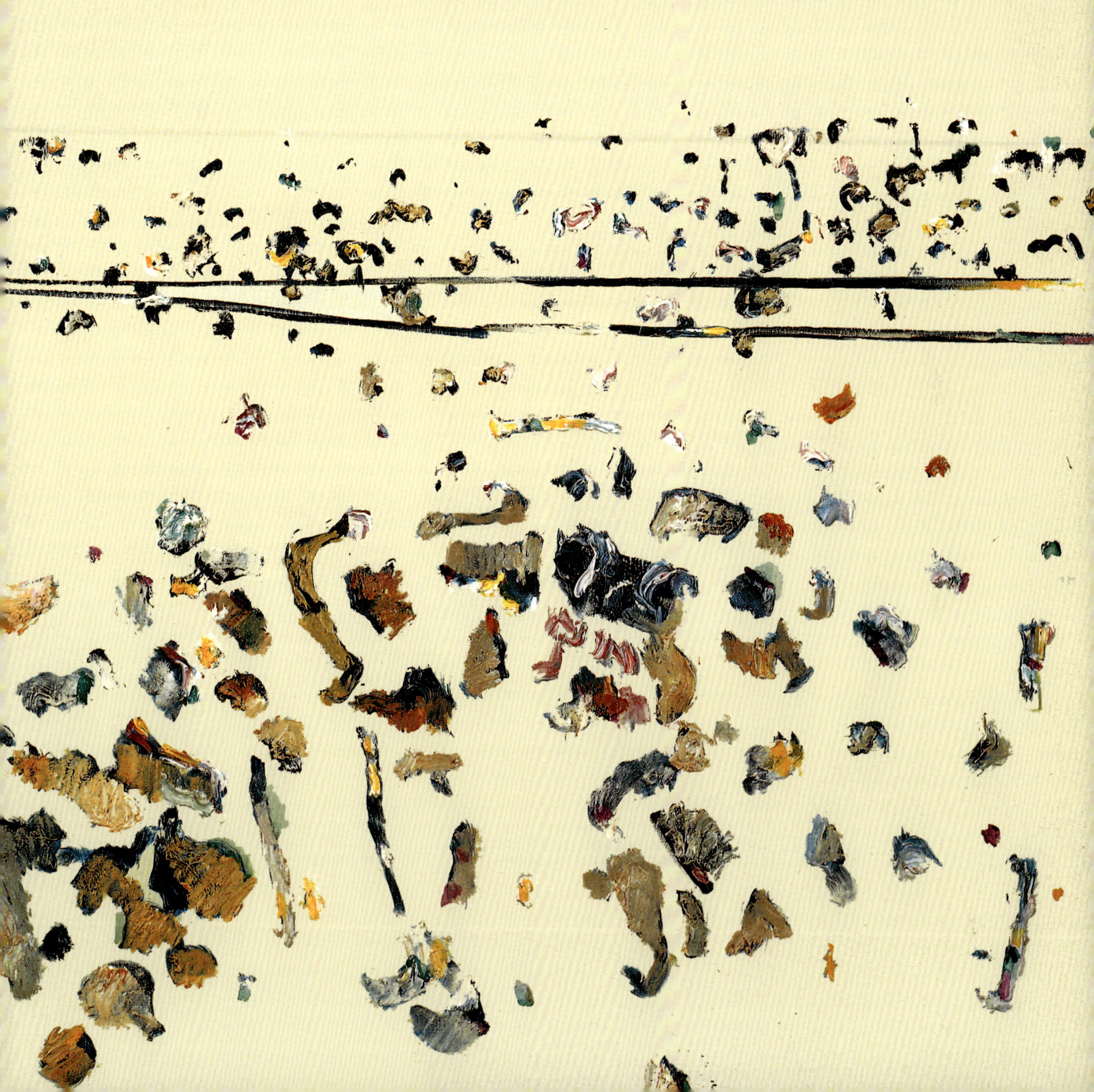

In 2013, in the present selection of works for the Royal Academy, half of those made during the reign of Queen Elizabeth II are by Aboriginal artists, and many settler and immigrant artists are influenced by Aboriginality. Already in 1954, during the first of Her Majesty's sixteen tours of Australia, she was asked to receive, in Canberra, the Aboriginal artist Albert Namatjira. He was a celebrity in the popular media, but to art insiders Namatjira's watercolour views of his desert country in the remote Red Centre were 'tourist art', and imitative of more fluent pastorals by Hans Heysen. (For the Queen's subsequent visit to Australia, organisers arranged a presentation by Heysen of his own *White Gums, Summer Afternoon* of 1963 (Royal Collection)[1].) Modernists preferred 'authentic' Aboriginal art, the creation myths and land-care stories from tropical coasts of the Northern Territory, painted on rough sheets of gum-tree bark. However, after Postmodernism taught us to accept hybridity and popularity, we reconsidered Namatjira's (and Heysen's) watercolours, and new Conceptualists honoured them by appropriation. Imants Tillers's *Untitled* (1978), comprising huge photographic blow-ups on canvas of a small Heysen gum-tree *Summer* (1909; Art Gallery of New South Wales, Sydney), was on view when the Queen opened the National Gallery of Australia, Canberra, in 1982.

The Elizabethan period began just after Australians had become, in 1949, Australian citizens as well as British subjects; during her tenth visit, in 1986, Queen Elizabeth proclaimed the Australia Act that formalised independence from the United Kingdom and confirmed direct access to the Crown. Though Australian artists in the first years of the young monarch's reign were less interested in nationalism than with catching up with post-war modernity, few abandoned landscape. Young painters in the 1950s, John Brack and Fred Williams among them, drew upon the classic Modernism of Seurat and Cézanne to express timeless aspects of Australian life and landscape. A somewhat later cohort, typified by John Olsen, took up the Abstract Expressionist style but seldom abandoned all reference to landscape. From the 1970s onwards, postmodern postcolonialist ideas encouraged widespread familiarity and engagement with Indigenous issues, and today Australian Aboriginal culture and Australian nature have equal weight as signifiers of Australianness in art.

ABORIGINALITY

Within the mainstream Euro-Australian art world, Sydney Long in around 1905 had painted Symbolist compositions in which Aboriginal figures were spirits of the land. Margaret Preston in the 1920s had been a lone pioneer in appreciation of Aboriginal aesthetics and, later, one of several expressing social concern for Aboriginal people.

G. W. Bot in the 1980s decided 'to be an Aborigine'. The first description of a wombat in French scientific writing, 'le grand Wam Bot', led to her playful nom de plume, a way of adopting an Aboriginal-style totemic relationship with the marsupials that flourish in her Canberra suburb.

Contrariwise, some artists of Aboriginal descent decline to be categorised as makers of 'Aboriginal art'. Two in the present exhibition are Tracey Moffatt and Gordon Bennett.

Moffatt insists she doesn't even make 'Australian art', just art about 'the human condition ... desperation and longing'.[2] She prefers ignorance of the wasteland location shoot for *Up in the Sky* (1997; cat.191), a narrative series of 25 photolithographs.[3] The retro technique, printed in monochrome blue, grey or sepia, recalls old film stills, once made to tempt customers into cinema screenings. Ambiguities are intended: white nuns who hold an unhappy black baby up to the sky could be at loving play, or else celebrating their well-intentioned theft of a neglected child. Says Moffatt, 'I'm not trying to be overtly political ... too boring to do and too boring to look at. I'm just trying to make images that "hold", using beauty and composition.'[4]

Bennett's *Possession Island* (1991; cat.176) appropriates an old schoolbook illustration – of Captain Cook taking possession of Australia's Pacific coast for the British Empire – veiled in Aboriginal dots and a whiplash of Abstract Expressionist drip painting. At the centre of the composition, with emphatic clarity, stands an inserted figure: a black Aboriginal servant dressed in red and yellow.

Black, red, yellow. Signifying Indigenous 'Blak' pride, red earth and sunlight, these are the colours of the Aboriginal flag, designed in 1971 by a Central Australian artist of Luritja/Wombia origin for Aboriginal land-rights activism and in 1995 recognised by Parliament as a statutory Flag of Australia. Bennett's *Possession Island* paints a story of subservience to and dispossession by land-takers (figs 37, 38).

Tim Johnson, visiting Papunya, asked the elders for permission to fill his own paintings with dots, and also invited Aboriginal artists to collaborate on his canvases. Permission was granted but, as they earlier told Hossein Valamanesh, 'as long as you paint your own story'.[5] Johnson saw a similarity between Aboriginal culture and Buddhism. So both in his *Dewachen* (1987; cat.177), named after the Tibetan 'Land of Bliss', and in a companion painting, *Yuelamu* (1988; Queensland Art Gallery, Brisbane), named after a Central Australian community, monks and Aborigines meditate in a shared space. The shimmer suggests enlightenment.

Hossein Valamanesh's installation *Longing/Belonging* (1997; cat.201) links nomadic Persians with nomadic Australians. In 1974 a theatre-in-community company took the Iranian new arrival to inland desert country. Says Valamanesh, 'witnessing our connection to nature and the universe ... The effects on my practice were both physical, through the use of natural materials, and metaphysical by recognition of such a connection'.[6] For *Longing/Belonging* a rug made by Qashqa'i pastoralists in southern Iran and used in their temporary home places, has landed – a fairytale Persian carpet – in arid mallee-gum scrubland by the big Murray River in Australia. Campfires signified home for Aborigines; fire burning on the carpet introduces two ancient cultures to each other.

Imants Tillers, son of a family displaced by war from Latvia to Australia, felt a need to see connections between different places, identities and ideas but also to accept unsystematic and unexpected mutations, extinctions and coincidences. His *Shadow of the Hereafter* (2007; cat.193) includes an aggrandised 284.5 cm appropriation of a readymade image, an inaccurately golden but preferred reproduction of Hans Heysen's watercolour, *The Land of the Oratunga* (1932; cat.127).

Words float over the land. Ghost-white stencilled letterings recite the names of white settlers' ghost towns or of Aboriginal tribes who no longer haunt these inland ranges. The dark semi-circles, fragments of lettering appropriated from Rosalie Gascoigne's relief construction *Monaro* (1989; cat.178), resemble the Aboriginal-art ideogram for a seated figure and, besides signifying former inhabitants, can be read as a muttering of lost meanings, and misunderstandings. Mallarmé's poem title *A Throw of the Dice Will Never Abolish Chance* provides a blue border for *Shadow of the Hereafter*. When he first exhibited the painting, alongside appropriations from Namatjira as well as Heysen, Tillers wrote: 'I seem to be in two minds as to where I should locate my psyche – next to the Central Australian ghost gum or the Latvian birch tree – in Europe or the Antipodes.'[7]

Shaun Gladwell's *Approach to Mundi Mundi* (2007; cat.197) is a video projection of ecstatic hands-free motorbike riding on the edge of an inland plain near Broken Hill, a present-day dreaming into existence of a red-earth world. 'Mundi Mundi' specifies the Aboriginal name of the plain, so we infer a homage to Rover Thomas's *Roads Meeting* (1987; cat.29),

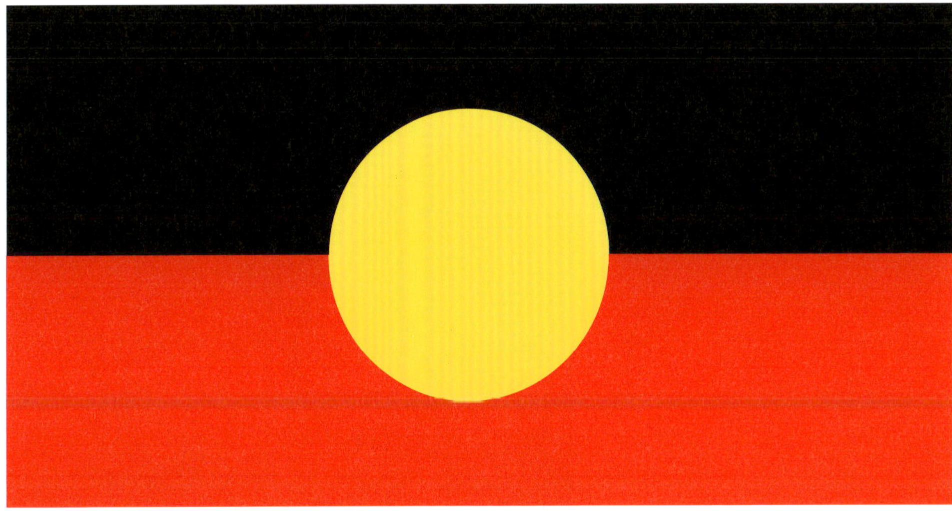

Fig. 37
The Australian Aboriginal flag, designed by HAROLD JABADA THOMAS, 1971

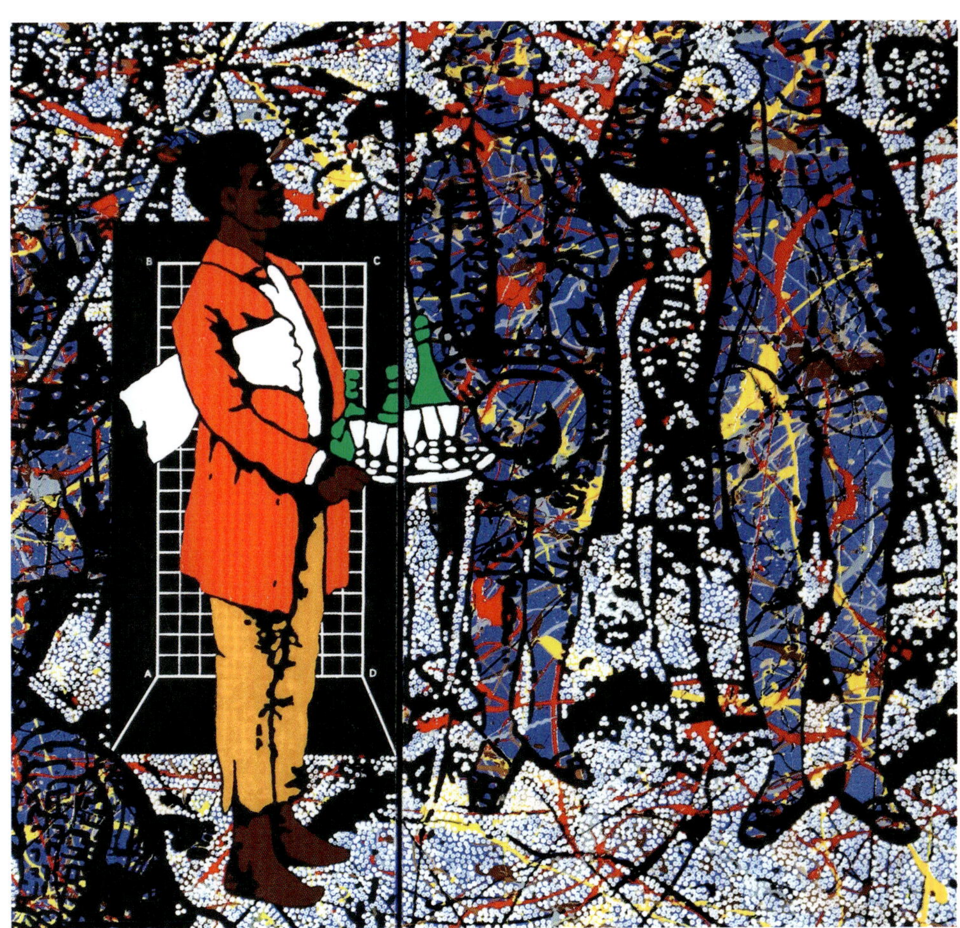

Fig. 38
GORDON BENNETT, **Possession Island**, 1991 (detail of cat.176). Oil and synthetic polymer paint on canvas, 162 × 260 cm

Museum of Sydney, Historic Houses Trust of New South Wales, Sydney. Purchased with funds from the Foundation for the Historic Houses Trust, Museum of Sydney Appeal, 2007

Fig. 39
DARREN SIWES, **Biyi Marrkidj**, 2011. Inkjet pigment print, 90 × 90 cm
National Gallery of Australia, Canberra. Purchased 2012

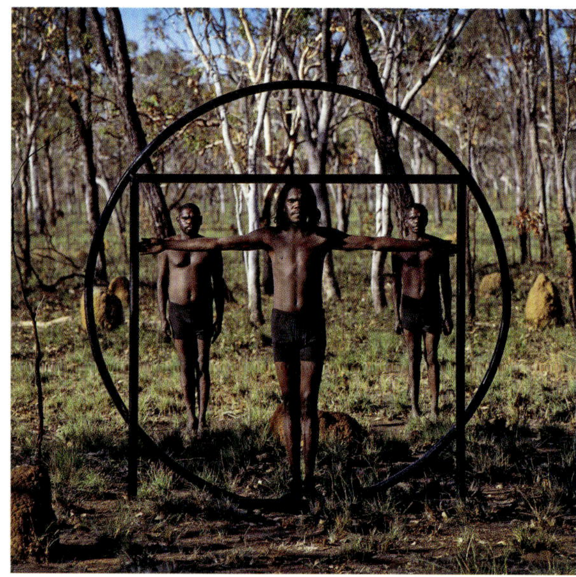

Fig. 40
SHAUN GLADWELL, **Approach to Mundi Mundi 1**, 2009. Marker pen on Polaroid photograph, 8.5 × 10.8 cm
Private collection, Sydney

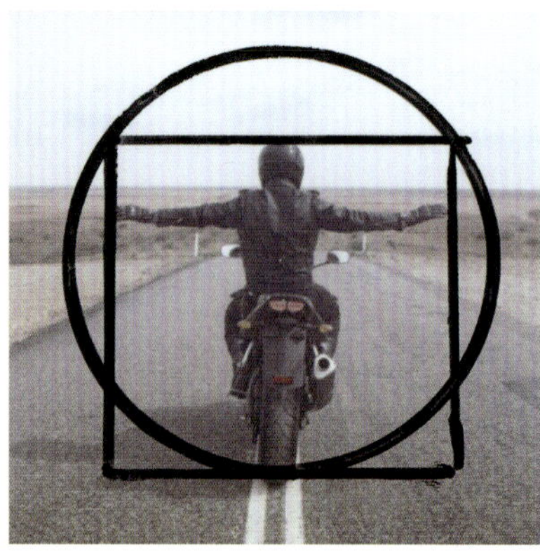

a crossing of red earth and black bitumen marked by Aboriginal hand-stencil stop signs. The trance-like effect of an apparently stationary moving image evokes the balanced concentration of skateboarding (a sport in which Gladwell is expert) or surfboard riding. Since the Aboriginal word 'Mundi' is also Latin for 'of the world', the rider's outstretched arms evoke Christ on the Cross and Leonardo's Vitruvian Man. *Approach to Mundi Mundi* is an immersion in here-on-earth spirituality (figs 39, 40).

ENVIRONMENTALISM

Nature creates culture: geography rules. Tim Flannery's book *The Future Eaters: An Ecological History of the Australasian Lands and People* (1994) gave focus to rising eco-fright. Since Australia has the world's poorest soils and most erratic climate, environmentalism became the other big idea in Australian art of the current Elizabethan period. It is interlinked with Aboriginality, which emphasises custodianship of country.

The geology of the vast, sparsely populated outback is mostly haematite-iron red, and, by the mid-twentieth century, well before the current iron-mining boom, red earth had become symbolic of Australia. The red shift followed an earlier gold-mining and wool-growing ('Golden Fleece') period that favoured golden yellow.

Green rainforests, however, survive from remote geologic and climatic eras, but only in very small areas, both subtropical and temperate, and are much used as cool summertime retreats for city dwellers. More than ecological sustainability, it was natural beauty lost to industrial development that caused Tasmanian state electors to form, in 1972, the world's first political 'Green' party. During a later federal election campaign, *Morning Mist, Rock Island Bend* (1981; cat.171), a magical forest photograph taken on Tasmania's Franklin River by the Latvian immigrant Peter Dombrovskis, helped to change an Australian government. The wild river was to be drowned for a hydroelectric dam: a protest poster used the Dombrovskis image to ask 'Could you vote for a party that will destroy this?' (fig.41). Many could not, and a government fell.

The subtropical rainforest in William Robinson's topographically entitled *Twin Falls and Gorge* (2000; cat.181) is a land of heavenly bliss. Archaic vegetation surges and swirls in multi-directional perspectives like the angels and draperies on Baroque church ceilings. Robinson's elevated tableland, above the Gold Coast and Surfers Paradise, is volcanic and hence fertile, filled with a teeming diversity of rocks and plants, cooling airs and birds.

Present-day artists add ironies to the nature study that all Australians learn. Fiona Hall made her *Paradisus Terrestris* (1989–90; cat.175), a suite of 23 miniature sculptures of plants, while living near the Adelaide Botanic Garden. Since Linnaean classification of the plant kingdom was based on stamens and pistils, the plants' male and female sexual organs, Hall's earthly paradise pairs each species with a display of human sexual stimulation.

The botanical images are based on antique engravings, the human on details from 1980s New York pornographic photographs.[8] Exclusion of the faces that were in the photographs, the miniaturisation (little peepshows inside sardine cans), the apparently precious material beauty of silvery metalwork in tin and aluminium, the elegant rendering of sexualities all somehow produce a chastely scientific air. *Paradisus Terrestris* would be at home in a seventeenth-century *Wunderkammer*, or cabinet of curiosities.

Simryn Gill, who divides her life between Malaysia and Australia, looks back botanically to Asian homelands in her *Rampant* (1999; cat.188). The work grew from wondering if she 'could find friends among the local Australian flora'.[9] Only too successful, in northern New South Wales she found groves of introduced bamboo, bananas, sugar cane and camphor laurels, some of which, lacking natural biological controls, had gone feral. Gill dressed up her plants in tropical Asian clothes: Indian and Malayan lungis and sarongs. In the black-and-white gelatin-silver prints these garments become pale Asian ghosts, aliens.

Howard Arkley's imposing canvases of everyday suburban houses began as an affectionate post-Pop classificatory project of Melbourne suburbia. *Superb + Solid* (1998; cat.185) was based on an estate agent's snapshot of a by then middle-aged three-car house in upmarket Brighton Beach – but the artist 'liked the way the image could be pushed around to suggest instead that it was a standard brick walk-up of three heat-baked flats' in a suburb well away from the bay.[10] The salesman's slogan no longer has any credibility; the image has become environmentally critical, of barely liveable housing. Callum Morton's digital print *Tomorrowland* (2004; cat.189), an imaginary theme park that failed, similarly foreshadows the melancholy future of once idealistic but eventually unloved or unlovable modernist developments.

SEEING AND FEELING

When Aboriginal painters encounter work by Fred Williams they recognise his dotted, no-horizon landscapes as like their own. Because flatland Australia generally lacks distant geographical features, European perspective becomes irrelevant. Artists look downward onto close-up ground-level intimacies, or else at endlessness from aircraft far above.

His all-over images suggest an unbounded, timeless nature in which we are as seamlessly embedded as are Indigenous Australians, whose art was not only micro-regional in content but also traditionally made from their own close-at-hand earths and ochres. Williams's materialities too – the pigments handled with care, the only partly mixed colours sparkling within each tree-blob, the harmonious intervals, the concern for temperature – all suggest that nature is to be understood as much by touch as by gaze. In his *Snow Storm, Kosciusko* (1976–77; cat.166) an upright format and the presence of sky help to emphasise the symbolic altitude of this unspectacular, uncraggy upland that happens to be Australia's highest mountain, where the artist encountered snow surviving into midsummer January. Both the perhaps summery *Yellow Landscape* (1968–69; cat.164), in which the horizon is no more than a dwindling of tree dots and dabs into nothingness, and the perhaps wintry *Silver and Grey* (1969; cat.165), in which lines suggesting a middle-ground fence or road are abstracted bits of Melbourne-fringe farmland near Williams's home.

The date of John Brack's *The Car* (1955; cat.160) makes it the Australian start of new Elizabethan post-war modernism, and also illustrates a new way of living: a Melbourne family has a new car; automobile ownership had long been necessary in the bush but only now had suburban sprawl overtaken metropolitan tram and railway systems. The sky is near-city white, not clean country blue. This is a Sunday drive through unprepossessing countryside exactly like the land Fred Williams would soon transform. The car, a Triumph

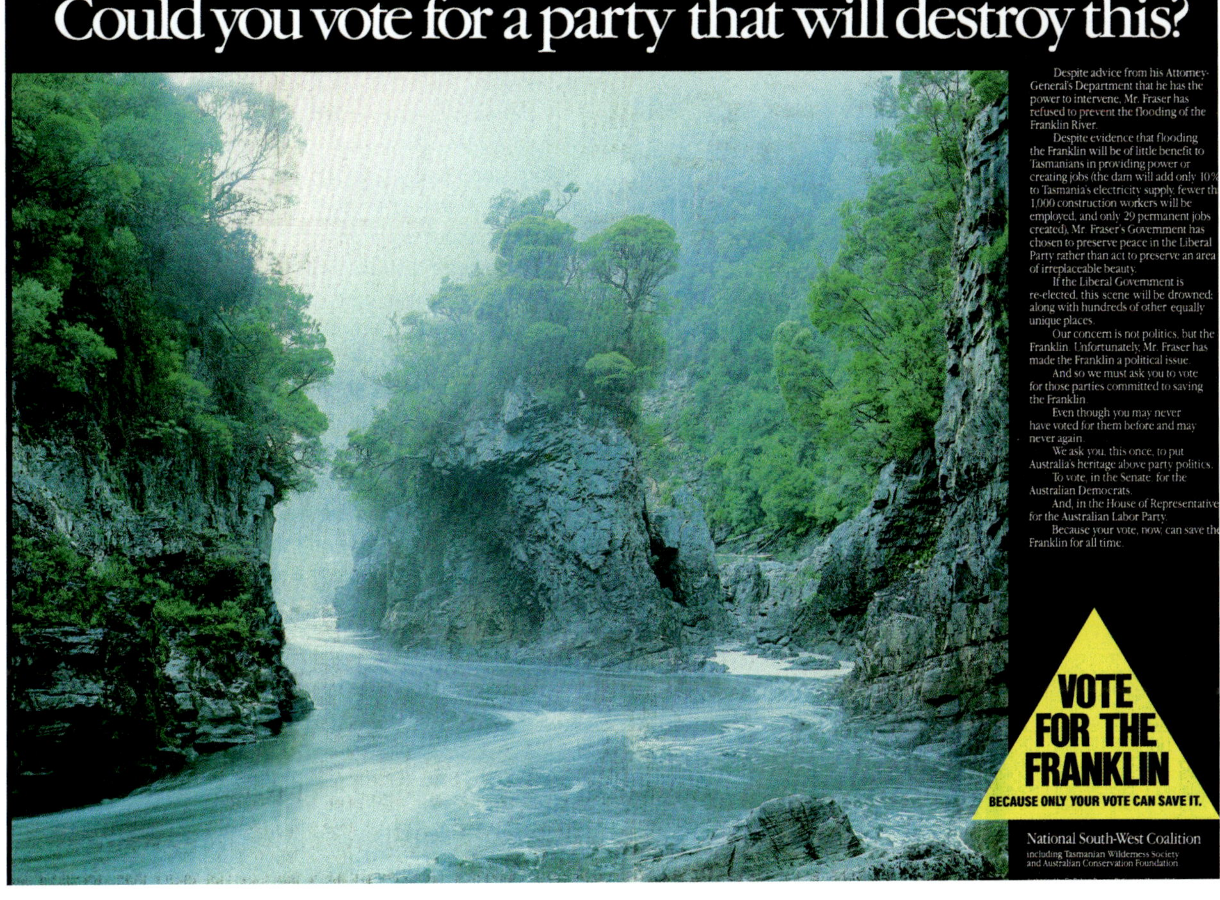

Fig. 41
Campaign poster used in the 1983 Australian federal election, authorised by Tasmanian Greens state parliamentarian Bob Brown, *Could you vote for a party that will destroy this? VOTE FOR THE FRANKLIN*; image from Peter Dombrovskis photograph (cat.171). Glossy rotogravure print, 44.2 × 55.3 cm, designed by Alan Marshall at Clemenger advertising agency, Melbourne
The Wilderness Society, Hobart

Mayflower, affordable, but stylish and British, had an angular, razor-edge look that many considered ugly. Brack loved working, wittily, at the edge of ugliness. The sudden, close glimpse of a family framed by car windows took place in a suburban street not in a rural landscape, so he put the landscape into the car, a mental prospect of a holiday excursion miniaturised in the mind.[11]

From the earlier generation of Expressionists, Arthur Boyd, nine years after settling in England in 1959, revisited Australia for a summer fellowship at the Australian National University in Canberra, and found the inland light strange: 'the blueness of the sky ... so intense compared to [Melbourne]'. His wife said of the 'landscapes with blue skies, he liked the way the ground was lighter than the brilliant sky'.[12] In his self-loathing 'Caged Painter' series, painted back in London, the Canberra grassland blazes white outside a chicken-wired studio window. As well as remembering a bone-clean Australia, in the extraordinary composition *Paintings in the Studio: 'Figure Supporting Back Legs' and 'Interior with Black Rabbit'* (1973–74; cat.169), Boyd was thinking about our kindness and unkindness to animals, and our own animality.

The many arms of Sydney Harbour are unusually twisty, indeed tentacular. John Olsen was living near the seaport entrance, looking inland, when he painted a centralised *Sydney Sun* (1965; cat.161) for installation as a ceiling decoration. A few years earlier he had sailed into the harbour after time in Europe and, he later recalled, 'the surrounding hills seemed to cradle the sun's light – like a benevolent bath, bubbling and effervescent. [The painting is an] image of things growing, pullulating from the sun's source.'[13]

Brett Whiteley, too, was recently back from Europe and America and living on Sydney Harbour when he painted the near-monochrome *Big Orange (Sunset)* (1974; cat.168 and see fig.42) that turned out to require a complementary colour-flash companion sculpture, of ultramarine palm trees. Whereas Olsen's yellow *Sydney Sun* pulls us upwards to the centre of the sky, this waterscape – low western light is coming from the right-hand side – invites us to look downwards into the warmth of Lavender Bay. Whiteley said such paintings were 'points of optical ecstasy, where romanticism and optimism overshadow any form of menace or foreboding'.[14] If 40 years ago there was no sense of menace, today the orange colour is prophetic of bushfire infernos that have since reached leafy suburbs, or red dust storms reaching the centre of Sydney from outback drought country.

Rosalie Gascoigne, a New Zealander accustomed to a land of smooth green pastures and a geology of sudden volcanic upthrusts, came to live in Canberra and discovered slow-rolling rough grasslands immediately to the south of the city. She became an assemblage sculptor, using scavenged, worn materials. Her long horizontal wall-hung *Monaro* (cat.178), named after the blond sheep-pasture region, is made from cut-up timber crates for fizzy drinks. Fine slivers and fragmented lettering become undulant vegetation as the motorist Gascoigne sweeps past and swoops up, and almost achieves momentary lift-off at each crest on the road. It's a haptic as well as a visual experience.

Unkempt small-farming Gold Coast hinterland is where Mike Parr grew up, obsessing about an unexplained bodily disability – a truncated arm. Besides his major works of performance art about his disability, and later about political injustice, he also draws or engraves huge distorted self-images. His drawing tended to facility so he roughed-up the techniques. An extremely rare occurrence of landscape is found in his series of 24 savagely engraved drypoints *Great Distances between Small Towns* (1990–91; cat.183). Here Parr endures tedium during the ten-hour drive from Sydney to Melbourne: plenty of time for thoughts to rise again about a newborn's deformed body, while passing endless worn-down hills and stoic tree trunks and stumps.

The need to classify and thereby grasp a world not widely available in mass imagery no doubt accounts for

Fig. 42
BRETT WHITELEY, **Big Orange (Sunset)**, 1974 (cat.168). Oil and collage on wood, 244 × 305 cm. **(Free-standing ultramarine) Palm Trees**, 1974. Painted fibreglass sculpture, 274 × 71 × 40.5 cm
Art Gallery of New South Wales, Sydney. Gift of Patrick White, 1975

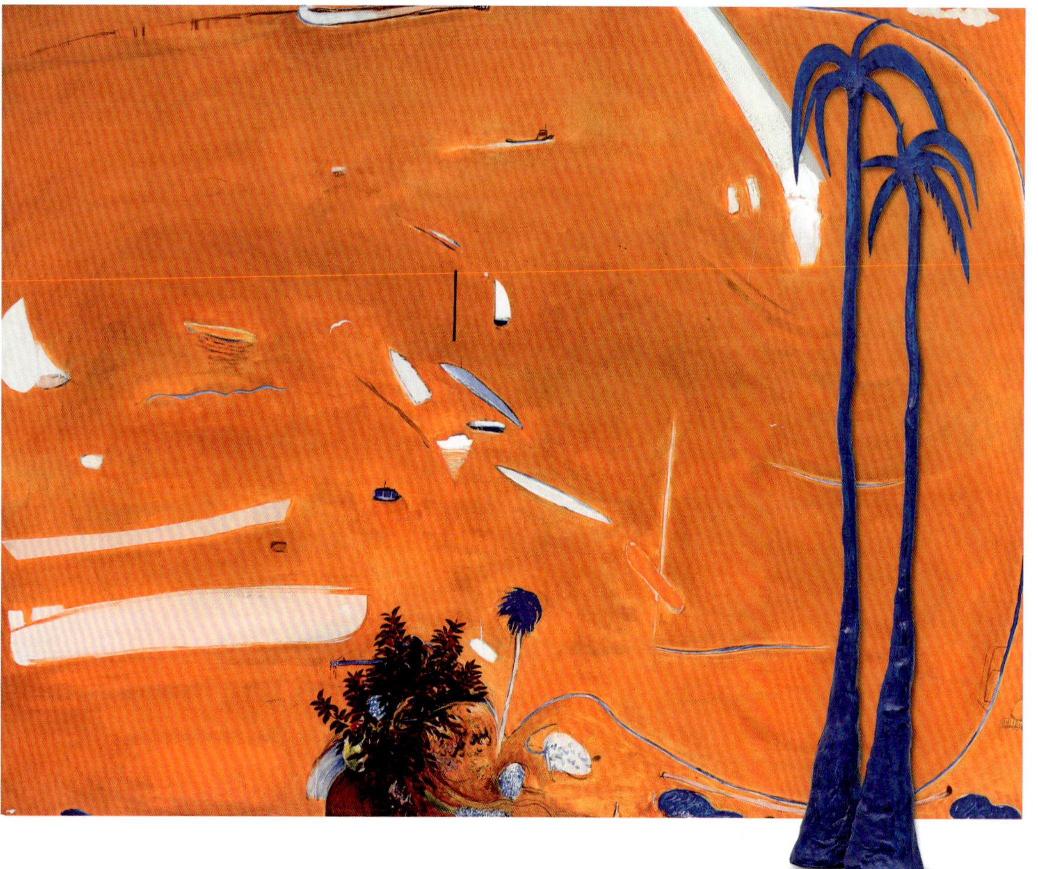

the frequency in Australian art of serial works. The most extended is Wesley Stacey's *The Road* (1973–75; cat.170), a suite of 280 small, snapshot-sized colour photographs, the unbeautified face of city, suburb, beach, bush and outback.

The photographic artist Bill Henson never tells the location of what the New York reviewer Bill Cooper described as 'abandoned buildings, vacant lots and deserted back roads' that form the turf of 'introverted, compellingly beautiful teenage outsiders'.[15] Seeking context for Henson's *Untitled* (1998–99; cat.190) in his monograph *Mnemosyne* (2005), we recognise a zone of mid-Victorian inner-Melbourne suburbs where railways still have level crossings, and find that the book pairs wasteland habitats with images of their nocturnal denizens: naked youths drunk on alcohol and eroticism, at the mysterious cusp of adulthood and loss of short-lived beauty (fig.43).

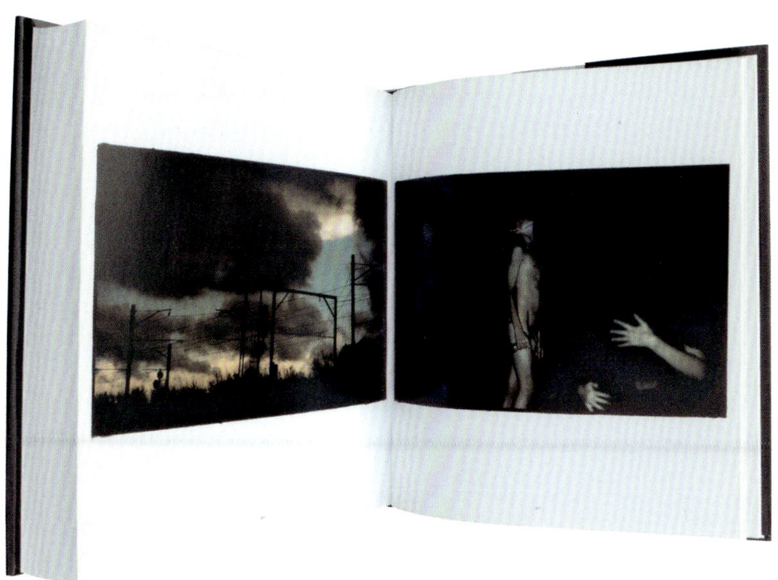

Fig. 43
Double-page spread showing Bill Henson's photograph *Untitled*, 1998–99 (cat.190) with his characteristic pairing of landscape and figurative images within his series

Double-page spread in Judy Annear, *Mnemosyne: Bill Henson*, exh. cat., Art Gallery of New South Wales, Sydney, 2005, pp. 466–7

IMMIGRANTS

In the current Elizabethan period many Australian artists were born elsewhere. Some – Valamanesh, Dombrovskis and Gill from Iran, Latvia and Malaysia – have been mentioned already. All carry their homelands with them.

Ian Fairweather was one of many British Empire children who felt abandoned and unloved when parents spent years away, looking after Egypt, India or the Far East. After restless years in China, the Philippines and Bali, in 1953, aged sixty-one, he settled on an undeveloped island backwater near Brisbane and achieved a beachcomberish serenity. *Monsoon* (1961–62; cat.163), one of very few landscapes by this philosopher of the human condition, was prompted by a tremendous storm that flattened thirteen trees around his self-built hut.[16] (Locals later remembered the intelligent cyclone-proof design of his fragile structure.) The reticent colours of mud grey, post-bushfire charcoal and casuarina-blossom orange are typical of Bribie Island. The work, a fusion of classic drab-coloured interlocking Cubism with Chinese calligraphy, is an astonishing image of thunder and lightning.

Sent back, by a Suez Canal pilot father, to boarding school in England aged eight, and both parents dead not long after, Tony Tuckson had an RAF posting to Australia in 1942 that resulted in love and marriage, and happiness and a life in Sydney. Landscape seldom entered his generally humanist Abstract Expressionist painting, but *Watery* (*c.*1960; cat.162), an intimate sublimity, is delicately inscribed with memories of rapidly dividing waters. It came from close re-encounters with J.M.W.Turner in exhibitions of oil paintings from the Tate Gallery and watercolours from the British Museum in London that toured Australia in 1960 and 1961.

Other immigrants have retained more of their Britishness, notably Brian Blanchflower, who arrived in Perth in 1972 aged thirty-three. His works favour ancient (natural) materials such as soil, sand, stone-grit, tar or chalk. Stonehenge and druidic rituals therefore come to mind when we note the materials of his *Nocturne 3 (Whale Rock)* (1982; cat.173): white chalk for stars marked large on a depicted megalith and small in the sky; black bitumen and sand in the oil paint; coarse canvas.

Peter Booth, aged seventeen when he arrived in Melbourne, retains childhood memories of blitzed houses burning in wartime Sheffield. Not landscape but mutating monsters, as much comical as sinister, characterise his usual imagery, which derives from a belief that the natural world is at risk from human nature. Even if humans cause their own self-extinction, he says: 'One thing I am not pessimistic about is the ability of nature to heal itself.'[17] His *Mangroves* (2002; cat.180), a dramatic pastel based on sketches made in the coastal Daintree Rainforest of tropical North Queensland, suggests a 'healing' in which roots and branches become arms and marching legs of crab- or spider-men: botany evolves to fill an emptied biological niche.

The son of a forester in Latvia, Jan Senbergs landed in Melbourne in 1950 aged ten, after a childhood in shifting war zones and displaced persons' camps. Growing up culturally isolated, he read a lot – Kafka was a favourite – and eventually found an image-scavenging style in which fragments of machinery, photocopied from book illustrations, become unstable monuments. In his *Fort* (1973; cat.179), theatre curtains have opened to reveal a ridiculously ramshackle guardian of wilderness, inspired by walks around Port Melbourne, where he sensed a tremendous presence in big black piles of rubbish.[18]

SONGS OF AUSTRALIA

The Song of Australia (1859), once proposed as a national anthem, begins: 'There is a land where summer skies / Are gleaming with a thousand dyes, / Blending in witching harmonies', and ends 'And FREEDOM's sons the banner bear, / No shackled slave can breathe the air, / Fairest of Britain's daughters fair – Australia!'

The Australia of Elizabeth II is a land of subtle, summery colours and easy lifestyle, and a society of unusual democratic temper and many freedoms. We conclude with four renderings of Australian landscape that contain ideas about Britain. Australian-born Bea Maddock, Philip Wolfhagen, Rosemary Laing and Robert MacPherson still think of the motherland.

Before considering the four, we should acknowledge keen British eyes observing difference. Here is Agatha Christie, accompanying her husband on a British Empire trade mission in 1922:

> What startled me principally, as we came into Melbourne, was the extraordinary ... difference Australian gum trees make to a landscape.... In England one becomes used to trees having dark trunks and light leafy branches; the reverse in Australia was quite astonishing. Silvery white-barks everywhere, and the darker leaves, made it like seeing the negative of a photograph.[19]

Many artists have relished such reversals, most notably Fred Williams in his forest interiors and Bea Maddock in her coastal panoramas.

Kenneth Clark, on his first days in Australia, in Sydney at midsummer in January 1949, was struck by another quality: the overall luminosity, 'the whole impression very light [with] no forest darkness'.[20] That was when he met Sidney Nolan, whose landscapes he greatly admired for their truth of tone.

Similar luminosity, based on similar direct, intense observation, is found in Elisabeth Cummings's *Wedderburn Spring* (1993; cat.182), an Abstract Expressionist landscape of her bush country near Sydney.

Bea Maddock, the daughter of an Anglican country parson in Tasmania, lost her faith during postgraduate study at the Slade School of Fine Art in 1960s London but never lost her belief in the seriousness of good work and social morality. Her *TERRA SPIRITUS ... with a Darker Shade of Pale* (1993–98; cat.184) is an almost forty-metre overall panoramic profile of the entire coast of Tasmania, as if observed from a circumnavigating vessel. First European explorers of the good country in south-eastern Australia all sailed past the southern end of Tasmania, and commercial shipping from Britain continued that way until well into the twentieth century; it was the starting point for much two-way gazing between black and white cultures. *TERRA SPIRITUS* is red and white, the red ochre a pigment used by Aborigines for both sacred ceremonial and everyday cosmetics.

Maddock's 'drawing' is in fact linear incision into which ochre is rubbed. The technique is a delicate counterpart to Tasmanian Aboriginal body adornment by scarification. The artist dug her own clay from near her studio, and prepared her own ochre sticks.[21] Hand-drawn Aboriginal words float above the sea, confidently naming important Aboriginal places inland; small letterpress-imprinted English words diffidently name places on the edge, assigned by settlers. The work was a private act of Aboriginal recognition and restitution, triggered by the High Court of Australia's 1992 repudiation, in *Mabo v. Queensland*, of the past land-takers' concept of *terra nullius*.[22] In depicted landscape, distances are normally pale and foregrounds dark but here the closest landscape headlands are the whitest, and many are scarified: the land and its Indigenous people are fused in spirit (fig.44).

Philip Wolfhagen lives in a beautiful, well-watered farming region of acclimatised oaks, elms and hawthorn hedgerows in northern Tasmania, known for two centuries as the Norfolk Plains. He acknowledges Constable's practices in Suffolk as ancestral to his own. His *Autumn Equinox: The Loss of the Sun* (2009; cat.198) employs the conventionally poetic season and time of day, and the twilight bonfire of tree-loppings across the river, to reinforce a note of melancholia in a land of convict and immigrant exiles, and dispossessed Aborigines. The botany is specific and significant: English oaks planted beside Wolfhagen's house are thriving; a silver birch from northern Europe did not survive an early-twenty-first-century drought but its skeleton was retained in the artist's garden.[23]

Ideas of 'leakage between the past of idyllic pastoral landscape and ... suburban-to-global landscape' generated Rosemary Laing's series of five photographs entitled *leak*.[24] In 2010 Laing placed a specially constructed timber frame for a mean suburban house on a stony rise among noble storm-damaged gum trees – but it was upside down and horizontally askew. Because the novelist Patrick White had been a young jackeroo (trainee stockman) in this Monaro region, Laing gave her photographs titles after characters in White's *The Twyborn Affair* (1979), in which a stockman called Jim was a minor presence. The upside-down *leak* shot entitled *Jim* (2010; cat.200) acknowledges a general amused awareness that Australia is 'Down Under', at the bottom of the world.

Robert MacPherson, a descendant of the pastoralist MacPhersons of Dagworth Station, in outback Queensland, where Australia's unofficial national anthem 'Waltzing Matilda' originated, was a stockman before he switched identity, aged twenty-one, and decided to be an artist. A proud autodidact, he is just as pleased by the presence of his plaited-leatherwork stock whips in the Australian Stockman's Hall of Fame in Longreach, Queensland, as being rated, by the star German curator René Block in the 1990 Biennale of Sydney, as a Duchampian Marxist and as artistically significant as Warhol, Beuys and Koons.[25]

Childhood in pineapple-plantation country near Brisbane lies behind MacPherson's *Mayfair: Bethonga Gold, for B.T.O.'s* (1995–2006; cat.186). The image pretends to be a two-panel roadside sign selling an unusually flavoursome real variety of pineapple called Bethonga Gold. Roughly punctuated but well-spaced words honour cheerfully untrained skills at lettering and layout, and 'beautiful scumbling of line and paint surface'; the eye-catching red panel, a motorists' stop sign, is an abstraction of segmented pineapple skin.[26] Identification of the 'B.T.O.' dedicatee(s) is withheld; his working-class mates will know who they are if they ever enter an art museum and read the label beside their artist-mate's work. 'Mayfair' is a teasingly irreverent series title for works about small business enterprise; in Brisbane, MacPherson once haunted a modest sandwich bar that had named itself after London's glamorous neighbourhood. The phrase 'rough end of the pineapple' is an Australianism for a raw deal, the worst part of a bargain, but Bethonga's advertising spiel of 'no rough ends' is not entirely about the convenience of buying fruit with rough spiky leaves already removed: it also concerns protection of a genetic monopoly; a buyer could plant a rough end in his own back yard and grow his own Bethongas. Moralist MacPherson notices hypocritical half-truths in advertising.

Maddock and MacPherson admire each other's work. One highly trained, the other not; one solemn, the other voluble; one essentially a draughtsman, the other a Greenbergian hard-edge painter – they share a love of eloquent words as well as lines, textures, forms and images. Their laconic, pared-down forms and strong moral stance express a long-standing idea of what it is to be Australian.

But those ways of Protestant Christianity, Westminster constitutional monarchy and rule of law all came from Britain. And, as we have seen, Australian artists live and work not only in places with Aboriginal names, such as Canberra and the Monaro, but also in their own Wedderburn, Newcastle, Norfolk and Mayfair.

Australian geography might be the prime source of Australianness, but the English language and British place names have an unusually strong presence in Australian visual art. Invocation and assertion of potent words as well as cultural evolution of Church, state and law will always preserve a British element in Australian art.

Fig. 44
BEA MADDOCK, **Terra Spiritus … with a Darker Shade of Pale**, 1993–98 (detail of cat. 184). From the 52-sheet series of stencils, 28.4 × 75.9 (each sheet). *Peemingen (Havelock Bluff)* from the third and southernmost of 51 coastal-profile sheets circling Tasmania: the stencilled incisions in paper rubbed with red ochre
National Gallery of Australia, Canberra. Gordon Darling Australasian Print Fund, 1998

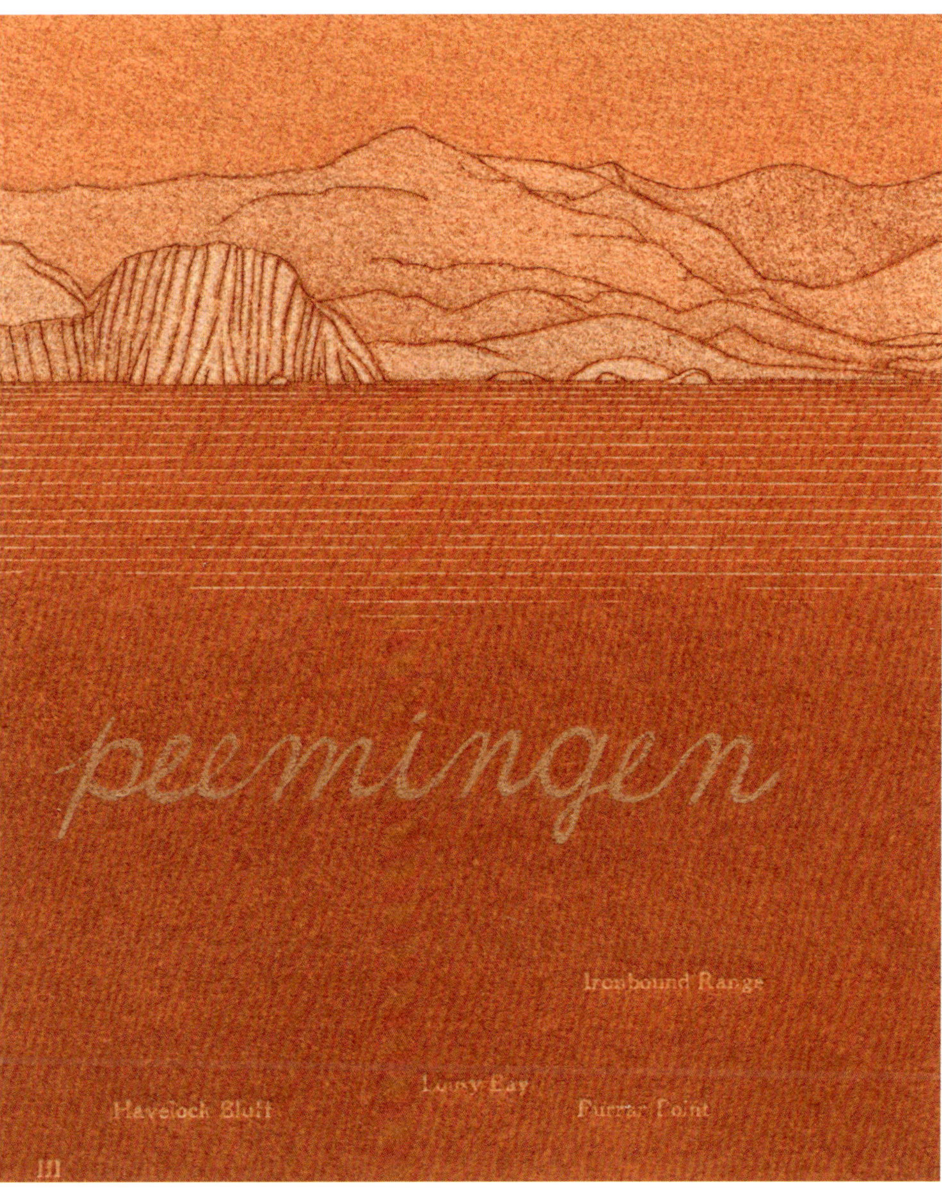

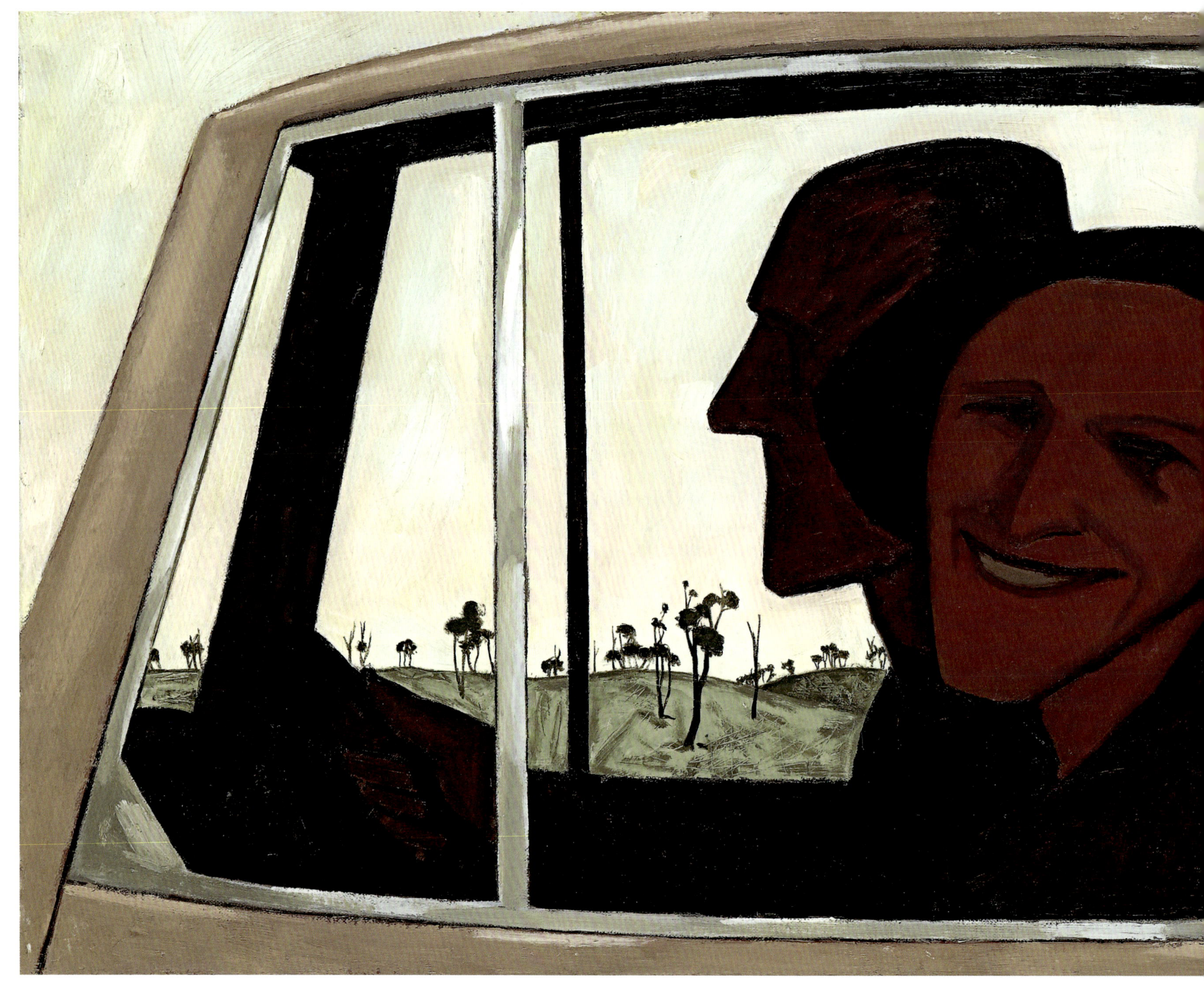

160

JOHN BRACK
The Car, 1955
Oil on canvas, 41 × 102.2 cm
National Gallery of Victoria, Melbourne.
Purchased 1956

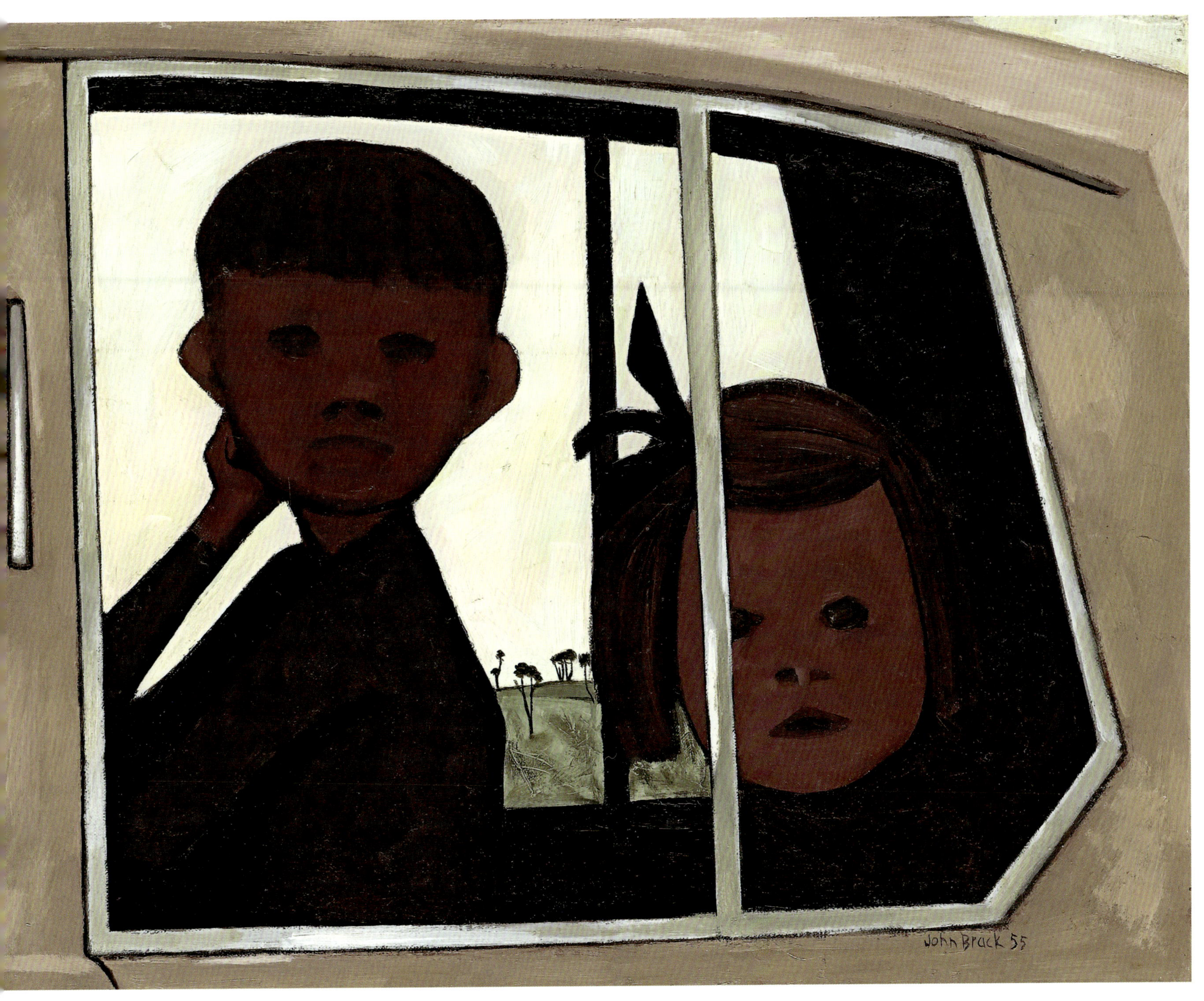
John Brack 55

161

JOHN OLSEN
Sydney Sun, 1965
Oil on three plywood panels,
305 × 412.5 cm (overall)

National Gallery of Australia, Canberra.
Purchased with funds from the Nerissa Johnson Bequest, 2000

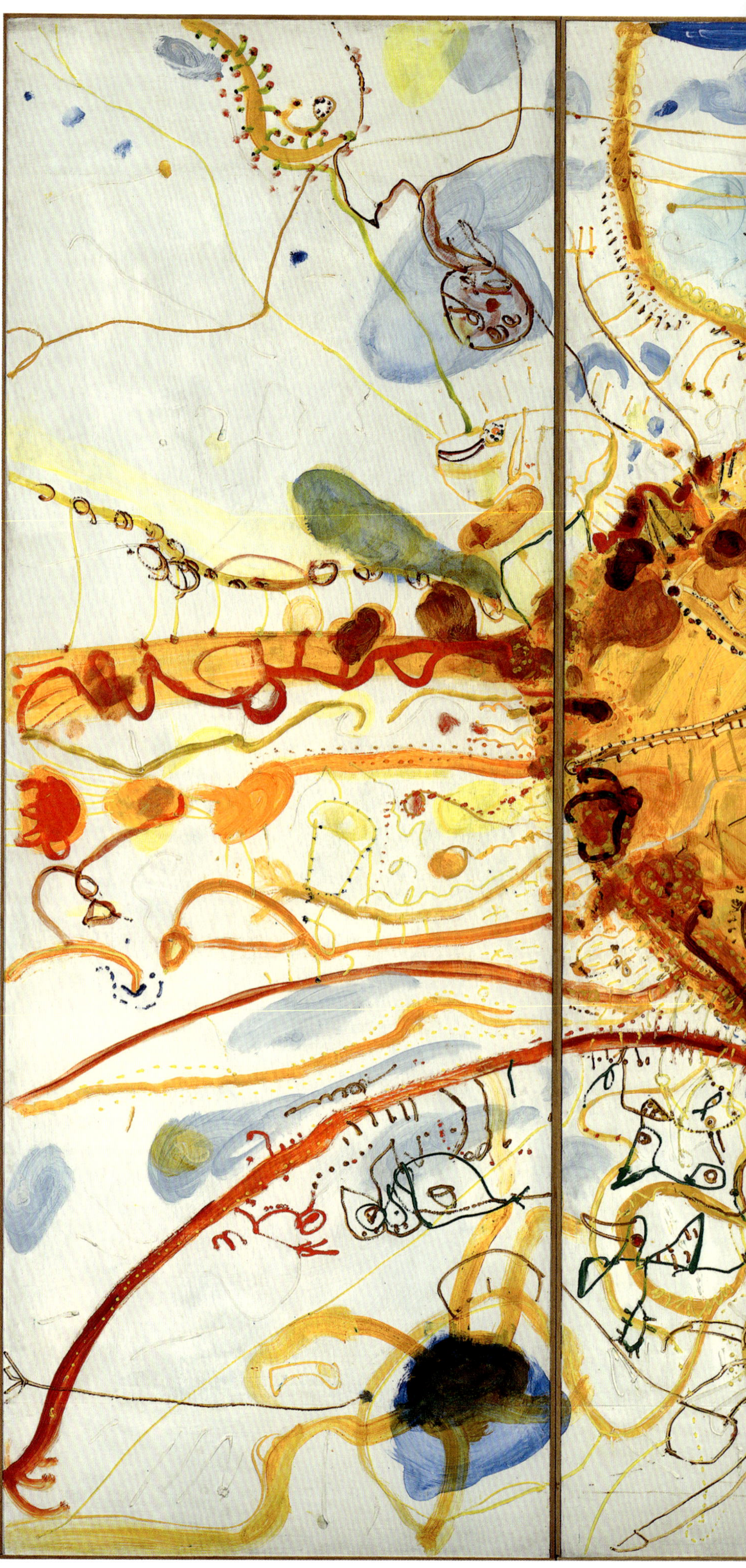

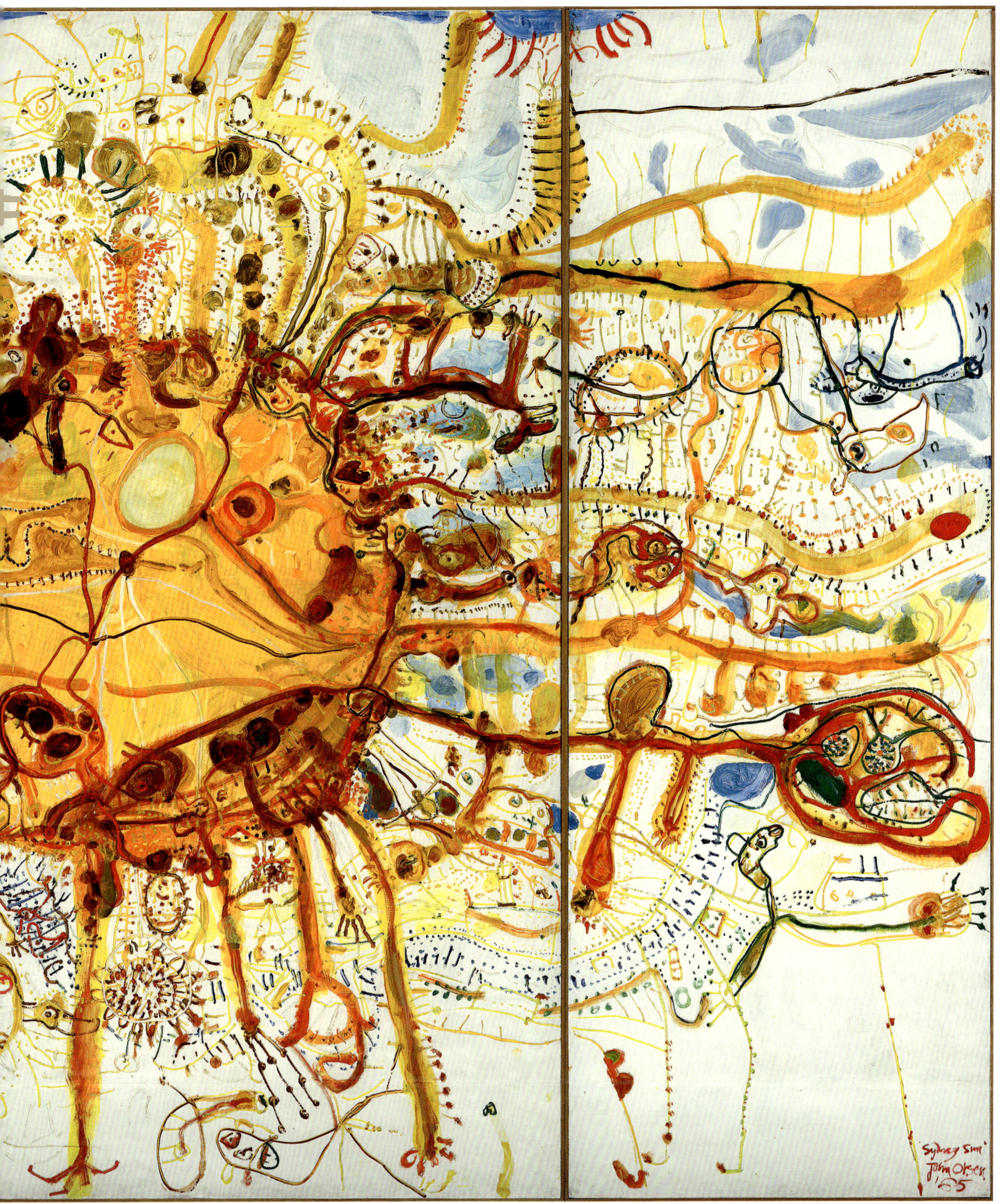
'Sydney Sun'
John Olsen
'65

162

TONY TUCKSON
Watery, *c.* 1960
Oil on composition board,
122.2 × 183 cm
National Gallery of Australia, Canberra.
Gift of Margaret Tuckson, 2002

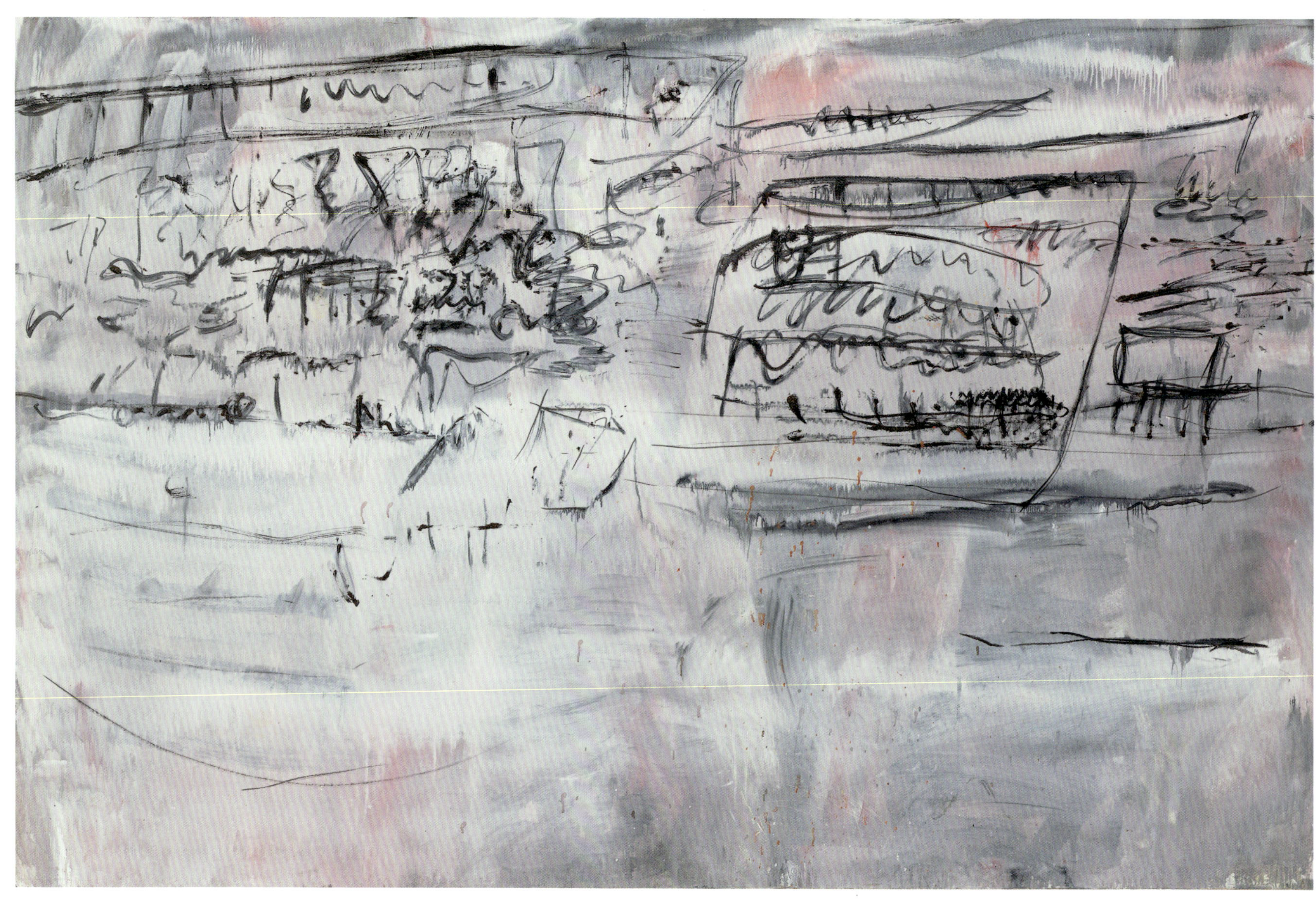

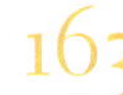

163

IAN FAIRWEATHER
Monsoon, 1961–62
Synthetic polymer paint and gouache on card, lined onto hardboard, 98.3 × 188.9 cm

State Art Collection, Art Gallery of Western Australia, Perth. Purchased 1983

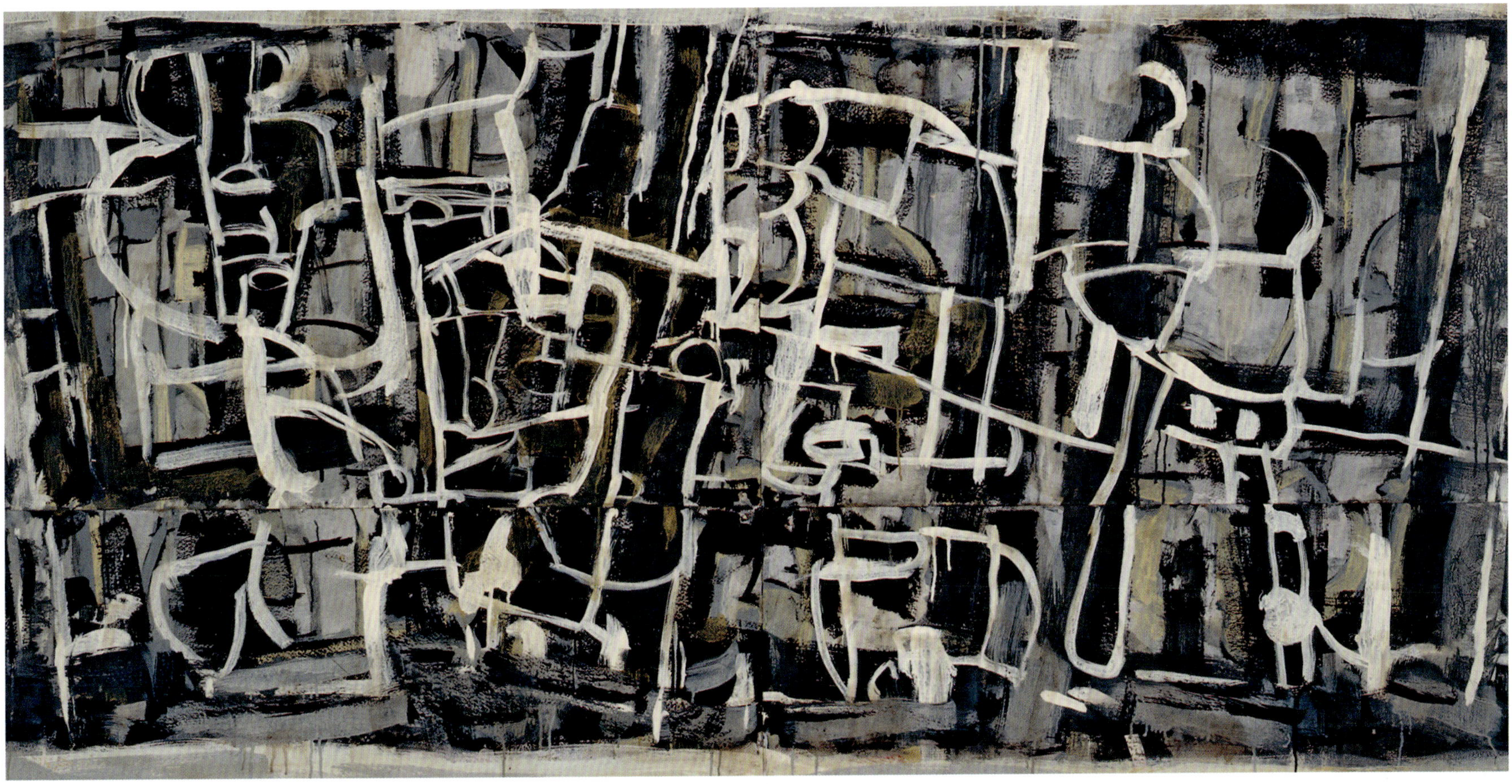

164

FRED WILLIAMS

Yellow Landscape, 1968–69

Oil on canvas, 141.7 × 193 cm

Geelong Gallery, Victoria.
Purchased 1976

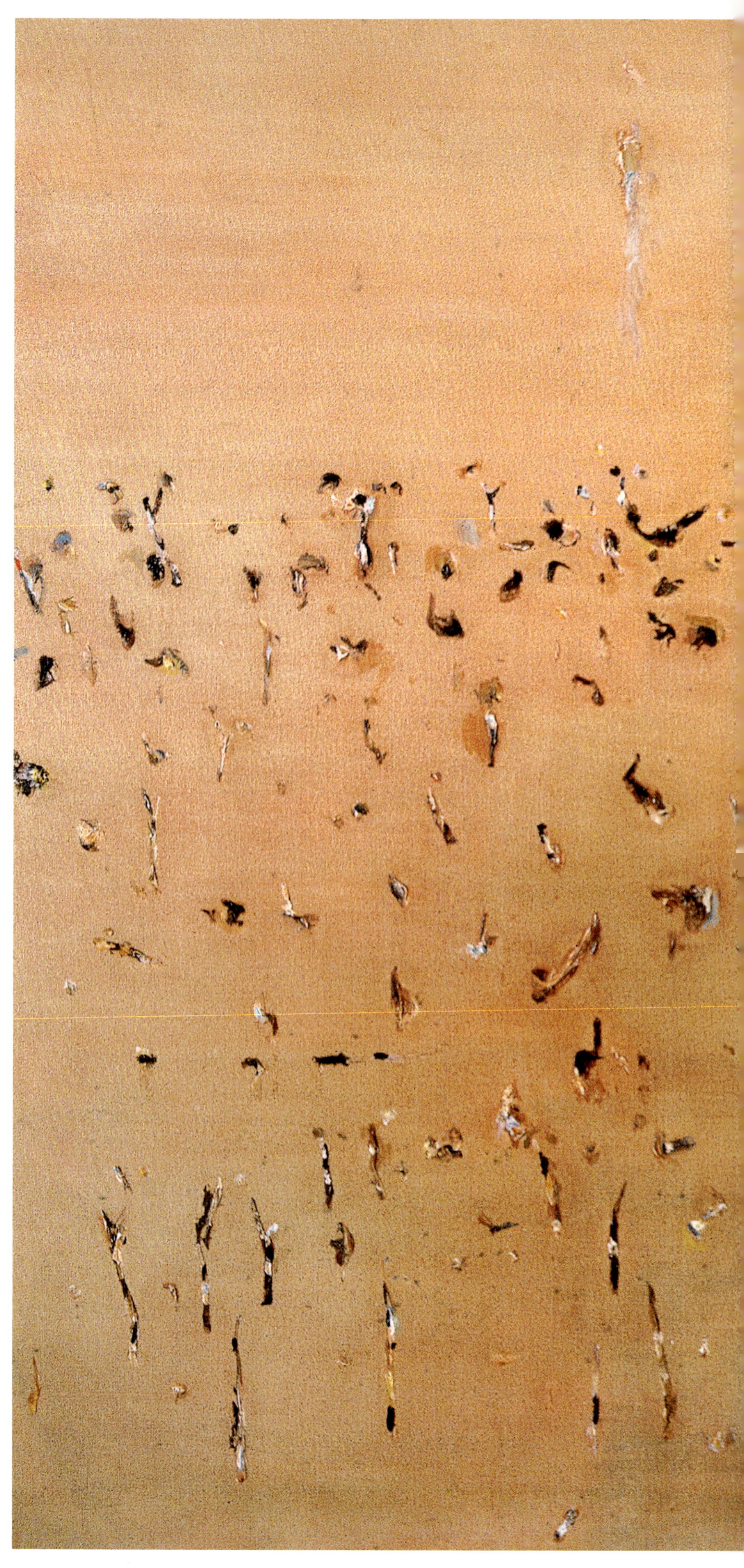

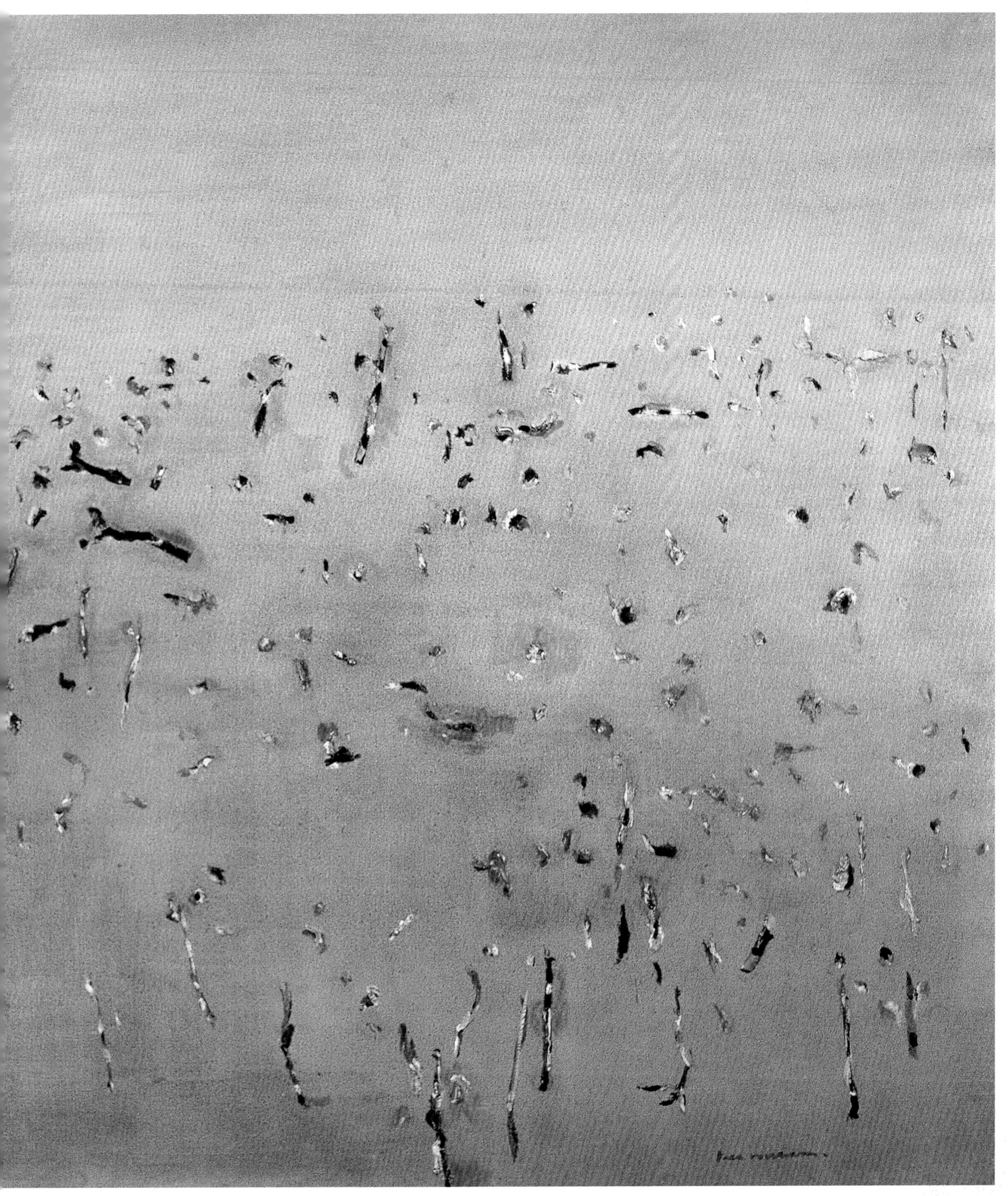

165

FRED WILLIAMS
Silver and Grey, 1969
Oil on canvas, 137.2 × 152.3 cm
Art Gallery of South Australia, Adelaide.
Gift of Howard and Christine Michell, 1992

166

FRED WILLIAMS
Snow Storm, Kosciusko, 1976–77
Oil on canvas, 183 × 101.6 cm
National Gallery of Australia, Canberra.
Purchased with funds from the Ruth Komon Bequest, 2013

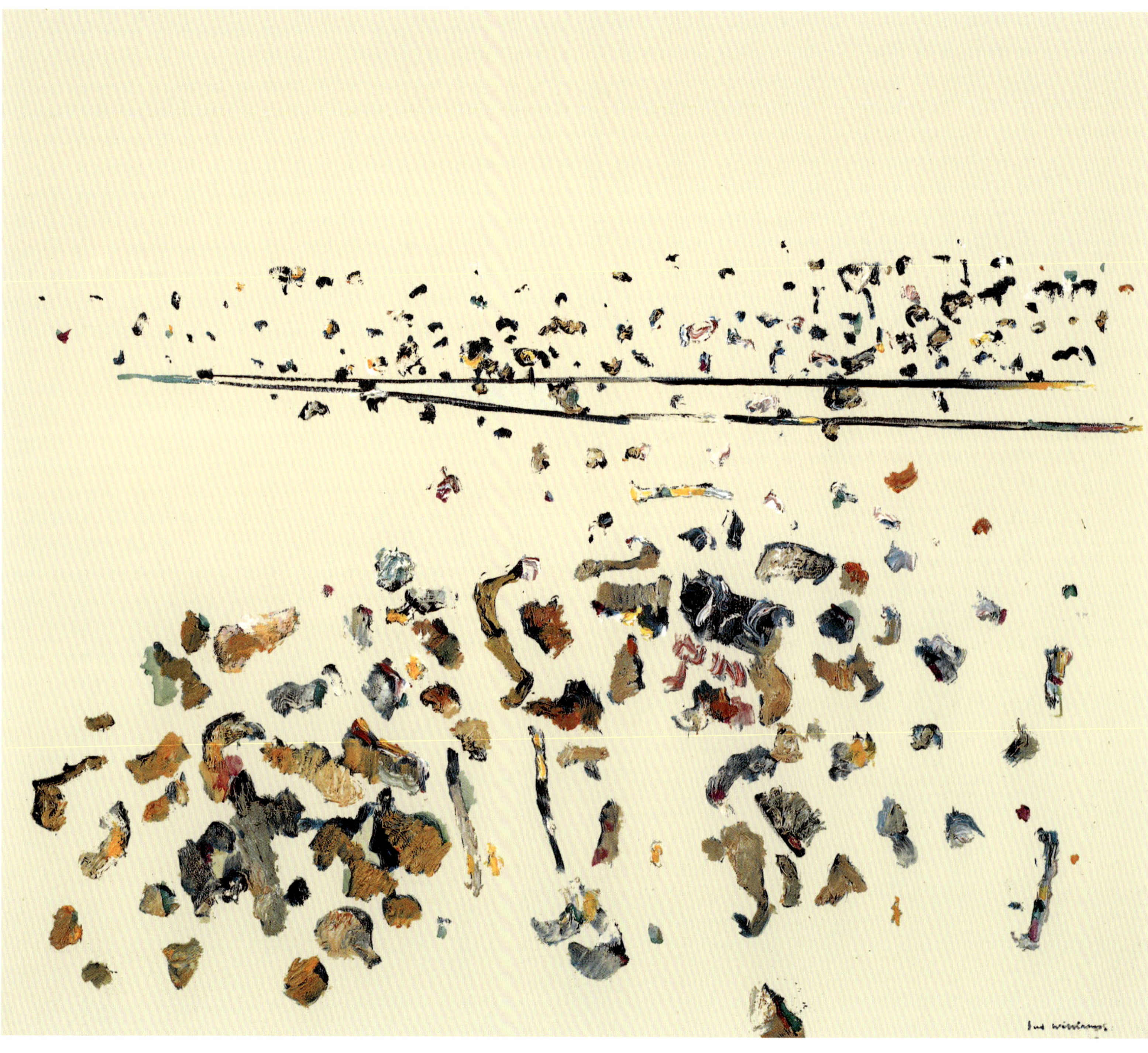

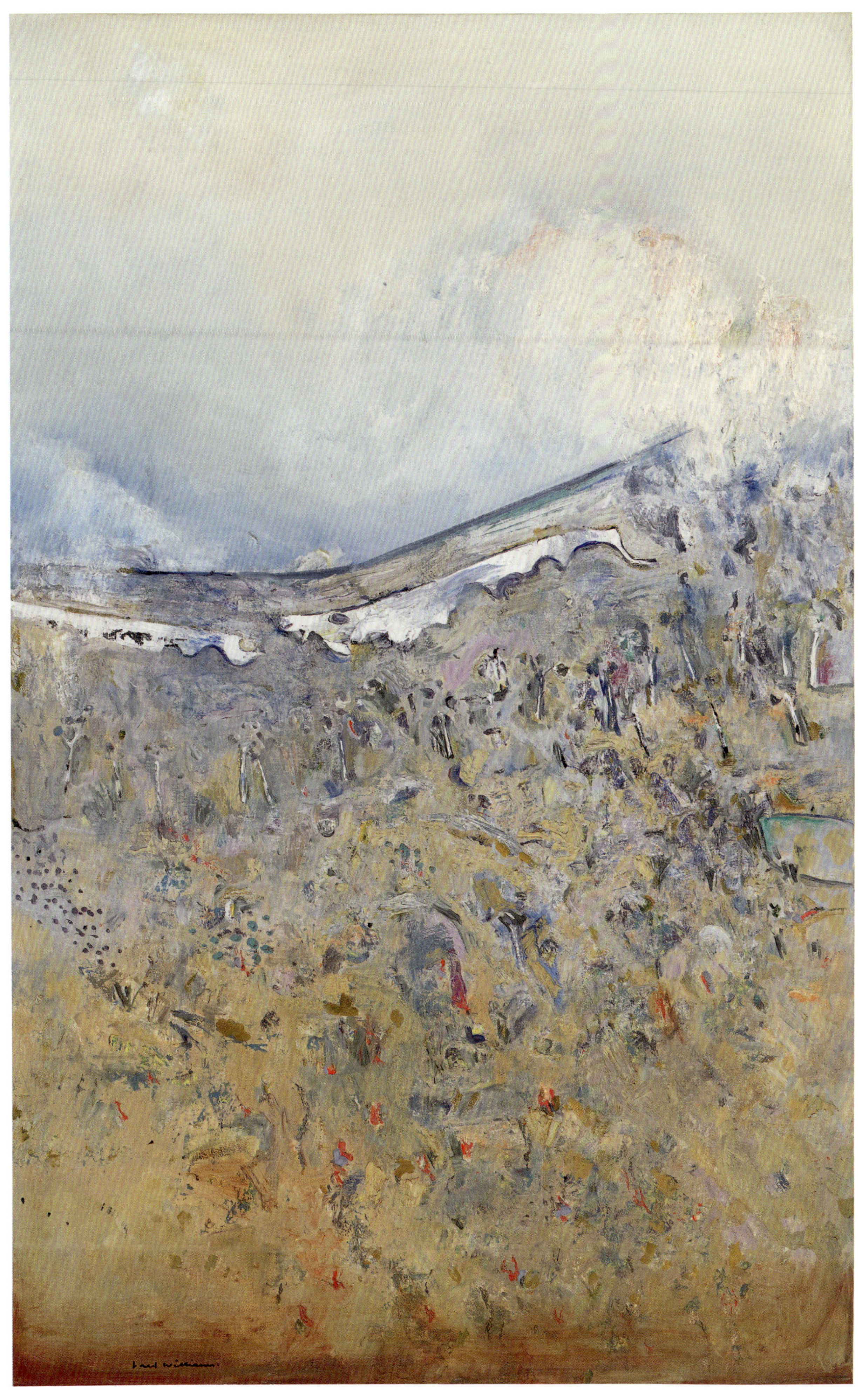

167

KEN WHISSON

Jean's Farm, 1972

Oil on composition board,

81 × 109.3 cm

National Gallery of Australia, Canberra.
Gift of the Philip Morris Arts Grant, 1982

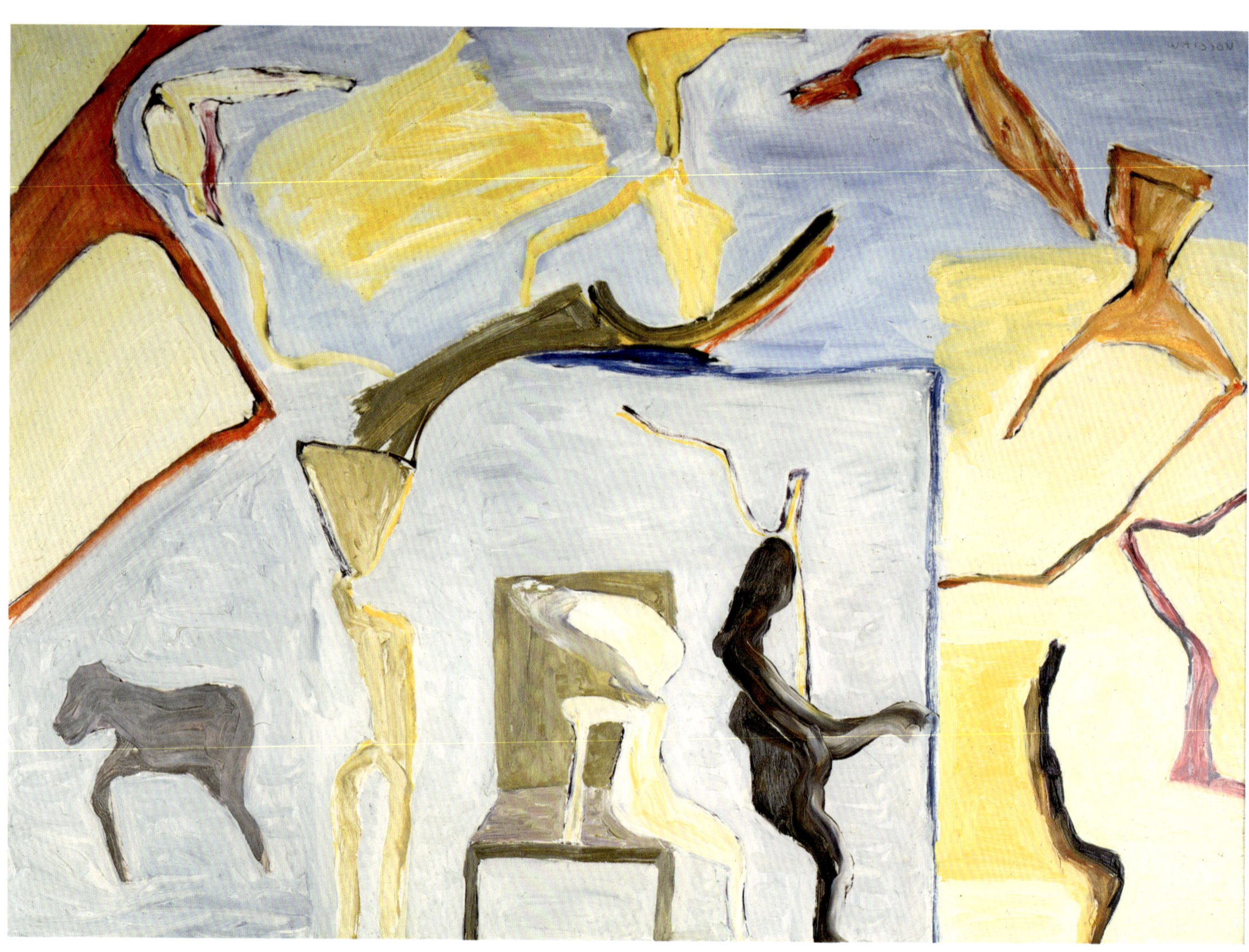

168

BRETT WHITELEY
Big Orange (Sunset), 1974
Oil and collage on wood, 244 × 305 cm
Art Gallery of New South Wales, Sydney.
Gift of Patrick White, 1975

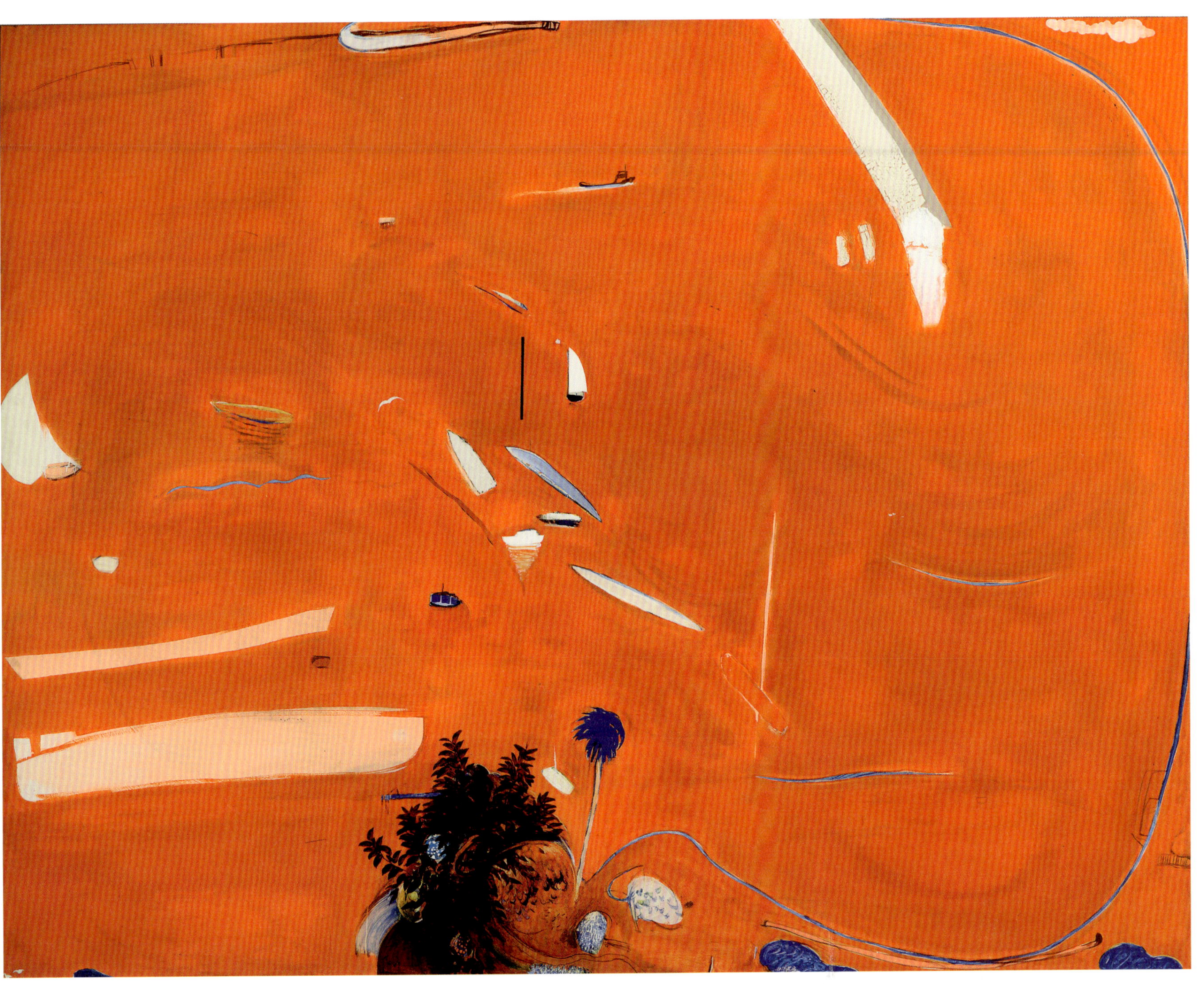

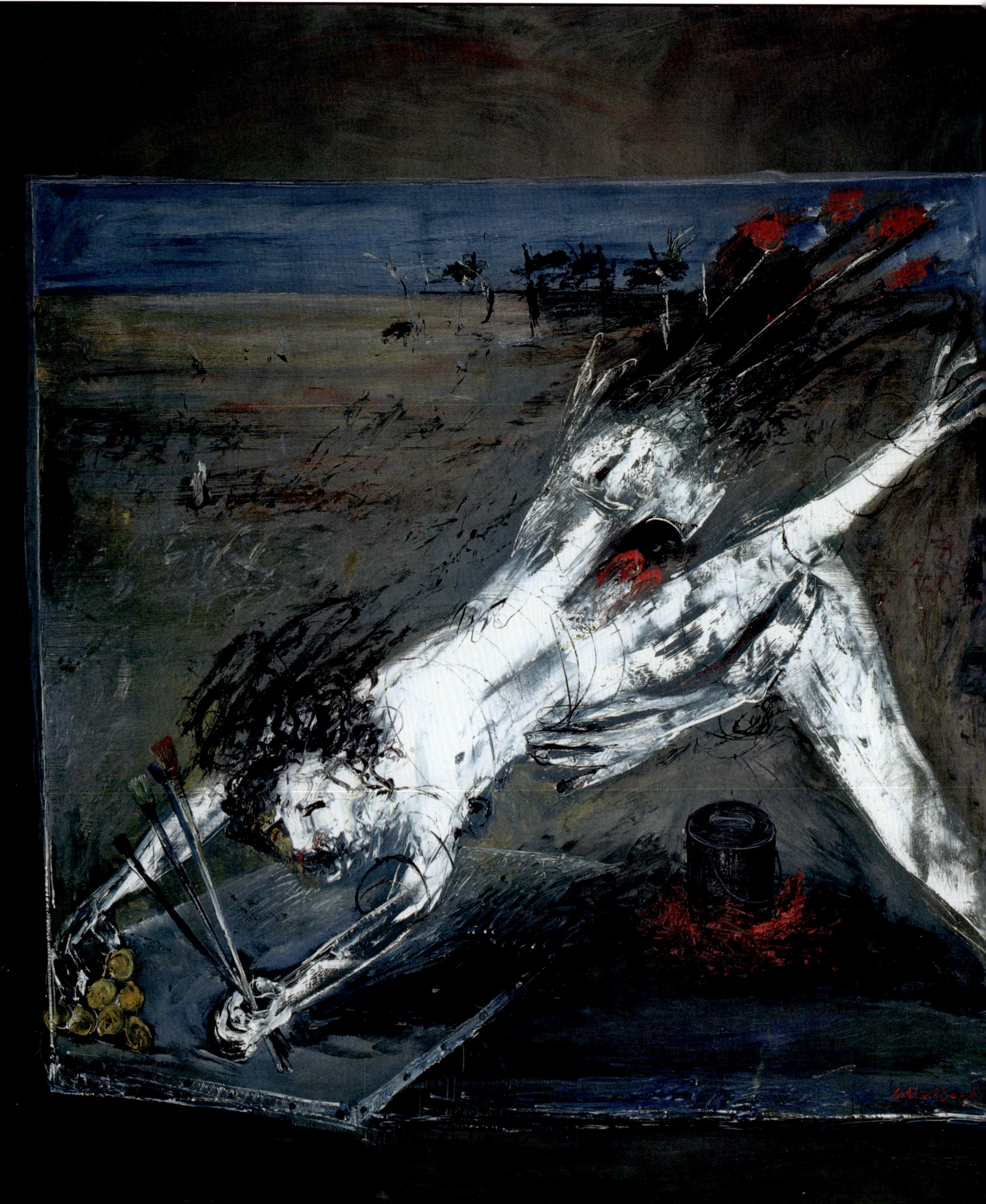

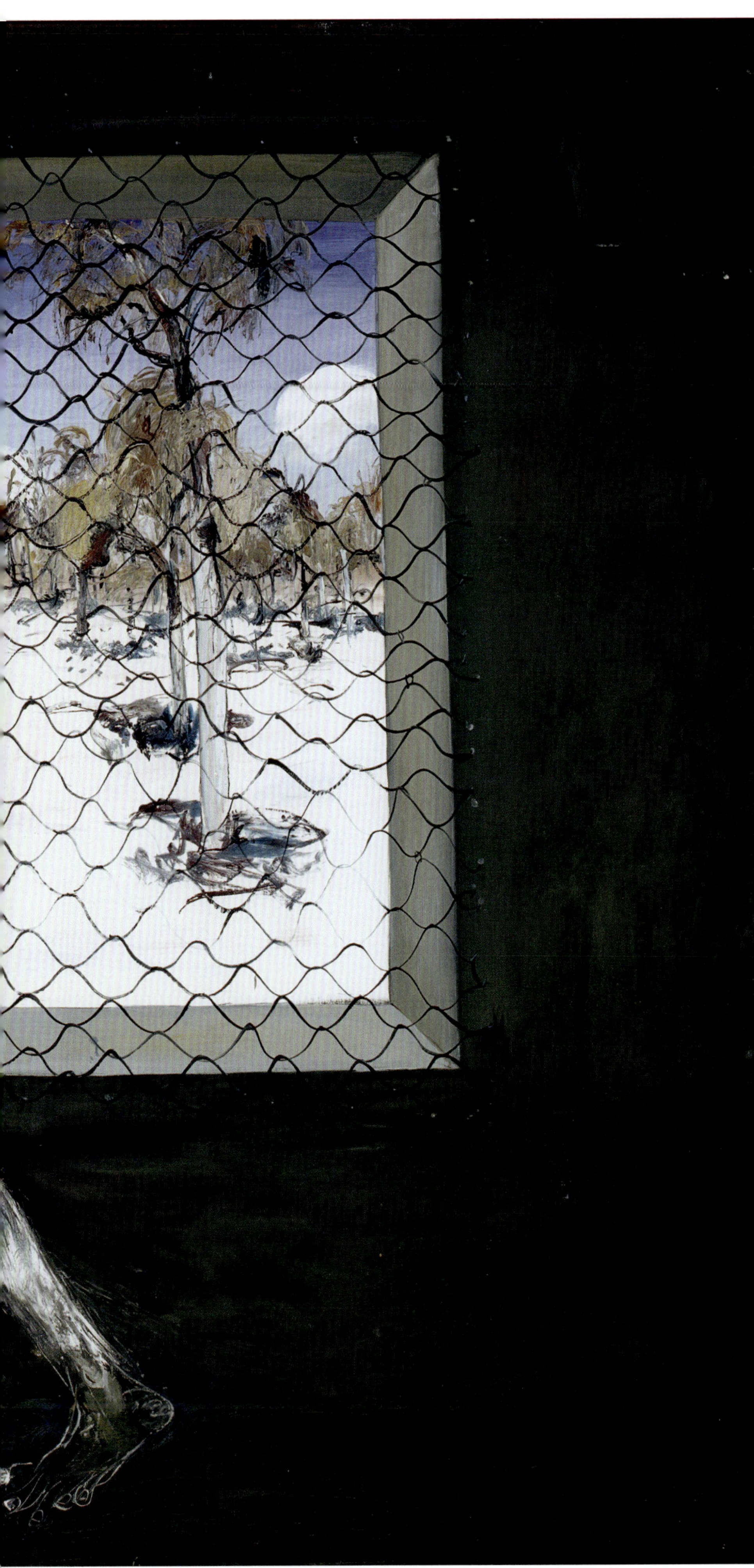

169

ARTHUR BOYD
Paintings in the Studio: 'Figure Supporting Back Legs' and 'Interior with Black Rabbit', 1973–74
Oil on canvas, 313.5 × 433.2 cm
National Gallery of Australia, Canberra.
The Arthur Boyd Gift, 1975

170 *overleaf*

WESLEY STACEY
The Road (Outback to the City 4; Kalgoorlie to Port Hedland, WA; Perth Fun City; Kalgoorlie to Port Headland, WA; Paraburdoo and Tom Price, The Pilbara, WA; Up the Centre, SA to NT; The Gulf to Burdekin, QLD; Work Day Roads 6; Roads to the Red Brick Home, Sydney; Night Roads, Sydney; Sydney to Canberra; Sydney to Canberra), 1973–75
A selection of twelve from a series of 280 C-type colour photographs, 9 × 12.6 cm
National Gallery of Australia, Canberra. Purchased 1984

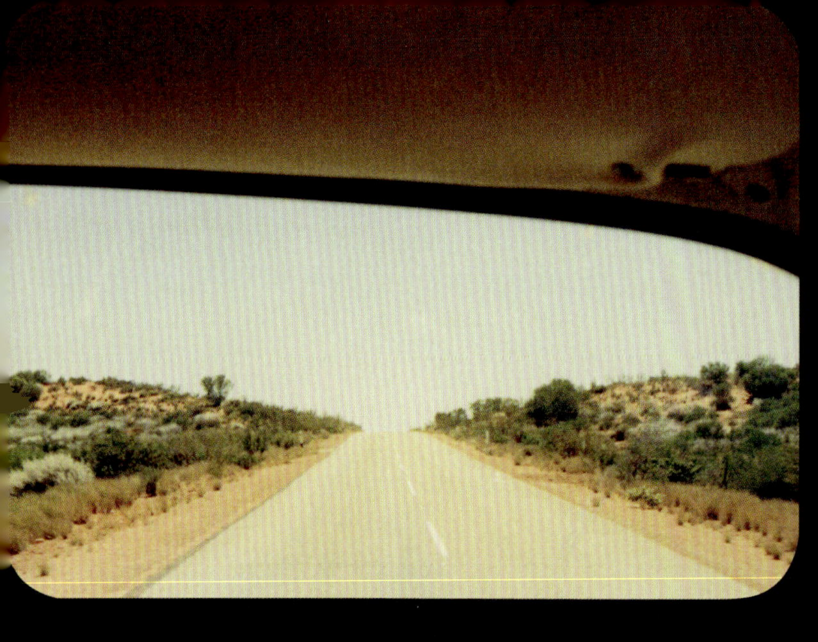

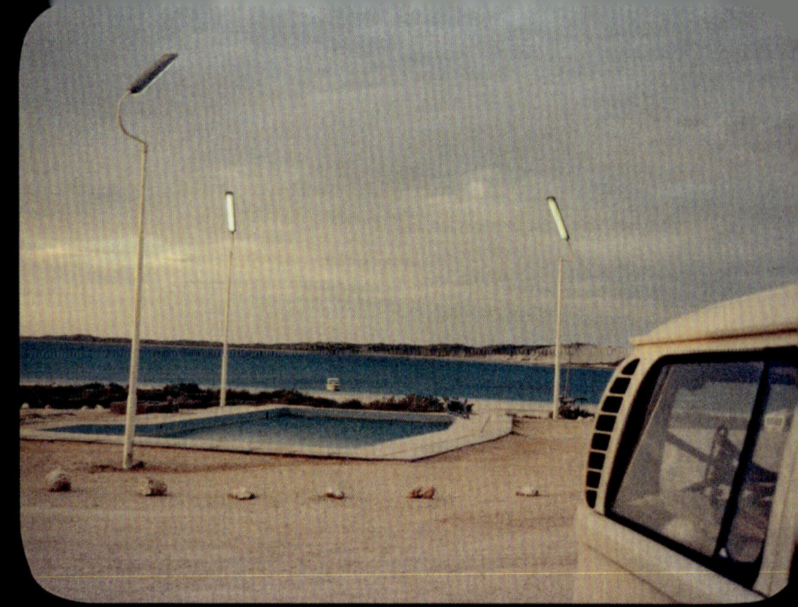

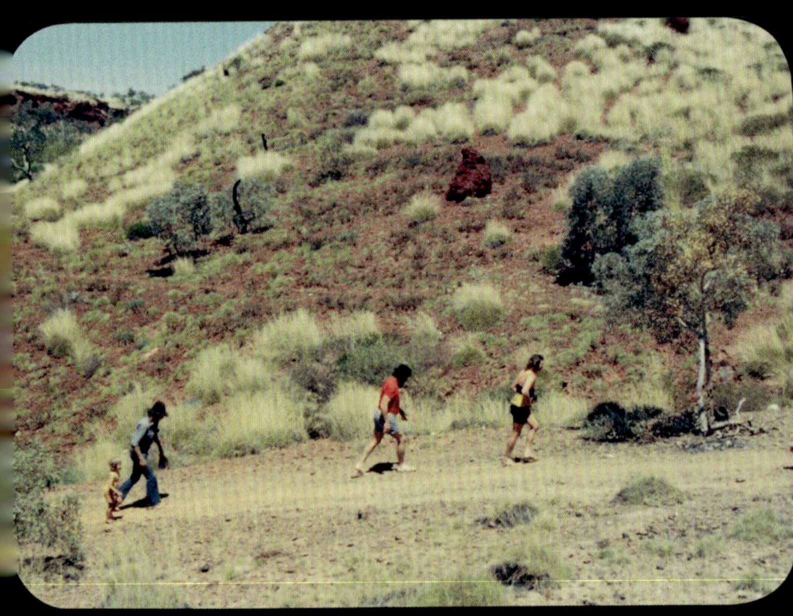

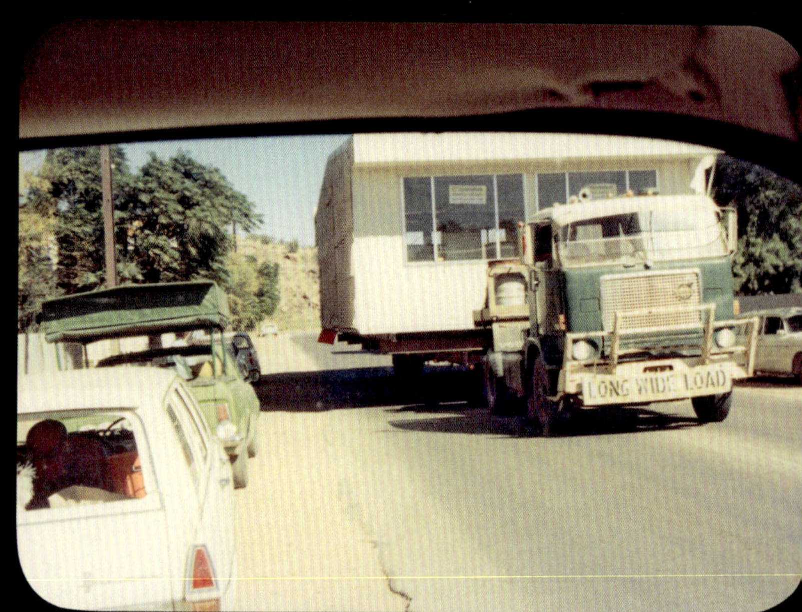
LONG WIDE LOAD

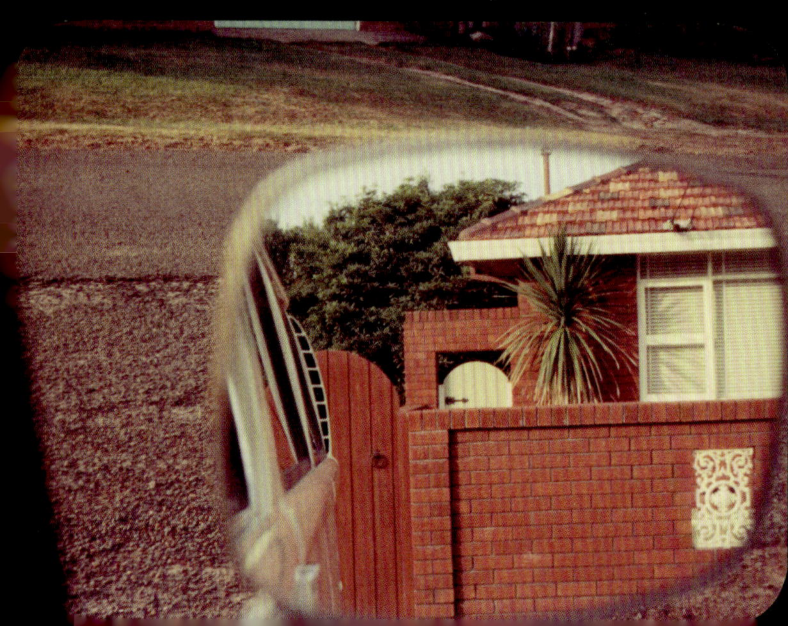

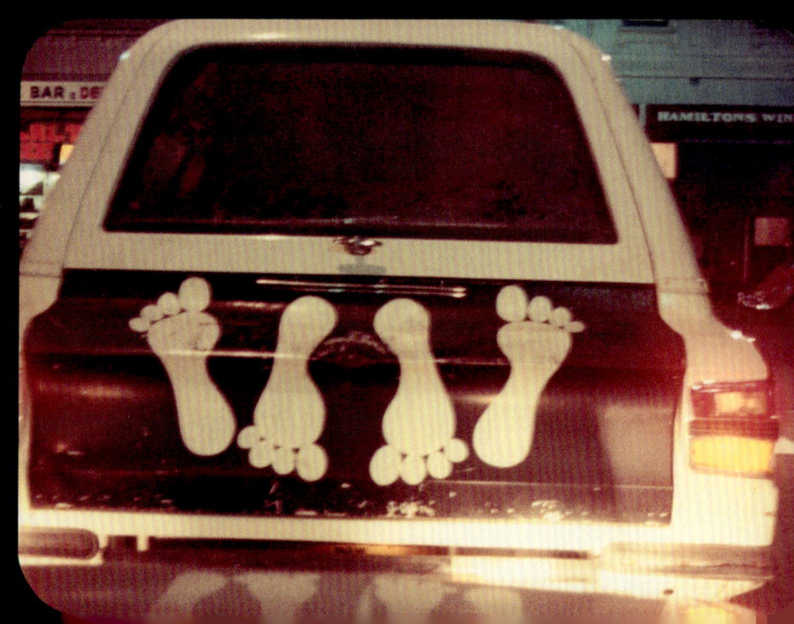

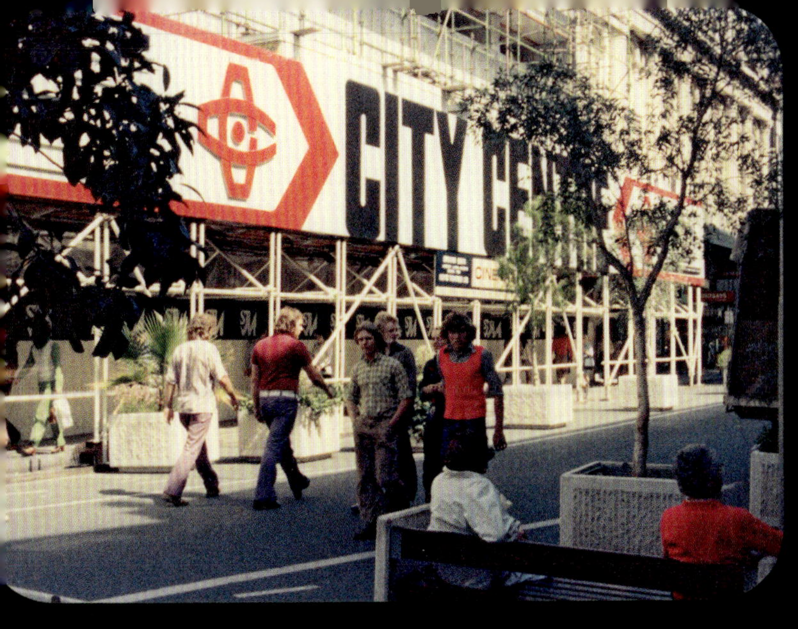
CITY CE

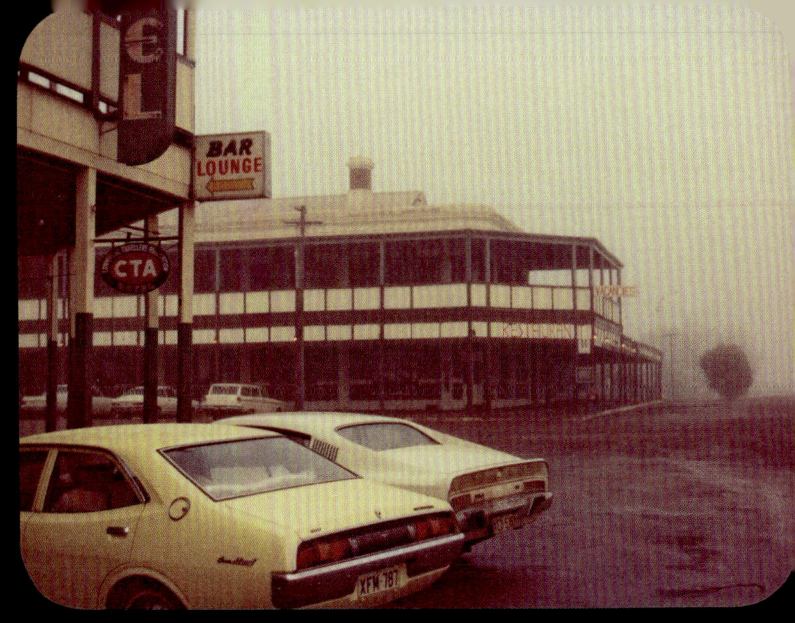
BAR
LOUNGE
CTA

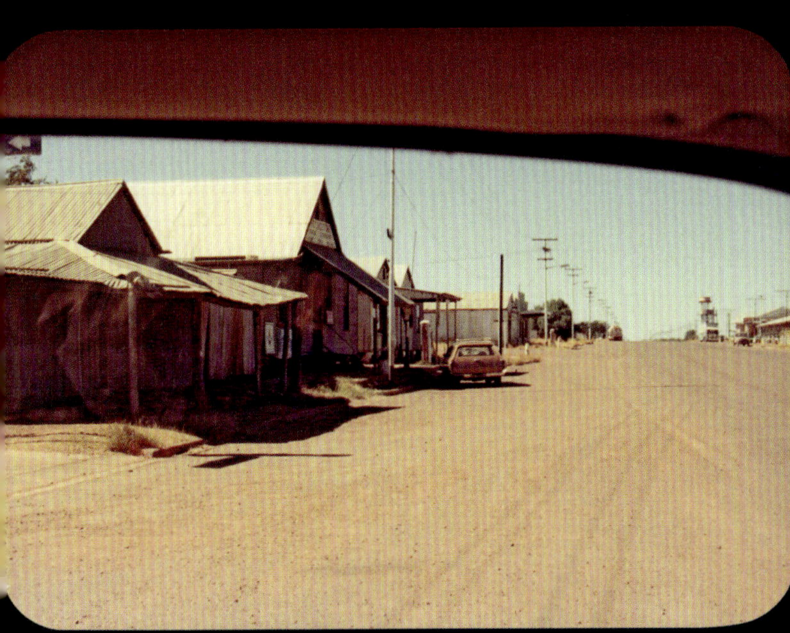

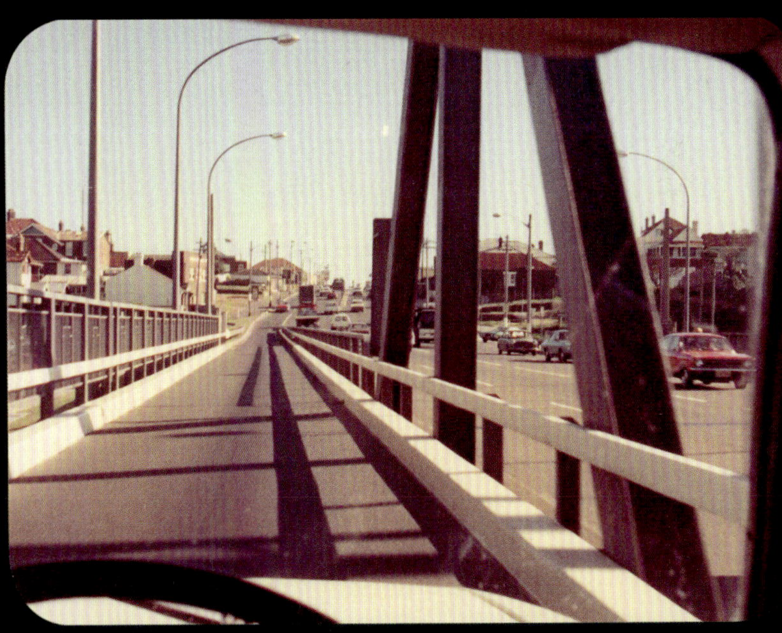

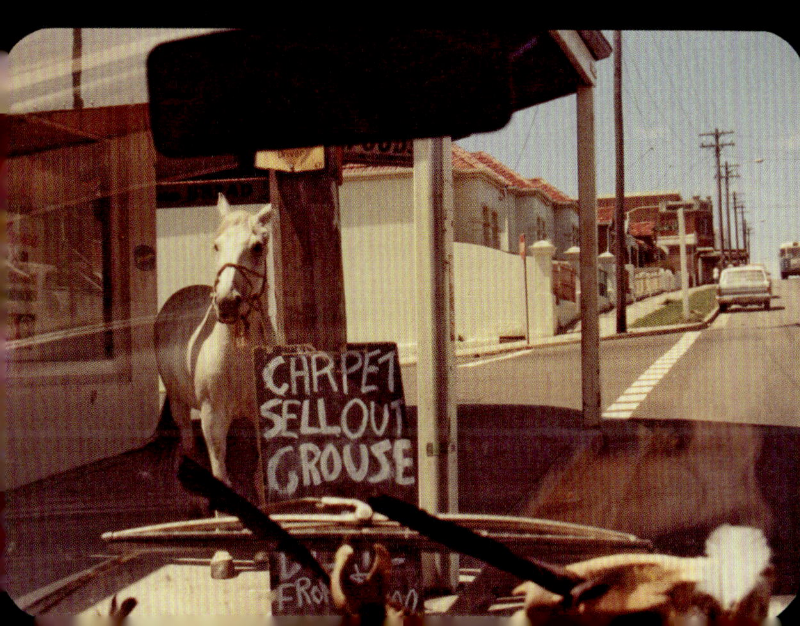
CARPET
SELLOUT
GROUSE

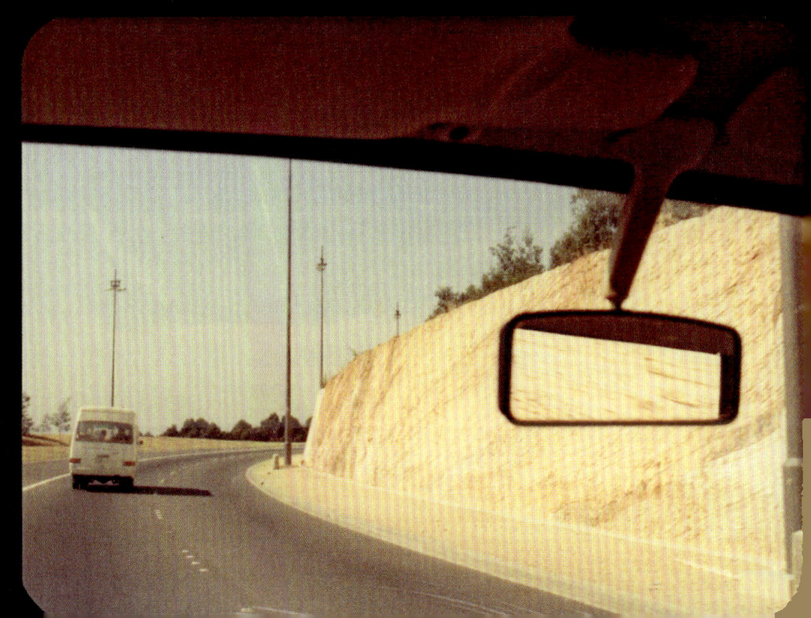

171

PETER DOMBROVSKIS

Morning Mist, Rock Island Bend, 1981, printed 2000

C-type colour photograph, 100 × 150 cm

National Gallery of Australia, Canberra.
Purchased 2002

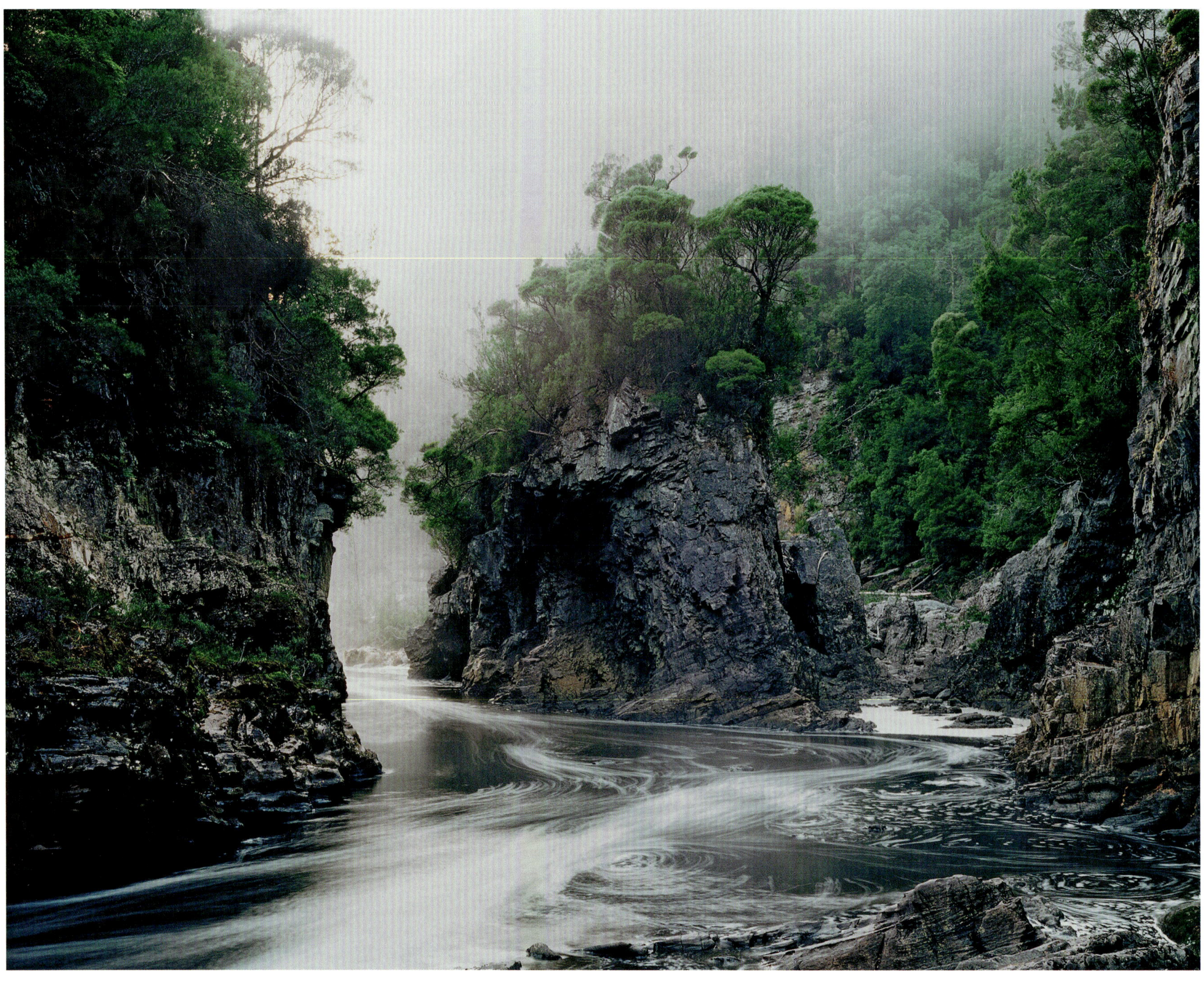

172

DAVID STEPHENSON

Self-portrait Looking Down a Survey-cut Proposed Site of Gordon below Franklin Dam, Tasmania, 1982

Mosaic of 9 gelatin silver photographs, 62.5 × 80.8 cm (overall)

Museum of Contemporary Art, Sydney.
Donated by the artist through the Australian Government's Cultural Gifts Program, 2010

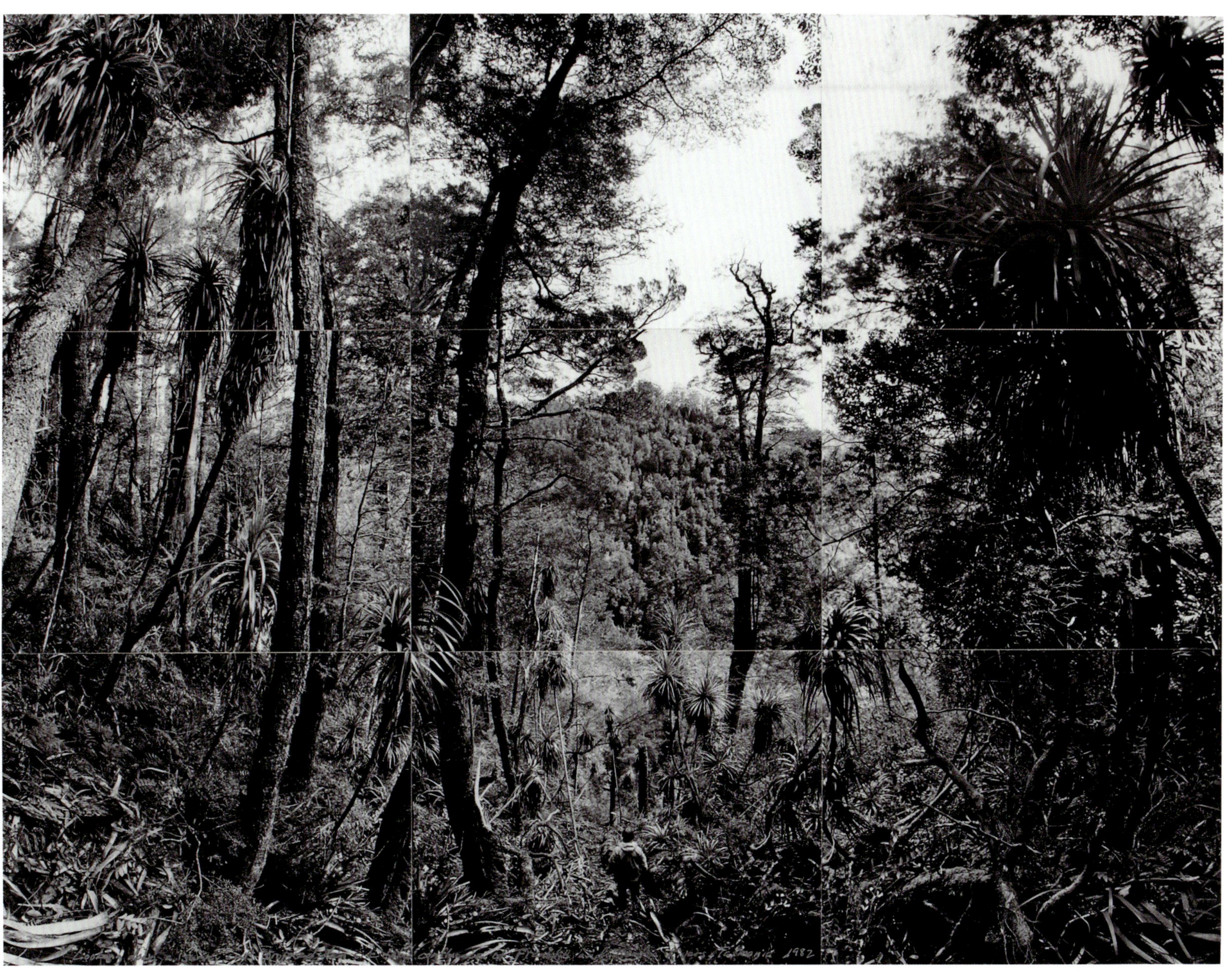

173

BRIAN BLANCHFLOWER

Nocturne 3 (Whale Rock), 1982

Oil, bitumen, sand, chalk on canvas,
178 × 255 cm

Art Gallery of South Australia, Adelaide.
Elder Bequest Fund, 1983

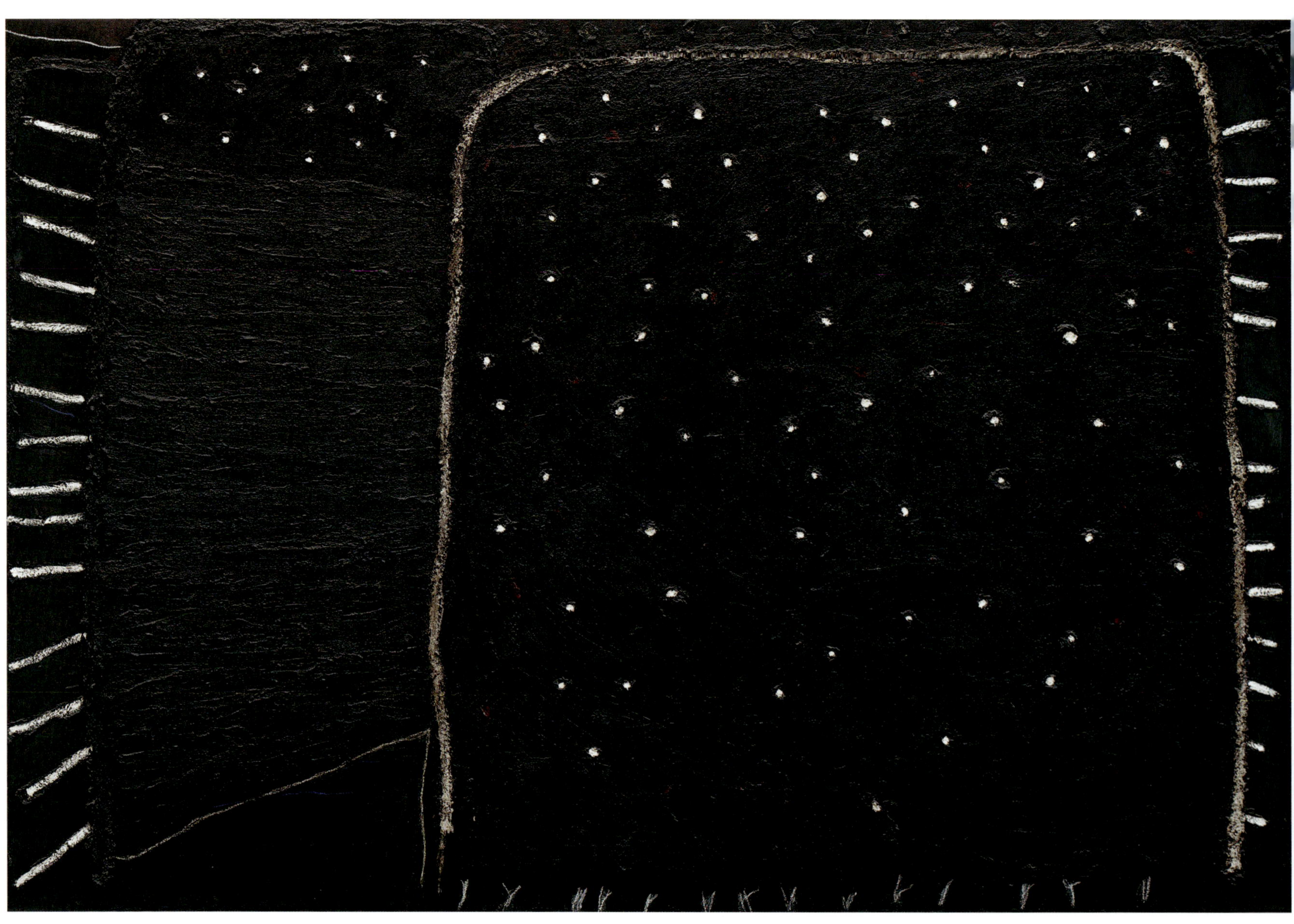

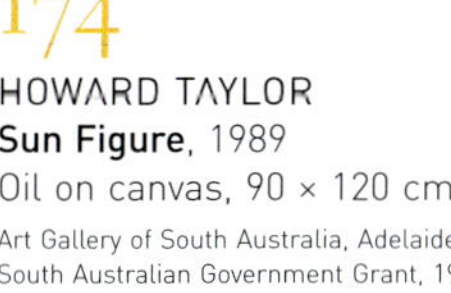

174
HOWARD TAYLOR
Sun Figure, 1989
Oil on canvas, 90 × 120 cm
Art Gallery of South Australia, Adelaide.
South Australian Government Grant, 1991

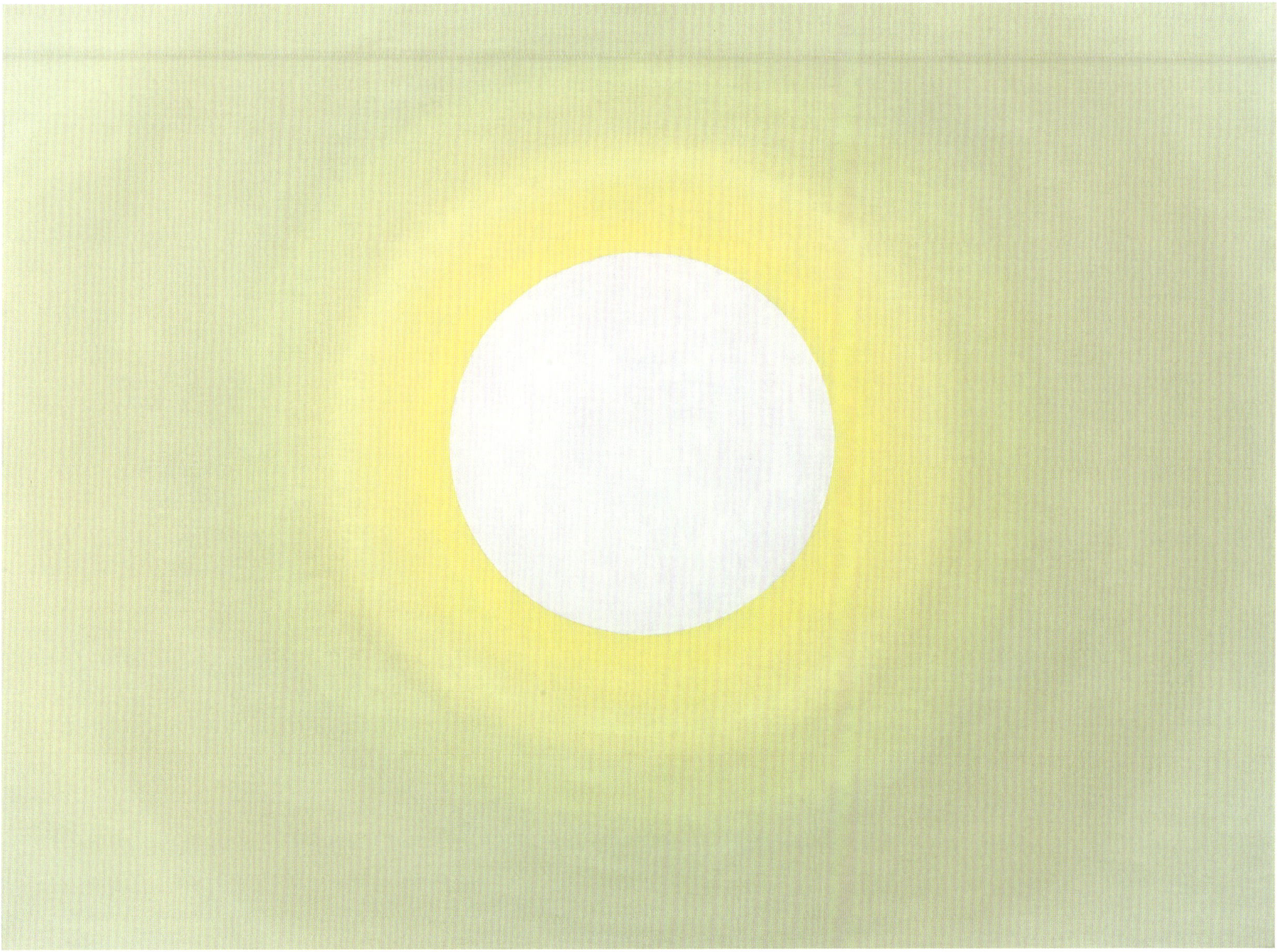

175 *overleaf*
FIONA HALL
Paradisus Terrestris, 1989–90
23 cut and moulded sardine tins;
aluminium, tin and steel, 24.5 × 11 cm
(each approximately)
National Gallery of Australia, Canberra.
Purchased 1994

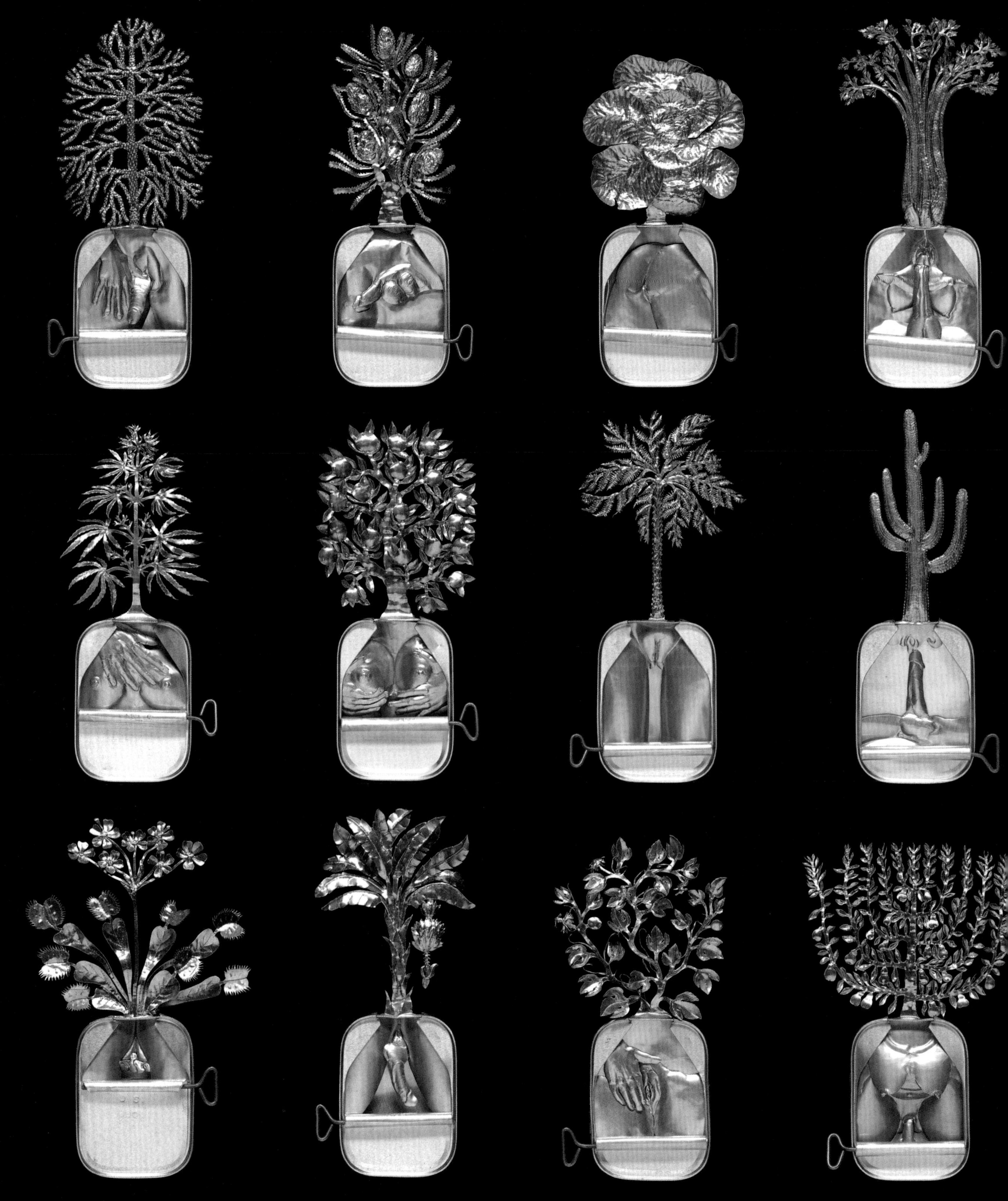

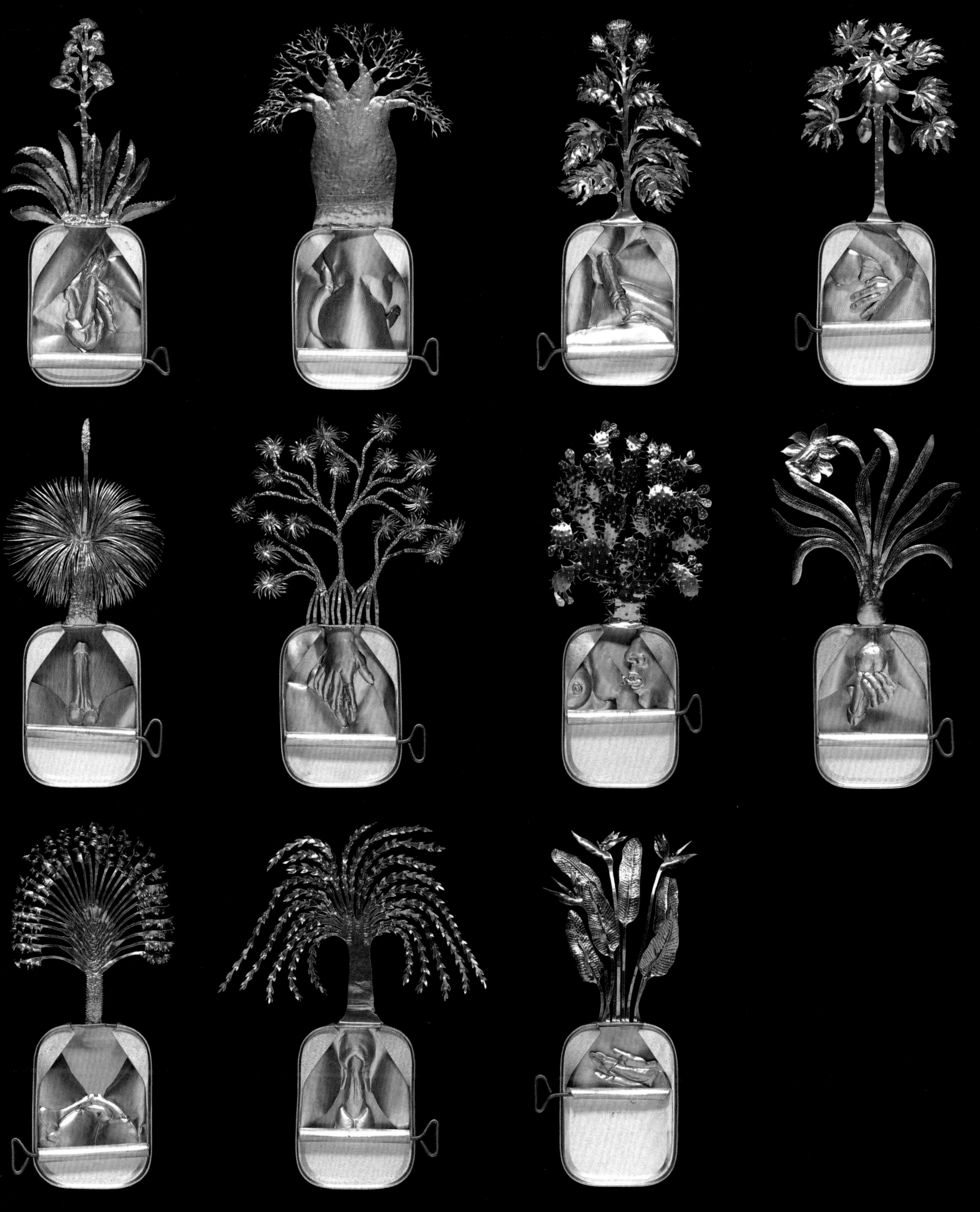

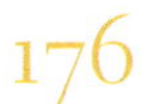

176

GORDON BENNETT
Possession Island, 1991
Oil and synthetic polymer paint on canvas, 162 × 260 cm

Museum of Sydney, Historic Houses Trust of New South Wales, Sydney.
Purchased with funds from the Foundation for the Historic Houses Trust, Museum of Sydney Appeal, 2007

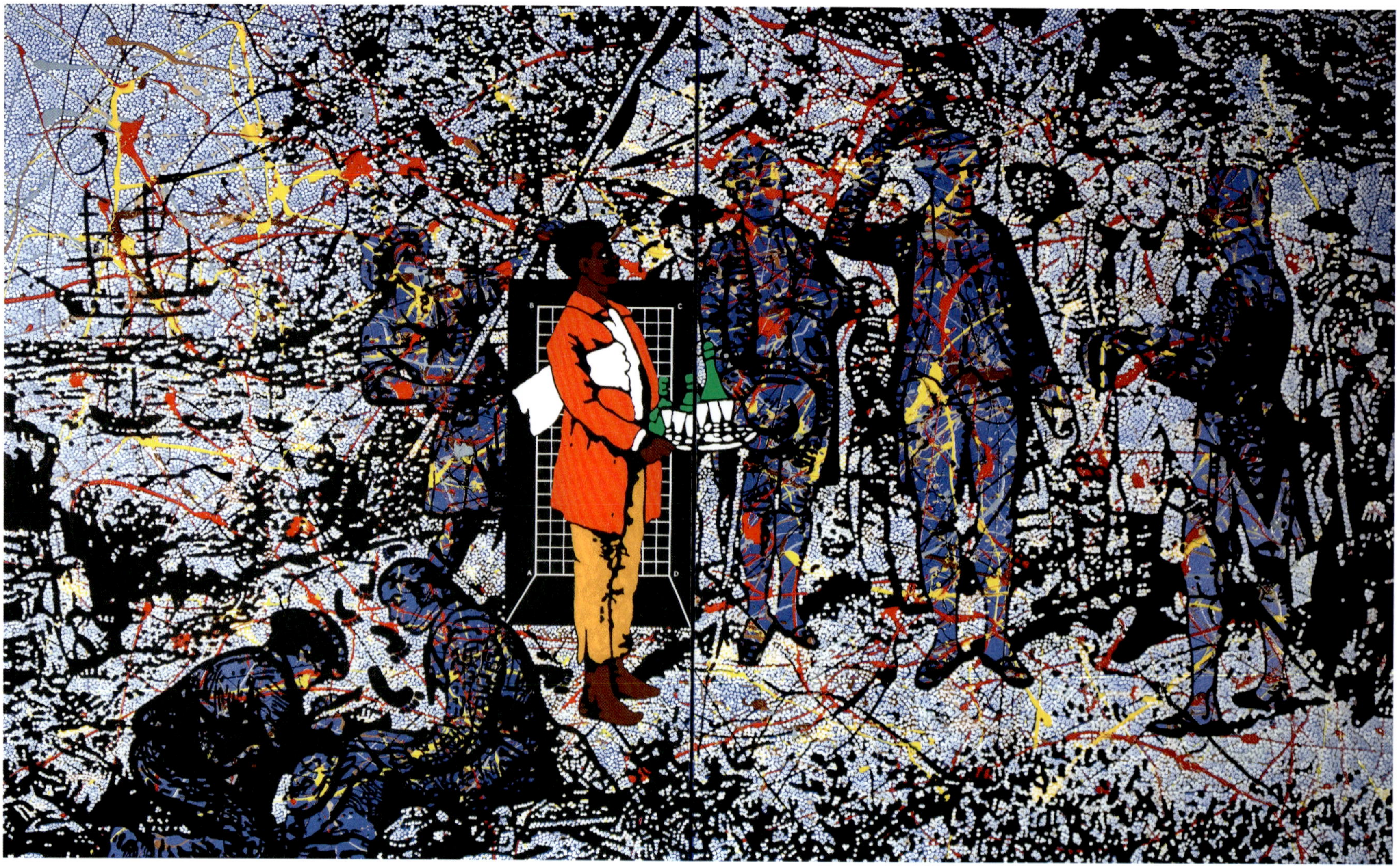

177

TIM JOHNSON

Dewachen, 1987

Synthetic polymer paint on linen, 182 × 243 cm

Museum of Contemporary Art, Sydney.
Gift of Lotti Smorgan AO and Victor Smorgan AC, 1995

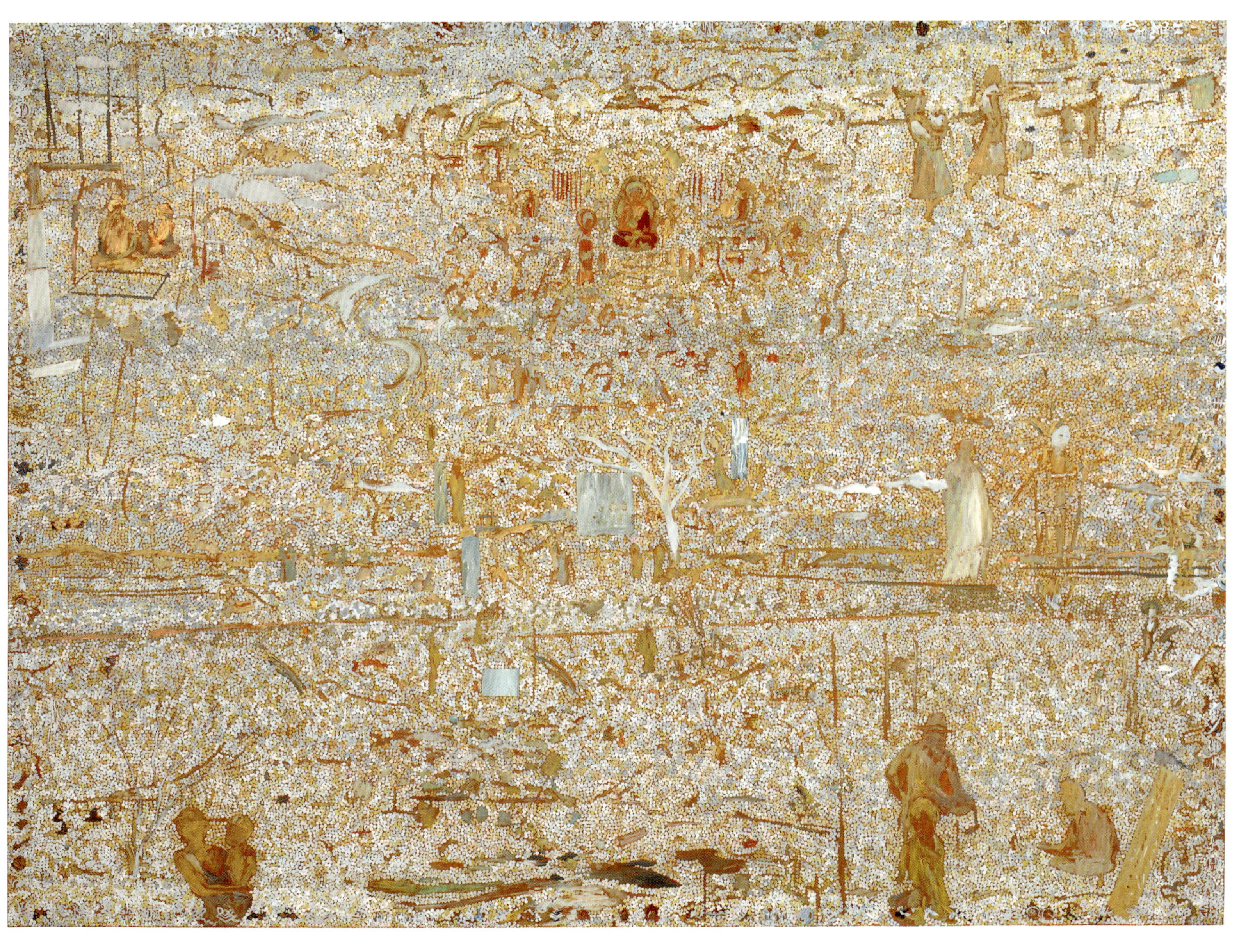

178

ROSALIE GASCOIGNE

Monaro, 1989

Synthetic polymer paint on soft-drink crates on plywood, 131 × 457 cm (overall)

State Art Collection, Art Gallery of Western Australia, Perth. Purchased 1989

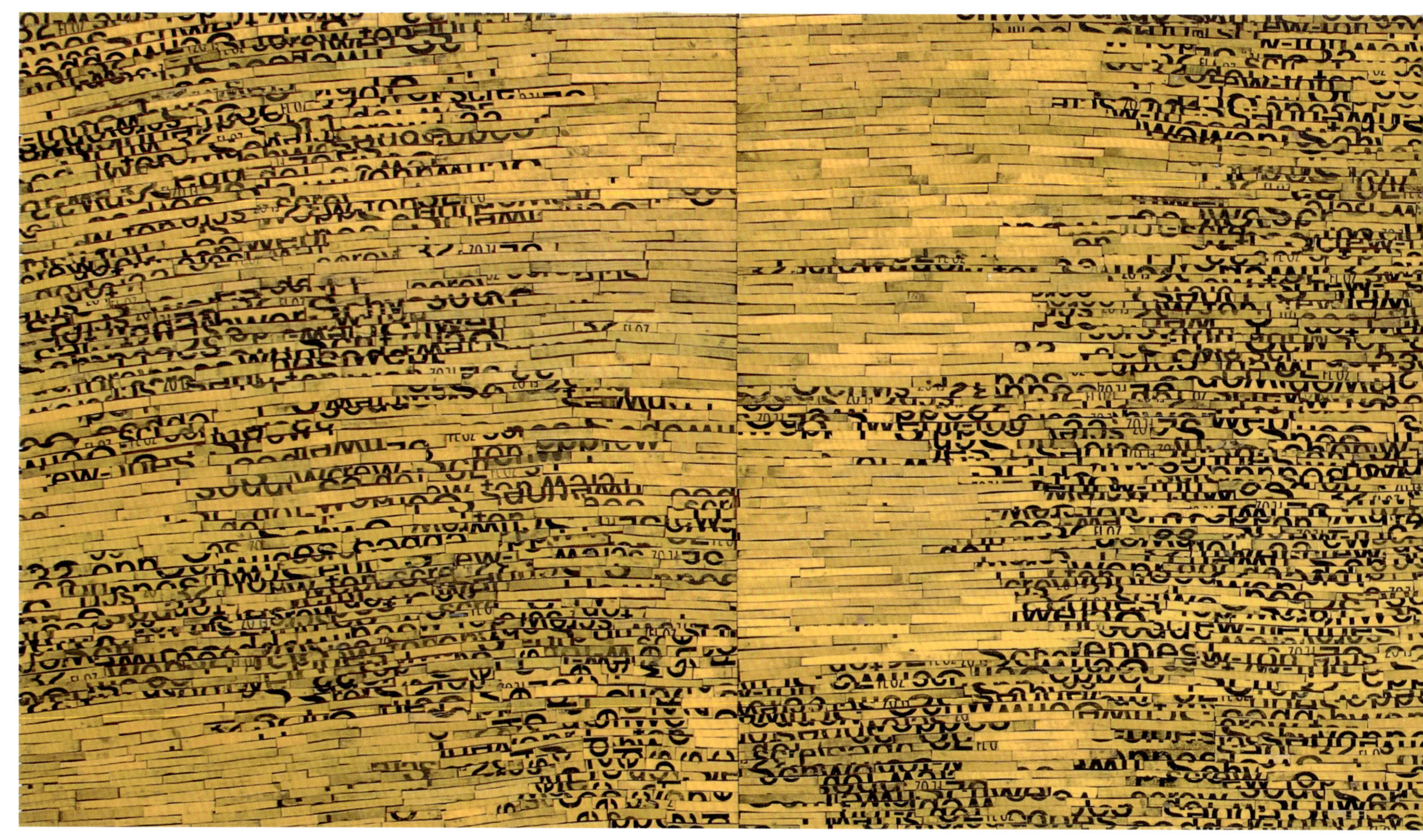

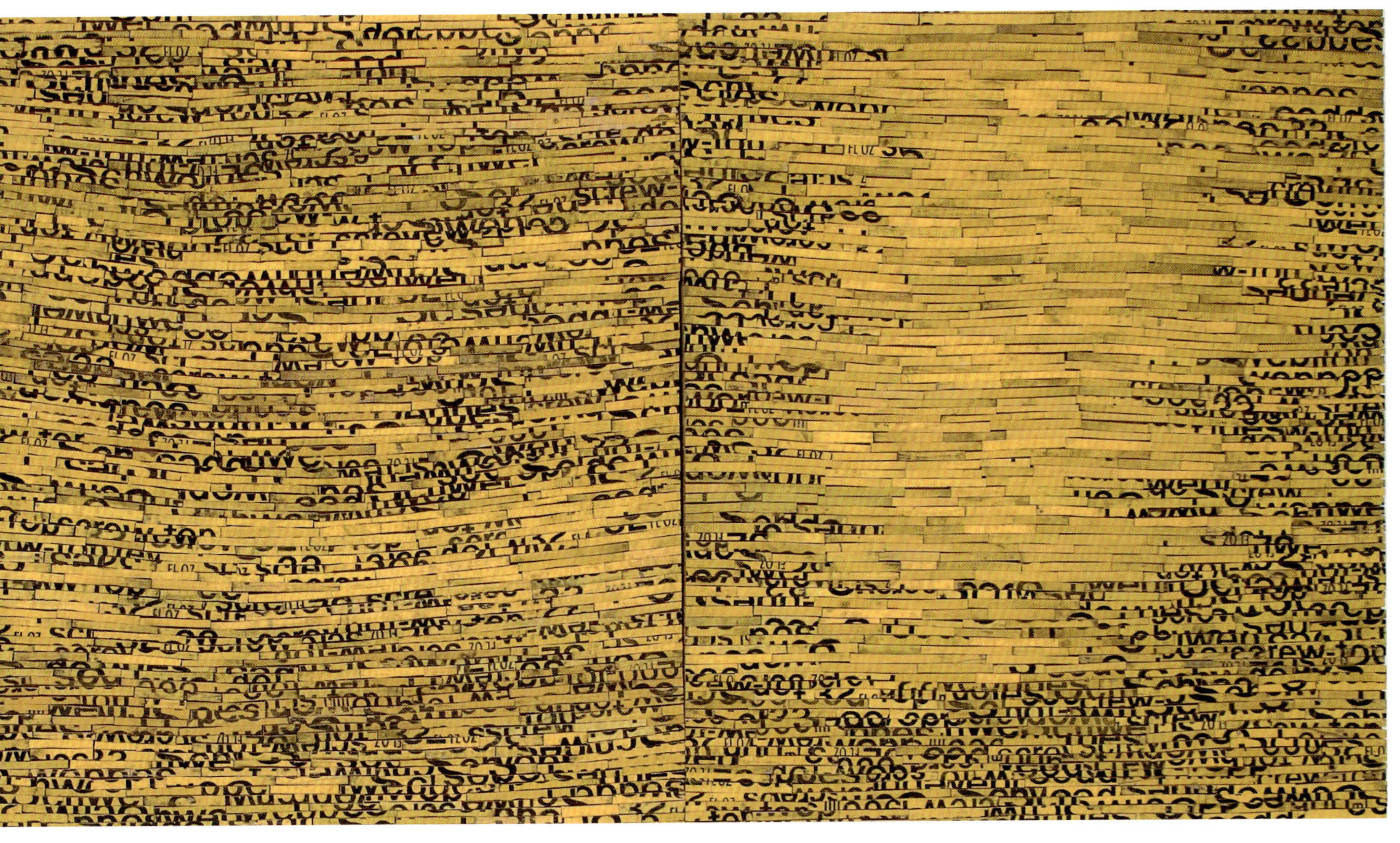

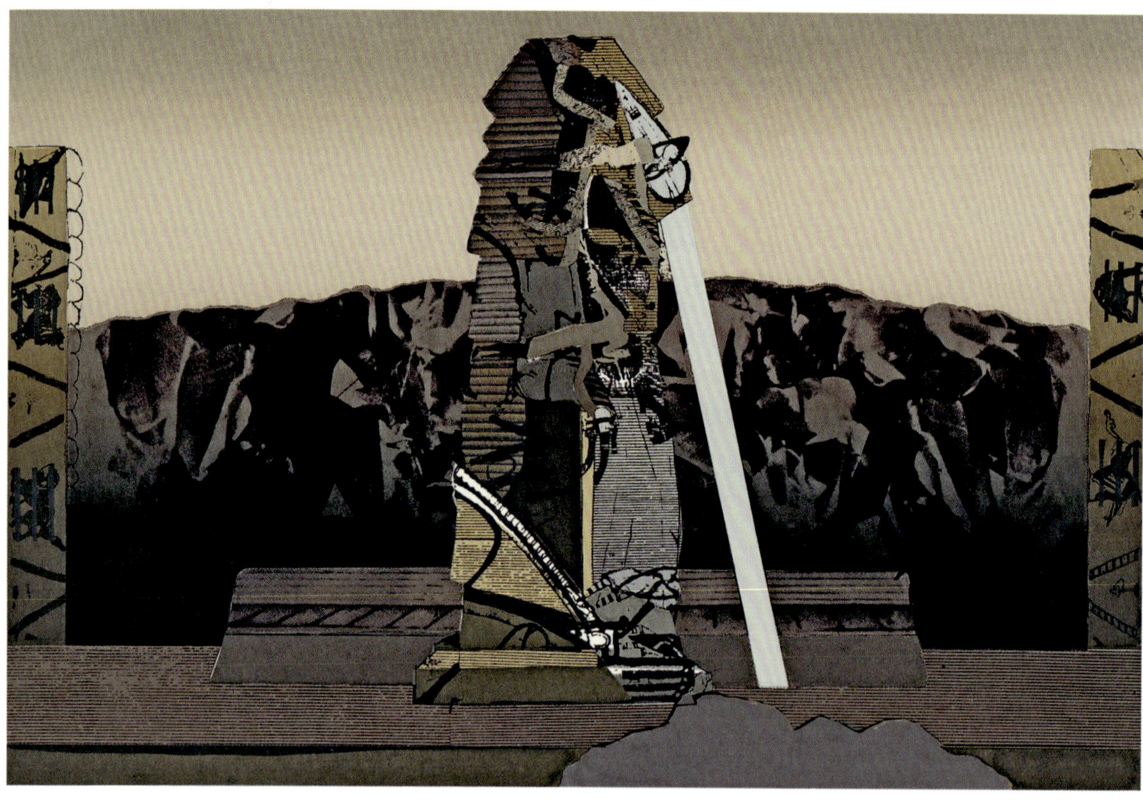

179

JAN SENBERGS
Fort, 1973
Screen-print, printed in colour, from multiple stencils, 55.9 × 81.5 cm
National Gallery of Australia, Canberra. Purchased 1973

180

PETER BOOTH
Mangroves, 2002
Pastel, 62 × 101 cm
National Gallery of Australia, Canberra. Purchased 2013

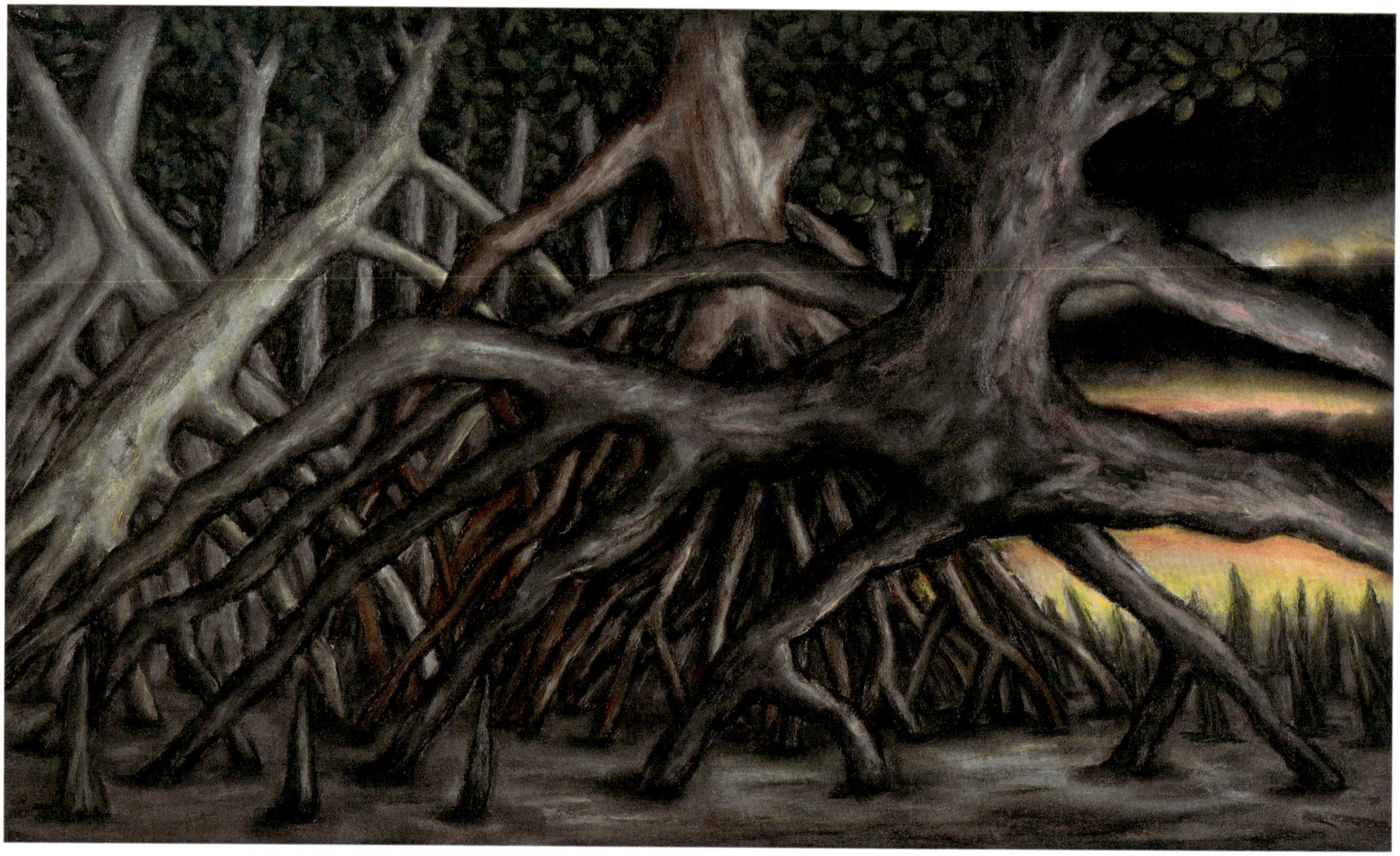

181

WILLIAM ROBINSON

Twin Falls and Gorge, 2000

Oil on canvas, 137 × 183 cm

National Gallery of Australia, Canberra.
Gift of Ray and Diana Kidd, 2013

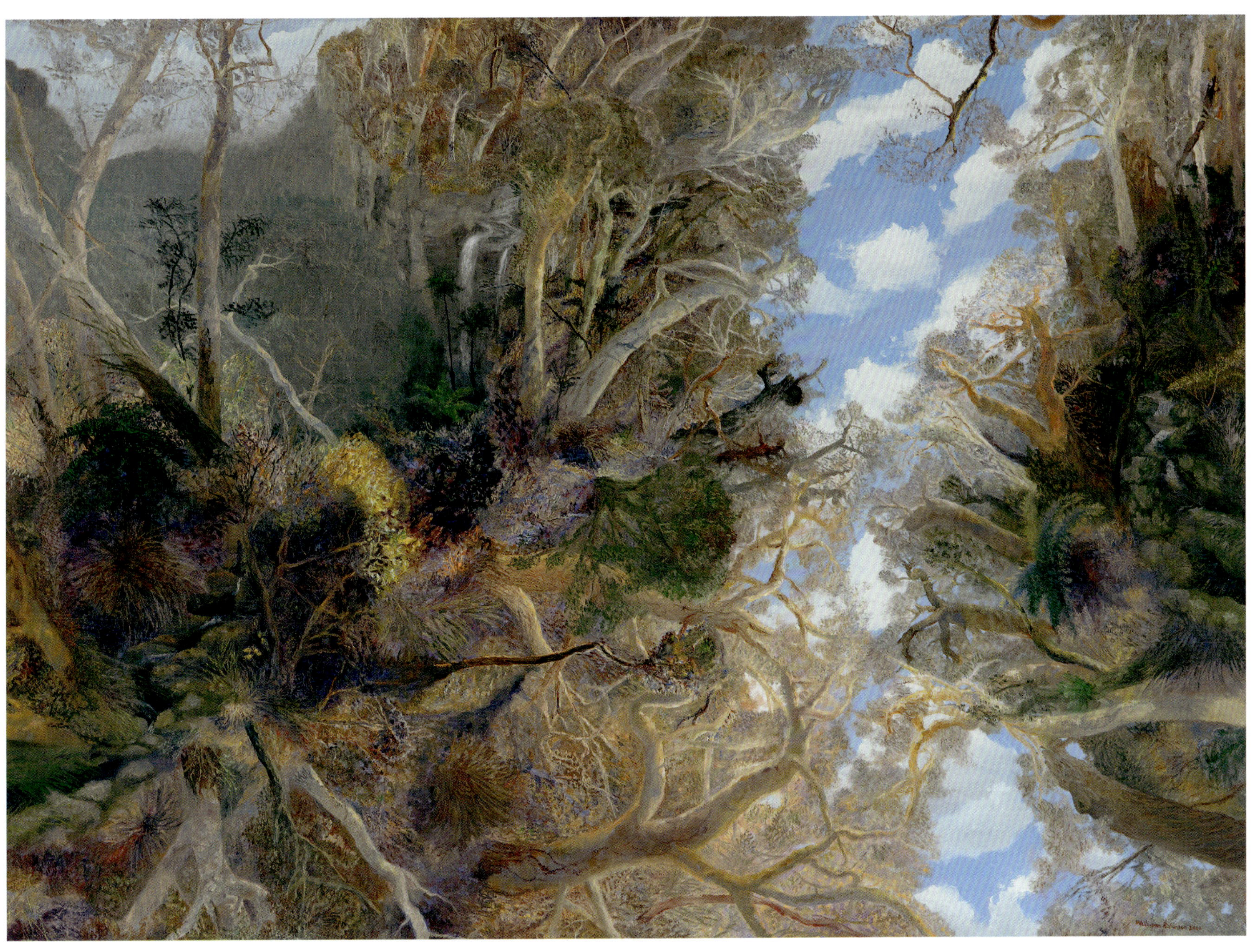

182

ELISABETH CUMMINGS

Wedderburn Spring, 1993

Oil on canvas, 173 × 196 cm

Campbelltown City Bicentennial Art Gallery, New South Wales. Purchased 1993

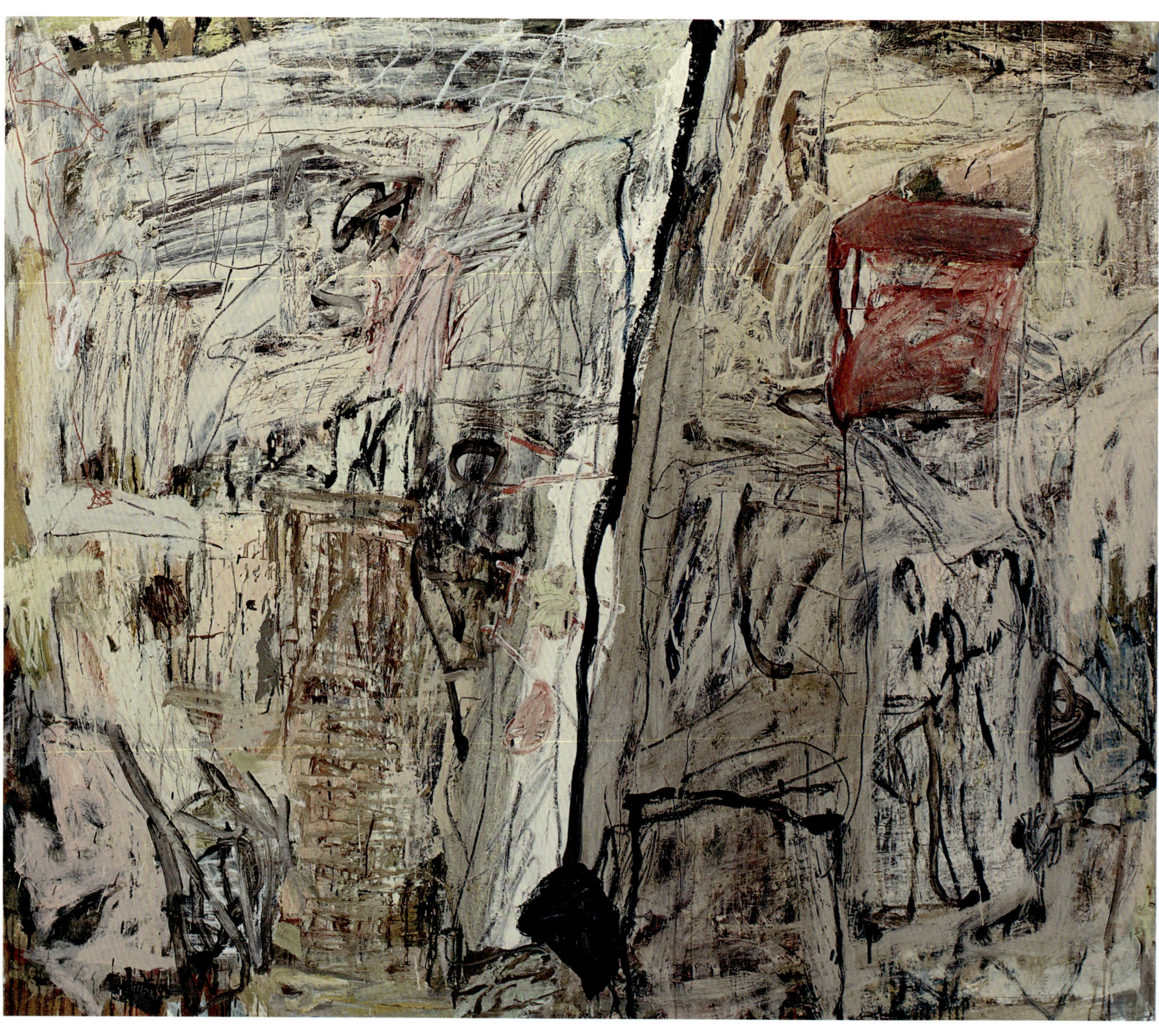

183
MIKE PARR
Great Distances between Small Towns, sheets 4–6, 11–13, 1990–91
A selection of six from the series of twenty-four drypoints, printed in black ink, each one from one plate, 76.2 × 106.4 cm (each sheet), printed by John Loane, at Viridian Press, Melbourne
National Gallery of Australia, Canberra. Purchased 2012

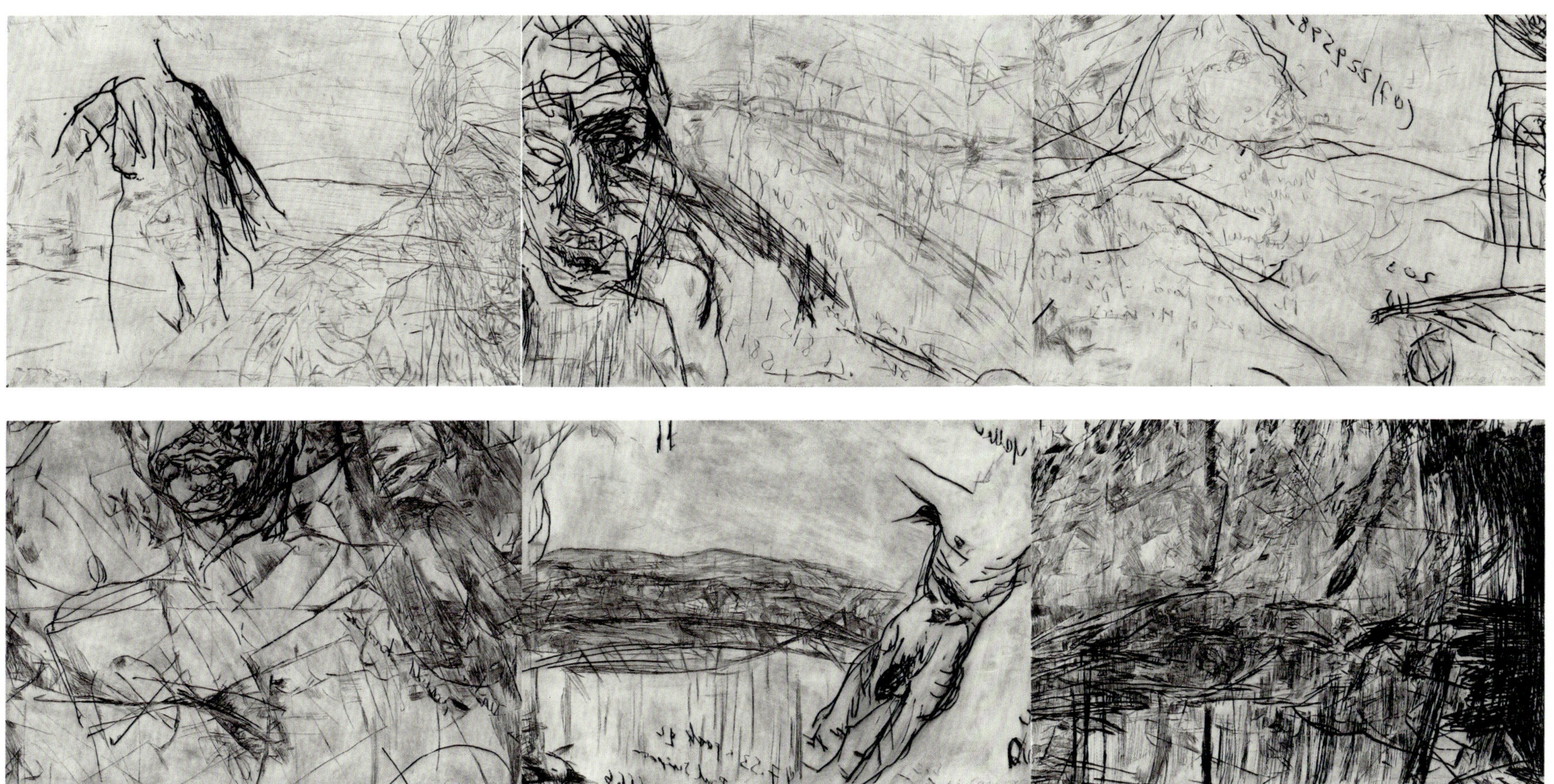

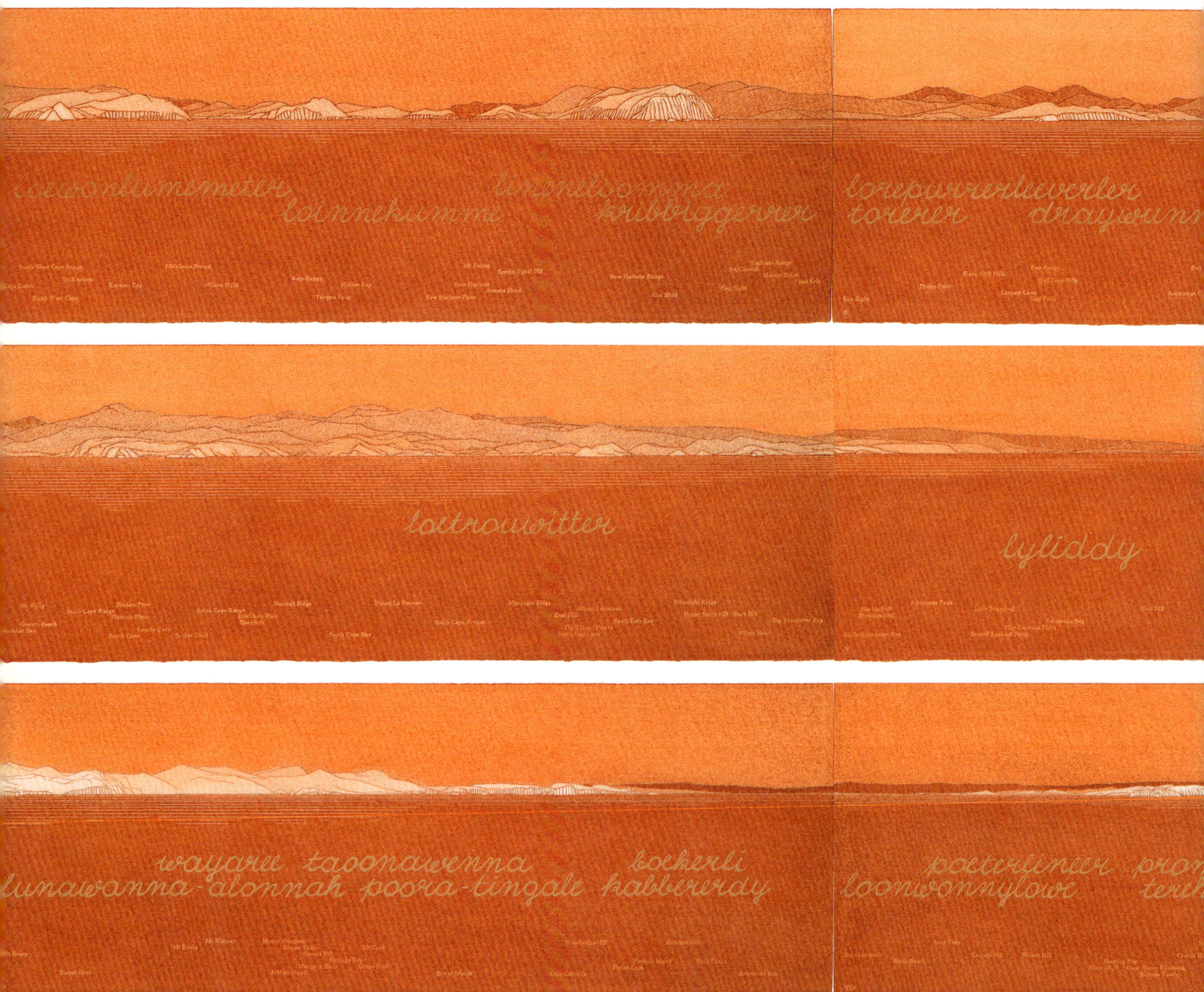

184

BEA MADDOCK

Terra Spiritus ... with a Darker Shade of Pale, 1993–98
From the 52-sheet series of stencils, printed in hand-ground Launceston ochre, each from multiple mylar stencils, blind printed letterpress and handwritten script, 28.4 × 75.9 cm (each sheet)

National Gallery of Australia, Canberra.
Gordon Darling Australasian Print Fund, 1998

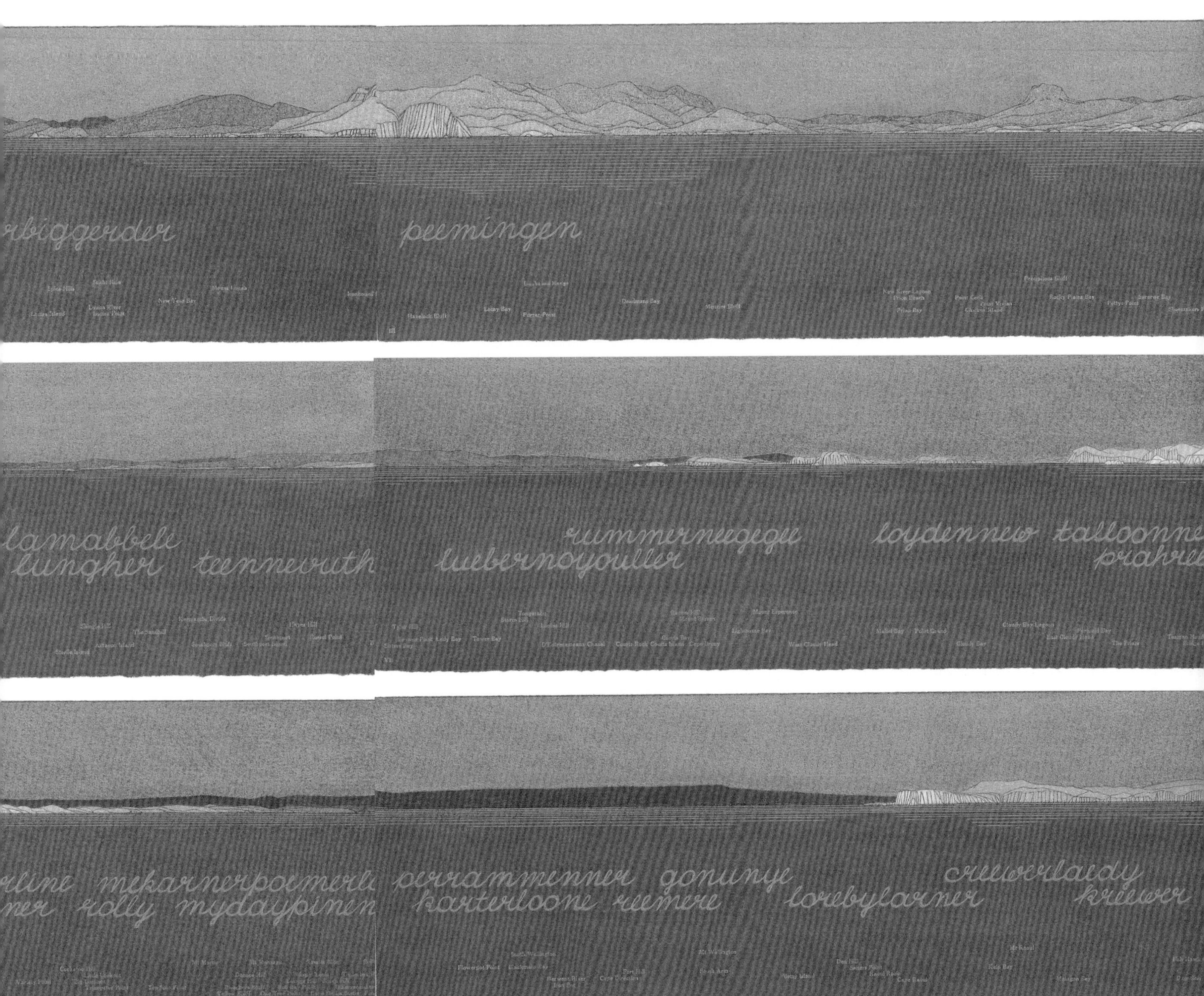
peemingen
teennevruth
rummerneegegee
luebernoyouller
loydennew
rolly
perrammenner
gonunye
karterloone
reemere
lorebylarner
creewrlaidy

185

HOWARD ARKLEY

Superb + Solid, 1998

Synthetic polymer paint on canvas, 200 × 300.6 cm

Art Gallery of New South Wales, Sydney. Purchased with funds from the Contemporary Collection Benefactors, 1998

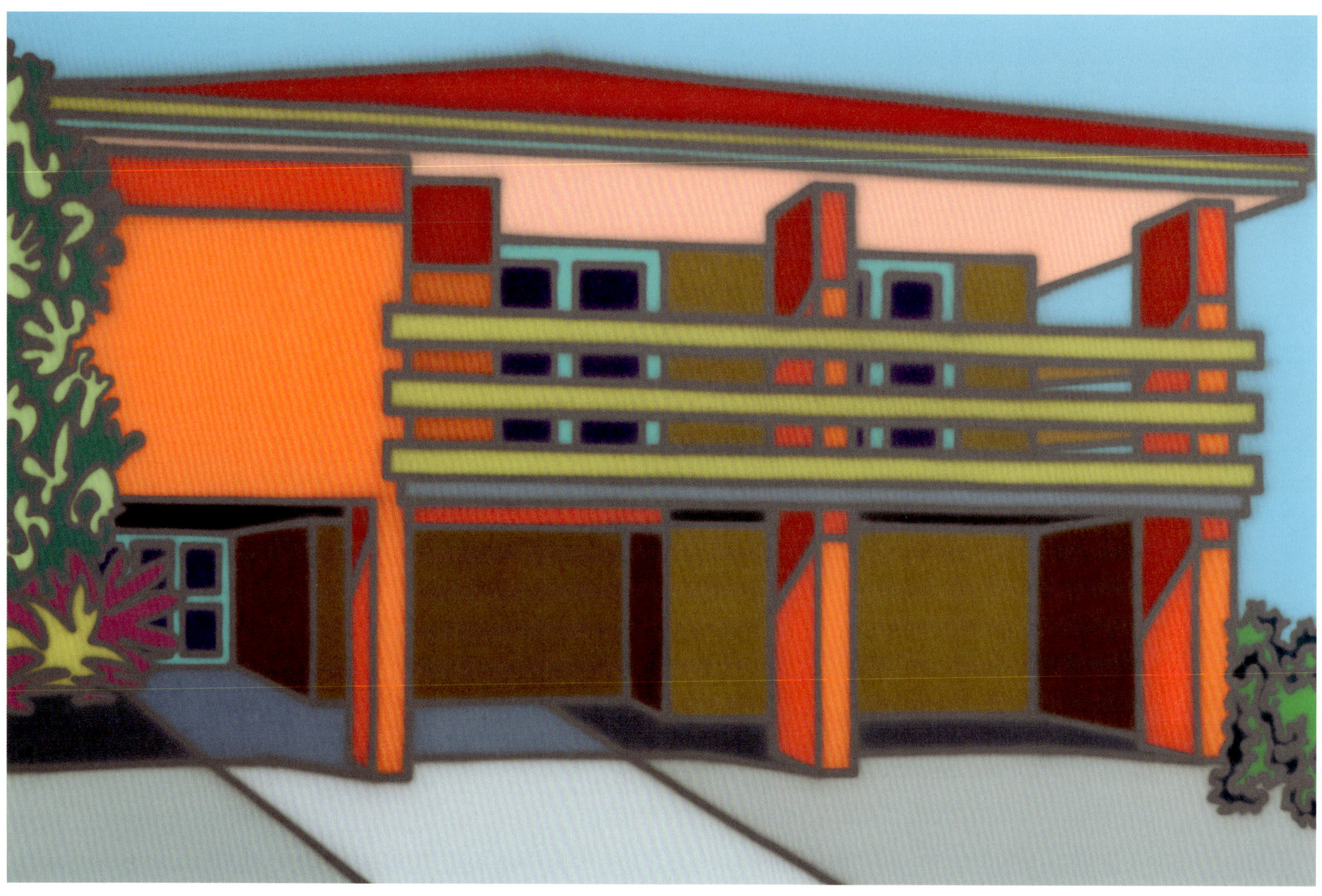

186

ROBERT MACPHERSON
Mayfair: Bethonga Gold, for B.T.O.'s,
1995–2006
Synthetic polymer paint on
three composition boards,
244 × 190 cm (overall)
National Gallery of Australia, Canberra.
Purchased 2012

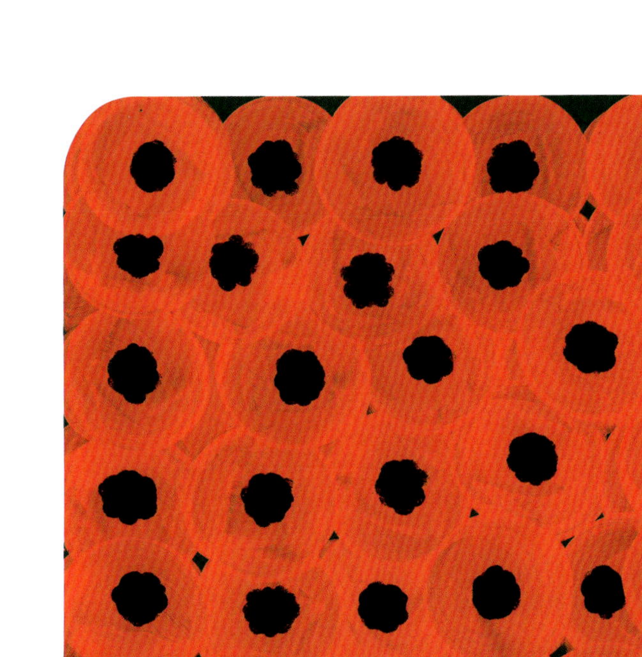

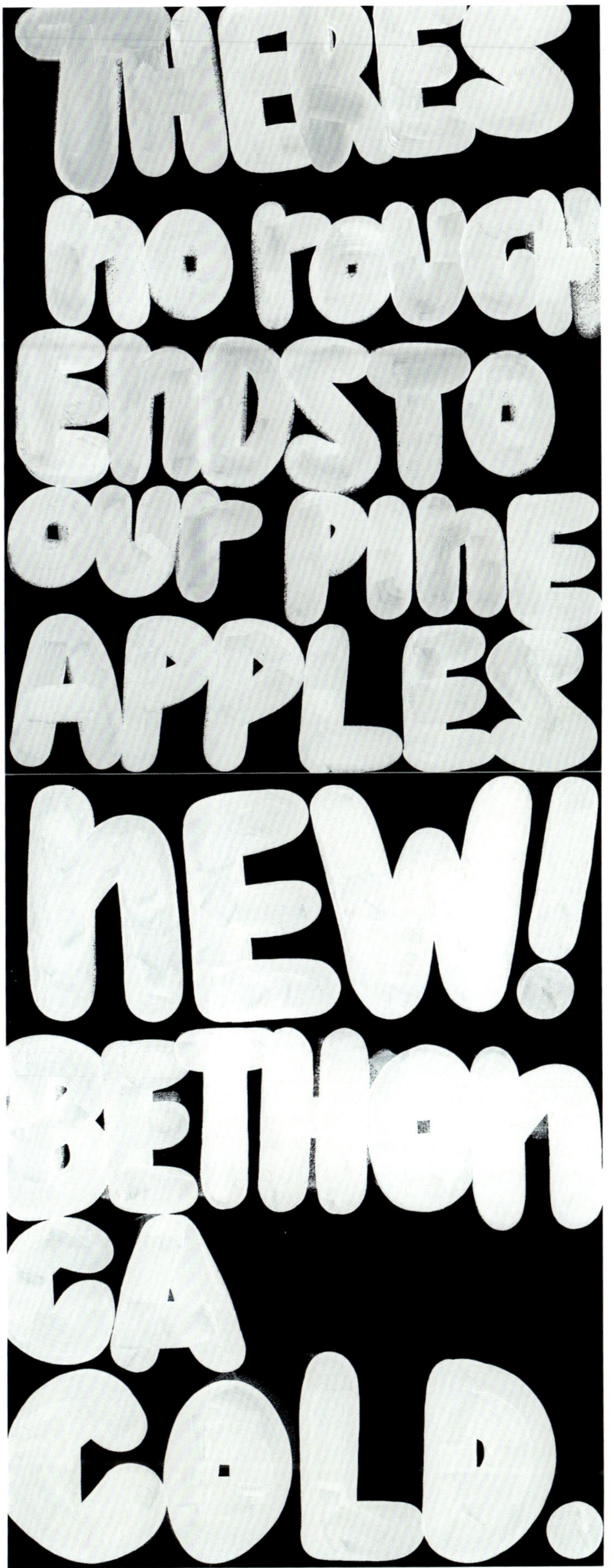

187

G.W. BOT

Garden of Gethsemane I, 2000

Linocut, printed in colour from multiple blocks, hand-coloured on thin tapa cloth, 98 × 50.8 cm

National Gallery of Australia, Canberra. Purchased with the generous assistance of the artist, 2011

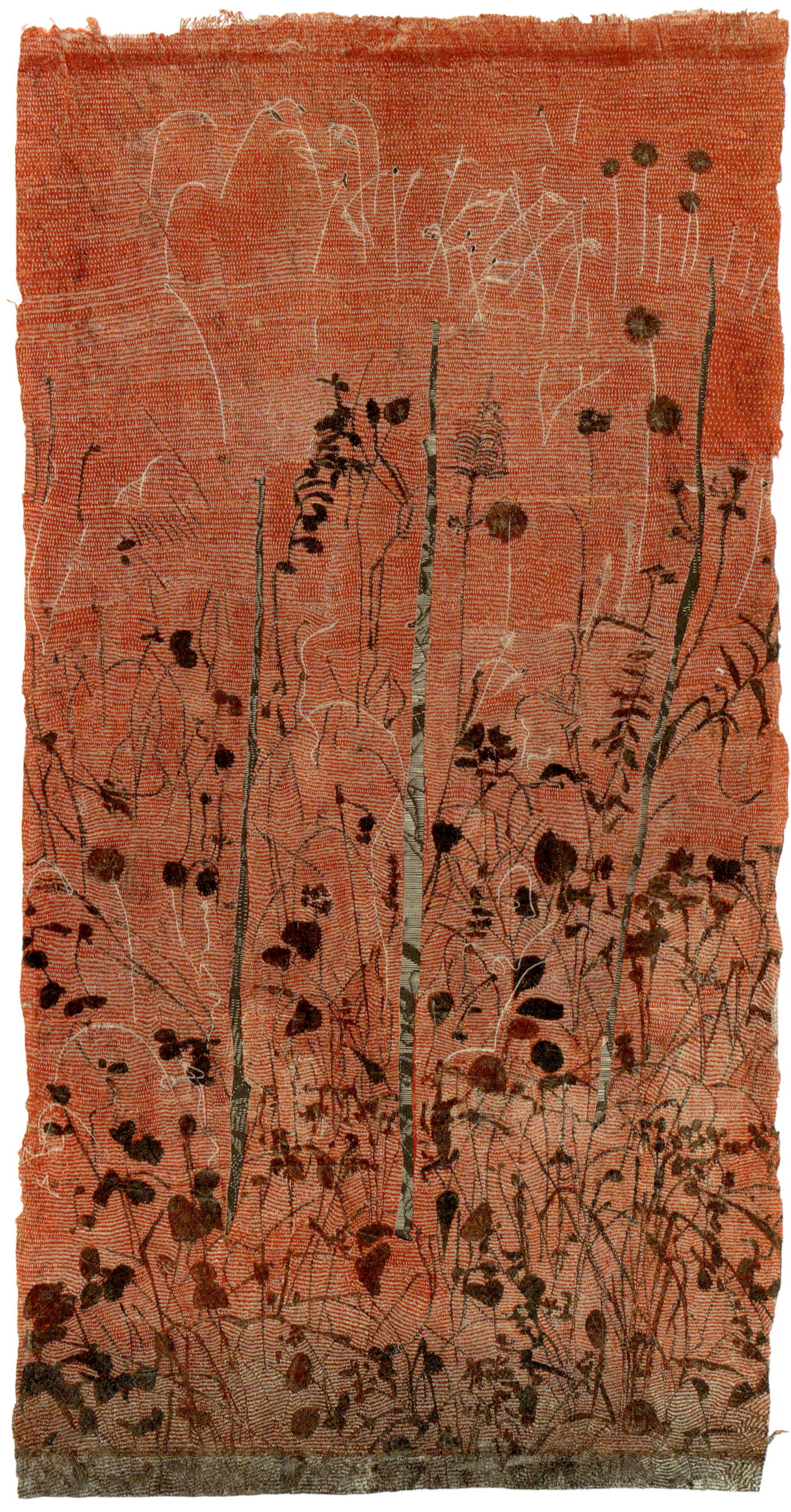

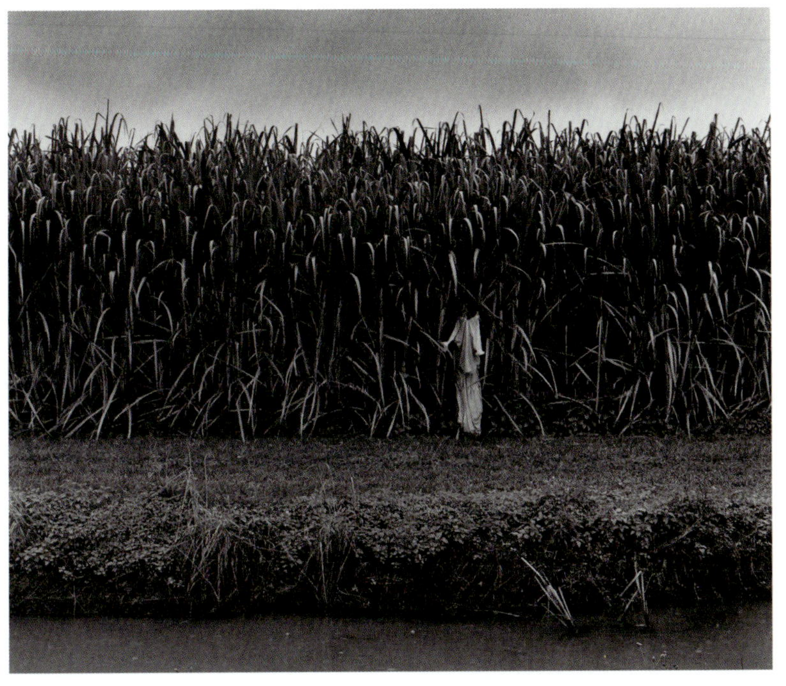

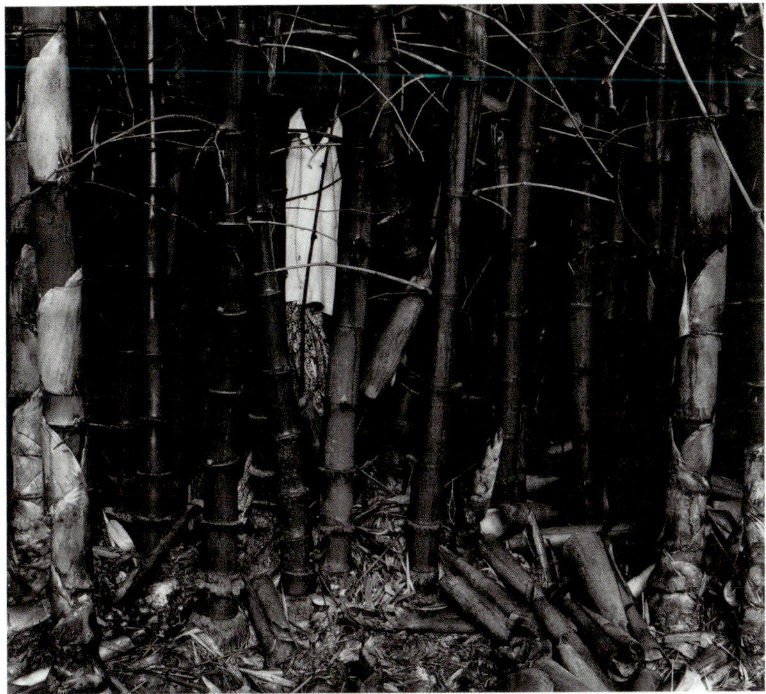

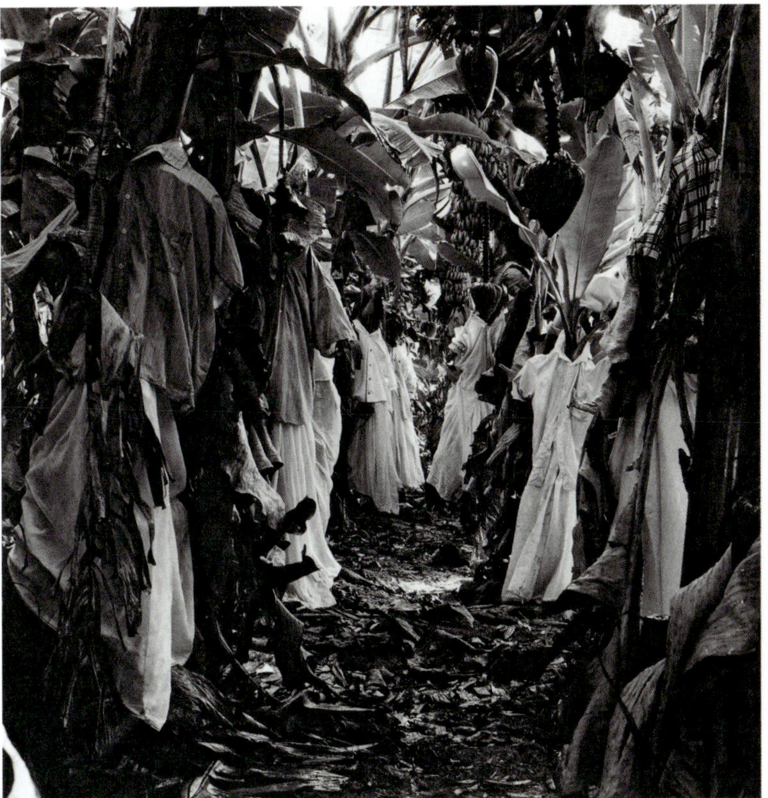

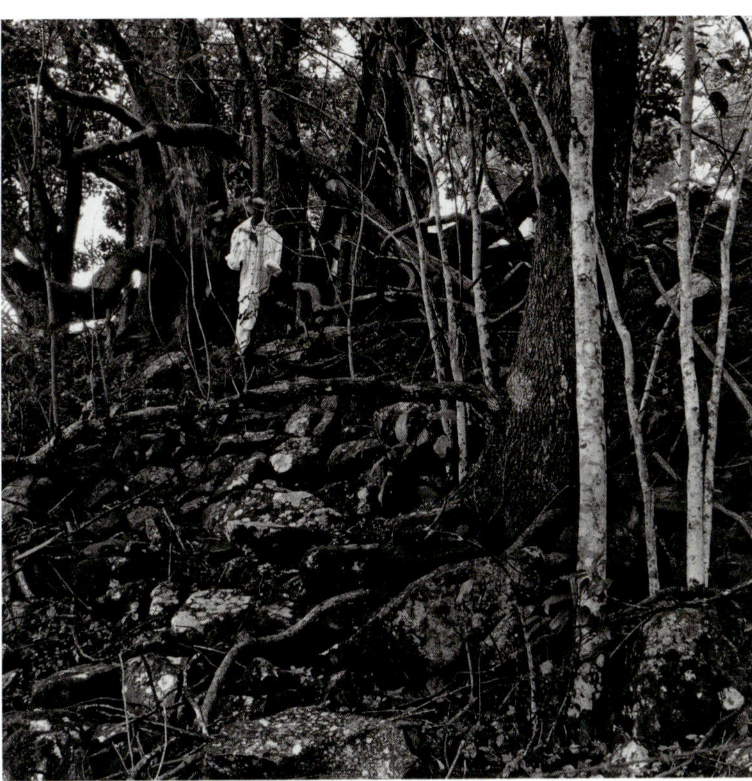

188

SIMRYN GILL
Rampant, 1999
A selection of four from a series of seven gelatin silver photographs, 23 × 26 cm, 23.5 × 25.6 cm, 25.4 × 23.9 cm, 24.5 × 23.6 cm

Art Gallery of New South Wales, Sydney.
Gift of the artist, 2005

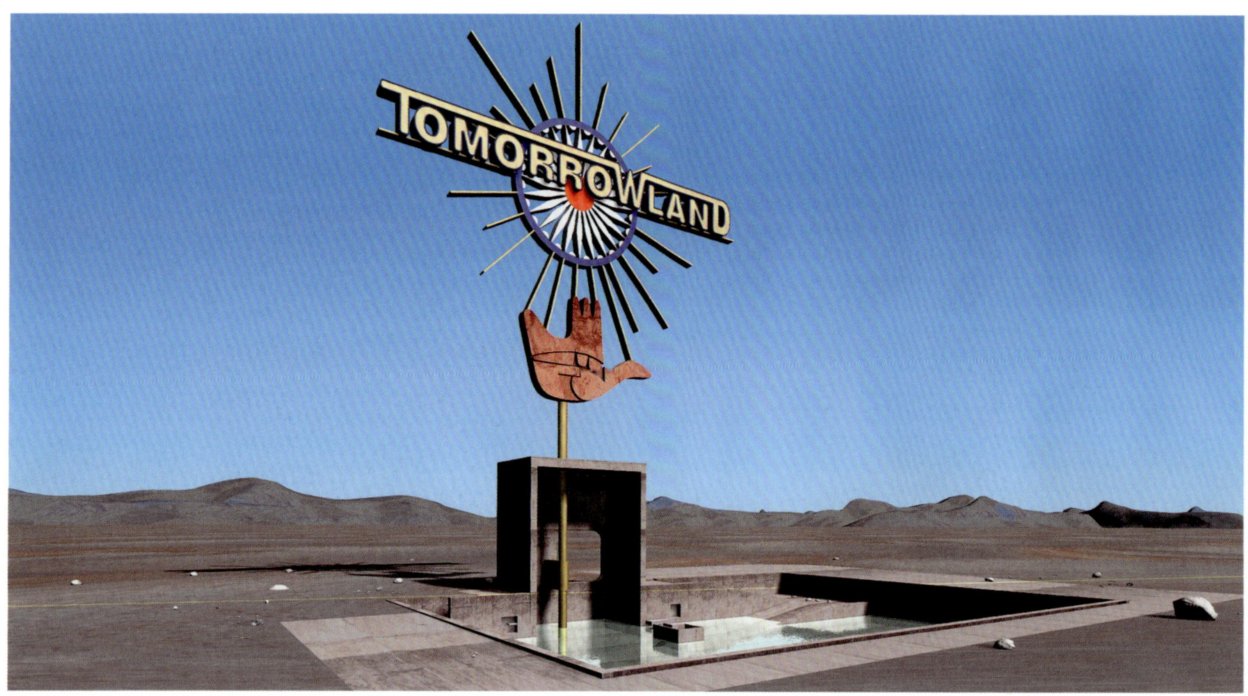

189
CALLUM MORTON
Tomorrowland, 2004
Digital print, 94.5 × 170 cm
National Gallery of Australia, Canberra.
Gift of Naomi Milgrom AO, 2013

190
BILL HENSON
Untitled, 1998–99
Inkjet pigment print,
127 × 180 cm
National Gallery of Australia, Canberra.
Purchased with funds from the Honorary Exhibition Circle Patrons, 2013

191
TRACEY MOFFATT
Up in the Sky #1, #2, #6, #8, #14, #24, 1997
A selection of six from the series of twenty-five lithographs
61.5 × 76 cm (each image)
Tate, London.
Purchased 1998

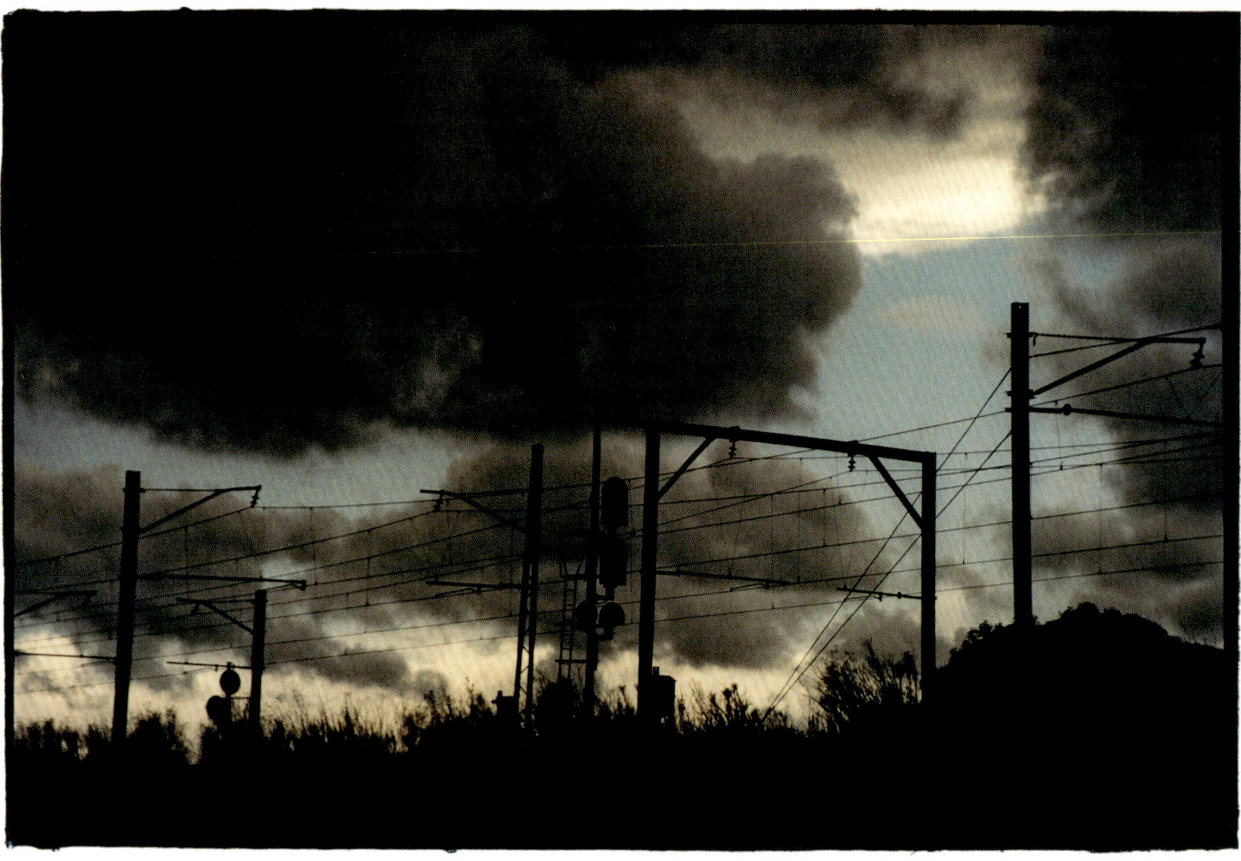

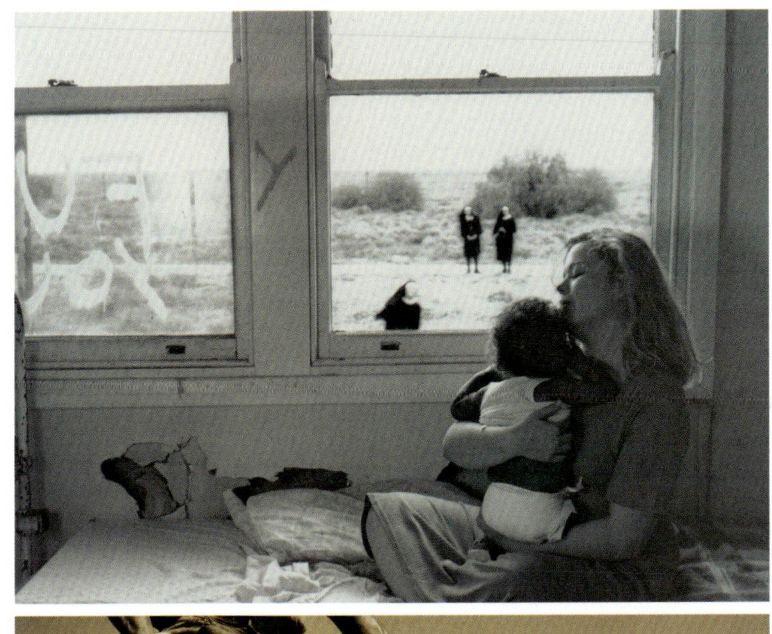

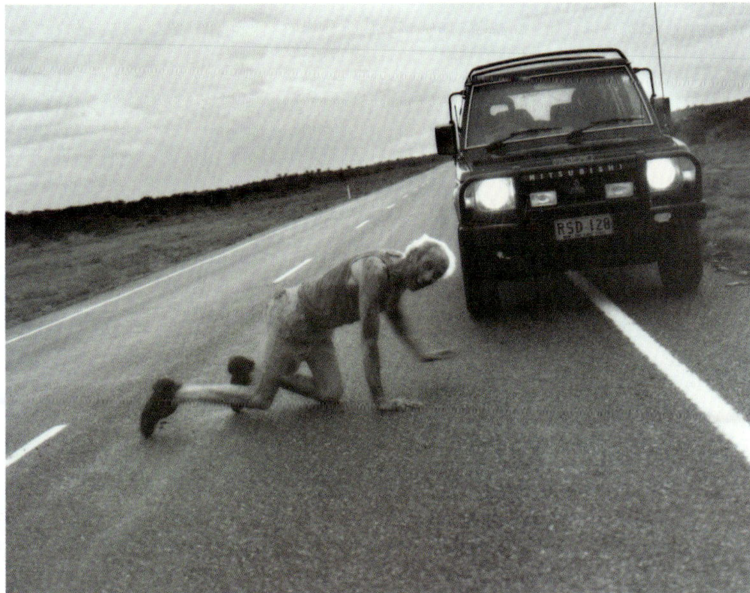
MITSUBISHI
RSD 128

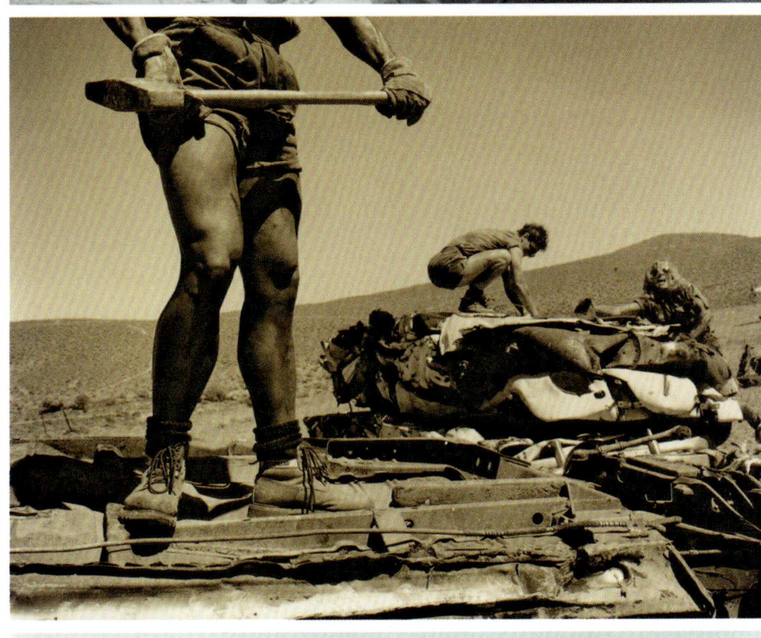

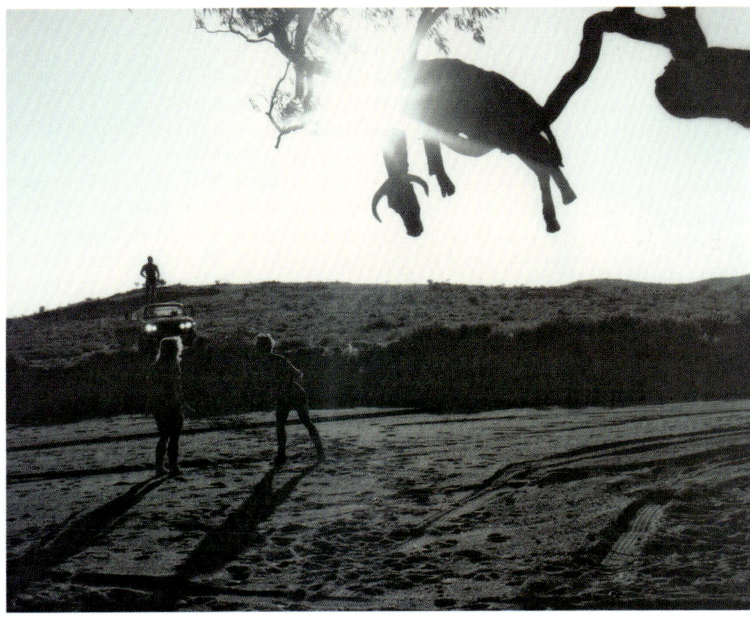

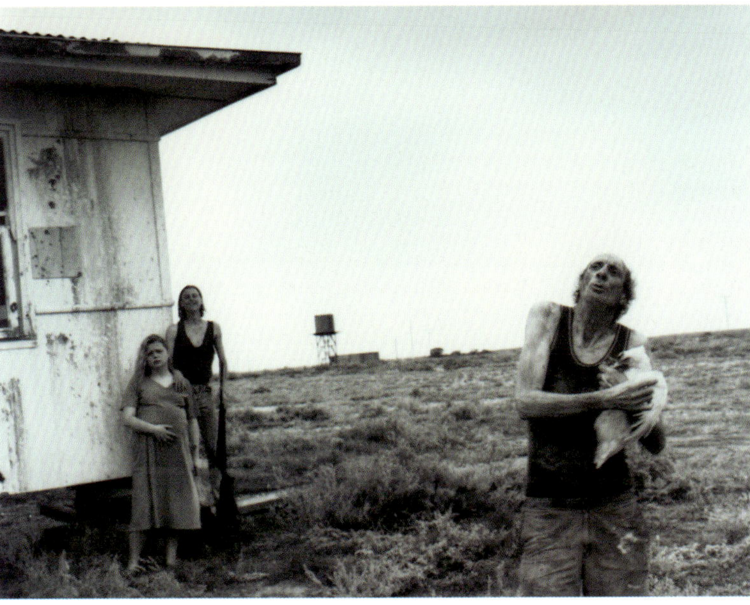

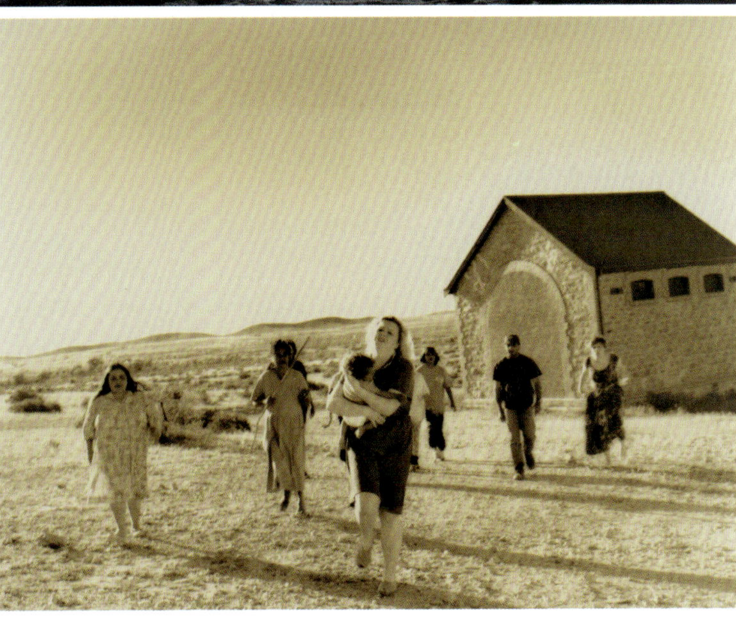

192

JOHN BEARD
Uluru 8, 2002
Oil and wax on linen,
180 × 262 cm

Australian National University, Canberra.
Gift of James Erskine through the Australian Government's Cultural Gifts Program, 2009

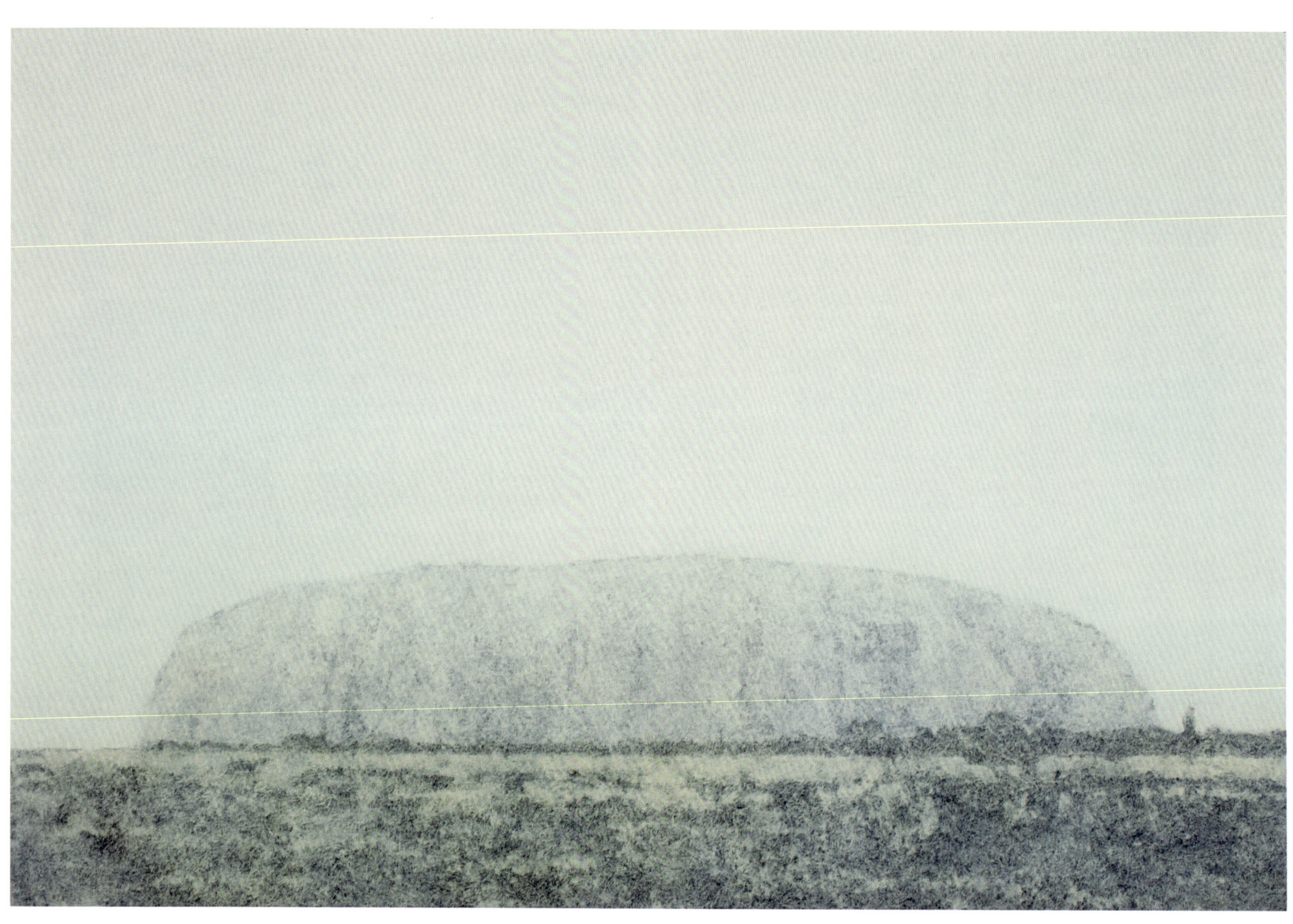

193

IMANTS TILLERS

Shadow of the Hereafter, 2007

Synthetic polymer paint and gouache on 72 canvas boards, 228.5 × 284.5 cm (overall)

Art Gallery of South Australia, Adelaide. Gift of the Art Gallery of South Australia Contemporary Collectors, Gosia Kudra-Schild and Taliangis family, 2007

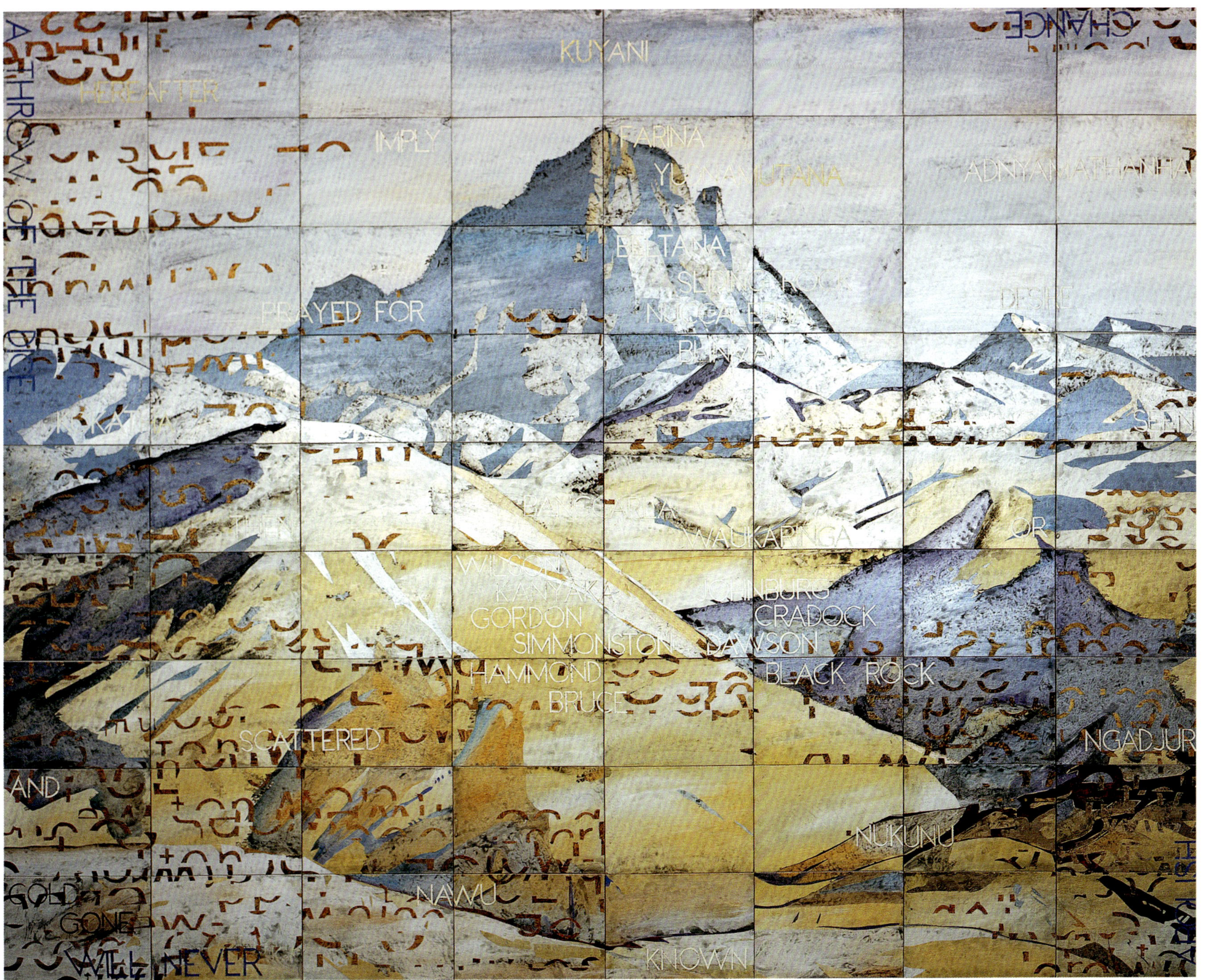

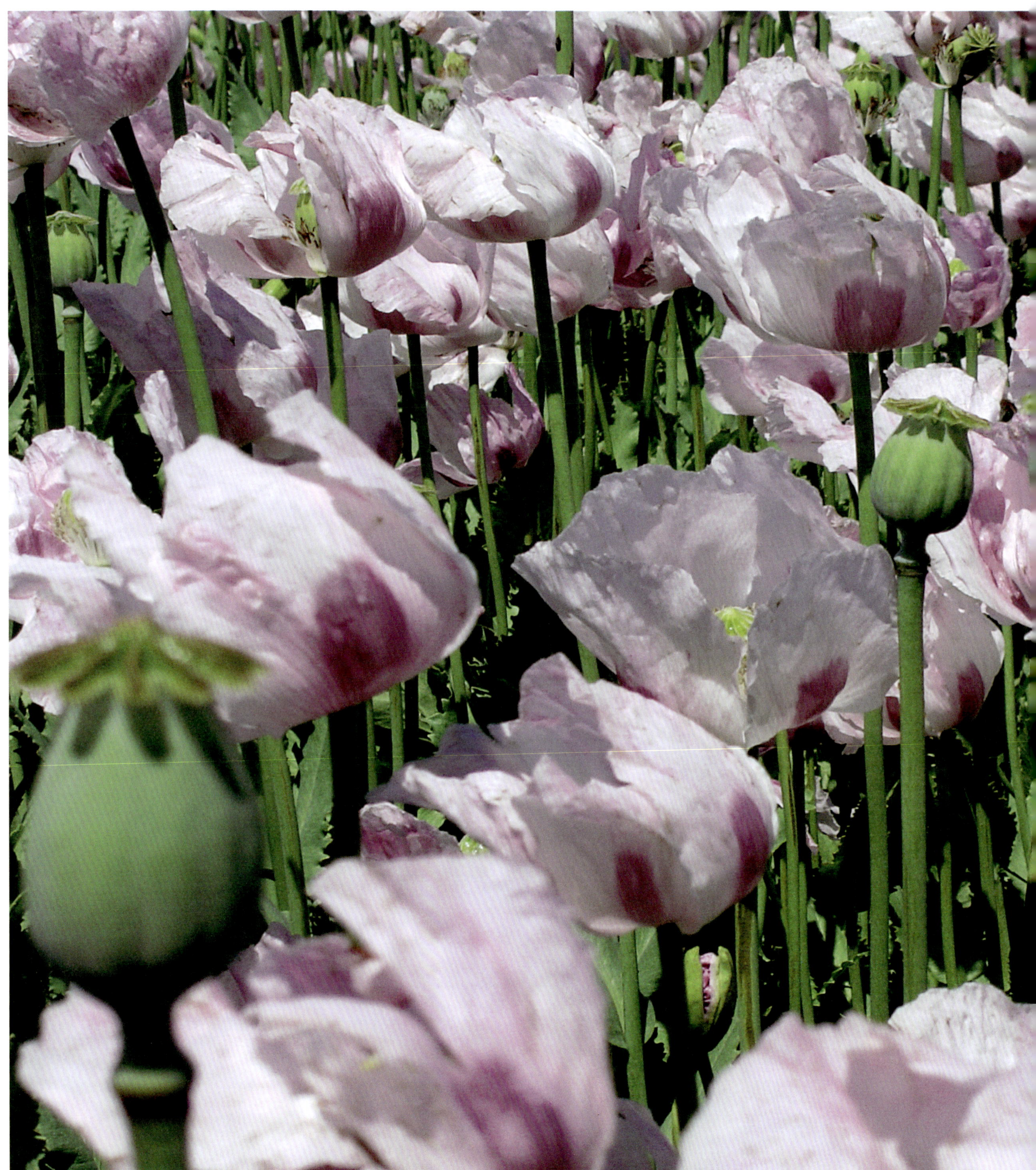

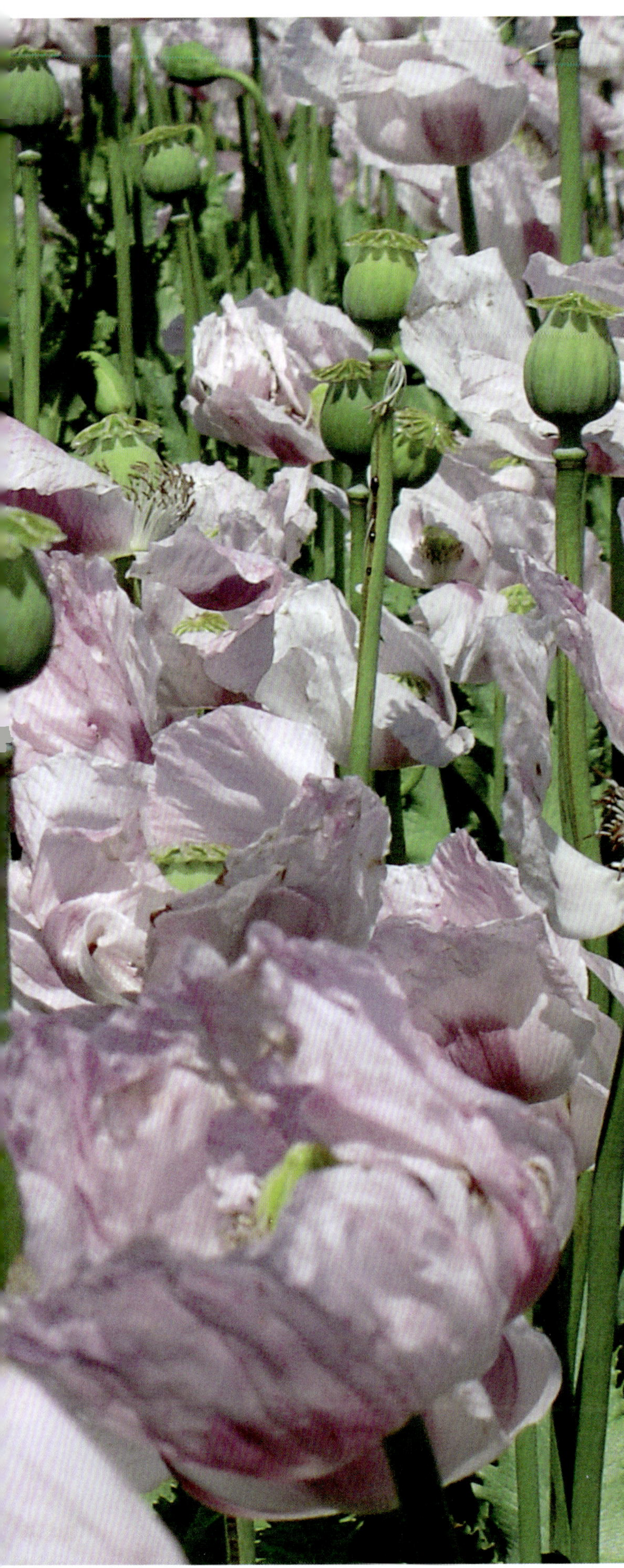

194
FIONA FOLEY
Bliss, 2006
Single-channel HD/DVD: 16:9,
ratio colour, sound 11 minutes, 20 seconds
Museum of Contemporary Art, Sydney.
Purchased with funds provided by the
Coe and Mordant families, 2009

195 *overleaf*
DENNIS NONA
Mutuk, 2009
Etching, printed in colour,
133 × 430 cm
National Gallery of Australia, Canberra.
Purchased 2009

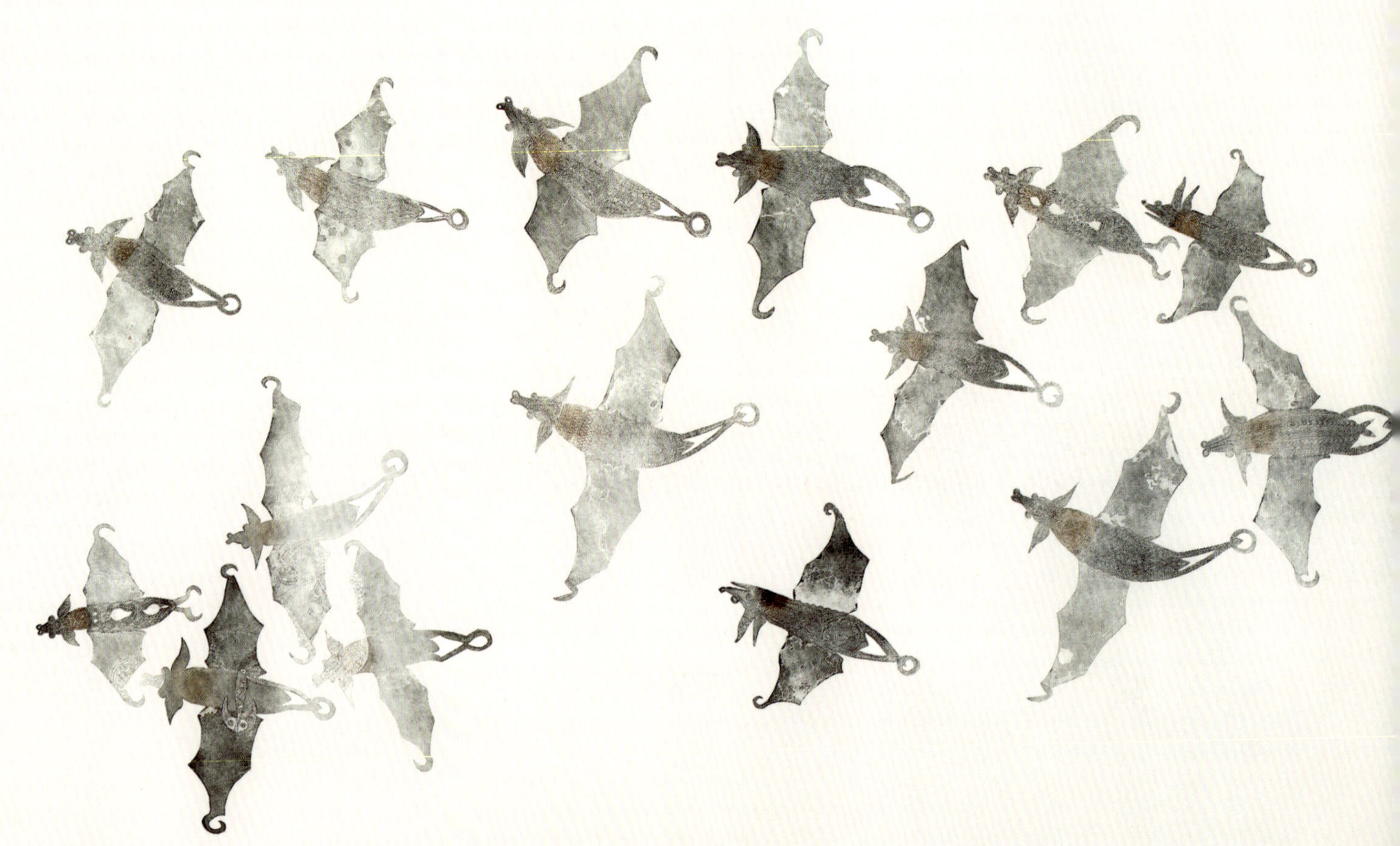

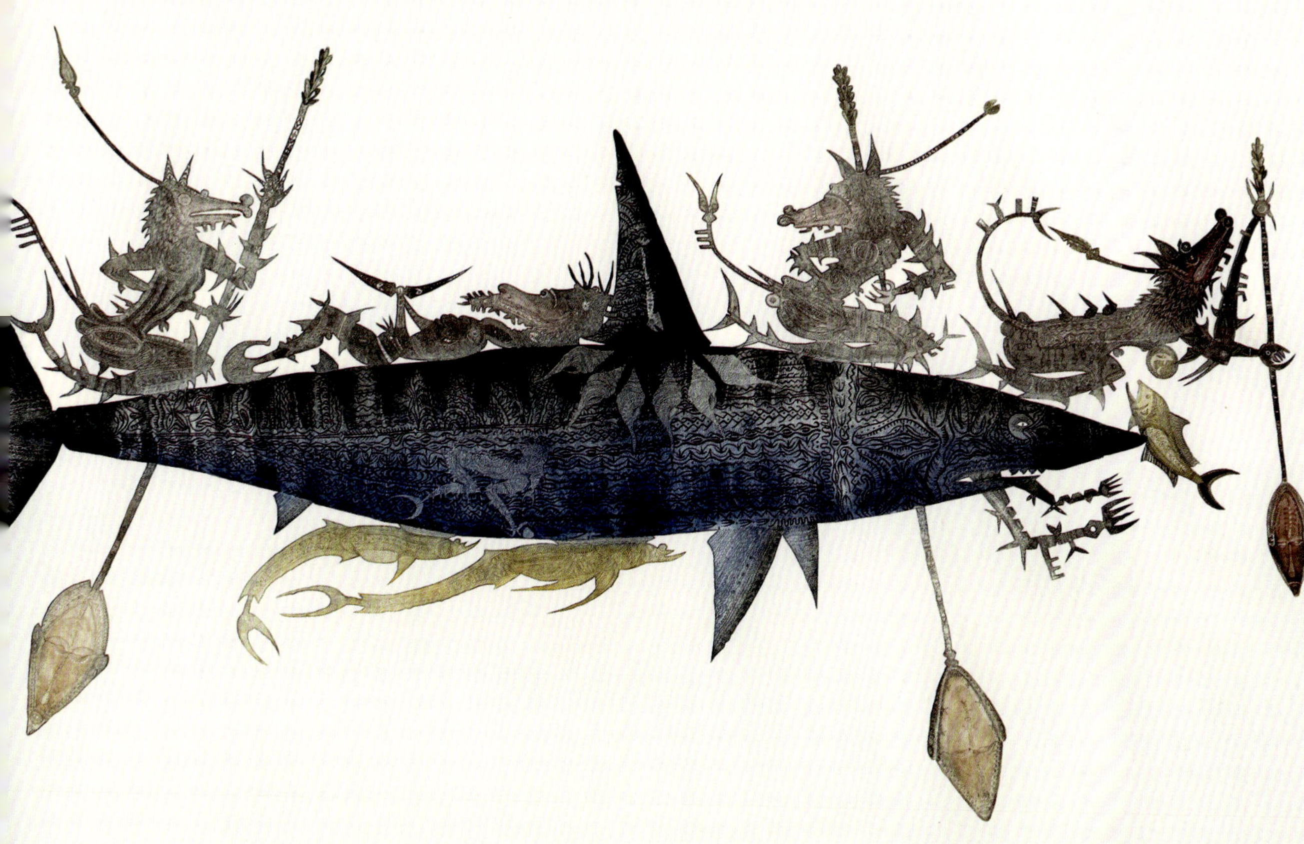

196
VERNON AH KEE
Can't Chant (wegrewhere) #2, 2009
Inkjet pigment print, 76 × 114 cm
National Gallery of Australia, Canberra.
Purchased 2009

197
SHAUN GLADWELL
Approach to Mundi Mundi, 2007
From the series *MADDESTMAXIMVS*
Single-channel HD/DVD, 16:9
ratio colour, silent 8 minutes,
37 seconds
Art Gallery of New South Wales, Sydney.
John Kaldor Family Collection

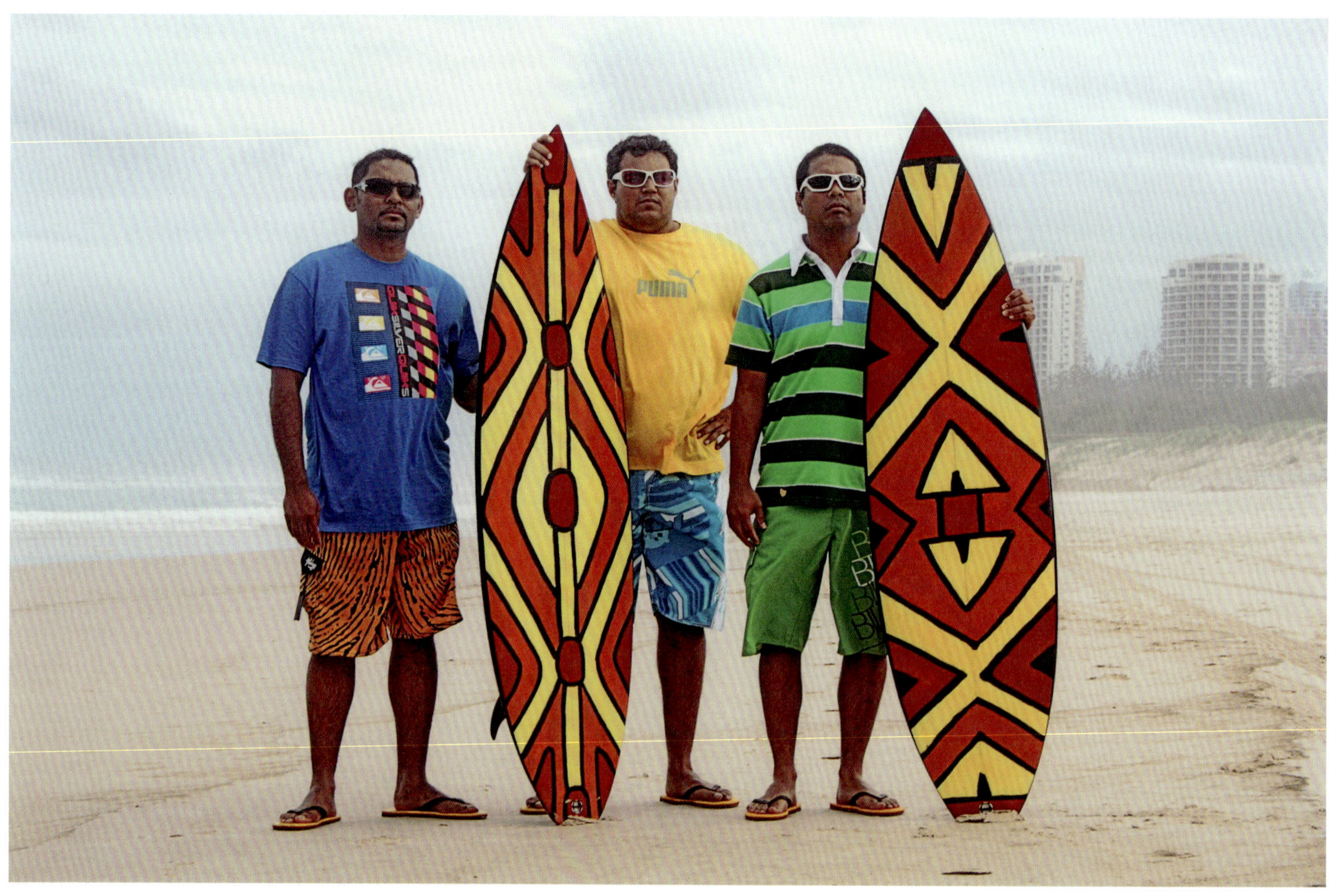

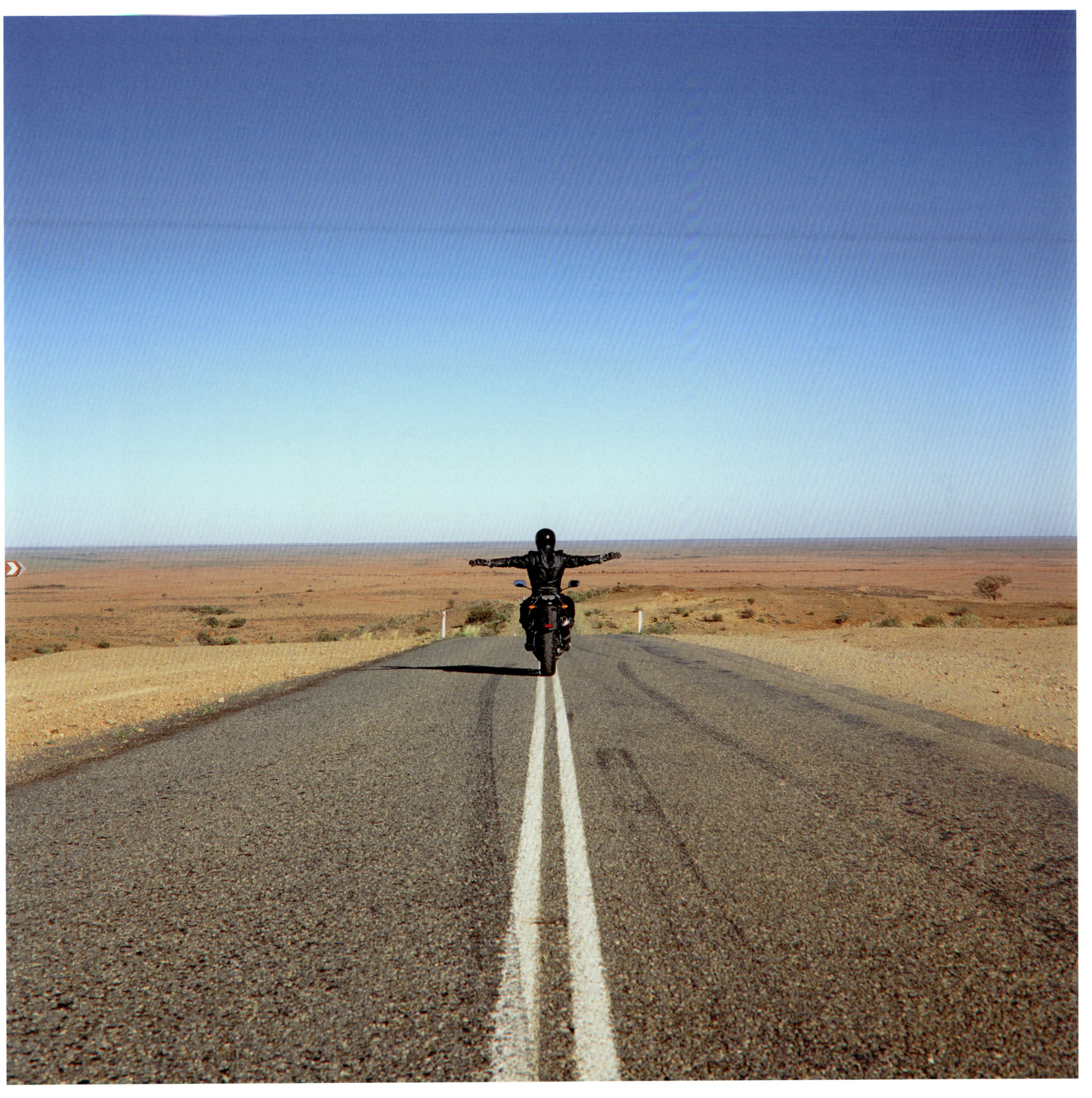

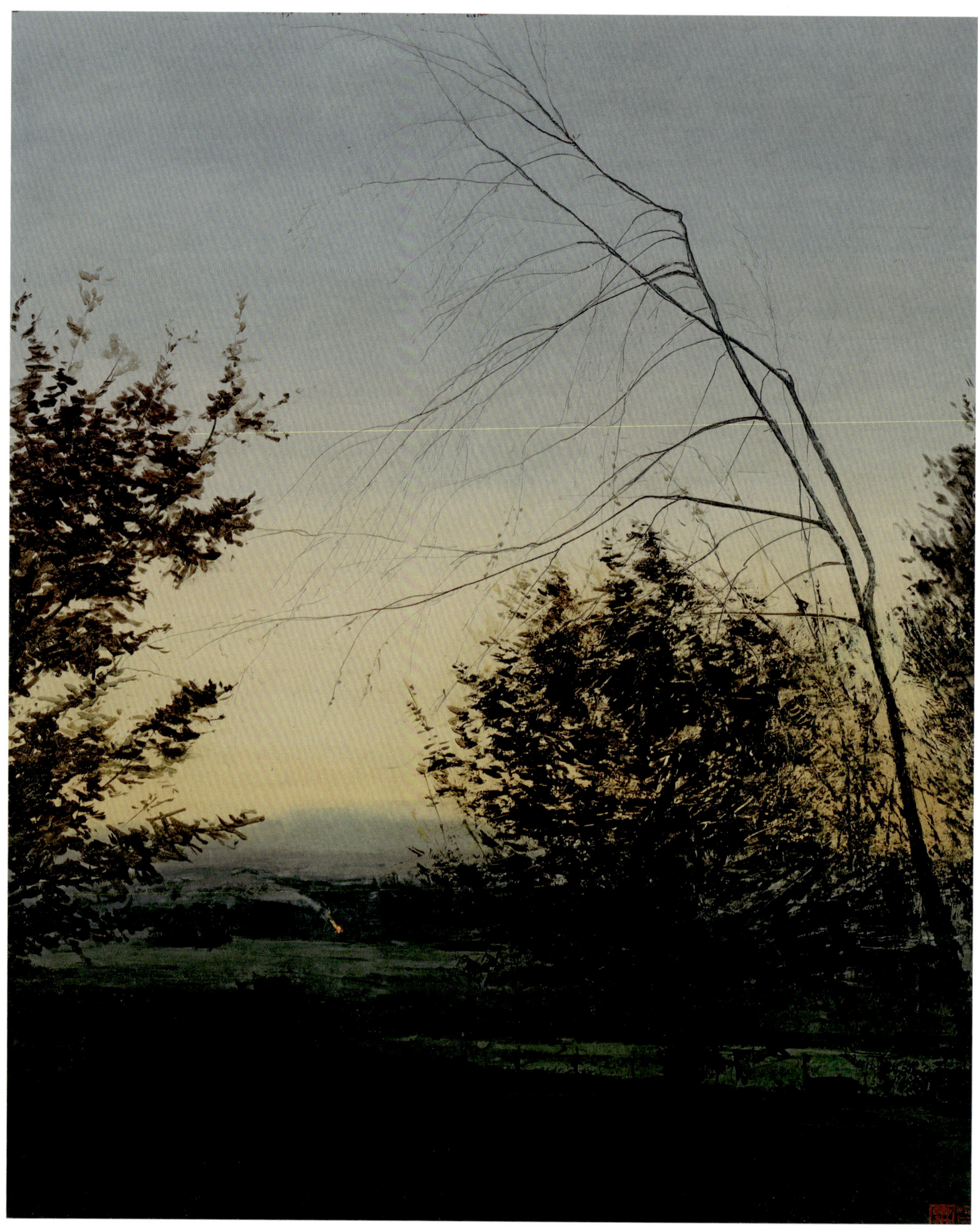

198
PHILIP WOLFHAGEN
Autumn Equinox: The Loss of the Sun, 2009
Oil and beeswax on canvas,
200.4 × 160.3 cm
National Gallery of Australia, Canberra.
Purchased 2009

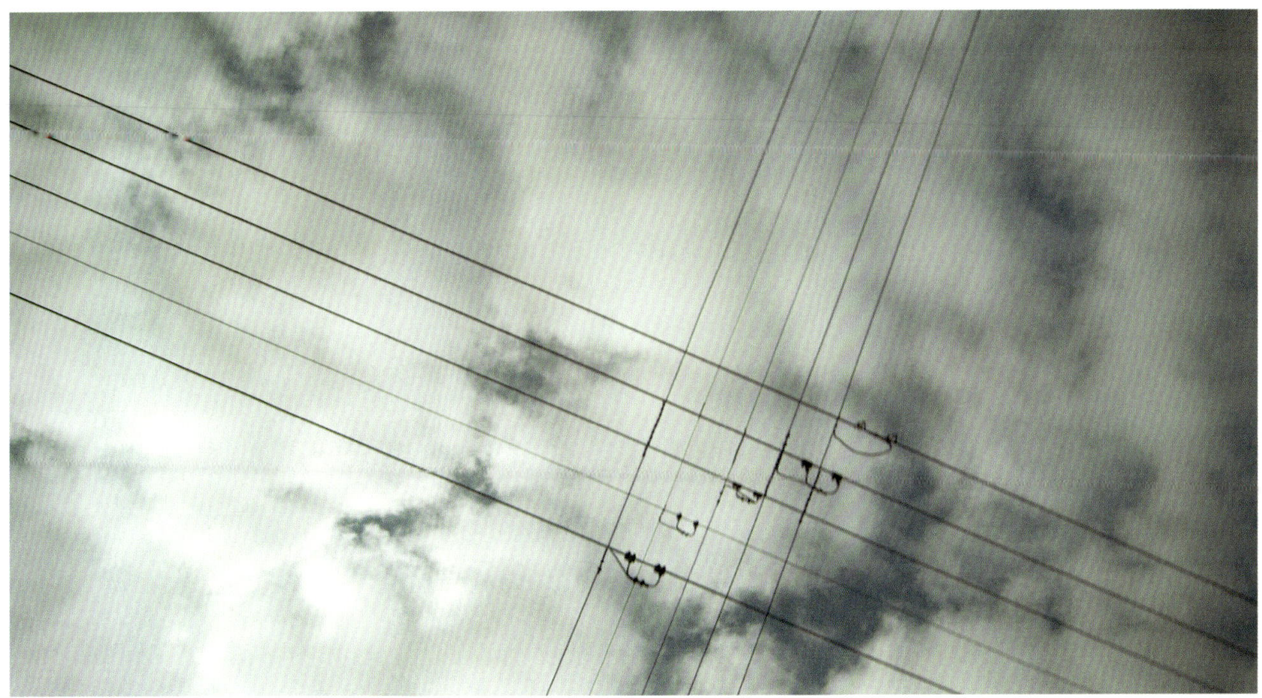

199
DANIEL CROOKS
Cloud Atlas (Fitzroy 1:23), 2012
Single-channel HD/DVD 16:9, ratio colour, silent, 21 minutes
National Gallery of Australia, Canberra. Purchased 2012

200
ROSEMARY LAING
Jim from the series **leak**, 2010
C-type colour photograph, 110 × 237.6 cm
National Gallery of Australia, Canberra. Purchased 2013

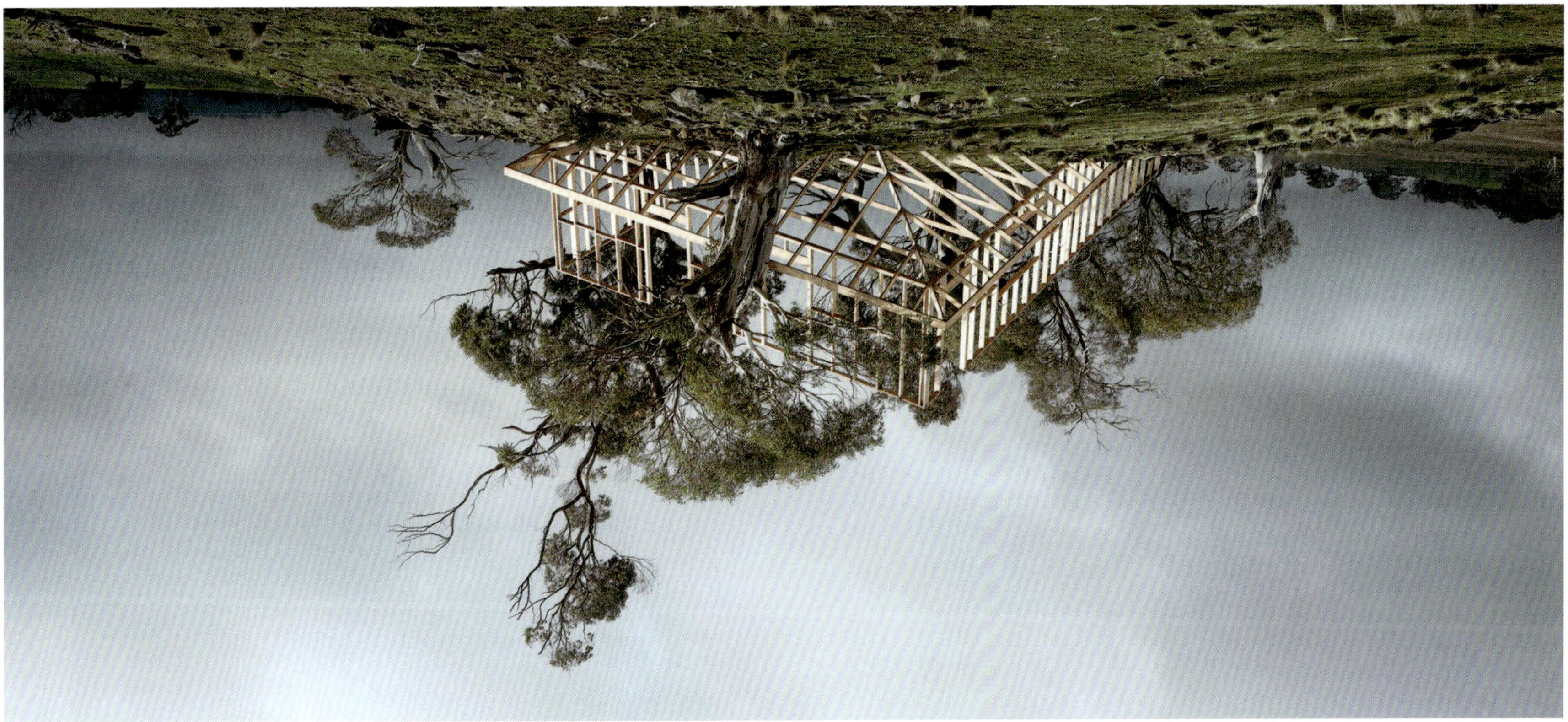

201

HOSSEIN VALAMANESH
Longing/Belonging, 1997
Direct colour positive photograph,
99 × 99 cm; carpet, velvet, 215 × 305 cm
Art Gallery of New South Wales, Sydney.
Purchased with funds from the Contemporary
Collection Benefactors, 2002

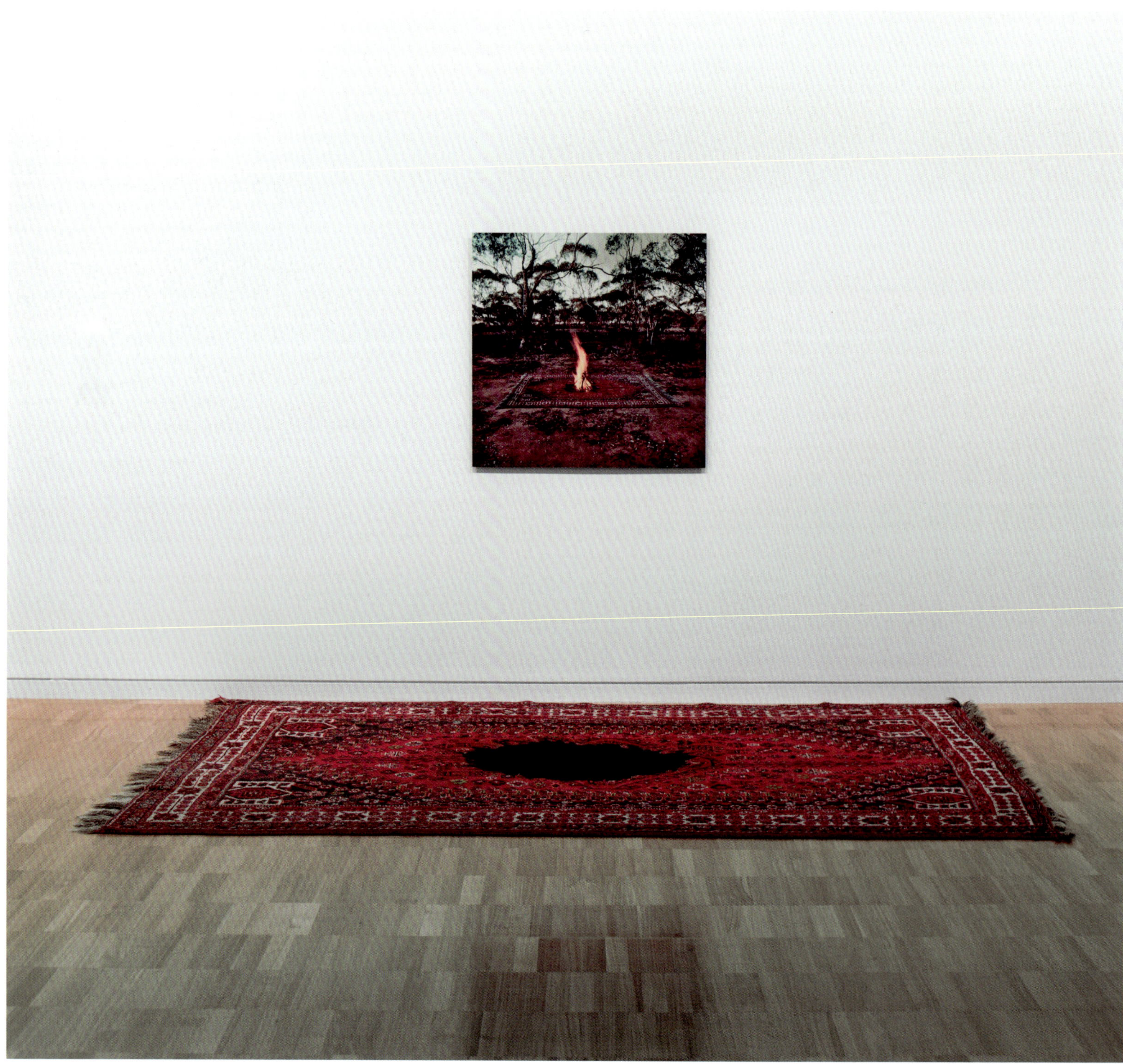

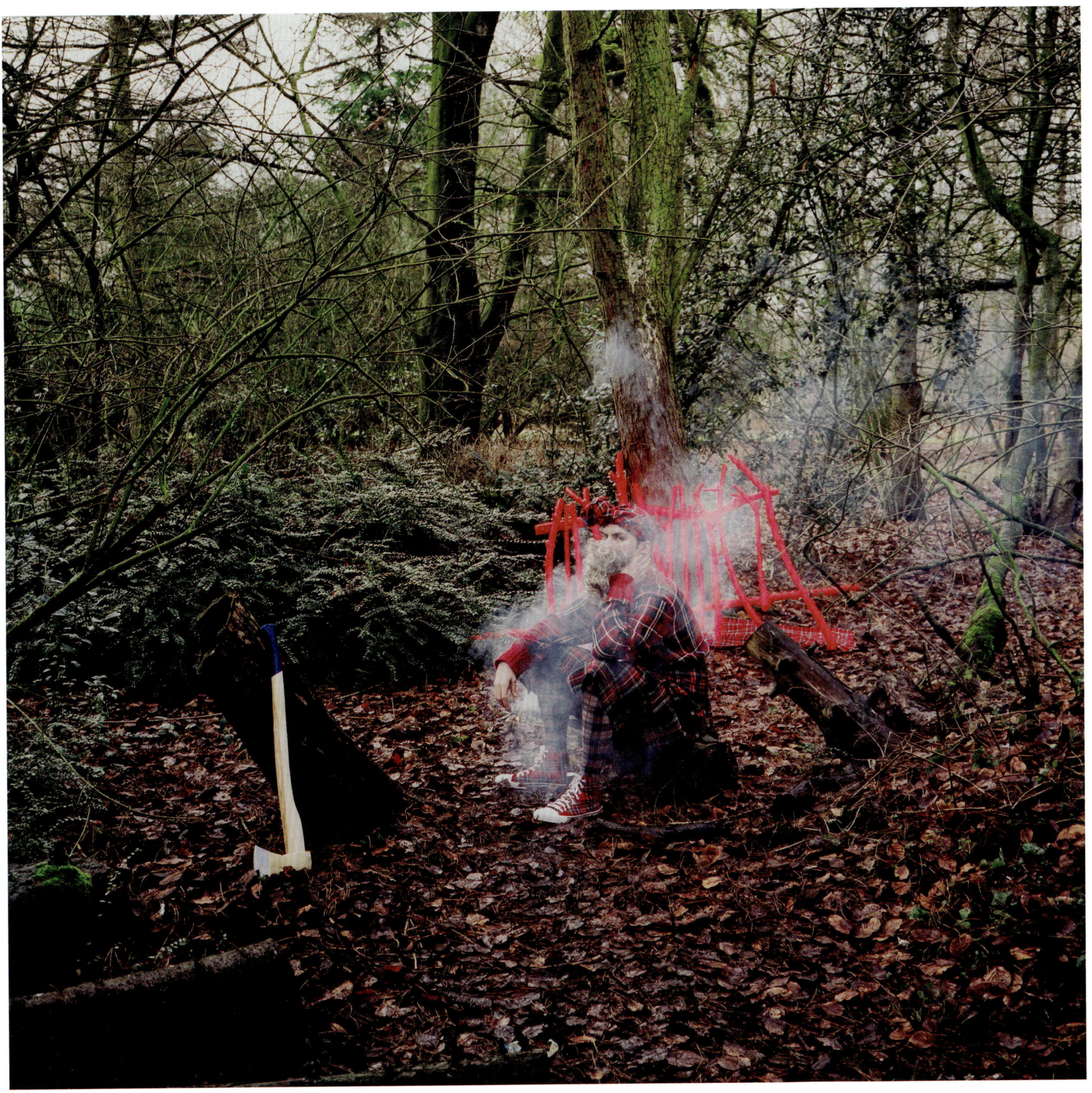

202

CHRISTIAN THOMPSON
Dead as a Door Nail, 2008
C-type colour photograph,
100 × 100 cm

National Gallery of Australia, Canberra.
Purchased 2012

203

DANIE MELLOR

An Elysian City (of Picturesque Landscapes and Memory), 2010
Pastel, pencil and wash with glitter and Swarovski crystal, 143 × 186 cm
National Gallery of Australia, Canberra. Purchased 2011

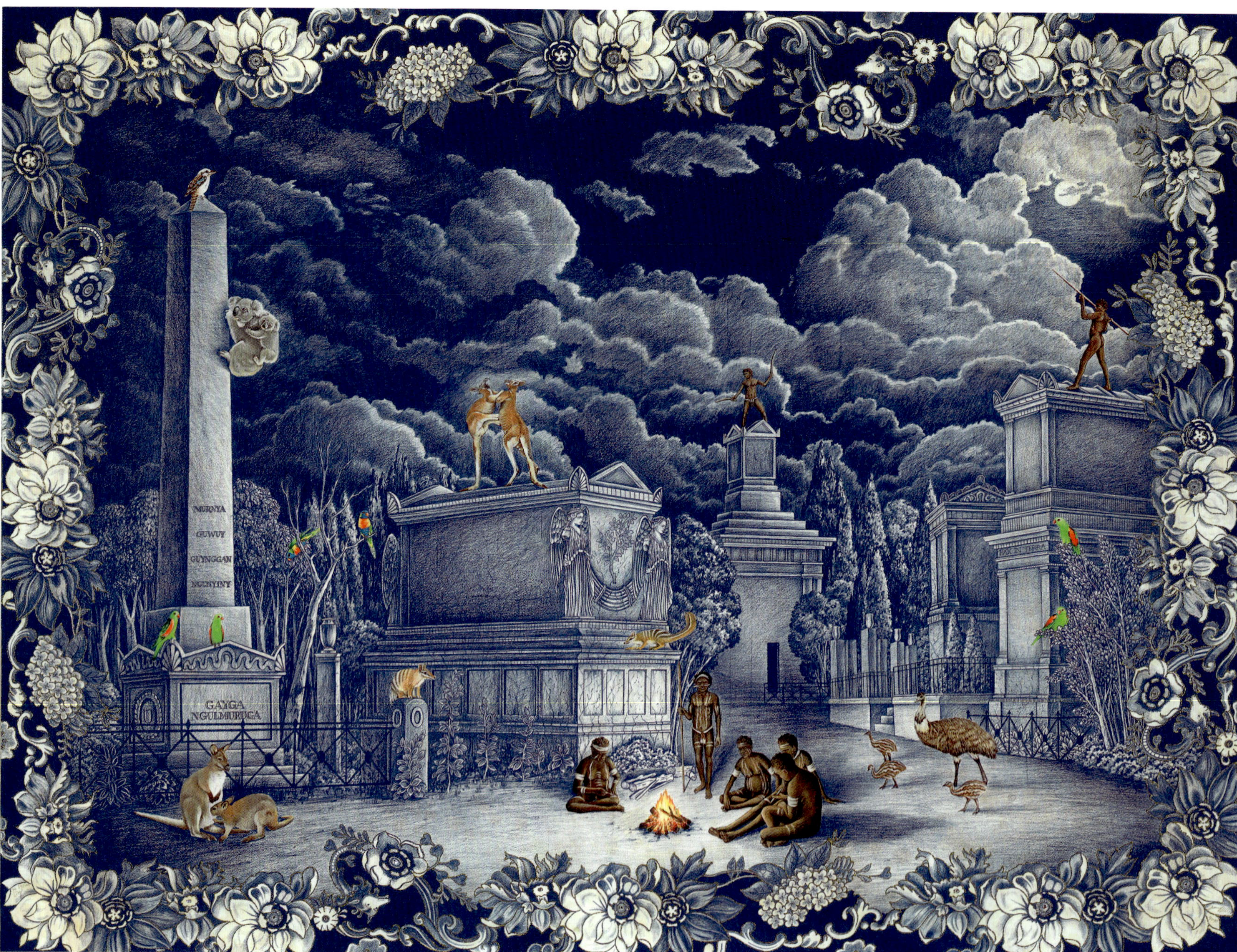

204

KATHY TEMIN

Tombstone Garden, 2012

Synthetic fur, synthetic polymer paint, synthetic stuffing, steel, composition board, 230 × 429 × 180 cm (overall)

National Gallery of Australia, Canberra. Purchased 2012

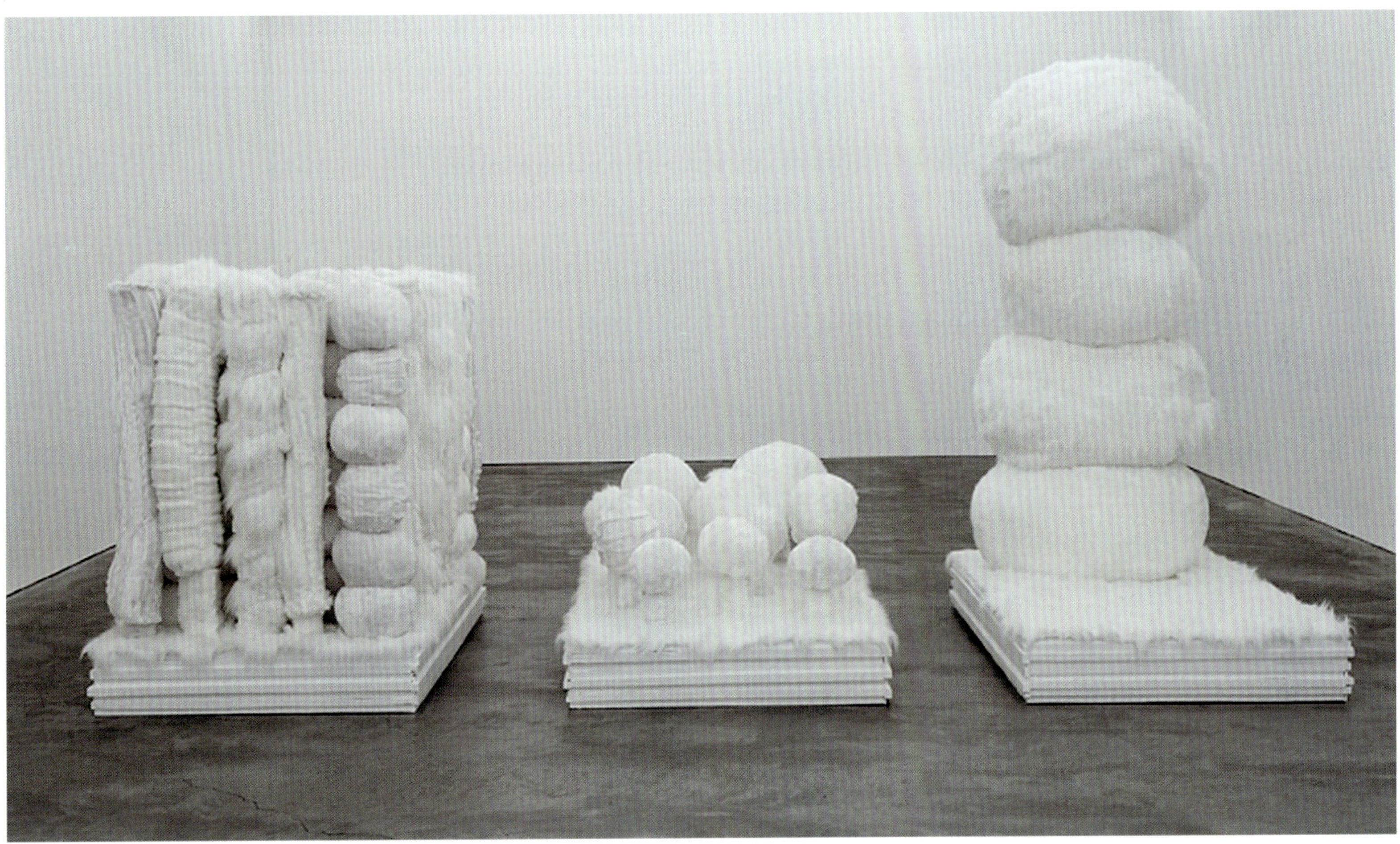

205

JUDY WATSON
fire and water, 2013
Sculptural installation,
600 × 750 × 1050 cm

Courtesy the Artist and Milani Gallery, Brisbane. Fabrication by Urban Art Projects, Australia, and Shanghai, China

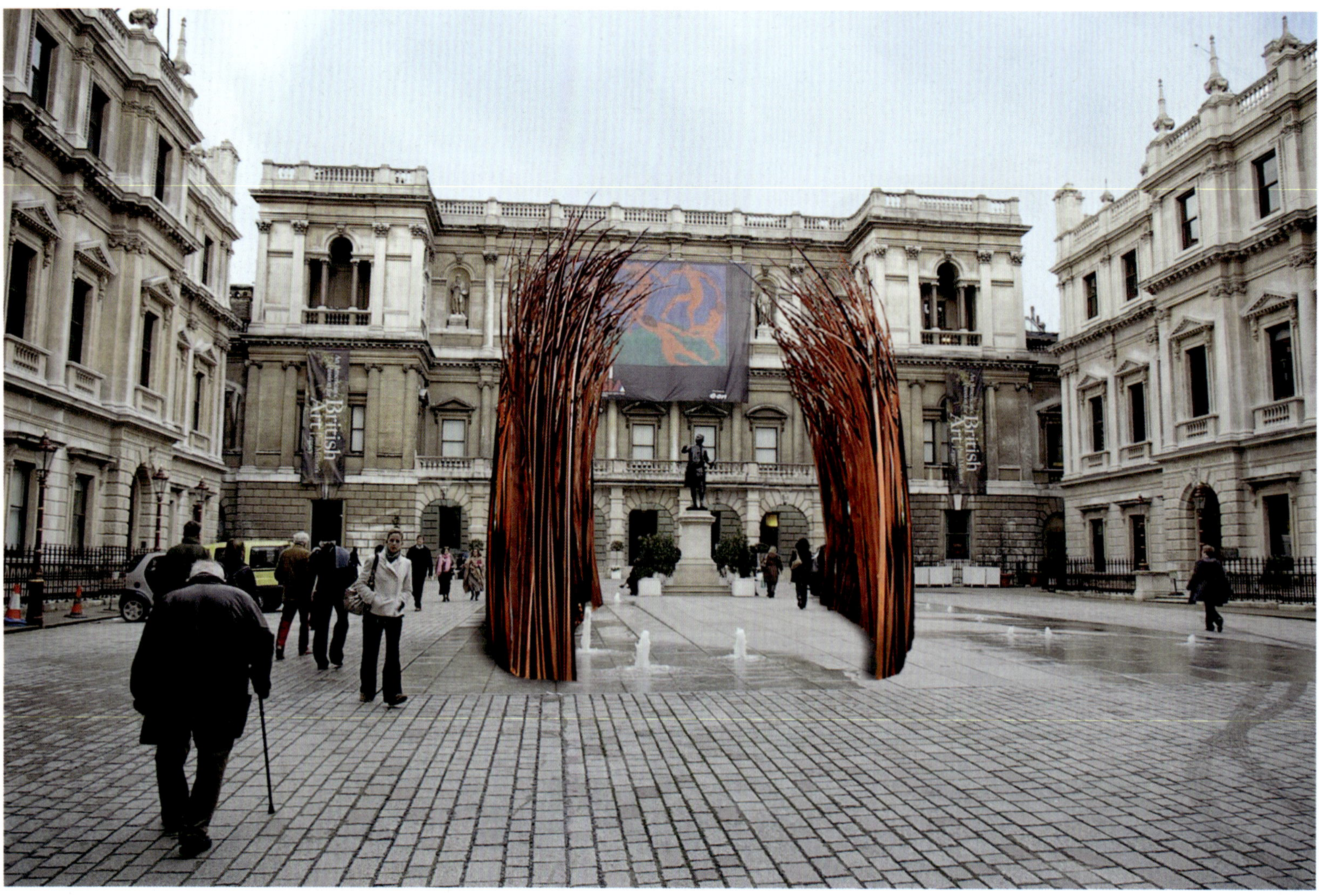

ARTISTS' BIOGRAPHIES

These artists are well represented in Australian public collections. The emphasis here is on their inclusion in major British, European and American collections. Only the most recent survey exhibitions have been mentioned. Books on the artist have been included when there is no major retrospective or survey exhibition.

VERNON AH KEE (b. 1967)
Kuku Yalandji, Yidindji, Waanji, Gugu Yimithirr, Koko people. Born Innisfail, North Queensland, 1967; moved to Brisbane, Queensland, 1991; lives in Brisbane

As a contemporary artist Vernon Ah Kee is moved by situations and circumstances in which he finds himself. Identity politics and race relations between black and white Australians are eloquently represented in a forthright and confrontational manner. Ah Kee is a versatile artist who works in several media: printmaking, photography, digital media, installation, text, painting and drawing. He studied Screen-printing at the Cairns College of TAFE (Technical and Further Education), North Queensland, and Visual Arts at Queensland College of Art, Griffith University, Brisbane, and is currently completing a Doctorate in Visual Arts there. Along with other local Aboriginal artists, Ah Kee formed the Queensland-based art collective ProppaNOW in 2004. He was selected for the first National Indigenous Art Triennial, 'Culture Warriors', at the National Gallery of Australia, Canberra, from 2007 to 2008 and the Venice Biennale in 2009.

GEORGE FRENCH ANGAS (1822–1886)
Born Newcastle upon Tyne, Northumberland, 25 April 1822; arrived Adelaide, 1844; visited New Zealand, 1844; returned to London, 1845–50; travelled in South Africa, 1846–47; lived in Australia, 1850–63; returned to London, 1863; died London, 4 October 1886

George French Angas was one of South Australia's leading watercolourists and a skilled naturalist. The eldest son of George Fife Angas, one of the founders of South Australia, he took sketching lessons in London under Benjamin Waterhouse Hawkins. During the first half of 1844 he travelled extensively in South Australia, sketching images of the Aborigines and their customs and making watercolour sketches for *South Australia Illustrated* (1846–47). Later in 1844 he travelled widely in New Zealand, making many watercolours of the Maoris and subsequently published *The New Zealanders Illustrated* (1846–47). He then spent time in Sydney, before returning to South Australia to exhibit his watercolours. In the 1850s he visited the New South Wales, Victorian and Queensland goldfields and was Secretary and accountant to the Australian Museum, Sydney, from 1853 to 1860. His work is held by the British Museum and was included in the exhibition 'Australian Painting' at the Tate Gallery in 1963. A book on his art, *George French Angas: Artist, Traveller and Naturalist 1822–1886* by John Tregenza was published in 1980.

DECLAN APUATIMI (1930–1985)
Tiwi people. Born Iminulapi, Bathurst Island, Northern Territory, 1930; spent most of his life at Nguiu, Bathurst Island, Northern Territory; died Nguiu, January 1985

Declan Apuatimi Allariki was a highly accomplished sculptor and a gifted ceremonial dancer and singer, known for his innovative carved and painted figures and tutini (Tiwi burial poles). When the first Tiwi art centre, Tiwi Pima Art was established in 1972 on Bathurst Island, Declan began to paint ceremonial regalia on bark. In the last decade of his life he was the face of Tiwi art, exhibiting widely and promoting his fellow Tiwi artists. In 1983 the collector Lord McAlpine of West Green commissioned an entire suite of his carvings that are now in the collection of the National Gallery of Australia, Canberra. He was the first Tiwi artist to have a retrospective exhibition in 1987 and his work was included in 'Aratjara: Art of the First Australians' at the Hayward Gallery, London, in 1993.

HOWARD ARKLEY (1951–1999)
Born Melbourne, 5 May 1951; travelled widely, including visits to Paris and New York, 1977–78; died Melbourne, 22 July 1999

Howard Arkley challenged the orthodoxy of Australian landscape painting during the late twentieth century, merging high and low art, and combining popular culture with the suburban home and garden. Rather than parodying the banality of suburbia, Arkley faced reality head-on, intensifying it (often with vibrant colour and a post-Pop sensibility) in his best-known airbrushed paintings of the 1990s. Born to a Jewish mother and a German father, he was impressed at an early age by Sidney Nolan's use of household enamel paints. He completed his studies at Prahran College of Advanced Education in 1975. His subjects include factories, cityscapes, masks and portraits. His extraordinary fifteen-panelled *Fabricated Rooms* (1997–99) was the centrepiece of his Venice Biennale exhibition in 1999, the year of his untimely death. A touring retrospective was organised by the National Gallery of Victoria, Melbourne, from 2006 to 2007. His work is held by the Metropolitan Museum of Art, New York.

WILLIAM BARAK (c. 1824–1903)
Woiworung people. Wurundjeri clan. Born Brushy Creek (present-day Croydon, Melbourne), Victoria, c. 1824; moved to Coranderrk Aboriginal Reserve, Victoria, 1863; died Coranderrk Aboriginal Reserve, Victoria, 15 August 1903

William Barak (also known as Beruk) was born prior to European settlement and saw the encroachment of non-Aboriginal populations onto his land. As a young boy he witnessed his father and other elders sign over their land in a treaty with the settler farmer John Batman. Yet he adjusted remarkably as a town (Melbourne) grew up around him. Barak became a prominent and articulate cultural leader and advocate in Victoria and always sought for justice and the recognition of Aboriginal rights for his people. He helped establish Coranderrk Aboriginal Reserve, which became a remarkable example of a self-sufficient community, including Aboriginal farming and various enterprises (hops, wheat and crafts). William Barak fought to keep his heritage and culture alive through political endeavours and also through his art. In 2003 the National Gallery of Victoria, Melbourne, mounted a retrospective exhibition, 'Remembering Barak', on the centenary of his death.

JOHN BEARD (b. 1943)
Born Aberdare, Wales, 24 October 1943; arrived Perth, 1983; travelled widely, 1986–96; moved to Sydney, 1997; lives in Sydney and London

John Beard is a contemporary Welsh-Australian artist who is concerned with the structures of representation. He studied at Swansea College of Art, Wales, from 1962 to 1965, the University of London, from 1965 to 1966, Middlesex University, London, in 1975, and the Royal College of Art, London, from 1979 to 1981. In 1968 he participated in the *Man Made* programmes on art and design for the BBC. He taught Art in England between 1966 and 1983 and, following his move to Perth, Western Australia, between 1983 and 1989. He had a ten-week artist-in-residency at Tate St Ives, Cornwall, in 1998. Since the mid-1990s his paintings have explored the fugitive nature of reality, including vastly larger-than-life portraits. He has exhibited widely in Britain and Australia, including at the Royal Academy Summer Exhibition, London, in 1981 and a survey exhibition was held at the Australian National University Drill Hall Gallery, Canberra, in 2009. His work is represented in numerous international collections, including Tate's.

LUDWIG BECKER (1808–1861)
Born Rödelheim, Germany, 5 September 1808; arrived Launceston, 1851; moved to Bendigo, 1852; moved to Melbourne, 1854; died Bulloo, Queensland, 29 April 1861

Ludwig Becker was an accomplished German-born colonial explorer, naturalist and geologist. His brothers included a top-ranking soldier and a well-known landscape painter. In 1828 Becker worked in lithography at Frankfurt. He spent almost two years in Tasmania, painting miniatures and landscapes before joining the gold rush in Victoria, where he was unsuccessful prospecting but made meteorological observations and sketches. After his move to Melbourne, he painted Romantic landscapes, small watercolours full of detail and human interest, and natural-history subjects. He was the artist on the ill-fated Burke and Wills expedition that attempted to traverse the Australian continent from south to north for the first time between 1860 and 1861. Some of Becker's finest works include small drawings and watercolours made on this tragic expedition, during which he perished.

CLARICE BECKETT (1887–1935)
Born Casterton, Victoria, 21 March 1887; died Sandringham, Victoria, 7 July 1935

Clarice Beckett created some of the most evocative, poetic Australian landscapes in the early twentieth century. Her subjects include Melbourne's urban and suburban environments: trams, cars, power poles, streets, beaches and bush. The daughter of a bank manager, she settled in the bayside suburb of Beaumaris, an area her father had chosen for retirement. In 1919 she studied with Max Meldrum, who advocated a tonal approach. Influenced by his teachings, she often painted outdoors in the early mornings or at dusk. She cared for ailing parents from the late 1920s, though she managed to continue painting. In 1935, frail and susceptible to the elements, she contracted pneumonia and died at the age of forty-eight. A memorial exhibition was held at the Athenaeum Gallery in Melbourne in 1936. In 1999 interest in Beckett's work was reignited with a touring survey, organised by the Ian Potter Museum of Art, University of Melbourne.

GORDON BENNETT (b. 1955)
Born Monto, Queensland, 9 October 1955; travelled extensively during the 1990s, including a visit to Hautvillers, France, as the recipient of the Moët & Chandon Australian Art Fellowship, 1991–92; lives and works in Brisbane

Gordon Bennett is an internationally acclaimed contemporary artist who, in much of his art, has been concerned with mapping alternative histories and rejecting racial stereotypes. He is the son of an Indigenous Australian mother and an Anglo-Celtic father, and worked for a time as a fitter and turner and an electrical linesman. He graduated from the Queensland College of Art, Brisbane, in 1988. Issues of identity, Australian colonial and postcolonial history, racism and social injustice informed his works of the 1990s. By the mid-1990s he created an alter ego, John Citizen, 'the Australian Everyman', signifying his distaste for typecasting. He has also responded to the 9/11 terrorist attacks in New York and referenced the Iraq War and issues of secrecy. A major international touring exhibition was organised by Ikon Gallery, Birmingham, in 1999 and began its tour at the Brisbane City Gallery and toured throughout 2000 to Ikon Gallery, Arnolfini, Bristol and Henie-Onstad Kunstsenter, Oslo. A major retrospective in 2007 was organised by the National Gallery of Victoria, Melbourne, touring to other major State galleries throughout Australia. More recently, Bennett received further international acclaim when he was selected for 'dOCUMENTA (13)', Kassel. A major retrospective exhibition at the AAMU, Museum of Contemporary Aboriginal Art, in Utrecht in 2012 further exposed Bennett's art practice to a European audience.

DORRIT BLACK (1891–1951)
Born Adelaide, 23 December 1891; travelled to Europe, 1927–29 and 1934–35; worked in Sydney, 1929–33; died Adelaide, 13 September 1951

Dorrit Black was a leading Australian modernist during the interwar years. The daughter of an engineer and architect, she studied under H. P. Gill in Adelaide around

1910 and with Julian Ashton at the Sydney Art School from 1915 to 1923. As a mature artist, she studied linocut in London with Claude Flight at the Grosvenor School of Modern Art in 1927, academic Cubism in Paris with André Lhote between 1927 and 1928 and with Albert Gleizes in 1929. She produced linocuts, using simplified geometric forms and bright colours, and on her return to Sydney fostered an interest in the colour linocut in Australia. She ran the Modern Art Centre, Sydney, from 1931 to 1933 and in 1935 moved to Adelaide, where she concentrated on painting in a modernist manner. She taught at the South Australian School of Arts and Crafts from 1940. A touring retrospective of her work was organised by the Art Gallery of South Australia, Adelaide, in 1975 and a book on her art, *The Art of Dorrit Black* by Ian North, was published in 1979.

BRIAN BLANCHFLOWER (b. 1939)
Born Brighton, East Sussex, 4 October 1939; moved to Perth, 1972; lives in Perth

Brian Blanchflower is a leading contemporary Western Australian artist, with an interest in cosmology. His contemplative paintings portray the constant flux and energy of nature. In the late 1950s he studied at Brighton College of Art and worked in Britain before moving to Australia in 1972. From 1972 to 1981 he taught Fine Art at Western Australian Institute of Technology, Curtin University (WAIT) and was artist-in-residence at AIR and SPACE studio in London between 1983 and 1984 and Pier Art Centre, Orkney, in 1984. Trips to south coast Western Australia and the salt-lake region north-east of Perth formed the basis for many works during the 1970s and 1980s. His work has become increasingly abstract. He uses the material presence of a painting to create an emotional force and an object for meditation. He has had numerous solo exhibitions, including surveys organised by the Art Gallery of Western Australia, Perth, in 1990 and the Lawrence Wilson Art Gallery, Perth, in 2010.

PETER BOOTH (b. 1940)
Born Sheffield, Yorkshire, 2 November 1940; moved to Melbourne, December 1957, aged seventeen; lives in Melbourne

Peter Booth first exhibited geometric abstract compositions, covered in lush black-and-red paintwork, under whose surfaces lay dreams and nightmares. His works reveal both a comical and an apocalyptic side: human/animal mutations are seen as part of universal evolution and recovery as well as punishment for destroying nature. Booth studied for two years at the Sheffield College of Art before he emigrated to Australia, where he graduated in 1965 from the National Gallery Art School, Melbourne. Showing many influences, including Goya's 'Black Paintings', to which his father had drawn his attention, and Neo-Expressionism, his work is in fact highly personal. It includes early childhood memories of fiery furnaces and bombings in wartime Sheffield, where his father was a steelworker, as well as hallucinatory images that emerged after a violent break-in in Melbourne in 1975, which caused Booth to develop epilepsy. He has produced numerous drawings, which are as significant as his paintings. His work was shown at the Australian Pavilion at the 1982 Venice Biennale and is held by the Metropolitan Museum of Art and the Museum of Modern Art in New York. He has had a number of solo exhibitions and a retrospective was organised by the National Gallery of Victoria, Melbourne, from 2003 to 2004.

G. W. BOT (b. 1954)
Born in Quetta, Pakistan, 12 December 1954; moved to Australia, 1956, aged two; lives in Canberra

G. W. Bot (the exhibiting name of Chrissie Grishin) is a contemporary Australian printmaker and sculptor who has created her own signs and glyphs to capture her close personal relationship with the landscape and gardens around Canberra. The daughter of an Australian army officer, she was educated in London, where she learnt to make linocuts. She studied Medieval English and History at the Australian National University, Canberra, between 1974 and 1982. Her artist's name derives from 'le grand Wam Bot', after the early French explorers' term for the wombat, which she has adopted as a totemic animal. She has held five solo exhibitions in London and a touring survey was organised by the Goulburn Regional Art Gallery from 2010 to 2013. Her work is held by the British Museum and the Victoria and Albert Museum in London and was included in the exhibition 'Out of Australia' at the British Museum in 2011.

ARTHUR BOYD (1920–1999)
Born Murrumbeena, Victoria, 24 July 1920; lived in London, 1959–71; lived between England and Australia, 1972–99; died Melbourne, 24 April 1999

Arthur Boyd made a highly significant contribution to Australian art in diverse media. Best known for expressive, psychologically intense images, he was most interested in the human condition and environmental and political issues. Son of the potter Merric Boyd and the painter Doris Boyd, he spent much of his adult life between Australia and England. His reputation in London emerged with his first retrospective at the Whitechapel Art Gallery in 1962, the same year that he created the set and costume designs for Elektra at the Royal Opera House, Covent Garden. In 1975 he presented a major gift of his art to the National Gallery of Australia, Canberra, and in 1993 gifted properties at Bundanon and Riversdale, New South Wales, to the Australian people. He represented Australia twice at the Venice Biennale (in 1958, with Arthur Streeton, and in 1988) and his work was included in exhibitions of Australian art in London at the Whitechapel Art Gallery (1961), the Tate Gallery (1963), the Victoria and Albert Museum (1972) and the British Museum (2011). It is held by the British Museum, Tate and the Victoria and Albert Museum in London. He has been the subject of several surveys and a touring retrospective was organised by the Art Gallery of New South Wales, Sydney, in 1993.

JOHN BRACK (1920–1999)
Born Melbourne, 10 May 1920; travelled to Europe and Mexico City, 1973; visited Europe, 1976; died Melbourne, 11 February 1999

John Brack's contribution to Australian art resides in his profound interest in modern life and the human condition. From a working-class background (his father worked in a brewery), he attended the National Gallery Art School, Melbourne, in the 1940s before and after serving in the Army. He was a generous, exemplary teacher and Head of the National Gallery Art School from 1962 to 1968. His crisply delineated images of people in everyday contexts are depicted with wry humour and insight. Brack also invested seemingly ordinary objects such as pens and pencils with life as active participants in allegorical paintings. While his art of the 1950s and 1960s began with his local environment, his later works concentrated on themes such as past civilisations, war, political difference and religious or philosophical beliefs. His work was included in Australian art exhibitions in London at the Whitechapel Art Gallery (1961), the Tate Gallery (1963) and the British Museum (2011). He has been the subject of several surveys and a touring retrospective was organised by the National Gallery of Victoria, Melbourne, in 2009.

OSWALD BRIERLY (1817–1894)
Born Chester, Cheshire, 19 May 1817; worked near Sydney, 1842–51 and 1868; died London, 14 December 1894

A noted British marine painter and the son of the amateur artist Dr Thomas Brierly, Oswald Brierly studied in London with Henry Sass, exhibited at the Royal Academy of Arts between 1839 and 1871 and regularly with the Society of Painters in Oil and Watercolours. Brierly sailed to Sydney on Ben Boyd's yacht *Wanderer*, and joined him in his whaling operations at Twofold Bay on the south coast of New South Wales. He also accompanied Captain Owen Stanley on his exploratory voyage in 1848 through northern Australian waters on HMS *Rattlesnake*. These adventures in Australian waters had a lasting effect on his art. The artist returned to England in 1851, but revisited Australia in 1868 on the *Galatea* during the Duke of Edinburgh's world cruise. Brierly was appointed as marine painter to Queen Victoria in 1874. His work is held by the British Museum, the Victoria and Albert Museum and the Royal Collection in London.

JACK BRITTEN (*c.* 1922–2002)
Gija people. Born Garndawarranginy (Alice Downs), Western Australia, *c.*1922; moved to Wurreranginy (Frog Hollow), Western Australia; died Eastern Kimberley, Western Australia, 2002

Jack Britten (Aboriginal name Warnngayirriny) was known for his paintings of Purnululu National Park or the Bungle Bungles, a spectacular range of sandstone canyons near Turkey Creek. As with most of his contemporaries in the Kimberley, Britten spent much of his adult life working as a stockman on a number of cattle stations in the region, allowing him access to his ancestral lands, and he continued to participate in ceremonies. He also spent time trapping dingoes and panning for gold. Britten began painting on canvas about 1987 and favoured the use of natural-earth pigments mixed with the dark-red gum of the bloodwood tree as a binder, although in the Ninth National Aboriginal Art Award in Darwin of 1992 he won in the section for Best Painting in a European Medium.

LOUIS BUVELOT (1814–1888)
Born Morges, Switzerland, 3 March 1814; worked in Bahia, Brazil, 1835–40; worked in Rio de Janeiro, Brazil, 1840–52; returned to Switzerland, 1852; arrived Melbourne, 1865, aged fifty-one; died Melbourne, 30 May 1888

Louis Buvelot was the leading landscape painter in Victoria during the 1870s, depicting rural landscapes that reflect an interest in tone and light. The son of a Swiss public official, he studied Art in Lausanne and Paris. After a period in Brazil, he arrived in Australia in 1865 as a mature and experienced artist and found fresh inspiration in the local landscape. Influenced by the French Barbizon tradition of outdoor painting, he made extensive sketching tours around Victoria and depicted the gentle landforms and settled, domesticated countryside. In contrast to the style of Eugene von Guérard and Nicholas Chevalier, his free handling of paint and his sense of being at home in the land inspired the young Melbourne painters, Tom Roberts, Frederick McCubbin and Arthur Streeton. His work is held by Tate and was included in the exhibition 'Australian Painting' at the Tate Gallery, London, in 1963. A retrospective of his work was held at the Bendigo Art Gallery, Victoria, in 1975.

NICHOLAS CAIRE (1837–1918)
Born Guernsey, Channel Islands, 28 February 1837; arrived Adelaide, 1858; moved to Victoria, 1870; died Melbourne, 13 February 1918

Nicholas Caire was the finest photographer of an Antipodean Arcady set in the temperate bushland of Victoria. The son of an agricultural labourer from Guernsey, he trained and worked as a photographer in Adelaide in the mid-1860s. In 1870 he relocated to Melbourne, where he found a lucrative market for his work from the tourists attracted by the rainforest scenery in the mountains to the east of the city. He was also deeply interested in the giant trees growing in Victoria's mountains, searching them out and photographing them during the 1880s and early twentieth century, when they were being progressively destroyed by logging, bushfires and storms. Reflecting the themes of contemporary painters, he photographed bush characters. He also photographed Aboriginal settlements, recording the mix of agricultural and traditional pursuits. His work is held in the Royal Collection in London. A touring survey of his work was organised by the Art Gallery of New South Wales, Sydney, from 1980 to 1981.

ROBERT CAMPBELL JNR (1944–1993)
Dhungutti people. Ngaku clan. Born Kempsey, New South Wales, 1944; died Kempsey, 13 July 1993

Robert Campbell Jnr belongs to a group of urban-based Aboriginal artists, including Trevor Nickolls (1949–2012) and Lin Onus (1948–1996), who emerged in the 1980s and are considered to be the resistance freedom fighters of Aboriginal art. They grew up in an environment where Aboriginal people were striving on a national platform for the recognition of their human rights and sovereignty over their traditional lands. Campbell's work reflects an Aboriginal perspective of Australian history and society. It tackles issues of racism, oppression, dispossession, massacres, deaths in police custody, alcohol and violence. Campbell left school at an early age and sought seasonal work. However, painting became his saving grace. Campbell's work has been shown in various exhibitions: 'Stories of Australian Art', at the Commonwealth Institute, London, and the Usher Art Gallery, Lincoln, in 1988; 'Tagari Lia', at the Third Eye Centre, Glasgow, in 1990; and 'Aratjara: Art of the First Australians' at the Hayward Gallery, London, in 1993.

ETHEL CARRICK (1872–1952)
Born Uxbridge, Middlesex, 7 February 1872; worked in Australia intermittently, 1908–52; died Melbourne, 17 June 1952

Working in a French Impressionist manner, British-born Ethel Carrick produced works celebrating a leisured and elegant way of life during the Edwardian period. She studied in London at the Guildhall School of Music and the Slade School of Fine Art from 1898 to 1899, and from 1902 to 1903. Between *c.*1904 and 1905 she worked in the artists' colony in St Ives, Cornwall, where she met the Australian painter E. Phillips Fox, whom she married in 1905. The couple then travelled widely from a base in Paris. Carrick exhibited at the Royal Academy of Arts, London, between 1907 and 1937 and was an associate of the Société Nationale des Beaux-Arts, Paris. Her work is characterised by broad brushstrokes and vibrant colours and depicts markets, parks and flower gardens, beaches, intimate views of families, women and children, and flower-pieces. A survey exhibition of her work and that of her husband was organised by the Queensland Art Gallery, Brisbane, in 2011.

JEFF CARTER (1928–2010)
Born Melbourne, 5 August 1928; died Berry, New South Wales, 25 October 2010

Jeff Carter produced often laconic and witty Australian images that have become emblematic of a way of life connecting the colonial and Indigenous past with post-war immigration. The son of a railway man, he was self-taught, and styled himself 'as photographer to the poor and unknown', particularly in the Australian rural heartlands, bush and desert outback regions, as well as in towns and beaches. His travel writing and photography career began in 1946. Numerous magazine stories, books and films followed in the 1960s and 1970s as he journeyed across Australia and Europe. He also made documentary films. From the 1990s he focused on retrospectives, monographs and films. A survey of his work was published by the State Library of New South Wales in 2005. His work was the subject of a documentary, *Inland Heart*, in 2010 and a major exhibition, 'Beach, Bush and Battlers', at the State Library of New South Wales in 2011, touring from 2012 to 2014.

HAROLD CAZNEAUX (1878–1953)
Born Harold Cazneau, Wellington, New Zealand, 30 March 1878; arrived Australia, *c.*1886, aged about eight; moved to Sydney, 1904; died Sydney, 19 June 1953

Harold Cazneaux was Australia's most renowned Pictorialist photographer, known for adapting the European movement's Impressionistic style to the characteristic beauty of Australian light, life and landscapes. The son of British photographers, he trained in the 1890s in Adelaide, where he was inspired by exhibitions of Pictorial photography. He moved to Sydney in 1904, held the first one-man photographic art exhibition in Australia in 1909, was a founder of the Sydney Camera Circle in 1916 and opened his own studio in 1919. Cazneaux was official photographer for the chic magazine *The Home* from 1920, which provided him scope for both his commercial and salon photography. He exhibited award-winning works overseas and was correspondent for the British *Photograms of the Year.* A survey exhibition was organised by the Art Gallery of New South Wales, Sydney, in 2008.

NICHOLAS CHEVALIER (1828–1902)
Born St Petersburg, Russia, 9 May 1828; moved to Lausanne, Switzerland, 1847; moved to London, 1851; lived in Italy, 1852–54; arrived Melbourne, 1854; visited New Zealand, 1865–66; returned to London, 1870; died London, 15 March 1902

During the second half of the nineteenth century Nicholas Chevalier depicted dramatic mountains and waterfalls and tranquil rivers, painted with meticulous detail. The son of a Swiss overseer of estates and his Russian wife, he studied Art in Lausanne, Munich and Rome. In 1851 he moved to London, where he worked as an illustrator, moving to Italy from 1852 for two years, and then to Australia from 1854 for six years. Between 1852 and 1895 he exhibited at the Royal Academy of Arts, London. He was stirred by the untamed Australian landscape and by the art of Eugene von Guérard, whom he accompanied on sketching treks into the wilderness. In 1869 he joined HMS *Galatea* as an artist with the Duke of Edinburgh and in 1874 he was commissioned by Queen Victoria to depict the marriage of the Duke. His work is held by the Victoria and Albert Museum and the Royal Collection in London. A travelling survey exhibition was organised by the Gippsland Art Gallery, Victoria, from 2011 to 2012.

CHARLES CONDER (1868–1909)
Born Tottenham, Middlesex, 24 October 1868; arrived Sydney, 1884, aged fifteen; moved to Melbourne, 1888; moved to Paris, 1890; moved to London, 1894; died Virginia Water, Surrey, 9 February 1909

Charles Conder was a prominent Impressionist and Symbolist painter in Australia during the late 1880s. In 1884 he was sent to Sydney by his engineer father to stay with his uncle. He attended painting classes with Alfred Daplyn and Julian Ashton from 1887 to 1888 and sketched landscapes outdoors in the Hawkesbury region of New South Wales and around Sydney's beaches. In late 1888 he moved to Melbourne, where he worked with Tom Roberts and Arthur Streeton. In 1889 he contributed to the famous '9 by 5 Impression Exhibition' in Melbourne. He returned to Europe in 1890, studied the nightlife of Paris and became a friend of Toulouse-Lautrec. There he studied at the Académie Julian and at Fernand Cormon's atelier. He painted many watercolours on silk and exquisite designs for fans that evoke the spirit of *fêtes galantes*. His work is held by the British Museum, Tate and Victoria and Albert Museum in London. It has been exhibited widely, including in the shows of Australian art in London at the Grafton Galleries (1898) and the Tate Gallery (1963) and in a touring retrospective organised by the Art Gallery of New South Wales, Sydney, in 2003.

DANIEL CROOKS (b. 1973)
Born Hastings, New Zealand, 31 January 1973; arrived Melbourne, 1994; lives in Melbourne

Daniel Crooks is a leading contemporary digital media artist and photographer who works with non-linear time structures, breaking up the flow of time and space. He was brought up in Auckland, where he studied Graphic Design at the Auckland Institute of Technology in 1994. He studied Animation at the Victorian College of the Arts School of Film and Television, Melbourne, in 1993, and was a resident artist at the Australia Council Studio, London, in 2005. Crooks taught at the Royal Melbourne Institute of Technology (RMIT) from 2001 to 2002, and worked as a motion graphic designer from 2002 to 2008 at the Australian Centre for the Moving Image, Melbourne, since 2004. Confronting yet captivating, his digital images stretch and distort the familiar urban world and landscape while questioning our perception of it. The Anne & Gordon Samstag Museum of Art, Adelaide, will hold a survey of his work in 2013.

ELISABETH CUMMINGS (b. 1934)
Born Brisbane, 3 June 1934; lived in Europe, 1959–68; travelled widely in Australia; moved to Wedderburn, New South Wales, 1990; lives in Wedderburn

The work of the contemporary artist Elisabeth Cummings is notable for its sensuous painterly touch, inspired by Pierre Bonnard and Ian Fairweather. From 1953 to 1957 she attended East Sydney Technical College. A travelling scholarship enabled her to travel in 1959 to Europe, where she lived for almost a decade, mainly in Italy and France. She studied with Oskar Kokoschka in Salzburg in 1961. She has travelled widely in Australia: to the Pilbara, Flinders Ranges and Arnhem Land, as well as to Currumbin in Queensland and northern New South Wales. A mud-brick and wood house in the Wedderburn bush south of Sydney has been her home since 1990, a respite from city life. Outdoor paintings are mostly studies for works painted in her studio, where she can take time to develop them in quiet contemplation. The S. H. Ervin Gallery, Sydney, organised a survey of her work in 2012.

NICI CUMPSTON (b. 1963)
Barkindji people. Born Adelaide, South Australia, 1963; lives in Adelaide

Nici Cumpston is a visual artist, curator and academic. Her photographic work captures the degradation of her people's country in the Lower Murray River region of South Australia. Cumpston's conceptual framework dates back to the time when she worked in the photographic department of the South Australian Police Force, where she was responsible for processing images of devastating scenarios. The black-and-white documentary nature and melancholic renditions of her landscape photographs are tenderly brought back to life through the gentle use of hand-colouring, a technique she mastered at the South Australian School of Art, Adelaide. Cumpston was selected for the second National Indigenous Art Triennial, 'unDisclosed', at the National Gallery of Australia, Canberra, in 2012.

RICHARD DAINTREE (1832–1878)
Born Hemingford Abbots, Huntingdonshire (now Cambridgeshire), 13 December 1832; arrived Victorian goldfields, 1852; moved to Melbourne, 1854; visited London, 1857; moved to Queensland, 1864; returned to London, 1871; died Beckenham, Kent, 20 June 1878

Richard Daintree was the first to understand the potential of photography to promote the Australian colonies overseas. The son of a British farmer, he worked as a prospector, then as an assistant geologist in the Victorian Geological Survey from 1852 to 1856, before further study at the Royal School of Mines Laboratory, London, where he learned wet-plate photography. Back in Melbourne in 1857, Daintree became a commercial photographer with French journalist Antoine Fauchery, publishing the first album of Australian views and portraits, entitled *Australia.* Daintree rejoined the Geological Survey in 1859, pioneering the use of photography in official reports and displays, as he did as the government geologist in North Queensland from 1868 to 1871. He showed his photographs in various international exhibitions in London from 1872 to 1876, while Agent-General for Queensland. The Daintree Rainforest in Queensland was named after him.

ROBERT DALE (1810–1853)
Born Winchester, Hampshire, November 1810; arrived Fremantle, Western Australia, 1829; returned to England, 1833; died Bath, Somerset, 20 July 1853

Lieutenant Robert Dale was an early nineteenth-century topographical draughtsman, explorer and soldier. He was posted to the Swan River Colony in Western Australia as an ensign with the British Army's 63rd Regiment of Foot and was seconded to assist Surveyor-General John Septimus Roe. He spent four years in the Survey Department, surveying, clearing roads and exploring. He was the first European explorer to cross the Darling Range in Western Australia and to see and describe the numbat. He was stationed at King Georges Sound in 1832, and his highly accurate drawings made from the summit of Mount Clarence near the present-day town of Albany were the basis of *The Panoramic View of King Georges Sound, Part of the Colony of Swan River*, printed and published in London in 1834 (cat. 54).

DAVID DAVIES (1864–1939)
Born Ballarat, Victoria, 21 May 1864; travelled to Europe, 1890–93; returned to Melbourne, 1893; moved to England, 1897; worked in Dieppe, 1908–32; died Looe, Cornwall, 26 March 1939

David Davies is known for his nocturnal Australian landscapes of the 1890s and for his early twentieth-century Dieppe watercolours. The son of a Welsh-born miner, he studied at the Ballarat School of Design and at the National Gallery Art School, Melbourne, from 1886 to 1890. In the late 1880s he painted restrained, low-toned works, capturing the effects of early evening light at Eaglemont. He studied at the Académie Julian in Paris from 1890 to 1891 and started to paint outdoors at St Ives between 1892 and 1893. On his return to England in 1897, he again worked in Cornwall, and then in Dieppe. He exhibited at the Royal Academy of Arts, London, from 1899 to 1906 and the Royal Institute of Painters in Oil Colours from 1919 to 1931, and his work was included in the exhibitions of Australian art in London at the Grafton Galleries (1898), Burlington House (1923) and the Tate Gallery (1963). A touring survey of his work was organised by the Art Gallery of Ballarat, Victoria, from 1984 to 1985.

ROY DE MAISTRE (1894–1968)
Born Bowral, New South Wales, 27 March 1894; visited Europe, 1923–26; moved to London, 1930; died London, 1 March 1968

Roy de Maistre was a leading exponent of early Modernism in Australia. The son of a pastoralist, he studied the viola and violin at the Conservatorium of Music and Art at the Royal Art Society of NSW with Antonio Dattilo-Rubbo in Sydney. From 1917 to 1919 he experimented, together with Roland Wakelin, with 'colour-music' and was one of the first Australian artists to paint abstracts, characterised by high-key colour, large areas of flat paint and simplified forms. In 1930 he left Australia for London. His friends included Francis Bacon, with whom he lived for a short time in the 1930s. From the 1930s onwards his paintings are generally figurative with a Cubist structure and, with his conversion to Roman Catholicism in 1951, he turned to religious subjects. He exhibited at the Royal Academy of Arts, London, from 1941 to 1967 and a retrospective was organised by the Whitechapel Art Gallery, London, in 1960. A project exhibition of his work was shown at the Art Gallery of New South Wales, Sydney, in 1976 and books on his life and work, *Roy de Maistre: The Australian Years 1894–1930*, were published in 1988 and *Roy de Maistre: The English Years 1930–1968* in 1995, both by Heather Johnson. His work is held by Tate and was included in the exhibitions of Australian art in London at the Whitechapel Art Gallery (1961) and the Tate Gallery (1963).

PETER DOMBROVSKIS (1945–1996)
Born Wiesbaden refugee camp, Germany, 2 March 1945; arrived Australia, 1950, aged five; moved to Hobart, 1951; died Western Arthur Range, Southwest Tasmania, 20 March 1996

The late twentieth-century photographer and photo publisher Peter Dombrovskis sought to reverence nature by revealing the strange almost prehistoric beauty of his Tasmanian homeland. Of Latvian parentage, Dombrovskis was raised by his mother in Hobart and taught himself photography. He was partially inspired not only by earlier colonial landscape painters and photographers, but also by Lithuanian–Australian conservationist and wilderness photographer Olegas Truchanas, who mentored him at the outset of his career in the 1960s in Tasmania and provided models for his high-quality publishing projects in the 1980s and 1990s. His bestselling book *Wild Rivers* (1983), with text by conservationist Dr Bob Brown, whom he had met in the late 1970s, was published at the height of Australia's largest environmental campaign.

RUSSELL DRYSDALE (1912–1981)
Born Bognor Regis, Sussex, 7 February 1912; visited North Queensland, 1919–21; migrated to Melbourne, 1923, aged eleven; visited Europe, 1932–34; returned to Melbourne, 1935; travelled to London and Paris, 1938–39; moved to Sydney, 1940; moved to Hardy's Bay, New South Wales, 1966; died Sydney, 29 June 1981

Russell Drysdale created an original vision of the Australian landscape during the 1940s and 1960s, portraying the emptiness and loneliness of the Australian outback and country townships. The son of an Anglo-Australian pastoralist, he studied with George Bell in Melbourne from 1935 to 1938 and travelled to London, where he attended Iain Macnab's Grosvenor School of Modern Art, and Paris between 1938 and 1939. He travelled numerous times to the interior of Australia, including a trip to record the drought devastation in south western New South Wales in 1944 and a journey through the north-west of Australia in 1958. His work was singled out by Kenneth Clark in 1949 as being among the most original in Australian art, and his exhibition at the Leicester Galleries, London, in 1950 convinced British critics that Australian artists had an original vision. In 1954 he represented Australia at the Venice Biennale. He continued to exhibit in London until 1972. His work is held by Tate in London, and the Metropolitan Museum of Art, New York, and was included in the exhibitions of Australian art in London at the Whitechapel Art Gallery (1961) and the Tate Gallery (1963). He has been the subject of several surveys and a touring retrospective was organised by the National Gallery of Victoria, Melbourne, in 1997.

MAX DUPAIN (1911–1992)
Born Sydney, 4 April 1911; died Sydney, 27 July 1992

Max Dupain was the first Australian photographer to turn from Pictorialist idealism to the formal design of Modernism in the mid-1930s, and later to the disruptive tableaux of Surrealism. His bold and intense images were a fusion of these influences. The son of an Australian pioneer of physical education, Dupain trained in Sydney with Cecil Bostock, established his own highly successful commercial studio and exhibiting career in 1934 and was a founder of the Contemporary Camera Groupe in 1937. From the late 1950s Dupain specialised in architectural work. His *Sunbaker* (1937; cat. 138) was not shown in public until a retrospective in 1975, which was followed five years later by another exhibition at the Art Gallery of New South Wales, Sydney. A survey of his work was held by the Art Gallery of New South Wales in 1992. His work is included in the collection of the Victoria and Albert Museum, London.

AUGUSTUS EARLE (1793–1838)
Born London, 1 June 1793; travelled widely; worked in Tasmania, 1825; worked in Sydney, 1825–28; worked in New Zealand, 1827–28; returned to London, 1830; died London, 10 December 1838

Augustus Earle, artist and traveller, was the most interesting artist working in New South Wales during the 1820s. The son of an American-born artist, he studied Art in the Neoclassical tradition with Benjamin West. He exhibited at the Royal Academy from 1806 to 1838, showing his *A Bivouac of Travellers in Australia in a Cabbage-Tree Forest, Day Break* in 1838. He was an adventurous artist and travelled widely, creating a significant record of the effects of European contact and colonisation in the Pacific. In Sydney he showed his versatility by painting landscapes and local genre subjects, sympathetic studies of Aborigines, portraits of colonial notables and was commissioned to undertake Neoclassical decorations. He also opened an art gallery and gave painting lessons. His work is held by the British Museum, the National Maritime Museum and the Royal Collection in London. A book on his art, *Augustus Earle, Travel Artist: Paintings and Drawings in the Rex Nan Kivell Collection, National Library of Australia* by Jocelyn Hackforth-Jones, was published in 1980.

G. W. EVANS (1780–1852)
Born London, 5 January 1780; worked in South Africa, 1798–1802; arrived Sydney, 1802; worked in Tasmania intermittently, 1812–17; moved to Tasmania, 1818–26; visited London, 1826–32; returned to Sydney, 1832; moved to Hobart, 1844; died Hobart, 16 October 1852

G. W. Evans was a competent early nineteenth-century surveyor, resolute explorer and accomplished landscape artist. The son of the Secretary to the Earl of Warwick, he served a short apprenticeship as an engineer and architect. He worked as a surveyor in New South Wales and Tasmania, and participated in an expedition with the first Europeans to cross the Great Dividing Range. For brief periods he farmed land in New South Wales and in Tasmania. After his return to Sydney in 1832, he set up as a bookseller and then became Drawing Master at the King's School, Parramatta, New South Wales, before settling in Hobart. His topographical views of Parramatta, Sydney Harbour and Hobart are some of the most interesting watercolours of the early settlements and newly explored territory in Australia.

IAN FAIRWEATHER (1891–1974)
Born at Bridge of Allan, Stirlingshire, Scotland, 29 September 1891; travelled extensively, living in England, Asia and Australia; lived on Bribie Island, Queensland, from 1953; died Brisbane, 20 May 1974

Ian Fairweather made a major contribution to Australian art with work that is characterised by a spiritual sensibility and calligraphic linearity. Over years of study during a peripatetic life he developed a profound connection with Asian culture. The son of a Surgeon-General posted to India six months after his birth, he lived with his aunts for the first ten years of his life. At eleven, following his father's retirement, the family moved to Jersey, where Fairweather developed a liking for islands and the solitary life. After studies at the Slade School of Fine Art in the early 1920s, serving in both the First and Second World War and travelling widely, he finally settled in 1953 on Bribie Island, where he painted consistently. For the next two decades he lived a spartan, relatively isolated existence, becoming an inspiration to many Australian artists. His work was included in the Australian art exhibitions in London at the Whitechapel Art Gallery (1961) and the Tate Gallery (1963). Touring retrospectives were organised by the Queensland Art Gallery, Brisbane, in 1965 and 1994.

ADRIAN FEINT (1894–1971)
Born Narrandera, New South Wales, 28 June 1894; died Sydney, 25 April 1971

Adrian Feint was a mid-twentieth-century Sydney painter and printmaker, best known for his bookplate designs. Many of his still-life and landscape paintings have affinities with Surrealism. He studied with Julian Ashton at the Sydney Art School both before and after serving in the Australian Imperial Force (AIF) in France and Belgium during the First World War. Known for his impeccable taste, Feint was co-director and manager of the Grosvenor Gallery, Sydney, from 1924 to 1928 and worked with the commercial art studio, Smith & Julius from 1928 to 1940, contributing many illustrations to *Art in Australia* and the magazine *The Home*. After the Second World War he took up flower painting, taking advice from Margaret Preston. An exhibition of his bookplates was held at the Library of Congress, Washington DC, in 1930 and a touring survey was organised by Carrick Hill, Adelaide, in 2009.

FIONA FOLEY (b. 1964)
Badtjala people. Wondunna clan. Born Maryborough, Queensland, 1964; lives in Brisbane, Queensland

Fiona Foley's people come from the world's largest sand island, Thoorgine (Fraser Island). Her interrogation of the historical record of black and white engagement on the Queensland frontier has revealed some harrowing stories of the colonial past. Foley belongs to the 'first wave' of urban-based Aboriginal artists. She studied at the Sydney College of the Arts, specialising in sculpture, and is one of the founding members of the first city-based Aboriginal artists' co-operative, Boomalli, established in Sydney in 1987. She works in several media, including photography, etching, digital media, installation and public art. Foley is also a curator, academic and writer. She has been awarded several international residencies. Her work has been displayed in many exhibitions, including: the landmark 'Koori Art '84' at Artspace, Sydney, in 1984; in 'Aratjara: Art of the First Australians' at the Hayward Gallery, London, in 1993; in 'In Place (Out of Time)', at the Museum of Modern Art, Oxford, in 1997; and in 'Continuity and Change: Cultural Dynamism in the Modern World', at the British Museum, London, in 2009.

E. C. FROME (1802–1890)
Born Gibraltar, 7 January 1802; arrived Adelaide, 1839; returned to England, 1849; died Ewell, Surrey, 12 February 1890

E. C. Frome was an amateur colonial watercolour painter, soldier, surveyor and explorer. The son of an English clergyman, he was orphaned early in life, and at the age of fifteen entered the Royal Military Academy, Woolwich. In 1825 he was commissioned into the Royal Engineers. As Surveyor-General of South Australia, he surveyed large areas of the colony, exploring and mapping new territory to the north as far as the Flinders Ranges, and easterly towards the Murray and south-east to Lake Alexandrina and the Coorong. He was the first European artist to record many of the more remote areas of South Australia, including the dramatically beautiful Flinders Ranges and the inland deserts. He captured the character of the landscape and its physical features in a graphic, direct style, showing the inherent beauty of the country.

ROSALIE GASCOIGNE (1917–1999)
Born Auckland, New Zealand, 25 January 1917; moved to Canberra, 1943; died Canberra, 23 October 1999

Rosalie Gascoigne's art was a unique form of assemblage sculpture, mostly to be hung on a wall or viewed on a table top or plinth, but some floor-based installations allowed even more variations in viewpoint. The materials were readymade, occasionally dried plant material, bones or feathers, but usually scavenged artefacts from local dumps and building sites, well-used and weathered, and hence as poetic of the Canberra region as the strange natural world that demanded intense scrutiny on her arrival from New Zealand. With a family background in engineering and teaching, the arts graduate and teacher of English was at first, after her marriage (to astronomer Ben Gascoigne), a restless housewife and mother in Australia. Her artistic flair emerged in the 1960s through her study of an avant-garde school of Ikebana. In 1974, at the age of fifty-seven, she held her first solo exhibition in Canberra. By the following year an exhibition of her work in Sydney brought wide acclaim, with the Australian art world recognising a remarkable, distinctive talent. In 1982 she represented Australia at the Venice Biennale. Her work can be found in numerous museums, including the Metropolitan Museum of Art, New York. Retrospectives were organised by the City Gallery Wellington in 2004 and the National Gallery of Victoria, Melbourne, from 2008 to 2009.

S. T. GILL (1818–1880)
Born Periton in the parish of Minehead, Somerset, 21 May 1818; arrived Adelaide, 1839; moved to Victoria; died Melbourne, 27 October 1880

S. T. Gill was an acute observer of daily life and the first artist to record and celebrate mining in colonial Australia. The son of a Baptist minister, teacher and amateur artist, he was educated in Plymouth and worked in London as a draughtsman and watercolour painter. In Adelaide he painted landscapes and city views and important events as well as depicting people, animals and houses and taking some of the first photographs. In over 40 years in Australia, he travelled extensively throughout South Australia, Victoria and New South Wales. In 1846 he accompanied John Horrocks's exploration party through the rugged Flinders Ranges as far north as Lake Dutton. Six years later he went to the goldfields in Victoria and became renowned for his goldfield images. He produced thousands of records of life in colonial Australia. His work was included in the exhibition 'Australian Painting' at the Tate Gallery in 1963. In 1986 the Art Gallery of South Australia, Adelaide, held a retrospective of his South Australian works.

SIMRYN GILL (b. 1959)
Born Singapore, 12 July 1959; moved to Kuala Lumpur; moved to Adelaide, 1987; moved to Sydney, 1996; lives in Sydney and Port Dickson, Malaysia

Simryn Gill is an Australian and Malaysian-based contemporary artist, who considers questions of place and history and how they might intersect with personal, cultural and collective experience. She was raised in Port Dickson, Malaysia, and educated in Jaipur, India and Britain. Gill works with a range of materials, including books, plant materials and other found objects, as well as photographs, drawing and installations. There is a strong sense of narrative in her work, in which she juxtaposes items in a different way, creating new possibilities and considering how we experience a sense of place, while often using humour as a mischievous device. The displacement of objects within her work echoes the journeys of people. Her work has been included in international exhibitions, including 'Face Up: Contemporary Art from Australia' at the Hamburger Bahnhof, Berlin, from 2003 to 2004, and a solo show at Tate Modern, London, in 2006 and the Smithsonian, Washington DC, from 2006 to 2007. An exhibition of her work was organised by the Queensland Art Gallery, Brisbane, in 2010 and she represented Australia at the Venice Biennale in 2013. Her works are held in the Tate collection.

SHAUN GLADWELL (b. 1972)
Born Sydney, 13 December 1972; worked in London, 2001–02; lives in Sydney and London

Shaun Gladwell is a leading contemporary artist who works in performance, painting and sculpture, but is best known for his video installations depicting improvised and choreographed performances, which he describes as 'performance landscapes'. Concerned with depicting bodies in motion – speed and gravity, bodies and machines – and with creating rhythmic and poetic imagery, he uses filmic devices such as slow motion and long pans to capture performances by breakdancers, skateboarders and BMX bike riders. The son of a soldier, he studied at the Sydney College of the Arts and the College of Fine Arts, University of New South Wales, and Goldsmiths College, University of London, under an Anne & Gordon Samstag International Visual Arts Scholarship between 2001 and 2002. In 2009 he represented Australia at the Venice Biennale and travelled to Afghanistan as an Australian Official War Artist.

JOHN GLOVER (1767–1849)
Born Houghton on the Hill, Leicestershire, 18 February 1767; arrived Hobart, 18 February 1831, aged sixty-four; died Deddington, Tasmania, 9 December 1849

John Glover was Australia's finest colonial artist in the 1830s and 1840s and one of the most significant landscape painters of his generation working outside Europe. The son of a farmer, he exhibited at the Royal Academy of Arts, London, between 1795 and 1812. A prolific watercolourist, he helped to promote the medium, becoming a founding member of the Society of Painters in Water Colours in 1804 and a founder of the Society of British Artists in 1823. Profoundly influenced by the art of Claude Lorrain, he was labelled an 'English Claude'. After a successful career in England, Glover emigrated at the age of sixty-four to Tasmania, where he found fresh inspiration in the local landscape. He painted images suffused with light, showing Australia as an Arcady and a land of plenty, and including depictions of Aboriginal people. His British work is held by the British Museum, the Courtauld Institute of Art, Tate, the Victoria and Albert Museum in London, the Metropolitan Museum of Art in New York and the National Gallery of Art in Washington DC, while his Australian work is represented in the Musée du Louvre in Paris. His work was included in the exhibition of Australian art in London at the Tate Gallery in 1963. Touring retrospectives were organised by Queen Victoria Museum and Art Gallery, Launceston, in 1977 and the Tasmanian Museum and Art Gallery, Hobart, from 2003 to 2004.

ELIOTH GRUNER (1882–1939)
Born Gisborne, New Zealand, 16 December 1882; arrived Sydney, 1883, under one year old; visited Europe, 1923–25; returned to Sydney, 1925; died Sydney, 17 October 1939

Elioth Gruner painted landscapes bathed in a gentle, subtle light during the early twentieth century. The son of a poor working family, he began his studies when he was about twelve years old with Julian Ashton in Sydney, where he met George W. Lambert, who inspired his painting. Based in Sydney, he made many painting excursions throughout New South Wales. He exhibited at the Royal Academy of Arts, London, in 1922. The following year he travelled to London, where he managed the Australian art exhibition at Burlington House, in which some of his work was included. On his return to Sydney after his travels he began to paint smaller pictures, thinning his paint to give the surface a drier and more pastel-like appearance, while presenting his subjects from above and using flatter forms. A retrospective was organised by the Art Gallery of New South Wales, Sydney, in 1983.

FIONA HALL (b. 1953)
Born Sydney, 14 November 1953; worked in London, 1976–78 and 1999; lived in Rochester, New York State, 1978–82; moved to Adelaide, 1983; visited India and Pakistan 1997; travelled to London, 1998; visited Sri Lanka, 1999; lives in Adelaide

One of Australia's most thought-provoking contemporary artists, Fiona Hall incorporates profound social and moral issues in her work, including the shared genetic ancestry of humans and plants and the nexus between botany and economics. Her mother, who studied physics and is thought to be the first woman radio astronomer, encouraged her daughter's artistic interests and inculcated an enduring intellectual curiosity in her. Hall studied at the East Sydney Technical College from 1972 to 1978, and in Rochester from 1978 to 1982, and taught Photo Studies at the South Australian School of Art from 1983 to 2002. Hall's reputation was confirmed with the *Paradisus Terrestris* series (1989–90). In 1999, on a residency in London, she regularly visited Kew Gardens, which had first inspired her in the 1970s. The National Gallery of Australia, Canberra, has a major outdoor work, *Fern Garden* (1998). Hall's first solo exhibition was at the Creative Camera Gallery, London, in 1977. Her work has since been included in many national and international exhibitions, including 'Face Up: Contemporary Art from Australia' at the Hamburger Bahnhof, Berlin, from 2003 to 2004, 'dOCUMENTA (13)' in Kassel in 2012, as well as touring surveys organised by the Queensland Art Gallery, Brisbane, in 2005 and the Museum of Contemporary Art, Sydney, in 2008.

EDMUND HENDERSON (1821–1896)

Born Mudeford, Christchurch, Dorset, 19 April 1821; arrived Perth, 1850; returned to England, 1863; died London, 8 December 1896

Topographical artist and engineer, Edmund Henderson arrived in Western Australia in 1850 with the first convicts in the position of Comptroller-General in charge of convicts. The son of a Vice-Admiral in the Royal Navy, he was educated at the Royal Military Academy, Woolwich. In Western Australia he was responsible for the construction of the convict prison, barracks and officers' quarters. The initial success of the convict system in Western Australia was largely due to his wise administration. A talented amateur artist, the finest in nineteenth-century Western Australia, Henderson painted atmospheric drawings and watercolours that express his response to the Western Australian landscape.

BILL HENSON (b. 1955)

Born Melbourne, 7 October 1955; lives in Melbourne

Bill Henson is one of Australia's most internationally acclaimed contemporary artists. He studied at the Prahran College of Advanced Education between 1974 and 1975, followed by self-education in the cities and museums of Europe during the 1980s. His first solo exhibitions at the National Galley of Victoria in Melbourne (1975) and the Photographers' Gallery in London (1981) revealed the dark romanticism of his work as a counter to the documentary photographic art then dominant. Henson characteristically works in series (untitled since 1984) of darkly illuminated tableaux of crowds, isolated figures and haunted adolescent faces, interiors and indeterminate urban spaces with echoes of a heroic past but suggestive of a modern melancholy in the human condition. His recent landscape works set at twilight in empty semi-industrial spaces, often in suburban Melbourne, are momento mori. Henson has had numerous exhibitions and represented Australia at the 1995 Venice Biennale. A touring survey of his work was organised by the Art Gallery of New South Wales, Sydney, in 2005.

HANS HEYSEN (1877–1968)

Born Hamburg, Germany, 8 October 1877; arrived Adelaide, 1884, aged seven; lived in Europe, 1899–1903; moved to Hahndorf, South Australia, 1908; died Mount Barker, South Australia, 2 July 1968

Hans Heysen is one of the best-loved Australian landscape painters, known for his Federation-period images of majestic gum trees, through which cattle or sheep move. Heysen emigrated to Australia when he was seven. He studied Art in Adelaide with James Ashton at the Norwood Art School from 1893 to 1898, under H. P. Gill at the South Australian School of Design in 1898, and in Paris at the Académie Julian, Académie Colarossi and Ecole des Beaux-Arts and later in Italy from 1899 to 1903. From 1904, after his return to Adelaide, he began to make the monumental Australian gum tree of the Adelaide Hills the heroic motif of his oils and watercolours. (Australian trees had been depicted by earlier artists, but Heysen was the first to pay homage to the grandeur of the Australian eucalypt and to capture the specifics of their individual species.) He exhibited with the Royal Academy of Arts, London, in 1922. In 1926 Heysen made the first of many trips to the Flinders Ranges, depicting the arid, strong forms and clear contours of the mountains. His work was included in the exhibitions of Australian art in London at the Grafton Galleries (1898) and Burlington House (1923) and is held by the British Museum and the Royal Collection. He exhibited widely and touring retrospectives were organised by the Art Gallery of South Australia, Adelaide, to mark his centenary in 1977 and from 2008 to 2009.

J. J. HILDER (1881–1916)

Born Toowoomba, Queensland, 23 July 1881; moved to Sydney, April 1904; died Sydney, 10 April 1916

J. J. Hilder was the principal Sydney watercolour painter during Australia's Federation period. He worked in a bank and painted in his free time. He studied Art in Sydney with Julian Ashton from *c.*1904 to 1907. In 1906 Hilder was diagnosed with tuberculosis, and, with seriously declining health, resigned his position in the bank in 1909. His watercolour cityscapes, bush scenes and seascapes have a sense of light-filled harmony. He had a remarkable ability with watercolour wash, creating large areas of vibrating colour. In 1916 the monograph *J. J. Hilder: Water-colourist* was one of the first significant art books to be published in Australia. Hilder's work was included in the exhibition of Australian art in London at Burlington House in 1923. A survey exhibition was organised by the Queensland Art Gallery, Brisbane, in 1966.

PADDY JAMINJI (c.1912–1996)

Gija people. Born Bedford Downs, Western Australia, *c.*1912; moved to Warmun (Turkey Creek), Western Australia, 1975; died Wyndham, Western Australia, 1996

Paddy Jaminji (also known as Jampijin) was the first artist to paint the boards carried in the Kurirr Kurirr ceremony about the cyclone that destroyed Darwin in 1974. Jaminji played a seminal role in the development of the Eastern Kimberley painting movement throughout the 1980s. He was raised on Bedford Downs cattle station on his ancestral lands in the Eastern Kimberley, where he spent most of his life as a cattle drover. His paintings, featuring surfaces of textured natural pigments, reflect a desire to preserve the conservative aspects of his Gija culture in the face of great social and cultural change. His work was included in the exhibition 'Aratjara: Art of the First Australians' at the Hayward Gallery, London, in 1993.

PADDY JAPALJARRI SIMS (c.1917–2010)

Warlpiri people. Born Kunajarrayi (Mount Nicker), Northern Territory, *c.*1917; died Yuendumu, Northern Territory, 2010

Paddy Japaljarri Sims is regarded as the doyen of the modern painting movement at Yuendumu, where he lived since the settlement was built in 1947. He was one of the senior Warlpiri artists to paint the doors of the school at Yuendumu with traditional Dreaming designs in 1983, and was instrumental in establishing the local art collective, Warlukurlangu Artists, in 1986. In 1989 Sims led a group of Warlpiri artists to create a sand mosaic, *Yarla*, in the exhibition 'Magiciens de la Terre' at the Centre Georges Pompidou and the Grande Halle de la Villette, Paris. His work has featured in major exhibitions in Australia and abroad, including 'Dreaming the World' at St Mungo Museum of Religious Life and Art, Glasgow, in 1993 and 'Aratjara: Art of the First Australians' at the Hayward Gallery, London, in 1993.

TIM JOHNSON (b. 1947)

Born Sydney, 1 September 1947; visited India and South East Asia, 1974–75; visited Alice Springs, Papunya and Kintore, 1980s; lives in Sydney

Central to the practice of contemporary artist Tim Johnson is a personal, meditative search and an interest in cross-cultural collaboration, revealed in shimmering landscapes of association. The son of a professor of architecture, he studied at the University of New South Wales and the University of Sydney between 1966 and 1970. In the early 1970s he co-founded the artist-run co-operative Inhibodress and experimented in diverse media. After returning to painting, he started to take a deep interest in Aboriginal and Buddhist art and philosophies. In the 1980s he visited Aboriginal artists at Papunya and collaborated with Clifford Possum Tjapaltjarri and Michael Nelson Tjakamarra. He has also worked with Tibetan and Vietnamese artists. His work has been exhibited nationally and internationally, including a solo exhibition in Glasgow in 1994. A touring retrospective was organised by the Art Gallery of New South Wales, Sydney, and the Queensland Art Gallery, Brisbane, in 2009.

H.J. JOHNSTONE (1835–1907)

Born Birmingham, West Midlands, 1835; arrived Melbourne, 1853; returned to England, late 1870s; died London, 1907

H. J. Johnstone was a popular nineteenth-century painter and professional photographer. The son of a photographer, he studied at the Birmingham School of Design and later worked with his father. In 1853 he travelled to the Victorian goldfields, but, after prospecting unsuccessfully, he became part-owner of Melbourne's most fashionable photographic studio. He attended the National Gallery Art School, Melbourne, in 1870 and took private lessons with Louis Buvelot. A prolific and conservative artist, he continued to produce Australian landscapes from his photographs after he left Australia in the late 1870s. Majestic river red gum trees glowing in the light of early morning or evening dominate his landscapes, sometimes populated by Aboriginal figures. He became a member of the Royal Society of British Artists in London from 1886 and exhibited with the Royal Academy of Arts, London, between 1881 and 1900. His *Evening Shadows, Backwater of the Murray, South Australia* (1880; cat. 90) was the first work of art that the Art Gallery of South Australia, Adelaide, acquired.

LARRY JUNGURRAYI SPENCER (c.1919–1990)

Warlpiri people. Born Yirripirlangu, Northern Territory, *c.*1919; died Yuendumu, Northern Territory, 1990

Larry Jungurrayi Spencer had a brief artistic career in the public sphere. From 1953 to 1954 he was one of several Warlpiri artists who made crayon drawings at the request of the American anthropologist Mervyn Meggitt at Lajamanu (Hooker Creek), Northern Territory. His main subjects are Ngalyipi Jukurrpa (Snake Vine Dreaming) and Ngarrka Jukurrpa (Initiated Men Dreaming). In 1983 Spencer was one of five Warlpiri artists to paint the doors of the school at Yuendumu with traditional Dreaming designs.

PADDY JUPURRURLA NELSON (c.1920–1999)

Warlpiri people. Born Napanangkajarra, Northern Territory, *c.*1920; died Yuendumu, Northern Territory, 1999

Paddy Jupurrurla Nelson was one of five senior Warlpiri artists to paint the doors of the school at Yuendumu with traditional Dreaming designs in 1983. The *Yuendumu Doors* acted as a catalyst for the establishment of a modern painting movement in the community. The American anthropologist Mervyn Meggitt had collected crayon drawings by Nelson and other Warlpiri artists at Lajamanu (Hooker Creek) from 1953 to 1954. Nelson's work has featured in a number of international exhibitions, including 'Art & Aboriginality' at Aspex Gallery, Portsmouth, in 1987, and 'Dreamings' at the Asia Society Galleries, New York, in 1988. Nelson was one of five Warlpiri artists to create a sand mosaic, *Yarla*, in the exhibition 'Magiciens de la Terre' held at the Centre Georges Pompidou and the Grande Halle de la Villette, Paris, in 1989.

MIRDIDINGKINGATHI JUWARNDA (SALLY GABORI) (b.c.1924)

Kaiadilt people. Born Bentinck Island, South Wellesley Island group, Gulf of Carpentaria, Queensland, *c.*1924; removed by government officials to Mornington Island, South Wellesley Island group, 1948; returned to her Bentinck Island homelands, 1980s

Mirdidingkingathi Juwarnda (also commonly known as Sally Gabori) is a senior woman of the Kaiadilt people, Bentinck Island. She is widely recognised for her bold and confident paintings and colourful articulations of her country. In her youth she learnt the traditions of her Kaiadilt people, including the cultural significant of particular Dreaming sites, and has long been an accomplished producer of women's traditional craft, both in wood and natural fibres. In 2005, as part of a workshop at the Mornington Island Art centre, she began to paint powerful and emotive renditions of her sacred country. In less than a decade she has become an acclaimed artist whose work appears in many national and international exhibitions, including the second National Indigenous Art Triennial, 'unDisclosed', at the National Gallery of Australia, Canberra, in 2012.

EMILY KAME KNGWARREYE (c. 1910–1996)
Anmatyerr people. Born Alhalker, Utopia Station, Northern Territory, *c.*1910; died Alice Springs, Northern Territory, 2 September 1996

Emily Kame Kngwarreye first painted on canvas in 1988 and quickly rose to prominence as one of Australia's most renowned and prolific painters of the late twentieth century. The constant theme of her art is the country of her birth, Alhalker. She spent most of her working life on cattle stations but learnt very little English, preferring to speak her native tongue, Anmatyerr. Kngwarreye was a respected ceremonial leader throughout her life. She was a founding member of the Utopia Women's Batik Group in 1977. Retrospective exhibitions of her work toured Australia in 1998, and to Japan in 2008. She was awarded an Australian Artists' Creative Fellowship in 1992 in recognition of her contribution to the cultural heritage of the nation, and she represented Australia posthumously at the Venice Biennale in 1997.

ROSEMARY LAING (b. 1959)
Born Brisbane, 16 August 1959; moved to Hobart, 1982; moved to Sydney, 1990; lives in Sydney

Rosemary Laing is a sophisticated contemporary Conceptual artist producing intriguing, dramatic large-scale colour photo-media works, mostly of installations and performances in the Australian landscape. She trained at the College of Advanced Education, Brisbane, and the colleges of art in the Universities of Tasmania, Sydney and New South Wales from 1979 to 1996. Since the late 1980s Laing has made photo series, testing out points of interface between technology and nature, politics and philosophy. Her *groundspeed* series presented deceptively innocent images of floral carpet painstakingly laid on the Australian forest floor. Most recently she has photographed suburban house-frames inverted into pastoral hillocks. Her work is held in various international collections, and she has been included in international exhibitions, including 'Face Up: Contemporary Art from Australia' at the Hamburger Bahnhof, Berlin, from 2003 to 2004 and the Venice Biennale in 2007. Surveys of her work were organised by the Australian Centre for Photography, Sydney, in 2000 and the Museum of Contemporary Art, Sydney, in 2005.

GEORGE W. LAMBERT (1873–1930)
Born St Petersburg, 13 September 1873; moved to Württemberg, Germany, 1875; moved to Yeovil, Somerset, 1881; arrived Sydney, 1887, aged thirteen; worked in Europe, 1900–21 (London, 1902); died Sydney, 29 May 1930

George W. Lambert ARA was one of Australia's most capable portrait painters, war artists and sculptors of the early twentieth century, with considerable finesse and wit. The posthumous son of an American railway engineer working in Russia, he studied Art in Sydney with Julian Ashton from 1894 to 1900. In his early paintings he expressed a nationalist sentiment, but his principal work was in portraiture, painted with bravura. During the First World War he served as an Australian Official War Artist, and produced a group of desert landscapes with strong forms creating rhythmical patterns. In the 1920s he completed several significant sculpture commissions and major war paintings. He exhibited at the Royal Academy of Arts, London, from 1904 to 1930, was elected an Associate of the Royal Academy in 1922, and his work was included in a commemorative exhibition of late members in 1933, as well as in the exhibitions of Australian art in London at the Grafton Galleries (1898) and Burlington House (1923). His work is held by the National Portrait Gallery, London. He has been the subject of several surveys, and a retrospective was organised by the National Gallery of Australia, Canberra, in 2007.

TIM LEURA TJAPALTJARRI (c. 1929–1984)
Anmatyerr people. Born Laramba (Napperby Creek), Northern Territory, *c.*1929; died Alice Springs, Northern Territory, 1984

Tim Leura Tjapaltjarri was a prolific artist known for creating atmospheric pictures by applying paint onto a wet ground, and for the calligraphic quality of his brushstrokes. He was a nephew of Albert Namatjira, and a cousin of Clifford Possum Tjapaltjarri, with whom he collaborated on several major canvases. Like Clifford, Tim was a master woodcarver who had produced paintings for sale before the Papunya painting movement began in 1971. Leura spent many of his adult years working as a stockman until injury forced him to retire. In the last years of his life Leura lamented the dispossession of Aboriginal people and the degradation of the environment in a series of brooding, melancholy paintings dominated by washes of sombre colour. His work has been shown in major exhibitions, including 'Aratjara: Art of the First Australians' at the Hayward Gallery, London, in 1993.

JOHN LEWIN (1770–1819)
Born London, 29 March 1770; arrived Sydney, 1800; lived at Parramatta, 1800–08; died Sydney, 27 August 1819

John Lewin, Australia's first free-settler professional artist, was an acute observer of the Australian landscape, vegetation and light, capturing the nature of both pastoral landscapes and wilderness. The son of a natural-history artist, he was trained by his father in London. In New South Wales he painted and etched images of native birds and animals, insects, fish, as well as portraits of the Aboriginal people and settlers. In 1801 his etchings for a publication on birds were the first documented printing of images in the colony. He published *Prodomus Entomology: Natural History of Lepidopterous Insects of New South Wales* in 1805, while his *Birds of New South Wales* (a first edition was published in Britain in 1808) became the first illustrated book to be published in Australia in 1813. He participated in several expeditions, including one with Governor Macquarie across the Blue Mountains in 1815. He was an Associate of the Linnean Society of London and his work is held by the British Library, the British Museum, the Linnean Society and the Natural History Museum in London. A touring retrospective was organised by the State Library of New South Wales, Sydney, in 2012.

JAMES W. R. LINTON (1869–1947)
Born London, 14 June 1869; arrived Perth, 1896; visited London, 1907–08; died Perth, 29 August 1947

Painter, craftsman and teacher, James W. R. Linton was the foremost Western Australian artist and teacher of the early twentieth century, who had a prolonged influence on the visual arts in Perth. The son of the English watercolourist, James Dromgole Linton, he studied Art in London at the Slade School of Fine Art from 1885 to 1888, at Westminster School from 1891 to 1892 and Metalwork at the Sir John Cass Technical Institute from 1907 to 1908. He exhibited in London at the Royal Institute of Painters in Water Colours from 1890 to 1903 and the Royal Institute of Oil Painters from 1890 to 1909. After working on the Western Australian goldfields, he settled in Perth and taught at the Linton School of Art, which he had founded, from 1899 to 1938, at Perth Technical School from 1902 to 1931, and at the University of Western Australia from 1927 to 1932. In his paintings he was principally interested in depicting nature defined by light, applying the colour in small dabs over a densely worked surface. He painted many landscapes of his property at Parkerville, in which he often dramatically divided the composition into light and shade, and used colour contrasts of rust against green. A book on his art, *Line, Light and Shadow: James W. R. Linton, Painter, Craftsman, Teacher* was published in 1986.

SYDNEY LONG (1871–1955)
Born Goulburn, New South Wales, 20 August 1871; moved to Sydney, *c.*1888; worked in London, 1910–21; returned to Sydney, 1921–22; stayed in London, 1922–24; returned to Sydney, 1925; returned to London, 1951; died London, 23 January 1955

Australia's foremost Art Nouveau painter and a major Symbolist, Sydney Long was a significant watercolourist and painter-etcher at the turn of the twentieth century. The putative posthumous son of an Irish commission agent, Long studied Art with Julian Ashton in Sydney between 1892 and 1900, and at the South London School of Technical Art from 1913 to 1914 and the Central School of Arts and Crafts, London, from 1918 to 1921. Long's Art Nouveau paintings capture the spirit of the Australian bush. In 1905 he published an article, 'The Trend of Australian Art Considered and Discussed'. He exhibited at the Royal Academy of Arts, London, from 1913 to 1928 and was elected an Associate of the Royal Society of Painter-Etchers and Engravers, London, in 1921. His work was included in the exhibition of Australian art in London at the Grafton Galleries in 1898 and '1900: Art at the Crossroads' at the Royal Academy in London in 2000. His etchings are held in London by the British Museum, the Victoria and Albert Museum and the Royal Collection. A retrospective was organised by the National Gallery of Australia, Canberra, in 2012.

JOSEPH LYCETT (1774–1828)
Born Staffordshire, 1774; arrived Sydney, 1814; returned to London, 1823; died Birmingham, West Midlands, February 1828

Joseph Lycett was a convict artist, best known for his images of the settlement's progress. Transported to New South Wales for forgery, where he repeated his original offence, he was sent to the penal colony of Newcastle, where he attracted the patronage of Captain James Wallis. He painted watercolours of the Aboriginal (Awabakal) people, a few distinctive oil paintings, botanical studies and decorated two collector's chests. After his return to London, he made a series of aquatints based on his watercolours, showing the Australian landscape as a fertile land. In Britain he again forged notes and, on being arrested, cut his throat, and died from an infection. His work is held by the National Maritime Museum, London. A touring retrospective was organised by the Museum of Sydney from 2006 to 2007.

FREDERICK MCCUBBIN (1855–1917)
Born Melbourne, 25 February 1855; visited Europe, 1907; died Melbourne, 20 December 1917

Prominent Australian Impressionist and outstanding Federation-period painter, Frederick McCubbin is noted for his narrative images of pioneers and for his Impressionist landscapes. The son of a baker, he studied at the National Gallery Art School, Melbourne, between 1872 and 1886 and became an associate of Tom Roberts, Arthur Streeton and Walter Withers. After his only trip to Europe in 1907, he produced his most brilliant works, sparkling Impressionist landscapes. From 1886 to 1917 McCubbin was Drawing Master at the National Gallery Art School, where he had a prolonged influence. In 1916 the monograph *The Art of Frederick McCubbin* was one of the first significant art books to be published in Australia. His work was included in the exhibitions of Australian art in London at the Grafton Galleries (1898), Burlington House (1923) and the Tate Gallery (1963). He has been the subject of several surveys, including touring retrospectives organised by the National Gallery of Victoria, Melbourne, in 1991 and the National Gallery of Australia, Canberra, from 2009 to 2010.

QUEENIE MCKENZIE (c. 1912–1998)
Gija people. Born Old Texas Downs Station, Western Australia, *c.*1912; moved to Warmun (Turkey Creek), Western Australia, mid-1970s; died Warmun, 1998

Queenie McKenzie (also known as Nakarra) was born of an Aboriginal mother and a white father. As a young child, she was rescued by her mother from adoption, a policy enforced by the state for such children. McKenzie worked as a camp cook on cattle stations, where she befriended Rover Thomas. In about 1950 she saved his life after he had been thrown from a horse. McKenzie was the first woman to join the Eastern Kimberley painting movement initiated by Paddy Jaminji and Thomas. Her paintings are characterised by a palette that includes pink and violet ochres that she mined herself. The government of Western Australia declared her a State Living Treasure in 1998.

ROBERT MACPHERSON (b.1937)
Born Brisbane, 14 February 1937; childhood in Nambour, Queensland; moved to Brisbane 1949, aged twelve; lives in Brisbane

Robert MacPherson is a proud autodidact, focused on the processes of making and understanding. His father worked on a farm and Robert, on leaving convent school at fourteen, similarly worked with cattle, then sugar cane, until, at the age of twenty-one, he decided to become an artist. Making a living from painting ships at the Brisbane docks, he read about art at the public library and, by the mid-1960s, was experimenting with American-style colour field abstraction. In 1973, aged thirty-six, he eventually exhibited his work and was immediately perceived as a leading practitioner of Conceptual Art, formalist but satirical. His work is characterised by serial images and permutation of form, a look of ease and a celebration of the languages and concerns of small communities. His paintings, installations and prolific drawings all celebrate the poetic beauty of simple materials, gestures and ideas, especially those found among the working classes. His work has been included in international exhibitions, including 'Face Up: Contemporary Art from Australia' at the Hamburger Bahnhof, Berlin, from 2003 to 2004. A touring retrospective was organised by the Art Gallery of Western Australia, Perth, in 2001.

KENNETH MACQUEEN (1897–1960)
Born Ballarat, Victoria, 8 April 1897; moved to Brisbane, 1909; lived in Europe, 1916–19; died Millmerran, Queensland, 21 June 1960

Kenneth Macqueen was a significant Queensland modernist, a distinctive landscape watercolourist who adopted a modernist approach in which rhythm, shape and colour play a dominant role. The son of a Presbyterian clergyman, he served in the Australian Imperial Force (AIF) during the First World War and after the war studied Art in London and night classes at the Westminster School of Art under Bernard Meninsky and later full-time study at the Slade School of Fine Art with Henry Tonks. After the war he worked on sheep stations in New South Wales, and in 1922 settled on a property near Millmerran, Queensland, where he divided his time between farming and landscape painting in watercolour. His watercolours reflect a close observation of the landscape he farmed and painted. He exhibited at the Royal Academy of Arts, London, in 1931 and his work is held by the Metropolitan Museum of Art, New York. A retrospective was organised by the Queensland Art Gallery, Brisbane, from 2007 to 2008.

TOMMY McRAE (c.1842–1901)
Kwatkwat people. Born Albury, Victoria, *c.*1842; lived and worked around the Wahgunyah region, upper Murray River, Victoria; died Wahgunyah, 15 October 1901

Tommy McRae or Yackaduna (also known as Tommy Barnes) lived at a time when Aboriginal people suffered the full impact of colonial settlement and yet he remained strong and forthright in his culture and beliefs. He spent his adult life engaging with non-Indigenous people and worked as a stockman and drover. In his retirement he turned to illustrating the sights he had seen in his lifetime. His artistic capacity was recognised at a local level and he made a good living from commissions from many settlers to produce his unique ink and pencil sketches. For the last two decades of his life he filled copious numbers of sketchbooks with his drawings. Five of McRae's drawings were exhibited at the Chicago World's Fair in 1893, and three in the exhibition 'Art of Australia 1788–1941' that toured North America in 1941.

BEA MADDOCK (b.1934)
Born Hobart, Tasmania, 13 September 1934; studied in England and Italy, 1959–61; moved to Launceston, Tasmania, 1962; worked in Melbourne, 1970–83; returned to Launceston, 1983; lives in Launceston

Bea Maddock is one of Australia's finest contemporary printmakers, and is also a significant painter, notably of multi-panel panoramic landscapes. The daughter of an Anglican country parson, after studying painting in Hobart, she turned to printmaking in London, while a student at the Slade School of Fine Art, from 1959 to 1961. Reversals of dark and light, mirror-imaging and highly simplified linear designs are characteristic of her highly serious art, which has recently explored post-colonial Indigenous presence in her own place of birth. The British Museum, London, and the Museum of Modern Art, New York, hold examples of her prints and drawings. In 1982 an embossed-paper mural of solemn words and photo-based images was installed in a new building for the High Court of Australia, Canberra. In 1991 the National Gallery of Australia, Canberra, presented a retrospective of her prints, drawings and paintings and in 2013 the National Gallery of Victoria, Melbourne, organised a survey exhibition. Her work was included in exhibitions of Australian art in London at the Victoria and Albert Museum (1972) and the British Museum (2011).

NANDABITTA MAMINYAMANDJA (c.1911–1981)
Anindilyakwa people. Born Groote Eylandt, Northern Territory, *c.*1911; died Groote Eylandt, 1981

Nandabitta Maminyamandja was born before a Christian mission was established on Groote Eylandt in 1921 at the time the anthropologist Norman Tindale first collected bark paintings from the area. Nandabitta's painting style is characteristic of the art of the Anindilyakwa people; it relates to the rich array of figurative rock paintings dating back approximately 2,700 years found across the islands, and his paintings have a ground of black manganese, of which there are large deposits on the island. His subjects include ancestral narratives about the creation of features of the land by the ancestral Sawfish, Manta Ray and Shovel-nosed Shark. A prolific painter, he is also known for his paintings of historical events, such as the annual seasonal visits by the Macassan fishing fleets from Sulawesi, Indonesia, that date back to the 1700s.

DJAMBAWA MARAWILI (b.1953)
Madarrpa clan. Born north-east Arnhem Land, Northern Territory, 1953; lives at Yilpara, north-east Arnhem Land

Djambawa Marawili AM is a cultural activist, Madarrpa clan leader and chairman of several Aboriginal organisations. He was taught to paint by his father, Wakuthi Marawili (1921–2005), and his uncle, the celebrated painter Narritjin Maymuru (*c.* 1914–1981). He was one of seven Aboriginal artists who presented the Barunga Statement to the Prime Minister of Australia, Bob Hawke, in 1988. Djambawa won the Telstra National Aboriginal and Torres Strait Islander Art Bark Painting Award in 1996. In 2006 he was a recipient of the Member of the Order of Australia in 2006, and was instrumental in the Australian High Court's landmark decision to grant Australian Indigenous Sea Rights in 2008. His work featured in 'Tagari Lia' at the Third Eye Centre, Glasgow, in 1990, the Biennales of Sydney in 2006 and 2010, and the 3rd Moscow Biennale of Contemporary Art in 2009.

MAWALAN MARIKA (c.1908–1967)
Rirratjingu people. Born north-east Arnhem Land, Northern Territory, *c.*1908; moved to Yirrkala, north-east Arnhem Land, 1935; died Darwin, Northern Territory, 1967

Mawalan Marika was the senior Rirratjingu clan leader who negotiated the establishment of the Methodist Mission at Yirrkala in 1935. A great visionary, he advocated the need to teach the newcomers about the strength and profundity of Aboriginal culture, especially through art. Mawalan was a prolific and innovative artist and worked closely with anthropologists and collectors, including Donald Thomson, Ronald and Catherine Berndt, and Tony Tuckson. He was instrumental in fighting for the recognition o Aboriginal land rights and was a signatory to the Aboriginal Bark Petition presented to the Commonwealth government in 1963. He also participated in the Yirrkala Church Panel paintings. In the 1960s Mawalan was the first man to teach his daughters to paint sacred clan designs. His work has been included in several international exhibitions, such as: 'Australian Aboriginal Bark Paintings 1912–1964', Commonwealth Arts Festival, Walker Art Gallery, Liverpool, in 1965; 'Dreamings' at the Asia Society Galleries, New York, in 1988; and 'Aratjara: Art of the First Australians' at the Hayward Gallery, London, in 1993.

CONRAD MARTENS (1801–1878)
Born London, 21 March 1801; arrived Sydney, 1835; died Sydney, 21 August 1878

After his arrival in Sydney in 1835, Conrad Martens was the leading landscape artist in New South Wales for over 40 years. The son of a merchant and Austrian Consul to London, he studied watercolour painting in London under Anthony Vandyke Copley Fielding. Before he was resident in Sydney, he was employed on the scientific voyage of the *Beagle* to the Southern Hemisphere with Charles Darwin. Not intending to stay in Australia, he was enchanted by the picturesque and prosperous seaport city and almost immediately received strong patronage to depict Sydney Harbour views and pastoral homesteads. His earliest watercolours of Sydney are full of light and atmosphere. By the 1850s Martens's watercolours became distinctly Turneresque, often depicting the changing weather and the time of day. His work is held by the British Museum, London, and the Metropolitan Museum of Art, New York, and was included in the exhibition of Australian art in London at the Tate Gallery in 1963. A survey of his work, *Conrad Martens: Life and Art* by Elizabeth Ellis, was published by the State Library of New South Wales, Sydney, in 1994.

JOHN MAWURNDJUL (b.1952)
Kuninjku people. Kurulk clan. Born Mumeka, central Arnhem Land, Northern Territory, 1952; moved to Milmilngkan outstation, central Arnhem Land, 1980s

John Mawurndjul is one of Australia's most renowned artists on the world stage, yet he lives a traditional life in the Tomkinson River flood plains and shuns settlements and townships. His older brother, Jimmy Njiminjuma (1947–2004) taught him to paint in the 1980s and he was influenced by Yirawala and Peter Maralwanga (1916–1987). Mawurndjul won the Clemenger Contemporary Art Prize in 2003 and a retrospective of his work was held at the Museum Tinguely, Basel, in 2005. Mawurndjul was commissioned to design a ceiling piece for the Musée du Quai Branly, Paris, that opened in 2006. His work has featured in several major exhibitions, including: 'Magiciens de la Terre' at the Centre Georges Pompidou and the Grande Halle de la Villette, Paris, in 1989; 'Aratjara: Art of the First Australians' at the Hayward Gallery, London, in 1993; and the first National Indigenous Art Triennial, 'Culture Warriors', at the National Gallery of Australia, Canberra, from 2007 to 2008.

RICKY MAYNARD (b.1953)
Ben Lomond/Big Rivers people. Born Launceston, Tasmania, 1953; studied at the International Center of Photography, New York, 1990; lives on Flinders Island, Bass Strait, Tasmania

Ricky Maynard's passion for photography began at the age of sixteen when he was employed at a film processing company in Melbourne. A brief excursion into aerial landscape photography convinced him to pursue photography as an art form. In 1983, as a trainee photographer at the Australian Institute of Aboriginal and Torres Strait Islander Studies, Canberra, he was confronted with the powerful nature of the medium and how it can oppress the vulnerable. He determined that he would spend substantial time with his subjects so that the work became a collaboration between equal parties. In 1990 Maynard trained at the International Center of Photography, New York, and, on his return to Australia, produced a remarkable series of photographs of his culture, his people and his homeland. He has won many awards, including the Mother Jones International Fund for Documentary Photography Award, New York, in 1994, and the Australian Human Rights Commission Award for Photography in 1997.

CHARLES MEERE (1890–1961)

Born London, 6 December 1890; worked in Sydney, 1927–30; returned to Sydney, 1933; died Sydney, 17 October 1961

Charles Meere was one of a group of Sydney artists who depicted national life during the interwar period using a modernised classical approach. Born in London of Irish parents, Meere studied Design and Mural Painting in London at the Royal College of Art from 1919 to 1922 and the Atelier Colarossi, Paris, from *c.*1923 to 1927. He visited Australia in 1927 in search of employment as a commercial artist, and, following his return in 1933, he established a commercial art studio. He was an influential teacher at the East Sydney Technical College in the late 1930s. He is best known for his stylised Art Deco paintings of Australian life in the 1930s and 1940s, in particular *Australian Beach Pattern* (1940; cat. 139). He worked as an illustrator for the *Daily Telegraph* from 1942, and for the *Sydney Morning Herald* from 1945 to 1949.

DANIE MELLOR (b.1971)

Mamu, Ngagen people. Born Mackay, North Queensland, 13 April 1971; lives in Bowral in the Southern Highlands, New South Wales

Danie Mellor's art investigates the history of the colonisation of Australia through reconstructed images from the Ages of Enlightenment and Exploration, and of the land of his Aboriginal ancestors, the rainforests of the Atherton Tablelands, Queensland. Mellor studied at North Adelaide and Canberra Schools of Art, completed a Master in Fine Art at Birmingham Institute of Art and Design, and was awarded a Ph.D. from the Australian National University, Canberra, in 2004. He now teaches Art Theory at the Sydney College of the Arts. Mellor works mainly in drawing, printmaking and ceramics. In 2009 he won both the Telstra National Aboriginal and Torres Strait Islander Art Award and the Shepparton Indigenous Ceramic Art Award. Mellor was selected for the first National Indigenous Art Triennial, 'Culture Warriors', at the National Gallery of Australia, Canberra, from 2007 to 2008.

MICKEY OF ULLADULLA (c.1820–1891)

Yuin Dhurga people. Born on the south coast of New South Wales, *c.*1820; lived in an Aboriginal reservation at Ulladulla, New South Wales, 1880s; died Ulladulla, 13 October 1891

We may never know the Aboriginal name of Mickey of Ulladulla (also known as Mickey the Cripple), who was named after the port of Ulladulla. The first known reference to him dates back to 1875 in an illustration 'Drawn by Mickie, An old crippled blackfellow of Nelligen [a nearby river port]' held in the Mitchell Library, Sydney. His figurative drawings describe Aboriginal ceremonies, domestic activities such as fishing and hunting, and European endeavours in the region. Some of his most accomplished works depict sailing ships. Mickey was encouraged to draw by a non-Aboriginal woman who lived close to the reserve at Ulladulla. His rare historical drawings can be found in state and national libraries, museums and galleries around Australia.

TRACEY MOFFATT (b.1960)

Born Brisbane, 12 November 1960; moved to Sydney, 1984; worked in New York, 1990–2010; lives in New York and Sunshine Coast, Queensland

Tracey Moffatt is one of the most internationally exhibited and acclaimed contemporary Australian artists. The daughter of an Indigenous mother, she was born in Brisbane and raised in foster care. She graduated from Queensland College of Art, Brisbane, in 1982. Moffatt moved to Sydney in 1984, where she initiated the first exhibition of Aboriginal and Torres Strait Islander photographers in 1986. She came to prominence in the 1990s with vibrant theatrical, quasi-narrative photo series, film and video compilation works addressing gender, popular culture, racial politics and stereotypes, ambition, childhood, sexual abuse and sadomasochism. Her later photo series became more enigmatic, heavily rendered with painterly texture and open to multiple readings. Recent works also address winning, losing, fame and celebrity. Her work is held by Tate, London, the Museum of Modern Art and the Solomon R. Guggenheim Museum, New York, and the Museum of Contemporary Art, Los Angeles. Surveys were organised by the Museum of Contemporary Art, Sydney, from 2003 to 2004, the Art Gallery of South Australia, Adelaide, in 2011 and the Museum of Modern Art, New York, in 2012.

CALLUM MORTON (b. 1965)

Born Montreal, Canada, 1965; arrived Melbourne, 1967; lives in Melbourne

Callum Morton's art reveals a persistent interest in modernist architecture as an area for open-ended critical reflection. During the 1980s and 1990s in Melbourne, he studied Architecture and Fine Arts. In drawings, installations and digital prints of houses, cinema screens, monuments and vortexes, Morton combines pathos and deadpan humour. He often adds sound and film recordings, weaving disjointed stories in urban or suburban theatres of mind. His work has been included in international exhibitions, such as 'Face Up: Contemporary Art from Australia' at the Hamburger Bahnhof, Berlin, from 2003 to 2004. For the Venice Biennale in 2007 he reconstructed a life-size version of his family home *Valhalla*, which was designed by his father and never finished, revealing his ongoing fascination with the built environment as a site of lost and found dreams. Morton has taught and exhibited nationally and internationally and in 2012 was appointed as Head of Fine Arts at Monash University, Melbourne. A survey of his work was held at the Heide Museum of Modern Art, Melbourne, in 2011.

BARDAYAL NADJAMERREK (c.1926–2009)

Kuninjku people. Mok clan. Born Kukkurlumurl, Mann River region, Western Arnhem Land, *c.*1926; died Kabulwarnamyo outstation, Western Arnhem Land, Northern Territory, 16 October 2009

(Lofty) Bardayal Nadjamerrek was taught the art of rock painting by his father Yanjorluk in the 1940s. As an adult he worked in the mining, pastoral and buffalo industries and also participated in the war effort. Nadjamerrek began to produce bark paintings at the end of the 1960s. In 1999 he won the Work on Paper Award at the Telstra National Aboriginal and Torres Strait Islander Art Awards. He received the Order of Australia in 2004 in recognition of his contribution to Australian culture through his art and rock art research. Nadjamerrek was selected for the first Australian Indigenous Art Triennial, 'Culture Warriors', which opened at the National Gallery of Australia, Canberra, in 2007. The Museum of Contemporary Art, Sydney, mounted a retrospective exhibition of his work from 2010 to 2011.

DOREEN REID NAKAMARRA (c.1955–2010)

Pintupi people. Born near Warburton, Western Australia, *c.*1955; moved to Papunya, Northern Territory, early 1960s; moved to Kiwirrkura, Western Australia, *c.*1990; died Kiwirrkura, 2010

Doreen Reid Nakamarra is renowned for paintings of her ancestral desert lands that dazzle the eye through the optical effects created by repeated sections of narrow, parallel undulating lines. The daughter of the painter Pirrmangka Reid Napanangka (*c.*1940–2001), Reid led a traditional semi-nomadic life with her extended family before settling first at Papunya, then at Kiwirrkura, where she commenced her artistic career. Reid's work was selected for the first National Indigenous Art Triennial, 'Culture Warriors', at the National Gallery of Australia, Canberra, from 2007 to 2008, the 3rd Moscow Biennale of Contemporary Art in 2009 and 'dOCUMENTA (13)' in Kassel, Germany, in 2012.

MICK NAMARARI TJAPALTJARRI (c.1926–1998)

Pintupi people. Born Marnpi, Northern Territory, *c.*1926; moved to Papunya, Northern Territory, late 1960s; died Alice Springs, Northern Territory, 16 August 1998

Mick Namarari Tjapaltjarri was one of the most innovative and influential painters of the Western Desert movement. He first encountered white people as a child: the anthropologist Norman Tindale records Namarari at Yamunturrngu (Mount Liebig) in 1932. In about 1940 his family went to Hermannsburg, where he attended the mission school. Namarari was a founding member of the Papunya painting group in 1971. Two years later he painted *Sacred Caves*, now in the collection of the National Gallery of Australia, Canberra, using desert symbolism in a work about Stonehenge. Namarari won the National Aboriginal and Torres Strait Islander Art Award in 1991. He was the first recipient of the Australia Council's prestigious Red Ochre Award in 1994 for his contribution to Aboriginal culture at home and abroad. His work featured in a several major exhibitions, including 'Aratjara: Art of the First Australians' at the Hayward Gallery, London, in 1993 and the Biennale of Sydney in 2000.

ALBERT NAMATJIRA (1902–1959)

Western Arrarnta people. Born Ntaria (Hermannsburg), Northern Territory, 28 July 1902; died Alice Springs, Northern Territory, 8 August 1959

Albert (Elea) Namatjira is one of Australia's best-known Aboriginal artists. In the 1930s he was taught to paint watercolour landscapes by the non-Aboriginal artist Rex Battarbee (1893–1973), who guided his career in later years. Namatjira's outstanding ability was to capture the natural features and the shifting light of the desert in paint. He held his first solo exhibition at the Fine Arts Society Gallery, Melbourne, in 1938, followed by a series of sell-out exhibitions. The Art Gallery of South Australia, Adelaide, was the first major public art museum to acquire the work of an Aboriginal artist when it bought Namatjira's *Illum-baura (Haasts Bluff), Central Australia*, in 1939. He was presented to Her Majesty Queen Elizabeth II in 1954. In 1957 he was the first Aboriginal person to be granted full Australian citizenship. A major touring exhibition of his work was mounted by the National Gallery of Australia, Canberra, from 2002 to 2003.

DOROTHY NAPANGARDI (c.1950–2013)

Warlpiri people. Born Mina Mina, Northern Territory, *c.*1950; moved to Yuendumu, Northern Territory, *c.*1957; moved to Alice Springs, Northern Territory, by 1987; died 1 June 2013

Dorothy Napangardi Robinson is known for minimally painted black-and-white canvases of her ancestral lands around the salt lakes of Mina Mina in the Tanami Desert. As a child she led a traditional life and remembers seeing a white person for the first time when she was about seven years old. She began her painting career in Alice Springs in 1987 with brightly coloured canvases of native food plants. In 1997 her subject matter focused on the ancestral Women's Digging Stick Dreaming at Mina Mina. Napangardi won the Telstra National Aboriginal and Torres Strait Islander Art Award in 2001 and the Museum of Contemporary Art, Sydney, mounted a retrospective from 2002 to 2003.

SIDNEY NOLAN (1917–1992)
Born Melbourne, 22 April 1917; moved to England, 1953; died London, 28 November 1992

Arguably Australia's most internationally celebrated painter of the twentieth century, Sidney Nolan RA is noted for portraying Australian legends and the sparse landscape of central Australia. The son of a Melbourne tram driver, he studied Art at Prahran Technical College and the National Gallery Art School in Melbourne during the 1930s. Although his first work was abstract, during the Second World War he began to depict the flat, scrubby Wimmera landscape in central Victoria. Between 1946 and 1947 he completed a series of paintings about the bushranger Ned Kelly, which have become seminal images in Australian art (cats 154, 155, 156, 157). He subsequently made personal interpretations of other historical and legendary figures such as the explorers Burke and Wills. His work was singled out by Kenneth Clark in 1949 as being among the most original in Australian art. In 1954 he represented Australia at the Venice Biennale. He was elected a Royal Academician in 1991. His work is held by the British Museum, Tate and the Victoria and Albert Museum in London and the Metropolitan Museum of Art in New York. It was included in the exhibitions of Australian art in London at the Whitechapel Art Gallery (1961), the Tate Gallery (1963) and the British Museum (2011) and his Ned Kelly series was shown at the Metropolitan Museum of Art in New York in 1994 and at the Irish Museum of Modern Art in Dublin from 2012 to 2013. He has been the subject of several surveys, including touring retrospectives organised by the National Gallery of Victoria, Melbourne, in 1987 and by the Art Gallery of New South Wales, Sydney, in 2007.

DENNIS NONA (b. 1973)
Kala Lagaw Ya (Western Torres Strait Island) people. Born Waiben (Thursday Island), Torres Strait Islands, 1973; lives on Badu (Mulgrave Island), Torres Strait Islands

Dennis Nona is recognised as one of the most significant Torres Strait Islander artists in Australia. He comes from a rich carving tradition and was taught from a very early age. In the 1980s he studied at the Cairns College of TAFE (Technical and Further Education), North Queensland, where he made the transition from carver to linocut printmaker. He also studied Printmaking at the Canberra School of Art. Nona's mastery of the technique is evident in the complex, detailed and occasionally monumental prints that depict th ancestral narratives of the people of the Torres Straits. In 2007 he won the Telstra National Aboriginal and Torres Strait Islander Art Award and featured in the first National Indigenous Art Triennial, 'Culture Warriors', at the National Gallery of Australia, Canberra, from 2007 to 2008.

JOHN OLSEN (b. 1928)
Born Newcastle, New South Wales, 21 January 1928; moved to Sydney, 1935; lived in Europe, 1957–60 and 1965–66; lived in Cottles Bridge, Victoria, 1969–71; lived in Sydney, 1971–81; lived in Clarendon, South Australia, 1981–87; lived in Sydney, 1987–88; lived in Blue Mountains, 1988–90; lived in Rydal, New South Wales, 1990–99; lives and works in the Southern Highlands of New South Wales

John Olsen is a leading contemporary Australian artist whose work is characterised by an enquiring, robust line and an ability to convey a 'totality of experience' in which all living things are interconnected. He attended art classes in Sydney from 1947 to 1956. Growing up in Sydney provided a basis for later works relating to the city and its harbour. From the 1960s he introduced a freshness and vitality into Australian art, informed by Zen philosophy, literature and poetry, and a distinctive sense of place. In the 1970s his travels to remote areas introduced new perspectives into his art. His work is held by the British Museum and the Royal Collection in London. It was included in Australian art exhibitions in London at the Whitechapel Art Gallery (1961) and the Tate Gallery (1963). He has had numerous solo exhibitions and a touring retrospective was organised by the National Gallery of Victoria, Melbourne, from 1991 to 1992.

OTTO PAREROULTJA (1914–1973)
Western Arrarnta people. Born Ntaria (Hermannsburg), Northern Territory, 24 March 1914; died Ntaria, 1973

Otto Pareroultja was one of three brothers, including Reuben (1916–1984) and Edwin (1918–1986), who were part of the first group of watercolour painters led by Albert Namatjira at Hermannsburg. Although influenced by Namatjira, the brothers took a less naturalistic approach to painting. Otto in particular developed a style of robust application of paint in rhythmic spiralling lines to create landscapes that pulsate with ancestral forces. His linear patterns recall the designs engraved into the surfaces of sacred objects. After Albert Namatjira's works, Otto Pareroultja's paintings are the most highly sought after by collectors of the Hermannsburg School of watercolour painting.

MIKE PARR (b. 1945)
Born Sydney, 19 July 1945; grew up in south-east Queensland; moved to Sydney, in the late 1960s

Mike Parr is Australia's best-known performance artist. He also makes installations and, from the 1980s, large drawings and prints, and also sculptures. All works are self-referential, about psychosocial distortion, control, ethics, violence, confusion and endurance: immediately after his birth the doctor amputated most of one arm without consulting Parr's mother. The subject was never discussed in the family, and he was treated as if he had been born that way. After abandoning Arts/Law at the University of Queensland, Brisbane, Parr briefly studied Painting in 1968 at East Sydney Technical College. In the early 1970s he helped establish, with Tim Johnson, Inhibodress, a short-lived artists' co-operative which became Australia's first space for Conceptual text works, performance art, sound art and video art. Since then his work has been presented worldwide, most often in Europe and in 1980 he represented Australia at the Venice Biennale. His work is held by the British Museum, London, and the Metropolitan Museum of Art, New York, and was shown in London in the exhibition of Australian art at the British Museum in 2011. Survey exhibitions have been organised by the Newcastle Art Gallery, NSW (2005), the Museum of Contemporary Art, Sydney (2006), and the Kunsthalle Vienna (2012–13).

TIMMY PAYUNGKA TJAPANGARTI (c. 1940–2000)
Pintupi people. Born Parayirpilynga, Western Australia, c. 1940; died Alice Springs, Northern Territory, 2000

Timmy Payungka Tjapangarti belonged to the Pintupi group, although he also identified with the Kukatja. He was an important ceremonial leader and was among the first of the Pintupi to settle at Papunya in 1961, where, a decade later, he became a member of the first painting group. Payungka was heavily involved in the establishment of the Pintupi settlements of Walungurru (Kintore) and Kiwirrkura in the 1980s. His extensive ancestral knowledge enabled him to produce paintings of great spiritual vitality exemplified by the exquisite *Sacred Sandhills* (cat. 19). His work has been included in such major exhibitions as 'Dreamings' at the Asia Society Galleries, New York, in 1988, and the touring exhibition 'Tjukurrtjanu: Origins of Western Desert Art', organised by the National Gallery of Victoria, Melbourne, from 2011, moving on to the Musée du Quai Branly, Paris, from 2012 to 2013.

LONG JACK PHILLIPUS TJAKAMARRA (b. c. 1932)
Pintupi/Luritja people. Born Kalipinypa, Northern Territory, *c.* 1932; moved to Papunya, Northern Territory, 1962

Long Jack Phillipus Tjakamarra is one of two surviving members of the original men's painting group that was formed at Papunya in 1971. He was born at the Water Dreaming site of Kalipinypa in his mother's country, grew up in the Mount Farewell area, near Wilkinkarra (Lake Mackay), and spent some years at the Ikuntji (Haasts Bluff) settlement. For a time he was a community councillor at Papunya and participated in painting the murals on the walls of the Papunya school that were the catalyst for the painting movement. Tjakamarra painted some of the first large canvases to emerge from the community. He also served on the Aboriginal and Torres Strait Islander Arts Board of the Australia Council. He won the Northern Territory Golden Jubilee Award in 1983 and the Alice Springs Caltex Art Award in the following year.

W. C. PIGUENIT (1836–1914)
Born Hobart, 27 August 1836; moved to Sydney, 1880; visited Europe, 1898 and 1900; died Sydney, 17 July 1914

The son of a convict, W. C. Piguenit was Australia's first locally born professional landscape painter. Known for his majestic Romantic paintings, Piguenit worked during the late colonial and Federation periods. He took painting lessons in Hobart from the Scottish painter Frank Dunnett, worked as a draughtsman with the Survey Department in Hobart between 1850 and 1873 and accompanied several expeditions into the Tasmanian wilderness. In 1880 he moved permanently to Sydney. In 1898 and 1900 he visited Europe, exhibiting at the Salon in Paris. Piguenit emphasised the grandeur of the wilderness in his paintings, and in his later work he was increasingly concerned with depicting atmospheric effects. His work was included in the 1898 'Exhibition of Australian Art' at the Grafton Galleries, London, and a retrospective was organised by the Tasmanian Museum and Art Gallery, Hobart, from 1992 to 1993.

AXEL POIGNANT (1906–1986)
Born Leeds, West Yorkshire, 12 December 1906; worked in Sweden, 1919–25; returned to England, 1925; arrived Sydney, 1926; moved to Perth, 1930; returned to Sydney, 1943; returned to England, 1956; died London, 5 February 1986

Axel Poignant was a major early twentieth-century documentary photographer best known for his extensive essays of outback Western Australia and Indigenous life and culture in the Northern Territory. Poignant emigrated to Australia in 1926 and turned to photography to make a living in 1929. He set up a studio in Perth in 1930, and made his first photoessays on outback workers, settlers and Indigenous people. He photographed Indigenous communities at Liverpool River, Northern Territory, in 1952, the source of his popular children's photo book, *Piccaninny Walkabout* (1957). Poignant returned to England in 1956, where he worked as a photojournalist. In 1980 Poignant's photographs were included in the Royal Anthropological Institute's exhibition, 'Observers of Man', in London. Surveys of his work were organised by the Art Gallery of New South Wales, Sydney, in 1982 and from 2007 to 2008.

CLIFFORD POSSUM TJAPALTJARRI (c. 1932–2002)
Anmatyerr people. Born Laramba (Napperby Creek), Northern Territory, *c.* 1932; moved to Alice Springs, Northern Territory, 1985; died Alice Springs, 21 June 2002

Clifford Possum Tjapaltjarri is the best-known artist of the Papunya painting group. Innovative and imaginative, Clifford produced some of the most complex narrative paintings of the movement. He was chairman of the Papunya Tula Artists' co-operative from 1980 to 1985, after which he worked independently. Clifford's experience among Europeans, working as a stockman, engendered a keen interest in their perception of land, and in the late 1970s he created a series of monumental canvases that conceptually married the creative travels of Anmatyerr ancestors with European methods of mapping. The execution of the first of these,

Warlugulong (1976; Art Gallery of New South Wales, Sydney), was filmed for the BBC documentary *Desert Dreamers*. Retrospectives of his work were shown at the Institute of Contemporary Arts, London, in 1988, and another toured Australia between 2003 and 2005. In 1990 he was presented to Her Majesty Queen Elizabeth II.

MARGARET PRESTON (1875–1963)
Born Adelaide, 29 April 1875; lived in Europe, 1904–07 and 1912–19; moved to Sydney, 1920; died Sydney, 28 May 1963

A leading Sydney modernist in the interwar years, Margaret Preston made many paintings, woodcuts and stencil prints displaying strong design and simplified forms. The daughter of a marine-engineer, she studied Art in Melbourne, Adelaide, Paris, and later Pottery at the Camberwell School of Arts and Crafts, London. She mainly produced still-lifes using flattened areas of colour and strong lines. In the 1940s she reduced her palette to earth colours, reflecting the influence of Aboriginal art. Adept at promoting her art and ideas, Preston contributed many articles to *Art in Australia* and *The Home*. She proposed that Australian artists should look at Aboriginal art as a basis for their work and suggested that Australians should actively exchange ideas with their Asian neighbours. Her work was included in 'Exhibition of Australian Art in London' at Burlington House, London, in 1923. She has been the subject of several surveys, including retrospectives organised by the Art Gallery of South Australia, Adelaide, in 1980, by the National Gallery of Australia, Canberra, in 2004 and the Art Gallery of New South Wales, Sydney, in 2005.

JOHN SKINNER PROUT (1805–1876)
Born Plymouth, Devon, 19 December 1805; arrived Sydney, 1840; moved to Hobart, 1844; visited Port Phillip, 1847; returned to Britain, 1848; died London, 29 August 1876

The colonial artist John Skinner Prout produced freely painted, light-filled watercolours, delighting in the effects of mist and mountain, sea and shore. It is believed that he received some training from his uncle, the English watercolourist, Samuel Prout. Before emigrating with his family, he painted topographical views of English monuments and was elected as a member of the new Society of Painters in Water Colours. In Australia, he sketched in New South Wales, Tasmania and Victoria, working up his sketches into finished watercolours and occasional oil paintings. A lithographic press was among the possessions that he brought with him to Australia, which he used to produce lithographic views in Australia, such as *Sydney Illustrated* (1842–44), *Tasmania Illustrated* (1844–46) and *Views of Melbourne and Geelong* (1847). He also taught, presented lectures on art and helped to arrange exhibitions. In 1848 he returned to Britain, leaving an artistic vacuum in Hobart. His work is held by the British Museum and the Victoria and Albert Museum in London. A touring retrospective was organised by the Tasmanian Museum and Art Gallery, Hobart, from 1986 to 1987.

PUNMU COLLABORATIVE
JAKAYU BILJABU (b.*c.*1937); YIKARTU BUMBA (b.1940s); DOREEN CHAPMAN (b.1970s); MAY CHAPMAN (b.1940s); NYANJILPAYI NANCY CHAPMAN (b.*c.*1941); LINDA JAMES (b.1984); MULYATINGKI MARNEY (b.1941); REENA ROGER (b.1950s); BEATRICE SIMPSON (b.*c.*1966); RONELLE SIMPSON (b1988); MUNTARARR ROSIE WILLIAMS (b.*c.*1943)

The Punmu collaborative is one of six communities of Martu people that span a large section of the Canning Stock Route in Western Australia. The communities are represented by the collective Martumili Artists that was established in 2006, based in the mining town of Newman. Although the work of several individual Martu artists has been known for some time, Martu artists came to public attention through a major exhibition detailing the Aboriginal history of the Canning Stock Route, 'Yiwarra Kuju', at the National Museum of Australia, Canberra, from 2010 to 2011. The strong communal attachment to the country of the Martu people is reflected today in the painting of large collaborative canvases.

LLOYD REES (1895–1988)
Born Brisbane, 17 March 1895; moved to Sydney, 1917; moved to Hobart, 1986; died Hobart, 2 December 1988

Lloyd Rees is known for his landscapes celebrating the environment of Sydney and the south coast and for his masterly drawings. He studied Art at Brisbane's Central Technical College and then worked as a commercial artist in Sydney. For 40 years, between 1946 and 1986, Rees taught Art at Sydney University's Faculty of Architecture. He made many trips to Europe, and was particularly inspired by the French and Italian countryside. Most of Rees's work is concerned with depicting the effects of light and the harmony between human beings and nature. In later years it became increasingly experimental, semi-abstract impressions with lighter tones, showing the influence of Turner. His work was included in the exhibitions of Australian art in London at Burlington House (1923) and the Tate Gallery (1963). He has been the subject of several surveys, including retrospectives organised by the Art Gallery of New South Wales, Sydney, in 1995 and 2013 and an exhibition at Queensland Art Gallery, Brisbane, in 2011.

TOM ROBERTS (1856–1931)
Born Dorchester, Dorset, 9 March 1856; arrived Melbourne, 1869, aged thirteen; lived in Europe, 1881–85; returned to Melbourne, 1885; moved to Sydney, 1891; worked in England, 1903–23; returned to Australia, 1923; died Kallista, Victoria, 14 September 1931

Australia's foremost artist of the late nineteenth century, Tom Roberts promoted outdoor landscape painting, depicted important rural subjects of a national character and was Australia's leading portrait painter. The son of a newspaper editor, he came to Australia with his widowed mother, studied at the National Gallery Art School, Melbourne, from 1874 to 1880 and attended the Royal Academy Schools in London between 1881 and 1883. He exhibited at the Royal Academy of Arts, London, from 1883 to 1919. Following his return to Melbourne in 1885, he established *plein-air* painting camps around Box Hill, Beaumaris and Eaglemont and was the major instigator of the 1889 '9 by 5 Impression Exhibition' in Melbourne. In 1891 he moved to Sydney and visited sheep stations in rural New South Wales to paint, before going back to London in 1903. He returned to Australia permanently in 1923 and painted intimate landscapes in a low-key palette. His work is held by the British Museum and the Royal Collection in London and was included in the exhibitions of Australian art in London at the Grafton Galleries (1898) and the Tate Gallery (1963). He was the subject of a touring exhibition organised by the Art Gallery of South Australia, Adelaide, from 1996 to 1997.

WILLIAM ROBINSON (b. 1936)
Born Brisbane, 16 April 1936; travelled extensively in Europe, 1990–2000; lives in Brisbane

Contemporary artist William Robinson has taken a fresh approach to the Australian landscape, portraying the natural world, and especially the Queensland rainforest, from multiple viewpoints. His work takes into account time-space relationships, daily fluctuations in nature and cycles of life, death and renewal. He studied Art at the Central Technical College, Brisbane, from 1955 to 1956, and taught Art in various tertiary institutions from 1957 to 1989. A move in 1984 to an area of eucalypt forest and subtropical rainforest marked a turning point, and his *Mountain* series (1992–93), painted after his personal loss in his family convey a profound inner life. He has an abiding passion for music. Robinson is also known for wry portraits and radiant still-lifes. Surveys of his work were held at the Queensland Art Gallery, Brisbane, from 2001 to 2002 and the Queensland University of Technology, Brisbane, in 2011. His work is held by the Metropolitan Museum of Art, New York.

JULIUS SCHOMBURGK (1819–1893)
Born Freyburg (Unstrut), Germany, 27 September 1819; arrived Adelaide, 1850; moved to South Africa, 1892; died Durban, South Africa, March 1893

Julius Schomburgk made some of the most spectacular centrepieces and silver objects in colonial Australia. The son of a Lutheran pastor, he was apprenticed in Nordhausen, Germany, in 1834 before coming to Adelaide in 1850. He appears to have earned his living as a jeweller in Melbourne between 1852 and 1853. From 1854 he worked in various partnerships with silversmiths in Adelaide, under his own name as J. Schomburgk from 1858 to 1862, and in 1863 transferred his business to J.M.Wendt, for whom he worked for many years. Schomburgk is celebrated for his work in the naturalistic style using Australian motifs, his inventive designs and the outstanding quality of his craftsmanship. He exhibited work at major international exhibitions, including the London International Exhibition of 1862.

ALEXANDER SCHRAMM (1813–1864)
Born Berlin, 18 December 1813; arrived Adelaide, 1849; died Adelaide, 6 November 1864

Alexander Schramm was the most significant artist working in oils in colonial South Australia in the mid-nineteenth century across a range of subjects. Schramm was an established artist in Germany before emigrating to Adelaide in 1849. The son of a bookseller, he trained in the German Beidermeier milieu in Berlin, and studied in Rome, where he became acquainted with the work of the German Nazarenes. He subsequently lived in Warsaw for six years. Schramm painted genre scenes, group and single portraits of colonists and the most important Christian religious painting, *Madonna and Child* (1851), in Australian colonial art. However, most of his creative energy was devoted to the sympathetic portrayal of the South Australian Indigenous people in typical local landscapes. He was the first professional artist to depict in oils the dry landscape and distinctive gum trees of his adopted South Australian homeland. Although no examples have been found, Schramm also (infrequently) produced sculpture. He is represented in the Märkisches Museum, Berlin.

JAN SENBERGS (b. 1939)
Born rural Latvia, 29 September 1939; arrived Melbourne, March 1950, as a refugee, aged ten; lives in Melbourne

Jan Senbergs is a contemporary Australian artist who creates imaginative reinterpretations of modern cities that reflect his fascination with technology. The émigré son of a Latvian forester, he became a silk screen-printing apprentice in 1955, studying under Leonard French. In 1966 he was the recipient of the Helena Rubinstein Travelling Art Scholarship and subsequently studied in Europe and England. He taught Screen-printing at Royal Melbourne Institute of Technology (RMIT) from 1967 to 1980. Between 1989 and 1990 he held the post of Visiting Professor – Chair of Australian Studies at Harvard University. He constructs fragmented environments from a montage of disparate sources, including newspapers and photographic segments of objects. His work is held by the British Museum, London, the Museum of Modern Art, New York, and the National Gallery of Art, Washington DC. It was included in exhibitions of Australian art in London at the Victoria and Albert Museum (1972) and the British Museum (2011) and in numerous solo exhibitions, including a survey of his prints organised by the Art Gallery of New South Wales, Sydney, in 2008.

JEFFREY SMART (1921–2013)

Born Adelaide, 26 July 1921; moved to Sydney, 1951; moved to Italy, 1965; moved to his farmhouse Posticcia Nuova, near Arezzo, Italy, 1971; lives in Italy

Jeffrey Smart is an expatriate Australian painter, known for his stark, almost hyperreal urban landscapes. The son of a businessman, he studied in Adelaide at the South Australian School of Art from 1937 to 1941 and in Paris from 1948 to 1949. He paints images that are enigmatic and ambiguous and sometimes surreal, often focusing on the built environment, highways and airports, factories and road signs. Although his work is always firmly based in reality, he is concerned with structure in his paintings, using form and colour as the basis of his precisely conceived compositions. His work is held by the Metropolitan Museum of Art, New York, and was included in the exhibitions of Australian art in London at the Whitechapel Art Gallery (1961) and the Tate Gallery (1963). He has been the subject of several surveys, including retrospectives organised by the Art Gallery of New South Wales, Sydney, in 1999 and the Anne & Gordon Samstag Museum of Art, University of South Australia, Adelaide, in 2012.

GRACE COSSINGTON SMITH (1892–1984)

Born Sydney, 20 April 1892; lived in England, 1912–14; visited Europe, 1949–50; died Sydney, 20 December 1984

Grace Cossington Smith is one of Australia's first Post-Impressionists and an innovative modernist who conveyed a luminous spiritual presence underlying the world she painted. Encouraged by her solicitor father and her mother, she studied with Antonio Dattilo-Rubbo in Sydney and was inspired by reproductions of Van Gogh and Cézanne. She also attended drawing classes at the Winchester School of Art, England, from 1912 to 1914. In the 1920s and 1930s she painted memorable images of the Sydney Harbour Bridge as well as landscapes, still-lifes and the objects she knew and loved. She lived in Turramurra on Sydney's North Shore for most of her adult life and her remarkable late paintings of interiors of her house confirm her fascination with colour 'vibrant with light'. In 1950 she exhibited her work in London, both at the New English Art Club and the Royal Academy of Arts. A touring retrospective was organised by the National Gallery of Australia, Canberra, from 2005 to 2006.

WESLEY STACEY (b. 1941)

Born Sydney, 10 February 1941; worked in London, 1965–66; returned to Sydney; lives on south-east coast of Australia

Wesley Stacey is a significant environmental Australian photographer of the 1960s and 1980s. He started taking photographs from around 1959 while studying and working as a graphic designer in Sydney and London. In London from 1965 to 1966 he mounted an exhibition of Australian vernacular architecture at the Royal Institute of British Architects. As a freelance photographer in Australia he published several landmark books of architectural heritage and the natural environment. He left commercial work in the mid-1970s and became a founder of the Australian Centre for Photography, Sydney. His panoramic 1980s and 1990s work reflects on the span of the land and Indigenous cultural history. A retrospective of his work was organised by the National Gallery of Australia, Canberra, in 1991.

HENRY STEINER (1835–1914)

Born Rodenberg, Germany, 1835; arrived Adelaide, 1858; returned to Germany, 1884; lived in Adelaide, 1886–89; returned to Germany, 1889; died Hanover, Germany, 24 July 1914

Henry Steiner is noted for his presentation silver objects, including trowels and testimonial centrepieces, ceremonial objects, sporting trophies (several gold horseracing trophies) and mounted emu eggs, but he also produced smaller silver objects and gold jewellery. Trained in Germany, he settled in Adelaide in 1858. He ran a successful gold- and silversmithing business that traded under his name from 1862 until 1884, when he returned to Germany, shortly after his wife and two daughters had died from typhoid. Steiner exhibited his work in international exhibitions in Philadelphia (1876), Paris (1878), Sydney (1879–80), Melbourne (1880–81), where he received several awards. His early work followed the fashionable naturalistic style of mid-century, but from 1879 he developed a supremely elegant Neoclassical style in his pieces that were often finely engraved.

DAVID STEPHENSON (b. 1955)

Born Washington DC, USA, 8 April 1955; moved to Hobart, Tasmania, 1982; lives in Hobart

Contemporary photographer David Stephenson has developed one of the most extensive bodies of Australian landscape photography. The son of scientists, he studied at the University of Colorado and the University of New Mexico, completing a Master of Fine Arts (MFA) in Photography in 1982. In the same year he moved to Hobart to teach Photography at the University of Tasmania, attracted by its wilderness landscapes. His early work, often multi-panel assemblages, was shaped by 1970s and 1980s New Topographics American West Coast photography. Since the 1990s Stephenson's work has a planetary perspective, and most recently consists of large-scale colour digital photographs of cities at night. His work is held by the Museum of Modern Art and the Metropolitan Museum of Art in New York. A retrospective was organised by the National Gallery of Victoria, Melbourne, in 1998.

ARTHUR STREETON (1867–1943)

Born Mount Duneed, Victoria, 8 April 1867; moved to Sydney, 1891; worked in England, 1897–1923; returned to Melbourne, 1923; moved to Olinda, Victoria, 1938, died Olinda, 1 September 1943

Arthur Streeton is one of Australia's best-known Impressionist painters whose 'gold and blue' paintings have defined an image of Australia. The son of a schoolteacher, he studied Art at the National Gallery Art School, Melbourne, from 1882 to 1888. In 1888, along with Tom Roberts and Charles Conder, he established a sketching camp at Eaglemont and in 1889 contributed to the famous '9 by 5 Impression Exhibition' in Melbourne. In 1891 he moved to Sydney, where he painted spontaneous, lyrical views of Sydney Harbour before moving to London in 1897. He exhibited with the Royal Academy of Arts between 1891 and 1904. In Australia in the 1920s and 1930s he painted sunny pastoral landscapes and purple-blue hazy vistas, and campaigned to preserve native forests. His work is held by the Victoria and Albert Museum and the Royal Collection in England, and was included in the exhibitions of Australian art in London at the Grafton Galleries (1898), Burlington House (1923) and the Tate Gallery (1963). He represented Australia at the 1958 Venice Biennale (together with Arthur Boyd), and has been the subject of numerous surveys, including a touring retrospective organised by the National Gallery of Victoria, Melbourne, in 1995.

HOWARD TAYLOR (1918–2001)

Born Hamilton, Victoria, 29 August 1918; moved to Adelaide, 1918; moved to Perth, 1932, aged fourteen; lived in Europe, 1938–49; moved to Northcliffe, Western Australia, 1967; died Perth, 19 July 2001

Howard Taylor is one of the most innovative Australian artists of the late twentieth century. Working in Western Australia, he was concerned with the dynamics of light and the forms and patterns in landscape. He was the son of an architect. In 1940, while on active service with the RAF, he was captured and became a German prisoner of war. He studied at the Birmingham College of Art from 1946 to 1948 and taught Art at Perth Further Education Centre (later Perth Technical College) from 1951 to 1965 and at the School of Architecture and Planning, Western Australian Institute of Technology, Curtin University (WAIT) from 1965 to 1969. From 1960 he made many significant public sculptures, and was committed to communicating his art to a broad non-art audience. He took a close interest in observing the natural environment around him, creating symbolic, sculptural and abstract works. The government of Western Australia declared him a State Living Treasure in 1998. A touring retrospective was organised by the Art Gallery of Western Australia, Perth, from 2003 to 2006.

KATHY TEMIN (b. 1968)

Born Sydney, 13 March 1968; worked in London, 1996–97; lived in New York, 1997–99; lived in Epernay, France, 1999–2000; lives in Melbourne

Contemporary artist Kathy Temin has become best known for her visceral soft sculptures that blur the boundaries of public and private, presence and absence. As a daughter of Jewish émigrés – her father was a Hungarian-born survivor of the Holocaust – Temin engages with this past and a broader adversity. Her work includes idealised landscape sculptures as sites of reflection and memory, contrasted with the emotional content found in soft-toy imagery and the minimalism of monochrome. She has exhibited widely, including with such kindred spirits as Eva Hesse and Louise Bourgeois, as well as a survey exhibition held at the Heide Museum of Modern Art, Melbourne, in 2009 and the project *My Monument: Black Garden* at the Art Gallery of New South Wales, Sydney, in 2011. In 1996 she studied at Goldsmiths College, University of London, and in 2007 was awarded a Ph.D. from the Victorian College of the Arts, University of Melbourne. She is currently an Associate Professor at Monash University, Melbourne.

ERIC THAKE (1904–1982)

Born Melbourne, 8 June 1904; died Melbourne, 3 November 1982

Eric Thake was a Melbourne modernist who sometimes used elements of Surrealism to depict the Australian landscape and often created images using witty visual puns. He studied briefly at the National Gallery Art School, Melbourne, between 1921 and 1922 and with George Bell between 1925 and 1928, developing an interest in simplified form. He worked as a commercial artist in advertising for 30 years, from 1926 to 1956. He was a founding member of the Contemporary Art Society in Melbourne in 1938. During the Second World War he served as an artist with the Royal Australian Air Force (RAAF), and produced images with strong abstract designs. The city of Melbourne was a constant inspiration for his cool, refined graphic-style images. His prints are held by the British Museum and the Victoria and Albert Museum in London, and were included in the exhibition 'Out of Australia' at the British Museum in 2011.

ROVER THOMAS (c. 1926–1998)

Wangkajunga/Kukatja people. Born Kunawarritji (Well 33, Canning Stock Route), Western Australia, *c.*1926; moved to the Eastern Kimberley, *c.*1937; died Warmun (Turkey Creek), Western Australia, 11 April 1998

Rover Thomas (also known as Joolama) was one of the most influential Australian painters of the twentieth century who instigated a modern painting movement in the Eastern Kimberley. Taken up the Canning Stock Route to the Kimberley as a boy, Thomas became a cattle stockman and fencer. He travelled across the Eastern Kimberley and into the Northern Territory, before settling in the Aboriginal community of Warmun, where, in the late 1970s, the Kurirr Kurirr Dreaming and its ceremony were revealed to him. In 1990 Thomas was the first Aboriginal artist, along with Trevor Nickolls (1949–2012), to represent Australia at the Venice Biennale; the National Gallery of Australia, Canberra, mounted an exhibition of his work in 1994; and a retrospective toured Australia from 2003 to 2005.

CHRISTIAN THOMPSON (b. 1978)
Bidjara people. Born Gawler, South Australia, 1978; based in Oxford

Christian Thompson is a contemporary artist who has engaged with the national and, more recently, the international art community since he left art school in 1996. He works in photography and digital media installations (including soundscapes), engaging with identity politics and his own personal position – often placing himself within the work. He is a visual arts graduate from the University of Southern Queensland, Brisbane, and the Royal Melbourne Institute of Technology, Melbourne. He studied theatre at DasArts Advanced Studies in Performing Arts, Amsterdam, the Netherlands, and is currently undertaking a Doctorate of Philosophy (Fine Art) at the University of Oxford. Thompson's work was selected for the first National Indigenous Art Triennial, 'Culture Warriors', at the National Gallery of Australia, Canberra, from 2007 to 2008, and for the Biennale of Sydney in 2010.

IMANTS TILLERS (b. 1950)
Born Sydney, 30 July 1950; lived in Paris and Vence, France, 1976; lives in Cooma, New South Wales

Imants Tillers is one of Australia's most internationally acclaimed contemporary artists. His parents migrated from Latvia to Australia before he was born. Over the years, issues of migration, fragmentation and reclamation have been persistent currents in his work. In the early 1980s he developed a unique way of working on small canvas boards that come together on the wall and fragment back into stacks on the floor. Tillers represented Australia at the Venice Biennale in 1986. In the 1990s he tackled issues of displacement in his *Diaspora* series. In the twenty-first century his interest in landscape has intensified and he has collaborated with Aboriginal artist Michael Nelson Tjakamarra. His work is held by the Metropolitan Museum of Art, New York. He has exhibited widely, including at the Institute of Contemporary Arts, London, in 1988 and the Museum of Modern Art, Oxford, in 1997. He has had numerous solo exhibitions, including a survey exhibition of his work organised by the National Gallery of Australia, Canberra, in 2006.

ANATJARI TJAMPITJINPA (c. 1927–1999)
Pintupi people. Born Gibson Desert, Western Australia, *c.* 1927; moved to Papunya, Northern Territory, 1964; moved to Kiwirrkura, 1985; died Kiwirrkura, Western Australia, 1999

Anatjari (No. 1) Tjampitjinpa spent the early part of his life in the Gibson Desert and first saw a white person in 1963. He and his family were taken to Papunya a year later. In the early 1970s he produced some pencil drawings and watercolours for Geoffrey Bardon, the art teacher at the local school. Tjampitjinpa took up painting regularly at Papunya in 1976. He moved around a number of communities and, while at Balgo, in the early 1980s, he taught local artists to paint in acrylic on canvas. In 1985 he settled at Kiwirrkura. Tjampitjinpa was one of the main Pintupi artists to paint about the esoteric teachings of the Tingari ancestors, a recurring theme in his work.

UTA UTA TJANGALA (c. 1926–1990)
Pintupi people. Born Yumari (Dover Hills), Western Australia, *c.* 1926; moved to Papunya, Northern Territory, *c.* 1970; then to Walungurru (Kintore), Northern Territory, early 1980s; died Alice Springs, Northern Territory, December 1990

Uta Uta Tjangala was one of the original painters at Papunya in 1971. During the great drought of the late 1950s, he and his family had made the epic trek across hundreds of miles of desert from the west to the settlement of Ikuntji (Haasts Bluff), arriving in late 1956. Tjangala was a man of high ritual status and the major theme in his work concerned the Tingari ancestors, particularly in relation to events around his place of birth. Tjangala became a master of monumental paintings about the Tingari, often made in collaboration with other artists. His work has been included in several major exhibitions, such as the São Paolo Biennale in 1983, 'Dreamings' at the Asia Society Galleries, New York, in 1988, 'Tagari Lia' at the Third Eye Centre, Glasgow, in 1990, and 'Aratjara: Art of the First Australians' at the Hayward Gallery, London, in 1993.

TURKEY TOLSON TJUPURRULA (c. 1942–2001)
Pintupi people. Born near Ikuntji (Haasts Bluff), Northern Territory, *c.* 1942; moved to Papunya, Northern Territory, 1959; moved to Walungurru (Kintore), Northern Territory, 1983; died Alice Springs, Northern Territory, 2001

Turkey Tolson Tjupurrula was one of the youngest artists to join the Papunya painting co-operative, which he chaired from 1985 to 1995. In this role he championed the rights of Aboriginal artists. Tolson is renowned for a series of large canvases about making spears at a site called Ilyingaungau in his ancestral lands: the hypnotic austerity of repeated lines of stippled paint in these works was adopted by other Pintupi painters in the 1990s to allude to highly restricted themes about the Tingari ancestors. His work has been shown in several major exhibitions, including 'Aratjara: Art of the First Australians' at the Hayward Gallery, London, in 1993.

JESSIE TRAILL (1881–1967)
Born Melbourne, 29 July 1881; worked in England, 1906–09; died Emerald, Victoria, 15 May 1967

Jessie Traill forged a radical path in printmaking in Australia in the first half of the twentieth century, producing insightful views of the Australian bush and dynamic images of industry. The daughter of a wealthy banker, she studied at the National Gallery Art School, Melbourne, from 1902 to 1906 and with John Mather around 1903, becoming one of the first women to practise etching in Australia. She studied in Paris in 1907 and in London with Frank Brangwyn from 1908 to 1909. She exhibited in London with the Royal Academy of Arts from 1909 to 1914, the Society of Graphic Art from 1925 to 1938 and in the Australian art exhibition at Burlington House in 1923. She regularly travelled overseas, and, from 1927 to 1932, often visited Sydney. Influenced by Japanese woodcuts and Art Nouveau, she experimented with unusual decorative formats. Her prints are held in the collection of the British Museum, London. A touring survey of her prints was organised by the National Gallery of Australia, Canberra, in 2013.

HORACE TRENERRY (1899–1958)
Born Adelaide, 5 December 1899; visited Sydney, 1922–23; moved to Port Willunga, South Australia, 1934; died Adelaide, 10 January 1958

Trenerry was one of the major South Australian modernists during the 1930s and 1940s. He studied Drawing at night classes and with James Ashton and Fred Britton in Adelaide, and with Julian Ashton in Sydney. Elioth Gruner inspired Trenerry to depict the effects of light on the landscape, and in the late 1920s he developed a friendship with Hans Heysen, who encouraged him to visit the Flinders Ranges. In 1934 Trenerry moved to Port Willunga, South Australia, where he began to use dry textured colours and bold, dynamic compositions, painting with a rich impasto surface and a calligraphic approach. He lived there in relative isolation and poverty, and later ill health, until 1951. His work was included in the exhibition 'Australian Painting' at the Tate Gallery in 1963. A touring retrospective was organised by Carrick Hill, Adelaide, in 2010.

ALBERT TUCKER (1914–1999)
Born Melbourne, 29 December 1914; travelled to Hiroshima and Nagasaki, Japan, 1947; travelled extensively in England and in Europe, 1947–56; moved to New York, 1958–60; visited London, New York, Mexico City and San Francisco, 1967–68; returned to Melbourne, 1960; died Melbourne, 3 October 1999

Albert Tucker made a significant contribution to Australian post-war Modernism. The son of a railway worker, he attended life-drawing classes at the Victorian Artists' Society from 1933 to 1937. In the late 1930s and early 1940s he was a member of the Contemporary Art Society, Melbourne, and a contributor to the *Angry Penguins* journal, promoting avant-garde ideas. Viewing maimed soldiers and psychiatric patients at the Heidelberg Military Hospital during the war made an indelible impression. His mature work was informed by European Modernism and influenced by his experiences in wartime Melbourne. In Italy in 1954 he developed his imagery of Antipodean heads (one was acquired by the Solomon R. Guggenheim Museum, New York). In 1956 he represented Australia at the Venice Biennale. Tucker had a solo exhibition at the Imperial Institute, London (1957), and his work was included in Australian art exhibitions in London at the Whitechapel Art Gallery (1961), the Tate Gallery (1963) and the British Museum (2011). It is held by the British Museum in London and the Museum of Modern Art in New York. He has been the subject of several surveys, including a retrospective organised by the National Gallery of Victoria, Melbourne, in 1990 and an exhibition of his *Images of Modern Evil* series (1943–48) at the Heide Museum of Modern Art, Melbourne, in 2011.

TONY TUCKSON (1921–1973)
Born Ismailia, Egypt, 18 January 1921; sent to school in England, 1929, at the age of eight; RAF posting to Australia, 1942, aged twenty-one; died Sydney, 24 November 1973

The son of a Suez Canal pilot, Tony Tuckson was Australia's finest Abstract Expressionist. Art studies in London at Hornsey and Kingston were interrupted by war service as a Spitfire pilot, although he later resumed them in Sydney. After graduating with the highest honours, the brilliant student accepted a position, in 1950, at the Art Gallery of New South Wales, Sydney, where he remained for the rest of his life. There he encouraged Australia's art museums to take Aboriginal art seriously. He seldom exhibited his own work until his two solo shows in 1970 and 1973. His reading of Herbert Read's *Art Now* (1933), and seeing work by Cézanne, Picasso and Matisse, and later Pollock, influenced his art, which expresses raw emotion and haptic knowledge of the body. The British Museum, London, which has seventeen of his drawings, held an exhibition 'Out of Australia' in 2011, in which his work was included. A touring survey exhibition of his work was organised by the National Gallery of Australia, Canberra, from 2000 to 2001.

HOSSEIN VALAMANESH (b. 1949)
Born Tehran, Iran, 2 March 1949; lived at Khash, Baluchestan, 1953–60; moved to Perth, Western Australia, 1973, aged twenty-four; moved to Adelaide, 1975; lives in Adelaide

Hossein Valamanesh, the son of a public servant who worked in local government, studied Art and Theatre in Tehran but, unhappy with the Shah's undemocratic regime, he left for Australia, following friends who had settled in Perth. Early childhood in remote Baluchestan prepared him for a cultural-exchange project with Indigenous Australians in the Western Desert at Papunya. In 1975 he settled in Adelaide, graduated from the South Australian School of Art and married a fellow-student, Angela Carter (now Valamanesh), with whom he has collaborated on various public sculptures. His art looks back from Australia at Iranian culture, in installations of everyday household goods and personal clothing, and natural materials such as plant matter, earth, water and fire, plus mystic Persian poetry. He has held numerous residencies in Europe and Asia, especially Japan. His work is held by the British Museum, London. Major surveys of his work were organised by the Art Gallery of South Australia, Adelaide, in 2001 and the Museum of Contemporary Art, Sydney, in 2002.

EUGENE VON GUERARD (1811–1901)
Born Vienna, 17 November 1811; lived and worked in Italy, 1830–38; lived and worked in Germany, 1838–52; arrived Victoria, 1852; moved to Europe, 1882; moved to England, from 1891; died London, 17 April 1901

Arguably Australia's most significant colonial landscape artist and the son of a Viennese court miniature painter, Eugene von Guérard trained as a painter in the European art centres of Rome, Naples and Düsseldorf. His meticulous paint application and painstaking attention to detail were a result of the influence of German Romantic painters, with whom he came into contact in Düsseldorf. His artistic endeavours in Australia were informed by his interest in the geography, geology and biology of the Australian 'New World', travelling and sketching throughout Victoria, Tasmania, New South Wales, South Australia and New Zealand, sometimes with scientific expeditions. Although he meticulously recorded geological wonders, he was also interested in the Romantic association of his subjects. His pastoral scenes showing the properties and substantial houses of landholders and his sublimely beautiful and yet implicitly ominous landscapes are some of the most magnificent in Australian colonial art. He sent works to be exhibited at the Royal Academy of Arts, London, in 1865 and the London International Exhibition of 1873. Von Guérard was Painting Master at the National Gallery Art School, Melbourne, from 1870 to 1881. A touring retrospective was organised by the National Gallery of Victoria, Melbourne, from 2011 to 2012.

ROLAND WAKELIN (1887–1971)

Born Greytown, New Zealand, 17 April 1887; moved to Sydney, 1912; worked in London, 1922–24; returned to Sydney, 1924; worked in Europe, 1956–57; died Sydney, 28 May 1971

Roland Wakelin was a leading exponent of early Modernism in Australia. The son of an English-born timber merchant, he studied at the Wellington Technical School, New Zealand, between 1902 and 1903 and then under Antonio Dattilo-Rubbo in Sydney from 1913 to 1915. Together with Roy de Maistre, he experimented from 1917 to 1919 with 'colour-music' and adopted a form of abstraction with simplified shapes and a restricted palette. From 1934 he painted scenes of domestic life with sonorous colour. He supplemented his income from his art by working as a commercial artist and later by teaching art at the National Gallery Art School, Melbourne, in 1951 and at the Faculty of Architecture, University of Sydney, from 1952 to 1967. His work was included in the exhibition 'Australian Painting' at the Tate Gallery in 1963. A touring survey of his work was organised by the Art Gallery of New South Wales, Sydney, in 1967.

ALICE WAMBA (*c.* 1907–1975)

Tiwi people. Born Paru, Melville Island, Northern Territory, *c.* 1907; died Melville Island, 1975

Alice Wamba Tukuruinga grew up on Paru on Melville Island away from the influence of the Catholic Church across the Apsley Strait on Bathurst Island. Consequently, her art practice was developed according to cultural parameters related to ceremony and daily life. The symbols and patterns in her work are associated with the imagery painted on ceremonial objects and people's bodies as part of ritual. A common feature of her work, and the bark paintings from other female artists of the region, is that they reference women's activities, such as collecting food from coral outcrops along the coastal shoreline at low tide.

JOHNNY WARANGKULA TJUPURRULA (*c.* 1918–2001)

Pintupi people. Born Minjirrpirri, Northern Territory, *c.* 1918; moved to Papunya, Northern Territory, 1957; died Alice Springs, Northern Territory, February 2001

Johnny Warangkula Tjupurrula developed a style of painting that incorporated layers of dotting and stippling to create animated and atmospheric surfaces relating to the great Pintupi Rain or Water Dreaming sites. In 1954 he was introduced to Her Majesty Queen Elizabeth II on a royal tour. Warangkula was a community councillor at Papunya when he joined the initial group of painters in 1971. In 1997 his *Water Dreaming at Kalipinypa* (1972; the John and Barbara Wilkerson Collection, New York), sold at auction for AU$206,000 – at the time a record for a work by an Aboriginal artist and more than 1,000 times the sum he had earned on the initial sale of the painting. Three years later the same painting sold for nearly AU$500,000. These sales prompted the Australia government to pass resale royalty legislation for all Australian artists. Warangkula's work was included in major exhibitions such as 'Aratjara: Art of the First Australians' at the Hayward Gallery, London, in 1993, and the touring exhibition 'Tjukurrtjanu: Origins of Western Desert Art', organised by the National Gallery of Victoria, Melbourne, from 2011, moving on to the Musée du Quai Branly, Paris, from 2012 to 2013.

THOMAS WATLING (1762–*c.* 1814)

Born Dumfries, Scotland, 19 September 1762; arrived Sydney, 1792; worked in Calcutta, 1801–03; returned to Dumfries, 1803; died, *c.* 1814

Thomas Watling was Australia's first convict painter and illustrator. The son of a soldier, he worked as a portraitist and coach painter and taught Drawing before being convicted for forging hand-drawn banknotes and transported to New South Wales. He was assigned to the Surgeon-General John White, an amateur naturalist, who put his artistic skill to good use. In 1796 he was given a conditional pardon, made absolute the following year. He practised as a miniature painter in Calcutta from 1801 to 1803 before returning to Dumfries, where he worked as an artist and teacher and was again tried for forgery (but discharged 'not proven'). His landscapes, studies of Aboriginals and a large number of natural-history drawings are held by the Natural History Museum, London, as part of the Watling collection.

JUDY WATSON

Waanyi people. Born Mundubbera, Queensland, 9 October 1959. Lives in Brisbane

Judy Watson is a painter, printmaker and sculptor who explores historical connections to her people's land in the Gulf Country of north-west Queensland. In 1995 Watson won the Moët & Chandon fellowship for emerging Australian contemporary artists and a residency in France. In 1997 her work was shown in 'In Place (Out of Time): Contemporary Art in Australia' at the Museum of Modern Art, Oxford, and in the same year she represented Australia at the Venice Biennale with two other Indigenous artists, Emily Kame Kngwarreye and Yvonne Koolmatrie. Around this time she conducted intensive research into the Aboriginal collections at the Horniman Museum and the British Museum in London. In 1999 the Melbourne Museum commissioned Watson to create a fifty-metre-long etched zinc wall. Watson made an etched glass façade and ceiling works for the Musée du Quai Branly, Paris, in 2006, the year she was awarded the Clemenger Contemporary Art Award. In 2011 her work was shown in 'Out of Australia: Prints and Drawings from Sidney Nolan to Rover Thomas' at the British Museum.

WILLIAM WESTALL (1781–1850)

Born Hertford, Hertfordshire, 12 October 1781; worked in Australia waters, 1801–03; died London, 22 January 1850

William Westall ARA was the first professional landscape artist to work in Australia. The son of a brewery manager, he was taught drawing by his half-brother Richard Westall RA, and entered the Royal Academy Schools in London in 1799. Aged nineteen, he was appointed as landscape artist with Matthew Flinders's mapping voyage that circumnavigated Australia on HMS *Investigator* from 1801 to 1803. In Australian waters Westall made numerous sensitive landscape drawings, a few watercolours and many coastal profiles. The Admiralty subsequently commissioned a series of oil paintings, which were exhibited at the Royal Academy of Arts in 1810 and 1812. Mainly on the strength of these views, he was elected as an Associate of the Royal Academy in 1812. These paintings and the engravings based on them for Matthew Flinders's *A Voyage to Terra Australis* (1814) were the first public images of the South Seas continent presented to the general British public. His work is held by the British Museum, the Courtauld Institute of Art, Tate, the Victoria and Albert Museum, the Royal Academy and the Royal Collection in London and by the Metropolitan Museum of Art in New York.

KEN WHISSON (b. 1927)

Born Lilydale, Victoria, 1927; worked in Europe, 1954–56; lived in England, 1968–1970; moved to Perugia, Italy, 1977; lives in Italy

Ken Whisson is an expatriate contemporary Australian artist known for his independent, uncompromising style of figurative Expressionism. The son of a greengrocer, he attended Swinburne Technical College, Melbourne, from 1944 to 1945 and then studied Art with Russian émigré painter Danila Vassilieff, who had a great influence on his work, from 1945 to 1946. He has lived in Italy since 1977, but returns to Australia every year. He has developed an increasingly linear and abstract graphic approach, featuring searching lines and small jagged planes of vivid colour. His work is often playful and makes reference to remembered landscapes of both natural and built environments in which the components seem to jostle and overlap. His work is held by the British Museum, London, and was included in the exhibition 'Out of Australia' at the British Museum in 2011. A touring retrospective was organised by the Heide Museum of Modern Art, Melbourne, in collaboration with the Museum of Contemporary Art, Sydney, in 2012.

ISAAC WHITEHEAD (1819–1881)

Born Dublin, Ireland, 1819; arrived Melbourne, 1857; died Melbourne, 1881

Isaac Whitehead was colonial Victoria's most skilful picture framer and a painter of romantic beauty spots, with an eye for detail. The son of a carver and gilder, he worked as a picture framer in Dublin from 1848 to 1851. By 1860 he had established himself as the principal picture framer in Melbourne, creating frames that were elaborately decorated with floral motifs, supplying fine gilt frames to Eugene von Guérard, Louis Buvelot and others. He was largely trained as a painter in Melbourne especially under the influence of von Guérard, depicting a number of views of the forest scenery of Victoria, with large trees, tree-fern gullies and clear springs. He exhibited in Melbourne, Sydney and Paris and his work was included in the London Colonial and Indian Exhibition of 1886.

BRETT WHITELEY (1939–1992)

Born Sydney, 7 April 1939; worked in Europe and USA, 1960–69; returned to Sydney, 1969; died Thirroul, New South Wales, 15 June 1992

Brett Whiteley is one of Australia's most prodigious and extrovert late twentieth-century artists, known for his sensuous Sydney Harbour views, as well as his virtuoso use of sweeping line. The son of a publisher, he was mostly self-taught and studied Art informally at the National Art School, Sydney, from 1956 to 1959. His career was launched in London in the early 1960s after the Tate Gallery purchased one of his paintings. He incorporated Pop imagery and social protest in his paintings. He was a talented draughtsman and the *enfant terrible* of Australian art, becoming increasingly dependent on alcohol and heroin before his premature death in 1992. His work is held by Tate and the British Museum in London and by the Metropolitan Museum of Art in New York. It was included in the exhibitions of Australian art in London at the Whitechapel Art Gallery (1961), the Tate Gallery (1963) and the British Museum (2011). He has been the subject of several surveys and a touring retrospective was organised by the Art Gallery of New South Wales, Sydney in 1995, which manages his former workplace and home as a museum.

FRED WILLIAMS (1927–1982)

Born Melbourne, 23 January 1927; worked in London, 1952–56; returned to Australia, 1957; travelled extensively, 1967–82; died Melbourne, 22 April 1982

Australia's foremost twentieth-century painter and printmaker, Fred Williams had a fresh way of looking at Australian landscape that was informed by his immersion in early European Modernism. A passion for *making* was matched by an enthusiasm for art history and museums. The son of an electrical engineer, he attended the National Gallery Art School and classes with George Bell in Melbourne. In London in the 1950s, he attended the Chelsea School of Art and, briefly, the Central School of Arts and Crafts, and exhibited at the Royal Academy of Arts in 1952. In the groundbreaking works painted back in Australia he distilled the essence of localities to convey a wider sense of place. He had numerous solo exhibitions, including one at the Museum of Modern Art, New York (1977) and another at the British Museum, London (2003), as well as several retrospectives in Australia, including a touring exhibition organised by the National Gallery of Australia in 2011. His art was included in the exhibitions of Australian art in London at the Whitechapel Art Gallery (1961), the Tate Gallery (1963), the Victoria and Albert Museum (1972) and the British Museum (2011). His work is held by the British Museum, the Victoria and Albert Museum and the Royal Collection in London and by the Metropolitan Museum and the Museum of Modern Art in New York. A touring retrospective of his work was organised at the National Gallery of Australia, Canberra, in 2012.

WALTER WITHERS (1854–1914)
Born at Aston Manor, Warwickshire, 22 October 1854; arrived Melbourne, 1883; visited Europe, 1887–88; died Melbourne, 13 October 1914

Walter Withers was an Australian Impressionist, known for his poetic landscapes with a gentle light. The son of a roper, he studied in London at the Royal Academy of Arts and the South Kensington Schools from 1870 to 1882, before being sent to Australia by his father. After a period as a farm labourer, he worked as a lithographer and studied at the National Gallery Art School, Melbourne, becoming a friend of Frederick McCubbin and Tom Roberts. He continued his studies in Paris from 1887 to 1888. On his return to Australia he worked at the mansion Charterisville, near Heidelberg, where he taught Art, and later at the outer Melbourne suburb of Eltham. His work was included in the exhibitions of Australian art in London at the Grafton Galleries (1898), Burlington House (1923) and the Tate Gallery (1963). A survey exhibition was held in 1975 at the Geelong Gallery, Victoria.

PHILIP WOLFHAGEN (b. 1963)
Born Launceston, Tasmania, 10 March 1963; moved to Sydney, 1990; moved back to Tasmania, 1996; lives in Longford, near Launceston

Philip Wolfhagen is one of Australia's leading contemporary landscape painters. He creates images that are mysterious and sombre in mood, produced with thickly applied pigment. They are inspired by the atmospheric landscape of northern Tasmania and the emotive qualities of light and weather. The son of a woolgrower, he grew up in the Tasmanian Midlands. He studied at the Tasmanian School of Art, Hobart, from 1983 to 1984 and from 1986 to 1987, and at the Sydney College of the Arts, the University of Sydney, in 1990. His art frequently makes reference to the work of John Constable, seeking to transpose Constable's oil sketches into a contemporary idiom. Like Constable, he likes to paint the places he knows best, a landscape that is personal, located nearby his home. His work has been included in several group exhibitions and a survey exhibition was held at the Newcastle Art Gallery, New South Wales, in 2013.

YIRAWALA (c. 1897–1976)
Kuninjku people. Born clan. Born Marrkolidjban region on the Liverpool River, Western Arnhem Land, *c.* 1897; moved to Minjilang (Croker Island), Northern Territory, 1950s; died Minjilang, 17 April 1976

Yirawala is recognised as the master bark painter of Western Arnhem Land. His authoritative cultural status and his innovative style had a major influence on subsequent generations of Western Arnhem Land painters, including John Mawurndjul (b. 1952). In the early 1960s his work followed the ancient rock art traditions of Western Arnhem Land, and developed to include sacred clan designs previously only ever seen in ritual. While at Minjilang (Croker Island) he produced sorcery paintings featuring multi-limbed figures in contorted positions. His bark painting style culminated in detailed variations on sacred clan designs that cover the entire surface of the bark. Yirawala was appointed a Member of the Order of the British Empire in 1971 for his services to Aboriginal art. Yirawala's work has appeared in several international exhibitions, including: 'Dreamings' at the Asia Society Galleries, New York, in 1988; and 'Aratjara: Art of the First Australians' at the Hayward Gallery, London, in 1993.

BLAMIRE YOUNG (1862–1935)
Born Londesborough, Yorkshire, 9 August 1862; arrived Australia, 1885; lived in England, 1893–95 and 1912–23; died Montrose, Victoria, 14 January 1935

Blamire Young was the leading practitioner of watercolour in Melbourne during the Federation period. The son of a land agent, he studied Mathematics at the University of Cambridge and first came to Australia to teach Mathematics. Changing course, he studied in London at Hubert von Herkomer's art school at Bushey in 1893 and participated in the innovative poster work of J. & W. Beggarstaff with William Nicholson and James Pryde. In Australia in the late 1890s he became prominent as a poster artist. In his watercolours he often used an experimental approach. He exhibited at the Royal Academy of Arts, London, from 1918 to 1922 and his work is held by the Victoria and Albert Museum and the Royal Collection in London. It was included in the exhibition of Australian art in London at Burlington House in 1923. A touring retrospective was organised by the National Gallery of Victoria, Melbourne, in 1983.

GULUMBU YUNUPINGU (c. 1945–2012)
Gumatj clan. Born Biranybirany, north-east Arnhem Land, *c.* 1945; died Gunyangara (Ski Beach), north-east Arnhem Land, Northern Territory, 9 May 2012

Gulumbu Yunupingu's signature theme focuses on the constellations of Garak the universe that she painted on sheets of bark and on larrakitj (memorial poles) in a public art career lasting only one decade. She belonged to an artistic dynasty: her father was the renowned artist Munggurrawuy Yunupingu; her sisters Nyapanyapa and Barrapu Yunupingu are artists too. In 2004 Gulumbu won the Telstra National Aboriginal and Torres Strait Islander Art Award. Her work featured in the first National Indigenous Art Triennial, 'Culture Warriors', at the National Gallery of Australia, Canberra, from 2007 to 2008, and the 2010 Biennale of Sydney. Gulumbu was commissioned to design a ceiling piece for the Musée du Quai Branly, Paris, that opened in 2006.

MUNGGURRAWUY YUNUPINGU (c. 1905–1979)
Gumatj people. Born north-east Arnhem Land, Northern Territory, *c.* 1905; moved to Yirrkala, north-east Arnhem Land, 1935; died Yirrkala, 12 April 1979

Munggurrawuy Yunupingu was a senior Gumatj cultural leader who, along with his contemporaries, developed the modern north-east Arnhem Land bark painting style featuring episodic vignettes. Munggurrawuy was one of the artists involved in the creation of the Yirritja Yirrkala Church Panels from 1962 to 1963, and was also a signatory to the Aboriginal Bark Petition presented to the Commonwealth government in 1963. His legacy is seen in the careers of three of his daughters, who all became artists – Gulumbu, Nyapanyapa and Barrapu Yunupingu – and of his sons, the politician Galarrwuy Yunupingu and the musician Mandawuy Yunupingu. Munggurrawuy's work has appeared in several international exhibitions, including: 'Australian Aboriginal Bark Paintings 1912–1964', Commonwealth Arts Festival, Walker Art Gallery, Liverpool, in 1965; 'Dreamings' at the Asia Society Galleries, New York, in 1988; and 'Aratjara: Art of the First Australians' at the Hayward Gallery, London, in 1993.

NOTES

AUSTRALIA: AN INTRODUCTION
KATHLEEN SORIANO

1 Kenneth Clark, 'Foreword', in *Recent Australian Painting*, exh.cat., Whitechapel Art Gallery, London, 1961, p.4.

2 Thomas M. Messer, 'Preface and Acknowledgements', in Australian Visions, exh.cat., Solomon R. Guggenheim Museum, New York, 1984, p.8.

3 Memory Holloway, 'Bleak Romantics', in *Australian Visions*, exh.cat., Solomon R. Guggenheim Museum, New York, 1984, pp.11–21.

4 Quoted in Bill Gammage, *The Biggest Estate on Earth: How Aborigines Made Australia*, London, 2011, pp.14–15.

5 William Light, quoted in Bill Gammage, op.cit., pp.270–71.

6 Howard Taylor, quoted by Gary Dufour, 'Visual Experience and Pictorial Structure', in *Howard Taylor: Phenomena*, exh.cat., Art Gallery of Western Australia, Perth, Museum of Contemporary Art, Sydney, 2003, p.37.

7 Dorothea Mackellar, extract from 'My Country', first published in 1908.

8 Sidney Nolan, quoted in Andrew Sayers, 'Art, Myth and Society: The Australian Avant-garde 1939–50', *Australian Art* (Oxford History of Art series), Oxford and New York, 2001, pp.155–74.

9 Sidney Nolan, quoted in Andrew Sayers, 'Sidney Nolan', in *Australian Art in the National Gallery of Australia*, Canberra and London, 2002, pp.202–03.

10 Bryan Robertson, 'Preface', in *Recent Australian Painting*, exh.cat., Whitechapel Art Gallery, London, 1961, pp.5–12.

DEAD HEART / LIVE HEART
THOMAS KENEALLY

1 Barron Field, 'The Kangaroo', first published 1819.

2 A. D. Hope, 'Australia', first published on the eve of the Second World War.

COUNTRY: ABORIGINAL ART
WALLY CARUANA AND FRANCHESCA CUBILLO

1 The continent of Australia was declared *terra nullius*, land belonging to no one or the empty land, by its colonial overlords in the early nineteenth century, effectively denying Aboriginal people the legal right to own land.

2 Bill Gammage, *The Biggest Estate on Earth: How Aborigines Made Australia*, Sydney, 2011, p.5.

3 Galarrwuy Yunupingu, 'The Black/White Conflict', in Wally Caruana (ed.), *Windows on the Dreaming: Aboriginal Paintings in the Australian National Gallery*, Australian National Gallery, Canberra, and Sydney, 1989, p.13.

4 *Shorter Oxford English Dictionary*.

5 Robert Hughes, *The Art of Australia*, Ringwood, 1970 edition, p.75. Nonetheless, Aboriginal art encompasses human emotions as well.

6 Despite its currency, the English term 'Dreaming' fails to capture the all-encompassing nature of the concept.

7 Peter Sutton, 'Icons of Country', in D.Woodward and G.M.Lewis (eds), *The History of Cartography*, vol. 2, Book Three, Chicago, 1998, p.360.

8 In this, they are akin to Scottish clans and their tartan patterns.

9 See, for example, the description of Long Jack Phillipus Tjakamarra's *Kalipinypa Water Dreaming* (cat.17), later on.

10 Now, some 50 languages and dialects languages are spoken on a daily basis.

11 Two bark paintings from Port Essington entered the collection of the British Museum in the mid-nineteenth century.

12 The practice of mural painting continues to this day alongside the tradition of portable bark paintings.

13 This is the term used in Western Arnhem Land.

14 Yolngu is the collective term for the people of Eastern Arnhem Land.

15 The technique is known as 'firestick farming'.

16 G.Bardon and J.Bardon, *Papunya, A Place Made After the Story: The Beginnings of the Western Desert Painting Movement*, Melbourne, 2004, p.7.

17 As with the Fire Dreaming in Arnhem Land, the desert Fire Dreaming connects a number of language groups over a vast area. Apart from the religious and social imperatives for these connections, Gammage (op.cit., p.185) suggests they are also necessary to maintain a coordinated fire regime over large expanses of country.

18 Similarly, the placement of other elements in the painting does not reflect their correct geographic locations.

19 This is somewhat comparable to the schematic map of the London Underground.

20 The writing of Aboriginal languages is a modern phenomenon. In the Western Desert, orthographies vary: for example the word for Dreaming is written as *Tjukurrpa* in most languages, but *Jukurrpa* by the Warlpiri.

21 Ancestral Rainbow Serpents are usually associated with the storms, rain and lightning of the wet season.

22 Robert Campbell Jnr deliberately used the racist term 'Abo' in the title of the work to underscore the prejudicial nature of official Australian histories.

23 The practice became so widespread and destructive that the Queensland government introduced *The Aboriginal Protection and Restriction of Sale of Opium Act 1897*, which allowed the state to control Aboriginal people and place them on government reserves and missions.

24 Galarrwuy Yunupingu, op.cit., p.14.

25 In *The Art of Australia* (op cit., p.62), Robert Hughes attributes these sentiments to Streeton.

LAND AND LANDSCAPE: THE COLONIAL ENCOUNTER 1800–80

RON RADFORD

1 Bernard Smith (ed.), *Documents on Art and Taste in Australia*, Melbourne, 1975, pp.11 and 14. The now obsolete word 'off-scape' means a distant prospect that needs improvement.

2 Ron Radford in Sarah Thomas (ed.), *The Encounter, 1802: Art of Flinders and Baudin Voyages*, exh.cat., Art Gallery of South Australia, Adelaide, 2002, p.112.

3 T.M.Perry and Donald H.Simpson (eds), *Drawings by William Westall*, London, 1962, p. 62. Others have suggested that the object in the cave is a decorated shield.

4 The Proclamation of Governor Bourke, 10 October 1835, implemented the doctrine of *terra nullius* upon which British settlement was based, reinforcing the notion that the land belonged to no one prior to the British Crown taking possession of it.

5 Bernard Smith (ed.), *Documents on Art and Taste in Australia*, Melbourne, 1975, p.13.

6 Fifteen of these are now held by the State Library of New South Wales, Sydney. The other five are unaccounted for; see also Richard Neville, *Mr J.W.Lewin: Painter and Naturalist*, Sydney, 2012, pp.194–215.

7 John Lewin, Letter to Alexander Huey, November 1812. Belfast Public Records Office, D3220/2/4.

8 Acknowledged for some time, this theme is explored in much detail in Bill Gammage's recent book *The Biggest Estate on Earth: How Aborigines Made Australia*, Sydney, 2011.

9 Ron Radford and Jane Hylton, *Australian Colonial Art 1800–1900*, Adelaide, 1995, pp.46–8.

10 John McPhee (ed.), *Joseph Lycett. Convict Artist*, exh.cat., Museum of Sydney, Sydney, 2006, pp.97–121.

11 Radford and Hylton, op.cit., pp.68–70.

12 Radford and Hylton op.cit., pp.71–4.

13 In the early 1840s, Glover sent six paintings to King Louis-Philippe of France. Two of these – *A Corroboree of Natives in Van Diemen's Land* and *Ben Lomond Setting Sun* – were transferred to the Louvre in 1848. Elizabeth Johns (ed.), *New Worlds from Old: Nineteenth-century Australian and American Landscapes*, exh.cat., National Gallery of Australia, Canberra, 1998, pp.128–9.

14 In their enthusiasm to embrace Australia's landscape art, the most interesting development in Australian art, Australian art historians overlook (or are ignorant of) the fact that from the second half of the 1820s to the first half of the 1850s, there were infinitely more professional portrait painters working in the Australian colonies than professional landscape painters. Indeed, in the comparatively lively art scene in South Australia, figure and portrait painting remained prominent until the 1890s.

15 Tasmania also produced Australia's first two locally trained artists. The first was the portrait and figure painter Robert Dowling, who painted professionally from 1850 and later worked in London, exhibiting at the Royal Academy. More relevant to this exhibition was W.C.Piguenit, who was born of a convict father in Hobart in 1836 and was Australia's first locally born and trained landscape painter.

16 Ron Radford, in *Turner from the Tate: The Making of a Master*, exh.cat., Art Gallery of South Australia, Adelaide, 2013, pp.71–2.

17 Radford and Hylton, op.cit., pp.98–100.

18 Daniel Thomas in Ruth Pullin, *Eugene von Guérard: Nature Revealed*, exh.cat., National Gallery of Victoria, Melbourne, 2011, p.158.

19 W.C.Piguenit, in his first two decades in Sydney from 1880, was the most popularly admired and best-represented living artist in the Art Gallery of New South Wales. Indeed, his *Mount Olympus, Lake St Clair, Tasmania, the Source of the Derwent* (1875; fig.25) was one of the first paintings acquired by that gallery. In the present exhibition, he is represented by *The Flood in the Darling, 1890* (1895; cat.92), which is not discussed in the body of this essay because it falls outside the colonial period up to 1880. This radiant painting of water and sky has the optimism of an almost Biblical cleansing and does not hint at the human and natural devastation that this and other floods bring to Australia almost annually.

20 Jane Hylton, *Reflections: H.J.Johnstone's Evening Shadows, Australia's Most Copied Painting*, exh.cat., Art Gallery of South Australia, Adelaide, 1999.

ART NATION: AUSTRALIAN LANDSCAPE 1880–1920

ANNE GRAY

1 Sydney Long, 'The Trend of Australian Art Considered and Discussed', *Art and Architecture*, 1905; Frederick McCubbin, 'Some Remarks on the History of Australian Art', in James MacDonald, *The Art of Frederick McCubbin*, Melbourne, 1916; Arthur Streeton, 'Eaglemont in the Eighties: Beginnings of Art in Australia', *Argus*, Melbourne, 16 October 1934.

2 Julian Ashton, 'Art in Australia and Its Possibilities', *Table Talk*, 27 January 1888, p.3, and 'An Aim for Australian Art', *Centennial Magazine*, 1, August 1888, pp.31–2; Henry Laurie, 'Speech to the Victorian Artists' Society', *Table Talk*, 7 June 1889, p.5; Sidney Dickinson, 'What Should Australian Artists Paint?', *Australasian Critic*, 1 October 1890, p.22.

3 'Editorial', *Argus*, 24 August 1895, p.6.

4 Whistler's 'Notes' – 'Harmonies' – 'Nocturnes' were shown at Messrs Dowdeswell, London, in May 1884; Constable's small outdoor sketches were displayed at the Victoria and Albert Museum, London, from April 1880 to October 1882.

5 Percy Bysshe Shelley, 'Queen Mab', Book VIII, 1813.

6 The high viewpoint and horizon line and the flattened perspective and carefully placed figures all recall Japanese art, which was much admired at this time.

7 Arthur Streeton, 'Eaglemont in the Eighties: Beginnings of Art in Australia', *Argus*, Melbourne, 16 October 1934.

8 *Table Talk*, 26 April 1899, p.5.

9 'An effect is only momentary; so an impressionist tries to find his place. Two half-hours are never alike, and he who tries to paint a sunset on two successive evenings must be more or less painting from memory.'

10 Arthur Streeton to Frederick McCubbin, October 1891, quoted in R.H.Croll (ed.), *Smike to Bulldog: Letters from Arthur Streeton to Tom Roberts*, Sydney, 1946, p.21.

11 *The Age*, Melbourne, 27 May 1892.

12 Lloyd Rees, *The Small Treasures of a Lifetime: Some Early Memories of Australian Art and Artists*, Sydney, 1969, p.52.

13 Tom Roberts's talk to the Society of Artists, Sydney, quoted in *Sydney Morning Herald*, 21 October 1895, p.3, quoted in Jane Clark and Bridget Whitelaw, *Golden Summers: Heidelberg and Beyond*, Melbourne, 1985, p.129.

14 Like Roberts, Davies had seen Whistler's 'Nocturnes' in London and had absorbed ideas from Japanese art.

15 Robert Hughes, *The Art of Australia*, Ringwood, Victoria, 1966, p.77.

16 See Ron Radford, *Our Country: Australian Federation Landscapes, 1900–1914*, exh.cat., Art Gallery of South Australia, Adelaide, 2001.

17 Ibid., p.20.

18 W. Baldwin Spencer, *Wanderings in Wild Australia*, London, 1928, p.794, quoted in Andrew Sayers, *Australian Art*, Oxford, 2001, p.101.

19 Sydney Long, 'The Trend of Australian Art Considered and Discussed', *Art and Architecture*, 1905, p.10.

20 James MacDonald, op.cit., p.84.

21 Colin Thiele, *Heysen of Hahndorf*, Adelaide, 1968, p.109.

22 Letter from Heysen to Lionel Lindsay, in Lionel Lindsay, 'The Art of Hans Heysen', *Art in Australia*, Sydney, special number, 1920, p.8.

23 Ron Radford, op.cit., p.96.

24 Roy de Maistre, in *Colour in Art*, exh.cat., Gayfield Shaw Art Salon, Sydney, 1919.

25 Tom Roberts's talk to the Society of Artists, Sydney, quoted in *Sydney Morning Herald*, 21 October 1895, p.3, quoted in Jane Clark and Bridget Whitelaw, op.cit., p.129.

26 Melbourne and Sydney had opened their public art galleries in the 1860s and 1870s, but it was not until 1880 that the Fine Arts Annexe was officially opened as the Art Gallery of New South Wales, and not until the 1880s and 1890s that other state capitals and major regional towns in Victoria followed.

27 In 1897 the Art Gallery of South Australia received a bequest of £25,000 from Sir Thomas Elder, the first significant bequest to a major art museum in Australia. And in 1904 the National Gallery of Victoria received the Felton Bequest, the largest acquisition fund for an art museum in Australia, which enabled the gallery to make significant purchases on the international art market, such as Camille Pissarro's *Boulevard Montmartre* (1897), as well as at home in Australia.

28 Writers included the novelists Miles Franklin, Joseph Furphy and Henry Handel Richardson and the poets Christopher Brennan, Henry Lawson, Dorothea Mackellar and Banjo Paterson. Australia's first cinema opened in Pitt Street, Sydney, in 1896, and the Australian-made film *The Story of the Kelly Gang* was first shown at the Athenaeum Hall, Melbourne, in 1906.

AUSTRALIAN LANDSCAPE: PATHWAYS INTO THE MODERN WORLD 1920–50

DEBORAH HART

1 First published by the George M.Hill Company, Chicago and New York, 1900.

2 Curated by Basil Burdett, the exhibition included works by Cézanne, Picasso and Matisse, and toured to Adelaide, Melbourne, Sydney, Brisbane, Hobart and Launceston.

3 See Anne Gray, *Australian Art in the National Gallery of Australia*, Canberra, 2002, pp.136, 137.

4 Drusilla Modjeska, *Stravinsky's Lunch*, Sydney, 1999, p.217.

5 See Anne Gray, http://nga.gov.au/Exhibition/Lambert/Detail.cfm, viewed 15 January 2013.

6 Quoted in Rosslyn D.Haynes, *Seeking the Centre: The Australian Desert in Literature, Art and Film*, Cambridge, 1988, p.17.

7 Quoted in Lionel Lindsay, 'Heysen's Recent Watercolours', *Art in Australia*, series 3, no.24, June 1928 (unpaginated). See also Rebecca Andrews, *Hans Heysen*, exh.cat., Art Gallery of South Australia, Adelaide, 2008.

8 Gael Newton, *Shades of Light* online, www.photo-web.com.au/ShadesofLight/11-pictorial.htm, viewed 15 January 2013.

9 John Slater, *Through Artists' Eyes: Australian Suburbs and Their Cities, 1919–1945*, Carlton, Victoria, 2004, p.74.

10 For discussion of Beatrice Irwin's theories, see Deborah Hart, *Grace Cossington Smith*, exh. cat., National Gallery of Australia, Canberra, 2005, pp.28, 30. Mary Eagle, *Modern Australian Painting Between the Wars, 1914–1939*, Sydney, 1990, gives alternative approaches around the First World War.

11 Kenneth Macqueen, *Adventure in Watercolour: An Artist's Story*, Sydney, p.3.

12 Ibid., p.2.

13 Clarice Beckett was the most gifted student of Max Meldrum, who advocated Tonalism in painting.

14 See John Slater, *Through Artists' Eyes: Australian Suburbs and Their Cities, 1919–1945*, Carlton, Victoria, 2004, p.119.

15 Renée Free, *Lloyd Rees*, Sydney, 1979, p.53.

16 These anthropologists included Frederick McCarthy and Leonard Adam. In 1940 Preston travelled to Oenpelli in Arnhem Land, Bathurst and Melville Islands and Wandjina sites in the Kimberley, which made a profound impression. See Deborah Edwards, *Margaret Preston*, exh. cat., Art Gallery of New South Wales, Sydney, 2005, pp.278, 279.

17 Ian North, in Deborah Edwards, *Margaret Preston*, exh.cat., Art Gallery of New South Wales, Sydney, 2005, p.194.

18 Australian involvement in the war was centred on two arenas of conflict: against Germany and Italy, and against Japan in alliance with the United States and Britain.

19 Arthur Boyd, *Australian Eye* series, Australian National Gallery, Canberra, and Film Australia, Victoria, 1981, part 3, series 4.

20 In 1892 Henry Lawson wrote a short story entitled *The Drover's Wife*. Drysdale's drawing is reproduced in Lou Klepac, *Russell Drysdale*, Kensington, New South Wales, 1983, p.85.

21 Joseph Burke, *The Paintings of Russell Drysdale*, Sydney, 1951, p.12.

22 Gael Newton, 'In the Outback', in John McDonald (ed.), *Federation: Australian Art and Society, 1901–2001*, exh.cat., National Gallery of Australia, Canberra, 2000, p.63.

23 Numerous performers wearing outfits based on Nolan's *Ned Kelly* appeared against an enormous backdrop of the painting.

24 Quoted in Patrick McCaughey (ed.), *Bert and Ned: The Correspondence of Albert Tucker and Sidney Nolan*, Carlton, Victoria, in association with Heide Museum of Modern Art, Bulleen, Victoria, 2006: Letters, p.110.

25 Ibid.

26 The exhibition opened at David Jones's Art Gallery on 8 March 1949. See Geoffrey Smith, *Sidney Nolan: Desert and Drought*, exh.cat., National Gallery of Victoria, Melbourne, 2003, p.12, and Cynthia Nolan, quoted on p.15.

ELIZABETHAN POST-COLONIAL 1950–2013

DANIEL THOMAS

1 The Royal Collection website gives a descriptive title, *Oxen and Gum Trees*.

2 Elizabeth Ann Macgregor, 'Tracey Talks...', in Glenn Barkley et al., *Volume One: MCA Collection*, Sydney, 2012, p.345.

3 It was Silverton, not quite a ghost town, near Broken Hill in outback New South Wales, a frequent location for major movies, among them *Wake in Fright* (1971) and the *Mad Max* series (1979 on).

4 Elizabeth Ann Macgregor, op cit., p.348.

5 Ian North, 'Profiling Hossein: A Conversation with the Artist', in Mary Knights and Ian North, *Hossein Valamanesh: Out of Nothingness*, Adelaide, 2011, p.12.

6 Ibid., p.13.

7 *Imants Tillers: In Two Minds*, exh.cat., Greenaway Art Gallery, Adelaide, 2007, p.3.

8 Julie Ewington, *Fiona Hall*, exh.cat., Annandale, 2005, pp.101–09, 120, note 2.

9 Blair French and Daniel Palmer, *Twelve Australian Photo Artists*, Sydney, 2009, p.61.

10 Daniel Thomas, 'Howard Arkley', in Laura Murray Cree and Nevill Drury (eds), *Australian Painting Now*, North Ryde, 2000, p.32.

11 Ian Burn, 'The Car, the Family, the Landscape', in Daniel Thomas (ed.), *Creating Australia: 200 Years of Art, 1788–1988*, exh.cat. for the Australian Bicentennial Authority's 'Great Australian Art Exhibition 1788–1988' (curator Ron Radford), Art Gallery of South Australia, Adelaide, and the five other State Galleries, 1988, pp.182–83, 239.

12 Mary Eagle, *Three Creative Fellows: Sidney Nolan, Arthur Boyd, Narritjin Maymuru*, exh.cat., Drill Hall Gallery, Australian National University, Canberra, 2007, pp.19, 21.

13 Letter, 2000, Olsen acquisition file, National Gallery of Australia, Canberra; Deborah Hart in Anne Gray (ed.), *Australian Art in the National Gallery of Australia*, Canberra, 2002, p.267.

14 Exhibition statement, 1974, in Sandra McGrath, *Brett Whiteley*, Sydney, 1979, p.168.

15 *Artforum*, 2002, in Judy Annear, *Mnemosyne: Bill Henson*, exh.cat., Art Gallery of New South Wales, Sydney, 2005, p.436.

16 Murray Bail, *Fairweather*, Millers Point, 2009, p.257.

17 Ashley Crawford, 'View from the Booth', *The Age*, 29 November 2003 (preview article for Jason Smith's exhibition 'Peter Booth: Human/Nature' at the National Gallery of Victoria, Melbourne, 2003).

18 National Gallery of Australia Research Library, Canberra, 'James Gleeson Interviews: Jan Senbergs', 1 April 1979.

19 Agatha Christie, *An Autobiography*, London, 1977, excerpted in Mathew Prichard (ed.), *Agatha Christie: The Grand Tour. Letters and Photographs from the British Empire Expedition*, London, 2012, p.133.

20 Simon Pierse, *Australian Art and Artists in London, 1950–1965: An Antipodean Summer*, Farnham, 2012, p.1.

21 Alisa Bunbury, *Bea Maddock*, exh.cat., National Gallery of Victoria, Melbourne, 2013, p.31.

22 Irena Zdanowicz, 'Geography with a Purpose: Bea Maddock's TERRA SPIRITUS', *Print Quarterly*, vol. 28, no. 4, 2011.

23 Wolfhagen acquisition file, 2009–13, National Gallery of Australia, Canberra.

24 Abigail Solomon-Godeau, *Rosemary Laing*, Munich, 2012, p.32.

25 René Block, *The Readymade Boomerang: Certain Relations in Twentieth-century Art: The Eighth Biennale of Sydney*, exh.cat., Biennale of Sydney and Museum of Contemporary Art, Sydney, 1990, p.17.

26 Pineapple skin via the artist's gallerist, Kerry Crowley, Yuill/Crowley, Sydney, January 2013; Mayfair signage, Trevor Smith, *Robert MacPherson*, exh.cat., Art Gallery of Western Australia, Perth, 2001, pp.73–5.

SELECT BIBLIOGRAPHY

Brian Adams, *Sidney Nolan: Such Is Life, A Biography*, London, 1987

Christopher Allen, *Art in Australia: From Colonization to Postmodernism*, London, 1997

Jaynie Anderson (ed.), *The Cambridge Companion to Australian Art*, Port Melbourne, 2011

Rebecca Andrews, *Hans Heysen*, exh.cat., Art Gallery of South Australia, Adelaide, 2008

Judy Annear, *Mnemosyne: Bill Henson*, exh.cat., Art Gallery of New South Wales, Sydney, 2005

Ron Appleyard, Barbara Fargher, Ron Radford, *S. T. Gill: The South Australian Years, 1839–1852*, exh.cat., Art Gallery of South Australia, Adelaide, 1986

Aratjara: Art of the First Australians, exh.cat., Kunstsammlung Nordrhein-Westfalen, Düsseldorf, Hayward Gallery, London, Louisiana Museum, Humlebaek, and National Gallery of Victoria, Melbourne, 1993–94

Murray Bail, *Fairweather*, Millers Point, 2009

Geoffrey Bardon, *Papunya Tula: Art of the Western Desert*, Melbourne, 1999

Geoffrey Bardon and James Bardon, *Papunya, A Place Made After the Story: The Beginnings of the Western Desert Painting Movement*, Melbourne, 2004

Glenn Barkley et al., *Volume One: MCA Collection*, Sydney, 2012

Glenn Barkley and Lesley Harding, *Ken Whisson: As If*, exh.cat., Heide Museum of Modern Art, Bulleen, 2012

John Beard, Stephen Bann, Anthony Bond and Charles Saumarez Smith, *John Beard*, Neutral Bay, 2011

Roger Benjamin and Andrew C. Weislogel (eds), *Icons of the Desert: Early Aboriginal Paintings from Papunya*, New York, 2009

Ronald M. Berndt, Catherine H. Berndt and John E. Stanton, *Aboriginal Australian Art: A Visual Perspective*, Melbourne, 1992

René Block, *The Readymade Boomerang: Certain Relations in Twentieth-century Art: The Eighth Biennale of Sydney*, exh.cat., Biennale of Sydney and Museum of Contemporary Art, Sydney, 1990

Lissant Bolton, *Baskets and Belonging: Indigenous Australian Histories*, exh.cat., British Museum, London, 2011

Tim Bonyhady, *Australian Colonial Paintings in the Australian National Gallery*, Canberra, 1986

Tim Bonyhady, *The Colonial Earth*, Carlton, 2000

Tim Bonyhady, *Images in Opposition: Australian Landscape Painting 1801–1890*, Melbourne, 1985

Carl Bridge et al., *Australians in Britain*, Clayton, 2009

Anne Marie Brody, *Larrakitj: Kerry Stokes Collection*, West Perth, 2011

Anne Marie Brody (ed.), *Stories: Eleven Aboriginal Artists, Works from the Holmes à Court Collection*, Sydney, 1997

David Bromfield, *Brian Blanchflower*, Nedlands, 1989

Candice Bruce, *Eugen von Guérard*, exh.cat., Australian National Gallery, Canberra, 1980

Buku-Larrngay Mulka Centre, *Saltwater: Yirrkala Bark Paintings of Sea Country*, Neutral Bay, 1999

Alisa Bunbury, *Bea Maddock*, exh.cat., National Gallery of Victoria, Melbourne, 2013

Darleen Bungey, *Arthur Boyd: A Life*, Crows Nest, 2007

Joseph Burke, *The Paintings of Russell Drysdale*, Sydney, 1951

Ian Burn, *National Life and Landscapes: Australian Painting 1900–1940*, Sydney, 1991

David Burnett et al., *Story Place: Indigenous Art of Cape York and the Rainforest*, exh.cat., Queensland Art Gallery, Brisbane, 2003

Roger Butler (ed.), *Printed: Images in Colonial Australia, 1801–1901*, Canberra, 2007

Roger Butler (ed.), *Printed: Images by Australian Artists, 1885–1955*, Canberra, 2007

Roger Butler, *The Prints of Margaret Preston: A Catalogue Raisonné*, Canberra, 1987

Roger Butler, *Prints by Mike Parr*, exh.cat., Australian National Gallery, Canberra, 1990

Roger Butler (ed.), *Stars in the River: The Prints of Jessie Traill*, exh.cat., National Gallery of Australia, Canberra, 2013

Roger Butler and Anne Kirker, *Being and Nothingness: Bea Maddock: Work from Three Decades*, exh.cat., National Gallery of Australia, Canberra, 1992

Edmund Capon, with Barry Pearce and Peter Quartermaine, *Jeffrey Smart Retrospective*, exh. cat., Art Gallery of New South Wales, Sydney, 1999

Belinda Carrigan (ed.), *Rover Thomas: I Want to Paint*, exh.cat., Holmes a Court Gallery, Perth, 2003

Paul Carter, *Hossein Valamanesh*, Roseville East, 1996

Wally Caruana, *Aboriginal Art*, London and New York, 2003

Wally Caruana (ed.), *Windows on the Dreaming: Aboriginal Paintings in the Australian National Gallery*, Australian National Gallery, Canberra, 1989

Wally Caruana et al., *Roads Cross: The Paintings of Rover Thomas*, exh.cat., National Gallery of Australia, Canberra, 1994

Wally Caruana, Susan Jenkins and Djon Mundine et al., *Le Mémorial: un chef-d'œuvre d'art aborigène*, exh.cat., Musée Olympique, Lausanne, 1999

George Chaloupka, *Journey in Time, The World's Longest Continuing Art Tradition: The 50,000-Year Story of the Australian Aboriginal Rock Art of Arnhem Land*, Reed, 1993

Jane Clark, *Sidney Nolan, Landscapes and Legends*, exh.cat., National Gallery of Victoria, Melbourne, 1987

Jane Clark and Bridget Whitelaw, *Golden Summers: Heidelberg and Beyond*, exh.cat., National Gallery of Victoria, Melbourne, 1985

Jane Clark et al., *Town and Country: Portraits of Colonial Homes and Gardens*, exh.cat., Bendigo Art Gallery, 2005

Kenneth Clark, Colin MacInnes and Bryan Robertson, *Sidney Nolan*, London, 1961

Kenneth Clark, Robert Hughes and Bryan Robertson, *Recent Australian Painting*, exh.cat., Whitechapel Art Gallery, London, 1961

Roberta Colombo Dougoud and Barbara Muller (eds), *Dream Traces: Australian Aboriginal Bark Paintings*, exh.cat., Musee d'Ethnographie de Geneve, Geneva, 2010

Colour in Art, exh.cat., Gayfield Shaw Art Salon, Sydney, 1919

Peter Conrad, *At Home in Australia*, New York and London, 2003

Stephen Coppel, *Out of Australia: Prints and Drawings from Sidney Nolan to Rover Thomas*, exh.cat., British Museum, London, 2011

Brenda Croft, *Culture Warriors: National Indigenous Triennial*, exh.cat., National Gallery of Australia, Canberra, 2007

R. H. Croll (ed.), *Smike to Bulldog: Letters from Arthur Streeton to Tom Roberts*, Sydney, 1946

Isobel Crombie, *Body Culture: Max Dupain, Photography and Australian Culture 1919–1930*, Mulgrave, 2006

Crossing Country: The Alchemy of Western Arnhem Land Art, exh.cat., Art Gallery of New South Wales, Sydney, 2004

Franchesca Cubillo and Wally Caruana, *Aboriginal and Torres Strait Islander Art: Collection Highlights*, National Gallery of Australia, Canberra, 2010

Nici Cumpston, *Desert Country*, exh.cat., Art Gallery of South Australia, Adelaide, 2010

Eva Czernis-Ryl (ed.), *Brilliant: Australian Gold and Silver, 1851–1950*, Sydney, 2011

Carly Davenport et al., *Yiwarra Kuju: The Canning Stock Route*, exh.cat., National Museum of Australia, Canberra, 2010

Alan Davies, Sandra Byron, Theresa Willsteed and Jeff Carter, *Beach, Bush + Battlers: Photographs by Jeff Carter*, Sydney, 2010

Jeff Doring (ed.), *Gwion Gwion: Dulwan mamaa, Secret and Sacred Pathways of the Ngarinyin Aboriginal People of Australia*, Cologne, 2000

Gary Dufour, *Howard Taylor Phenomena*, exh.cat., Art Gallery of Western Australia, Perth, 2003

Mary Eagle, *Australian Modern Painting Between the Wars 1914–1939*, Sydney, 1990

Mary Eagle, *The Oil Paintings of Arthur Streeton in the National Gallery of Australia*, Canberra, 1994

Mary Eagle, *The Oil Paintings of Charles Conder in the National Gallery of Australia*, Canberra, 1997

Mary Eagle, *The Oil Paintings of Tom Roberts in the National Gallery of Australia*, Canberra, 1997

Mary Eagle, *Three Creative Fellows: Sidney Nolan, Arthur Boyd, Narritjin Maymuru*, exh.cat., Drill Hall Gallery, Australian National University, Canberra, 2007

Deborah Edwards, *Margaret Preston*, exh.cat., Art Gallery of New South Wales, Sydney, 2005

Deborah Edwards and Denise Mimmocchi (eds), *Sydney Moderns: Art for a New World*, exh.cat., Art Gallery of New South Wales, Sydney, 2013

Elizabeth Ellis, *Conrad Martens: Life and Art*, Sydney, 1994

Helen Ennis and Phillip Adams, *Harold Cazneaux: The Quiet Observer*, Canberra, 1997

Helen Ennis, *Intersections: Photography, History and the National Library of Australia*, exh.cat., Canberra, 2004

Helen Ennis, *Olive Cotton*, exh.cat., Art Gallery of New South Wales, Sydney, 2000

Helen Ennis, *Photography and Australia*, London, 2007

Julie Ewington, *Fiona Hall*, exh.cat., Annandale, 2005

Julie Ewington and Wayne Tunnicliffe (eds), *Tim Johnson: Painting Ideas*, exh.cat., Art Gallery of New South Wales, Sydney, 2009

Tim Fisher, *Painting Forever: Tony Tuckson*, exh.cat., National Gallery of Australia, Canberra, 2001

Fiona Foley: Forbidden, exh.cat., Museum of Contemporary Art, Sydney, 2009

Renée Free, *Lloyd Rees*, Sydney, 1979

Alison French, *Seeing the Centre: The Art of Albert Namatjira 1902–1959*, exh.cat., National Gallery of Australia, Canberra, 2002

Blair French, *Shaun Gladwell: Videowork*, exh.cat., Artspace, Sydney, 2007

Blair French and Daniel Palmer, *Twelve Australian Photo Artists*, exh.cat., Sydney, 2009

Ann Galbally, *Charles Conder: The Last Bohemian*, Carlton, 2005

Ann Galbally, *Frederick McCubbin*, Melbourne, 1981

Ann Galbally and Anne Gray (eds), *Letters from Smike: The Letters of Arthur Streeton, 1890–1943*, Melbourne, 1989

Ann Galbally and Barry Pearce, *Charles Conder*, exh.cat., Art Gallery of New South Wales, Sydney, 2003

Bill Gammage, *The Biggest Estate on Earth: How Aborigines Made Australia*, London, 2011

Kelly Gellatly, *Gordon Bennett*, exh.cat., National Gallery of Victoria, Melbourne, 2007

Kelly Gellatly, *Rosalie Gascoigne*, exh.cat., National Gallery of Victoria, Melbourne, 2008

Shaun Gladwell, *MADDESTMAXIMVS: Planet and Stars Sequence*, Melbourne, 2009

Shaun Gladwell, *Stereo Sequences*, exh.cat., Australian Centre for the Moving Image, Melbourne, 2011

Angela Goddard et al., *Art, Love and Life: Ethel Carrick and E. Phillips Fox*, exh.cat., Queensland Art Gallery, Brisbane, 2011

Kirsty Grant (ed.), *John Brack*, exh.cat., National Gallery of Victoria, Melbourne, 2009

Anne Gray, *Art and Artifice: George Lambert 1873–1930*, Roseville East, 1996

Anne Gray (ed.), *Australian Art in the National Gallery of Australia*, Canberra, 2002

Anne Gray, *Face: Australian Portraits 1880–1960*, exh.cat., National Gallery of Australia, Canberra, 2010

Anne Gray, *George Lambert (1873–1930). Catalogue Raisonné: Paintings and Sculpture, Drawings in Public Collections*, Perth, 1996

Anne Gray, *G.W.Bot: The Australian Wilderness and Garden: Language, Calligraphy and Semantics*, exh.cat., Hart Gallery, London, 1999

Anne Gray, *George W. Lambert Retrospective: Heroes and Icons*, exh.cat., National Gallery of Australia, Canberra, 2007

Anne Gray, *Line, Light and Shadow: James W.R.Linton, Painter, Craftsman, Teacher*, Fremantle, 1986

Anne Gray, *Out of the West: Western Australian Art 1830s–1930s*, exh.cat., National Gallery of Australia, Canberra, 2011

Anne Gray, *Sydney Long: The Spirit of the Land*, exh.cat., National Gallery of Australia, Canberra, 2012

Anne Gray and Ron Radford, *McCubbin: Last Impressions, 1907–17*, exh.cat., National Gallery of Australia, Canberra, 2009

Simon Gregg, *Nicholas Chevalier: Australian Odyssey*, exh.cat., Gippsland Art Gallery, Sale, 2011

John Gregory, *Carnival in Suburbia: The Art of Howard Arkley*, Port Melbourne, 2006

Sasha Grishin, *The Art of John Brack*, Melbourne, 1990

Grazia Gunn, *Arthur Boyd, Seven Persistent Images*, exh.cat., Australian National Gallery, Canberra, 1985

Jocelyn Hackforth-Jones, *Augustus Earle, Travel Artist: Paintings and Drawings in the Rex Nan Kivell Collection, National Library of Australia*, Canberra, 1980

Jocelyn Hackforth-Jones, *The Convict Artists*, South Melbourne, 1977

David Hansen, *John Glover and the Colonial Picturesque*, exh.cat., Tasmanian Museum and Art Gallery, Hobart, 2003

Deborah Hart, *Fred Williams: Infinite Horizons*, exh.cat., National Gallery of Australia, Canberra, 2011

Deborah Hart, *Grace Cossington Smith*, exh.cat., National Gallery of Australia, Canberra, 2005

Deborah Hart (ed.), *Imants Tillers: One World, Many Visions*, exh.cat., National Gallery of Australia, Canberra, 2006

Deborah Hart, *John Olsen*, St Leonards, Sydney, 2000

Deborah Hart et al., *William Robinson: The Transfigured Landscape*, exh.cat., William Robinson Gallery, Queensland University of Technology, 2011

Nic Haygarth, *The Wild Ride: Revolutions that Shaped Tasmanian Black and White Wilderness Photography: From the Sublime to the Skyline*, Hobart, 2008

Peter Haynes, *G.W.Bot Gardens*, exh.cat., Canberra Museum and Gallery, 2003

Rosslyn D. Haynes, *Seeking the Centre: The Australian Desert in Literature, Art and Film*, Melbourne, 1998

Richard Heathcote (ed.), *Adrian Feint: Cornucopia*, exh.cat., Carrick Hill, Adelaide, 2009

Margot Hilton and Graeme Blundell, *Brett Whiteley: An Unauthorised Life*, Sydney, 1996

Ursula Hoff, *Charles Conder*, Melbourne, 1972

Rosalind Hollinrake, *Clarice Beckett: Politically Incorrect*, exh.cat., Ian Potter Museum of Art, University of Melbourne, 1999

Jeanette Hoorn, *The Lycett Album: Drawings of Aborigines and Australian Scenery*, National Library of Australia, Canberra, 1990

Frannie Hopkirk, *Brett: A Portrait of Brett Whiteley by His Sister*, Sydney, 1996

Robert Hughes, *The Art of Australia*, Ringwood, 1966; 1970

Robert Hughes, *The Fatal Shore: The Epic of Australia's Founding*, New York, 1986

Jane Hylton, *Modern Australian Women: Paintings and Prints 1925–1945*, exh.cat., Art Gallery of South Australia, Adelaide, 2000

Jane Hylton, *Reflections: H. J. Johnstone's Evening Shadows, Australia's Most Copied Painting*, exh.cat., Art Gallery of South Australia, Adelaide, 1999

Jane Hylton, *South Australia Illustrated: Colonial Painting in the Land of Promise*, exh.cat., Art Gallery of South Australia, Adelaide, 2012

Jane Hylton and John Neylon, *Hans Heysen: Into the Light*, Kent Town, 2004

Jennifer Isascs, Judith Ryan et al., *Emily Kngwarreye Paintings*, Roseville East, 1998

Jennifer Isaacs, *Tiwi: Art, History, Culture*, Carlton, 2012

Christa E. Johannes and Anthony V. Brown, *W.C.Piguenit 1836–1914 Retrospective*, exh.cat., Tasmanian Museum and Art Gallery, Hobart, 1992

Elizabeth Johns (ed.), *New Worlds from Old: Nineteenth-century Australian and American Landscapes*, exh.cat., National Gallery of Australia, Canberra, National Gallery of Victoria, Melbourne, Wadsworth Atheneum, Hartford, Corcoran Gallery of Art, Washington DC, 1998–99

Heather Johnson, *Roy de Maistre: The Australian Years, 1894–1930*, Roseville, 1988

Heather Johnson, *Roy de Maistre: The English Years 1930–1968*, Roseville, 1995

Vivien Johnson, *Clifford Possum Tjapaltjarri*, exh. cat., Art Gallery of South Australia, Adelaide, 2003

John Jones, *Robert Dowling: Tasmanian Son of Empire*, exh.cat., National Gallery of Australia, Canberra, 2010

Christian Kaufmann (ed.), *'Rarrk': John Mawurndjul, Journey Through Time in Northern Australia*, exh.cat., Museum Tinguely, Basel, 2005

Thomas Keneally, *A Commonwealth of Thieves: The Improbable Birth of Australia*, New York 2005

Thomas Keneally, *Australians: Volume 1, Origins to Eureka*, Crows Nest, 2009

Thomas Keneally, *Australians: Volume 2, From Eureka to the Diggers*, Crows Nest, 2011

Sylvia Kleinert and Margo Neal (eds), *The Oxford Companion to Aboriginal Art and Culture*, Melbourne, 2000

Lou Klepac, *The Life and Work of Russell Drysdale*, Kensington, 1983

Lou Klepac, with Barry Pearce and Jeffrey Smart, *Horace Trenerry*, Roseville, 2009

Mary Knights and Ian North, *Hossein Valamanesh: Out of Nothingness*, Kent Town, 2011

Hendrik Kolenberg, *Jan Senbergs, Complete Screenprints 1960–88*, exh.cat., Art Gallery of New South Wales, Sydney, 2008

Hendrik Kolenberg and Anthony Brown, *Skinner Prout in Australia, 1840–48*, exh.cat., Tasmanian Museum and Art Gallery, Hobart, 1986

Kasper König, Emily Joyce Evans and Falk Wolf (eds), *Remembering Forward: Australian Aboriginal Painting Since 1960*, exh.cat., Museum Ludwig, Cologne, 2010

Karel Kupka, *Un Art à l'état Brut, Peintres et Sculptures des Aborigènes d'Australie*, Lausanne, 1962

Karel Kupka, *Dawn of Art: Painting and Sculpture of Australian Aborigines*, Sydney, 1965

Carly Lane and Franchesca Cubillo (eds), *Undisclosed: Second National Indigenous Art Triennial*, exh. cat., National Gallery of Australia, Canberra, 2012

Terence Lane et al., *Australian Impressionism*, exh.cat., National Gallery of Victoria, Melbourne, 2007

Colin Laverty, *Beyond Sacred: Recent Painting from Australia's Remote Aboriginal Communities, The Collection of Colin and Elizabeth Laverty*, Prahran, 2008

Colin Laverty, *Beyond Sacred: Australian Aboriginal Art, The Collection of Colin and Elizabeth Laverty*, Prahran, 2011

Sandra Le Brun Holmes, *Yirawala: Painter of the Dreaming*, Sydney, 1994

Samantha Littley, *Making It Modern: The Watercolours of Kenneth Macqueen*, exh.cat., Queensland Art Gallery, Brisbane, 2007

Elwyn Lynn, *Sidney Nolan: Myth and Imagery*, London, 1967

Patrick McCaughey (ed.), *Bert and Ned: The Correspondence of Albert Tucker and Sidney Nolan*, Carlton, 2006

Patrick McCaughey, *Fred Williams*, Sydney, 1980, revised 1987, 1996, 2008

Patrick McCaughey, *Voyage and Landfall: The Art of Jan Senbergs*, Carlton, 2006

Pamela McClusky, Wally Caruana, Lisa Graziose Corrin and Stephen Gilchrist, *Ancestral Modern: Australian Aboriginal Art*, New Haven and London, 2012

John McDonald, *Art of Australia*, Sydney, 2008

John McDonald (ed.), *Federation: Australian Art and Society, 1901–2001*, exh.cat., National Gallery of Australia, Canberra, 2000

John McDonald, *Jeffrey Smart: Paintings of the '70s and '80s*, Roseville, 1990

Sandra McGrath, *Brett Whiteley*, Sydney, 1979

Janet McKenzie, *Arthur Boyd: Art and Life*, London, 2000

Andrew Mackenzie, *Frederick McCubbin 1855–1917: 'The Proff' and His Art*, Lilydale, 1990

Andrew Mackenzie (ed.), *Walter Withers: The Forgotten Manuscripts*, Lilydale, 1987

Andrew Mackenzie, *Walter Withers 1854–1914: A Biographical Sketch*, Moorebank, 1989

Ian McLean, *The Art of Gordon Bennett*, Roseville East, 1996

Ian McLean (ed.), *How Aborigines Invented the Idea of Contemporary Art: Writings on Aboriginal Art*, Sydney, 2011

John McPhee (ed.), *Joseph Lycett: Convict Artist*, exh.cat., Museum of Sydney, Sydney, 2006

John McPhee, *The Art of John Glover*, South Melbourne, 1980

Humphrey McQueen, *Tom Roberts*, Sydney, 1996

Kenneth Macqueen, *Adventure in Watercolour: An Artist's Story*, Sydney, 1948

Filippo Maggia (ed.), *Tracey Moffatt: Between Dreams and Reality*, exh.cat., Spazio Oberdan, Milan, 2006

David Malouf, *A Spirit of Play: The Making of Australian Consciousness*, Sydney, 1998

Banduk Marika et al., Margie West (ed.), *Yalangbara: Art of the Djang'kawu*, exh.cat., Museum and Art Gallery of the Northern Territory, Darwin, 2008

Linda Michael, *Callum Morton: In Memoriam*, exh.cat., Heide Museum of Modern Art, Bulleen, 2011

Drusilla Modjeska, *Stravinsky's Lunch*, Sydney, 1999

James Mollison and Nicholas Bonham, *Albert Tucker*, South Melbourne, 1982

James Mollison and Jan Minchin, *Albert Tucker: A Retrospective*, exh. cat., National Gallery of Victoria, Melbourne, 1990

Alan Moorehead, *Coopers Creek: The Story of the Ill-fated Burke and Wills Expedition into the Burning Interior of Central Australia*, London, 1963

Howard Morphy, *Aboriginal Art*, London, 1998

Howard Morphy, *Ancestral Connections: Art and an Aboriginal System of Knowledge*, Chicago, 1991

Howard Morphy, *Becoming Art: Exploring Cross-cultural Categories*, Sydney, 2008

Howard Morphy and Rebecca Coates (eds), *In Place (Out of Time): Contemporary Art in Australia*, exh.cat., Museum of Modern Art, Oxford, 1997

Howard Morphy and M. Smith Boles (eds), *Art from the Land: Dialogues with the Kluge-Ruhe Collection of Australian Aboriginal Art*, University of Virginia, Charlottesville, 1999

Tom Mosby et al., *Ilan Pasin (This Is Our Way): Torres Strait Art*, exh.cat., Cairns Regional Gallery, 1998

Djon Mundine et al., *They Are Meditating: Bark Paintings from the MCA's Arnott's Collection*, exh.cat., Museum of Contemporary Art, Sydney, 2008

Keith Munro et al., *Bardayal 'Lofty' Nadjamerrek AO*, exh.cat., Museum of Contemporary Art, Sydney, 2010

Laura Murray Cree and Nevill Drury (eds), *Australian Painting Now*, North Ryde, 2000

Dorothy Napangardi et al., *Dancing Up Country: The Art of Dorothy Napangardi*, exh.cat., Museum of Contemporary Art, Sydney, 2002

Richard Neville, *Mr J. W. Lewin: Painter and Naturalist*, Sydney, 2012

Gael Newton, *Max Dupain*, Sydney, 1980

Gael Newton, *Simply Peter Dombrovskis*, Sandy Bay, 2006

Gael Newton, *Shades of Light: Photography and Australia 1839–1988*, Canberra, 1988

Gael Newton, *Tracey Moffatt: Fever Pitch*, Annandale, *c.* 1995

Cynthia Nolan, *Outback*, London, 1962

Rachel Nolan et al., *The Torres Strait Islands*, exh.cat., Queensland Art Gallery and Gallery of Modern Art, Brisbane, 2011

Dennis Nona et al., *Sesserae: The Works of Dennis Nona*, Brisbane, 2005

Ian North, *The Art of Dorrit Black*, Adelaide, 1979

Michael O'Ferrall, *1990 Venice Biennale: Australia: Rover Thomas, Trevor Nickolls*, exh. cat., Art Gallery of Western Australia, Perth, 1990

John Olsen, *Drawn from Life*, Sydney, 1997

Barry Pearce, *Arthur Boyd Retrospective*, exh. cat., Art Gallery of New South Wales, Sydney, 1993

Barry Pearce, *Elioth Gruner, 1882–1939*, exh.cat., Art Gallery of New South Wales, Sydney, 1983

Barry Pearce (et. al.), *Sidney Nolan, 1917–1992*, exh.cat., Art Gallery of New South Wales, Sydney, 2008

Barry Pearce, *Jeffrey Smart*, Roseville, 2005

Barry Pearce, Bryan Robertson and Wendy Whiteley, *Brett Whiteley: Art and Life*, exh.cat., Art Gallery of New South Wales, Sydney, 1995

Hetti Perkins (ed.), *Crossing Country: The Alchemy of Western Arnhem Land Art*, exh.cat., Art Gallery of New South Wales, Sydney, 2004

Hetti Perkins, Brenda Croft and Victoria Lynn, *Fluent: Emily Kame Kngwarreye, Yvonne Koolmatrie, Judy Watson: XLVII Esposizione Internazionale d'Arte, La Biennale di Venezia 1997*, exh.cat., Art Gallery of New South Wales, Sydney, 1997

Hetti Perkins and Margie West (eds), *One Sun One Moon: Aboriginal Art in Australia*, exh.cat., Art Gallery of New South Wales, Sydney, 2007

T. M. Perry and Donald H. Simpson (eds), *Drawings by William Westall*, London, 1962

Georges Petitjean, *Outsider/Insider: The Art of Gordon Bennett*, exh.cat., Museum of Contemporary Aboriginal Art, Utrecht, 2012

Georges Petitjean, *Contemporary Aboriginal Art: The AAMU and Dutch Collections*, Utrecht, 2010

Simon Pierse, *Australian Art and Artists in London, 1950–1965: An Antipodean Summer*, Farnham, 2012

Anne Pitkethly, *N. J. Caire, Landscape Photographer*, Rosanna, 1988

John Douglas Pringle, *Australian Painting Today*, London, 1963

Ruth Pullin, *Eugene von Guérard: Nature Revealed*, exh.cat., National Gallery of Victoria, Melbourne, 2011

Ron Radford, *Ocean to Outback: Australian Landscape Painting, 1850–1950*, exh.cat., National Gallery of Australia, Canberra, 2007

Ron Radford, *Our Country: Australian Federation Landscapes, 1900–1914*, exh.cat., Art Gallery of South Australia, Adelaide, 2001

Ron Radford, 'Turner and Australia', in *Turner from the Tate: The Making of a Master*, exh.cat., Tate, London, 2013

Ron Radford and Jane Hylton, *Australian Colonial Art 1800–1900*, exh.cat., Art Gallery of South Australia, Adelaide, 1995

Ron Radford et al., *Tom Roberts*, exh.cat., Art Gallery of South Australia, Adelaide, 1996

Robert Reason, *Bounty: Nineteenth-century South Australian Gold and Silver*, exh.cat., Art Gallery of South Australia, Adelaide, 2012

Lloyd Rees, *The Small Treasures of a Lifetime: Some Early Memories of Australian Art and Artists*, Sydney, 1969

T. G. Rosenthal, *Sidney Nolan*, London and New York, 2002

John Rothenstein, *The Life and Death of Conder*, London, 1938

Judith Ryan and Kim Akerman (eds), *Images of Power: Aboriginal Art of the Kimberley*, exh.cat., National Gallery of Victoria, Melbourne, 1993

Judith Ryan, Carol Cooper and Joy Murphy-Wandin, *Remembering Barak*, exh.cat., National Gallery of Victoria, Melbourne, 2003

Judith Ryan, Philip Batty, John Kean et al., *Tjukurrtjanu: Origins of Western Desert Art*, National Gallery of Victoria, Melbourne, 2011

Andrew Sayers, *Australian Art*, Oxford, 2001

Andrew Sayers, Sarah Engledow and Wally Caruana, *Open Air: Portraits in the Landscape*, exh.cat., National Portrait Gallery, Canberra, 2008

Andrew Sayers, *Aboriginal Artists of the Nineteenth Century*, Melbourne, 1994

Andrew Sayers, *Drawing in Australia: Drawings, Watercolours, Pastels and Collages from the 1770s to the 1980s*, Australian National Gallery, Canberra, 1989

Andrew Sayers, *Sidney Nolan's Ned Kelly: The Ned Kelly Paintings in the National Gallery of Australia*, National Gallery of Australia, Canberra, 2002

Andrew Sayers, Sarah Engledow and Wally Caruana, *Open Air: Portraits in the Landscape*, exh.cat., National Portrait Gallery, Canberra, 2008–09

Edward Scheer, *The Infinity Machine: Mike Parr's Performance Art 1971–2005*, Melbourne, 2010

Lynne Seear (ed.), *Darkness and Light: The Art of William Robinson*, exh. cat., Queensland Art Gallery, Brisbane, 2001

Lynne Seear and Julie Ewington (eds), *Brought to Light: Australian Art, 1850–1965: From the Queensland Art Gallery Collection*, 1998

John Slater, *Through Artists' Eyes: Australian Suburbs and Their Cities, 1919–1945*, Carlton, 2004

Bernard Smith (ed.), *Documents on Art and Taste in Australia*, Melbourne, 1975

Bernard Smith, *Australian Painting, 1788–1960*, London, 1962; expanded editions, Melbourne, to 1970 (1971), to 1990 (1991, with Terry Smith), and to 2000 (2001, with Christopher Heathcote)

Geoffrey Smith, *Arthur Streeton, 1867–1943*, exh.cat., National Gallery of Victoria, Melbourne, 1995

Geoffrey Smith, *Russell Drysdale, 1912–1981*, exh.cat., National Gallery of Victoria, Melbourne, 1998

Geoffrey Smith, *Sidney Nolan: Desert and Drought*, exh.cat., National Gallery of Victoria, Melbourne, 2003

Jason Smith, *Peter Booth: Human/Nature*, exh.cat., National Gallery of Victoria, Melbourne, 2003

Jason Smith and Sue Cramer (eds), *Kathy Temin*, exh.cat., Heide Museum of Modern Art, Bulleen, 2009

Trevor Smith, *History and Memory in the Art of Gordon Bennett*, exh.cat., Ikon Gallery, Birmingham, 1999

Trevor Smith, *Robert MacPherson*, exh.cat., Art Gallery of Western Australia, Perth, 2001

Ted Snell, *Howard Taylor: Forest Figure*, South Fremantle, 1995

Michael Snelling, *Tracey Moffatt*, exh.cat., Institute of Modern Art, Brisbane, 1999

Abigail Solomon-Godeau, *Rosemary Laing*, Munich, 2012

Virginia Spate, *Tom Roberts*, Melbourne, 1972

Baldwin Spencer, *Wanderings in Wild Australia*, London, 1928

Russell Storer et al., *Simryn Gill*, exh.cat., Museum of Contemporary Art, Sydney, 2008

Lara Strongman and Paula Savage (eds), *Tracey Moffatt*, exh.cat., Wellington City Gallery, 2002

Catherine Summerhayes, *The Moving Images of Tracey Moffatt*, Milan, 2007

Peter Sutton (ed.), *Dreamings: The Art of Aboriginal Australia*, New York, 1988

Luke Taylor (ed.), *Painting the Land Story*, exh.cat., National Museum of Australia, Canberra, 1999

Luke Taylor, *Seeing the Inside: Bark Painting in Western Arnhem Land*, Oxford, 1996

Colin Thiele, *Heysen of Hahndorf*, Adelaide, 1968

Daniel Thomas (ed.), *Creating Australia: 200 Years of Art, 1788–1988*, exh.cat., Art Gallery of South Australia, Adelaide and Australian Bicentennial Authority, Sydney, 1988

Daniel Thomas (ed.), *Bea Maddock: Catalogue Raisonné Vol. 1, 1951–1983*, Launceston, 2011

Sarah Thomas (ed.), *The Encounter, 1802: Art of Flinders and Baudin Voyages*, exh.cat., Art Gallery of South Australia, Adelaide, 2002

John Tregenza, *George French Angas, Artist, Traveller and Naturalist, 1822–1886*, Adelaide, 1980

John Turner, *Joseph Lycett: Governor Macquarie's Convict Artist*, Newcastle, 1997

Christopher Uhl, *Albert Tucker*, Melbourne, 1969

Nancy Underhill (ed.), *Nolan on Nolan: Sidney Nolan in His Own Words*, Camberwell, Victoria, 2007

Nancy Underhill et al., *Eureka!: Artists from Australia*, exh.cat., Institute of Contemporary Arts, London, 1982

Susanna de Vries, *Ethel Carrick Fox: Travels and Triumphs of a Post-Impressionist*, Brisbane, 1997

Diane Waldman, *Australian Visions*, exh.cat., Solomon R. Guggenheim Museum, New York, 1984

Leslie Walton, *The Art of Roland Wakelin*, Seaforth, 1987

Warlukurlangu Artists, *Kuruwarri = Yuendumu Doors*, Canberra, 1992

Jonathan Watkins, *Stories of Australian Art*, exh.cat., Commonwealth Institute, London, and Usher Gallery, Lincoln, 1988

Judy Watson and Louise Martin-Chew, *Judy Watson: Blood Language*, Carlton, 2009

Margaret K. C. West, *Declan, a Tiwi artist*, Perth, 1987

Tim Winton et al., *Illumination: The Art of Philip Wolfhagen*, exh.cat., Newcastle Art Gallery, 2013

Irena Zdanowicz, 'Geography with a Purpose: Bea Maddock's TERRA SPIRITUS', *Print Quarterly*, vol. 28, no. 4, 2011

Irena Zdanowicz and Stephen Coppel (eds), *Fred Williams: An Australian Vision*, exh.cat., British Museum, London, 2003

LENDERS TO THE EXHIBITION

ADELAIDE

Art Gallery of South Australia

Royal Agricultural and Horticultural Society of South Australia

South Australian Museum

University of Adelaide Visual Art Collection

ARMIDALE, NEW SOUTH WALES

New England Regional Art Museum

BALLARAT

Art Gallery of Ballarat

BRISBANE

Courtesy Judy Watson and Milani Gallery

Queensland Art Gallery

CAMPBELLTOWN, NEW SOUTH WALES

Campbelltown City Bicentennial Art Gallery

CANBERRA

Australian National University

National Gallery of Australia

National Library of Australia

GEELONG

Geelong Gallery

HOBART

Tasmanian Museum and Art Gallery

LONDON

Ministry of Defence Art Collection

Tate

MELBOURNE

National Gallery of Victoria

State Library of Victoria

NEWCASTLE, NEW SOUTH WALES

Newcastle Art Gallery

PERTH

State Art Collection, Art Gallery of Western Australia

SYDNEY

Art Gallery of New South Wales

Art Gallery of New South Wales. John Kaldor Family Collection

Australian National Maritime Museum

Manly Art Gallery and Museum

Museum of Contemporary Art

Museum of Sydney, Historic Houses Trust of New South Wales

State Library of New South Wales

PHOTOGRAPHIC ACKNOWLEDGEMENTS

Adelaide, Art Gallery of South Australia, Photos Saul Steed: cats 4 (© Estate of the artist licensed by Aboriginal Artists Agency Ltd), 20 (© Estate of the artist licensed by Aboriginal Artists Agency Ltd), 25 (© Estate of the artist licensed by Aboriginal Artists Agency Ltd), 42, 44, 49, 55, 56, 57, 63, 64, 66, 67, 68, 72, 76, 88, 90, 100, 106, 108, 111, 117 (© DACS 2013), 127 (© DACS 2013), 128 (© estate of Kenneth Macqueen), 133 (© DACS 2013), 136, 137, 141, 140 (© courtesy of the Trenerry family), 141, 142 (© DACS 2013), 150 (© Jeffrey Smart), 165 (© Estate of Fred Williams), 173 (© Art Gallery of South Australia), 174 (Courtesy The Howard H Taylor Estate. Represented by Galerie Düsseldorf Perth Western Australia), 193 (Courtesy the artist and Greenaway Art Gallery).

Adelaide, © South Australian Museum: fig. 14 (Archives, Leske Coll.), fig. 20 (© DACS 2013).

Armidale, New England Regional Art Museum, © Karen P. Clune: cat. 148.

Ballarat, Art Gallery of Ballarat, photo Ben Cox: cats 81, 112; fig. 26.

Brisbane, © Judy Watson c/o Milani Gallery: cat. 205.

Brisbane, Queensland Art Gallery: cat: 110 (© Reproduced with kind permission of the Ophthalmic Research Institute of Australia), cat. 118 (Natasha Harth, QAGOMA).

Cambelltown, Cambelltown Arts Centre, courtesy the artist / Jagath Dheerasekara: cat. 182.

Canberra, Australian National University, © John Beard / Australian National University Art Collection: cat. 192.

Canberra, © House of Representatives. By permission of the Yirrkala community, Buku-Larrnggay Mulka Centre: fig. 16.

Canberra, National Gallery of Australia: cats 2 (© Estate of the artist licensed by Aboriginal Artists Agency Ltd), 3 (© DACS 2013), 5 (© Estate of the artist licensed by Aboriginal Artists Agency Ltd), 6–7 (© DACS 2013), 9 (© Buku-Larrnggay Mulka Centre), 10 (© Estate of the artist licensed by Aboriginal Artists Agency Ltd), 11 (© Gulumbu Yunupingu), 12 (© Anindilyakwa Land Council), 13 (© DACS 2013), 14 (© Estate of the artist licensed by Aboriginal Artists Agency Ltd), 16–19 (© Estate of the artist licensed by Aboriginal Artists Agency Ltd), 21 and back cover (© Estate of the artist licensed by Aboriginal Artists Agency Ltd), 22 (© DACS 2013), 24 (© Estate of the artist licensed by Aboriginal Artists Agency Ltd), 26 (Courtesy the estate of Jack Britten), 27 (Courtesy of the Estate Queenie Mckenzie), 29–30 (© the artist's estate courtesy Warmun Art Centre), 31 (© Doreen Reid Nakamarra / Papunya Tula Artists / Aboriginal Artists Agency), 32 (© DACS 2013), 37 (© Estate of the artist licensed by Aboriginal Artists Agency Ltd), 38 (Courtesy of the artist and Roslyn Oxley9 Gallery, Sydney), 39 (© DACS 2013), 40 (© Nici Cumpston), 41 (Image courtesy of the Artist, Mornington Island Art, Queensland & Alcaston Gallery, Melbourne), 122 (© Caroline de Maistre Walker), 123 (© J. Murray), 124 (© J. Murray), 129–31 (© Estate of Grace Cossington Smith), 135 (© the artist), 143 (© DACS 2013), 144 (© Eric Thake Estate), 145 (© Barbara Tucker), 147 (reproduced with permission of Bundanon Trust), 152–3 (© Estate of Russell Drysdale), 159 (© Sidney Nolan Trust / Bridgeman Art Library), 161–2 (© DACS 2013), 166 (© DACS 2013), 170 (© Wesley Stacey), 171 (© Liz Dombrovskis), 175 (© Fiona Hall), 179–80 (© DACS 2013), 181 (© William Robinson), 183 (© Mike Parr), 184 (© Bea Maddock), 186 (© the artist), 187 (© G.W. Bot), 189–90 (Courtesy of the artist and Roslyn Oxley9 Gallery, Sydney), 195 (© Dennis Nona / Print published by The Australian Art Print Network), 196 (© Vernon Ah Kee. Courtesy Milani Gallery), 198 (Photo courtesy of the artist), 199 (Courtesy the artist and Anna Schwartz Gallery Australia), 200 (© Rosemary Laing), 202 (Courtesy of the artist and Gallery Gabrielle Pizzi, Melbourne, Australia), 203 (© Danie Mellor), 204 (Image courtesy of the artist and Anna Schwartz Gallery, Melbourne / John Brash); figs 1 (© Polixeni Papapetrou / image courtesy of the artist), 2 (© the artist), 6 (© DACS 2013 / Julie Dowling), 7 (Courtesy of the artist and Gallery Gabrielle Pizzi, Melbourne, Australia), 8 (Courtesy of the artist and Gallery Gabrielle Pizzi, Melbourne, Australia), 9 (Courtesy of the artist and Roslyn Oxley9 Gallery, Sydney), 12 (© Estate of the artist licensed by Aboriginal Artists Agency Ltd), 18 (© Michael Jensen), 21 (© the artist's estate, courtesy Warmun Art Centre), 35 (Courtesy of the Cazneaux Family), 36 (© Sidney Nolan Trust / Bridgeman Art Library), 43.

Canberra, National Library of Australia, courtesy of the Cazneaux Family: cat. 132.

Canberra, courtesy National Museum of Australia / Licensed by Aboriginal Artists Agency: fig. 19.

© Bill Gammage: fig. 4.

© Shaun Gladwell. Photo Josh Raymond / Cinematographer Gotaro Uematsu / Courtesy the artist and Anna Schwartz Gallery Australia: fig. 40.

Geelong, Geelong Gallery, courtesy of the Estate of Fred Williams: cat. 164.

Hobart, courtesy of The Wilderness Society Collection, 2013: fig. 41

London, © Getty Images / Oxford Scientific. Photo: Daniel Cox: fig. 15.

London, Ministry of Defence Art Collection / Roy Fox: cat. 46.

London, © Tate, London 2013 / Courtesy of the artist and Roslyn Oxley9 Gallery, Sydney: cat. 191.

Melbourne, National Gallery of Victoria, NGV Photo Services: cats 15 (© Estate of the artist licensed by Aboriginal Artists Agency Ltd), 23 (© DACS 2013), 33 (© courtesy Martumili Artists), 82, 87, 91, 94–7, 113, 116 (© DACS 2013), 160 (© National Gallery of Victoria); figs 5, 11, 17 (By permissión of the Bardon Family. Photo: Allan Scott), 27 (NGV Photo Services), 29 (NGV Photo Services), 31, 44 (© Bea Maddock).

Mulgrave, Carroll & Richardson, by permission of Harold Thomas: fig. 37.

Newcastle, Newcastle Art Gallery, photo courtesy Newcastle Art Gallery Collection: cat. 50.

Perth, Art Gallery of Western Australia / Bo Wong, Art Gallery of Western Australia: cats 28 (© the artists estate, courtesy Warmun Art Centre), 163 (© Estate of Ian Fairweather. All rights reserved, DACS 2013), 178 (© DACS 2013).

Sydney, Art Gallery of New South Wales / photo AGNSW: cats 8 (© Djambawa Marawili, Buku Laarngay Arts Centre Yirrkala), 92, 99, 104–5, 109, 139 (© DACS 2013), 114 (Photo AGNSW), 149 (© Margaret Rose Preston Estate), 151 (© AGNSW), 158 (© AGNSW), 168 (© Wendy Whiteley), 185 (© The Estate of Howard Arkley. Licensed by Kalli Rolfe Contemporary Art), 188 (© Simryn Gill), 201 (© Hossein Valamanesh / Courtesy the Greenaway Art Gallery); figs 2 (© Anne Zahalka. Licensed by Viscopy, Sydney/DACS, 2013), 9 (© Estate of the artist licensed by Aboriginal Artists Agency Ltd / © Wendy Whiteley), 10 (© Sidney Nolan Trust/Bridgeman Art Library), 25, 30 (© Estate of Sydney Long. Courtesy Ophthalmic Research Institute of Australia / AGNSW), 34 (© Anne Zahalka. Licensed by Viscopy, Sydney / DACS, 2013), 42 (© Wendy Whiteley / AGNSW).

Sydney, Art Gallery of New South Wales, © Shaun Gladwell, Josh Raymond / Cinematographer Gotaro Uematsu / Courtesy the artist and Anna Schwartz Gallery Australia: cat. 197.

Sydney, Australian National Maritime Museum, photo reproduced courtesy of the National Maritime Museum: cat. 62.

Sydney, Historic Houses Trust of New South Wales, © Gordon Bennett / photo Jenni Carter: cat. 176; fig. 38.

Sydney, Museum of Contemporary Art: cats 172 (© the artist), 177 (© the artist), 194 (© Fiona Foley / Photo courtesy Andrew Baker Art Dealer, Brisbane).

Sydney, Powerhouse Museum. Photo: Marinco Kojdanovski: fig. 33 (© DACS, 2013).

Sydney, State Library of New South Wales: cats 43 (Mitchell Library. State Library of NSW - Call no. PXD 388/f.1), 48 (Mitchell Library. State Library of NSW – Call no. PXE 888/11), 73 (Mitchell Library. State Library of NSW - Call no. PXD 75 / 7); fig. 24 (Dixson Galleries. State Library of NSW – DG 24/16); fig. 32 (Mitchell Library. State Library of NSW – Ephemera).

© Isambard Thomas: pp.20–21

INDEX

All references are to page numbers; those in **bold** type indicate catalogue plates, and those in *italic* type indicate essay illustrations

A

Aboriginal people
- bark paintings 27, 35, 43–4
- Barunga Statement 39
- ceremonial art 42–3, *43*
- and colonial settlement 49–50
- Dreaming 23, 26, 35, 42–3
- Federation landscapes 151–2
- flag 228, *229*
- influence of 26
- languages 43
- mainstream art world and 228–30, 234
- Papunya Tula Artists' Co-operative 26, 33, 35
- relationship with the land 23, 33, 42, 50
- rock art 32–3, 44
- sand paintings 33–5
- urban artists 26
- Yirrkala Bark Petitions 39

Abstract Expressionism 150, 228, 233, 234
Adelaide 23, 96, 98, 188
Ah Kee, Vernon, *Can't Chant (wegrewhere) #2* 50, **280**
Angas, George French 97–8
- *Port Lincoln from Winter's Hill* 97–8, **127**
- *Scene Showing Emus in a Plain (Coorong)* 97, **127**

Apuatimi, Declan, *Pamijini* 45, **61**
Arkley, Howard, *Superb + Solid* 231, **268**
Arnhem Land 33, 43–5
Art Nouveau 151
Ashton, Julian 101, 148
Australian Alps 99
Australian bush 23, 24
Australian Impressionists 24, 101, 148, 150
Awabakal people 95

B

Bacon, Francis 26, 153
Banks, Joseph 30, 93
Barak, William 43, 49, 151–2
- *Corroboree* **84**

Barbizon school 24, 101
Bardon, Geoffrey 26, 33, 35, 46
bark paintings 27, 35, 43–4
Baru 45
Bathurst Island 45
Bathurst Plains 95
Battarbee, Rex 33
Beard, John, *Uluru 8* **274**
Beaumaris 149, 187
Becker, Ludwig 97, 98
- *Border of the Mud Desert near Desolation Camp, 9 March* **129**
- *Mallee Sand Cliffs at the Darling, 12 October* **128**
- *Meteor Seen by Me on 11 October* 97, **128**

Beckett, Clarice 187–8
- *Morning Shadows* 188, **203**
- *Passing Trams* 188, **203**

Beckett, Samuel 189
Bennett, Gordon 26, 228
- *Possession Island* 228, 229, **258**

Beuys, Joseph 235
Black, Dorrit 188–9, 191
- *The Olive Plantation* 188–9, 191, **207**

Blake, W. S., *A View of the Town of Sydney in the Colony of New South Wales* *93*
Blanchflower, Brian 233
- *Nocturne 3 (Whale Rock)* 233, **254**

Bligh, William 95
Block, René 235
Blue Mountains 95, 150
bone-burial ceremonies 44
Booth, Peter 233
- *Mangroves* 233, **262**

Bot, G. W. 228
- *Garden of Gethsemane* **270**

Botany Bay 92
Box Hill 148
Boyd, Arthur 25, 35, 186, 189–90, 191, 232
- 'Caged Painter' series 232
- *The Hunter I* 189–90, **212**
- *The Mining Town (Casting the Money Lenders from the Temple)* 189, **213**
- *Paintings in the Studio: 'Figure Supporting Back Legs' and 'Interior with Black Rabbit'* 232, **248–9**

Boyd, Daniel, *Treasure Island* *23*
Brack, John 228
- *The Car* 25, 231–2, **236–7**

Bradman, Donald 30
Bribie Island 233
Brierly, Oswald 97
- *Amateur Whaling, or a Tale of the Pacific* 97, **122–3**

Brisbane 96, 235
Britten, Jack, *Purnululu (Bull Creek Country)* **74–5**
Bruegel, Pieter, *Tower of Babel* 189
Burke and Wills expedition 32, 97
Buvelot, Louis 98, 99, 101
- *Summer Afternoon, Templestowe* 149, *149*
- *Winter Morning near Heidelberg* 101, **141**

C

Caire, Nicholas, *Fairy Scene at the Landslip, Blacks' Spur, Victoria* 100, **143**
Campbell, Robert Jnr 26, 49–50
- *Abo History (Facts)* 50, **87**

Canberra 232
Canning Stock Route 48
Cape Leeuwin 92–3
Carrick, Ethel, *Manly Beach – Summer Is Here* 153, **179**
Carter, Jeff, *Tobacco Road, Ovens Valley* **202**
Cazneaux, Harold 187
- *Arch of Steel* 187, **200**
- *The Spirit of Endurance* 187, *189*

Cézanne, Paul 186, 228
Chevalier, Nicholas 98, 99, 101
- *Mount Arapiles and the Mitre Rock* 101, **140**

Chinese art 189, 233
Christianity 44
Christie, Agatha 234
Clark, Kenneth 22, 190–1, 234
Colac tribe 98
'colour-music' 153
Conceptualism 228
Conder, Charles 24, 101, 148, 149, 151
- *Bronte Beach* 149, **160**
- *Departure of the Orient – Circular Quay* 153, **160**
- *Herrick's Blossoms* 150, **167**
- *A Holiday at Mentone* 149, **161**
- *How We Lost Poor Flossie* 150, **167**
- *Impressionists' Camp* *150*

Constable, John 23, 148, 188, 234
Cook, Captain James 30, 228
Corot, Camille 148
Cronulla Beach 50
Crooks, Daniel, *Cloud Atlas (Fitzroy 1:23)* **283**
Cubism 186, 188, 233
Cummings, Elisabeth, *Wedderburn Spring* 234, **264**
Cumpston, Nici 50
- *Campsite V, Nookamka Lake* 50, **88**

Cyclone Tracy 49

D

Daintree, Richard, *Gold Diggers' Sale, Queensland* **140**
Dale, Robert, *Panoramic View of King Georges Sound, Part of the Colony of Swan River* 96, **114–15**
Darwin 49, 189
Davies, David 148, 149, 151
- *Moonrise* 151, **171**

De Maistre, Roy 153
- *Forest Landscape* 153, **182**

Depression (1890s) 24, 151
Depression (1930s) 187, 190, 191
Dickens, Charles, *David Copperfield* 32
Dickinson, Sidney 148
Docker River 35
Dombrovskis, Peter 233
- *Morning Mist, Rock Island Bend* 230, *231*, **252**

Dowling, Julie, *Walyer* *26*
Dreaming 23, 26, 35, 42–3, 44
Drysdale, Russell 25, 50, 190, 191
- *The Drover's Wife* 190, **218**
- *Emus in a Landscape* 190, **219**

Dupain, Max, *Sunbaker* 188, **204**

E

Earle, Augustus 95
- *A Native Camp of Australian Savages near Port Stevens, New South Wales* 95, **113**
- *View from the Summit of Mount York, Looking towards Bathurst Plains, Convicts Breaking Stones, New South Wales* 95, **113**

Eliot, T.S. *The Waste Land* 189
Elizabeth II, Queen 228, 234
Enlightenment 30, 42
environmentalism 230–1
Evans, G.W. 95
- *A View of Sydney New South Wales on Entering the Heads* 92, 95, **104**

Expressionism 186

F

Fairweather, Ian 233
Monsoon 233, **241**
Federation period 25, 151–3
Feint, Adrian, *The Jetties, Palm Beach* 188, **214**
'fernmania' 100
Field, Barron 30–1, 32
Field Island 44
First World War 186, 187, 191
Flannery, Tim, *The Future Eaters* 230
Flight, Claude 188
Flinders, Matthew 92
Flinders Island 50, 96
Flinders Ranges 97, 186, 189, 190
Foley, Fiona 26, 50
Bliss 50, **276–7**
Folingsby, George 101
Franklin River 230, *231*
Frome, E. C. 97
First View of the Salt Desert – Called Lake Torrens 97, **126**

G

Gascoigne, Rosalie 232
Monaro 229, 232, **260–1**
Gija people 48
Gill, H. P. 101
Gill, S. T. 97, 101, 233
Diggings in the Mount Alexander District of Victoria in 1852 **125**
Looking SW from Table Land, August 22nd 97, **124**
North Terrace, Adelaide, Looking South-east from Government House Guardhouse 98, **124**
Gill, Simryn 27
Rampant 230–1, **271**
Gladwell, Shaun
Approach to Mundi Mundi 229–30, **281**
Approach to Mundi Mundi I 230
Gleeson, James 190
Gleizes, Albert 188
Glover, John 96
Cawood on the Ouse River **119**
A Corroboree of Natives in Mills Plain 96, 101, **116**
A View of the Artist's House and Garden, in Mills Plains, Van Diemen's Land 96, **118**
View of Mills Plains, Van Diemen's Land 96, **117**
gold rush 98, 99
Green parties 230, *231*
Gregory, J. W., *The Dead Heart of Australia* 31
Groote Eylandt 45
Group 9 188
Gruner, Elioth, *The Wave* 153, **178**
Guggenheim (Solomon R.) Museum, New York 23
Gulidjan people 98
Gumatj clan 45

H

Hall, Fiona, *Paradisus Terrestris* 230, **256–7**
Havell, Robert, Jnr, *Panoramic View of King Georges Sound, Part of the Colony of Swan River* 96, **114–15**
Hawkesbury River 95
Heidelberg 149–50
Henderson, Edmund 97
Perth, West Australia **121**
Henson, Bill 233
Mnemosyne 233, *233*
Untitled 233, *233*, **272**
Heysen, Hans 97, 101, 152, 186–7, 189, 190, 228
The Land of the Oratunga 186–7, **194**, 229
Midsummer Morning 152, **176**
Red Gold 152, **177**
Summer 228
White Gums, Summer Afternoon 228
Hilder, J. J. 148, 152
Dry Lagoon 152–3, **174**
Hobart 96, 97, 98, 101
Holloway, Memory 23
Hope, A. D. 31
Horrocks expedition 97
Hughes, Robert 151

I

immigrants 27, 31, 233–4
Indonesia 45
Irwin, Beatrice, *New Science of Colour* 187

J

Jaminji, Paddy 26–7
Kimberley Landscape **77**
Japaljarri Sims, Paddy, *Yanjilypiri Jukurrpa (Star Dreaming)* 48, **69**
Japanese art 150, 189
Jeffries, Richard 187
Johnson, Tim 228–9
Dewachen 228–9, **259**
Yuelamu 229
Johnstone, H. J., *Evening Shadows, Backwater of the Murray, South Australia* 50, 101, **144–5**, 153
Joyce, James, *Ulysses* 189
Jungurrayi Spencer, Larry, *Yanjilypiri Jukurrpa (Star Dreaming)* 48, **69**
Jupurrurla Nelson, Paddy
Yanjilypiri Jukurrpa (Star Dreaming) 48, **69**
Wardilykakurlu manu Yankirrikirlli – Bush Turkey and Emu 48

K

Kakadu 33
Kaltukatjara 35
Kame Kngwarreye, Emily 26, 30, 48
Anwerlarr Anganenty (Big Yam Dreaming) **70–1**
Kangaroo Service: Sydney to London by Air (poster) *187*
Kelly, Ned 23, 25, 32, 190
the Kimberley 33, 43, 48–9
Koons, Jeff 235
Kuku Yalandji people 50
Kundaagi 44
Kurirr Kurirr ceremonial cycle 48–9

L

Laing, Rosemary 234–5
Jim 235, **283**
Lambert, George W.
A Sergeant of the Light Horse 186, *186*
The Squatter's Daughter 186, **192**
Laurie, Henry 148
Lawson, Henry 148
Leonardo da Vinci 230
Leura Tjapaltjarri, Tim, *Fatal Love Dance* **65**
Lewin, John 94
Evans's Peak 95, **110**
Fish Catch and Dawes Point, Sydney Harbour 95, **111**
View from Governor Bligh's Farm, Hawkesbury, New South Wales 94, 95, **105**
Lhote, André 188
Light, William 23
Linton, James W. R. 152
Falls Road, Late Evening **193**
Long, Sydney 148, 151, 152, 228
The Music Lesson 152, *152*
The Spirit of the Plains 151, **170**
Lungkata 47
Lycett, Joseph 92, 95, 99
Aborigines Hunting Kangaroos 42
Aborigines Using Fire to Hunt Kangaroos 42, 95, **112**
Inner View of Newcastle 92, 95, **112**
'The Lycett Album': Drawings of Aborigines and Scenery, New South Wales 42, 95, **112**

M

Macassan people 45
McCaughey, Patrick 32
McCubbin, Frederick 24, 101, 148–9, 150, 152, 153
Collins Street 153, **180**
Down on his Luck 50
Lost 149, **154**
The Pioneer 152, 153, **172–3**
Violet and Gold 152, 153, **180–1**
Mackellar, Dorothea, 'My Country' 25
McKenzie, Queenie, *Gija Country* **76**
MacPherson, Robert 234, 235
Mayfair: Bethonga Gold, for B.T.O's 235, **269**
Macquarie, Lachlan 95
Macqueen, Kenneth 152, 186, 187
Birds and Sheep, Darling Downs 187, **195**
McRae, Tommy 43, 49, 151–2
Victorian Blacks – Melbourne Tribe Holding Corroboree after Seeing Ships for the First Time **84**
Maddock, Bea 234, 235
Terra Spiritus ... with a Darker Shade of Pale 234, *235*, **266–7**
Mallarmé, Stéphane 229
Manifold family 98–9
Marawili, Djambawa 27
Source of Fire 45, **57**
Marika, Mawalan 44
The Milky Way 45, **58**
Martens, Conrad 96–7, 99, 101, 150
Campbell's Wharf 97, **120**
View of Sydney from Neutral Bay 96–7, **120**
Martumili Artists, *Ngayarta Kujarra* **82–3**
Mawurndjul, John 27
Mardayin Design at Dilebang 44, **56**
Milmilngkan **56**
Rainbow Serpent's Antilopine Kangaroo 44, **53**
Maymuru, Narritijn 44
Maynard, Ricky
The Healing Garden, Wybalenna, Flinders Island, Tasmania 50, **88**
Portrait of a Distant Land 50
Meere, Charles
1938 Empire Games poster 187, 188
Australian Beach Pattern 188, 189, **204–5**
Melbourne 96, 98, 149, 150–1, 187, 189, 233, 234
Mellor, Danie, *An Elysian City (of Picturesque Landscapes and Memory)* 50, **286**
Melville Island 45
Menzies, Robert 191
Messer, Thomas M. 23
Mickey of Ulladulla 43, 49
Fishing, Native Flora and Fauna **85**
Mirdidingkingathi Juwarnda (Sally Gabori), *My Country* **89**
Modernism 186, 190, 228
Moffatt, Tracey 27, 228
Selling Aluminium Siding 27
Up in the Sky 228, **273**
Monet, Claude 150, 152
Moore, Henry 190
Morton, Callum, *Tomorrowland* 231, **272**
Mount Eccles *24*
Murray River 50, 101, 229
Musée du Louvre, Paris 96
Muslim Australians 50

N

Nadjamerrek, Bardayal
The Artist's Country, Liverpool River 44, **55**
Dead Man **54**
Nadubi Spirit-Woman, with Possum, Magpie Goose and Fish 44, **51**
Nakamarra, Doreen Reid, *Untitled* **80**
Namarari Tjapaltjarri, Mick 26
Rain Dreaming at Nyunmau 48, **72**
Namatjira, Albert 27, 33, 46, 189, 228, 229
Nandabitta, Maminyamandja, *Macassan Prau and Trepang Curing* 45, **60**
Napangardi, Dorothy, *Sandhills of Mina Mina* **81**
Napangardi clan 35
National Gallery of Australia, Canberra 228
New South Wales 92, 96, 190, 230
Nicholson, William 153
Nickolls, Trevor 27, 49–50
'9 by 5 Impression Exhibition', Melbourne (1889) 150
Nolan, Cynthia 190
Nolan, Sidney 25, 31–2, 50, 97, 186, 190–1, 234
Burke 32, *32*
The Burning Tree **222**
Glenrowan 190, **220**
Inland Australia 190, 191, **225**
Kiata 190, *191*
Ned Kelly series 25, 32, 190, **221**
Pretty Polly Mine 191, **224**
Quilting the Armour 190, **223**
Nona, Dennis, *Mutuk* **278–9**
North, Ian 189
Northern Territory 228

O

Olsen, John 26, 35, 188, 228
Sydney Sun 232, **238–9**
Olympic Games, Sydney (2000) 190
Onus, Lin 49
Orpheus 32

P

Papapetrou, Polixeni, *The Wimmera* 22
Papunya people 45–7, *46*, *47*, 48
Papunya Tula Artists' co-operative 26, 33, 35
Pareroultja, Otto, *Central Australian Landscape with Ghost Gums* **86**
Parr, Mike 232
Great Distances between Small Towns 232, **265**
Parramatta 95
Paterson, Banjo 148, 190
Payungka Tjapangarti, Timmy, *Sacred Sandhills* 47, **65**
Perth 96
Phillipus Tjakamarra, Long Jack 26
Kalipinypa Water Dreaming 46, **64**
Pictorialist movement 187
Piguenit, W. C. 101, 148
The Flood in the Darling, 1890 153, **155**
Mount Olympus, Lake St Clair, Tasmania, the Source of the Derwent *100*
Pintupi people 47–8
Poignant, Axel, *Swagman on the Road to Wilcannia* 190, **202**
Port Lincoln 98
Port Phillip District 95
Possum Tjapaltjarri, Clifford 26, 32
Bushfire II *34*
Warlugulong 47, **68**
Post-Impressionism 186
Postmodernism 228
Preston, Margaret 26, 189, 191, 228
Aboriginal Landscape 189, **208**
The Expulsion **215**
Flying over the Shoalhaven River 189, **209**
Prout, John Skinner 97
Maria Island from Little Swanport, Van Diemen's Land 97, **130**
Shipwreck off Cape Pillar 97, **131**
South Bank of the Yarra, near Melbourne 97, **130**
Pryde, James 153
Purrumbete 98–9

Q

Queensland 50, 96

R

Radford, Ron 152
Rainbow Serpent 33, 49
rarrk patterns 44
Rees, Lloyd 189
The Road to Berry 188, **217**
Roberts, Tom 24, 50, 101, 148–9, 150, 151
Allegro con brio, Bourke Street West 148, **156–7**
The Artists' Camp 148–9, **158**
A Break Away! 24, 151, 153, **168**
Evening Train to Hawthorn 150, **166**
'Evening, when the quiet east flushes faintly at the sun's last look' 149, **159**
Shearing the Rams 24, *25*
Slumbering Sea, Mentone 149, **158**
A Summer Morning Tiff *148*, 149
The Sunny South 149, **159**
Robertson, Bryan 26
Robinson, William, *Twin Falls and Gorge* 230, **263**
rock art 32–3, 44, 45
Romanticism 24, 98, 101, 149
Rousseau, Henri 'Le Douanier' 190
Royal Academy of Arts 24, 25, 93, 94, 150

S

sand paintings 33–5
Schomburgk, Julius
Duncan Challenge Trophy **139**
John Ridley Testimonial Candelabrum 100, **139**
Schramm, Alexander 98
Adelaide, A Tribe of Natives on the Banks of the River Torrens **131**
Second World War 189, 191
Senbergs, Jan 234
Fort 234, **262**
Seurat, Georges 228
Shelley, Percy Bysshe 149
shields *47*
Siwes, Darren, *Biyi Marrkidj* *230*
Smart, Jeffrey 25, 35, 97
Holiday Resort 189, **216**
Smith, Grace Cossington 186, 187, 191
The Bridge in Building 187, **199**
Eastern Road, Turramurra 187, **198**
Four Panels for a Screen 187, **196–7**
The Song of Australia 234
South Australia 95–6, 97, 98
South Sulawesi 45
Spencer, Baldwin 44, 152
Stacey, Wesley, *The Road* 233, **250–1**
Steiner, Henry, *Inkwell* **138**
Stephenson, David, *Self-portrait Looking Down a Survey-cut Proposed Site of Gordon below Franklin Dam, Tasmania* **253**
Streeton, Arthur 24, 50, 101, 148, 149–51
Fire's On 150–1, 153, **169**
Golden Summer, Eaglemont 94–5, 150, **164–5**
The National Game 150, **166**
The Selector's Hut (Whelan on the Log) 150, **162**
Sirius Cove 150, **163**
'sunshine school', photography 187
Surrealism 186, 189
Sutherland, Graham 190
Sutherland, Jane 150
Field Naturalists *151*
Swan River District 95
Sydney 26, 96–7, 101, 153, 232
Sydney Harbour 92, 150, 187, 232
Sydney Harbour Bridge 25, 187, 191
Symbolists 228

T

Tasmania 50, 95, 96, 97, 230, 234
Tate Gallery, London 22, 191
Taylor, Howard 23–4
Sun Figure **255**
Temin, Kathy, *Tombstone Garden* **287**
Terry, Samuel 23
Thake, Eric, *Brownout* 189, **210**
Thomas, Dylan 189
Thomas, Harold Jabada, Australian Aboriginal Flag *229*
Thomas, Rover 26–7, 48–9
Cyclone Tracy **79**
Roads Meeting 49, **78**, 229–30
Ruby Plains Killing 2 49, *49*
Thompson, Christian
Black Gum 1 *27*
Dead as a Door Nail 50, **285**
Tillers, Imants 229
Shadow of the Hereafter 229, **275**
Untitled 228
Tingari ancestors 47–8
Tiwi people 45
Tjampitjinpa, Anatjari, *Ceremonial Ground* **63**
Tjangala, Uta Uta 47
Old Man's Dreaming 47, **66–7**
Tjapaltjarri clan 35
Tolson Tjupurrula, Turkey, *Straightening Spears at Ilyingaungau* 48, **73**
Toulouse-Lautrec, Henri de 151
Traill, Jessie 187
Building the Harbour Bridge IV **201**
Trenerry, Horace, *The Road to Maslins* 188, **206**
Tucker, Albert 190
Sunbathers 189, **211**
Tuckson, Tony 233
Watery 233, **240**
Turner, J.M.W. 23, 94, 95, 96, 97, 152, 233

U

Ubirr Rock 33
Uluru *44*
Utopia 48

V

Valamanesh, Hossein 228, 233
Longing/Belonging 229, **284**
Van Diemen's Land 95
Venice Biennale 27
Victoria 95, 98–9, 190
Von Guérard, Eugene 98–100, 101
Bushfire 99–100, **137**
The Crater of Mount Eccles *24*
Ferntree Gully in the Dandenong Ranges 100, **133**
From the Verandah of Purrumbete 98–9, **135**
North-east View from the Northern Top of Mount Kosciusko 99, **136–7**
Purrumbete from across the Lake 98–9, **134**
Sketch for Bushfire *99*, 100
Stony Rises, Lake Corangamite 98, 101, **132**

W

Wakelin, Roland 153
Barn near Tuggerah 153, **183**
Houses at Hunters Hill 153, **183**
Wallis, Captain James 92
'Waltzing Matilda' 190, 235
Wamba, Alice, *Coral* 45, **61**
Warangkula Tjupurrula, Johnny 26
A Bush Tucker Story 46, **62**
Warhol, Andy 235
Warlpiri people 48
watercolours 152–3
Watling, Thomas 92, 94
View of the Town of Sydney in the Colony of New South Wales 92, **102–3**
Watson, Judy, *fire and water* **288**
Westall, Richard 92
Westall, William 92–4
Chasm Island, Native Cave Painting 93, **106–7**
Hawkesbury River (View no. 7) *94*
View in Sir E. Pellew's Group, Gulph of Carpentaria, Discovered by Captain Flinders, 1802 93, **108**
View of Cape Townsend and of the Islands in Shoal-Water Bay, Taken from Mount Westall, 1802 94, **109**
Western Australia 95, 96
Western Desert 43, 45–8, 99
Whisson, Ken, *Jean's Farm* **246**
Whistler, J. M. 148, 149, 150
White, Patrick 31
The Twyborn Affair 235
Whitechapel Art Gallery, London 22
Whitehead, Isaac 98, 100
In the Sassafras Valley, Victoria 100, **142**
Whiteley, Brett 26, 31, 188
The Balcony 2 *31*
Big Orange (Sunset) 232, *232*, **247**
(Free-standing ultramarine) Palm Trees *232*
Wilde, Oscar, *The Importance of Being Earnest* 32
Williams, Fred 26, 32, 97, 228, 231–2, 234
Silver and Grey 231, **244**
Snow Storm, Kosciusko 231, **245**
Upwey Landscape *33*
Yellow Landscape 231, **242–3**
Wimmera 190
Withers, Walter 149, 150, 151
The Last of Summer 151, **171**
Wolfhagen, Philip 234
Autumn Equinox: The Loss of the Sun 234, **282**
Wybalenna 50

Y

Yidinji people 50
Yirawala, *Kundaagi – Red Plains, Kangaroo* 44, **52**
Yolngu people 44–5, *45*
Young, Blamire 152
Dry Weather 153, **175**
Yuendumu 35, 48, *48*
Yunupingu, Gulumbu, *Garak the Universe* **59**
Yunupingu, Munggurrawuy, *Fire Story at Caledon Bay* 45, **58**

Z

Zahalka, Anne, *The Bathers* 188, *188*

SUPPORTERS OF THE ROYAL ACADEMY

MAJOR BENEFACTORS

The President and the Trustees of the Royal Academy Trust are grateful to all its donors for their continued loyalty and generosity. They would like to extend their thanks to all those who have made a significant commitment, past and present, to the galleries, the exhibitions, the conservation of the Permanent Collection, the Library collections, the Royal Academy Schools, the Learning programme and other specific appeals.

HM The Queen
Her Majesty's Government
The 29th May 1961 Charitable Trust
The Aldama Foundation
The American Associates of the Royal Academy Trust
The Annenberg Foundation
Barclays Bank
BAT Industries plc
Sir David and Lady Bell
The late Tom Bendhem
The late Brenda M Benwell-Lejeune
John Frye Bourne
British Telecom
The Brown Foundation
John and Susan Burns
Mr Raymond M Burton CBE
Sir Trevor Chinn CVO and Lady Chinn
The Trustees of the Clore Foundation
The John S Cohen Foundation
Sir Harry and Lady Djangoly
The Dulverton Trust
Alfred Dunhill Limited
The John Ellerman Foundation
The Eranda Foundation
Ernst & Young
Esso UK plc
Esmée Fairbairn Charitable Trust
The Fidelity UK Foundation
The Foundation for Sports and the Arts
Friends of the Royal Academy
Jacqueline and Michael Gee
The Getty Grant Programme
Mr Thomas Gibson
Glaxo Holdings plc
Diane and Guilford Glazer
Mr and Mrs Jack Goldhill
Maurice and Laurence Goldman
The Horace W Goldsmith Foundation
HRH Princess Marie-Chantal of Greece
Mr and Mrs Jocelin Harris
The Philip and Pauline Harris Charitable Trust
The Charles Hayward Foundation
Heritage Lottery Fund
IBM United Kingdom Limited
The Idlewild Trust
Lord and Lady Jacobs
The JP Jacobs Charitable Trust
The Japan Foundation
Gabrielle Jungels-Winkler Foundation
Mr and Mrs Donald Kahn
The Lillian Jean Kaplan Foundation
The Kresge Foundation
The Samuel H Kress Foundation
The Kirby Laing Foundation
The Lankelly Foundation
The late Mr John S Latsis
The David Lean Foundation
The Leverhulme Trust
Lex Service plc
The Linbury Trust
Sir Sydney Lipworth QC and Lady Lipworth CBE
John Lyons Charity
Ronald and Rita McAulay
McKinsey and Company Inc
John Madejski OBE DL
The Manifold Trust
Marks and Spencer
The Paul Mellon Estate
The Mercers' Company
The Monument Trust
The Henry Moore Foundation
The Moorgate Trust Fund
The late Mr Minoru Mori HON KBE
 and Mrs Mori
Museums and Galleries Improvement Fund
National Westminster Bank
Stavros S Niarchos
Simon and Midge Palley
The Peacock Charitable Trust
The Pennycress Trust
PF Charitable Trust
The Pidem Fund
The Pilgrim Trust
The Edith and Ferdinand Porjes Trust
The Porter Foundation
John Porter Charitable Trust
Rio Tinto
John A Roberts FRIBA
Sir Simon and Lady Robertson
The Ronson Foundation
Rothmans International plc
RTZ Corporation plc
Dame Jillian Sackler DBE
Jillian and Arthur M Sackler
Mr Wafic Rida Saïd
Mrs Jean Sainsbury
The Saison Foundation
The Sammermar Trust
The Basil Samuel Charitable Trust
Mrs Coral Samuel CBE
Sea Containers Ltd
Shell UK Limited
Miss Dasha Shenkman
William and Maureen Shenkman
The Archie Sherman Charitable Trust
The late Pauline Sitwell
The Starr Foundation
Sir Hugh Sykes DL
Alfred Taubman
Sir Anthony and Lady Tennant
Ware and Edythe Travelstead
The Trusthouse Charitable Foundation
The Douglas Turner Trust
Unilever plc
The Weldon UK Charitable Trust
The Welton Foundation
The Weston Family
The Malcolm Hewitt Wiener Foundation
The Maurice Wohl Charitable Foundation
The Wolfson Foundation

and others who wish to remain anonymous

PATRONS

The Royal Academy is extremely grateful to all its Patrons, who generously support every aspect of its work.

Chair
Robert Suss

Platinum
Celia and Edward Atkin CBE
Mr and Mrs Christopher Bake
Mr and Mrs Patrick Doherty
Ms Ghizlan El Glaoui
Mr Denis Korotkov-Koganovich
Mr and Mrs Jake Shafran
David and Sophie Shalit

Gold
Christopher and Alex Courage
Mr and Mrs Andrew Higginson
Mrs Elizabeth Hosking
Miss Joanna Kaye
Lady Rayne Lacey
Jacqueline and Marc Leland
The Licensing Company, London
Sir Sydney Lipworth QC and Lady Lipworth CBE
Mr and Mrs Ronald Lubner
Sir Keith and Lady Mills
Jean and Geoffrey Redman-Brown
Mrs Stella Shawzin
Mr Kevin Sneader and Ms Amy Munter
Jane Spack
David Stileman
Mr and Mrs Pierre Winkler
Mr Robert John Yerbury

Silver
Lady Agnew
Miss H J C Anstruther
Lord Ashburton
Mr and Mrs Simon Bamber
Jane Barker
Ms Catherine Baxendale
The Duke of Beaufort
Mrs J K M Bentley, Summers Art Gallery
Mr Nigel Boardman
Eleanor E Brass
Mr and Mrs Richard Briggs OBE
Mrs Elie Brihi
Mrs Marcia Brocklebank
Sir Francis Brooke Bt
Mrs Joyce Brotherton
Lady Brown
Jeremy Brown
Lord Browne of Madingley
Mr Martin Burton
Mr F A A Carnwath CBE
Sir Roger Carr
Jean and Eric Cass
Sir Charles and Lady Chadwyck-Healey
Sir Trevor Chinn CVO and Lady Chinn
Mr and Mrs George Coelho
Denise Cohen Charitable Trust
Sir Ronald Cohen
Ms Linda Cooper
Mark and Cathy Corbett
Mr and Mrs Ken Costa
Julian Darley and Helga Sands
The Countess of Dartmouth
Mr Daniel Davies
Peter and Andrea De Haan
The de Laszlo Foundation
Mrs Anita Dinkin
Dr Anne Dornhorst
Lord Douro
Mr and Mrs Jim Downing
Ms Noreen Doyle
Janet and Maurice Dwek
Mrs Sheila Earles
Lord and Lady Egremont
Bryan Ferry
Benita and Gerald Fogel
Mr Sam Fogg
Mrs Rosamund Fokschaner
Mrs Jocelyn Fox
Mrs Anthony Foyle
Mr and Mrs Eric Franck
Mr Simon Freakley
Arnold Fulton
The Lord Gavron CBE
Jacqueline and Jonathan Gestetner
Lady Getty
Mr Mark Glatman
Lady Gosling
Mr Stephen Gosztony
Piers Gough CBE RA
Mr Gavin Graham
Mrs Mary Graves
Mrs Margaret Guitar
Sir Ewan and Lady Harper
Mrs Melanie Harris
Richard and Janeen Haythornthwaite
Sir John Hegarty and Miss Philippa Crane
Michael and Morven Heller
Lady Heseltine
Mr and Mrs Alan Hobart
Mr Philip Hudson
Mr and Mrs Jon Hunt
Mrs Deanna Ibrahim
S Isern-Feliu
Mrs Caroline Jackson
Mr Michael Jacobson
Sir Martin and Lady Jacomb
Mrs Raymonde Jay
Fiona Johnstone
Mr Nicholas Jones
Mrs Ghislaine Kane
Dr Elisabeth Kehoe
Mr Duncan Kenworthy OBE
Princess Jeet Khemka
Mr and Mrs Naguib Kheraj
Mr D H Killick
Mr and Mrs James Kirkman
Mrs Aboudi Kosta
Mr and Mrs Herbert Kretzmer
Norman A Kurland and Deborah A David
Joan H Lavender
Mr George Lengvari and Mrs Inez Lengvari
Lady Lever of Manchester
Mr Peter Lloyd
Miss R Lomax-Simpson
The Hon Mrs Virginia Lovell
Mr and Mrs Henry Lumley
Mrs Josephine Lumley
Gillian McIntosh
Andrew and Judith McKinna
Mr Nicholas Maclean
Sir John Mactaggart
Madeline and Donald Main
Mrs Inge Margulies
Mr Charles Martin
Mr and Mrs Richard Martin
Zvi and Ofra Meitar Family Fund
Professor Anthony Mellows OBE TD
 and Mrs Anthony Mellows
Mrs Joy Moss
Dr Ann Naylor
Mr Stuart C Nelson
Ann Norman-Butler
North Street Trust
Mr Michael Palin
John H Pattisson
Nicholas B Paumgarten
Mr and Mrs D J Peacock
Mr and Mrs A Perloff
Mr Philip Perry
David Pike
Mr Maurice Pinto
Mr and Mrs Anthony Pitt-Rivers
Mr Basil Postan
John and Anne Raisman
Mr David Reid Scott
Lady Renwick
Rothschild Foundation
Miss Elaine Rowley
Mr and Mrs K M Rubie
The Lady Henrietta St George
Mr Adrian Sassoon
H M Sassoon Charitable Trust
Mr and Mrs Christopher Satterthwaite
Carol Sellars
Mr and Mrs Kevin Senior
Christina Countess of Shaftesbury
Mr Robert N Shapiro
Major General and Mrs Jonathan Shaw
Richard and Veronica Simmons
Alan and Marianna Simpson
The Tavolozza Foundation
Lady Tennant
Anthony Thornton
Mr Anthony J Todd
Miss M L Ulfane
John and Carol Wates
Mrs Angela Webb
Edna and Willard Weiss
Anthony and Rachel Williams
Christopher G Williams Esq
Mr William Winters

Patron Donors
Stephen Barry Charitable Settlement
Mr and Mrs William Brake
Mr Peter Lloyd
Mrs Bianca Roden
The Michael H Sacher Charitable Trust

and others who wish to remain anonymous

Benjamin West Group Patrons
Chair
Lady Judge CBE

Platinum
Mr Tony Davis
David Giampaolo
Charles and Kaaren Hale
Ms Dambisa Moyo
Mr and Mrs John R Olsen

Gold
Marco and Francesca Assetto
Lady Judge CBE
Mr Christian Levett
Ms Alessandra Morra
Mr John Peter Williams

Silver
Lady J Lloyd Adamson
Mr Dimitry Afanasiev
Poppy Allonby
Mrs Spindrift Al Swaidi
Mrs Ruth Anderson
Ms Sol Anitua
Mr Andy Ash
Mrs Leslie Bacon
Naomi and Ted Berk
Mrs Michal Berkner Jenrick
Jean and John Botts
Mrs Olga But-Gusaim
Mrs Sophie Cahu
Brian and Melinda Carroll
Mr and Mrs Paul Collins
Vanessa Colomar de Enserro
Ms Karla Dorsch
Mr and Mrs Jeff Eldredge
Mr David Fawkes
Mrs Stroma Finston
Cyril and Christine Freedman
Mrs Mina Gerowin Herrmann
Ms Moya Greene
Mr David Greenwald
Mr and Mrs Timothy Hart
Mr Andrew Hawkins
Ms Alexandra Hess
Mr Rashid Hoosenally
Katie Jackson
Suzanne and Michael Johnson
Syrie Johnson
Lord and Lady Leitch
Mrs Stephanie Léouzon
Charles G Lubar
Ted and Patricia Madara
Cornelius Medvei
Mrs Victoria Mills
Scott and Christine Morrissey
Neil Osborn and Holly Smith
Lady Purves
Mr James B Sherwood
Mr Stuart Southall
Sir Hugh and Lady Sykes
Mr Ian Taylor
Miss Lori Tedesco
Mr and Mrs Julian Treger
Frederick and Kathryn Uhde
Mr Craig D Weaver
Prof Peter Whiteman QC
Mr and Mrs John Winter
Ms Regina Wyles

and others who wish to remain anonymous

Schools Patrons
Chair
Clare Flanagan

Platinum
Mrs Sarah Chenevix-Trench
Matthew and Sian Westerman

Gold
Sam and Rosie Berwick
Christopher Kneale
Mr William Loschert
Mr Keir McGuinness

Silver
Lord and Lady Aldington
Mrs Elizabeth Alston
Mr Nicholas Andrew
Dr Anne Ashmore-Hudson
Mr Jonathan and Mrs Sarah Bayliss
Mrs Gemma Billington
Tatiana Cherkasova
Rosalind Clayton
Mr Richard Clothier
Ms Davina Dickson
Mrs Dominic Dowley
John Entwistle OBE
Mrs Catherine Farquharson
Ian and Catherine Ferguson
Ms Clare Flanagan
Mr Mark Garthwaite
Mrs Michael Green
Mr Lindsay Hamilton
Mrs Lesley Haynes
Rosalyn Henderson
The Hon Tom Hewlett
Prof Ken Howard OBE RA and Mrs Howard
Mark and Fiona Hutchinson
Mrs Susan Johns
Ms Karen Jones
Mrs Marcelle Joseph
Mr and Mrs S Kahan
Mr Paul Kempe
Ms Nicolette Kwok
Mrs Anna Lee
Mr and Mrs Mark Loveday
Mrs Nicola Manby
Philip and Val Marsden
The Mulberry Trust
Lord and Lady Myners
Peter Rice Esq
Anthony and Sally Salz
Brian D Smith
Mr Simon Thorley QC
Mr Ray Treen
Mrs Carol Wates
Mrs Diana Wilkinson
Mr and Mrs Maurice Wolridge

and others who wish to remain anonymous

Contemporary Circle Patrons
Chair
Susie Allen-Huxley

Platinum
Robert and Simone Suss

Gold
Mrs and Mrs Thomas Berger
Mr Jeremy Coller
Helen and Colin David
Mrs Alison Deighton
Matthew and Monika McLennan
Mr and Mrs Scott Mead
Ms Miel de Botton
Mr and Mrs Simon Oliver
Mr and Mrs Paul Phillips
Richard Sharp

Silver
Joan and Robin Alvarez
Mrs Charlotte Artus
Jeremy Asher
Mr David Baty
Ms Sara Berman
Viscountess Bridgeman
Dr Elaine C Buck
Ms Debra Burt
Nadia Crandall
Mrs Georgina David
Mrs Elizabeth Davydova
Mr Patrick De Nonneville
Mollie Dent-Brocklehurst
Mrs Sophie Diedrichs-Cox
Mr and Mrs Gerard Dodd
Chris and Angie Drake
Mrs Jennifer Duke
Mr Timothy Ellis
Lady Polly Feversham
Mr Stephen Garrett
Simon Gillespie
Mrs Susan Hayden
Margaret A Jackson
Mr Gerald Kidd
Mrs Fiona King
Anna Lapshina
Mrs Sarah Macken
Mr Penelope Mather
Dr Carolina Minio Paluello
Sophie Mirman
Victoria Miro
Mr and Mrs Jeremy Nicholson
Mrs Tessa Nicholson
Mrs Yelena Oosting
Veronique Parke
Mr Tremayne Carew Pole
Mrs Tineke Pugh
Mrs Catherine Rees
Mrs Karen Santi
Edwina Sassoon
Omar Shah
Richard and Susan Shoylekov
Ms Ana Stanic
Jeffery C Sugarman and Alan D H Newham
Anna Watkins
Cathy Wills
Manuela and Iwan Wirth
Mr and Mrs Maurice Wolridge
Ms Cynthia Wu

Patron Donors
Mrs Karen Santi

and others who wish to remain anonymous

Library and Collections Circle
Patron Donors
Mr Mark W Friend
Mr Loyd Grossman
Miss Jo Hannah Hoehn
Mr and Mrs Robert Hoehn
Lowell Libson
Pam and Scott Schafler
Mr and Mrs Bart Tiernan
Jonny Yarker

and others who wish to remain anonymous

Young Patrons
Kalita al Swaidi
Miss Maria Allen
Miss Joy Asfar
Rosanna Bossom
May Calil
Mr and Mrs Tom Davies
Mr Stefano Donati
Mr Rollo Gabb
Miss Fernanda Gilligan
Laura Graham
Soliana Habte
The Hon Alexandra Knatchbull
Marc C Koch
Julie Lawson
Lilly Le Brun
Mr Lin Lei
Mr Mandeep Singh
Mr Stephen Sobey
Miss Annabelle Wills
Miss Burcu Yuksel

Patron Donor
Mr Haakon Lorentzen

and others who wish to remain anonymous

TRUSTS AND FOUNDATIONS
Artists Collecting Society
The Atlas Fund
The Albert Van den Bergh Charitable Trust
The Bomonty Charitable Trust
The Charlotte Bonham-Carter Charitable Trust
William Brake Charitable Trust
R M Burton 1998 Charitable Trust
C H K Charities Limited
P H G Cadbury Charitable Trust
The Carew Pole Charitable Trust
The Clore Duffield Foundation
John S Cohen Foundation
The Evan Cornish Foundation
The Sidney and Elizabeth Corob Charitable Trust
The Dovehouse Trust
The Gilbert and Eileen Edgar Foundation
The John Ellerman Foundation
The Eranda Foundation
Lucy Mary Ewing Charitable Trust
The Margery Fish Charity
The Flow Foundation
The Garfield Weston Foundation
Gatsby Charitable Foundation
The Golden Bottle Trust
The Gordon Foundation
Sue Hammerson Charitable Trust
The Charles Hayward Foundation
Heritage Lottery Fund
Hiscox
Holbeck Charitable Trust
The Harold Hyam Wingate Foundation
The Ironmongers' Company
The Emmanuel Kaye Foundation
The Kindersley Foundation
The de Laszlo Foundation
The David Lean Foundation
The Leche Trust
The Leverhulme Trust
The Maccabaeans
The McCorquodale Charitable Trust
The Machin Foundation
The Paul Mellon Centre
The Paul Mellon Estate
The Mercers' Company
Margaret and Richard Merrell Foundation
The Millichope Foundation
The Mondriaan Foundation
The Monument Trust
The Henry Moore Foundation
The Mulberry Trust
The J Y Nelson Charitable Trust
The Old Broad Street Charity Trust
The Peacock Charitable Trust
The Pennycress Trust
PF Charitable Trust
The Stanley Picker Charitable Trust
The Pidem Fund
The Edith and Ferdinand Porjes Charitable Trust
Mr and Mrs J A Pye's Charitable Settlement
Rayne Foundation
The Reed Foundation
T Rippon & Sons (Holdings) Ltd
Rootstein Hopkins Foundation
The Rose Foundation
Schroder Charity Trust
The Sellars Charitable Trust
The Archie Sherman Charitable Trust
Paul Smith and Pauline Denyer-Smith
The South Square Trust
Spencer Charitable Trust
Oliver Stanley Charitable Trust
Peter Storrs Trust
Strand Parishes Trust
The Joseph Strong Frazer Trust
The Swan Trust
Thaw Charitable Trust
Sir Jules Thorn Charitable Trust
The Bruce Wake Charity
Celia Walker Art Foundation
Warburg Pincus International LLC
Weinstock Fund
Wilkinson Eyre Architects
The Spencer Wills Trust
The Maurice Wohl Charitable Foundation
The Wolfson Foundation
The Worshipful Company of Painter-Stainers

AMERICAN ASSOCIATES OF THE ROYAL ACADEMY TRUST
Burlington House Trust
Mrs James C Slaughter

Benjamin West Society
Mrs Deborah Loeb Brice
Mrs Nancy B Negley

Benefactors
Mr Michael Moritz and Ms Harriet Heyman
Mrs Edmond J Safra
The Hon John C Whitehead

Sponsors
Mrs Drue Heinz HON DBE
David Hockney OM CH RA
Mr Arthur L Loeb
Mr and Mrs Hamish Maxwell
Mr and Mrs Richard J Miller Jr
Diane A Nixon
Ms Joan Stern
Dr and Mrs Robert D Wickham

Patrons
Mr and Mrs Steven Ausnit
Mr and Mrs E William Aylward
Mr Donald A Best
Mrs Mildred C Brinn
Mrs Benjamin Coates
Lois M Collier
Mr and Mrs Stanley De Forest Scott
Mr and Mrs Lawrence S Friedland
Mr and Mrs Leslie Garfield
Ms Helen Harting Abell
Dr Bruce C Horten
Mr William W Karatz
The Hon Eugene A Ludwig and Dr Carol Ludwig
Miss Lucy F McGrath
Mr and Mrs Wilson Nolen
Mrs Mary Sharp Cronson
Ms Louisa Stude Sarofim
Martin J Sullivan OBE
Mr Robert W Wilson

Donors
Mr James C Armstrong
Ms Naja Armstrong
Laura Blanco
Mr Constantin R Boden
Dr and Mrs Robert Bookchin
Laura Christman and William Rothacker
Ms Alyce Faye Cleese
Mr Richard C Colyear
Mr and Mrs Howard Davis
Ms Zita Davisson
Mr Gerry Dolezar
Ms Maria Garvey Dowd
Mrs Beverley C Duer
Mrs June Dyson
Mr Robert H Enslow
Mrs Katherine D Findlay
Mr and Mrs Gordon P Getty
Mr and Mrs Ellis Goodman
Mrs Oliver R Grace
Sir Jeremy and Lady Greenstock
Mr and Mrs Gustave M Hauser
Mrs Judith Heath
Ms Elaine Kend
Mr and Mrs Nicholas L S Kirkbride
Ms Jeanne K Lawrence
The Hon Samuel K Lessey Jr
Mr Henry S Lynn Jr
Ms Clare E McKeon
Ms Christine Mainwaring-Samwell
Ms Barbara T Missett
The Hon and Mrs William A Nitze
Mrs Charles W Olson III
Ms Jennifer Pellegrino
Cynthia Hazen Polsky and Leon B Polsky
Ms Wendy Reilly
Donna Rich
Mr and Mrs Daniel Rose
Mrs Nanette Ross
Mrs Martin Slifka
Mr Albert H Small
Mr and Mrs Morton I Sosland
Mrs Frederick M Stafford
Mr and Mrs Alfred Taubman
Ms Evelyn Tompkins
Mr Peter Trippi
Mrs Judith Villard
Ms Lucy Waring

Corporate and Foundation Support
American Express Foundation
The Blackstone Charitable Foundation
British Airways PLC
The Brown Foundation
Crankstart Foundation
Fortnum & Mason
Gibson, Dunn & Crutcher
The Horace W Goldsmith Foundation
Hauser Foundation
Kress Foundation
Leon Levy Foundation
Loeb Foundation
Henry Luce Foundation
Lynberg & Watkins
Edmond J Safra Philanthropic Foundation
Siezen Foundation
Sony Corporation of America
Starr Foundation
Thaw Charitable Trust

CORPORATE MEMBERS OF THE ROYAL ACADEMY
Launched in 1988, the Royal Academy's Corporate Membership Scheme has proved highly successful. Corporate membership offers benefits for staff, clients and community partners and access to the Academy's facilities and resources. The outstanding support we receive from companies via the scheme is vital to the continuing success of the Academy and we thank all members for their valuable support and continued enthusiasm.

Premier Level Members
American Express
A T Kearney Limited
Barclays plc
Bird & Bird
Catlin Group Limited
CBRE
Christie's
Deutsche Bank AG
FTI Consulting
GlaxoSmithKline plc
Insight Investment
JM Finn & Co
Jones Lang LaSalle
JTI
KPMG
Linklaters
Neptune Investment Management
Schroders Private Banking
Smith & Williamson
Sotheby's

Corporate Members
The Boston Consulting Group UK LLP
British American Tobacco
Brunswick
Capital International Limited
Clifford Chance LLP

Essex Court
F & C Asset Management plc
GAM
Lazard
Lindsell Train
Marie Curie
Moelis & Company
Oracle Capital Group
The Royal Society of Chemistry
Slaughter and May
Tanya Baxter Contemporary
Tiffany & Co.
Trowers & Hamlins
UBS
Vision Capital Limited
Weil, Gotshal & Manges

Associate
All Nippon Airways
Bank of America Merrill Lynch
BNP Paribas
Bloomberg LP
Bonhams 1793 Ltd
Credit Agricole CIB
Ernst & Young
Generation Investment Management LLP
Heidrick & Struggles
John Lewis Partnership
Lubbock Fine Chartered Accountants
Morgan Stanley
Pentland Group plc
Rio Tinto
Sykes & Sons Limited
Timothy Sammons Fine Art Agents

SUPPORTERS OF PAST EXHIBITIONS

The President and Council of the Royal Academy would like to thank the following supporters and benefactors for their generous contributions towards major exhibitions in the last ten years:

2013
Richard Rogers RA: Inside Out
Ferrovial Agroman
Heathrow
Laing O'Rourke
Mexico: A Revolution in Art, 1910–1940
2009–2013 Season supported by JTI
Conaculta
Visit Mexico
Sectur
Mexican Agency for International Development Cooperation
Art Mentor Foundation Lucerne
Catherine and Franck Petitgas
James and Clare Kirkman
Mercedes Zobel
245th Summer Exhibition
Insight Investment
George Bellows
2009–2013 Season supported by JTI
Edwards Wildman
Premiums 2013, RA Schools Annual Dinner and Auction and RA Schools Show 2013
Newton Investment Management
Manet: Portraying Life
BNY Mellon, Partner of the Royal Academy of Arts

2012
Mariko Mori
JTI
RA Now
JTI
Bronze
Christian Levett and Mougins Museum of Classical Art
Daniel Katz Gallery
Baron Lorne Thyssen-Bornemisza
John and Fausta Eskenazi
The Ruddock Foundation for the Arts
Tomasso Brothers Fine Art
Jon and Barbara Landau
Janine and J. Tomilson Hill
Embassy of the Kingdom of the Netherlands
Eskenazi Limited
Lisson Gallery
Alexis Gregory
Alan and Mary Hobart
Richard de Unger and Adeela Qureshi
Rossi & Rossi Ltd
Embassy of Israel
244th Summer Exhibition
Insight Investment
From Paris: A Taste for Impressionism – Paintings from the Clark
2009–2013 Season supported by JTI
Edwards Wildman
The Annenberg Foundation
Premiums, RA Schools Annual Dinner and Auction and RA Schools Show 2012
Newton Investment Management
Johan Zoffany RA: Society Observed
2009–2013 Season supported by JTI
Cox & Kings
Building the Revolution: Soviet Art and Architecture 1915–1935
2009–2013 Season supported by JTI
The Ove Arup Foundation
The Norman Foster Foundation
Richard and Ruth Rogers
David Hockney RA: A Bigger Picture
BNP Paribas
Welcome to Yorkshire: Tourism Partner
Visit Hull & East Yorkshire: Supporting Tourism Partner
NEC

2011
Degas and the Ballet: Picturing Movement
BNY Mellon
Region Holdings
Blavatnik Family Foundation
Eyewitness: Hungarian Photography in the Twentieth Century. Brassaï, Capa, Kertész, Moholy-Nagy, Munkácsi
2009–2013 Season supported by JTI
Hungarofest
OTP Bank
243rd Summer Exhibition
Insight Investment
Premiums, RA Schools Annual Dinner and Auction and RA Schools Show 2011
Newton Investment Management
Watteau: The Drawings
2009–2013 Season supported by JTI
Region Holdings
Modern British Sculpture
American Express Foundation
The Henry Moore Foundation
Hauser & Wirth
Art Mentor Foundation Lucerne
Sotheby's
Blain Southern
Welcome to Yorkshire: Tourism Partner

2010
GSK Contemporary – Aware: Art Fashion Identity
GlaxoSmithKline
Pioneering Painters: The Glasgow Boys 1880–1900
2009–2013 Season supported by JTI
Glasgow Museums
Treasures from Budapest: European Masterpieces from Leonardo to Schiele
OTP Bank
Villa Budapest
Daniel Katz Gallery, London
Cox & Kings: Travel Partner
Sargent and the Sea
2009–2013 Season supported by JTI
242nd Summer Exhibition
Insight Investment
Paul Sandby RA: Picturing Britain, A Bicentenary Exhibition
2009–2013 Season supported by JTI
The Real Van Gogh: The Artist and His Letters
BNY Mellon
Hiscox
Heath Lambert
Cox & Kings: Travel Partner
RA Outreach Programme
Deutsche Bank AG

2009
GSK Contemporary
GlaxoSmithKline
Wild Thing: Epstein, Gaudier-Brzeska, Gill
2009–2013 Season supported by JTI
BNP Paribas
The Henry Moore Foundation
Anish Kapoor
JTI
Richard Chang
Richard and Victoria Sharp
Louis Vuitton
The Henry Moore Foundation
J W Waterhouse: The Modern Pre-Raphaelite
2009–2013 Season supported by JTI
Champagne Perrier-Jouët
GasTerra
Gasunie
241st Summer Exhibition
Insight Investment
Kuniyoshi. From the Arthur R. Miller Collection
2009–2013 Season supported by JTI
Canon
Cox & Kings: Travel Partner
Premiums and RA Schools Show
Mizuho International plc
RA Outreach Programme
Deutsche Bank AG

2008
GSK Contemporary
GlaxoSmithKline
Byzantium 330–1453
J F Costopoulos Foundation
A G Leventis Foundation
Stavros Niarchos Foundation
Cox & Kings: Travel Partner
Miró, Calder, Giacometti, Braque: Aimé Maeght and His Artists
BNP Paribas
Vilhelm Hammershøi: The Poetry of Silence
OAK Foundation Denmark
Novo Nordisk
240th Summer Exhibition
Insight Investment
Premiums and RA Schools Show
Mizuho International plc
RA Outreach Programme
Deutsche Bank AG
From Russia: French and Russian Master Paintings 1870–1925 from Moscow and St Petersburg
E.ON
2008 Season supported by Sotheby's

2007
Paul Mellon's Legacy: A Passion for British Art
The Bank of New York Mellon
Georg Baselitz
Eurohypo AG
239th Summer Exhibition
Insight Investment
Impressionists by the Sea
Farrow & Ball
Premiums and RA Schools Show
Mizuho International plc
RA Outreach Programme
Deutsche Bank AG
The Unknown Monet
Bank of America

2006
238th Summer Exhibition
Insight Investment
Chola: Sacred Bronzes of Southern India
Cox & Kings: Travel Partner
Premiums and RA Schools Show
Mizuho International plc
RA Outreach Programme
Deutsche Bank AG
Rodin
Ernst & Young

2005
China: The Three Emperors, 1662–1795
Goldman Sachs International
Impressionism Abroad: Boston and French Painting
Fidelity Foundation
Matisse, His Art and His Textiles: The Fabric of Dreams
Farrow & Ball
Premiums and RA Schools Show
The Guardian
Mizuho International plc
Turks: A Journey of a Thousand Years, 600–1600
Akkök Group of Companies
Aygaz
Corus
Garanti Bank
Lassa Tyres

2004
236th Summer Exhibition
A T Kearney
Ancient Art to Post-Impressionism: Masterpieces from the Ny Carlsberg Glyptotek, Copenhagen
Carlsberg UK Ltd
Danske Bank
Novo Nordisk
The Art of Philip Guston (1913–1980)
American Associates of the Royal Academy Trust
The Art of William Nicholson
RA Exhibition Patrons Group
Vuillard: From Post-Impressionist to Modern Master
RA Exhibition Patrons Group

Other Supporters
Sponsors of events, publications and other items in the past five years:

Carlisle Group plc
Castello di Reschio
Cecilia Chan
Country Life
Guy Dawson
Derwent Valley Holdings plc
Dresdner Kleinwort Wasserstein
Lucy Flemming McGrath
Foster and Partners
Goldman Sachs International
Gome International
Gucci Group
Hines
IBJ International plc
John Doyle Construction
Harvey and Allison McGrath
Martin Krajewski
Marks & Spencer
Michael Hopkins & Partners
Morgan Stanley Dean Witter
The National Trust
Prada
Radisson Edwardian Hotels
Richard and Ruth Rogers
Rob van Helden
The Wine Studio